P9-BBQ-430

Children's Thinking
Developmental Function and Individual Differences

Children's Thinking

Developmental Function and Individual Differences

David F. Bjorklund

Florida Atlantic University

Brooks/Cole Publishing Company
Pacific Grove, California

Brooks/Cole Publishing Company
A Division of Wadsworth, Inc.

© 1989 by Wadsworth, Inc., Belmont, California, 94002.
All rights reserved.
No part of this book may be reproduced, stored in a retrieval system, or transcribed,
in any form or by any means—electronic, mechanical, photocopying, recording,
or otherwise—without the prior written permission of the publisher,
Brooks/Cole Publishing Company, Pacific Grove, California 93950,
a division of Wadsworth, Inc.

Printed in the United States of America

10 9 8 7 6 5 4 3 2 1

Library of Congress Cataloging in Publication Data
Bjorklund, David F.
    Children's thinking : developmental function and individual
differences / David F. Bjorklund.
        p.   cm.
    Bibliography: p.
    Includes index.
    ISBN 0-534-09384-1
    1. Cognition in children. 2. Individual differences in children.
I. Title.
BF723.C5B48 1988   88-22241
155.4′ 13—dc 19   CIP

Sponsoring Editor: *Phil Curson*
Marketing Representative: *Bob Podstepney*
Editorial Assistant: *Amy Mayfield*
Production Editor: *Penelope Sky*
Production Assistant: *Dorothy Bell*
Manuscript Editor: *William Waller*
Permissions Editor: *Carline Haga*
Interior and Cover Design: *Roy R. Neuhaus*
Art Coordinator: *Sue C. Howard*
Interior Illustration: *Maggie Stevens-Huft*
Typesetting: *TypeLink, Inc., San Diego, California*
Printing and Binding: *R. R. Donnelley & Sons Company, Harrisonburg, Virginia*

Credits continue on page 355.

This book is dedicated to my teachers, with much appreciation and fondness:

Eliot J. Butter
Peter A. Ornstein

Preface

The wonders of cognitive development fascinate me, and I try to convey my enthusiasm to my readers. Development can be appreciated on a variety of levels. Philosophers have pondered the nature of development from the time of the ancients. Is the child born inherently good or inherently evil? Is the course of development predestined—fixed by biology or the position of planets at the time of birth—or does the social and physical environment play a vital role in dictating one's developmental outcome? Development can also be viewed from a less grand perspective. For example, many people believe that an understanding of who we are as adults requires an understanding of where, developmentally speaking, we came from. On a more practical level, knowledge about development can be applied to the important tasks of child rearing and education. This book addresses issues on each of these levels.

Academic interest in intellectual development is nearly as long-standing as the field of psychology itself. However, research into children's thinking accelerated in the United States during the 1960s and 1970s and continues unabated today. Many issues of intellectual development have venerable histories, but much of our understanding of how children think is new. This is an exciting and controversial area, with much ground remaining to be explored. In this book I have covered developmental topics ranging from classic Piagetian theory and information processing approaches to children's thinking, perception, and memory. Unique to this volume

is the inclusion of the origins of individual differences in cognition, cognitive styles, and sex differences.

Traditionally, researchers who studied cognitive development (the age-related changes in thinking common to all children) and those who studied individual differences in children's thinking rarely talked to one another. This has changed over the last decade, with the realization that individual differences in children's thinking often reflect the children's varying levels of cognitive development. This is the first textbook to integrate these two related fields of developmental psychology. As such, it provides the student with a broader view of the development of intelligence than can be achieved when the two topics are taught separately. I do discuss the standard topics that are included in other texts at comparable depth. In fact, I have given equal attention to classic Piagetian theories and interpretations of development and contemporary information processing approaches. I have provided a critical review that includes research findings whenever possible, as well as a summary of research and theory.

The book is intended for use in upper-level undergraduate courses in psychology and education, and can be appreciated by readers of varying levels of expertise, from first and second year psychology majors to beginning graduate students.

There are many topics worthy of inclusion in a book such as this, and because of space limitations and the necessity of making the topics fit into a manageable framework, not all could be included. I apologize to the many authors whose important work is not cited.

☐ Acknowledgements

Anyone who writes a book such as this does so with the help of many people. I must first thank Marc Frankel, who assisted me in writing 3 of the 14 chapters. It was Marc who convinced me to start the book, and without his confidence in the project I might still be weighing the pros and cons of textbook writing without having set a word to paper. I owe a special thanks to Dan Curtiss, who helped me at the last minute with the most difficult part of the book: Chapter 13, on cognitive styles. Dan's strong experimental background and his experience as a school psychologist enabled him to provide a much needed perspective.

My editors at Brooks/Cole, Phil Curson, C. Deborah Laughton, and Penelope Sky, were wonderful to work with every step of the way, as was everyone else up and down the line. Bill Waller did an excellent job of copyediting and taught me something about writing along the way. Conscientious professional reviewers included Mary Attig, Pennsylvania State University; Ruth Ault, Davidson College; Jerrold Barnett, Northeast Missouri State University; David Carson, North Dakota State University; Roberta Corrigan, University of Wisconsin; Gordon Greenwood, University of Florida; John Hagen, University of Michigan; Dorothea Halpert, City University of New York; Nora Newcomb, Temple University; Michael Rabinowitz, Memorial University; and Hoben Thomas, Pennsylvania State University.

I would like to thank the following colleagues who took the time to read earlier drafts of the manuscript and to provide constructive criticism: Charles Brainerd, University of Arizona; Eliot Butter, University of Dayton; David Perry, Florida Atlantic University; and Paula Schwanenflugel, University of Georgia. Several students provided helpful comments and assistance: Jean Bernholtz, John Buchanan, Kathy Harnishfeger, Brandi Green, Katie Lyon, Jacqueline Muir, Hanna Neufeld, Kathy Raynovic, and Randi Wiener. I am grateful to the psychology department secretaries at the Boca Raton campus of Florida Atlantic University, who had the patience to muddle through my seemingly endless set of references: Ann Fox, Silvia Friedman, Susan McDonough, and Ruth Murray. I also wish to thank Judy Bub and Joanne Picca, from the Fort Lauderdale campus, who carefully proofread the manuscript.

Finally, I would like to thank my wife, Barbara, for her compassion and assistance during the 3 years I spent writing and editing this book. In addition to being an understanding and supportive wife, Barbara is also my best colleague. Her criticisms and opinions about which topics and research data to include and about writing style were invaluable. She was the first person other than me to use the book as a guide for lectures in a college course, and her comments and those of her students concerning what worked and what did not were vital. She also picked up some of the slack, both around the house and around the word processor. In sum, my deepest thanks and love go to Barbara.

David F. Bjorklund

Brief Contents

1   An Introduction to Children's Thinking   1

2   Piaget's Theory   15

3   Information Processing Approaches   45
with Marc T. Frankel

4   Perception   67

5   Sensorimotor Intelligence   86

6   Thinking in Symbols   107

7   Language and Thought   134

8   Memory   152

9   Social Cognition   173

10   Individual Differences in Intelligence   199

11   Experience and Intelligence   226
with Marc T. Frankel

12   Stability of Intelligence over Infancy and Childhood   248

13   Cognitive Styles   263
      with Daniel D. Curtiss

14   Sex Differences   285
      with Marc T. Frankel

Contents

1 An Introduction to Children's Thinking   1

  ☐ Basic Concepts in Children's Thinking   3
    Cognition   3
    Development   4

  ☐ Issues in Children's Thinking   5
    Stages of Development   5
    Nature and Nurture   7
    The Stability and Plasticity of Human Intelligence   8
    Important Research Issues   10

  ☐ Overview of the Remainder of the Book   13
  ☐ Summary   14

2 Piaget's Theory   15

  ☐ Piaget's Theory of Intelligence   17
    Some Assumptions of Piaget's Theory   17
    Functional Invariants: Organization and Adaptation   20
    Equilibration   21
    Stages of Development   22
    Are Operations Reasonable?   38

  ☐ An Alternative to Piaget: Fischer's Skill Theory   40
  ☐ Summary   42
  ☐ Notes   43

3 Information Processing Approaches   45
with Marc T. Frankel

  ☐ Assumptions of the Information Processing Approaches   46

Limited Capacity   46
The Information Processing System   46
Representation of Knowledge   46
Automatic and Effortful Processes   47
Components of Information Processing   48

☐ Information Processing Theories of Development   50
Sensory Register   50
Short-Term Store   51

☐ Developmental Differences in Information Processing Components   54
Metacognitive Components   55
Performance Components   55
Knowledge-Acquisition Components   57

☐ The Role of Strategies in Cognitive Development   59
Mediational and Production Deficiencies   59
What Are Production Deficient Children Doing?   60

☐ The Contributions of Children's Knowledge Base to
    Cognitive Development   61
Knowledge Base and Memory Development   61
Knowledge of Rules   64
Children's Belief about What Is Alive   64

☐ Summary   66

☐ Note   66

4   Perception   67

☐ Basic Perceptual Abilities of Young Infants   69
Skin and Body-Orientation Senses   69
Chemical Senses   69
Hearing   69
Vision   70

☐ The Development of Visual Perception   71
Discrimination and Attention   71
The Development of Visual Preferences in Infancy   72
Infant Categorization   78

☐ Auditory Perception in Infancy   81

☐ Intermodal Integration in Infancy   82

☐ Summary   84

5 | Sensorimotor Intelligence   86

☐ Stages of the Sensorimotor Period 87
Piaget's Description of Development in the Sensorimotor Period 87
Non-Piagetian Research into the Stages of Sensorimotor Intelligence 93

☐ Imitation 94
Piaget's View of Imitation in the Sensorimotor Period 94
Non-Piagetian Research into Imitation in the Sensorimotor Period 95

☐ Object Permanence 100
Piaget's Description of the Development of Object Permanence 101
Non-Piagetian Research into the Development of Object Permanence 102

☐ Summary 106

6 | Thinking in Symbols   107

☐ Transitions in Symbolic Representation 108
From Sensorimotor to Symbolic Representation 108
From Literal to Conceptual Representation 109
From Action-Based to Conceptual Representation 111
From Conceptual to Abstract Representation 112

☐ Some Phenomena That Vary as a Function of Children's Use of Symbols 113
Classification 113
The Appearance/Reality Distinction 122
Children's Number and Arithmetic Concepts 124

☐ Children's Development of Representational Abilities 130

☐ Summary 132

7 | Language and Thought   134

☐ Language Acquisition 135
Precursors to Language 135
From Words to Sentences 136

☐ The Development of Communication Skills 137
Communication and Egocentrism 137
Metacommunication 138
Preschoolers' Communication Competence 139

☐ Language and Thought 140
The Self-Regulatory Function of Language 140
The Development of Inner Speech 141

☐ The Development of Semantic Memory   143

The Development of Word Meaning   143
The Development of Natural Language Categories   144
How Does Semantic Memory Develop?   149

☐ Summary   150

8   Memory   152

☐ The Structure of Memory   153

☐ The Development of Memory in Children   154

Memory Development in Infancy   154
Recognition   155
Recall   157
Constructive Memory   158

☐ The Development of Memory Strategies   161

Rehearsal   161
Organization   162
Retrieval   163
Other Strategies   164

☐ Factors That Influence Children's Use of Memory Strategies   165

Encoding   165
Knowledge Base   166
Efficiency of Cognitive Processing   167
Metamemory   168

☐ Summary   171

☐ Note   172

9   Social Cognition   173

☐ Taking the Perspective of Another   174

☐ Social Information Processing   176

☐ Children's Humor   179

Humor and Mental Effort   179
Humor and Cognitive Development   180

☐ Cognitive Bases of Gender Identity   183

Kohlberg's Theory of Gender Identification and the Concept of Gender Constancy   183
Gender Schemas   188
Children's Theories of Gender   189

☐ Cognitive Bases of Early Social Functioning   190

The Nature of Mother/Infant Attachment   190

Perceptual and Cognitive Bases of Attachment   191
Mental Models of Attachment   194
Can Individual Differences in Quality of Attachment Be Responsible for Individual
    Differences in Cognitive Competence?   195
☐ Summary   197

10 Individual Differences in Intelligence 199

☐ Approaches to the Study of Intelligence   200
The Psychometric Approach   200
Information Processing Approaches   206
Piagetian Approaches   213
Sternberg's Triarchic Theory   214

☐ The Heritability of Intelligence   218
The Concept of Heritability   218
Elementary Cognitive Tasks and Intelligence   219
Familial Studies of Intelligence   220
Scarr and McCartney's Genotype → Environment Theory   222

☐ Summary   224

11 Experience and Intelligence 226

with Marc T. Frankel

☐ Establishing Intellectual Competence   227
Institutionalization Studies   227
A Transactional Approach to the Study of Parent/Child Interaction   228
Parents as Teachers   231
The Home Environment   232
The Role of Family Configuration   238

☐ Modification and Maintenance of Intellectual Functioning   238
Modification of Retardation Caused by Early Experience   239
Maintenance of the Beneficial Effects of Early Experience on Intelligence   243
How Modifiable Is Human Intelligence?   245

☐ Summary   246

12 Stability of Intelligence over Infancy and Childhood 248

☐ The Relationship between Developmental Function and
    Individual Differences   250

☐ Predicting Later Intelligence from Tests in Infancy   251
Discontinuity with Instability   253

Continuity with Stability   254
Can Later Intelligence Be Predicted from Infancy?   257

☐ The Stability of IQ Scores over Childhood   257
Prediction of Adult IQ Level from Childhood Data   257
Patterns of IQ Change over Childhood   258

☐ Summary   261

13   Cognitive Styles   263

with Daniel D. Curtiss

☐ Why Study Cognitive Styles?   264

☐ Field Dependence/Field Independence   265
The Definition and Measurement of FD/FI   265
Developmental Change and Stability of FD/FI   267
Implications of FD/FI for Children's Intellectual Performance   268

☐ Reflection and Impulsivity: The Significance of Conceptual Tempo   270
Definition, Measurement, and Development of Reflection/Impulsivity   271
Implications of Conceptual Tempo for Children's Task Performance   274

☐ Convergent and Divergent Thinking   276
Definitions and Distinctions   276
Measurement of Divergent Thinking   277
Stability of Divergent Thinking over Childhood   278
Correlates and Consequences of Divergent Thinking   279
Is the Distinction between Convergent and Divergent Thinking a Distinction
   of Cognitive Style?   279

☐ Hemisphericity: Left-Brain versus Right-Brain Processing   280
Cerebral Lateralization   280
Successive versus Simultaneous Processing   281
Hemisphericity and Creativity   282
Is Hemisphericity a Cognitive Style?   283

☐ Summary   283

14   Sex Differences   285

with Marc T. Frankel

☐ Some Background on the Study of Sex Differences   286

☐ Sex Differences in Cognition   286
Sex Differences in Mathematical Ability   287
Sex Differences in Spatial Abilities   288
Sex Differences in Verbal Behavior   292

☐ Theories of the Origins of Sex Differences 293
  Gender Differentiation and the Effects of Prenatal Hormones on Cognitive Functioning 294
  Pubertal Hormones and Changes in Cognitive Functioning 295
  Patterns of Hemispheric Specialization 295
  Sex-Linked Inheritance 296
  The Interaction of Biological and Experiential Factors in Sex Differences
    in Children's Thinking 296

☐ How Important Are Sex Differences in Cognition? 297

☐ Summary 298

☐ Note 299

☐ References 300

☐ Author Index 333

☐ Subject Index 344

Children's Thinking

Developmental Function and
Individual Differences

1

An Introduction to Children's Thinking

Basic Concepts in Children's Thinking
□ Cognition □ Development

Issues in Children's Thinking
□ Stages of Development □ Nature and Nurture □ The Stability and Plasticity of Intelligence
□ Important Research Issues

Overview of the Remainder of the Book

Summary

Intelligence is our species' most important tool for survival. Evolution has provided other species with greater speed, coats of fur, camouflage, or antlers to help them adapt to changing environments. Human evolution is different. It has provided us with powers of discovery and invention by which we change the environment or develop techniques for coping with environments we cannot change. Although we are not the only "thinkers" in the animal kingdom, no other species has our powers of intellect. The way in which we think separates us from all other species and has altered the principles of natural selection that govern the evolution of life on this planet.

This remarkable intelligence does not arise fully formed in the infant, however. Because human intelligence is flexible, we require substantial experience to master the cognitive feats that typify adult thinking, and we spend the better part of two decades developing an adult nervous system. Little in the way of complex thought patterns is built into the human brain, ready to go at birth, although biology obviously predisposes us to develop the ability for complex thought. Our mental prowess develops gradually over childhood, changing in quality as it does.

Our impressive intellectual skills are not uniform among members of the species. Some people, at every age, make decisions more quickly, perceive relations among events more keenly, or think more deeply than others. Such individual differences in thinking have developmental histories. Some of these differences have their origin in biology, others in the environment. For some thinking skills these differences are stable over time. Young children and even infants who are advanced in some forms of intelligent functioning will continue to display this superiority as older children and adults. For other skills such stability is not observed.

Most books dealing with children's thinking have approached the topic primarily from the perspective of *developmental function*, the form that cognition takes over time. In the present context, the study of developmental function is synonymous with the study of *cognitive development*, and refers to age-related differences in thinking. What are the mental abilities of infants? What is a 2-year-old's understanding of numbers, words, and family relations? What about that of a 4- or 6-year-old? How do school-age children and adolescents conceptualize cause and effect? What types of jokes do they find funny? How do they evaluate the relative worth of two products in the grocery store? In the first part of this book I deal with data and theory pertaining to developmental function. What differentiates the book from most others is its second part, in which I examine *individual differences* in children's thinking. In the present context, individual differences refer to patterns of intellectual aptitudes that differ among children of a given age. How can differences in intelligence among same-age children best be described and conceptualized? What is the nature of these differences? Once differences have been established, to what extent can they be modified? Will differences observed in infancy and early childhood remain stable, or are some intellectual differences limited to a particular time in development?

Although the people who study individual differences in thinking have traditionally not been the same people who study developmental function (Cronbach, 1957), the picture is changing, and I will attempt, where possible, to integrate the two concepts. I believe that individual differences in children's thinking can best be understood by appreciating how the nature of thought changes over time. I will argue that factors that influence such differences vary as a function of when they occur. The same environmental or genetic factors that drastically affect the thought of a 16-year-old may have no apparent consequence for a toddler of 16 months. Thus, questions concerning how nature and nurture interact to yield a particular level of intelligence must be evaluated from a developmental perspective. Individual differences, like thought itself, have developmental histories, making the relationship between developmental function and individual differences and between nature and nurture dynamic ones.

In this first chapter I introduce the topic of cognitive development—how children's thinking changes over time. In addition to describing developmental and individual differences in cognition, scientists who study children's thinking are also concerned with the mechanisms that underlie cognition and its development. Is cognitive development achieved primarily by an expression of the genetic code, or does experience in a social environment play a major role in the form that cognition takes? Do children develop all of their intellectual skills uniformly, or do some skills develop at faster rates than others? Is development relatively continuous and gradual over childhood, or are there major disruptions in its course? These and other issues are introduced in this chapter. Before delving too deeply into these issues, however, I need to define some basic terms. These definitions are followed by a look at some of the issues that have dominated the field of cognitive development over the last century and other issues that are of concern to the contemporary scientist.

☐ Basic Concepts in Children's Thinking

We all know what thinking is. When used in our day-to-day parlance, it refers to what we do to solve problems or to ponder the great questions of our age and to what we don't do when we behave impulsively, making decisions before evaluating all the alternatives. Thinking involves the use of symbols, such as words or numbers. Yet, when psychologists speak of thinking, they use the term a bit differently. The impulsive, "thoughtless" act that resulted in the purchase of a 1958 Edsel may not have been wise, but it was not truly thoughtless. Also, the trial-and-error efforts of a 15-month-old girl as she repeatedly attempts to fit her doll between the bars of her crib may not be based on the symbols of language or mathematics, but they are a form of thinking nonetheless. Because the terms *thinking* and *thought* already have definite meanings to us, psychologists often use other terms to describe what goes on during problem solving or other acts of intelligence. The most frequently used term is *cognition*.

Cognition

Cognition refers to the processes or faculties by which knowledge is acquired and manipulated. Cognition is usually thought of as being *mental*. That is,

cognition is a reflection of a mind. It is not directly observable. We cannot "see" the process whereby an 8-month-old discovers that the Mickey Mouse doll hidden under the blanket continues to exist even though it is out of his sight; nor can we directly assess the steps a 7-year-old child takes to compute the answer to the problem $15 - 9 = ?$. Although we cannot see or directly measure what underlies children's performance on these and other tasks, we can infer what is going on in their heads by assessing certain aspects of their behavior. That is, cognition is never measured directly but is inferred from the behaviors we can observe.

What psychologists can observe and quantify are things such as the number of words children remember from a list of 20, the number of seconds it takes to identify well-known pictures or words, or the amount of time 6-month-olds spend looking at a picture of a familiar face relative to an unfamiliar one. For the most part, however, cognitive developmentalists are not interested in these overt, countable behaviors. What they are interested in are the processes or skills that underlie these behaviors. What mental operations does a 6-year-old engage in that are different from those performed by a 4-year-old or an 8-year-old? How does speed in identifying words reflect how information is stored in the minds of children of different ages? What kind of mental picture has the infant formed of the familiar face of her mother that allows her to tell it apart from all other faces? How are such mental pictures created? How are they modified?

This is not to say that cognitive psychologists are unconcerned with "important" phenomena such as reading, adding numbers, or communicating effectively. Many are, and they have developed research programs aimed at fostering in children these and other intellectual skills critical for success in a technological society. But the behaviors themselves are seen as secondary. What are important and what need to be understood are the mechanisms that underlie performance. By discovering the mental factors that mediate intelligent behavior, we can better understand that behavior and its development, which in turn can yield a better understanding of children.

Cognition includes not only our conscious and deliberate attempts at solving problems but also the unconscious and nondeliberate processes that are involved in routine daily tasks. We are not aware of the mental activity that occurs when we recognize a familiar tune on the radio or even when we read the morning paper. Yet, much in the way of cognitive processing is going on. Reading for most of us has become nearly automatic. We can't drive by a billboard without reading it. It is something we just *do* without giving it any thought. But the mechanisms involved in reading are complex, even in the well-practiced adult.

Cognition involves mental activity of all types. It includes activity that is geared toward acquiring, understanding, and modifying information. Cognition includes such activities as developing a plan for solving a problem, executing that plan, and evaluating the success of the plan, making modifications as needed. It also involves the initial encoding of a stimulus (that is, how a physical stimulus is defined so it can be "thought" about) and classifying what kind of thing it is ("Is this a letter, a word, a picture of something familiar?"). Both the macro-mechanisms involved in strategy deployment and the micro-mechanisms involved in the initial registration and evaluation of a single stimulus are examples of cognition.

Cognition, then, reflects knowledge and what one does with it; and one of the main points of this book is that cognition develops.

Development

Change over Time

Development refers to changes in structure or function over time. *Structure* refers to some substrate of the organism. Thus, structure may refer to actual nervous tissue, muscle, or limbs, or, in cognitive psychology, to the mentalistic knowledge base that underlies intelligence. When speaking of cognitive development, we use structure to mean some hypothetical mental construct, faculty, or ability that changes with age. For example, children's knowledge of terms such as *dog, violin,* and *liberty* could be construed as existing in some sort of mental structure, with the meanings of these words changing over time. Or one could hypothesize some form of mental organization that permits children to place objects in serial arrays according to height.

In contrast to structure, *function* is used to denote actions related to the structure. These include factors external to the actual structure being studied, such as neurochemical or hormonal secretions, and other exogenous factors that can best be described as "experience"—that is, external sources of stimulation. The source of function can also be endogenous, or internal, in terms of the activity of the structure itself. For example, function can refer to the exercise of a muscle, the firing of a nerve cell, or the activation of a cognitive process. With respect to cognitive development, function refers to some action by the child, such as retrieving the definition of a word from memory, making comparisons between two stimuli, or adding two numbers to arrive at a third.

Development is characteristic of the species and has its basis in biology. Its course, therefore, is relatively predictable. Development can be contrasted with *learning*, which also is reflected by changes in behavior over time. Learning, however, usually occurs over relatively brief periods, whereas development occurs over longer periods. Furthermore, learning is a direct function of specific experience, making it difficult to predict what any particular child will learn and when he or she will learn it, unless we know many details about that child. In comparison, all children go through development in approximately the same way at approximately the same time.

Despite this predictability, individual differences do exist at all developmental levels, so that, at any age, some children will be more advanced with respect to some cognitive skills than others. For the most part, developmental psychologists average the performance of children at a given age to yield a mean level or style of performance. This does not preclude the consideration of individual differences. Generally, although children of a specified age may differ in terms of cognitive abilities, it is usually assumed that the course of development is similar for children of varying levels of aptitudes. In other words, patterns of individual differences are conceptually independent of patterns of development.

Structure, Function, and Development

Development is usually conceived in terms of a relationship between structure and function. This relation is typically expressed in terms of an interaction, in that the activity of the structure itself and stimulation from the environment can contribute to changes in the structure, which in turn contribute to changes in how that structure operates. Function does more than just maintain a structure (that is, prevent atrophy); it is necessary for proper development to occur. Function is limited, of course, to the actions that structures are capable of performing. The result is a *bidirectional*, or reciprocal, relationship between structure and function, which can be expressed as *structure* ↔ *function*. Other theories propose a *unidirectional* relationship between structure and function. A strong environmentalist position, for example, would contend that function (experience) can directly cause changes in structure (that is, *function* → *structure*). In contrast, a strong "nature" view would contend that structure dictates function (*structure* → *function*), with development being seen as the unfolding of genetic sequences unperturbed by variations in environment.

The bidirectional effect of structure and function can best be illustrated with work in embryology. Chick embryos, for example, display spontaneous movement before muscle and skeletal development is complete. When embryonic chicks are given a drug to temporarily paralyze them for as little as one to two days, deformations of the joints of the legs, toes, and neck develop (Drachman & Coulombre, 1962). In other words, the spontaneous activity (function) of the skeletal structures is necessary for the proper development of joints.

With respect to cognitive development, the activity of mental "structures" facilitates or induces changes in the structure from which the activity emanates. This view is most clearly reflected in the work of the Swiss psychologist Jean Piaget. He believed that the activity of the child (or of the child's structures) is a necessary condition for development to occur. That is, in order for structures to change,

they must be active. It is the structures' making contact with the external world that is responsible, to a large extent, for their development. Such a viewpoint makes children important contributors to their own development. It is not simply the environment that is shaping children's intellects or a particular level of intellectual ability that has been dictated by genes, but an active interaction between thinking children and their world that is responsible for cognitive growth. (More will be said of Piaget's theory in Chapter 2.)

☐ Issues in Children's Thinking

Most of the issues central to cognitive development are issues central to developmental psychology in general. For example, stages of development, the nature/nurture issue, and the stability of behavior over time are of equal significance to social and personality development as they are to cognitive development. Yet, each area has its own way of expressing these concerns and of defining the questions that stimulate research and theory. An introduction to some of the issues at the heart of inquiry into cognitive development is provided next.

Stages of Development

When speaking of children, we frequently refer to stages. The "terrible twos" is a stage reserved for 2-year-olds, and we may speak of a stubborn child who refuses to wear anything but "Masters of the Universe" underwear as being in a stage, a stage we hope will be over by wash day. In everyday conversation, we use the term *stage* to refer to a period of time in which a child displays a certain type of thought or behavior. Stages during childhood are not permanent, but are transitory times as a child makes his or her way to adulthood. Stages are related to age. When we see children engaging in behavior appropriate to a younger child, we often say that they have regressed to an earlier stage.

The epitome of stage theories in cognitive development belongs to Piaget. Piaget proposed four major periods of cognitive development. The earliest, which he called sensorimotor, typifies the hands-on problem solving of infants and toddlers. All later stages involve the use of mental symbols, permitting children to represent objects and ideas via symbols such as language. Differences between these later stages are somewhat more subtle than the drastic difference between the infant and the symbol user, but they reflect striking differences in the quality of thinking just the same. When an apple is divided into four pieces, for instance, a 4-year-old will probably think that the result is more "apple." The 8-year-old knows that this notion is ridiculous.

Not all age-related changes constitute changes in stages of development, however. Flavell (1971) listed several attributes of stages, the first being that stages entail *qualitative* rather than *quantitative* differences. Another characteristic of stages is that the change from one to another is relatively abrupt. In other words, development is *discontinuous* and not *continuous*. Children's thinking within a stage is also proposed to be relatively even, or *homogeneous*. That is, all stage-related skills are integrated with one another, resulting in a child whose cognitive functioning is similar across a wide range of tasks. These characteristics of stages are now examined briefly.

Qualitative versus Quantitative Differences

Stages are based on the belief that children's thinking in each stage is qualitatively different from the thinking of children in earlier or later stages. Qualitative differences are those of type, or kind. These can be contrasted with *quantitative* differences, which are differences in things that can be counted. Contrast, for example, the differences in the way a 14-month-old and a 20-month-old play with a toy telephone. The activities of most 14-month-olds toward the phone are based on seeing how it responds to them. They pull on the elastic cord, pound indiscriminately on the buttons with their palms to hear the bell ring, and shake the receiver, swinging the rest of the toy around them. What are important to their play are the perceptual consequences of their actions on the toy. Within half a year another approach to playing with this same toy can be observed. Most 20-month-old children recognize the phone as a toy that represents something else in the adult world, and they behave toward it accordingly.

Although having few words, they pick up the receiver and "talk" into it, even though much of their talk is gibberish. They hold the phone to the ear of their mother, expecting her to play along and to say something into the phone. Dogs and cats may even be asked to play along with the phone game. The game can also be expanded to include other objects to substitute for the toy phone, such as a shoe or a banana. What underlie these differences in play are the ways in which children conceptualize objects and how they interact with them, and these differences seem to be qualitative in nature.

Problems arise when it comes to defining what constitutes a qualitative change. The difference between the perceptually based play of the 14-month-old and the symbolically based play of the 20-month-old certainly appears to be qualitative. The older child doesn't do "more" with the toy or do it faster than the younger child; the entire nature of the play is different. The same can be said for the difference between the 4-year-old and the 8-year-old, who hold different beliefs about the amount of "apple" as a function of how many pieces it is cut into. In other words, when one cannot see, on the surface, ways in which the different approaches to a problem vary quantitatively, they must vary qualitatively. Qualitative differences are subjective ("It certainly looks like a different type of behavior to me") and reflect our inability to describe the change in ways that can be more easily quantified.

Yet, does the surface appearance of a qualitative change mean that the mechanisms underlying development are also qualitative in nature? Remember that cognition deals with unobservables. Behavior serves only as the outward manifestation of what we are really interested in. Perhaps, for instance, changes in the amount of information that children can consider at any one time are responsible for the drastically different behavior observed in the 4-year-old and the 8-year-old described above. Four-year-olds know that 4 is greater than 1. They also know that any particular object can be divided into pieces and, in some cases, be put back together again. Yet, these are different pieces of knowledge, and coordinating them at one time requires greater memory capacity than they can muster. Or possibly it takes them so long to process one piece of information that by the time a second piece needs to be considered, it is too late. The first piece has been dealt with and is lost from their immediate memory. The 8-year-old, by comparison, can hold on to two thoughts at once and can think about things sufficiently quickly that the first item of information is still available by the time the second piece becomes conscious. Such changes in the amount of information that can be remembered and the speed with which that information can be processed are quantitative. It is possible that these or related quantitative changes are responsible for the apparent qualitative changes that are observed in overt behavior.

The issue of the extent to which cognitive development is qualitative or quantitative is much debated. Many argue that it is both (Flavell & Wohlwill, 1969). Surely many changes *within* a stage are quantitative in nature. A 30-month-old girl plays with the toy telephone in much the same way as the 20-month-old does, yet she uses more words and includes more aspects to the game (such as knowing how to dial and to mimic real phone conversations) than does the younger child. The two children are doing the same *type* of thing, but the older child is doing it better. More controversial is whether the underlying causes of cognitive change are quantitative or qualitative. Most concur that the transition from infancy to early childhood involves a qualitative change. More controversy exists concerning later development.

Continuity versus Discontinuity

Stated simply, changes from one stage to another are theorized to be reasonably abrupt. There is little in the way of a transition period from one stage to the next. So the qualitatively different behaviors appear suddenly and function at maturity from their onset. Furthermore, all stage-related skills make the jump at once. Note that as defined here, discontinuity refers to the suddenness of the change in observed functioning and not necessarily to the changes that underlie the intelligent behavior.

Homogeneity of Cognitive Function

Stage theories propose that all stage-related functions are well integrated, so that how children solve one problem is similar to how they solve other problems. A 2-year-old acts like a 2-year-old in all she says and does, and an 8-year-old is every inch an 8-year-old in all of his activities. In other words, cognition is relatively uniform, or homogeneous, within an individual.

Many developmental psychologists would agree with the general statement that cognition is highly integrated within a given child at any one time. But development is not quite as even as some stage theories would have us believe. It is not unusual for a child to excel at one intellectual skill but be average or even below average at others. Some 6-year-olds, for example, seem to know all there is to know about dinosaurs. They know their eating habits, their approximate size, and the type of armament they had. These same children may find it difficult to remember their phone number or to brush their teeth every morning. Another child may do very well at reading and the language arts in general but have great difficulty in mastering the basics of mathematics. Motivation is certainly one reason for some discrepancies of these types. Yet, it is not uncommon to find less glaring differences in many children. Children, as well as adults, often have pockets of expertise that are seemingly inconsistent with the remainder of their cognitive skills. Many stage theories have difficulty explaining these discrepancies. In general, there is substantial homogeneity of cognitive functioning but not quite as much as classic stage theorists propose. One of the tasks of researchers in cognitive development is to explain how development can appear so even most of the time and for most tasks and yet so uneven at other times and for other tasks.

Nature and Nurture

Historically, perhaps the central issue of all psychology has been that of nature versus nurture. To what extent are behavior, personality, psychopathology, thought, or patterns of development a function of one's biological constitution or of one's social and physical environment? As will be seen, however, the appropriate question is not to what extent behavior or development is a function of nature or nurture but, rather, how nature and nurture interact to produce a particular pattern of behavior or development.

In the area of children's thinking, the controversy is most apparent with respect to individual differences. The psychological literature abounds with studies, reviews, and theoretical statements on both sides of the issue. The genetic view held sway for most of the early 20th century. Leaders of the young American science of psychology such as Yerkes, Terman, and Brigham believed that the newly developed tests of intelligence accurately measured one's innate intellectual aptitudes. Influential educational psychologists such as Britain's Sir Cyril Burt interpreted the patterns of relationships among the IQs of people of various degrees of genetic similarity (for example, identical twins versus siblings versus unrelated people) as strong evidence that the bulk of one's intelligence was inherited (see Kamin, 1974).

As the mood of American society shifted in the 1950s and 60s, however, so did the best considered opinion of the nature of individual differences. Environment, particularly early environment, was seen as having hindered intellectually slow children. J. McVicker Hunt's 1961 book, *Intelligence and Experience*, fueled an already raging fire of professional concern for the underprivileged, leading to government programs such as Head Start that aimed to improve the educational standing of poverty-stricken children. By the mid- to late 1960s biology was given only lip service as a significant cause of individual differences within the wide range of normal intelligence.

The pendulum began to swing back, however, in the years that followed. The shift away from a strong environmental position stemmed mainly from research in neuroscience and behavioral genetics. Discoveries of genes predisposing one to depression and obsessive behavior, for example, made more credible the possibility that intellectual skills such as a facility with language or the ability to mentally rotate three-dimensional figures have a genetic basis. Similarly, the findings of recent adoption studies demonstrate that the likelihood of becoming an alcoholic is better predicted by one's biological parents' behavior (alcoholic or nonalcoholic) than by the behavior of one's adoptive parents. Such results indicate a substantial genetic basis for a condition that was previously believed to be environmentally caused. Surely

individual differences in intelligence can be similarly interpreted.

The pendulum seems not to be swinging as widely during this oscillation as it did in the past. The current perspective gives biology a large role in influencing individual differences for a wide range of behaviors, including those reflecting intelligence. But environment has not been relegated to a back shelf, waiting for another shift in perspective to occur. The environment is seen as playing a critical role in interaction with one's biological constitution. Stated another way, there is a *transaction* between children's biology and their environment.

At one level it is trivial to state that nature and nurture interact. There is really no other alternative. It's *how* nature and nurture interact to yield a particular pattern that is of significance. The currently popular transactional view holds that children's genetic constitutions will influence how they experience the environment. A highly active toddler, for example, will make it difficult for her mother to confine her to a playpen, resulting in a child who has a greater number of experiences outside of her playpen than a less active child. A child who processes language easily may be more apt to take advantage of the reading material that surrounds him than a child whose genetically based talents lie in other areas, such as the ability to comprehend spatial relations. Environment is thus seen as very important from this perspective; but it is one's biology that influences which environments are most likely to be experienced and, possibly, how those experiences will be interpreted. These issues will be discussed in greater detail in the chapters on individual differences, particularly in Chapter 10, where the heritability of intelligence will be explored, and Chapter 11, where the role of experience in affecting individual differences in intelligence will be examined.

The Stability and Plasticity of Human Intelligence

Given that a particular level of intellectual competence has been established, to what extent will it remain constant over time? Will a precocious infant become a bright 3-year-old and later a talented adult? Or is it more likely that a slow-witted 5-year-old will become an above-average high school student and a sluggish infant a whiz kid computer jock? Once patterns have been established, what does it take to change them? Can they be modified by later experience? How plastic, or pliable, is the human intellect?

The stability and plasticity of intelligence are related. Stability refers to the degree to which children maintain their same relative rank order over time in comparison with their peers in some aspect of cognition. Does the high-IQ 3-year-old maintain her position in the intellectual pecking order at age 8 or 18? Plasticity concerns the extent to which children can be shaped by experience. More specifically with respect to cognition, once a pattern of intellectual competence is established, to what extent can it be altered? Is our cognitive system highly flexible, capable of being bent and rebent; or once an intellectual pattern has been forged, is it relatively resistant to subsequent manipulation?

For the better part of this century, it was believed that individual differences in intelligence were relatively stable over time and not likely to be strongly modified by subsequent environments. These views were held both by people who believed that such differences were mainly inherited and those who believed that they were mainly a function of environment, but for different reasons. People on the "nature" side assumed that intelligence was primarily an expression of one's inheritance and that this expression would be constant over one's lifetime. People on the other side of the fence emphasized the role of *early* experience in shaping intelligence. Experience was the important component affecting levels of intelligence, with experiences during the early years of life being most critical.

Kagan (1976) referred to this latter view as the tape recorder model of development. Every experience was seen as being recorded for posterity, without the opportunity to rewrite or erase something once it had been recorded. Evidence for this view was found in studies of children reared in nonstimulating institutions (Skeels & Dye, 1939; Spitz, 1945). Infants receiving little in the way of social or physical stimulation showed signs of retardation as early as 3 or 4 months of age. These deleterious effects became exacerbated the longer children remained institutionalized, and they were maintained long after children left the orphanages (Dennis, 1973; Goldfarb, 1947). The finding of long-term consequences of early experience was consistent with Freudian theory, which held that experiences during the oral and anal stages of development (from birth to about 2 years) have important effects on adult personality.

Evidence of the permanence of the effects of early experience was also found in the animal literature. For example, Harry Harlow and his colleagues demonstrated in a number of classic studies that isolating infant rhesus monkeys from their mothers (and other monkeys) adversely affected their later social and sexual behaviors (Harlow, Dodsworth, & Harlow, 1965). Without steady interaction from other monkeys during infancy, young monkeys grew up to lack many of the social skills that facilitate important adaptive exchanges such as mating, cooperation with others, and play. Furthermore, their maladaptive behaviors apparently remained stable over the life of the animals.

Exceptions were found, however, and many began to believe that these exceptions were actually the rule. In one classic study, for instance, mentally retarded infants were removed from their overcrowded and understaffed orphanage to an institution for the mentally retarded (Skeels, 1966). There they received lavish attention at the hands of women inmates, and within the course of several years they were demonstrating normal levels of intelligence. In other work, isolated monkeys were placed in therapy sessions with younger, immature monkeys on a daily basis over a 6-month period. By the end of therapy, these isolates were behaving in a reasonably normal fashion and were able to become integrated into a laboratory monkey troop (Suomi & Harlow, 1972). Each of these studies demonstrates a plasticity on the part of a young organism and a resilience concerning the negative effects of early environments. (These studies will be discussed in greater detail in Chapter 11.)

Kagan (1976) proposed that one reason to expect

resilience is that development does not proceed as a tape recorder does. Rather, development is transformational, with relatively drastic changes occurring between adjacent stages. During these times the "tapes" are changed. Alternatively, methods of representing and interpreting the world change, so that the codes of the earlier tapes are "lost" to the child. The tapes of our infancy may still reside in our heads, but we've lost the ability to play them or, maybe, the ability to understand the code in which they were written. From this view, plasticity should be the rule rather than the exception, especially for the experiences of infancy and early childhood.

Note that from this perspective one would not predict that all forms of behavior or cognition are modifiable. If the cognitive ability under question does not go through transformations in its development, there is every reason to expect that early patterns will be maintained. That is, intellectual aptitudes that change quantitatively over time, and not qualitatively, should show relative stability. Similarly, if an environment responsible for establishing a particular pattern of behavior (for example, a nonstimulating institution) remains relatively constant over time, there is no reason to expect remarkable changes in children's relative mental functioning.

One thing worth noting here is that although the issues of stability and plasticity are concerned with individual differences in children's thinking, they are not unrelated to issues of developmental function. Kagan proposed plasticity for aspects of intelligence that undergo transformations in development. In other words, if development proceeds via qualitatively different stages, experiences at one stage need not have long-term consequences for functioning at a later stage. (They may, of course, but there is no compelling reason why they must.) Similar arguments can be made about the stability of intelligence. If a cognitive skill changes in quality over time, why should one predict stability of individual differences? Yet, if one believes that cognitive development is relatively continuous in nature, there is every reason to predict relative stability of individual differences. (These issues will be examined in greater depth in Chapters 11 and 12.)

Important Research Issues

In the previous sections, some general issues in children's thinking were introduced. In this section I briefly list some of the more specific issues that are central to the continuing study of children's thinking.

Changing Ways of Representing the World

One key issue that all theories of cognitive development must address concerns age differences in how children represent experience. There is more than one way to know a thing, and children of different ages seem to use different ways of representing their world.

Adults, as well, use a variety of techniques to represent knowledge. In providing directions to my house to a colleague over the phone, for instance, I must convey the information verbally, via a language code. But how is it represented in my head? I may be thinking of the route I take by generating visual images of the buildings and landmarks I pass and converting those into words. In fact, what I have done in the past is to sketch a map and then transform that map into words that can be understood by my listener. What the person on the other end of the phone must do is first interpret what I say. He must take my linguistic code and transform it into a form he can understand. He may keep it in a language code and try to remember street numbers and the verbal description of landmarks I provide. Or he may draw his own map, either on paper or mentally.

In the example above at least two forms of representation are involved. I must have some long-term representation of the route to my home. That representation may exist in any of a number of forms—visual, verbal, or even motoric, remembering the moves I make as I take turns and hit the accelerator and brake. In retrieving it, I must convert it to a verbal code so that I can convey it to the person on the other end of the line. That person must now *encode* this information. Encoding refers to the representation of a stimulus. At one level, my colleague could have attended only to the sounds of the words I spoke, encoding the acoustic properties of the words. If he did, he would probably be late for dinner. More likely, he attended to the *semantic*, or meaning, features of the words. Once a basic meaning had been derived, however, he might have converted the message to a mental (or physical) map, realizing that he would be better able to find my house if the relevant information was in the form of a visual image.

How children represent knowledge and how they encode events in their world change developmentally. Basically, infants and toddlers much younger than 18 months seem limited to knowing the world in terms of raw perception and their actions on things. There is little use of symbols to represent events. Once symbolic functioning does arise, however, it can be used in multiple ways, and these vary with development. In studies of audio-visual integration, for example, children are presented with an auditory pattern and are told to choose which of three dot patterns corresponds to the sounds they heard (Birch & Belmont, 1965). A child may hear "tap, tap, tap, [pause] tap," and be shown three patterns of dots: (1) •• ••; (2) ••• •; and (3) • •••. Which visual pattern goes with the auditory pattern they heard? Most 4- and 5-year-olds choose randomly. They may have counted the taps and then selected the first alternative that had the proper number. Older children have little difficulty with such problems. They can encode the auditory sequence as a 3–1 pattern and find a corresponding pattern among the dots. Note that there is no direct correspondence between the taps and the dots. One must be made. This process, according to some, requires encoding both messages in a verbal code, making it possible for them to be contrasted. Older children seem to do this spontaneously, but preschool children do not.

Most cognitive developmentalists agree that there are age differences in how children represent their world. They disagree, however, about the nature of these differences and whether they are quantitative or qualitative in nature. Can all children use all types of symbols, and do they simply use them with different frequencies? Or does representation develop in a stage-like manner, with the more advanced forms of symbol use being unavailable to younger children? Research and theory pertinent to

these and other issues related to changes in representation are central to the study of cognitive development, and they will be discussed in the pages ahead.

Changes in Strategies

Strategies are usually defined as deliberate mental operations that are aimed at solving a problem. We use strategies intentionally to help us achieve a specified goal. Strategies can be seen in the behavior of infants. Six-month-olds alter how hard they swing at mobiles over their cribs to yield slightly different movement from the inanimate object. Eighteen-month-old toddlers will deliberately stack boxes one on top of another so that they can reach the kitchen shelf and the chocolate chip cookies. These are no less willful strategies than is the rhyming mnemonic the sixth-grader uses to remember how many days there are in each month or the plan the 15-year-old uses as she plays all her trump cards first in a game of bridge. Yet, strategies do change with development, and children seem increasingly able to carry out successful strategies as they grow older. One of the key research questions in cognitive development concerns changes in the strategies children use and the situations in which they use them.

Children's strategies can be observed in simple games. For example, Mosher and Hornsby (1966) gave 6-, 8-, and 11-year-old children a variant of the parlor game Twenty Questions. Children were shown an array of 42 pictures of common objects and asked to find which one the experimenter had in mind. Children could ask only questions that could be answered with a yes or no. The pictures included objects from familiar categories, including food, transportation, and tools, but the objects could also be grouped on the basis of perceptual features (for example, things with red on them).

Mosher and Hornsby described two general types of strategies that can be used on this task. The first they called *constraint seeking*. Here, children attempt to constrain the number of alternatives by asking questions that eliminate large numbers of the pictures. Children may ask if the picture is in the top half of the array and follow this question by other location-limiting queries that further reduce the whereabouts of the correct picture. Alternatively, children may eliminate conceptual or perceptual groups of items. They may ask: "Can you eat it?" "Is it alive?" or "Does it have red on it?" Each question eliminates several possible alternatives. The second strategy Mosher and Hornsby described was that of *hypothesis scanning*. Here, each question tests a specific hypothesis. A child may ask: "Is it the duck?" then "Is it the firetruck?" and "Is it the chair?" Such a strategy is not very efficient, with each question being pertinent to only one item. The results of Mosher and Hornsby's study are shown in Figure 1-1. As can be seen, nearly all of the responses of the 6-year-olds were of the hypothesis-scanning type, whereas most of the 11-year-olds' questions were constraint seeking. Eight-year-olds fell nicely in the middle.

Mosher and Hornsby did a second study in which children were told a story and asked to derive a reason for the story's outcome. Children were told, for example, "A man is driving down the road in his car, and the car goes off the road and hits a tree." They were then told to figure out what had caused the accident, asking only questions that could be answered by yes or no. The pattern of results of this study was highly similar to that of their first. Older children asked constraint-seeking questions, such as "Was the man sick?" or "Was the weather bad?" In contrast, 6-year-olds zeroed in on the possible reason immediately. "Did the driver get stung in the eye by a bee and lose control and go off the road into the tree?" This question might be followed by a similar one involving a wasp or a blinding flash of light.

Other strategies, of course, are more subtle. What strategies do children use when reading, when attempting to remember the gist of a story, or when trying to solve an arithmetic problem? Can children who do not use strategies be taught to use them? Will children use them in some contexts but not others? Such questions have been central to research in cognitive development and will continue to be in the years to come.

Other Issues to Look For

Cognitive developmentalists are a varied lot with varied interests. Here are a few other contemporary

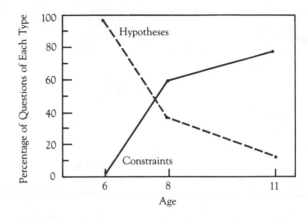

FIGURE 1-1 Percentage of constraint-seeking and hypothesis-scanning questions by 6-, 8-, and 11-year-olds (adapted from Mosher and Hornsby, 1966)

issues around which research, theory, and controversy abound.

1. To what extent do infants come into the world prepared to perceive and think? What perceptual and conceptual biases are built into the human brain that can be discerned shortly after birth?
2. How do age changes in the facts that children know about their world (their knowledge base) influence patterns of thinking?
3. Are developmental changes mainly changes in absolute limits or capacity, or are they changes in the efficiency with which information can be handled? Related to this question, to what extent does cognitive processing become *automatic*, requiring very little in the way of strategies, and how important is this process to cognitive development?
4. How does the social environment affect cognitive development, and how does children's level of cognitive development influence their social behavior?

Much has been covered in this chapter. You should now have some idea of what children's thinking is and what some of the important theoretical and research questions are. Most of these issues will be reiterated throughout the book.

☐ Overview of the Remainder of the Book

The rest of this book is divided into two major parts. In Chapters 2–9 I will deal with developmental function, or age-related changes in children's thinking. In Chapters 10–14 I will deal with individual differences within children of a given age and issues relating to the stability and plasticity of those differences.

The first two chapters on developmental function are devoted to major theoretical approaches to the study of cognitive development. In Chapter 2 I will describe the theory of Piaget. Piaget has unquestionably been the most influential person in the field of cognitive development, and any appreciation of contemporary research requires an understanding of the theory that, more than any other, stimulated interest in children's thinking. The chapter will include the principles and assumptions of Piaget's theory (his metatheory), although data describing his stages will also be presented. Because of the impact he has had on the field of cognitive development, his work and theory will surface continually through other chapters of the book. In Chapter 3 I will examine information processing approaches to children's thinking. They have replaced Piaget's theory as the most popular approaches to the study of cognitive development and present an important alternative to Piagetian theory.

The remaining chapters on developmental function will be devoted to specific topics of cognitive development. In Chapter 4 I will explore the perceptual abilities of infants. Chapter 5, on sensorimotor intelligence, will also be about infancy, but more from a Piagetian perspective. Topics will include infants' developing control of their own actions, imitation, and the belief that objects continue to exist even when they are out of one's immediate perception (object permanence). In Chapter 6 I will be concerned with children's use of symbols for thought. Although this topic could include most forms of cognition beyond infancy, I have selected only several topics to examine in detail. These include classification, the appearance/reality distinction, and children's number and early arithmetic concepts. Chapter 7 will be devoted to language and thought. In this chapter I will cover only briefly children's acquisition of their mother tongue and spend greater space on the more "cognitive" topics of communication, the developmental relationship between language and thought, and semantic memory, emphasizing children's acquisition of natural language categories, exemplified by concepts such as *animals, fruits, vegetables*, and *tools*. In Chapter 8 I will examine the development of memory in children, and in Chapter 9 the topic of social cognition. Social cognition is a reasonably new area of inquiry, although people have been doing research on the topic for years without having a name for it. More specifically, I will examine how developmental differences in cognition affect aspects of social development (such as gender identification and mother/infant attachment) and also how social and cognitive development are entwined, often making their separation for the purpose of study difficult.

The first chapter on individual differences will be devoted primarily to the assessment of them. How can differences in children's thinking best be conceptualized? Traditional psychometric approaches (for example, IQ tests) will be reviewed, as will information processing and Piagetian viewpoints and some contemporary alternative approaches to intelligence testing. The chapter will conclude with a discussion of the heritability of intelligence, or the degree to which differences in intelligence among people from a given population can be attributed to inheritance.

In Chapter 11 I will examine the opposite side of the nature/nurture coin, reviewing research concerning the role of experience in establishing, maintaining, and modifying intelligence. In Chapter 12 the stability of individual differences will be examined. To what extent will patterns of individual differences measured at one point in development (infancy, for example) be found at a later time? Is a bright, responsive 6-month-old likely to be a smart, verbally proficient 4-year-old? Current research into the stability of individual differences, perhaps more than that in any other area, points to the need to integrate concepts of developmental function with those of individual differences.

In Chapter 13 I will explore individual differences in what has come to be known as cognitive styles. Cognitive styles refer to differences in how people process information, tying it closely to information processing models of thinking. Rather than reflecting general modes of perception or learning as information processing theories of developmental function typically do, the cognitive styles approach examines relatively stable differences in children's preferences or techniques for processing information and how these differences relate to other aspects of thinking. In the final chapter, cognitive differences between the sexes are examined. Although there is some controversy over whether sex differences in cognition even exist, what is more controversial is their origin and whether they are of significant magnitude to have any real effect on day-to-day functioning.

□ Summary

The study of *cognitive development* involves an examination of how children's thinking changes over time. *Cognition* refers to the acquisition and manipulation of knowledge. It includes conscious, effortful processes, such as those involved in making important decisions, and unconscious, automatic processes, such as those involved in recognizing a familiar face, word, or object. Cognition cannot be observed directly but must be inferred from behavior.

Development refers to changes in structure or function over time. Development has its roots in biology, and its course is relatively predictable. Yet, within any given age or stage, there are individual differences in children's thinking. This book will investigate aspects of both *developmental function*,

the species-typical pattern that cognition follows over development, and *individual differences* in children's thinking.

Changes between stages of development are said to be *qualitative* rather than *quantitative* in nature. Qualitative differences are those of type, or kind, whereas quantitative differences are those of amount or speed. Shifts from one stage to another are theorized to occur abruptly, reflecting *discontinuity* rather than *continuity* in development. Stages require that children's abilities be highly integrated within a stage. Many (but not all) cognitive developmentalists agree that there is substantial *homogeneity* of cognitive function, although there is not as much homogeneity as is predicted by many stage theories.

The current perspective on the nature/nurture issue with respect to cognitive development and intelligence favors a *transactional* view, with children playing a critical role in their own development.

Stability refers to the degree to which children maintain their same rank order over time relative to their peers. *Plasticity* refers to the extent to which children can be shaped by the environment. For most of this century, it was believed that intelligence was relatively stable over time and that experiences later in life could not greatly affect patterns of intelligence established earlier. More recent research suggests that stability is found for some characteristics but not others and that human intelligence can be substantially modified under certain circumstances. It is important to consider the issues of stability and plasticity along with issues of developmental function. Among several other important research issues, the two most critical are developmental differences in how children *represent* information and the extent to which children use *strategies* to mediate their thinking.

2

Piaget's Theory

Piaget's Theory of Intelligence

☐ Some Assumptions of Piaget's Theory   ☐ Functional Invariants: Organization and Adaptation
☐ Equilibration   ☐ Stages of Development   ☐ Are Operations Reasonable?

An Alternative to Piaget: Fischer's Skill Theory

Summary

Notes

Jean Piaget (1896–1980) has had a greater impact on the field of developmental psychology than any other theorist in the brief history of our science. Trained as a biologist, the self-proclaimed experimental philosopher formulated a grand theory of intelligence that made children themselves, rather than their environments or their genetic constitutions, the primary force in the development of thought. Piaget changed the way we look at children. Following Piaget, we no longer view the young child as an incomplete adult. Piaget taught us that children's thinking at any given age reflects a unique way of interpreting the world. Development is more than the simple acquisition of skills and knowledge. The 4-year-old is not just a smaller-sized model of the 12-year-old who merely lacks the experience and knowledge of his older peer. Rather, in addition to quantitative differences in what these two children know (that is, changes in amount, degree, or speed) there are qualitative differences in how they know it (that is, changes in form or type). As a result of Piaget's work, it is difficult for us today to conceive of the child as a passive organism, shaped and molded by environmental pressures. At any given developmental level, children are seekers of stimulation who act on their environment as much as their environment acts on them. They determine to a large extent what experiences they will have and, thus, how their individual development will proceed.

Most contemporary theorists start with Piaget's theory (or at least phenomena brought to light by Piaget) and attempt to build upon the edifice he and his colleagues established in nearly 60 years of work. Many cognitive developmentalists hold great reverence for Piagetian theory because of the impact it has had and will continue to have well into the next century on the field of developmental psychology. A familiarity with this theory is essential for an understanding of cognitive development as it is studied today.

Piaget's formal training was in biology.[1] In the course of his doctoral studies on mollusks, he developed an interest in the philosophical study of knowledge. How is it that a species acquires the knowledge that it needs to survive? Piaget was interested in the acquisition of knowledge both in phylogeny (the

evolutionary development of knowledge in the species) and in ontogeny (the development of knowledge in the individual). It was while working in the laboratory of Theodore Simon, the co-inventor (with Alfred Binet) of the IQ test, that he decided he had found his perfect subject: the human child. In administering a test of reasoning to children, Piaget became somewhat disillusioned with the black-and-white nature of the instrument. The standardized form of the test obviously had many advantages, but its emphasis on the "right" answers minimized an understanding of how children were really thinking. What fascinated Piaget were children's incorrect answers. They were not random, for different children of a similar age provided similar erroneous responses, which they obviously had not been taught by adults (for example, a belief that the sun followed them as they were walking).

Piaget did not approach the task of understanding the development of knowledge as a traditional psychologist nor as a biologist. Rather, he created an experimental philosophy that sought answers to philosophical questions through empiricism. He called this new approach *genetic epistemology*. Epistemology is the study of knowledge and its acquisition. *Genetic*, as used here, does not refer to genes, DNA, or inheritance but is used as it was commonly applied during the early part of this century as a synonym for developmental. Thus, genetic epistemology is the experimental study of the development of knowledge.

In 1921 Piaget became Director of Studies at the J. J. Rousseau Institute in Geneva, and for the next 59 years he and his students delved into the issues surrounding the acquisition of knowledge in children. It is because of his long association with this institution that the phrase *Genevan psychology* is equivalent to Piagetian psychology. His studies ranged from observations of neonates to the development of abstract reasoning in adolescents. There are few topics in cognitive development that he did not formally address.

It should be remembered, however, that Piaget's theory is one of developmental function. His concern was with the development of intelligence in the species. Little of his work specifically addressed issues relating to individual differences, although he hoped that others would apply his theory to achieve a better understanding of mental retardation or to improve education. To assert that Piaget's theory is inadequate because it does not sufficiently explain individual differences in children's thinking, however, is akin to accusing Freud of not properly explaining cognitive development. In both cases, these issues relate to a theory the thinker did not propose. Piaget's theory (like Freud's) is broad and covers a great deal of ground, and he can be forgiven for leaving some areas of cognition for others to investigate.

☐ Piaget's Theory of Intelligence

Piaget was a stage theorist. He believed that cognition develops in a series of discrete stages, with children's thinking at any particular stage being qualitatively different from that which preceded it or that which will follow it. In other words, he did not view cognitive development as the gradual accretion of knowledge or skills. Rather, he saw it as a series of transformations, with children's thinking going through some relatively abrupt changes over relatively brief periods. Despite the discontinuous nature of changes in children's thinking, Piaget believed that the functions underlying cognitive development were continuous. New abilities did not just pop up but emerged from earlier abilities. Thus, Piaget hypothesized transitional or preparatory phases between stages, brief times when a child could have one foot in two qualitatively different cognitive worlds.

Some Assumptions of Piaget's Theory

Structures

Before describing Piaget's account of children's thinking at each stage of development, I must introduce several assumptions he made about the nature of development. One concept central to his theory is that of *structures*. According to Piaget, cognition develops through the refinement and transformation of mental structures (Piaget & Inhelder, 1969).

Structures refer to unobservable, mental knowledge that underlies intelligence and intelligent behavior. In a sense, all cognitive psychologists are concerned with unobservables and use behavior only to achieve an understanding of what goes on "in the head." Structuralism, however, is a specific orientation within cognitive psychology, and an appreciation of what Piaget meant by structures is essential for understanding his theory.

Unfortunately, it is easier to develop an appreciation of structures than it is to define them precisely in a way that is comprehensible to the uninitiated. Structures are most simply viewed as some enduring knowledge base by which children interpret their world. Structures, in effect, represent reality. Children know their world in terms of their structures. Structures are the means by which experience is interpreted and organized. For Piaget, cognitive development is the development of structures. Children enter the world with some reflexes by which they interpret their surroundings, and what underlie these reflexes are structures (or, more properly, schemes).[2] As development progresses, it is structures that change.

Brainerd (1978a) provides an analogy from linguistics that may make it easier to understand what Piaget meant by structure. Consider the following three sentences: "John kicked Bob," "Mary kissed Jim," and "Judy pushed Joey." Each has a different concrete (that is, observable) structure. However, each could be described as having a single, underlying abstract structure, namely an unmodified subject followed by a past-tense verb followed by an unmodified object. It is this level of abstraction that characterizes Piaget's structures. They are never seen but nonetheless underlie observable signs of intelligence.

Intrinsic Activity

A second central thesis of Piagetian theory is the notion that the child is *intrinsically active*. Children are not passive creatures, waiting to be stimulated by their surroundings before they behave. Rather, they are active initiators and seekers of stimulation. Of course, when Piaget spoke of a child being intrinsically active, he was actually referring to a property of structures. Structures are intrinsically active and must be exercised so that they can be strengthened, consolidated, and developed. Structures are most active when they are newly acquired, as any parent of a young child who has just learned a new game (such as rolling a ball back and forth with Daddy) can attest.

When thinking in terms of characteristics of children, we can view intrinsic activity as intrinsic curiosity. Children are not content with what they already know but seek to know more. Although a child can be enticed with external rewards to acquire certain information, such exogenous reinforcements are not necessary to motivate learning and development. The motivation for development is within the child.

Although there may seem to be nothing revolutionary in this position today, it was at considerable odds with the majority view of a generation ago. Even today, when few people question the intrinsic activity of children, Piagetian theory, with its emphasis on the child as an initiator, raises some eyebrows. When it is carried to its logical extreme, children who initiate interactions with objects and people in their world must play an important role in their *own* development. They are the movers and shakers of their own experience and thus are primarily responsible for their own development. This view is counter to traditional behavioral theory, which postulates the environment (and particularly the parents) as the major "cause" of intellectual development. It is also very different from most hereditarian viewpoints, which stress a particular level and pattern of genetically determined abilities, remaining relatively stable over time, as the primary source of intellectual growth. Piaget made the child not only the focus of development but also its major perpetrator. Therefore, the role of the psychologist is to explain how children's actions affect their own development. Environmental and genetic sources also play a role in influencing development, of course, and Piaget most explicitly believed that development is the result of an interaction between a biologically prepared child and his or her environment. Nevertheless, unlike most of his contemporaries, Piaget placed his emphasis squarely on the child.

The Constructive Nature of Cognition

Related to the notion of intrinsic activity is Piaget's belief that cognition is a *constructive* process. According to Piaget, when children act on their world, they interpret the objects and events that surround them in terms of what they already know. For Piaget, there is no such thing as objective reality. We interpret the world in terms of our personal perspective. Reality is a construction, based on information in the environment and information residing in our heads. Piaget believed that when we are confronted with environmental information, our interpretation process starts with what we already know. Our current state of knowledge guides this processing, substantially influencing how (and what) new information is acquired. In other words, the world is not out there for everyone to perceive in exactly the same manner. Knowing is an active, constructive process, an interaction between the environment and the individual.

Such a constructionist position is not unique to Piaget. Constructionist viewpoints have been adopted by numerous psychologists dating back to Bartlett (1932) and can be found in the contemporary work of researchers such as Bransford and Franks (1971) and Loftus and her colleagues (Loftus, 1975; Wells & Loftus, 1984). But Piaget's position has a distinct developmental perspective. If reality is a construction, children at different developmental levels must surely construct different realities. The same event experienced by a 2-, 7-, and 14-year-old will be interpreted very differently by each. This is true not only because of differences in the amount of knowledge possessed by these children (that is, quantitative differences) but also because of differences in how each can process information (that is, qualitative differences). For a 6-month-old whose rattle is hidden by a blanket, reality is that the rattle no longer exists. A 3-year-old boy believes that wearing girls' clothes or playing girls' games transforms him, temporarily, into a girl; and a 6-year-old is convinced that a baloney and cheese sandwich cut into quarters provides more to eat than the same sandwich cut into halves. An older child or adult believes none of this, but, for Piaget, reality is not an absolute but is a construction based on our past experiences and our current cognitive structures. (See the accompanying cartoon.)

Epigenesis

Piaget believed in the bidirectional relationship between structure and function (see Chapter 1). In other words, he believed that the activity emanating from the child (or the child's structures) influences subsequent development of those structures. This belief is best illustrated by his application of the concept *epigenesis*. Epigenesis has its origins in embryology. When used in that context, it refers to the well-established fact that an embryo's development proceeds by a series of transformations. New structures arise as a result of changes in the organization of earlier structures. When dealing with psychological or behavioral development, epigenesis refers to the fact "that all patterns of activity and sensitivity are not immediately evident in the initial stages of development and that the various behavioral capabilities of the organism become manifest only during the course of development" (Gottlieb, 1973, p. 8). In other words, development is gradual, with changes in the form that behavior (or cognition) takes occurring over time.

Piaget applied epigenesis to cognitive development, proposing that thinking develops gradually through a series of transformations. He used the term *genesis* to refer to the transformation of one structure into another, more advanced, structure (Piaget, 1967). A new cognitive skill does not arise fully formed. Rather, it has a history, in that the structure that underlies the new skill is a transformation of an earlier structure. Nothing starts out fully formed. To quote Piaget (1967):

> Whenever one is dealing with a structure in the psychology of intelligence, its genesis can be traced to other more elementary structures which do not constitute absolute beginnings themselves but have a prior genesis in even more elementary structures, and so on ad infinitum. . . . Every structure presupposes a construction. All these constructions originate from prior structures and revert, in the final analysis . . . to the biological problem [pp. 149–150].

(Piaget did not concern himself with development before birth but, as the quotation indicates, left that problem to biologists.) Thus, following the principle of epigenesis, the abstract reasoning of the adolescent can be traced back to the overt actions of the infant. Although Piaget's theory has come in for much criticism lately, variants of his epigenetic principle have been implicitly adopted by many cogni-

© 1985 North America Syndicate. Reprinted with special permission.

Children construct reality based on what they know and their current cognitive structures.

tive developmentalists (Case, 1985; Fischer, 1980; McCall, Eichorn, & Hogarty, 1977).

Functional Invariants: Organization and Adaptation

Piaget used the term *functional invariants* to describe processes that characterize all biological systems (including intelligence) and operate throughout the life span. He proposed two functional invariants: organization and adaptation.

Organization

Organization refers to the fact that every intellectual operation is related to all other acts of intelligence. Thus, one structure does not exist independently of other structures but is coordinated with them. Similarly, organization is used to refer to the tendency to integrate structures into higher-order systems or structures. For example, a week-old infant has a scheme for sucking and an independent scheme for hand and arm movements. It does not take long, however, for these two schemes to become coordinated, resulting in a thumb-sucking scheme. Thumb-sucking is not innate but represents the organization of two initially independent schemes into an integrated, higher-order scheme (even if these schemes become coordinated before birth).

Adaptation

The second functional invariant in Piaget's theory is *adaptation*. In its simplest form, adaptation refers to the organism's tendency to adjust its structures to environmental demands. Piaget defined two aspects of adaptation: *assimilation* and *accommodation*. Basically, assimilation refers to the incorporation of new information into already existing schemes. Assimilation, however, is not a passive process. It often requires that a child modify or distort the environmental input (hence, one source of cognitive errors) so that it can be interpreted by the child's current schemes. Assimilation does not reflect the mere registration of a stimulus but the active construction of external data to fit with the child's existing schemes.

Complementary to assimilation is the process of accommodation, which refers to the changing of a current scheme in order to incorporate new information. Accommodation occurs when children are confronted with information that cannot be interpreted by current cognitive schemes. It is obviously an active process, resulting in the modification of existing schemes as a result of those schemes' interaction with the environment.

Piaget stressed that every act of intelligence involves *both* assimilation and accommodation. However, some actions involve a predominance of one over the other. For example, Piaget proposed that play is the purest form of assimilation, with children modifying information in the environment to fit their make-believe actions. Conversely, he proposed that there is a relative predominance of accommodation in imitation, with children adjusting their schemes to match that of a model (see Chapter 5).

It is by these complementary processes of assimilation and accommodation that knowledge is constructed. In fact, Piaget viewed knowledge as an activity and not a state, per se. Furth (1969) has interpreted Piaget's position concerning the acquisition of knowledge by suggesting that knowledge "can be viewed as a structuring of the environment according to underlying subjective structures [assimilation] or as a structuring of the subject in living interaction with the environment [accommodation]" (p. 20).

As a simple example of assimilation and accommodation, consider the grasp of an infant. Babies reflexively grasp objects placed in their palms. This grasping scheme can be applied to a variety of objects that easily fit into the infant's hand. So, grasping the handle of a rattle, Daddy's finger, or the railing of the crib all involve (primarily) assimilation. The infant is incorporating information into an existing scheme. If this same infant is presented with a small ball, some slight alterations in his hand movements are required for him to apply his grasping scheme to this new object and to "know" it. These modifications constitute (primarily) accommodation, permitting the infant to incorporate new data by adjusting his current schemes.

Assimilation and accommodation also describe the functioning of older children. The 2-year-old who calls all men "Daddy," for example, is using the verbal label she acquired to refer to her father to refer to all adult males (assimilation). She must learn to restrict her use of the term *Daddy* to her father and develop new terms for other men (accommodation), lest she cause embarrassment to her mother. Likewise, many college students reading this chapter will need to alter their way of thinking about children and development in order to make sense of Piagetian theory. Piaget is not easily assimilated, and, typically, much accommodation is required before his theory is understood and appreciated.

Equilibration

Piaget stated that at least four major factors contribute to development: (1) maturation, the gradual unfolding of genetic plans; (2) the child's actions on objects in his or her world; (3) social transmission, the knowledge abstracted from people in the environment; and (4) equilibration, a concept unique to Piagetian theory. Piaget maintained that the first three factors are not sufficient to explain development and that development can be understood only when maturation, the child's actions on the world, and social transmission are integrated with equilibration.

Equilibration refers to the organism's attempt to keep its cognitive structures in balance. It is Piaget's explanatory concept for the motivation behind development. Why should we develop at all? Why do cognitive structures change? Piaget's answer is to be found in his equilibration model. When some information is encountered that does not match a child's current schemes, an imbalance, or disequilibrium, results. This disequilibrium can be thought of as cognitive incongruity, with the new information not quite fitting the child's current state of knowledge. States of disequilibrium are intrinsically dissatisfying, and there is an attempt to reinstate equilibrium.

How is this equilibration achieved? According to Piaget, equilibration is achieved by altering one's cognitive structures. That is, given the disconfirming information, accommodation can occur, with current schemes being slightly modified to match the environmental data. As a result, a new and more

stable structure develops. It is more stable because fewer intrusions will set it into a state of disequilibrium than was the case with the immediately preceding structure.

Although Piaget viewed the equilibration process as involving mainly accommodation on the part of the child, with only minor distortions, I believe that the process can be viewed as involving two other options. For example, the new information may be too discrepant from a child's current schemes, making accommodation impossible but also making assimilation unlikely. The alternative is to ignore (that is, not act on) the object, thus returning the structures to their original state. For instance, a first-grader given an algebra problem to solve will probably remain in a state of disequilibrium only briefly, realizing very soon that she does not have the foggiest idea what these symbols mean, and go on to something else.

Another alternative is to distort the new information by assimilation, making it compatible with the old structures. Here there is no qualitative change in the structures, only a possible broadening of the original schemes. Nevertheless, the environmental intrusion is dealt with effectively, although it may not appear that way to an outsider. For example, the same algebra problem given to a 12-year-old will probably be recognized as a math problem, and the child may apply his basic arithmetic schemes to derive an "answer." Such an answer will probably be wrong, but distorting algebra problems to arithmetic ones can serve to re-establish a temporary equilibrium. The equilibration process is schematically presented in Figure 2-1.

Let me provide one more hypothetical example of how the equilibration process might work. A 3-year-old in the bathtub is confronted for the first time by a bar of soap that floats. The child has no scheme for floating soap. Toy boats float, but soap sinks. This new information produces cognitive incongruity, or a state of disequilibrium. The child can distort somewhat the characteristics of the soap and assimilate it to her "toy boat" scheme. She also has the option of hiding it under the wash cloth and pretending it was never there. Her third option is to modify her current "soap scheme" (that is, accommodate), acting

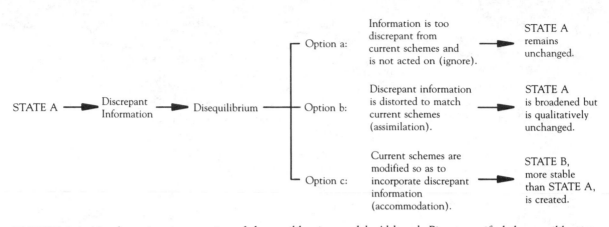

FIGURE 2-1 A schematic representation of the equilibration model. Although Piaget specified that equilibration involves accommodation (Option c), Options a and b reflect ways in which children may achieve temporary states of stability.

on the object so as to change slightly her knowledge of soaps and in the process incorporating this new information with other similar information.

Accommodation, and thus the attainment of more stable structures, is most apt to occur when the new information is only slightly discrepant from current structures. Information that exactly matches current structures can be assimilated into those structures, and information that is too different from what a child already knows is likely to be either distorted or ignored. Regardless, children remain active operators on their environments throughout and following the re-establishment of equilibrium.

Stages of Development

Piaget divided cognitive development into four major periods: *sensorimotor, preoperations, concrete operations*, and *formal operations*. A brief description of the major characteristics of children's thinking at each of Piaget's major periods is provided in Table 2-1. Piaget insisted that children progress through these stages in an invariant and culturally universal order. Stages cannot be skipped. So, from a Piagetian perspective, a precocious 8-year-old who has mastered analytic geometry acquired these skills by going through the same stage sequence as his much older adolescent peers. He just went through them at a faster rate.

This assumption of the invariant order of stages is a direct consequence of Piaget's belief that development is *epigenetic*. As discussed earlier, epigenesis refers to the fact that development proceeds gradually, with later developments being based on earlier ones. According to Piaget (1967), no structure in the psychology of intelligence arises fully formed. Instead, it develops from earlier structures. Thus, the abstract reasoning of the adolescent can be traced back to the overt actions of the infant. Children cannot display reasoning at the concrete operational level until they have mastered the prerequisites at the preoperational level. In a sense, development at earlier stages is all preparatory for development at later stages; "new" structures do not magically appear, nor do they lie dormant until the proper level of maturation has been achieved. Rather, in Piagetian psychology, structures are new only in the particular form or organization that they take. Each current structure can be traced to earlier and more primitive structures, which were necessary for the attainment of the more advanced structure. Piaget referred to this characteristic of development as *hierarchization*.

Sensorimotor Stage

The first major period in Piaget's stage theory is the sensorimotor, which lasts from birth to approximately 2 years of age (Piaget, 1952, 1954, 1962).

During the sensorimotor period, children's intelligence is limited to their own actions. Over the course of the first 18 months or so children develop some complex problem-solving skills, but they do it without the benefit of mental representation. They know the world only in terms of their direct actions (both sensory and motor) on it. For example, a 6-month-old baby moving toward a favorite toy will stop and act as if the toy no longer exists if it is covered by a cloth, even though the infant is watching as the toy is being covered. The baby "knows" the toy by her direct actions on it, and when it is out of sight, it is out of mind. Twelve-month-old infants are not fooled by such a simple ruse, but their knowledge of objects independent of their own actions on them is still limited. For instance, after dropping his bottle from the right side of his crib on three occasions (and having his mother retrieve it), 1-year-old Michael drops it from the left side of his crib. But he still leans to his right and looks all around to find the missing bottle. He "knows" the object in terms of his most recent actions on it, and that includes searching to his right despite having watched it fall to his left!

The description of sensorimotor intelligence is intentionally brief here. Piaget's observations and theory of intelligence in infancy have had such a profound impact on the field that they will be covered in a separate chapter, along with more contemporary research and theory into the nature of cognition in the first 2 years of life (Chapter 5).

The Development of Operations

The three periods that follow the sensorimotor stage are all similar in that the child has symbolic (that is, mental representational) abilities, but they differ in how children are able to use these symbols for thought (Piaget & Inhelder, 1969). As I have noted, Piaget labeled these next three periods *preoperations*, describing children's thinking between the ages of 2 and 7 years, *concrete operations*, occurring between the ages of 7 and 11, and *formal operations*, characterizing the advent of adult thinking beginning about age 11 (see Table 2-1). As the names denote, each period is characterized by *operations* or, in the case of the preoperational stage, the lack of them. Most of Piaget's work beyond the infancy period dealt, in one way or another, with the development

TABLE 2-1   Major Periods of Cognitive Development in Piaget's Theory

Period and approximate age range	Major characteristics
Sensorimotor: birth to 2 years	Intelligence is limited to the infant's own actions on the environment. Cognition progresses from the exercise of reflexes (for example, sucking, visual orienting) to the beginning of symbolic functioning.
Preoperations: 2 to 7 years	Intelligence is symbolic, expressed via language, imagery, and other modes, permitting children to mentally represent and compare objects out of immediate perception. Thought is intuitive rather than logical and is egocentric, in that children have a difficult time taking the perspective of another.
Concrete operations: 7 to 11 years	Intelligence is symbolic and logical. (For example, if A is greater than B and B is greater than C, then A must be greater than C.) Thought is less egocentric. Children's thinking is limited to concrete phenomena and their own past experiences; that is, thinking is not abstract.
Formal operations: 11 to 16 years	Children are able to make and test hypotheses; possibility dominates reality. Children are able to introspect about their own thought processes and, generally, can think abstractly.

of operations. Operations are particular types of cognitive schemes, and they describe general ways in which children act on their world.

Piaget specified four characteristics of operations. First of all, they are mental and thus require the use of symbols. Not all symbol users possess operations, however, as is apparent in Piaget's description of preschool children as preoperational.

Second, operations derive from action. In fact, they can be thought of as internalized actions. This should not be surprising given Piaget's belief that every form of cognition has its origins in earlier forms. With respect to operations, a child's overt actions for a particular cognitive function (counting, for example) serve as a necessary basis for the internalization of that process. Children first count on their fingers or physically line up red checkers with an equal number of black checkers, discovering through action that the one-to-one correspondence between the red and black checkers remains the same no matter where they start counting or how they arrange the pieces.

A third characteristic of operations is that they exist in an organized system. Piaget referred to this concept of overall integration as *structures d'ensemble*, or *structures of the whole*. Piaget believed that all cognitive operations are integrated with all other operations, so that a child's cognition at any particular time should be relatively even, or *homogeneous*. This assumption has met with substantial controversy, and data pertinent to this issue are presented in this and subsequent chapters.

Fourth, operations are logical, in that they follow a system of rules, the most critical of which are those of *reversibility*. Reversibility comes in two types: *negation* (or *inversion*) and *compensation* (or *reciprocity*). The negation rule states that an operation can always be negated, or inverted. In arithmetic, for example, subtraction is the inverse of addition. If 5 plus 2 equals 7, then 7 minus 2 must equal 5. Such a rule is obviously critical in children's learning of basic arithmetic. This brings to mind the 6-year-old who proudly announced to his mother that he had learned that day at school that 3 plus 2 equals 5. After praising him for his new knowledge, his mother asked him how much 2 plus 3 equaled. The

child answered that he didn't know; he hadn't learned that one yet.

The second type of reversibility, that of compensation, states that for any operation there exists another operation that compensates for the effects of the first. If water is poured from a short, fat glass into a tall, thin glass, for example, the increased height of the water level in the second glass is compensated for by a decrease in the breadth of the water.

In the sections to follow, a general account of Piaget's description of the thought of children in the preoperational, concrete operational, and formal operational stages is given. Some specific cognitive contents of these periods are also discussed, and both Piagetian and non-Piagetian research are examined. Many other topics relating to the development of operations in Piaget's theory will be discussed in later chapters, particularly Chapter 6.

The Transition from Preoperational to Concrete Operational Thought

Although based on symbols, preoperational thought as described by Piaget lacks the *logic* characteristic of concrete operations. By logic, Piaget meant that operations do not generate contradictions. In contrast to concrete operational children, preoperational children are greatly influenced by the appearance of things, and their thought is said to be *intuitive*. Thus, young children are less affected by what, according to logic, must be and more affected by what, according to appearance, seems to be.

An Illustrative Example: Conservation   Perhaps an example is the easiest way of presenting the distinction between preoperational and concrete operational thought. Conservation, the realization that an entity remains the same despite changes in its form, is the sine qua non of concrete operations. For Piaget, conservation was not just a convenient task to illustrate cognitive differences among children but represented the basis for all rational thinking (Piaget, 1965a).

The concept of conservation can apply to any substance that can be quantified, and conservation has been studied with respect to dimensions of length, number, liquid, mass, weight, area, and volume. In general, Piaget's conservation tasks take the following form:

$$A = B$$
$$B \rightarrow B'$$
$$A \; ? \; B'$$

In words, the equivalence between A and B is first established (for example, two balls of clay). Object B is then transformed while children watch (for example, by rolling one ball of clay into a sausage). Children are then asked to judge the equivalence of the transformed object with the initial, unchanged object and to provide a justification for their decision. Basically, children must realize that the quantitative relation between two objects remains invariant despite the perceptual deformation of one.

To illustrate, I describe children's performance on Piaget's conservation-of-liquid task in some detail (see Figure 2-2). A child is presented with two identical glasses containing equal amounts of water. A third glass is introduced that is taller and thinner than the original two containers. The water in one of the original glasses is then poured into the third, taller glass as the child watches. The water level in the new glass is, of course, higher than the level in the original glass. The child is then asked whether the two glasses have the same amount of water in them.

Most 5-year-old children answer this question by saying no, they are not the same anymore. There is more water in the new, taller glass. Ask them why this is so, and they will point out the difference in the height of the water. They will ignore the fact that the shorter glass is wider, and if this is pointed out to them, they will either dismiss it as insignificant or, in some cases, actually change their minds and tell you that there is more water in the shorter glass because it is so fat. They will admit that the amount of water in the two glasses was the same to begin with, and they do not believe that anyone is playing a trick on them. The difference in appearance between the water levels in the two glasses is too great for them to believe that the amount of water is still the same.

In contrast, most 8-year-olds given the same problem tell you that the two glasses contain the same

"Is there the same amount of water in the two glasses, or does one have more?"

Water is poured from one of the original glasses to a taller, thinner glass.

"Is there the same amount of water in the two glasses now, or does one have more? Why?"

FIGURE 2-2   Piaget's conservation-of-liquid problem

amount of water. When pressed to explain why, they say that all you did was pour water from one glass to the other and that you could just as easily pour it back to confirm equivalence. If you ask them "Why do they look so different then?" they will probably comment that although the water level is much higher in the tall, skinny glass, it is much wider in the short, fat glass and that the difference in height is made up by the difference in width. Children's responses to such questions are important, for in conservation problems it is not sufficient to provide the correct answer but also to provide a justification that involves the concept of reversibility.

This example demonstrates the intuitive thinking of the preoperational child. There really looks to be more in the tall, skinny glass. In fact, most objective adults would probably concur, although they know that this cannot be so. The young child's intuitive approach to the problem leads to some contradictions. What happens when the water in the tall glass is returned to its original container? Most preoperational children will tell you that the water in the two glasses is now the same, as it was to begin with. The contradiction, however, is one of objective fact; there is no apparent contradiction to the child.

Some cognitive discrepancy (disequilibrium) may be experienced by slightly older and cognitively more advanced children, who realize that something is not quite right but cannot figure out exactly what it is. For Piaget, these children are in a transition phase between preoperations and concrete operations. Their cognitive structures are thrown into a state of disequilibrium, and within a short time they will make the accommodations necessary to achieve conservation. For younger children no such disequilibration is experienced, as they assimilate the information to their preoperative schemes.

With a few, mainly laboratory-based exceptions, conservation is not something that children are taught. The notion of conservation develops gradually, and once it is acquired, most children assume that they have always thought that way. Ask most 8-year-old conservers if ever in their lives they thought the glass with the higher water level had more water, and they will answer no and often give you a funny look to think that an adult would ask such a question.

Piaget described three stages in the development of conservation. In Stage 1, corresponding to the preoperational period, children do not conserve at all. They cannot ignore the perceptual differences between the original and the transformed objects, and they assert that the actual amount of substance (clay, water, area, number, length) has changed. They center on a single dimension (for example, height), ignoring corresponding changes in a related dimension (for example, width). In Stage 2, which corresponds to a transition stage between the preoperational and concrete operational periods, children sometimes provide a conservation response when the perceptual differences are small, but they quickly switch back to nonconservation when the perceptual deformations are large. Children begin to consider two dimensions during this stage, but not consistently and not simultaneously. If one of two equal balls of clay is transformed into a sausage, for example, a child says that the longer sausage now has more clay than the ball. As the sausage is further lengthened, however, transforming it into a strand of spaghetti, the child reconsiders. The sausage is so

thin that the child now says that there is more clay in the fatter ball. This hypothetical child considered both the length and the thickness of the clumps of clay, but not at the same time. Piaget (1967) contended that this second stage is shorter than the first and in some cases may last only minutes. In Stage 3, corresponding to the concrete operational period, children consider both dimensions at once, demonstrate reversibility of thought, and generally display an operational knowledge of conservation. Although average ages for passing conservation tests vary as a function of what is being conserved (for example, length, number, liquid), Piaget's three-stage sequence has been replicated by other researchers (for example, Brainerd & Brainerd, 1972).

An operational knowledge of conservation does not develop simultaneously for all types of material; conservation of some substances develops before that of others. Piaget referred to this phenomenon as *horizontal décalage*. When children acquire the notion of conservation for one quantity—number, for instance—they do not realize that the same general principle applies for other quantities. Piaget asserted that the order in which conservation for different quantitative relations is acquired is constant across children. Thus, conservation of number is acquired before conservation of liquid or mass, and these are acquired before conservation of weight, which precedes the conservation of volume. This pattern of development has generally been confirmed by non-Genevan researchers (for example, Brainerd & Brainerd, 1972; Uzgiris, 1964).

Piaget's description of children's performance on conservation tasks illustrates the importance of the notion of reversibility. Preoperational children, he maintained, are unable to apply the reversibility rules of negation or compensation to arrive at correct solutions to conservation problems. Preoperational and concrete operational children also differ in other ways, however. Generally, Piaget described preoperational children as being more influenced by their immediate perceptions, more egocentric, and less likely to identify transformational relations between events than concrete operational children. Each of these factors is discussed briefly below.

Perceptual Centration versus Decentration Preoperational children's perception is said to be *centered*, in that they attend to and make judgments based on the most salient aspect of their perceptual field. They are highly attentive to particular portions of a perceptual array and are often unable to integrate various parts into a whole. In the conservation-of-liquid problem just discussed, their attention is directed only to the difference in height of the water levels, and they are unable (according to Piaget) to coordinate the two dimensions of height and width simultaneously. In contrast, concrete operational children's perception is said to be *decentered*, in that they can divorce themselves from specific aspects of a perceptual array and attend to and make decisions based on the entire perceptual field. Unlike their younger peers, they are able to consider two dimensions at once, in part because they are not so highly focused on one dimension that differences in the other escape their awareness.

The role of perceptual centration in young children's performance on conservation-of-liquid tasks is illustrated nicely in an experiment by Frank (cited in Bruner, Olver, & Greenfield, 1966). In this experiment, 4- to 7-year-old children were presented with different-sized, clear beakers. They were asked to pour water from one beaker (for example, a skinny one) into a second beaker (for example, a fat one). However, the second beaker was shielded by a screen so that the children could not see the water level of the second, wider beaker. When asked whether the second beaker held the same amount of water as the first had, most children gave conservation responses. When the screen was removed, revealing the difference in water levels, almost all 4-year-olds who had given a conservation response when the beaker had been screened changed their minds. They could not ignore the discrepancy in the size of the beakers or of the height of the water level and confessed to having been in error earlier.

Perceptual centration is not limited to young children's performance on laboratory tasks but is also reflected in their everyday thinking. Piaget (1969a) noted, for example, that preoperational children often use height as a means of estimating age.

Take, for example, the 5-year-old who told her 35-year-old, 4-foot 11-inch mother that she was the "youngest mommy in the whole neighborhood." In actuality, she was the *shortest* mommy in the whole neighborhood, and, if truth be known, one of the oldest among the mothers of her daughter's friends. (There is also the case of the 5-year-old who judged women's age to be a function of breast size, but that's another story.)

This age/height relation was illustrated in an experiment by Kratochwill and Goldman (1973). In their study, children between the ages of 3 and 9 years were shown realistic photographs of people from four age groups: infants, children, adolescents, and middle-aged adults. The size of the person's image in the photograph was varied, so that some photos were 3 inches tall and others were 5¼ inches tall. Children were given pairs of photos and asked to select the picture of the older person. Overall, the percentage of correct responses increased with age, but more interestingly, younger children were more likely than older children to choose incorrectly the taller, younger figure (for example, 5¼-inch picture of an infant versus a 3-inch picture of an adolescent). This does not mean that preschool children cannot evaluate the age of a person based on other factors such as facial characteristics. In fact, when children are not distracted by size and height cues, they do (Montepare & McArthur, 1986). Yet, when height cues are present, young children have a difficult time ignoring them despite often obvious age differences based on other characteristics (see also Looft, 1971).

Egocentricity Piaget described preoperational children as being, in general, more egocentric than older, concrete operational children. His description of preschool children as egocentric was not used disparagingly. By egocentric, Piaget was not referring to a personality trait whereby young children are self-centered and narcissistic. Rather, he used the term to describe young children's intellectual perspective. They interpret the world through preoperational eyes and generally assume that others see the world as they do. Their cognition is centered around themselves, and they have a difficult time putting themselves in someone else's shoes. Of course, they are less egocentric than sensorimotor children, who know objects and events only by direct action on them. Yet, they are more self-centered in cognitive perspective than concrete operational children.

According to Piaget, this egocentric perspective permeates young children's entire cognitive life, influencing their perceptions, their language, and their social interactions. Six-year-old Glenn, for example, assumes that all children in the first grade have older siblings and can never be the eldest child in their family. Glenn is in the first grade, and he has an older brother; therefore all first-graders, if they have siblings at all, must have older siblings.

Do not be misled, however, into believing that preschool children are so self-centered as to be oblivious of others in their environment. They can identify and empathize with the emotions of others (Hoffman, 1975) and realize that they possess knowledge that others do not share. In fact, research over the last decade has indicated that Piaget underestimated the perspective-taking abilities of young children and that egocentricity is far from an all-or-none matter.

The bulk of research on egocentricity has concentrated on two topics: (1) young children's abilities to assume the visual perspective of others and (2) communication, which will be discussed in Chapter 7. With respect to the former, Piaget and Inhelder's (1967) three-mountain problem served as the beginning of a long line of research. Children were seated in front of a three-dimensional display of three mountains. The mountains differed in size, color, and form, with each having a different object on its peak (a red cross, a snowcap, or a small house). A doll was then moved to different locations around the display, and the children were to select from a set of pictures the one that corresponded to the doll's point of view. Piaget and Inhelder reported that most children below the age of 8 years were unable to determine how the doll viewed the array but instead gave egocentric responses, choosing pictures that represented their own view of the mountains. That is, children stated that the doll saw what they saw.

Piaget and Inhelder's three-mountain task has been criticized as being unusually difficult, and more recent research has shown that children will show nonegocentric responding when provided with less complicated visual displays (Borke, 1975; Gzesh & Surber, 1985). Flavell and his colleagues (Flavell, Everett, Croft, & Flavell, 1981; Lempers, Flavell, & Flavell, 1977; Masangkay, McCluskey, McIntyre, Sims-Knight, Vaughn, & Flavell, 1974) have refined Piaget's original conceptions concerning visual perspective taking and proposed two developmental levels of knowledge about visual perception. At Level 1 children are able to determine that another person may see something that they do not. This ability is reflected in a task in which children are familiarized with a card having a different picture on each side (for example, a dog and a cat). The card is held upright between the child and the experimenter, and the child is asked what the experimenter sees. Children as young as 2½ years of age can consistently provide nonegocentric responses to this type of question, indicating that they realize that other people have different perceptions than they do. In fact, Rheingold, Hay, and West (1976) have observed the pointing behavior of toddlers, and they report that 18-month-old children will point to objects in their surroundings in order to direct an adult's attention to the objects. These young children wish to share their visual experiences, realizing that their perceptions are not necessarily the same as those of another.

In contrast to Level 1 perspective taking, Level 2 involves the knowledge that an object that is simultaneously viewed by two people may give rise to different visual impressions. At Level 2, children realize *how* another person may view the same object they are viewing, and they understand that the two views may differ. This realization is reflected by a task in which a picture is placed on a table so that it is right side up for the child but upside down for the experimenter seated on the opposite side of the table. The child is asked how the experimenter sees the picture. This is a more difficult task, and children typically do not solve Level 2 tasks consistently until 4 or 5 years of age. Nevertheless, the Level 2 tasks used by Flavell and his colleagues seem to be simplified versions of Piaget's three-mountain problem, and they indicate that the difficulty of the task greatly influences children's visual perspective-taking abilities.

States versus Transformations   According to Piaget, preoperational children center their attention on specific *states* and ignore the transformations between states. In the conservation-of-liquid example, young children fail to take into consideration the transformation of the water from one glass to the next, despite the fact that they observe it and possibly even do the pouring. Each event is viewed as a separate entity, and relations between entities are not considered.

An example can be found in a simple experiment in which children are asked to arrange (or draw) a series of sticks depicting "the successive movements of a bar that falls from a vertical, upright position to a horizontal one" (Flavell, 1963, p. 158). The correct depiction is shown in Figure 2-3. Although the solution of the task is easily accomplished by older children, preoperational children have considerable difficulty making (or sometimes even recognizing) the proper sequence. Each stick is treated independently of the others, making the notion of transformation from vertical to horizontal difficult. The preoperational child has been described as viewing the world as a series of still pictures, whereas the older child and adult see a movie.

Is Piaget's Account of Childhood Thinking Accurate?

Piaget's account of thinking during the preschool and elementary school years has stimulated more research than any other theory in cognitive development. As noted, however, there are considerable shortcomings in his theory. Piaget believed that he was assessing children's *competencies*, their actual abilities. The research cited previously into young children's visual perspective taking clearly demonstrates that they often have greater mental skills than Piaget attributed to them. Other researchers have shown that children who do not spontaneously

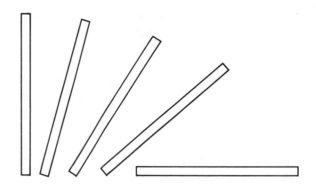

FIGURE 2-3   The falling sticks experiment. Children are to arrange the sticks to depict the successive movements of a stick falling from an upright to a horizontal position.

solve problems in a concrete operational way can be trained to do so. For example, although non-Genevan scientists have replicated the stages involved in the acquisition of conservation proposed by Piaget (Brainerd & Brainerd, 1972), many have also demonstrated that nonconservers as young as 4 years of age can be trained to conserve via a variety of techniques (Brainerd, 1974; Brainerd & Allen, 1971; Gelman, 1969). The magnitude of training effects is greater for older children (Brainerd, 1977a), with few studies revealing convincing evidence that 3-year-olds can be trained to conserve (Field, 1987). In a recent review of the conservation-training literature, however, Field (1987) concluded that 76% of all studies had successfully induced conservation in preschool children, with a smaller percentage of these studies demonstrating generalization to other materials and transfer over delayed periods (one week or longer).

One role of training experiments has been to test Piaget's assumption that development progresses best when children are allowed to discover on their own the principles underlying task performance (discovery learning), rather than being provided with explicit instructions on how to solve the task. The few studies that have made direct comparisons between instructional-learning and discovery-learning techniques in teaching conservation report larger effects for the *instructional* training (Botvin & Murray,

1975). Other conservation studies, using a variety of verbal and nonverbal procedures, have yielded significant training effects using a variety of direct instructional techniques (Brainerd, 1974; Siegler & Liebert, 1972; Zimmerman & Rosenthal, 1974). In contrast, studies done using the discovery method have been less successful in training nonconservers to conserve (Inhelder, Sinclair, & Bovet, 1974). Teaching conservation using discovery procedures is effective only for children in transition between pre-operations and concrete operations. Thus, Piaget's statement that training should be effective only when children are in a transition stage is confirmed if training is limited to discovery learning, which probably most resembles the conditions of children's real-world learning outside of school. When more explicit training techniques are used, even 4-year-old children can be taught to conserve.

One of the earlier successful conservation-training studies, which used neither the discovery method of learning nor direct instructions, was that of Gelman (1969). She hypothesized that one reason why preoperational children do not conserve is that they are attentive to the wrong dimension. If non-conserving children could be trained to attend to the proper dimension, they would display conservation. Gelman assessed 5-year-old children for their ability to conserve number, length, liquid, and mass. Groups of nonconserving children were then given training in which they were to select from among three stimuli the two that were the "same," with corrective feedback being given. Examples of the stimuli used in her experiment are shown in Figure 2-4. In the examples the three stimuli in any set can vary on the basis of several dimensions. In the right-hand column, two lines may "start" at the same position, may "end" at the same position, or may be the same length. The correct answer in each of these problems is based on length (or number of dots), with beginning and end points being irrelevant. Note that there is no explicit training of conservation on this task. The problem is one of simple discrimination, in which children must learn that the absolute length of the line (or number of dots) is the only invariant characteristic across the trials.

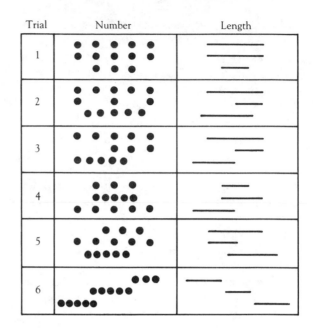

FIGURE 2-4   A schematic representation of stimuli used in a conservation-training study by Gelman. Children were to select the odd item based on the number of dots or the length of the lines (Gelman, 1969).

Children were retested for conservation several days after training and then again 2 to 3 weeks later. Control children, who received no training but only exposure to the test materials, were also retested at these times. Only a small percentage of the control children displayed conservation for any of the quantities (range 0% to 7.5%). In contrast, most children given training conserved the material on which they had been trained (number = 96%; length = 95%), and a majority of these children even transferred this conservation ability to other quantities (liquid = 55%; mass = 58%). What is equally impressive is that these children maintained their high levels of conservation 2 to 3 weeks later, actually showing a slight *increase* in conservation for their nontrained quantity (liquid or mass).

Gelman's study demonstrates not only that young children can be trained to conserve but also that one important component in conservation is attention to the relevant dimensions. Her research also shows that successful training on one quantity can result in transfer to other quantities. Despite the impressive training and transfer effects shown by Gelman and others (Brainerd & Allen, 1971), however, the training effects are confined to the laboratory. Will 4-year-old children who are taught to conserve in the lab be convinced that they have the same amount of sandwich regardless of whether it is cut into two pieces or four? Much recent work in cognitive development has been concerned with context specificity, or the extent to which cognitive competence is limited to a specific context (Chi, 1981). And future research should investigate the generality of conservation training beyond the laboratory and into the homes and schools of children.

Evidence that preoperational children have greater competencies than Piaget attributed to them have been reported for many of the phenomena that he investigated besides conservation. One of the most extensively studied has been *transitive inference*. Transitive inference is the process of inferring the relationship between two concepts or objects from a knowledge of their relationships to other concepts or objects. For instance, in a series of sticks arranged in increasing length (for example, A, B, C, D, and E), there is the implicit knowledge that any given element is both larger than the one immediately preceding it (for example, C > B) and smaller than the one immediately following it (for example, C < D). However, children do not necessarily know the relation between two items that have not been specifically compared. For instance, if D is longer than C, and C is longer than B, what is the relation between B and D? Although this is obvious to adults, it is not always apparent to children.

In Piaget's experiments on transitive inference (Inhelder & Piaget, 1964), children were asked to make judgments about a series of pairs of items; that is, which is longer, A or B? B or C? and so on. Children were then asked to make a judgment about two items that they had not seen together before (for example, which is longer, A or C?) and to provide a justification for their answer. Piaget reported that it was not until the advent of concrete operations, around 7 or 8 years of age, that children could successfully solve transitive-inference problems.

A number of researchers have questioned Piaget's methodology and his findings and have suggested alternative reasons for young children's failures on transitive-inference problems. The most extensive of this work has been done by Trabasso and his colleagues and deals with children's memory for the initial premises (Bryant & Trabasso, 1971; Riley & Trabasso, 1974; Trabasso, 1975). The paradigm used by Trabasso and his colleagues involved extensive training of all the premises. Sticks of different colors were used, and children were presented successive pairs of sticks and asked to judge which was the longer (for example, A or B, B or C, C or D, D or E). The children were later tested for their retention of the premises (for example, which was longer, the red stick A or the yellow stick B?). The children were then asked to make judgments concerning pairs of sticks that had not been presented together before (in the above example the critical pair would be sticks B and D). Given sticks B and D (the yellow and the blue sticks), which is longer? Unlike Piaget's subjects, children as young as 4 years of age in the Trabasso experiments were able to answer the critical transitive-inference question correctly, indicating that young children have the competence to solve such problems but that limitations of memory prevent them from displaying this competence under some circumstances.

Others have criticized Trabasso's experiments, contending that the extensive training given these children transformed the nature of the task, so that transitive inferences, as defined by Piaget, were not necessary. Rather, because the premises were overlearned, children had mentally constructed a seriated array and solved the problem by referring to this mental image, making an actual transitive inference unnecessary (Halford, 1984; Kallio, 1982). This interpretation is, in fact, supported by data from Trabasso's lab (Riley, 1976; Trabasso, Riley, & Wilson, 1975). However, this work also suggested that young children are not alone in taking an alternate route in solving transitive inferences and that even adults use a serial ordering strategy rather than a "true" transitive inference strategy. Furthermore, Trabasso counters that even if 4-year-olds are not truly making transitive inferences, they are forming a mental representation of a linear order to guide their performance, which, following Piaget, is an ability that is not supposed to be available to children until 7 or 8 years of age. Although Trabasso's interpretation of young children's transitive-inference abilities has been questioned recently (Brainerd & Kingma, 1984; Halford, 1984), most researchers agree that young children have greater cognitive competencies on these tasks than proposed by Piaget.

The Transition from Concrete Operational to Formal Operational Thinking

Concrete operational children are impressive thinkers. Given a set of data, they can arrive at an answer (generally) free of contradictions. They can solve reasonably complex problems, so long as the general form of the problem and of the solution are previously known to them. Their thought is directed to the objects and events that they are thinking about, and "thinking about things" suffices to get most people through most of the routine tasks of everyday life. However, most of us also recognize the change that takes place in early adolescence. Children are no longer tied to thinking about concrete objects. Their thought can roam to discover or invent objects, events, and relations independent of their previous experiences. Their thought can be applied inwardly, so that thinking is no longer restricted to things but can examine itself. As one Piagetian scholar has put it, "Concrete operations consist of thought thinking about the environment, but formal operations consist of thought thinking about itself" (Brainerd, 1978a, p. 215).

Hypothetico-Deductive Reasoning   The benchmark of formal operations is what Piaget referred to as *hypothetico-deductive reasoning* (Inhelder & Piaget, 1958). Deductive reasoning, which entails going from the general to the specific, is not, in itself, a formal operational process. Concrete operational children can arrive at a correct conclusion if they are provided with the proper evidence. However, their reasoning is confined to events and objects with which they are already familiar. "Concrete" operations are so named because children's thinking is limited to tangible facts and objects and not to hypotheses. Formal operational children, on the other hand, are not restricted to thinking about previously acquired facts but can generate hypotheses: what is possible is more important than what is real.

Thinking during the formal operational period can now be done solely on the basis of symbols, with no need for referents in real life. Although this ability may bring to mind a person whose head is perpetually in the clouds and who cannot carry on a conversation without getting into metaphysics, that was not Piaget's intention. Rather, he described a person who is not tied to actual facts in thinking but can postulate what might be as well as what is. The formal operational thinker can formulate ideas of things not yet experienced, accounting for the novel (to the child) and often grand notions that adolescents have about morality, ethics, justice, government, and religion. They are entering, cognitively, the adult arena and ponder many of the weighty issues of the day without having had to experience directly the things they think about. The theories of most adolescents are naive because of their limited knowledge; but for Piaget, these children are flexing their mental muscles, using their newly acquired symbolic skills to deal with "ideas" rather than with "things."

Hypothetical thinking is also critical for most forms of mathematics beyond arithmetic. If $2x + 5 = 15$, what does x equal? The problem does not deal with concrete entities such as apples or oranges, only with numbers and letters. Mathematics in general is based on hypotheses and not necessarily in reality. Let y be 22; or let it be 7, or -12, or 45 degrees, or the cosine of angle ABC. Once provided with a premise, formal operational thinkers can go on to solve the problem. They don't ask, "Is y *really 22*?" It is an arbitrary, hypothetical problem and one that can be answered only if it is approached abstractly, using a symbol system that does not require concrete referents.

Thinking like a Scientist   In addition to the development of deductive reasoning abilities, formal operational children are hypothesized to be able to think *inductively*, going from specific observations to broad generalizations. Inductive reasoning is the type of thinking that characterizes scientists, who make hypotheses and then systematically test them in experiments. By controlling for extraneous or potentially confounding factors, experiments lead to conclusions about nature. Inhelder and Piaget (1958) used a series of tasks to assess scientific reasoning, one of which, the pendulum problem, is discussed briefly here.

In the pendulum problem, children are given a rod from which strings of different length can be suspended. Objects of varying weight can be attached to the strings (see Figure 2-5). Children are shown how the pendulum operates (that is, by placing a weighted string onto the rod and swinging it) and are asked to determine the factors responsible for the speed with which the pendulum swings. The children are told that, in addition to the length of the string and the weight of the object attached to it, they may vary the height from which they drop the object and the force of the push they give it. Thus, in attempting to solve the problem of the oscillating pendulum, children can consider four possible factors (string length, weight of object, height of release, and force of push), with several levels within each factor (for example, three lengths of string, four weights of object). The children are given the opportunity to "experiment" with the apparatus before providing an answer. The correct answer is the length of the string; short strings swing faster than long strings, regardless of the other factors.

How might a scientist go about solving this problem? The first step is to make a hypothesis. It does not matter if the hypothesis is correct, merely that it can be tested and yield noncontradictory conclusions. This initial step is within the ability of concrete operational children. The next step is what separates the concrete from the formal operational thinkers: the testing of one's hypothesis. The trick is to vary a single factor while holding the others constant. For example, a child may examine the rate of oscillation for the 100-gram weight in combination with all other factors (that is, short string, high release, easy push; short string, high release, hard push; short string, low release, short push; and so

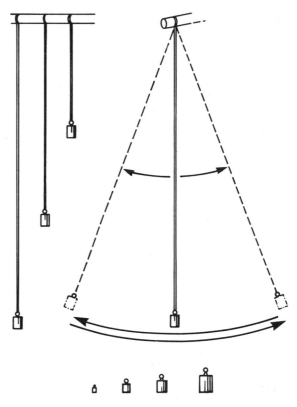

FIGURE 2-5 The pendulum problem. Children are to determine what factor or combination of factors is responsible for the rate at which the pendulum oscillates (Inhelder and Piaget, 1958).

on). This will then be done for other weights until the child has tested all of the various combinations. Table 2-2 (on page 34) presents the 16 possible combinations and their outcomes for a pendulum problem involving the four factors discussed above with only two levels for each factor (that is, long versus short string; heavy versus light weight; low versus high release; easy versus hard push).

Concrete operational children often get off to a good start on this problem, but they rarely arrive at the correct answer. Their observations are generally accurate (which is not the case for preoperational children), but they usually fail to isolate relevant variables and arrive at a conclusion before exhaustively testing their hypotheses. Children may observe that the pendulum swings fast with a short string and a heavy weight, for example, and conclude that both string length and weight are jointly responsible for rate of oscillation. According to Inhelder and Piaget (1958), it is not until the period of formal operations that children can test their hypotheses correctly, and, like a scientist, arrive at the only possible, logical solution.

Thinking about Thinking   A further formal operational characteristic involves the ability to examine the contents of one's thought. Concrete operational thinkers have available to them some powerful problem-solving skills. But, according to Piaget, they are not able to reflect on the content of their thinking to arrive at new insights. Concrete operational children gain knowledge from the outside world but cannot "learn" anything new by contemplating what they already know. In contrast, formal operational children can acquire new information as a result of internal reflection. Piaget (1971) used the term *reflective abstraction* to refer to "a rearrangement, by means of thought, of some matter previously presented to the subject in a rough or

immediate form" (p. 320). In other words, children can take knowledge they already possess and, without additional information from the external environment, reflect on that knowledge and arrive at a previously unknown "truth." Reflective abstraction is thinking about thinking, and it may allow children to more readily apply information they know to new situations or to discover alternative cognitive routes to old problems.

Egocentricity in Adolescence   One interesting observation by Piaget of adolescents that ties their cognition to that of much younger children concerns egocentricity. Egocentricity is usually associated with preoperational thought. However, Piaget defined egocentrism broadly as an inability to decenter, and he theorized that adolescents demonstrate their own form of centration. Piaget maintained that adolescents are concerned about their future in society and often with how they can transform society. Therefore, many of their grand social and political ideas may conflict with beliefs or attitudes of others (particularly people in authority). Adolescents may also believe that these abstract ideas are unique to them, making them impatient with the "stodgy and simple-minded" ideas of their elders. This view changes as the adolescent approaches adulthood, and many of us can identify with Mark Twain, who professed to be impressed by how much his father had learned between Twain's 14th and 21st birthdays.

Adolescence is a time when young people are trying to leave childhood behind and adopt adult roles, an attempt that often results in extreme self-consciousness. Adolescents' self-centered perspectives result in the mistaken belief that other people are as concerned with their feelings and behavior as they are, which, of course, serves only to increase their self-consciousness. Elkind (1967; Elkind & Bowen, 1979) has referred to adolescents' egocentrism as reflecting the feeling that they are constantly "on stage" or playing to an *imaginary audience*. This hypothesis has been confirmed in several studies, in which subjects' responses to potentially embarrassing situations and their tendencies to reveal aspects of themselves to others were related to

TABLE 2-2   Possible Combinations and Outcomes of Pendulum Problem

Weight of object	Height of drop	Force of push	Length of string	
			Short	Long
Light	Low	Easy	Fast	Slow
		Hard	Fast	Slow
	High	Easy	Fast	Slow
		Hard	Fast	Slow
Heavy	Low	Easy	Fast	Slow
		Hard	Fast	Slow
	High	Easy	Fast	Slow
		Hard	Fast	Slow

age and formal operational abilities (Adams & Jones, 1981; Elkind & Bowen, 1979; Gray & Hudson, 1984). Although there are some discrepancies in the results, the effect of the imaginary audience seems to peak in early adolescence and to decline as formal operational skills increase.

Elkind also proposed that the egocentrism of adolescence leads to what he called the *personal fable*, a belief in one's uniqueness and invulnerability. This belief is reflected in the often reckless behavior of adolescents and the assumption that bad things happen only to other people ("I won't get pregnant" or "I can get off the tracks before the train gets here").

Propositional Logic Piaget hypothesized that adults' mental operations correspond to a certain type of logical operation, specifically, propositional logic. Propositional logic is a form of symbolic logic that involves two or more factors (conventionally, P and Q), with each factor having two discrete values (for instance, true or false). Take, for example, two coins, a penny and a dime. Each coin has two and only two possible values, heads and tails. In flipping these coins we have four possible combinations: both the penny and the dime are heads (P and Q); the penny is heads and the dime is tails (P and not Q); the penny is tails and the dime is heads (not P and Q); and both the penny and dime are tails (not P and not Q).

These four alternatives can themselves be combined, resulting in 16 outcomes that are referred to as the *16 binary operations*.[3] Piaget postulated that these 16 binary operations correspond to *mental* operations characteristic of formal operational thought.[4] One of these operations, *implication*, is found frequently in human discourse and is expressed as "P implies Q." This means that Q is true if P is true, or P implies Q "if and only if no interpretation makes [P] true and [Q] false" (Quine, 1972, p. 40). In everyday language, implication is expressed in "if . . . then" statements. Tests of implication usually take the following form:

1. If there is a P, then there is a Q.
2. There is a P.
3. There is a Q.

Subjects are to determine the validity of the third statement, which in this example is true. Conversely, there is the invalid form of implications, and tests of this are usually expressed:

1. If there is a P, then there is a Q.
2. There is no P.
3. There is no Q.

In this case, the third statement is not necessarily true, for although P implies Q, the initial premise does not require that "not P implies not Q." For example, "If John passes calculus, then he will take his girlfriend out to dinner." Given this statement, the girlfriend can expect dinner if John passes calculus. Should John fail, however, dinner is not necessarily out of the question.

Based on observations from a variety of experimental tasks and the verbal reports of their subjects, Inhelder and Piaget concluded that concrete operational children are unable to use the 16 binary operations to solve problems, whereas formal operational thinkers can use each of the 16 operations as the tasks demand.[5]

Non-Piagetian Research into Formal Operations Many of the observations of Inhelder and Piaget (1958) have been replicated by others using either their original problems (Lovell, 1961) or modifications of their experimental tasks (Kuhn & Brannock, 1977). As with Piaget's research on concrete operations, however, subsequent research has indicated that Piaget underestimated children's intellectual abilities in many ways. Children much younger than the ages proposed by Inhelder and Piaget have been shown to display formal operational reasoning under some conditions. Subtle differences in how the instructions are given or in the task materials influence the likelihood of children successfully performing formal operational tasks (Danner & Day, 1977; Slater & Kingston, 1981), and a number of researchers have demonstrated that concrete operational children can be trained to solve formal operational problems (Siegler, Robinson, Liebert, & Liebert, 1973; Stone & Day, 1978). In general, research has indicated that young children have greater competencies with respect to some formal operational abilities than Inhelder and Piaget originally proposed, although they display these competencies only under limited conditions.

The restricted nature of young children's formal operational abilities is illustrated in a study by Hawkins, Pea, Glick, and Scribner (1984). They presented verbal syllogisms to 4- and 5-year-old children. Syllogisms are problems that require deductive reasoning and are of the form:

1. Socrates was a man.
2. All men are mortal.
3. Socrates was mortal.

Subjects are to discern the truth of the last statement, given the first two. Piaget proposed that the solving of syllogisms requires formal operational abilities in that the conclusions drawn from the premises "must be held to be true only by reason of the premises and quite independently of the empirical truth of these premises" (Piaget, 1969b, p. 32). Hawkins and his colleagues presented preschool children with syllogisms of three types: (1) *fantasy*, involving imaginary characters for which the children had no knowledge (for example, every banga is purple); (2) *congruent*, in which the premises were consistent with children's world knowledge (for example, bears have big teeth); and (3) *incongruent*, in which the premises were in contradiction to the children's knowledge (for example, glasses bounce when they fall). Examples of each of these three types of problems are as follows (Hawkins et al., 1984):

Fantasy Syllogisms

Every banga is purple.
Purple animals sneeze at people.
Do bangas sneeze at people?

Merds laugh when they're happy.
Animals that laugh don't like mushrooms.
Do merds like mushrooms?

Congruent Syllogisms

Bears have big teeth
Animals with big teeth can't read books.
Can bears read books?

Rabbits never bite.
Cuddly is a rabbit.
Does Cuddly bite?

Incongruent Syllogisms

Glasses bounce when they fall.
Everything that bounces is made of rubber.
Are glasses made of rubber?

Birds can fly.
Everything that can fly has wheels.
Do birds have wheels?

The children were given eight problems of each type, with some children being presented the set of fantasy problems first and others being presented the fantasy problems second or third.

In keeping with the theorizing of Piaget, children consistently failed the incongruent problems (13% correct), although their performance was very high on the congruent problems (94% correct). However, children can answer the congruent questions correctly without having to make any deductions, merely by assessing the truth of the statement with respect to their previous knowledge ("Can bears read books?" Of course not!). In fact, when children's justifications of their answers to the congruent problems were examined, most of them (81%) were described as *empirical*, with reference being made to their practical world knowledge. Very few of their responses (10%) were classified as *theoretical*, in which reference was made only to the information presented in the problem.

In contrast to the congruent and incongruent problems, answers to the fantasy problems are independent of children's past knowledge, for they pose questions about hypothetical characters, requiring, it would seem, hypothetico-deductive reasoning. Children's performance on the fantasy problems was very high, particularly when these problems were presented first (94% correct). The percentage of correct answers was lower on these problems when the congruent or incongruent problems preceded them (66% correct). Furthermore, children's justifications on the fantasy problems were likely to be classified as theoretical when the fantasy problems were presented first (58% theoretical), although nontheoretical explanations predominated when the fantasy problems were presented later in the session (92% nontheoretical explanations).

These findings indicate that 4- and 5-year-old children possess some rudiments of hypothetico-deductive reasoning, postulated by Piaget not to be available until around 11 years of age. However, this study also illustrates the tenuous nature of young children's hypothetical reasoning. They consistently failed the incongruous problems, being unable to think in terms of the hypothetical when the premises conflicted with their world knowledge. Yet, when imaginary characters were used, young children's responses and their justifications were indicative of true hypothetical deductions. Nevertheless, children were easily biased away from such deductions when the fantasy problems were preceded by the congruent or incongruent problems. Obviously, hypothetico-deductive reasoning is not a well-established ability in young children and is displayed only under optimal conditions. The findings of this study do not refute Piaget's observations of adolescent thought, but they do indicate that, under some circumstances, aspects of formal operational thinking can be found much earlier than suggested by Inhelder and Piaget.

In other situations, however, research has shown that Piaget's account of formal operations greatly *overestimates* how adults actually think. For example, Paris (1973) assessed the ability of children and adults to comprehend statements of propositional logic, including "If . . . then" implication statements, as discussed earlier. Paris reported that even 7-year-olds could answer correctly valid implications, for example: "If there is a P, then there is a Q. There is a P. There is a Q" (true or false?). However, both 7-year-olds and adults performed poorly on invalid implications, for example: "If there is a P, then there is a Q. There is no P. There is a Q" (true or false?). That is, not only can concrete operational children not solve the invalid form of implications, but neither can older children or adults. In other research, Kuhn, Langer, Kohlberg, and Haan (1977) interviewed 265 adolescents and adults who were participants in a longitudinal study. They administered a battery of formal operational tasks adapted

from Inhelder and Piaget. They reported that only about 30% of adults were classified as having completely achieved formal operations. Most adults were classified as being transitional between concrete and formal operations, with 15% demonstrating no formal operational abilities.

A study by Capon and Kuhn (1979) illustrates adults' tendencies to use formal operational abilities in a practical task. The researchers interviewed 50 women in a supermarket and asked them to judge which of two sizes of the same product was the better buy. One task involved two bottles of garlic powder: a smaller bottle, containing 1.25 ounces (35 grams) and selling for 41 cents, and a larger bottle, containing 2.37 ounces (67 grams) and selling for 77 cents. The women were provided with pencil and paper to use if they wished and were asked to justify their explanations. The most direct way to arrive at the correct answer is to compute the price per ounce (or gram) for each product and compare the two. This involves reasoning about proportions, which Inhelder and Piaget (1958) said was a scheme characteristic of formal operations. Fewer than 30% of the women used a proportional reasoning strategy, and at least 50% of the women used a strategy that yielded, at best, inconclusive evidence and was just as likely to be wrong as right. For instance, some women used a subtraction strategy, saying, for example, "With the bigger one you get 32 more grams for 36 more cents" and concluding that the bigger one was thus the better buy. Others merely relied on their past experiences, making statements such as, "The big one must be cheaper" without providing any justification for the statement. In general, formal operational reasoning was not observed for a majority of women on an everyday task. This does not mean that these adults might not have displayed formal reasoning under some other conditions, but it does suggest that formal operations are not a typical characteristic of adult thought in general.

Piaget's picture of adult intelligence is one of a reasonable, systematic, and logical thinker. This picture is shared by few psychologists who study adult cognition. We adults, in general, are not nearly so logical and systematic in our thinking as Piaget would have us be. We take shortcuts, make estimations, and arrive at conclusions before exhausting all the possible combinations of elements or considering all the facts. Formal operations as described by Piaget may reflect the best adults can do, but they fail to capture how grown-ups deal with real-world problems on a daily basis. To quote Wason and Johnson-Laird (1972): "At best, we can all think like logicians: at worst, logicians all think like us" (p. 245).

Are Operations Reasonable?

In this chapter I have discussed Piaget's account of operationality and examined some non-Piagetian research concerning the development of concrete and formal operations. How has Piaget's theory stood up to the onslaught of 50 years of research? Is Piaget's view of operations and their development reasonable?

What is implied by the concept *operations*? First of all, Piaget asserted that operations represent mentalistic and logical functioning. Operations are not available to the preschool-age child, and logical operations change in form between the concrete and formal operational periods. In other words, the development of operationality represents qualitative changes in thinking. The pattern of cognitive change that Piaget observed between the ages of 2 and 15 years has been replicated by many researchers using Piaget's original tasks. But others have reported that preoperational children can think "logically" (even hypothetically) under certain stimulus and instructional conditions. Are these children using primitive forms of operations, or are they circumventing the problem by using nonoperational techniques to arrive at "logical" answers? If the latter, might this not reflect an artificial solution to the problem and one that is not representative of the normal course of development? Or might it not reflect the possibility that even operational children do not use operations to solve these problems but, like their younger counterparts, find alternative paths without the need for logic? This seems to be the interpretation with respect to transitive inferences (Trabasso et al., 1975).

Second, the notion of operations implies substantial integration. Piaget's *structures of the whole* principle is concerned specifically with the organization of

operations. Discrepancies in cognitive abilities are found both within a given child and among different children, indicating that cognitive functioning is not so homogeneous as Piaget proposed. A particular child may display a highly egocentric attitude in one situation yet show impressive perspective-taking skills in another.

Such contradictory findings question Piaget's notion of stages, periods of development that represent qualitatively unique forms of thinking, with transitions between stages reflecting discontinuities in development. (See Brainerd, 1978b, and related commentaries for a thorough discussion of criticisms of Piaget's stage theory.) As Flavell (1978a) has written: "However much we may wish it otherwise, human cognitive growth may simply be too contingent, multiform, and heterogeneous—too variegated in developmental mechanisms, routes, and rates—to be accurately characterized by any single stage theory of the Piagetian kind" (p. 187). In response, a number of theorists have proposed that changes in children's thinking over time are primarily quantitative, with transitions from simpler to more complex forms of thinking reflecting continuities in development (Carey, 1985a; Klahr & Wallace, 1976; Trabasso, 1975). Others have maintained a belief in qualitative, stage-like developments in cognition but not in the lock-step way that Piaget proposed (Case, 1985; Fischer, 1980). It seems clear that stages of development are not as discrete and clear-cut as Piaget hypothesized. But what evidence do we need before we are willing to state that there are discontinuities in development? How stage-like is development?

Technically, to qualify for a stage, development must meet certain criteria. Among these criteria are that differences among stages are qualitative, that there is substantial homogeneity of functioning within a stage, and that the transition from one stage to the next is abrupt, with each cognitive item functioning at 100% efficiency as soon as it is functioning at all (see Chapter 1, Flavell, 1971). From the preceding discussion it seems apparent that development through the childhood years does not fit this definition of stages. Most notably, there is less homogeneity of function than stages require.

However, there may be more homogeneity of cognitive function, and thus more stage-like qualities to development, than initially meets the experimentalist's eye. This possibility has been discussed by Flavell (1982). First of all, a certain level of homogeneity is imposed by limits in children's information processing capacity. Although a given child's cognitive skills may vary, there is a limit of cognitive sophistication beyond which he or she cannot function. This limit, presumably dictated by maturational factors, expands with age, but at any given point in development it restricts the range of cognitive competencies that a child can display (see Chapter 3).

Second, the cognitive tasks that psychologists tend to study are relatively demanding, and such challenging tasks may yield greater heterogeneity of function than the more mundane tasks that constitute the vast majority of children's daily cognitive encounters. Children's cognition appears to be relatively even to an unobtrusive observer because most of the things children do are highly routine. It is primarily when children's cognitive competencies are pushed to their limits that we see unevenness in their abilities.

Third, there may be more homogeneity of function with respect to the *initial* cognitive treatment of a problem and more variability in how information is handled later in the task. Given a set of written problems to solve, for example, most adults and older children begin by reading them, attempting to discern what the nature of the task is. What happens after this "reading stage" is more likely to vary among individuals as a function of many factors. Similarly, when faced with a very difficult problem, children may adopt a "fallback" strategy that they use consistently. In the visual perspective-taking studies of Piaget and Inhelder (1967), for example, children may provide egocentric responses when the task's demands become too much for them to handle. They do not know what the answer is and so consistently give egocentric responses. I know college students who take multiple-choice exams in a similar fashion (for example, "When in doubt, guess C").

How stage-like cognitive development seems to be a function of where one looks for it. Nevertheless,

most developmental psychologists today believe that Piaget's account of operations attributes more stage-like properties to development than the data warrant. A fair statement concerning cognitive development is that average cognitive competencies increase with age, although there is a substantial range of cognitive abilities that children of any given age can display. Most of the cognitive functioning of children occurs within a relatively narrow range of competencies, with this range possibly broadening with age. However, children can display cognitive abilities substantially above (or below) the average, but only under optimal (or restrictive) conditions. This hypothetical relationship between age and range of cognitive abilities is graphically shown in Figure 2-6.

In sum, Piaget's account of the development of operations does not fully capture what actually occurs in development. New theories are needed to account for some of the discrepancies that researchers have found in Piaget's theory. Some of these theories will be discussed in Chapter 3, on information processing approaches to cognitive development. Before looking at these approaches, however, I would like to discuss a contemporary neo-Piagetian theory of cognitive development that ad-

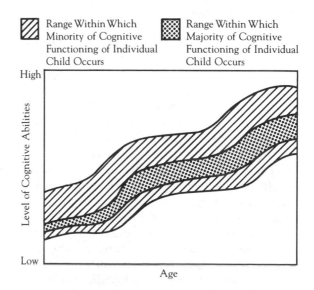

FIGURE 2-6 Hypothetical relationship between children's ages and their levels of cognitive ability.

dresses explicitly the issue of why development is often so uneven, the *skill theory* of Kurt Fischer.

☐ An Alternative to Piaget: Fischer's Skill Theory

Fischer (1980; Fischer & Bullock, 1981; Fischer & Pipp, 1984) has developed a theory of cognitive development that adopts many of the assumptions of Piaget's theory while incorporating many of the assumptions of traditional behavioral theories such as Skinner's. Fischer takes as his starting point the position that development is jointly defined by the organism and the environment. Piaget, of course, made the same assumption; but he gave the environment only a small role in affecting development. It is the child in active interaction with the environment who, for Piaget, is the principal "cause" of development. Fischer takes the environment more seriously than did Piaget. The consequence is a theory that is more equally weighted with respect to the contributions of the child and the environment in influencing development and one that predicts greater heterogeneity of cognitive functioning than was proposed by Piaget. (Other aspects of Fischer's theory will be examined in Chapter 6.)

Fischer theorizes that children develop *skills*, which are sets of actions (both physical and mental) by which they exercise control over sources of variation in their own behavior. An important aspect of Fischer's theory is that skills are jointly defined by the organism and the environment. Thus, only skills that are exercised in the most supportive of environments will be developed to their highest level. To the extent that a child's environment encourages development of various skills equally, there will be homogeneity (or evenness) of cognitive function. That is, if the environment is relatively homogeneous with respect to supporting all of a child's skills, development will proceed evenly. To the extent that one's environment is heterogeneous, however, with some skills being exercised more consistently or receiving more support than others, development will be relatively uneven. Since the world in which most children live is not homogeneous with respect to

opportunities to develop different skills, Fischer assumes, quite contrary to Piaget, that heterogeneity of cognitive function is the rule rather than the exception.

Fischer proposes that skills show an invariant developmental progression (à la Piaget) with respect to *optimal level* of performance. Optimal level refers to the maximum level of complexity of a skill that the individual can control, or, in other words, the best performance that a child can show. Consistent with Fischer's position that skills are jointly defined by the environment and the organism, the optimal level of performance is realized only for those skills practiced in the most supportive of environments.

Skills develop in a step-by-step sequence of ten hierarchical levels, with these levels being divided into three tiers (sensorimotor, representational, and abstract). Each tier reflects the general type of information that a child can control. In the *sensorimotor tier* (approximately 3 to 24 months) children's skills are limited to their actions on and perceptions of objects in their environments. In the *representational tier* (approximately 2 to 12 years) concrete objects can be represented mentally, and in the *abstract tier* (approximately 12 to 26 years) representational sets can be combined so that objects can be thought of in terms of general, intangible attributes. Each tier consists of four levels, with the highest skill level of one tier (for example, sensorimotor, Level 4) corresponding to the first level of the next tier (for example, representational, Level 1). A brief description of the sequence of Fischer's levels is presented in Table 2-3.

By stressing the role that the environment plays in the development of skills, Fischer's theory acknowledges the significance of experience far more than Piaget's does. However, Fischer's ten hierarchical levels and the cyclical, predictable nature of development are certainly reminiscent of Piaget, and Fischer's concept of optimal level is consistent with contemporary information processing viewpoints (see Chapter 3). What, then, is the contribution of this theory, and how is it similar to or different from other formulations, particularly that of Piaget?

Contrasts between Fischer's and Piaget's theories can most readily be made with respect to the basic structures of their theories: skills and schemes. *Schemes* are structures by which the child knows the world. They are based on action and, for Piaget, are the things that do the assimilating and accommodating. Schemes develop from earlier schemes (Piaget's epigenetic position) and have a high degree of generality in that they are integrated with one another (structures of the whole) and thus result in a high degree of homogeneity of cognitive functioning. *Skills* are also structures by which a child knows the world, and, like schemes, they are based in action and develop from earlier acquired skills. Similarly, skills are relatively well integrated and are characterized by the type of variations a child can control (sensorimotor, representational, abstract). Unlike schemes, however, most or all of a child's skills are *never* at the same level at a given time. Development of skills is induced by the environment in interaction with the child, and only skills that are induced most consistently operate at a child's optimal level. Skills are not generalizable but are specific to particular objects and tasks. Thus, unevenness of developmental function is the rule and not the exception.

Both schemes and skills are viewed as developing from simpler to more complex states or organization. For Piaget schemes are organized into stages, whereas for Fischer skills are organized into levels. The major difference between the two theorists is that Piaget's stages reflect a high degree of generality

and characterize the child. A child *is* a concrete operational thinker or *is in* the sensorimotor period. In contrast, levels characterize skills that are specific to particular objects and tasks. In Fischer's theory, children are not described as being at Level 4 or at Level 7. One can specify the optimal level of performance that a child is able to achieve, but this does not reflect a classification of the child. Accordingly, the range of expected behaviors for a given child is very broad, especially in comparison with the high degree of generality predicted for children at a particular stage in Piaget's theory.

One further difference is that, unlike Piaget, Fischer maintains that there are several different developmental routes to any particular outcome. That is, although all skills are based on earlier skills, it is not necessary for all children to progress through the same sequence of skills in exactly the same order. For example, a child may have achieved a Level 5 skill for conservation of length but have Level 6 skills for the more practiced conservation of number and solids. The child may coordinate these two Level 6 skills to arrive at a Level 7 skill and can then abstract the rule for Level 7 conservation of length without ever having attained the Level 6 skill for this particular content (Fischer, 1980, p. 512).

This theory and many other contemporary approaches to cognitive development take as their starting point many of the observations and assump-

TABLE 2-3 Description of Stages in Fischer's Skill Theory (Adapted from Fischer & Pipp, 1984)

Hierarchical level	Tier	Cyclical level	Characteristic structure	Estimated age range of emergence
1		1	Single set	3 to 4 months
2		2	Mapping	7 to 8 months
3	Sensorimotor skills	3	System	11 to 13 months
4	_____	4 = 1	System of systems	20 to 24 months
5		2		4 to 5 years
6	Representational skills	3		6 to 7 years
7	_____	4 = 1		10 to 12 years
8		2		14 to 16 years
9	Abstract skills	3		18 to 20 years
10		4		24 to 26 years

tions laid down by Piaget. Rather than viewing new theories of children's thinking as radical departures from Piaget's, it is more appropriate to view them as modifications and extensions of his approach. Not all new theories are neo-Piagetian. But few contemporary approaches ignore Piaget, making an understanding of Piagetian theory a necessary beginning for an appreciation of modern theories of cognitive development.

□ Summary

Piaget's theory of intellectual development has had a profound impact on how we view children, their thinking, and their development. He believed that abstract *structures* within the child underlie intelligence and that cognitive development is the development of these structures. He viewed children as being *intrinsically active* and thus responsible, to a large extent, for their own development. He believed that cognition is *constructive*, with our current state of knowledge influencing how we perceive and process new information. Development is *epigenetic* in nature, according to Piaget, with later forms of cognition developing from earlier, qualitatively different forms of thinking.

Piaget described the functions of *organization* and *adaptation* as invariant processes that are characteristic of all biological systems (including intelligence) and operate throughout the life span. Organization refers to the tendency of an organism to integrate structures into higher-order systems or structures. Adaptation refers to adjustments the organism makes in response to the environment, and it has two complementary components. *Assimilation* refers to structuring the environmental input to fit a child's current schemes, and *accommodation* refers to structuring the child's schemes to match the environmental data.

Piaget proposed *equilibration* as an explanatory mechanism for development. When confronted with information that cannot be assimilated into structures, the child is in a state of cognitive incongruity, or disequilibrium. When disequilibrium is resolved by accommodation, a new and more stable structure results. Structure B is said to be more stable than structure A if fewer things will throw structure B into disequilibrium (that is, if more things can be assimilated into B than A). Piaget stressed that equilibration is an active process, even when structures are relatively stable.

Piaget postulated four major periods of cognitive development. He hypothesized that these stages are (1) qualitatively different in form from each preceding or following stage; (2) culturally universal, so that all children progress through them in a single, invariant order; and (3) based on earlier, more primitive cognitive structures (*hierarchization*).

During the *sensorimotor* stage (from birth to about 2 years), children's thinking is limited to their own actions on objects. Commencing somewhere between 18 and 24 months, children begin to use *symbols*. From this point on, development consists of the development of *operations*. Piaget's account of the development of operations has produced more research than any other single topic in the history of cognitive development. He described three major periods occurring between the ages of approximately 2 and 15 years: *preoperations* (between 2 and 7 years), *concrete operations* (between 7 and 11 years), and *formal operations* (between 11 and 16 years). Piaget proposed four characteristics of operations: operations are (1) mental, (2) derived from action, (3) integrated with one another (structures of the whole), and (4) reversible. Piaget specified two types of reversibility: *negation* (or *inversion*) and *compensation* (or *reciprocity*).

Piaget described the thought of preoperational children as *intuitive* and the thought of concrete operational children as *logical*. Preoperational and concrete operational children were described as differing on the basis of several factors. Most critically, the thought of preoperational children was said to lack reversibility, the benchmark of operations. Piaget described the perception of preoperational children as *centered* on the most salient aspects of a perceptual array, whereas the perception of concrete operational children was described as *decentered*. Preoperational children were said to be *egocentric*, in that they have a difficult time assuming the perspective (visual, communicative, or social) of another person. Concrete operational children were described as being less egocentric, although recent research has indicated that even preschool-age children can easily take the perspective of another in certain situations. Finally, Piaget asserted that preoperational children attend to specific *states* and ignore *transformations* between states.

Piaget applied his theory to a number of different cognitive contents, the most critical of which is *conservation*. Conservation represents the cognitive constancy of quantitative relations, and it refers to the knowledge that an entity remains the same despite a perceptual transformation applied to that entity. Recent research on this topic has demonstrated, counter to Piaget's claims, that conservation can be accelerated by a variety of training techniques, although his description of the development of conservation has generally been confirmed.

The major factor in the transition from concrete to formal operations is the advent of *hypothetico-deductive reasoning*. The child can now think in terms of what is possible as well as what is real. With hypothetico-deductive reasoning, thinking can be done solely in terms of symbols, without the need for referents in real life. Piaget described the formal operational child as being able to think like a scientist, or to use *inductive reasoning*. Children can make a hypothesis and systematically test it, assessing one factor while controlling for others. Formal operational children are able to "think about thinking," or to reflect on the outcome of their own thought (*reflective abstraction*). Piaget also proposed that the thinking of formal operational children can be described by a system of logical rules.

Research into Piaget's account of formal operations has generally been critical. In some cases, even preschool children can solve simplified forms of formal operational tasks, whereas a majority of adults fail other formal operational problems. Piaget's emphasis on the logical properties of adult thought seems not to reflect the way most adults really think.

Overall, Piaget's account of the development of operations has generated tremendous interest over the last five decades. The findings from contemporary research seriously question some aspects of operations. Non-Piagetian research indicates that Piaget often underestimated the cognitive competencies of children. Young children can display sophisticated cognitive processing in certain situations and, in general, are less homogeneous with respect to cognitive functioning than he proposed.

Fischer's *skill theory* is a contemporary alternative to Piaget's theory. Fischer argues for a transaction of environmental and individual influences on development in an attempt to explain why cognitive development is so often uneven, counter to the prediction of Piaget's theory.

☐ Notes

1. Most of the biographical information in this section was obtained from Piaget's autobiography, published in Murchison & Boring (1952).
2. When discussing broad theoretical or philosophical issues, Piaget used the term *structure* to refer to any system within the child that underlies intelligence. When discussing a particular system reflecting some specific knowledge, however, he used the term *scheme*. Schemes reflect children's knowledge at all stages of development. When referring to some specific cognitive content, Piaget reserved the term *cognitive structure* to reflect a special type of scheme: that which is characterized by mental representation. By this definition, the organization that underlies sensorimotor intelligence is not in the form of cognitive structures but is in the form of schemes. In the remainder of this chapter I will try to use the term *scheme* whenever referring to the abstract organization that underlies some specific knowledge. I will use the term *structure* when referring to general aspects of Piaget's theory or his philosophical positions. In either case these terms are used to represent the abstract knowledge that underlies children's intelligence.

   One further clarification is in order. Earlier translations and reviews of Piaget's work used the term *schema* rather than *scheme*. Piaget had slightly different meanings for these terms and commented that the translations using *schema* were inaccurate (Piaget & Inhelder, 1969). To be consistent with Piaget's original intention, I will use the term *scheme* rather than *schema* throughout this and other chapters.
3. The 16 binary operations of propositional logic, follow-

ing Inhelder and Piaget (1958), are (1) affirmation: all combinations are possible; for example, P and Q, P and not Q, not P and Q, and not P and not Q are all possible; (2) negation: no combinations are possible; (3) conjunction: P is true and Q is true; (4) incompatibility: P is never true if Q is true, and vice versa; (5) disjunction: P is true or Q is true (or both are true); (6) conjunctive negation: P is false and Q is false; (7) implication: P implies Q; (8) nonimplication: P does not imply Q; (9) reciprocal implication: Q implies P; (10) negation of reciprocal implication: Q does not imply P; (11) equivalence: the effect of P is equal to the effect of Q; (12) reciprocal equivalence: the effect of P is not equal to the effect of Q; (13) affirmation of P: P is true independently of Q; (14) negation of P: P is false independently of Q; (15) affirmation of Q: Q is true independently of P; and (16) negation of Q: Q is false independently of P.

4. Piaget's particular brand of propositional logic has been criticized by logicians and mathematical psychologists as being faulty (see, for example, Ennis, 1975, 1976; Parsons, 1960). Although a full discussion of this criticism is not appropriate here, I will mention briefly some of the complaints lodged against Piaget's logical system. First of all, Piaget's logic is inefficient, in that he uses all 16 binary operations when, from the logician's standpoint, fewer are adequate. Second, Piaget's propositions, unlike the propositions of the logician, are not true abstract propositions but always refer to some interpretation of fact. Third, true logical propositions are independent of one another, whereas Piaget's propositions are not. Thus, Piaget's claim that concrete operational children cannot handle propositional logic must be viewed with caution, since, from the logician's point of view, Piaget's theory has little to do with true propositional logic.

5. Also important to Piaget's theory of formal operations is a system of logical operations called the INRC group. The group consists of four logical operations that can be applied to certain systems, including the 16 binary operations of propositional logic. The Identity operator (I) is an operation which when performed on the propositions leaves it unchanged. Take, for example, a penny and a dime, both showing heads. An Identity operation is one that leaves the situation as it was originally—for example, not turning over any of the coins. The Negation (N), or inverse, operation states that for every operation in the set there is another operation that will negate the effect of the first. If an operation is applied that turns the dime over once, the inverse operation involves turning the dime over a second time. The Reciprocal (R) operation involves an operation that is reciprocal to an earlier operation, such as turning the dime over if, in a previous operation, the penny was turned over. Finally, the Correlative (C) operation is the inverse of the Reciprocal. In the coins example, if the Reciprocal operation involves turning the dime over, the Correlative involves turning both the penny and the dime over. Piaget asserted that these logical operations are cognitive operations that formal operational thinkers apply to solving problems. Although the INRC group is important to Piaget's theory, he was less explicit about how the INRC group applies to the contents of formal operations than for other aspects of his theory, and for this reason the INRC group is mentioned only briefly here.

3

Information Processing Approaches
with Marc T. Frankel

Assumptions of the Information Processing Approaches
☐ Limited Capacity ☐ The Information Processing System ☐ Representation of Knowledge
☐ Automatic and Effortful Processes ☐ Components of Information Processing

Information Processing Theories of Development
☐ Sensory Register ☐ Short-Term Store

Developmental Differences in Information Processing Components
☐ Metacognitive Components ☐ Performance Components ☐ Knowledge-Acquisition Components

The Role of Strategies in Cognitive Development
☐ Mediational and Production Deficiencies ☐ What Are Production Deficient Children Doing?

The Contributions of Children's Knowledge Base to Cognitive Development
☐ Knowledge Base and Memory Development ☐ Knowledge of Rules
☐ Children's Belief about What Is Alive

Summary

Note

Although Piaget's approach to cognitive development stands as the major theoretical contribution of the past 50 years, the computer as a model for how the child handles knowledge has also contributed substantially to our understanding. Clearly, the child must manage an incredible array of information, which arrives almost constantly. Facts about people, things, and how they function must somehow be attended to, stored, and then recalled when needed to solve a problem or facilitate interaction with the environment.

☐ Assumptions of the Information Processing Approaches

There is no single information processing theory of cognition or cognitive development. Rather, information processing theories are built on a set of assumptions concerning how humans acquire, store, and retrieve information.

Perhaps the most obvious assumption of information processing approaches is that people process information. *Processing* refers to mentally acting on information in order to "know" it. We may act on an external stimulus in order to make sense of it (such as the writing on this page), or we may act on information that already resides in our heads. These mental actions can be referred to as operations, processes, procedures, strategies, information processing components, or programs. Each of these terms refers to mental actions taken by the individual in order to make sense of "input," or, in other words, to think.

Limited Capacity

Most central to the information processing approaches is the notion of *limited capacity*. We can deal with only so much information at any single time. This limited capacity to think is often discussed in terms of an energy metaphor (we only have so much mental energy to expend) or a space metaphor (we only have so much mental space in which to operate). So, for example, most of us have enough mental space to walk and chew gum at the same time. Add to these operations a nontrivial arithmetic

problem, however, and a noticeable change in our rate of gum chewing or walking will be discerned. We have added something else to do, and its successful execution will interfere with the execution of other operations.

The Information Processing System

Another assumption of information processing approaches is that information "moves" through the system. Human information processing is often represented with flow charts to depict schematically the pathways between input and storage (see Figure 3-1). The initial *multistore* models of the sort shown in the figure were first suggested as theories of memory (Atkinson & Shiffrin, 1968). At the risk of oversimplification, it may be said these theories assumed that information from the external world is initially represented, perceptually intact, in *sensory registers*. There are separate sensory registers for each sense modality (for example, visual, auditory, and haptic or active touch), and presumably they can hold large quantities of information—but for only a matter of milliseconds. From this initial registration, information is passed through to the *short-term store*, where capacity is smaller but the representations are more durable, lasting for seconds. The short-term store has also been referred to as the primary memory, working memory, and contents of consciousness. It is our short-term store that makes contact with the world, holding information long enough for us to evaluate it and to think about it. It is in the short-term store that we apply strategies, or control processes, for remembering or solving problems. The short-term store is where we live, mentally. Its capacity is limited, however, and if something is not done to the information once it is in the short-term store, it will be lost. If a person applies some cognitive operations to the information in the short-term store, it will be transferred to the *long-term store*, where presumably it is retained indefinitely.

Representation of Knowledge

Information processing approaches deal with knowledge and the processes we use to act upon that

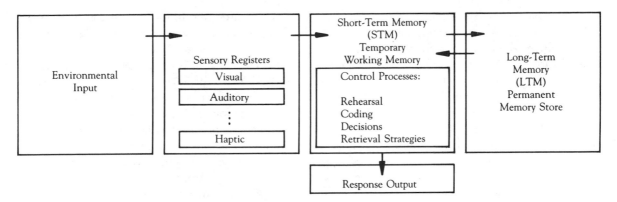

FIGURE 3-1   Flow of information through the memory system (Atkinson and Shiffrin, 1971)

knowledge. Knowledge can mean many things to a cognitive psychologist, including facts (Abraham Lincoln was president during the Civil War), structures for interpreting information (*à la* Piaget), awareness of the processes we have available for acting on information, and definitions of and relations among language terms. The latter type of knowledge has been termed *semantic memory*, and there have been many hypotheses about how people represent knowledge of words and familiar concepts in long-term memory. A currently popular approach holds that each item in semantic memory is represented by a *node* (Collins & Loftus, 1975). Each node is linked to other items in semantic memory (see Figure 3-2). In addition, each item has connections with features that characterize that item (for example, for the item *cat*, features may include *small, meows, drinks milk*). The strength of relations between items is graphically represented by the length of the line connecting them. So in Figure 3-2, for example, *Orange* and *Fire Engine* are more closely associated to *Red* than are *Apples* or *Sunsets*. Strength of association is important, because in this model once an item is *activated* (that is, entered into the short-term store), activation spreads to other items associated with it. The closer an item is to one that is currently activated, the more likely it also is to become activated, and the greater the likelihood that it will receive a sufficiently high degree of activation to be entered into the short-term store and become conscious.

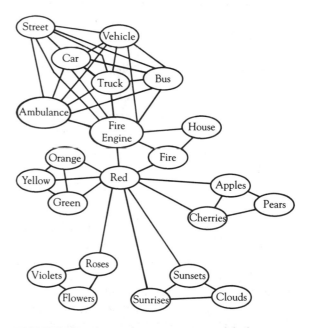

FIGURE 3-2   A spreading-activation model of semantic memory. The shorter the lines between two items, the less activation is needed for one item to be entered into the short-term store, given the activation of the other item (Collins and Loftus, 1975).

Automatic and Effortful Processes

With respect to methods for operating on knowledge, modern cognitive theorists assume that mental processes can be placed on a continuum in terms of how much of one's limited capacity each requires for its execution (Hasher & Zacks, 1979; Shiffrin & Schneider, 1977). At one extreme are *automatic* processes, which require none of the short-term store's limited capacity. At the other extreme are *effortful* processes, which make use of one's mental resources for their successful completion. In addition to not requiring any mental effort, truly automatic processes are hypothesized (1) to occur without intention and without conscious awareness, (2) not to interfere with the execution of other processes, (3) not to improve with practice, and (4) not to be influenced by individual differences in intelligence, motivation, or education (Hasher & Zacks, 1979). In contrast, effortful processes, which have also been called *strategies* or *controlled processes*, are hypothesized to (1) be available to consciousness, (2) interfere with the execution of other effortful processes, (3) improve with practice, and (4) be influenced by individual differences in intelligence, motivation, and education.

Although it is debatable whether any processes are truly automatic, requiring no mental effort for their execution (Cheng, 1985), most theorists agree that some mental operations involve more of one's attention (and limited capacity) than others. The automatic/effortful continuum of mental processes is illustrated in Figure 3-3.

Cognitive operations become less effortful with practice. The more frequently an operation is used, the more easily it can be executed, and, thus, the less mental space it requires for its proper functioning. I began dancing lessons not long ago, for example, and at first they were very effortful. "Hold your left arm this way, your right arm that way; step firmly; shift your weight from one foot to the other; keep your torso straight while you swing your hips this way; and don't forget the steps: one, two, slide, three, four, slide." With practice, less and less of my concentration was required for the execution of the proper sequences, permitting me the mental effort to add new moves. Jumping rope, playing golf, and riding a horse develop similarly, as do figuring in your head, retrieving people's names, and reading. In fact, once these highly developed skills do become relatively automatic, they can be disrupted by giving

too much attention to them. This can be noted by asking your tennis opponent to describe to you his very effective serve. Also, skills that were once highly efficient can become inefficient from lack of practice. Since the advent of calculators, for example, many adults probably do not do simple addition and subtraction as efficiently as they once did. The once smooth process has become more laborious, requiring relatively more mental effort. Thus, at their outset, most cognitive operations are very effort-consuming. With practice, they become executed with less and less expenditure of mental effort, leaving more mental space available for the execution of other operations.

Components of Information Processing

A number of cognitive theories extend these basic information processing assumptions in an attempt to formulate a model of how people think. One such model that has applications to development is the *componential theory* of Robert Sternberg (1977, 1985). In this theory, the *component* is the basic level of analysis and is defined as "an elementary information process that operates upon internal representations of objects or symbols" (Sternberg, 1985, p. 97).[1] Components have three properties: (1) duration, the amount of time it requires to execute a process; (2) difficulty, the probability of the process being executed without error; and (3) probability of execution, the likelihood that a process will be implemented in a particular situation. As will be seen in this and in later chapters, developmental differences exist in each of these three characteristics of components.

Sternberg further specifies three types of components: *metacomponents, performance components*, and *knowledge-acquisition components*. Metacomponents play an executive, decision-making role in cognition. They evaluate the problem at hand and select which lower-order components are needed to solve the problem. They are involved in allocating attentional resources to various aspects of task processing and in monitoring task solution (checking, for example, whether progress is being made toward a

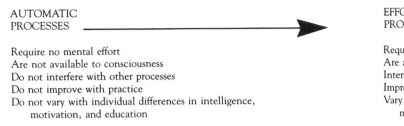

AUTOMATIC
PROCESSES

Require no mental effort
Are not available to consciousness
Do not interfere with other processes
Do not improve with practice
Do not vary with individual differences in intelligence,
    motivation, and education

EFFORTFUL
PROCESSES

Require mental effort
Are available to consciousness
Interfere with other processes
Improve with practice
Vary with individual differences in intelligence,
    motivation, and education

FIGURE 3-3 A hypothetical continuum of cognitive processes

correct solution or something different should be tried). Metacomponents are usually studied under the more general rubric of *metacognition*.

Performance components can be grouped into three types, each reflecting a different stage in task solution: (1) encoding components, in which the stimulus information is defined and represented in the information processing system; (2) components involved in the combination of or comparison between stimuli; and (3) response components, reflecting the retrieval of pertinent task information (that is, the answer to the problem).

The third category of components involves the processes used in the acquisition of knowledge and consists of selective encoding, selective combination, and selective comparison of information. This last set of components selects appropriate information relevant for task completion and relates the new information to previously stored knowledge.

These various components are obviously not independent of one another. Functioning of the metacomponents, for example, will influence the knowledge-acquisition and performance components, and the success of these latter components will be evaluated by the metacomponents, further modifying information processing routines. Figure 3-4 presents a graphic illustration of how these three components are proposed to interact. The metacomponents (M) directly activate knowledge-acquisition components (A, R, and T) as well as the performance components (P). This direct activation is denoted by solid double lines. The various knowledge-acquisition and performance components activate one another indirectly, as indicated by the solid single lines. Finally, the knowledge-acquisition and

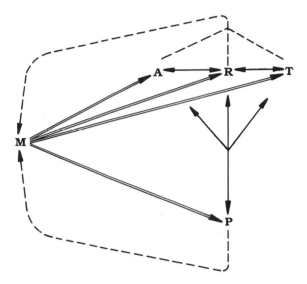

FIGURE 3-4 Interrelations among different components in Sternberg's componential theory. M refers to metacomponents; A, R, and T refer to the knowledge-acquisition components of acquisition, retrieval, and transfer; and P refers to the performance components. Direct activation of one component by another is depicted by solid double arrows. Indirect activation is represented by solid single arrows, and direct feedback is represented by single broken arrows (Sternberg, 1980).

performance components provide direct feedback to the metacomponents, reflected by the single broken lines. Thus, given feedback to the metacomponents, an evaluation of task progress can be made, and, if necessary, changes in the direct activation of the knowledge-acquisition and performance components can be accomplished, and so on. As should be apparent from this model, deficits in one component will have effects on the operation of other components in the system.

☐ Information Processing Theories of Development

Given the brief framework just outlined, where should a psychologist with an information processing point of view look to find developmental differences in children's thinking? One place to look is semantic memory, or children's knowledge base in general. Many developmental psychologists have examined age differences in the structure of children's language concepts, and these differences will be discussed in Chapter 7. However, the benchmark of information processing theories is the notion of limited mental capacity, and it is here that psychologists have searched for age differences that would explain developmental changes in children's thinking. There are apparently no capacity limitations to the long-term store. Children's ability to store and subsequently retrieve information from the long-term store will be the focus of Chapter 8. When looking for developmental differences in capacity, most researchers have limited their search to the sensory register and the short-term-store components of the multistore model described earlier.

Sensory Register

The initial registration of information can be studied in any sensory modality, but the most investigated sensory register in developmental work is that of vision (*iconic store*). When adults are flashed sets of letters or numbers for ⅒th of a second and then asked to remember them, they are typically able to recall only a few of the items, although they have the feeling that they know more. Sperling (1960) developed the *partial report technique*, in which subjects were shown a series of nine letters for a brief duration. After the visual display, a marker pointed to one row, with subjects having to recall the three items in that particular row. Performance under these conditions, in contrast to the total-recall task,

was nearly perfect, even though the subjects did not know ahead of time which row would be tested. Sperling's interpretation was that adults registered all the information but that it decayed so rapidly that by the time they could recall three or four items, the sensory memory for the remainder of the display had deteriorated, leaving them with the impression that they had seen more but the inability to remember exactly what.

Developmental research into the capacity of the iconic store has followed procedures similar to those used with adults. Sheingold (1973) used a circular array of seven geometric forms as stimuli (see Figure 3-5) with groups of children (ages 5, 8, and 11 years) and adults. The subjects were familiarized with the forms so that they could name each one quickly. Over a series of trials, the subjects were shown the array, with the position of the seven forms and a blank space rearranged on every trial. The stimuli remained visible for 100 milliseconds (⅒th of a second). Following the stimulus presentation, an indicator pointed to the position of one of the items, and the subject was to say which item had been in that position. Thus, subjects were to give a partial report (one of a possible eight), not knowing beforehand which of the eight positions would be tested.

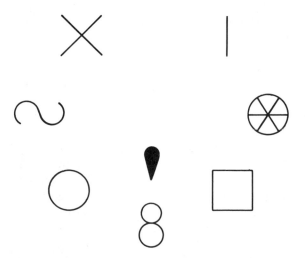

FIGURE 3-5　Stimuli used in Sheingold's developmental study of the capacity of the sensory register (Sheingold, 1973)

One factor manipulated in this experiment was the length of time between the display of the stimulus and the display of the indicator. On some trials, the indicator was shown simultaneously with the stimulus or immediately after it (no delay). On others, the delay between the stimulus and the indicator varied between 50 milliseconds (¹⁄₂₀th of a second) and 1000 milliseconds (1 second). The results of this experiment are shown in Figure 3-6, expressed in terms of the number of items the subjects had in memory (maximum = 8). The slight age differences observed at the simultaneous and no-delay intervals may have been due to the younger children being distracted by the indicator. But for the first delay that assessed memory (50 milliseconds), there were no age differences. The performance of the 5-year-olds was high and comparable to that of the older children and the adults. Age differences in memory performance began to appear as soon as 100 milliseconds, however, and these differences increased in magnitude as the length of the delay increased.

What do these data mean? First of all, the lack of developmental differences at 50 milliseconds indicates that even 5-year-olds are able to hold large quantities of information in iconic store over a brief interval. That is, as much visual information was getting into the sensory registers of 5-year-olds as those of adults. Yet, the dramatic decline in performance over delay for the 5- and 8-year-olds indicates that something other than the capacity of the iconic store was affecting performance. That something is apparently related to strategies or techniques used to get information from the sensory register to the more durable short-term store. Several possibilities that have been suggested are visual rehearsal, verbal encoding, and more focused attention to specific parts of the visual icon (Hoving, Spencer, Robb, & Schulte, 1978; Morrison, Holmes, & Haith, 1974). Although people may not be conscious of using these procedures to guide their performance, these strategies fall into the category of operations under the control of the individual. Thus, although the capacity of the sensory register shows minimal change from the preschool years through young adulthood,

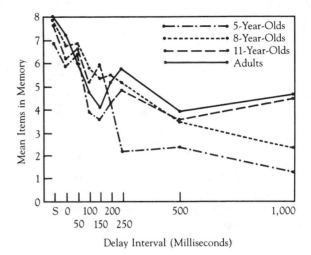

FIGURE 3-6 The number of items in visual (iconic) memory as a function of delay interval between display of a stimulus and presentation of a cue (Sheingold, 1973)

processes related to getting information from the sensory register to the short-term store do change with age.

Short-Term Store

Traditionally, the capacity of the short-term store has been assessed by tests of *memory span*. Memory span refers to the number of unrelated items that can be recalled in exact order. Presentation of items is done rapidly (usually one per second), so there is minimal time for the application of memory strategies to aid recall. A child's memory span has been used to reflect the size of the short-term store. Norms from the digit span subtests of the Stanford-Binet and Wechsler IQ scales show a regular increase in memory span with age. Similar findings have been provided by Dempster (1981). He reported, for example, that when digits are used, the memory span of 2-year-olds is about two items; of 5-year-olds, about four items; of 7-year-olds, about five items; and of 9-year-olds, about six items. The average memory span of adults is about seven items.

Pascual-Leone's Model of M-Capacity

These findings are consistent with a theory by Pascual-Leone (1970), who proposed maturational changes in memory capacity, called *M-space*. Pascual-Leone hypothesized that a child's cognitive capacity, represented by M, is an additive combination of a constant, called *a*, which is shared by all children, and a variable, labeled *k*, which changes with age. Thus, for any given child, mental capacity can be expressed as $M = a + k$, with the value of *k* increasing with age. Increments in *k* are, to Pascual-Leone, representative of transitions between Piagetian stages.

Tests of M-space are similar to tests of short-term memory span, the only difference being that some operation must be performed to transform the input before storing or retrieving it. An example is the counting span task (Case, Kurland, & Goldberg, 1982, Experiment 3). Children are presented cards with dots on them. The subjects are to count the dots and report the number. The task starts with one card. On subsequent trials the number of cards is incremented, increasing the memory load for the child. A child's M-space is defined as the level at which he or she can no longer maintain perfect recall. Typically, this level is about two items fewer than that found on standard memory span tasks.

Pascual-Leone proposed that the number of separate concepts a child can manipulate simultaneously is limited by M-space (that is, the amount of space available for cognitive processing). Seen in this light, the transition from preoperational to concrete operational thought, for example, involves an increase in M-space with a concomitant increase in the problem-solving capacity of the child (see Table 3-1). Rather than highlighting processes or structures that change between stages, Pascual-Leone proposed changes in cognitive performance as a function of changes in M-space. Since the constant *a* is identical for all children, estimation of M is accomplished through factor *k*. Pascual-Leone theorized that *k* corresponds to the amount of capacity required to deal with peripheral aspects of a task such as instructions and strategies. More specifically, *k* refers to the number of problem-solving schemes that a child can coordinate at any point. Thus, from Table 3-1, an early preoperational child can coordinate *a* + 1 schemes, a late preoperational child

a + 2 schemes, and so on. Basically, with age, children can keep more things in mind at once. As capacity expands with development, the child is increasingly able to consider new strategies or ideas and thus change stages. In Piaget's conservation problems, for example, young children typically make their decisions on the basis of a single dimension ("The water level's so high in this one that there must be more water in it"). To solve conservation problems, children must realize that a change in one dimension (height of water level, for example) is compensated for by a corresponding change in another dimension (width). From a point of view such as Pascual-Leone's, young children cannot keep two dimensions in mind at once. They can shift their attention from one dimension to another, but they do not have sufficient information processing capacity to coordinate two dimensions simultaneously.

Strategies, Speed of Processing, and Memory Span
Other researchers have proposed that changes in memory span are due to developmental differences in the use of strategies such as rehearsal—repeating the items to oneself (Samuel, 1978)—or chunking—recoding two or more items into a single memory unit (Dempster, 1978). However, Dempster (1981, 1985) and others have questioned both the capacity and strategy hypotheses of developmental changes in memory span. Concerning the role of strategies in memory span, Dempster (1981) concluded that "research offers little evidence that stra-

TABLE 3-1 M-Power as a Function of Age and Developmental Level (Case, 1974)

Piagetian substage	Age (years)	Modal value of M (a + k)
Early preoperational	(3–4)	a + 1
Late preoperational	(5–6)	a + 2
Early concrete	(7–8)	a + 3
Late concrete	(9–10)	a + 4
Early formal	(11–12)	a + 5
Middle formal	(13–14)	a + 6
Late formal	(15–16)	a + 7

tegic variables are a source of span differences, even though several—rehearsal, chunking and retrieval strategies—appear to be sources of performance differences in other tasks" (pp. 78–79). Of ten strategic and nonstrategic variables investigated by Dempster, only one, ease of item identification, appeared to be a major source of developmental differences in memory span.

Ease of item identification refers to speed of processing: how quickly can a child identify an item? Thus, speed of identification is an indication of processing efficiency. It is assumed that the faster an operation can be completed, the less mental effort it requires for its execution. In work by Chi (1977), 5-year-olds required more time to identify photographs of faces than did adults and showed corresponding differences in memory span for the faces. When the amount of time that adults were permitted to view the faces was limited, however, Chi reported drastic reductions in age differences in memory span. Thus, although maturational differences in the capacity of the short-term store appear to be small (few psychologists would say nonexistent), maturational differences are more substantial for speed of processing (Dempster, 1985; Kail, 1986), which in turn affects level of memory span.

Efficiency of Cognitive Processing

One contemporary theory of cognitive development that considers age differences in the efficiency with which information is processed is that of Robbie Case (Case, 1984, 1985; Case et al., 1982). Case proposed age-related declines in the amount of mental effort required to execute a cognitive process. Some of this improvement can be attributed to maturation. However, within each maturational stage (Case lists four, to be described in Chapter 6) children become increasingly adept at acquiring information and using strategies. This ability, in turn, fosters greater efficiency, resulting in heightened speed of processing.

Case distinguished between *storage space* and *operating space* when conceptualizing memory processes. Storage space refers to the hypothetical amount of space that an individual has available for storing

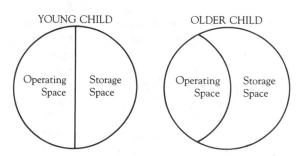

FIGURE 3-7 With age, children process information more efficiently, requiring less operating space and leaving more storage space.

information. Operating space is the amount of mental space that can be allocated to the execution of intellectual operations. Case also defined *total processing space* as the sum of storage and operating space.

Case proposed that there is a developmental *decrease* in the amount of operating space required for the execution of cognitive processes with a concomitant *increase* in operational efficiency. Simply put, as each new developmental skill is mastered and becomes practiced, the increase in *processing efficiency* frees attention for coordinating new strategies. Developmental changes in operating and storage space are displayed in Figure 3-7.

Support for Case's theory is illustrated in a study by Case and his colleagues (1982), who assessed the independent contributions of storage space and operating efficiency to memory performance. Storage space was measured by counting the number of items that children (ranging in age from 3 to 6 years) recalled under conditions that minimized the effects of memory strategies (for example, memory span tasks). Operating efficiency was reflected by the speed with which a set of cognitive operations such as identifying items could be performed. Case and his associates predicted that there would be a relationship between operational efficiency (as reflected by speed of identification) and storage space (as reflected by how much was remembered). Children who were slow in identifying items (thus requiring substantial amounts of operating space) should realize lower levels of memory performance for those items. The data supported this prediction, showing a relationship between storage space and operating efficiency that was also related to age. Furthermore, when the processing speeds of college subjects were reduced by changing the task so that they no longer benefited from being able to say the words quickly (unfamiliar nonsense words were used), their level of memory performance was comparably reduced. The results of this study are graphically presented in Figure 3-8. As processing efficiency increased (as reflected by speed of processing), memory performance increased. When adults were given a task reducing their processing efficiency to a level comparable to that of 6-year-olds, their memory performance was similarly modified.

An Alternative View of the Short-Term Store

Recent research has suggested yet another view of developmental differences in the information processing system that differs somewhat from the model adopted by Case and others. Brainerd and Kingma (1985), extending research done with adults by Klapp, Marshburn, and Lester (1983), suggested that there is no single, limited capacity information processing system but several. They proposed that working memory should be conceptualized as a series of independent stores, with each having its own resources and each being highly adapted for performing specific operations (for example, encoding stimulus information, retrieving information from memory). Brainerd and Kingma provided evidence for the *independent-process interpretation* of working memory by demonstrating that (1) young children's performance on several Piagetian reasoning tasks (for example, conservation) was not related to their ability to remember background information pertinent to the task; (2) modifications that affected children's performance on the reasoning tasks did not influence their short-term memory performance for task-related information; and (3) a manipulation that affected short-term memory performance for task information did not have a similar effect on children's reasoning performance. From these findings, Brainerd and Kingma suggested that a single "generic" information processing system, such as proposed by Case and others, is inappropriate and

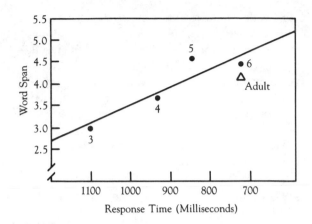

FIGURE 3-8 The relationship between word span and speed of word repetition at age levels from 3 to 6 years and adulthood. Younger children were generally slower to identify words and had shorter word spans than older children. When the identification times of adults were slowed to levels comparable to those of 6-year-olds, they showed a corresponding deficit in word span (Case, Kurland, and Goldberg, 1982).

that actually several different working memory systems develop independently of one another. Although this new approach differs radically from more traditional views, it still posits developmental differences in mental capacity but suggests that the information processing system is more complex than was initially believed. The results of future research, contrasting further the independent-processes and generic models, are needed before the value of this new approach to working memory can be evaluated.

☐ Developmental Differences in Information Processing Components

In an earlier section, Sternberg's (1977, 1985) componential theory was introduced as an information processing model that can be applied to development. Recall that he proposed three general types of information processing component: *metacomponents*, which make executive decisions and monitor task performance; *performance components*, which involve the encoding, comparison, and retrieval of stimulus information; and *knowledge-acquisition components*, which are processes involved in gaining new knowledge by selectively acting on the stimulus information and the information in one's long-term store. Although his theory has only recently been applied to children's cognitions (see Sternberg, 1985), developmental psychologists have long known of age differences in information processing abilities similar to those he describes.

Metacognitive Components

Age differences in metacomponents, or, more generally, metacognition, are the most recent discoveries of cognitive developmental psychologists. Metacognitive knowledge consists mainly of knowledge about what factors, or variables, influence thinking. Flavell and Wellman (1977) have described three major classes of metacognitive knowledge variables: *person, task,* and *strategy.* Person variables include people's knowledge of their own abilities and the abilities of other people with respect to thinking. For example, your knowledge that you can solve certain problems faster with visual information than with verbal information or that your grandfather remembers things from years ago more clearly than he does events from yesterday are examples of person variables. Task variables involve knowledge of the requirements of tasks. Is enough information provided to solve the task at hand, or is more needed? Is the task a familiar or a novel one? What variations in the task will make it more or less demanding? Strategy variables include a knowledge of which cognitive techniques one has available to solve a particular task and which strategies would be most appropriate for the task at hand. Does this task require my full concentration, or can it be accomplished with only a little study? What knowledge do I have that I can bring to bear to arrive at a solution?

One robust finding of the cognitive developmental literature over the past 15 years has been age differences in children's metacognitive knowledge. Metacognition has been investigated for a number of different cognitive domains, including memory (Flavell & Wellman, 1977), reading comprehension (Paris & Oka, 1986), attention (Miller, 1985), communication (Whitehurst & Sonnenschein, 1985), imitation (Green, Bjorklund, & Quinn-Cobb,

1988), and self-monitoring (Wellman, 1977). Some examples of the research findings include these: The ability to distinguish important from unimportant aspects of a written story improves with age (Brown & Smiley, 1978). An understanding of the factors that influence attention increases developmentally (Miller & Weiss, 1982). And young children do not effectively monitor information they have in memory, causing them to predict their memory performance poorly (Wellman, 1977). In general, age-related differences have been found in person, task, and strategy variables, with children becoming more cognizant with age of their own knowledge and how it can be applied. I will say more in later chapters about metacognitive development.

A good demonstration of developmental changes in metacognitive skills is seen in a study by Yussen and Levy (1975) in which children were asked to predict their memory spans. The researchers presented children and college students with a set of ten pictures, asking them to predict how many items they could recall in exact order (memory span task). Following the subjects' predictions, actual recall was assessed. Four-year-olds greatly overestimated their memory spans, predicting, on average, that they would recall slightly over eight of the ten items, whereas their actual recall was only somewhat greater than three items (level of overestimation = 152%). Twenty-four of 48 preschoolers (50%) predicted that they would recall all ten items. Predictions were closer to reality for third-grade and college students (overestimation = 40% and 6%, respectively), with only 5 of 48 third-graders (10%) and 1 of 48 college students (2%) predicting that they would recall all ten items. The preschoolers were aware of their failure on this task, but many were unperturbed, saying things such as "If you gave me a different list like that, I could do it" (Yussen & Levy, 1975, p. 507).

Performance Components

Developmental differences in performance components have been extensively studied in the past 20 years. With respect to encoding, age differences have been found in how children initially represent stimuli. For example, preschool children have been described as encoding objects primarily in terms of visual/imaginal properties of stimuli, whereas older children are more likely to represent an object in terms of abstract, symbolic features (Bruner, 1966; Kosslyn, 1978; see Chapter 6). In memory and learning tasks, young children have been found to use fewer features to encode an object than older children or adults, resulting in a more impoverished memory representation (Ackerman, 1984; Ceci & Howe, 1978).

Speed of Processing

With respect to overall speed of processing, young children require more time, and thus presumably use more of their limited capacity, to execute most cognitive processes than do older children (Dempster, 1981; Keating, Keniston, Manis, & Bobbitt, 1980; Whitney, 1986). Kail (1986) has reported that the general developmental changes in processing speed are similar across different tasks. Kail administered reaction time tasks to subjects ranging in age from 8 to 21 years. The subjects were presented a pair of letters in different orientation and were to determine, as quickly as possible, whether the two letters were identical or mirror images of each other. To do this, subjects must mentally rotate one letter into the same orientation as the other. In a name retrieval task the subjects were shown pairs of pictures and asked to determine whether they were physically identical or had the same name (for instance, different examples of a banana, one peeled and one unpeeled). Patterns of responses over these two tasks were highly similar, with reaction times becoming faster with age. Kail interpreted these data as reflecting age-related increases in the amount of processing resources available for the execution of cognitive operations, consistent with the position taken by Case (1985) discussed earlier in this chapter.

Yet, factors other than age affect speed of processing, most importantly familiarity with the to-be-processed information (Roth, 1983; Sperber, Davies, Merrill, & McCauley, 1982). For example, children in grades 2, 5, and 11 and mentally retarded adolescents were asked to name as quickly as possible pictures of familiar objects (Sperber et al., 1982).

Some of the pictures were preceded by a category prime (for example, "This is an animal"—COLLIE). Other items were preceded by a neutral cue ("There is no cue for this picture"—COLLIE). Half of the categories consisted of items that were perceptually similar to one another (for example, insects, animals), and the remaining half consisted of items that were perceptually dissimilar (for example, furniture, toys). The researchers found that decision times decreased as age and intelligence rose. They also reported that the facilitative effects of the category primes for the perceptual categories were significant for all but the second-grade children, but that a significant priming effect for the perceptually *dissimilar* categories was significant only for the eleventh-graders. Thus, processing speed was related to age and intelligence level but differed as a function of category (perceptually similar versus dissimilar). Response times were faster when children had more knowledge of the categories (the perceptual categories). From these findings, it can be concluded that one important factor in development that influences speed of processing is experience, or familiarity with the to-be-processed information.

The findings in this study do not lessen the contribution of maturation to speed of processing. Maturational changes surely underlie age changes in speed of processing. However, age differences in the degree of knowledge a child has for the information that is being requested are also important. People process familiar information faster (and thus with less mental effort) than they do less familiar information. Children can be viewed as universal novices. Almost everything is unfamiliar to them. With age, they become more experienced with the information and procedures involved in the assessment of cognitive ability and, in the process, quicken their speed of responding.

Retrieval

With respect to retrieval, developmental research indicates important age differences in the ease with which children can recall information they have in their memories. Once information has been encoded and entered into memory, younger children require more explicit promptings before that information can be retrieved (Howe, Brainerd, & Kingma, 1985; Kobasigawa, 1977).

Age differences in the efficiency of retrieval are illustrated in an experiment by Kobasigawa (1974). Children in grades 1, 3, and 6 were presented with sets of pictures to remember. The pictures were grouped by categories, and the children were given cue cards that served to classify the objects. Pictures of animals went with a picture of a zoo, for example, and food pictures went with a card showing a grocery store. Using this method, Kobasigawa ensured that the children encoded the items in terms of common category properties. Following presentation, the children were asked to recall as many of the items as they could under one of three conditions. Children in the free recall condition were asked to remember the items in any order that they liked. Children in the available-cue condition were shown the cue cards that had been paired with the items earlier (the zoo and grocery store) and were told that they could use these pictures to help them remember the other items. They were then asked to recall the items in any order they wished. Children in the directive-cue condition were shown each cue card, one at a time, were told how many items had been paired with it, and were asked to recall as many of those items as they could. Recall continued until children were tested on each of the cues.

The results of Kobasigawa's experiment are shown in Figure 3-9. Levels of memory performance increased with age for children in the free-recall condition, as would be expected. First- and third-grade children in the available-cue condition displayed no benefits relative to the children in the free recall condition, but some advantage was observed for the oldest children. Few first-graders in this second condition made any use of the cues, apparently being unaware that using them would aid their memory. In contrast, approximately 75% of the third-graders used the cues in this condition, but, as can be seen from their level of performance, they used them poorly. Results were strikingly different in the directive-cue condition, with developmental differences in the amount recalled being greatly minimized. These results indicate that the first- and third-graders had stored as much information about the to-

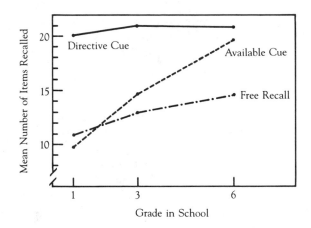

FIGURE 3-9 Children's mean levels of recall by grade and retrieval condition in an experiment by Kobasigawa (Kobasigawa, 1974)

be-remembered stimuli as the older children. Their problem was getting it out.

Knowledge-Acquisition Components
Selective Attention

Developmental differences in knowledge-acquisition processes have been found, with young children giving a disproportionate amount of attention to irrelevant task information and insufficient attention to critical features of the task (Lane & Pearson, 1982). These selective attention effects are illustrated in an experiment by Schiff and Knopf (1985). They presented 9- and 13-year-old boys with two tasks simultaneously. The primary task involved pressing a button every time a specified symbol (a star) was presented on a video screen. The secondary task involved remembering letters that were presented in the corners of the screen. Some children were instructed to ignore the letters and to attend only to the primary task, whereas other children were instructed to attend to both tasks. All children were asked to recall the letters in the corners, whether they had been instructed to attend to them or not. The researchers recorded not only responses to the primary and secondary tasks but also children's eye movements.

Schiff and Knopf reported that the older children performed better than the younger children on all tasks they were instructed to complete. In contrast, age differences on the secondary task (letter recall) when subjects were *not* instructed to attend to the letters were not significant, with the 9-year-olds actually remembering slightly more letters than the 13-year-olds. Examination of the children's eye movements indicated that the older children spent less time fixating the letters than the younger children in both the single and dual tasks. Schiff and Knopf interpreted these results as indicating that older children are better able to allocate attention in accordance with task demands and that they can store information more efficiently than younger children. This latter interpretation is based on the higher recall of letters on the secondary task for the 13-year-olds, despite their shorter fixation times. Schiff and Knopf concluded that "processing capacity increases during development, thereby allowing older children to attend and respond to more of the critical stimuli in a given period of time" and that "older subjects utilized a systematic strategy for allocating attention between two tasks to complete both with little decrement in performance" (p. 629).

Selective Comparisons

With respect to selective comparisons, young children are less likely than older children to relate newly acquired information to what they already know. For example, although young children may encode individual items in terms of similar category relations (for example, *dog, cow,* and *horse* are all encoded with the semantic feature ANIMAL), they are less likely than older children to make mental comparisons among these items and thus fail to use this single category feature to facilitate their performance in memory and learning tasks (Brainerd, Kingma, & Howe, 1986; Tighe, Tighe, & Schechter, 1975). This tendency is illustrated in a discrimination-learning experiment in which 7-year-old children and adults learned one of two responses for 16 different words (Tighe et al., 1975). Subjects were to decide whether each word "went with" a button on the left or one on the right. Half of the words were names of animals, for which one response was correct (for example, press the button on the right), and the remaining words were names of body

parts, for which another response was appropriate (for example, press the button on the left). The subjects continued at the task until they were able to classify each word correctly on two consecutive trials. Two to three weeks later the subjects were brought back to the laboratory and given an unexpected memory test for the words. They were shown triads of words, only one of which had been on the earlier learning task. As expected, the adults performed better than the children when the triads included one correct word from one of the task categories and two noncategory words (for example, *shoe, dog, chair*). However, the 7-year-olds showed greater retention than the adults when all the words in the triad were from the same category, with only one having been seen on the earlier discrimination learning task (for example, *arm, neck, finger*).

Why should 7-year-olds remember more than college students in this situation? The researchers proposed that the 7-year-olds had mastered the problem by learning a specific response for each individual exemplar (for example, press the right button for the word *cow,* left for *leg,* right for *dog,* right for *pig,* left for *arm*). Adults, in contrast, learned only two responses: ANIMAL word, press right; BODY PART word, press left. The adults were cognizant of the relationship among the words on the list, whereas the 7-year-olds, although being familiar with the categories ANIMALS and BODY PARTS, learned the problem instance by instance, ignoring the categorical relations among the items. Thus, the adults' memory for the items was excellent when only category information was necessary for making a decision (for example, of *shoe, dog,* and *chair,* only *dog* is a member of the ANIMALS category). In contrast, the 7-year-olds fared better when specific item information was necessary to solve the memory problem. Because the children generally failed to make comparisons among the category features of items when learning the discrimination task, they learned more about the specific words on the lists than the adults did.

As Sternberg (1985) has noted, the various types of components interact, so that deficits in one type of processing influence the effectiveness of other processes (see Figure 3-4). Also, improvements in one of these components can result in improvements in related ones. As children acquire more knowledge, for example, they develop a broader base for making selective comparisons among entries in memory. This development may lead not only to increased efficiency in the operation of the knowledge-acquisition components but also, indirectly, to greater ease in executing the various performance components. Thus, they will make greater gains in knowledge, resulting in a continuous feedback loop between knowledge-acquisition and performance components, with the individual moving from simpler to more complex levels of cognitive development.

☐ The Role of Strategies in Cognitive Development

As should be clear from the preceding paragraphs, strategies play an important role in children's developing cognitions. Many of the information processing components discussed in Sternberg's theory would qualify for the label *strategy*. Strategies are effortful cognitive operations that are directed at a goal. People carry them out deliberately to arrive at a solution to some problem (see Chapter 1).

During the 1960s, it became obvious to cognitive developmental researchers that young children (usually preschoolers) typically do not create the type of strategies that older children do. If strategies are so important to developmental differences in cognition, instructing a young child to use a strategy that is characteristic of an older child should, in some cases, result in changes in that child's cognitive performance.

Mediational and Production Deficiencies

Research using the logic of *training studies* flourished during the 1960s and 1970s and is still alive and well today. A three-step developmental progression of children's use of strategies was proposed. Early in development, children do not spontaneously generate a strategy to help them solve a task, and when

one is shown to them, they are unable to use it effectively to guide performance. This inability is referred to as a *mediational deficiency* (Reese, 1962). A potentially effective strategy does not mediate task performance for young children. Presumably, these children do not have the mental apparatus to effectively use the strategy. For slightly older children (or for slightly simpler strategies), the imposition of a strategy works wonders (or at least results in some improvement in task performance). In these cases, children do not produce the strategies spontaneously, but when shown what to do, they are able to follow instructions, with corresponding improvements. Thus, they still have a *production deficiency* (Flavell, 1970a). Children have the mental ability to use strategies but, for some reason, do not produce them without prompting. The stage of production deficiencies is followed by a stage in which children produce strategies on their own, not needing to have them imposed by an outsider.

Much cognitive developmental research through the 1970s focused on young children's production deficiencies. Many of the phenomena associated with concrete operations introduced by Piaget were examined from the viewpoint of production deficiency. Demonstrations abounded, with researchers showing that 4-, 5-, and 6-year-olds could be taught to conserve (Gelman, 1969), to solve transitive inferences (Bryant & Trabasso, 1971), and to take the visual perspective of another (Borke, 1975). Researchers examining concept formation and discrimination learning taught young children to use verbal labels as guides to classifying information, resulting in more mature problem solving (Kendler & Kendler, 1962). Memory research made extensive use of training studies, demonstrating that, under some conditions, young children could be trained to use reasonably complex strategies such as rehearsal, organization, and imagery, although the durability of such training was often short-lived (see Kail & Hagen, 1977; Chapter 8). It became clear that young children could be trained to use many of the strategies previously thought to be available only to older children. Tasks often had to be greatly simplified, and a trained 4-year-old rarely performed as well as an untrained 12-year-old; but younger children obviously had greater competence than psychologists had believed.

By showing that certain strategies could be taught to young children, researchers also illuminated something of the nature of what happens spontaneously in development. Thus, training studies were not done solely for their own sake (that is, to train children because they can be trained) but as a way of learning about the normal process of development.

What Are Production Deficient Children Doing?

The emphasis on production deficiencies and their laboratory remediation resulted in a science that had a good deal to say about what older children do and about how to train younger children to resemble older children (at least in the laboratory). But it had little to say about what young children do spontaneously (Brown & DeLoache, 1978). If young children are not using strategies (unless we train them), what *are* they doing?

In recent years, developmental psychologists have concentrated on what "production deficient" children do on their own. The answer is, basically, that they are also strategic. Preschool children, who do not spontaneously conserve liquid, make correct judgments on transitive inference problems, or organize sets of pictures according to taxonomic categories, nevertheless *do* do things to help them perform tasks (see Wellman, 1988, for a review). These strategies often result in incorrect answers, but they are strategies nonetheless.

Obviously, young children do not produce the sophisticated strategies used by older children and adults. Rather, they implement simpler goal-directed techniques. When trying to remember where the Big Bird doll was hidden minutes earlier, for example, 2-year-olds may point to the hiding location or simply look in the direction where it was hidden. These simple memory aids are not observed for 2-year-olds who are not asked to "remember where Big Bird was hidden," illustrating the goal-directed nature of these behaviors (DeLoache, Cassidy, & Brown, 1985).

Not only are the strategies used by young children not very sophisticated, they are not always effective.

For example, Baker-Ward, Ornstein, and Holden (1984) reported that 4-year-olds arranged pictures according to categories before a recall test (for example, putting all the pictures of animals in one pile and the pictures of clothing in another). But this organizational technique, which improves the memory performance of older children, did not have a beneficial effect for the 4-year-olds. Children who used this seemingly sophisticated strategy remembered no more of the pictures than children who did not. Similar findings have been reported by Miller and her colleagues for a selective-attention strategy (DeMarie-Dreblow & Miller, 1986; Miller, Haynes, DeMarie-Dreblow, & Woody-Ramsey, in press).

Miller and her colleagues suggested a transitional period, when children use a strategy but it does not facilitate their task performance (DeMarie-Dreblow & Miller, 1986; Miller et al., 1986). Miller has subsequently referred to this phenomenon as a *utilization deficiency* (Miller & Harris, in press). This state of affairs seems a bit perplexing. Why should young children who use a strategy not benefit from it? One speculation is that the execution of strategies requires substantial mental effort and that young children do not have enough information processing resources to execute the strategy and still perform other aspects of the task as well (Bjorklund & Harnishfeger, 1987; DeMarie-Dreblow & Miller, in press). That is, strategy use has a cost in terms of mental effort, and young children exert so much of their limited resources executing the strategy that they do not retain sufficient mental capacity to perform other aspects of the task efficiently.

This possibility was demonstrated in a memory training experiment by Bjorklund and Harnishfeger (1987). Third- and seventh-grade children were instructed in an organizational memory strategy (remembering all the words from a category together). In addition, the children were required to tap an index finger on the space bar of a microcomputer as fast as they could. Their tapping rate during the memory training was compared with their rate during a baseline period, when no memory task was given, and during a free-recall memory task, for which no training instructions had been provided. Decreases in tapping rate during the memory tasks were used as an indication of how much mental effort the children were expending on the tasks. The slower the children tapped (relative to when they were performing no memory task), the greater the mental effort that was required to perform the memory task. That is, the more mental effort required for the memory task, the more interference (measured in terms of decreased tapping rate) there should be on the secondary, tapping task.

Bjorklund and Harnishfeger reported that both the third- and seventh-graders showed increased interference as a result of the training, relative to the free-recall task. Furthermore, both groups later used the strategy that they had been shown during training. This use was indicated by increased *clustering* in recall, with children remembering words from the same category together (for example, remembering most of the ANIMAL words together, followed by the CLOTHING words, and so on). Only the seventh-grade children, however, showed a corresponding improvement in the number of words they recalled, relative to the free-recall task. The third-graders remembered no more words as a result of training than they did when no memory instructions had been given, despite the fact that they used the strategy and expended greater amounts of mental effort. Bjorklund and Harnishfeger interpreted these results as indicating that the third-graders used too much of their limited mental capacity in executing the strategy to have enough left over for other aspects of the memory task, such as retrieving specific words. Strategies are supposed to provide greater efficiency in processing, and had the third-grade children learned the strategy to a greater degree, their memory performance would probably have improved. Nevertheless, under the conditions of this experiment, it did not.

Strategies are effortful. Following the arguments of Case and others, discussed earlier in this chapter, processing becomes more efficient with age, allowing children to execute more strategies and to use them with greater effectiveness. The issue facing cognitive developmental psychologists is not whether children are being strategic. Rather, we are seeking to discover what strategies children of different ages use and how the simpler strategies used by young chil-

dren develop into the more sophisticated and effective strategies used by older children and adults.

☐ The Contributions of Children's Knowledge Base to Cognitive Development

Information processing approaches are concerned with the representation of knowledge and the processes applied to that knowledge. Recently, researchers have concentrated on how age differences in what children know, or their *knowledge base*, influence how they process information. Carey (1985a) has written that "the acquisition and reorganization of strictly domain-specific knowledge . . . probably account for most of the cognitive differences between 3-year-olds and adults" (p. 512). Young children are novices at most tasks, having less knowledge than older children about the to-be-processed information and about what it is they are supposed to do on the task itself (Brown & De-Loache, 1978). To what extent are young children's less sophisticated cognitive skills a function of limits on their abilities to process information, on the one hand, or limits on their knowledge about information relevant to the task, on the other?

Knowledge Base and Memory Development
Knowledge and Memory Span
An important demonstration of the role that differences in knowledge base can play in children's thinking was provided by Chi (1978). Chi assessed the memory span of a small group of children (average age 10.5 years) and of college-educated adults for two tasks. One task was to recall sets of digits (for example, remembering in exact order a series of quickly presented numbers). The other memory-span task was to recall the positions of chess pieces placed in plausible spots on a chess board. That is, subjects were shown the board for 10 seconds and then asked to reproduce the positions of the pieces. Typically, adults' memory span is greater than that of 10-year-olds. But these were not typical children: they were chosen from local chess tournaments and could be

considered experts. The adults, all above average in intelligence, knew how to play chess but not very well. The memory-span performance of the subjects in this experiment is shown in Figure 3-10. As can be seen, the children out-performed the adults when memory was for chess positions; but the customary developmental pattern was found when digits were the target stimuli, with adults showing higher levels of recall than the children.

These findings indicate that having a detailed knowledge base for a particular domain facilitates memory performance for information from that domain but not necessarily for information from other areas. Chess-expert children process chess-related information faster than less knowledgeable adults (Roth, 1983), but this increased efficiency is limited to the specific content for which the children are experts.

Knowledge and Free Recall

In studies of free recall, children are presented with a series of items (words, pictures, stories) and asked to recall those items in any order they wish. In comparison with tests of memory span, the rate of presentation of the items is relatively slow (for example, one word every 5 seconds), permitting the use of strategies to facilitate performance. Typically, levels of recall increase with age, with these improvements often being attributed to older children's use of strategies such as rehearsal (repeating the words to oneself) and organization (grouping and remembering items together, such as *dog* and *horse* or *shirt* and *dress*) (see Moely, 1977; Ornstein & Naus, 1978; Chapter 8).

In contrast to the usual interpretation, several researchers have proposed that most developmental improvements in memory functioning can be attributed to increases in children's knowledge of the information they are asked to remember. For example, Bjorklund (1985, 1987a) suggests that relations among items in semantic memory become stronger with age and that age differences in memory tasks can be attributed to differences in the ease with which these relations are activated. Thus, processing becomes increasingly automatic with age, resulting in higher levels of performance for older

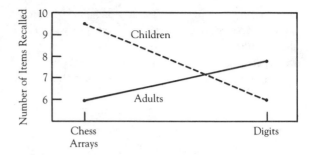

FIGURE 3-10 The average memory span for digits and chess arrays by chess-expert children and college-educated adults (adapted from Chi, 1978)

children. Rather than treating 10-year-olds as more strategic than 5-year-olds (that is, as intentionally using some memory strategy to help them remember), Bjorklund characterizes children as becoming *more automatic* with age, with sophisticated, deliberate strategies appearing sometime during adolescence.

In one series of experiments, Bjorklund and Zeman (1982) tested the recall of first-, third-, and fifth-grade children for two sets of materials. In the first set, the lists consisted of familiar words from well-known categories (for example, different members of the categories ANIMALS, FURNITURE, and TOOLS). Age differences in children's knowledge of these words and their category relations exist, and thus older children should find such sets easier to remember than younger children. For the second memory test, the subjects were asked to recall the names of the children from their current school class. Here, age differences in knowledge of the to-be-remembered information are minimized. All children had been in their classrooms for approximately 8 months, making the names of their classmates comparably familiar for children of all grade levels.

In addition to assessing the percentage of items (words or names) recalled, Bjorklund and Zeman also studied the extent to which children recalled the items in *clusters*. For the word task, a cluster was reflected by a child recalling several different items from the same category together (for example, *horse, dog, goat; hammer, drill, wrench*). For the class-recall task, clustering was reflected by a child recalling several different names together according to some organizational scheme apparent in the classroom (for example, seating arrangements or reading groups) or some characteristics inherent in the children themselves (for example, sex or race). Generally, levels of clustering (like levels of recall) increase with age and are associated with the use of memory strategies.

The recall and clustering results for the Bjorklund and Zeman study are shown in Figure 3-11. As can be seen, there were regular age-related improvements in recall and clustering for the word-recall task. Performance was higher overall for the class-recall task, and age differences in levels of performance were greatly reduced or eliminated.

On initial inspection of these data, it is tempting to conclude that having a detailed knowledge base for the information to be remembered caused all the children to process information *strategically*. That is, it appears as if children of all ages approached the class-recall task by selecting some scheme by which to organize their classmates (by where they sat, for instance), and then systematically used this scheme to recall the names. Bjorklund and Zeman doubted this interpretation, however. After the recall task, the children were asked a series of questions concerning how they had gone about recalling their classmates' names. Somewhat surprisingly, the majority of children at each grade were *unable* to describe the strategy apparent in their recall protocols. Most first-graders professed no strategy at all or said things such as "I used my brain." Third- and fifth-grade children were more likely to profess some strategy, but these strategies often did not conform to anything they had actually done in recalling the names. For example, many children said that they had recalled the names by alphabetical order. An examination of their protocols, however, revealed little or no evidence of clustering on this basis.

Bjorklund and Zeman interpreted these and related findings as indicating that the high levels of performance observed in class recall were not due to children being more strategic. Rather, they proposed that the strong associative links between the names of their classmates in semantic memory resulted in relatively efficient retrieval without the need for a strategy. Most children were telling the truth when

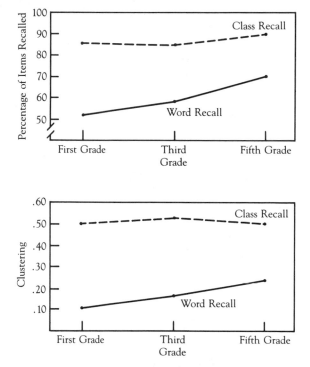

FIGURE 3-11 The average recall and clustering on class- and word-recall tasks by children in grades one, three, and five (based on data of Bjorklund and Zeman, 1982)

they said they had not used a strategy. What appeared to be a strategy was actually the relatively automatic activation of well-established relations among items in the children's semantic memories.

Bjorklund and Zeman went on to speculate that it is from such "automatic" retrieval that more deliberate and generalizable strategies develop. In the process of recalling names, children may identify some commonalities ("Hey, all those kids are in the Bluebirds reading group"). From here, they may decide to continue their recall efforts on the basis of the fortuitously discovered mode of organization. Thus, although most children do not begin the class-recall task with a plan, some discover one along the way. The strategy is discovered in the process of remembering.

Ornstein, Naus, and their colleagues (Ornstein, Baker-Ward, & Naus, 1988; Ornstein & Naus, 1985) have similarly argued that age-related increases in knowledge are responsible in part for developmental improvements in memory performance. But they stress the role that children's knowledge base plays in the instigation of strategic behavior. They propose that the use of memory strategies is facilitated by the automatic execution of certain parts of a task, even in very young children. Later in development, when children have a more sophisticated knowledge base and more experience, entire problem-solving routines may become automated. The difference between the positions of Bjorklund and of Ornstein and Naus is one of degree, with the researchers agreeing that what children know about a particular domain will substantially influence their ability to remember related information (cf. Chi, 1978).

Knowledge of Rules

Siegler (1981, 1983, 1986) has taken a somewhat different approach to interpreting differences in knowledge base among children. In his *rule assessment approach*, Siegler proposes that cognitive development can be characterized as the acquisition of increasingly powerful rules for solving problems. Siegler defines rules as "'if . . . then' statements linking particular conditions to actions to be taken if those conditions hold true" (Siegler, 1986, p. 88). Siegler maintains that developmental differences in the rules children possess are responsible in large part for age differences in cognitive functioning. In one study (Siegler, 1981), children between the ages of 5 and 17 years were found in over 90% of the trials to solve most Piagetian reasoning problems (for example, conservation, balance-scale problem) by applying one of several rules. In the balance-scale problem, for instance, children must determine which side of the balance will fall, considering the number of weights on each side of the balance and their distance from the midpoint. Children using Rule 1 consider only a single dimension: the amount of weight on each side. Children using Rule 2 similarly predict that the side with the most weights will drop, but when the number of weights is equal on both sides, they then consider the distance from the scale's midpoint. With Rule 3, children use both the weight and distance dimensions but have a difficult

time coordinating the two, resulting in their muddling through the problem. Finally, children using Rule 4 make the appropriate computations of weight and distance, thus deriving the correct answer regardless of how the weights are distributed across the scale. Siegler demonstrated that this progression of rules is highly similar for several Piagetian-type problems. Rules develop as children become increasingly able to encode or represent environmental events more precisely, permitting them to learn more advanced rules.

Siegler also contends that when the going gets mentally tough for children, they rely on *fallback* rules, procedures they apply when they are unfamiliar with the task at hand or when their limited information processing capacity is being strained. An example of a fallback rule was provided in the discussion in Chapter 2 of egocentric responding in visual perspective taking tasks. Given simple arrays of objects, young children can accurately take the visual perspective of another (Borke, 1975); but when the arrays become more complicated, as in Piaget and Inhelder's three-mountain problem, they give an egocentric response, saying that the other person sees the array exactly as they do. When pressed to make a decision about an overly complicated situation, in other words, they "fall back" to an earlier-acquired rule and use it consistently. Although on the surface Siegler's approach to cognitive development seems much different from the approaches of Chi or Bjorklund discussed above, all hold that what children know has a substantial impact on how they approach problems and arrive at solutions.

Children's Belief about What Is Alive

Differences in children's knowledge of a particular content area are not only important for memory and problem-solving tasks but may also affect children's thinking in ways that are not immediately obvious. Recent research has suggested, for example, that children's tendencies to attribute animate characteristics to inanimate objects is influenced by their degree of knowledge about the objects in question. Piaget (1969a) observed that young children often give life characteristics to nonliving things. He attributed this tendency to young children's inability to distinguish the psychological world from the physical world.

Movement or action seems to be the criterion in young children's determination of whether an object is alive. This way of thinking is illustrated in excerpts of interviews with children from Piaget (1969a):

Kenn (7½): "Is water alive?—Yes.—Why?—It moves. . . .—Is fire alive?—Yes, it moves. . . .—Is the sun alive?—Yes, it moves" [p. 200].

Vel (8½): "Is the sun alive?—Yes.—Why?—It gives light.—Is a candle alive?—No.—Why not?—(Yes) because it gives light. It is alive when it is giving light, but it isn't alive when it is not giving light.—Is a bicycle alive?—No, when it doesn't go it isn't alive. When it goes it is alive"* [p. 196].

Piaget asserted that at the earliest stages, children attribute animistic (particularly, human) characteristics to all objects. Later, they attribute life only to those objects that move spontaneously, and finally they distinguish between biologically animate and inanimate objects.

Research subsequent to Piaget's initial observations yielded equivocal findings. Several researchers have generally replicated Piaget's observations (Laurendeau & Pinard, 1962; Russell & Dennis, 1939); others have failed to find any significant degree of animism in young children (Johnson & Josey, 1931–32); and still others have presented evidence that animism persists into adulthood (see Looft & Bartz, 1969). One shortcoming of these early studies, as well as of Piaget's methodology, is that they relied primarily on children's decisions whether an object was alive, without specifying to the child what "being alive" actually means or evaluating what a child means when he or she says that an object is living. Several recent studies have improved upon the earlier methods by asking children to determine whether animate and inanimate objects possess particular features that are characteristic of either living or nonliving things (Bullock, 1985; Carey, 1985b; Dolgin & Behrend, 1984).

In the study by Bullock (1985), 3-, 4-, and 5-year-old children and adults were shown separate videotapes of four objects, two animate (a 2-year-old girl and a rabbit) and two inanimate (a plastic, wind-up worm and a set of wooden blocks). In each videotape, one of the four objects was initially stationary to the right and then moved to a bowl to the left of the screen. The subjects were asked a series of questions concerning the type of attributes each object possessed. Some attributes were appropriate for animate objects (for example, "Does X have a brain?" "Can X grow bigger?"), and others were appropriate for inanimate objects (for example, "If X breaks, can we fix it with glue?" "If we put X on a shelf, will it stay there?"). The subjects were later asked to justify their judgments and were also asked whether each of the four objects was "alive." Generally, the accuracy of children's judgments of attributes increased with age, with 5-year-olds being more similar to the adults than to the 3- and 4-year-old children. However, even the judgments of the 3-year-olds (which were often no better than expected by chance) did not reflect a general animistic orientation. The 3-year-olds were just as likely to attribute inanimate characteristics to animate objects (for example, "If you put the rabbit on the shelf, will it stay there?" "Yes") as they were to attribute animate characteristics to nonliving objects (for example, "Can the blocks grow bigger?" "Yes"). Movement did seem to be an important factor in influencing children's judgments of animacy, but the young children used it inconsistently. Bullock concluded that judgments of animateness by young children should not be attributed to an overall animistic attitude but reflect a "general uncertainty about the precise properties of many objects, regardless of object type" (p. 224).

These recent findings suggest that children's decisions about what is alive and what is not are a function of their degree of knowledge about objects (see Carey, 1985b). Given that young children have less detailed information about the nature of everyday objects in their environments than their older peers, they are less likely to make accurate decisions about the viability of those objects. On some occasions they err by assuming life where life does not exist; on other occasions they err by assuming no life when the object is indeed alive.

□ Summary

The information processing approaches to the study of cognition emphasize the flow of information through processing "systems," with the capacity of these systems being limited in terms of how much information they can hold and how quickly and elaborately they can process information. Cognitive operations are conceptualized as existing on a continuum with *automatic*, or *effortless*, processes at one extreme and *controlled*, *strategic*, or *effortful* processes at the other. Information processing theories are concerned with the acquisition and manipulation of knowledge. Knowledge of language terms and concepts has been referred to as *semantic memory*, with information in semantic memory being represented in terms of an interconnecting network of nodes.

Information processing approaches to cognitive development have yielded interesting elaborations of Piaget's theoretical framework. Initial information processing theories, as exemplified by Pascual-Leone's, stressed age-related changes in the capacity of the short-term store. More recent formulations, particularly that of Case, suggest that capacity remains relatively constant across development but that there are substantial age differences in the *efficiency* of information processing. Older children require less *operating space* for the execution of cognitive processes than younger children, leaving more space available for storage or for the execution of other cognitive operations. However, whether there is a single, "generic" pool of information processing resources, as suggested by Case and others, or separate, independent stores of resources, as suggested by Brainerd and Kingma, has yet to be determined.

Following Sternberg's componential theory, developmental differences have been found in *metacomponents*, processes responsible for monitoring task performance and making executive decisions, *performance components*, processes involved in the encoding, mental comparison, and retrieval of information, and *knowledge-acquisition components*, processes involved in gaining new information.

Children's *strategies* have been extensively studied in *training experiments*, in which young children who do not use a strategy spontaneously are instructed to use one. A three-stage sequence has been suggested. The earliest stage reflects children who cannot benefit from strategic instruction; these children are said to be illustrating a *mediational deficiency*. Slightly older children can benefit from a strategy when instructed but do not produce one spontaneously; they have a *production deficiency*. In the final stage children generate a strategy spontaneously and use it to facilitate performance. More recent work has indicated that even "production deficient" children use strategies spontaneously, although these strategies are not very sophisticated and may not facilitate performance. Two factors associated with children's successful use of strategies are the amount of mental effort the strategies require and the efficiency of children's information processing.

It is becoming increasingly clear that what children know, or their *knowledge base*, plays an important role in how they process information. Recent data indicate that the child's domain-specific knowledge, acquired continuously throughout development, accounts for many of the adult/child differences observed in cognition. The *rule-assessment approach* of Siegler holds that a child's knowledge and application of a small set of rules can account for developmental differences on Piagetian-type reasoning tasks. Although outwardly different from the knowledge base approaches of Chi and others, Siegler's theory also emphasizes the role that knowledge, in the form of rules, plays in affecting cognitive development. Age differences in children's knowledge base can also account for other developmental phenomena, such as their judgments of what is alive and what is not.

□ Note

1. In his most recent formulation, Sternberg (1985) has classified this theory as one of three subtheories in his broader triarchic theory of intelligence. The theory will be discussed in greater detail in Chapter 10.

Perception

Basic Perceptual Abilities of Young Infants
☐ Skin and Body-Orientation Senses ☐ Chemical Senses ☐ Hearing ☐ Vision

The Development of Visual Perception
☐ Discrimination and Attention ☐ The Development of Visual Preferences in Infancy
☐ Infant Categorization

Auditory Perception in Infancy

Intermodal Integration in Infancy

Summary

The beginning of all cognition lies in perception. Before we can make comparisons between two objects, categorize sets of items, retrieve a fact, or create an image, we must have the basic data from the external world with which to work. The theories of James and Eleanor Gibson (E. J. Gibson, 1969; J. J. Gibson, 1966) have greatly influenced the study of perception. The Gibsons viewed perception as an active process, whereby the organism extracts information from stimulation in the environment and, as a result, modifies its behavior. They, and developmental psychologists following their lead, have been less concerned with the individual's registration and preliminary interpretation of sensory input than with changes in an individual's behavior as a result of perception. In other words, the concern is with *perceptual learning* and not with perception for its own sake. Perceptual learning refers to:

> an increase in the ability to extract information from the environment, as a result of experience and practice with stimulation coming from it. . . . Perceptual learning is self-regulating, in the sense that modification occurs without the necessity of external reinforcement. It is stimulus oriented, with the goal of extracting and reducing the information in stimulation. Discovery of distinctive features and structure in the world is fundamental in the achievement of this goal [Gibson, 1969, pp. 3–4].

Although early developmental research in perception dealt with issues of basic sensory abilities (for example, whether babies can see and hear), most work of the past 25 years can properly be classified as investigations of perceptual learning. How is it that infants learn to discriminate the sounds of their language? What perceptual biases, if any, are they born with that make the learning process easier? How do infants come to recognize their mothers and, eventually, other people? How do they categorize experience? These questions deal with perception during infancy, and although perceptual development over childhood has not been ignored by developmental psychologists (see Gibson & Spelke, 1983; Smith, 1983), most research in the area has focused on the infant. Because of the wealth of information that has accumulated dealing with infant percep-

tion, I will restrict my discussion of perceptual development in this chapter to infancy.

Following from both the Gibsonian and Piagetian traditions, perceptual functioning in human infants is viewed today as an active process. Babies come into the world with dispositions to attend to certain classes of stimuli and with rules for acquiring information through their senses. These rules may change over the course of infancy, but even newborns are prepared to operate on their perceptual worlds and are not passive recipients of environmental stimulation. Haith (1980) summed up his study of vision in neonates by postulating five rules that they use in acquiring and processing visual information:

> *Rule 1:* If awake and alert and the light is not too bright, open your eyes.
> *Rule 2:* If it is dark, keep looking, scanning the environment broadly.
> *Rule 3:* If it is light and you see nothing, scan broadly, searching for edges.
> *Rule 4:* If an edge is found, cease the broad scanning and stay in the general vicinity of the edge. Implement eye movements that cross the edge.
> *Rule 5:* While in the proximity of edges, reduce the range of fixations perpendicular to the edges as the amount of contour in the area increases.

These rules for looking indicate that the newborn is well-equipped for the task of seeing. Newborns may not display the flexibility in visual processing that older infants do, but their visual scanning is not random, and they do show some selectivity in the things they choose to look at.

In the sections to follow, I examine infant perception, concentrating on vision, hearing, and sensory, or intermodal, integration. Keep in mind throughout the chapter that the infant is an active participant in the process of acquiring and interpreting perceptual information. Also keep in mind that infants are *learning* through their sensory perceptions. They are gaining knowledge, and this knowledge is being added to and is transforming their prior knowledge, which itself was gained from infants' senses.

☐ Basic Perceptual Abilities of Young Infants

No one expects much of newborns in the way of cognitive or perceptual abilities. In fact, the eminent American psychologist William James (1890) described the world of the young infant as "one great booming buzzing confusion." This view of young infants as passive "nonperceivers" was held by many psychologists and physicians well into the 1950s and '60s. In the past 30 years, we have learned much about the perceptual abilities of infants and realize that James's view was overstated. Newborns are far from mental giants, but they do enter the world able to perceive information from all of their senses and are somewhat selective in what they attend to. Furthermore, babies have some perceptual biases. Some sights, sounds, and smells are innately more pleasing to them than others, and they learn to prefer other sensations in the first weeks of life.

Skin and Body-Orientation Senses

Concerning the skin senses, newborns are sensitive to slight changes in temperature and are very receptive to touch. Sensitivity to touch is apparent early during the fetal period (Carmichael, 1970), and several studies have demonstrated more rapid development for groups of premature infants receiving tactile stimulation (for example, being stroked for four 15-minute periods per day over their first 10 days) than for those not being stroked (Solkoff, Yaffe, Weintraub, & Blase, 1969; White & LaBarba, 1976).

An awareness of the position of one's body in space (proprioceptive and vestibular senses) is also well developed. Newborns react to a sudden movement or a loss of support with a startle response, extending their forearms and later returning them to their chest (the Moro reflex). Also, one of the most effective techniques for soothing fussy babies involves regular alterations of their body position, usually accompanied by tactile stimulation (Korner & Thoman, 1972). That is, babies can be comforted by being rocked and held.

Chemical Senses

The chemical senses of taste and smell are reasonably well developed at birth. Newborns display different facial expressions, tongue movements, and physiological responses for each of the four basic tastes of sweet, sour, salty, and bitter and show a preference for sweet substances (Cowart, 1981; Steiner, 1979). Similarly, babies can discriminate among a wide variety of odors early in life (Steiner, 1979), and they develop preferences for certain odors within the first week. In a study by Macfarlane (1975), for example, 6-day-old nursing babies were able to discriminate the odor of their mothers from that of other women. Mothers wore breast pads in their bras between nursings. Two breast pads were placed on either side of an infant's head, one from the baby's mother and the other from another woman. Although there were no differences in infants' behaviors in this situation at 2 days of age, by day 6 babies were turning to their own mother's pad more often than to the pad of another woman. That is, not only can babies discriminate odors, they quickly learn to make associations with odors and to modify their behavior accordingly.

Hearing

Auditory perception is well developed in the newborn. Unlike visual stimulation, sound can be perceived in utero, and there is evidence that loud noises result in changes in the heart rates of 7-month-old fetuses (Bernard & Sontag, 1947). Infants appear to be more sensitive to high-frequency than to low-frequency tones (Trehub, Schneider, & Endman, 1980), and this may explain their seeming preference for the voices of women. As with smell, infants less than 1 week old have been shown to recognize their mothers on the basis of sound. DeCasper and Fifer (1980) measured the rate at which 1- to 3-day-old infants sucked on a pacifier. Then they conditioned the babies to alter their sucking rate (faster for one-half of the babies and slower for the other half) to the tape-recorded voices of their mothers and of an unfamiliar woman. DeCasper and Fifer reported that these young infants varied their sucking rates to hear their mothers' voices, indicating that they not only could discriminate the voices of their mothers from that of other women but also acquired a distinct preference for the voices of their mothers in a matter of days.

More recent research by DeCasper and Spence (1986) suggests that this preference may have its origins before birth. Pregnant women read aloud one of three passages twice a day during the last six weeks of their pregnancy. Shortly after birth, the neonates were tested for which passages, if any, would have more reinforcing value. Headphones were placed over babies' ears, and various passages were played to the infants. Nonnutritive sucking was assessed as a function of what passage was being played. First of all, a baseline of sucking rate was determined for each baby (that is, how rapidly the infant sucked on a nipple when no passage was being played). The babies then heard a familiar passage (the one their mothers had read during pregnancy) or a novel passage (one their mothers had not read) as a function of changes in their sucking rate. For some infants an increase in sucking rate was associated with the familiar passage, and a decrease in sucking rate was associated with the novel passage. The contingency was reversed for other infants. The general finding was that the familiar passage was more reinforcing than the novel passage. That is, infants were more likely to alter their sucking rate to hear the familiar passage than to hear the novel passage. Furthermore, the reinforcing value of the story was independent of who recited it, an infant's mother or another woman. These results present unambiguous evidence of prenatal conditioning to auditory patterns. The infants were able to discern the auditory characteristics of these often-repeated stories. These findings indicate not only that the auditory system in newborns is working well but also that babies are "learning" some things about the outside world while still in utero.

That young infants can learn to be soothed by music is indicated in tales of many parents of premature babies who were hospitalized for the first several months of life. A common practice on many premature nursery wards is to play the radio constantly. One parent reported that after three months in the hospital, her baby would fall asleep only if the radio was playing. This mother had planned on playing her daughter a musical diet of Mozart and Beethoven. Unfortunately, all she could find on all-night radio was country music. By the time the baby was 8 months old, her preference for country music had been decided, although her mother was working hard to change that preference.

Vision

Because of the absence of light in utero, vision does not function prenatally. Newborns can perceive light, as demonstrated by the pupillary reflex (constriction of the pupil to bright light and dilation to low levels of illumination), and they apparently see the world in color (Adams, Maurer, & Davis, 1986). However, *accommodation*, or focusing of the lens, is relatively poor at birth. Early research indicated that infants are born with a fixed lens, so that only stimuli approximately 20 centimeters away (about 8 inches) are in focus (Haynes, White, & Held, 1965). More recent work by Banks (1980) indicates that under favorable stimulus conditions accommodation is adult-like by as early as 2 months of age, with many younger infants displaying good accommodative ability. Newborns will visually track a moving object, but their eyes will not necessarily be moving in harmony. *Convergence* refers to both eyes looking at the same object, an ability apparently not possessed by newborns (Wickelgren, 1967). Convergence and *coordination* (both eyes following a moving stimulus in a coordinated fashion) improve over the first months of life and are adult-like by 6 months (Aslin & Jackson, 1979). Studies attempting to determine the *acuity* of infants, or the ability to see clearly, have yielded varied results, depending on the technique used. With normal acuity for adults being 20/20, estimates of newborn acuity range from 20/400 to 20/600, making the neonate legally blind in most states. Acuity improves over the next several months, and by some estimates it reaches adult levels by 6 months (see Walk, 1981).

Newborns have an impressive array of perceptual capabilities. They can see, hear, taste, and smell;

they have innate preferences for some stimuli and can make subtle discriminations among stimuli in some modes. Their perception is not so acute as that of the toddler or even the 6-month-old, but their world is also not merely a booming buzzing confusion.

In the sections to follow the development of visual and auditory perception and intersensory functioning in infancy are examined in greater detail. More research has been done on infant vision than on all the other senses combined, and it is my primary focus of discussion. The examination of auditory perception in infancy centers mainly on children's perception of language. The extent to which infants can coordinate information from two senses into an integrated whole is examined in the final section.

☐ The Development of Visual Perception

Discrimination and Attention

The research cited earlier indicated that newborns can discriminate differences in intensity of light, as reflected by their pupillary reflex, and can track a moving object. But what really interests most cognitive psychologists is the question of whether infants can really *see*: Can they discriminate form? Can they tell the difference between a checkerboard pattern and bull's-eye, for example? The issue of whether newborns can discriminate form is the basis of the philosophical argument concerning whether infants must *learn* to interpret sensory input (the *empiricist position*, as put forth by George Berekely and John Locke), or whether this ability is present at birth (the *nativist position*, as argued by René Descartes and Immanuel Kant). But how is one to tell? Infants cannot speak to us, nor can they make any sense of the things we say to them. As late as the 1960s many prominent psychologists believed that what a young infant knows and can perceive could not be discerned by scientific inquiry (Hochberg, 1962).

Robert Fantz developed a surprisingly simple technique for assessing *visual preferences* in young infants (Fantz, 1958, 1961; Fantz, Ordy, & Udelf, 1962). He placed alert babies in a *looking chamber* (see the

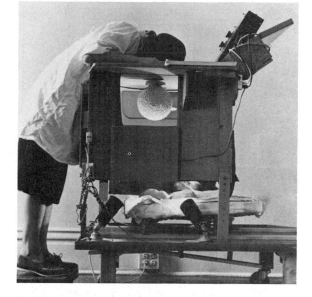

PHOTO 4-1   A looking chamber used to test visual preferences in human infants (Fantz, 1961)

accompanying photo). Series of visual stimuli were placed before infants' eyes, and an observer peeking through a hole in the chamber above the infant recorded which stimuli the baby looked at the most. If groups of infants spend significantly more time gazing at one pattern than another, it can be assumed that they can differentiate between the two patterns and *prefer* to look at one relative to the other. Using this technique, Fantz was able to show that babies less than 1 week old can tell the difference between stimuli such as a schematic face, a bull's-eye pattern, and an unpatterned disk (see Figure 4-1 on page 72). Because of the relatively poor acuity of young infants, stimuli must be reasonably discrepant before discriminations can be made, but such discriminations are made by newborns.

Infants' visual discrimination abilities increase over the first several months. For example, 3-month-olds prefer their mothers' faces to the faces of strangers (Barrera & Maurer, 1981), indicating that they can identify their mothers on the basis of vision alone. By 5 to 7 months, infants can make relatively fine discriminations among stimuli, including the socially important class of visual stimuli, human faces (Cohen & Strauss, 1979).

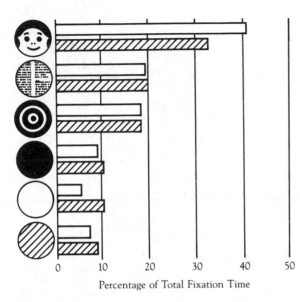

FIGURE 4-1 Infants' visual attention to different patterns. The dark bars show the results for 2- to 3-month-old infants, and the lighter bars, results for older infants (Fantz, 1961).

Fantz's results provided strong support for the nativist position. Babies come into the world prepared to see. But more important yet is the fact that they are biologically prepared to look at some things more than others. In the following section the visual preferences of newborns and how these preferences change over infancy are examined.

The Development of Visual Preferences in Infancy

What a baby, or anyone else for that matter, likes to look at depends on a variety of physical stimulus characteristics as well as psychological characteristics. Physical characteristics such as movement, amount of contour or contrast, complexity, symmetry, and curvature of the stimulus affect our looking behavior; familiarity and novelty determine the psychological significance of a stimulus for us. Familiarity and novelty become important determinants of infants' attention between 2 and 4 months. Until this time, babies' visual attention is affected chiefly by physical stimulus features.

Physical Stimulus Characteristics

Movement is a potent stimulus characteristic in influencing infants' visual attention. Everything else being equal, babies look more at a moving stimulus than at a comparable stimulus that is stationary. In an experiment by Haith (1966), newborns sucked on a nipple while watching a light display. On some trials, the light moved, tracing the outline of a triangle. Babies decreased their sucking on these trials, relative to those when the light did not move, indicating increased attention to movement.

Infants are also attracted to areas of high *contrast*, as reflected by the outline, or *contour*, of an object. In a pioneering study, Salapatek and Kessen (1966) assessed the visual scanning of newborns. Infants less than 1 week old were placed in a modified looking chamber with a white triangle painted on a black background situated before their eyes. The infants' eye movements were recorded and were contrasted with those when the triangle was not visible. Examples of the scanning patterns of the newborns when the triangle was present are shown in Figure 4-2. As can be seen, the infants' visual fixations were centered near the vertices of the triangles, the areas of most contrast; that is, those areas where visually scanning infants are most likely to encounter black/white contrasts.

Subsequent work by Salapatek and his colleagues

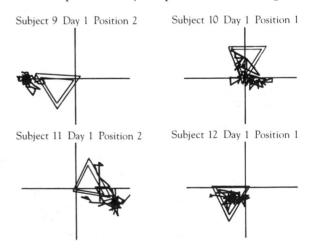

FIGURE 4-2 Examples of scanning patterns of newborns (Salapatek and Kessen, 1966)

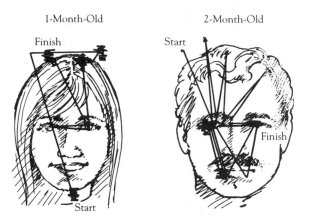

FIGURE 4-3 Examples of visual scanning of faces by 1- and 2-month-old infants

(Maurer & Salapatek, 1976; Salapatek, 1975) indicated that infants at 1 month of age direct their attention primarily to the outside of a figure and spend little time inspecting internal features. Salapatek referred to this tendency as the *externality effect*. By 2 months, however, most of infants' fixations are on internal stimulus features. An example of scanning patterns of 1- and 2-month-olds is shown in Figure 4-3.

Related to contour is *complexity*. Early researchers reported that a baby's preference for complexity increased with age. Young infants prefer to look at checkerboard patterns comprising a relatively few number of elements, for example, whereas older infants prefer patterns having a greater number of elements (Brennan, Ames, & Moore, 1966). In these and other experiments, however, complexity is confounded with amount of contour, because more complex stimuli have greater amounts of contour. Karmel and his colleagues reported data suggesting that the more complex patterns are preferred because they have more contour and that complexity, per se, has little to do with infants' visual preferences (Karmel, 1969; Karmel & Maisel, 1975).

More recently, Banks and his colleagues have proposed a *contrast sensitivity function* approach to infants' visual preferences (Banks & Ginsburg, 1985; Banks & Salapatek, 1981, 1983). This approach takes into consideration a number of factors, including spatial frequency (the number of pattern repetitions in a stimulus), orientation of a stimulus, and contrast, and it combines them in a mathematical model to predict visual preferences. Basically, a contrast sensitivity function describes the level of contrast a person needs to detect a pattern at a particular spatial frequency. Experiments by Banks and Salapatek (1981) demonstrated differences in the contrast sensitivity function among 1-, 2-, and 3-month-old infants. Infants were shown stimuli varying in spatial frequency, an example of which is shown in the accompanying photo. Infants' preferences for various spatial frequencies, as measured by visual fixation patterns, were then determined. Visual acuity (how clearly a stimulus can be seen, or how precisely stimuli can be discriminated) improved over the 1- to 3-month period, particularly with respect to high spatial frequencies (fine stripes). Based on these and related data, Banks and Salapatek proposed that previous developmental findings of infants' increasing preference for complexity may

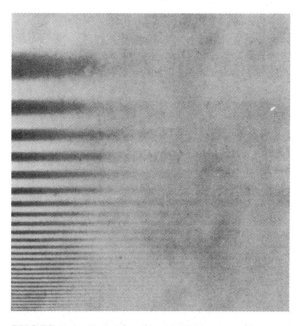

PHOTO 4-2 Example of a stimulus varying in spatial frequency used to assess contrast sensitivity function (Thanks to Martin Banks for making this photo available.)

instead be due to infants' improved visual acuity. More complex stimuli typically consist of more components with high spatial frequencies. Thus, as infants' visual acuity improves, they prefer to look at patterns with small elements (such as small checks in a checkerboard pattern), because these stimuli involve higher spatial frequencies than less "complex" stimuli (such as checkerboard patterns with larger checks).

Infants' preference for and processing of *symmetrical* stimuli have been shown for vertical stimuli. Although there seems to be no preference for vertical symmetry until the latter part of the first year, infants as young as 4 months process vertically symmetrical stimuli more efficiently than vertically asymmetrical or horizontal stimuli (Bornstein, Ferdinandsen, & Gross, 1981; Fisher, Ferdinandsen, & Bornstein, 1981; Humphrey, Humphrey, Muir, & Dodwell, 1986). Efficiency of visual processing in these studies was measured by rates of visual *habituation*, the decrease in attention as a result of repeated exposure to a stimulus. (See the discussion of habituation later in the chapter.) Four-month-old infants acquired information about vertically symmetrical stimuli more effectively than asymmetrical or horizontal information as reflected by their faster rates of habituation (that is, they looked at the symmetrical stimuli less on later trials than they did asymmetrical or horizontal stimuli). "The results . . . support the view that vertical has a special status in early perceptual development. . . . Whether innate, early maturing, or based on experience, the special quality of verticality generally may derive from the importance of the vertically symmetrical body and face" (Bornstein et al., 1981, p. 85).

One other physical stimulus feature of importance is that of *curvature*. Some of Fantz's original work demonstrated infants' preferences for curved stimuli, such as a bull's-eye, over linear (that is, straight-line) stimuli of comparable contour (Fantz, 1958). Ruff and Birch (1974) similarly observed a preference for curvilinear stimuli in 3- and 4-month-old infants, but they also found a preference for *concentric* stimuli, even if composed of straight lines (see Figure 4-4). This preference for curvature was reported even in a sample of newborns by Fantz and Miranda

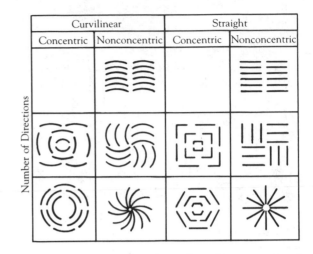

FIGURE 4-4   Examples of stimuli used to assess infants' preferences for curvature (Ruff and Birch, 1974)

(1975), although only when the stimuli differed in their outer perimeter (recall the externality effect). Such preferences for curvature may help explain young infants' seeming preference to attend to the human face.

One somewhat surprising visual preference recently found in young infants is that for *attractive faces* (Langlois et al., 1987). The researchers asked college men and women to judge the attractiveness of adult Caucasian women from photographs. From these ratings, eight attractive and eight unattractive photographs of faces were selected, although the distribution of attractiveness was relatively normal (that is, there were no extremely attractive or unattractive faces). The photographs were selected so that all women had neutral expressions, medium to dark hair, and did not wear glasses. In one condition of the study, 2- to 3-month-old and 6- to 8-month-old infants were shown pairs of faces varying in attractiveness (one attractive face and one unattractive one), and their looking time was measured. Both the younger and older infants spent significantly more time looking at the attractive faces than at the unattractive ones, with approximately two-thirds of the infants showing a preference for the more attractive faces. Furthermore, this effect was not mediated by the attractiveness of an infant's mother. The tendency to look longer at the attractive faces was observed irrespective of how attractive an infant's mother was judged to be.

Langlois and her colleagues speculated about the reasons for their results. One possibility is that attractive faces have more of the physical stimulus characteristics that attract infant attention than do unattractive faces. For example, attractive faces may be more curvilinear, concentric, and vertically symmetrical than unattractive faces, characteristics that would bias an infant's attention to them. A second alternative is that attractive faces may be more prototypical, or "face-like," than unattractive faces. Humans may have evolved to be particularly attentive to the socially significant stimuli of faces, with attractive faces having more features in common with the prototypical face than unattractive faces. In other words, infants are biologically prepared to attend to stimuli of certain proportions (Linn, Reznick, Kagan, & Hans, 1982), with attractive faces providing a closer match to those proportions than unattractive faces. Regardless of the reason, the data indicate that what was once believed to be a learned phenomenon (perceived attractiveness) may have its basis in biology (see also Samuels & Ewy, 1985).

Psychological Stimulus Characteristics

Movement, contour, complexity, symmetry, and curvature continue to affect the attention of people throughout life. As noted, however, beginning sometime around 2 to 4 months, the psychological characteristics of a stimulus exert an influence on whether and for how long it will be attended to. By psychological I refer to meaning. Stimuli that are *familiar* or *slightly novel* influence infants' attention. This implies some sort of memory for the stimulus event. For a stimulus to be regarded as familiar, it must be contrasted with some previous mental representation of that stimulus. Similarly, to be novel, a stimulus has to be slightly different from something that the perceiver already knows (Rheingold, 1985). The topic of infant memory will be discussed in Chapter 8. For now, keep in mind that the effect of these psychological features depends on infants forming representations of stimuli and using these memorial representations to influence their looking behavior.

Kagan (1971) proposed that beginning around 2 months infants form *schemas*, or sensory representations, and that it is the similarity of a stimulus to previously formed schemas that determines attention. A schema is not an exact copy of a stimulus but is "a representation of an event that preserves the temporal and spatial arrangement of its distinctive elements without necessarily being isomorphic with the event" (Kagan, 1971, p. 6). Kagan proposed the *discrepancy principle* to understand infants' attention to novel stimuli. According to Kagan, infants are most attentive to stimuli that are moderately discrepant from a schema. A stimulus that differs slightly from what a baby already knows (for example, a bearded face when the infant is familiar with nonbearded faces) is likely to maintain attention, whereas a highly familiar stimulus (a nonbearded face) or a highly discrepant one (a model of a face with its features scrambled) is likely to receive less of an infant's attention.

Support for the discrepancy principle has been provided by McCall and his colleagues (McCall & Kennedy, 1980; McCall, Kennedy, & Appelbaum, 1977). In these experiments, infants between 2 and 4 months old were familiarized with stimuli and were later shown new stimuli that varied in their similarity to the originals. The researchers reported an inverted-**U** relation for attention as a function of how similar the new stimulus was to the standard (see Figure 4-5). Stimuli that were highly similar to the original and those that were highly discrepant

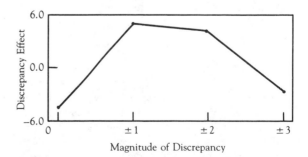

FIGURE 4-5 Relative amount of visual looking time (discrepancy effect) as a function of magnitude of discrepancy for 10-week-old infants (McCall, Kennedy, and Appelbaum, 1977)

received less attention than those of moderate discrepancy from the standard. This preference for novelty implies that some representation of the original stimulus was retained (a schema) and was used to guide subsequent visual processing.

Primary and Secondary Visual Systems

The shift from attention based primarily on physical stimulus features to attention based on psychological characteristics reflects underlying changes in the organization of the visual nervous system. Bronson (1974) cited behavioral and anatomical evidence suggesting that babies' vision during the first month of life is directed by the phylogenetically older *secondary visual system*. This system, which mediates visually guided behavior in simple animals, appears to be better developed in human newborns than the more sophisticated *primary visual system*. The secondary visual system operates mainly in the visual periphery (that is, nonfoveal) and serves to orient the infant toward a stimulus, providing information concerning *where* a stimulus is. Processing with the primary visual system is done by the fovea, the part of the retina where acuity is greatest, permitting the careful analysis of stimulus properties. With repeated exposure, infants can encode salient features of a stimulus, serving as the basis for perceptual representations (or schemas). In other words, the primary visual system provides information concerning *what* a stimulus is.

The primary visual system begins influencing babies' vision at around 2 months, and as visual experiences accumulate, they increasingly affect what infants choose to look at. According to Bronson (1974, p. 84),

> As memories accrue there is an increasing ability to utilize prior experience for the guidance of visual regard, and hence gaze no longer will be largely limited to the most salient aspects of a configuration. Around the third month babies are able to examine diverse aspects of a stimulus in a series of repeated refixations, and the development of this intentional scanning enables the infant to encode entire patterns where previously only isolated elements were recorded (for example, it is now a face that is smiled at, not just a pair of eyes).

Many parents can recognize this change. Babies during the first couple of months seem to stare at "things" even if those things happen to be located on a human face (such as eyes). By 3 or 4 months, however, many parents get the feeling that their baby is really looking at *them*. This feeling fits well with the research data.

Bronson's interpretation is that vision during the first few months of life is qualitatively different from subsequent vision. The earliest visual processing is under the control of subcortical portions of the brain, and it has different functions than does later visual processing, which is controlled chiefly by cortical brain structures. These differences in brain control of vision account for developmental changes in visual preferences observed over the first 3 or 4 months of life.

Depth Perception

One area of infant visual perception that has received considerable attention over the years is depth perception. At what age and under what conditions can infants discriminate visual patterns denoting depth? One reason for interest in the topic is that the ability to perceive depth appears to be innate for some species that are able to locomote shortly after birth, including chickens and goats (Walk & Gibson, 1961). Are human babies born with the ability to discriminate depth, or does the discrimination of depth require experience?

One factor that is important for the perception of depth concerns *binocular cues*. Because the two eyes are separated by several centimeters, the message one eye receives is slightly different from that received by its partner. This disparity produces information that is important for evaluating an object's distance from us. One ability critical for binocular depth perception is that of *bifoveal fixation*, the ability of the foveas of the two eyes to focus on the same object simultaneously. Aslin (1977) tested bifoveal fixation in 1-, 2-, and 3-month-old infants. A target was moved past the infants' eyes at one of two constant speeds, and eye fixations were photographed. Aslin reported that the infants' eyes did not consistently converge on the targets until 2 months and did not do so without delay until 3 months. Thus,

PHOTO 4-3 An infant on the visual cliff

binocular cues to depth perception are not likely to be functioning well until the second or third month of life.

One reason for the interest in the development of depth cues is their importance in early locomotion. Many parents have tales of their 6-month-old infants crawling off the side of the bed, sometimes to be caught by a watchful parent and sometimes not. What cues must infants attend to to avoid falling, and when and how do they develop? An apparatus designed to test these questions is the *visual cliff* (Gibson & Walk, 1960; Walk & Gibson, 1961). The visual cliff consists of a glass-topped table with a board in its center. On one side of the board the infant sees a checkerboard pattern situated directly under the glass. This is referred to as the "shallow"

side. On the other side the checkerboard pattern is several feet below the glass. This is referred to as the "deep" side (see the accompanying photo). Infants who can crawl (usually beginning around 7 or 8 months) are placed on the centerboard and called by their mothers from either side of the cliff. Will infants ignore the visual cues of depth on the deep side and crawl to their mothers, or will they fuss and refuse to traverse the deep side? Infants who crawl to their mothers on the shallow side but not on the deep side are said to be able to discriminate depth.

In general, early findings of Walk and Gibson indicated that babies rarely crawled to their mothers over the deep side. These findings suggest that once infants can crawl, they display fear, suggesting that little learning is necessary. However, more recent research by Campos and his colleagues found that the tendency to show fear on the visual cliff was related to the extent of previous locomotor experience (Campos, Haitt, Ramsay, Henderson, & Svejda, 1978). Infants with more locomotor experience were more likely to show fear than their less experienced peers, suggesting that such experience is related to depth perception.

Because tests of depth perception using the visual cliff require that an infant be able to crawl, the apparatus would seem to be inappropriate for assessing depth perception in younger infants. However, Campos and his colleagues used the visual cliff with babies who had not begun to crawl (2 and 3½ months) and were able to determine that locomotor experience is not necessary for the perception of depth (Campos, Langer, & Krowitz, 1970). The infants were placed on the centerboard of the cliff, and their heart rates were measured. They were later placed on the deep side, and changes in heart rates were assessed. Increases in heart rate reflect stress, and older infants placed on the deep side of a visual cliff showed such rises, indicating that they could discriminate depth and that they feared it. Younger infants in the study, however, showed *decreases* in heart rates relative to baseline. Decreases in heart rate reflect increased visual attention. Such a finding suggests that young infants can discriminate depth but have not yet learned to fear it. That, apparently, requires experience.

Infant Categorization

Babies have distinct preferences for what they like to look at and display a rudimentary form of visual memory, as reflected by the effects that novelty and familiarity have on their preferences. As important as these basic processes are, our ability to deal effectively with new information would be hopelessly impaired if we did not form *categories*. By the process of categorization, one can treat objects that are perceptually different as being the same kind of thing. Uncle Joe, Aunt Mary, Mommy, Daddy, and the stranger on the street are all unique individuals, but at one level they're all the same: they're all people. Our ability to categorize allows us to reduce an enormous diversity of information into manageable

units. A 6-month-old given a new stuffed animal, rattle, or bottle can identify each object and act toward it accordingly, even though she has never seen the object before. Each object is similar to something the child already knows, and the objects can be categorized and dealt with easily. The process of categorization is ubiquitous, permeating every aspect of our intellectual life, and the origins of categorization can be found in early infancy.

The Habituation/Dishabituation Paradigm

How does one tell if a preverbal baby has formed a category? One useful technique to assess categorization has been the *habituation/dishabituation* (or release from habituation) paradigm. Habituation refers to the decrease in response as a result of repeated presentation of a stimulus. The first day on the job in a noisy factory, for example, produces increased levels of physiological stress (heart rate, blood pressure). After a week in this environment, however, levels of stress decline, even though the noise remains. This is habituation. Dishabituation occurs when, following habituation, a new stimulus is presented that increases our level of responding. If we switch from factory A to factory B, for instance, our levels of physiological stress rise, even though the new factory is no louder than the old one. The noises are different, causing an increase in responding, or a release from habituation.

How does this notion relate to infant visual categories? The amount of time babies look at visual stimuli is analogous to the worker's physiological reactions to loud noise. The longer infants are exposed to a visual stimulus, the less time they spend looking at it. Habituation is said to occur when an infant's looking time is significantly less than it was initially (often defined as when visual fixation to the stimulus is 50% of what it was on the early trials). At that point, a new stimulus is presented. If attention (that is, looking time) increases from the level of immediately before, dishabituation is said to occur. Habituation and subsequent dishabituation have been reported for infants less than 2 days of age (Friedman, 1972; Slater, Earle, Morison, & Rose, 1985). A typical habituation/dishabituation curve is shown in Figure 4-6.

What does such a pattern mean? First of all, it

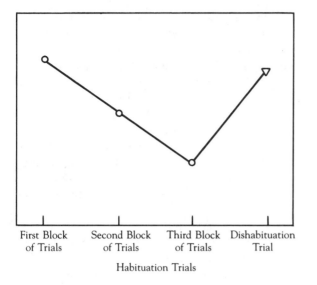

First Block | Second Block | Third Block | Dishabituation
of Trials | of Trials | of Trials | Trial

Habituation Trials

O – Looking time for familiarized stimulus presented during
    habituation trials

▽ – Looking time for novel stimulus presented following
    habituation

FIGURE 4-6 An example of results from an habituation/dishabituation experiment of infant visual attention. The amount of looking time decreases with repeated presentation of the same stimulus (habituation) but increases with the presentation of the new stimulus (dishabituation).

demonstrates that infants can discriminate between the two stimuli. Babies may not have a preference for one over the other, but the fact that they respond to the new stimulus with increased attention reflects that they can tell the difference between the two. In fact, this paradigm is very useful in determining infants' discrimination abilities when using stimuli for which they may not have a decided preference.

Habituation and dishabituation also indicate memory. Infants are making a discrimination between one stimulus that is physically present and another that is present only in memory. They are not choosing between two stimuli that are before them but between one stimulus that is in front of their eyes and another that is only in their minds. More will be said of the habituation/dishabituation paradigm with respect to infant memory in Chapter 8.

Given the basic habituation/dishabituation paradigm, how can it be used to assess infants' concepts? One way is by varying the stimuli that are presented

during the habituation trials. Rather than habituating infants to a picture of a face of a single individual (Sally), for example, pictures of different individuals can be presented (Sally, Mary, Barbara, and Joan). In both the single- and multiple-face cases, the amount of response declines with repeated exposure (that is, habituation). In the former case, infants are habituated to a specific stimulus (Sally), and in the latter case, to a *category* of stimuli (women's faces). After habituation has occurred, a new female face can be presented (Elizabeth). Infants who were habituated to a single face should recognize this new face as a novel stimulus and increase their attention to it (that is, show dishabituation). In contrast, infants who were habituated to women's faces in general should recognize it as just another example of a woman's face and continue to habituate. That is, even though they have never seen this face before, they should categorize it as familiar and direct relatively little of their attention to it.

The procedure and results described above are similar to those reported in an experiment by Cohen and Strauss (1979) for a group of 30-week-old infants. Cohen and Strauss interpreted their findings as evidence that such infants can abstract "appropriate conceptual categories regarding the human face" (p. 422). By continuing to habituate to the new stimulus, infants are, in effect, telling us that although the face is perceptually different from anything they have seen before, it is similar in general form to what they already know. They are telling us that they have acquired a category for female faces.

Research over the past 15 years has shown that infants 6 to 7 months of age can organize objects into perceptual categories during relatively brief experimental sessions (Cohen & Strauss, 1979; Cornell, 1974; Fagan, 1976). Such categorization is less frequently observed in younger infants, although it has been reported for 3- and 4-month-olds for "simpler" categories, such as classifying objects on the basis of shape independent of their orientation (Caron, Caron, & Carlson, 1979) or on the basis of a single common feature (Younger & Cohen, 1983). In related work, Schwartz and Day (1979) habituated infants 8 to 17 weeks old to geometric stimuli. They found that changing the angles of the figures produced dishabituation, whereas rotating the figures without changing the angles yielded only continued habituation. That is, infants as young as 2 months of age had formed concepts of simple geometric figures and were responding to more than line segments. These data do not mean that younger infants cannot form more complex perceptual categories based on everyday experiences; they do mean that the categorization process for infants during the first half of their first year is not well developed, although as seen from the Schwartz and Day research, infants are well prepared to form some simple types of visual categories.

The Structure of Infants' Categories

When infants form categories, how do they do it? This question is not restricted to infant researchers but also concerns scientists interested in concept formation in adults (Posner & Keele, 1970; Rosch, 1975). One popular way of describing adult concepts is in terms of *category prototypes*. A prototype is an abstract representation of a category. It reflects the central tendency, or "best example," of a category. Items that share many features in common with the prototype are said to be *typical* category exemplars (for instance, *robin* for the category BIRDS), whereas items that share fewer features with the prototype are said to be *atypical* category exemplars (for instance, *ostrich* for the category BIRDS) (see Rosch, 1975; Chapter 7).

Several researchers have demonstrated that infants form category prototypes much as adults do. In an experiment by Strauss (1981), for example, 10-month-old infants were habituated to a series of faces. The faces were derived from a prototype and varied in terms of four dimensions (length of face, separation of eyes, width of nose, and length of nose). The infants were not shown the prototype from which the stimulus faces had been derived. Following habituation, the infants were shown sets of category exemplars (that is, faces), including the category prototype. Based on the time they spent looking at the prototype and at other exemplars, infants displayed greater "memory" for the prototype (that is, continued to habituate to it), even though they had never been shown it during the habituation trials. This same pattern of "memory" for prototypes

is found in studies of adult concept formation (Homa, Cross, Cornell, Goldman, & Schwartz, 1973; Posner & Keele, 1970). A study by Bomba and Siqueland (1983) using dot patterns is perhaps even more impressive, in that they report evidence of prototype formation in 3- to 4-month-old infants. Finally, research by Roberts and Horowitz (1986) showed that 9-month-old infants formed a category for the concept BIRDS when habituated to highly typical exemplars of the category (for example, *sparrow*, *robin*, and *bluejay*). There was no evidence of concept formation, however, when atypical exemplars served as the habituation stimuli (for example, *turkey*, *ostrich*, and *chicken*). Like young children, infants are more apt to identify or form a category when provided with typical, as opposed to atypical, category exemplars (Anglin, 1977). The findings of these experiments are enlightening, suggesting that the categorization process of infants is qualitatively similar to that of older children and adults.

Color Categories

Although languages vary greatly in the number of terms they have to describe colors, people in all cultures seem to perceive colors similarly (Berlin & Kay, 1969). When subjects are given color chips to categorize into a specified number of groups, the outcomes are highly similar regardless of whether the person doing the sorting has 11 different basic color words in his or her language or only 2 (Heider, 1972).

The interesting developmental question is "Do infants categorize colors as adults do, or is there an age-related progression in the categorization of color?" Bornstein and his colleagues have investigated this question using the habituation/dishabituation paradigm (Bornstein, Kessen, & Weiskopf, 1976). Four-month-olds were habituated to a color patch corresponding to a wavelength of light of 480 nanometers. Adults classify this color as blue. After habituation the infants were presented with one of two different color patches, one corresponding to a wavelength 30 nanometers greater than the habituated stimulus (510 nanometers) and one corresponding to a wavelength 30 nanometers less than the habituated stimulus (450 nanometers). The two posthabituation stimuli were comparably discrepant from the standard stimulus but in opposite directions. Adults classify the 450-nanometer wavelength as blue, just as they classify the 480-nanometer wavelength. But adults classify the 510-nanometer wavelength as green. Thus, were adults to serve as subjects in this experiment, they would show dishabituation (increased visual attention) to the 510-nanometer wavelength, because they classify it as a color different from the standard blue. However, they would continue to habituate to the 450-nanometer wavelength of light because, although it is comparably different in terms of physical characteristics from the standard, it is perceived only as a different shade of the same color (both blue). How did the babies respond? The 4-month-old infants showed the same categorization responses as adults, habituating to the 450-nanometer stimulus and dishabituating to the 510-nanometer stimulus. The researchers reported similar results for other color boundaries. Although these findings do not prove that the way humans categorize the color spectrum is innate, they are strong evidence for that position.

□ Auditory Perception in Infancy

As noted earlier, infants can hear at birth, and within a matter of days they can develop a preference for their mother's voice (DeCasper & Fifer, 1980). In fact, recent evidence suggests that this preference may have its origins before birth (DeCasper & Spence, 1986). One particularly interesting aspect of infant auditory perception is the extent to which it is attuned to language. Speech consists of *phonemes*, the basic sounds of spoken language, and there is evidence that infants can discriminate among many phonemes soon after birth. For example, research by Eimas and his colleagues (Eimas, Siqueland, Jusczyk, & Vigorito, 1971) demonstrated that 1-month-old infants can tell the difference between phonemes such as *pah* and *bah*. The researchers conditioned babies to suck on a nipple in order to hear a sound (for example, *pah* for some infants). Infants continued to hear *pah* and, following the tenets of habituation described earlier for

vision, their sucking rate eventually declined. After a 2-minute period of decreased responding, a new phoneme was presented (*bah*). As with vision, an increase in responding to a novel stimulus following habituation reflects discrimination. Babies in the study showed dishabituation to the new sound by increasing their sucking rate, indicating that they could indeed differentiate between these two similar sounds.

A point worth making here is that sounds such as *pah* and *bah* are not discrete points on a sound continuum. Rather, there is a range of utterances that adults hear as *pah* and another range of utterances that adults hear as *bah*. That is, slightly different sounds are treated similarly, implying that adults form *categories* of speech sounds. Yet, there is a point on this continuum where, for adults, *pah* turns into *bah*. The work of Eimas and others indicates that such categorization of speech sounds is also found in young infants, implying that the ability is innate. (See Aslin, Pisoni, & Jusczyk, 1983, for a more extensive review.)

If infants can discriminate basic phonemes shortly after birth, how is it they acquire the language sounds peculiar to their mother tongue? English-speaking adults have a difficult time discriminating phonetic contrasts that occur in Czech but that are not found in English. Yet, babies from English-speaking homes have little difficulty with these contrasts, suggesting that they were born with the ability (Trehub, 1976). Other studies have similarly shown that infants can make discriminations among speech sounds that are *not* found in their mother tongues and that their parents cannot make (Lasky, Syrdal-Lasky, & Klein, 1975; Werker, Gilbert, Humphrey, & Tees, 1981). However, some phonetic discriminations are made only with experience. For example, Eilers and her colleagues reported that 6- to 8-month-old infants from English-speaking homes were unable to discriminate some phonetic contrasts that are found in Spanish but not in English (Eilers, Gavin, & Wilson, 1979). Babies from homes where Spanish was spoken had no trouble with such contrasts.

What these and other data suggest is that the process of acquiring the basic sounds of one's language is, at least, a two-way street. Babies can make some sound discriminations that adult speakers of their language communities cannot make; with time, they lose the ability to make these contrasts, because they rarely hear them. There are other sound discriminations, however, that infants cannot make that adults of their language cultures can. With experience, infants (and children) learn to make these discriminations. In sum, the development of perceiving (and producing) language sounds involves both (1) a loss of some discriminations that infants can make that are not found in adult language and (2) the acquisition of some discriminations that infants cannot make but that are made by adults (see Colombo, 1986; Walley, Pisoni, & Aslin, 1981).

Other studies have indicated that young infants can make discriminations among polysyllables under some situations. For example, research by Karzon (1985) has shown that 1- to 4-month-old infants can discriminate among three-syllable sequences (such as *marana* versus *malana*) if the exaggerated style of speaking to infants found in *"motherese"* is used. Motherese refers to the highly intonated speech that typifies mother-to-baby language. In the examples above, the middle syllable would be accented (*ma-rá-na* and *ma-lá-na*) in motherese, which would not be the case in normal adult-to-adult speech. Babies did not differentiate the syllables when they were spoken as in adult-directed speech. In related work by Stern and his colleagues (Stern, Spieker, & MacKain, 1982), mothers of 2-, 4-, and 6-month-old babies were found to use rising intonations when they wished to get a baby's attention and the down-up-down phrasing (as in the *malana* example above) when wishing to maintain an infant's attention. The results of these and other studies suggest that the auditory system of newborns is prepared to process certain types of language and that the sing-songy speech that adults often direct to infants is no accident but reflects the type of language that infants most readily discriminate and attend to.

One other study worth mentioning here is that of Condon and Sander (1974). They presented evidence that newborns are prepared to respond selec-

tively to human language. They reported that 1- and 2-day-old infants' movements were synchronized to speech sounds. It did not matter whether the language was English or Chinese. What was important was that it was language, for infants' movements were not synchronized to disconnected vowels or tapping sounds, suggesting to Condon and Sander that human infants have a template for recognizing human speech. Although provocative, these findings must be approached cautiously, because subsequent research has not always yielded the same findings (see Dowd & Tronick, 1986). Nevertheless, coupled with infants' seemingly innate ability to discriminate many language sounds and their preference for the human voice, the research evidence indicates that the roots of language are planted firmly in biology.

☐ Intermodal Integration in Infancy

Although we often think of each sense as being distinct from all others, as adults we do a great deal of coordinating information between senses. We direct our vision to a loud noise, and we are able to identify our slippers by touch alone when we are awakened in the middle of the night by a barking dog outside our window. Barbecued chicken can be identified by sight, smell, or taste, and we adjust the movements of our arms and hands in reaching for seen objects as a function of how far away they appear (to our eyes) to be. To what extent is such sensory integration available to infants?

At one level, *intermodal* (that is, between senses) integration is present at birth. Newborns move their heads and eyes in the direction of a sound, as if they wish to see what all the noise is about. In a series of experiments examining the effects of sound on visual scanning in newborns, Mendelson and Haith (1976) found that the presence of sound increased infants' visual attentiveness. They suggested that this response to sound increases the likelihood that infants will discover something to look at.

An interesting demonstration of intermodal integration in young infants was provided by Spelke

(1976). Spelke showed 4-month-old infants two films on side-by-side screens. On one screen was a film of a woman playing peekaboo; on the other screen was a hand holding a stick and striking a block of wood. A single sound track was played, corresponding either to the peekaboo or the drumming video. Babies somehow figured out which sound track went with which screen, devoting more looking time to the screen that matched the sound. That is, these 4-month-old infants realized that certain sound sequences go with certain visual displays and visually attended to those displays that provide such a match.

In somewhat related work, Bahrick and Watson (1985) investigated 5-month-olds' ability to integrate proprioceptive and visual information. The babies were seated in an infant seat equipped with a type of tray that prevented them from seeing their legs. Two video screens were placed before the infants. On one screen was displayed the infant's own legs, the picture being transmitted "live." On the other screen was a film of the legs of another infant (or in one experiment, the same infant's legs from a session recorded earlier). Thus, for one display, the movement of infants' legs was contemporaneous with their actual movement (contingent display), whereas for the other display, the movement of legs was independent of the infants' current activity. Bahrick and Watson reasoned that if infants are able to integrate proprioception (as reflected by their own leg movements) and vision, they should be able to discriminate between the two films and spend more time looking at one than the other. This was their finding. In three experiments, 5-month-olds spent, on average, 67% of their time looking at the noncontingent display. Presumably, the lack of contingency between their leg movements and those seen on the video produced some discrepancy, and this resulted in increased attention to the noncontingent display. In a fourth experiment, Bahrick and Watson tested 3-month-olds and found no overall preference for either the contingent or the noncontingent display. They concluded that proprioceptive/visual integration is well established by 5 months and that the ability to detect the congruency between one's

movements and their visual representation may play a fundamental role in an infant's perception of self, possibly underlying the development of visual self-recognition.

A seemingly more complex intermodal feat concerns *intermodal* (or *cross-modal*) *matching*. In intermodal matching, a child must be able to recognize an object initially inspected in one modality (touch, for example) via another modality (vision, for example). Rose, Gottfried, and Bridger (1981) have shown that 1-year-old babies can perform visual/tactual integration. The infants were presented an object (either by touch alone or vision alone) for 60 seconds (familiarization phase) and were later presented a small set of objects in the alternative mode (transfer phase). The researchers reported that the infants spent more time exploring the novel objects than the familiar ones (by manipulating or gazing at them) during the transfer phase. That is, the babies showed dishabituation by examining the novel stimuli more than the familiar ones, even though familiarization was done in a different sensory modality. Other studies using similar methods have demonstrated intermodal matching for 6-month-old infants (Bushnell, 1981; Gottfried, Rose, & Bridger, 1977). In related research, Meltzoff and Borton (1979) reported visual/tactual integration in infants less than 1 month old. In the latter study, the infants were familiarized with one of two pacifiers (a sphere or a sphere with knobs) and later shown three-dimensional models of the two pacifiers. In two experiments, the infants looked significantly longer at the visual display that corresponded to the pacifier they had orally (but not visually) inspected seconds earlier.

The available research on intermodal integration in infants suggests that there is much more of it going on than theorists such as Piaget proposed. But we must be cautious and not attribute too much sophistication to the young infant, for recognizing that a certain sight and sound go together, for example, is not the same skill as identifying an object from a two-dimensional picture after having only touched it (see Rose, Gottfried, & Bridger, 1983). Nevertheless, babies seem well equipped to handle information from several senses simultaneously and to coordinate that information to make sense of their world.

□ Summary

From birth, infants actively use their perceptual systems to acquire information from their surroundings. By 1 week of age babies can discriminate their mothers from other women by smell and by the sound of their voices. Recent evidence indicates that infants' preferences for their mothers' voices has its origins in the womb. Vision is not well developed at birth, although the abilities of convergence, coordination, and accommodation of the lens improve rapidly over the first 6 months.

The question of whether infants can discriminate form at birth was for centuries the center of a philosophical controversy between the empiricists and the nativists. A relatively simple procedure developed by Fantz of assessing *visual preferences* permitted resolution of this question. From birth infants look longer at some stimuli than others, indicating that they can discriminate between the stimuli and have a preference. Among the physical characteristics of a stimulus that attract infants' visual attention are *movement*, *contour* and *contrast*, certain levels of *complexity*, *curvature*, and *facial attractiveness*. Beginning around 2 months, infants' attention is also influenced by psychological factors such as the *familiarity* or *novelty* of a stimulus. Kagan proposed the *discrepancy principle* to explain infants' preferences for novel stimuli, stating that stimuli that are moderately discrepant from a previously acquired schema are most likely to be attended to. Developmental differences in the organization of the visual nervous system have been proposed to account for changes in infants' visual preferences over the first several months of life. At birth, the phylogenetically older *secondary visual system* is functioning better than the more sophisticated *primary visual system*. The secondary visual system mainly directs attention to a stimulus ("Where is it?"), whereas the primary visual system does fine-grain analyses ("What is it?").

The ability to perceive depth is affected by infants' ability to fixate both eyes on the same target (*bifoveal fixations*), which develops over the first 3 months. Depth perception has been extensively studied using the *visual cliff*. Infants who can crawl will not traverse the deep side of the cliff for fear of falling, although they will traverse the shallow side. Other research indicates that displaying fear on the visual cliff is related to one's amount of visual experience and that even prelocomotive infants can perceive depth but do not yet fear it.

Using the *habituation/dishabituation* paradigm, researchers have been able to demonstrate that infants can form visual *categories*. Habituation occurs when infants' looking time diminishes as a result of repeated presentation of a stimulus. Dishabituation occurs when looking time increases with the presentation of a new stimulus. Habituation and dishabituation to visual stimuli are found for newborns and reflect both discrimination and memory. Using the habituation/dishabituation paradigm in categorization studies, researchers have found that babies 7 months old form perceptual categories in terms of *prototypes*, much in the same way as adults and older children do. Three- and 4-month-old infants show categorization for "simpler" concepts such as orientation or for the presence of a single feature. Infants as young as 4 months categorize the color spectrum much as adults do, implying that this ability is innate.

Shortly after birth, infants show a preference for high-pitched voices, and they can develop a preference for their mothers' voice within the first few days of life. Using habituation/dishabituation techniques, researchers have shown that young infants can discriminate among *phonemes* and categorize language sounds much as adults do. Infants can make discriminations among some phonemes that adults of their language culture cannot, and they cannot make some discriminations that adults can. Development thus involves both a loss of some sound discriminations and the acquisition of others. Infants are able to discriminate among polysyllabic sequences best when they are spoken in *motherese*, and some research shows that infants synchronize their movements to language, suggesting that they are born with the ability to recognize human speech.

Intermodal integration refers to the coordination of information between two or more senses. Research has shown that 4-month-olds recognize that certain visual and sound sequences go together, and infants 6 months of age can match information from one sense to another. Some research suggests that *cross-modal matching* actually occurs in the first month of life under some conditions.

5

Sensorimotor Intelligence

Stages of the Sensorimotor Period
☐ Piaget's Description of Development in the Sensorimotor Period
☐ Non-Piagetian Research into the Stages of Sensorimotor Development

Imitation
☐ Piaget's View of Imitation in the Sensorimotor Period
☐ Non-Piagetian Research into Imitation in the Sensorimotor Period

Object Permanence
☐ Piaget's Description of the Development of Object Permanence
☐ Non-Piagetian Research into the Development of Object Permanence

Summary

Recently, I overheard a woman commenting about her 8-month-old nephew: "Wouldn't you like to know what he's thinking? How can babies think when they can't talk?" How indeed? The question of infant "thinking" has fascinated both casual and professional observers for years, and issues of pre-verbal thought continue to be of interest to psychologists, philosophers, and educators today.

Detailed studies of the perceptual skills of infants, discussed in the previous chapter, are relatively new to developmental psychology, not having appeared in any appreciable quantity until the 1960s. Yet, developmental psychologists have had a long-standing interest in the intellectual attainments of infants, going back to the turn of the century. James Mark Baldwin (1895) described the intelligence of infants as *sensorimotor* in nature, a term later adopted by Piaget. Baldwin meant that infants know their world only by their direct actions on it. They do not possess a representational system that allows them to "think" of objects that are not in their immediate perception, and they cannot make mental comparisons between objects. Piaget's work on infant intelligence, commencing in the 1920s, has served as the primary impetus for what is now a vast literature on cognitive functioning during the first 2 years of life.

Over the course of the first 2 years, cognition is transformed in two major ways. First, there is a progression from an action-based to a symbol-based intelligence, from sensorimotor to representational thinking. Second, there is a related change in personal perspective. Young infants, asserted Piaget, are unable to differentiate themselves from the external world. For young infants all the universe is one, with themselves at the center. This idea is similar to a notion of Piaget's contemporary Sigmund Freud, who described newborns' state of being unable to differentiate themselves from their environment as the "oceanic feeling." By the end of the sensorimotor period, infants not only can distinguish themselves from the objects they act upon but also realize that these objects have an existence independent of their actions on them. In general, over the course of infancy, children move increasingly from cognition centered on their immediate actions to cognition

that displaces them in time and space from the things they wish to think about.

In this chapter I examine the work of Piaget and others on the development of intelligence in infancy. First, I present an overview of Piaget's theory and observations of the development of sensorimotor intelligence, particularly the development of *intentionality*, or goal-directed behavior. Then I examine the cognitive contents of imitation and object permanence.

☐ Stages of the Sensorimotor Period

Piaget's Description of Development in the Sensorimotor Period

Piaget divided the sensorimotor period into six stages. A brief description of these stages is provided in Table 5-1. As with Piaget's theory in general, of course, infants progress through these increasingly complex stages in an invariant sequence, with the successful accomplishments of earlier stages being the basis for the accomplishments of later stages.

One comment should be made here concerning Piaget's methods of studying infant intelligence. His primary method was observation, and his sample was limited to his own three children. Piaget did conduct simple "experiments," such as removing his son's hand from his mouth and watching to see if the baby would resume sucking his thumb. Few psychologists today would dare propose a broad theory of infant intelligence based on so limited and biased a sample. The fact that Piaget's theory and observations have stood up so well over the past 60 years (although not without controversy) attests to his skills as an observer of children.

Stage 1: The Use of Reflexes (Birth to 1 Month)
Infants enter the world with a set of inherited action patterns, or reflexes, through which they interpret their experiences. Piaget used the term *reflex* broadly, so that infant reflexes include not only obvious behaviors such as sucking and grasping but also more subtle behaviors such as eye movements, orientation to sound, and vocalization. This is where

intellectual development begins, for, according to Piaget, it is from these basic reflexes that the child first makes contact with the world, acquiring knowledge of objects in the environment that later will serve as the basis for more complex accomplishments.

During this first stage, infants are primarily engaged in applying inherited reflexes to objects. If objects "fit" infants' reflexes (or, more appropriately, the schemes underlying these reflexes), the babies apply their reflexes to the object, assimilating it into their existing schemes. However, accommodation also occurs during the first weeks of life (that is, changing one's schemes in order to incorporate new information). For example, Piaget (1952) carefully observed his son, Laurent, making adjustments to nursing. He noted how Laurent would suck his hand, a quilt, or a coverlet even when not hungry, the reflex being released by almost anything that touched his lips. Piaget also observed that Laurent's ability to locate the nipple and nurse successfully improved gradually over the first 3 weeks of life as he learned to apply his sucking reflex selectively to the

nipple (rather than to the skin surrounding the nipple) when hungry.

Piaget's observations tell us a number of things about the cognitive abilities of infants during the first month of life. First of all, they demonstrate that during this time infants are highly restricted in what they can know. Behaviors are elicited by environmental events over which they have little control, and the range and flexibility of those schemes are highly limited. Second, young infants, although active, do not act on their environment in order to obtain specific outcomes. In other words, according to Piaget, they cannot separate *need* from *action* and thus cannot be said to behave intentionally. Third, Piaget's observations demonstrate adaptation on the part of the infants. This adaptation involves the assimilation of objects into inherited schemes and also the accommodation of those schemes.

With respect to assimilation, Piaget described three types. *Recognitory assimilation* refers to the selective use of a scheme. When the infant Laurent was hungry, his sucking was directed to the nipple.

TABLE 5-1 Major Characteristics of Children's Intelligence at Each Stage of Piaget's Sensorimotor Period

Stage and approximate age	Major characteristics
Stage 1 (basic reflexes): birth to 1 month	Cognition is limited to inherited reflex patterns.
Stage 2 (primary circular reactions): 1 to 4 months	Infant acquires first adaptations, extends basic reflexes; reflex is activated by chance (for example, thumb comes in contact with lips, activating sucking reflex); infant attempts to reproduce reflex, resulting in acquisition of new, noninherited behavior (thumb sucking) that can be activated at the infant's discretion; initial occurrence of behavior is by chance, so need follows action.
Stage 3 (secondary circular reactions): 4 to 8 months	By chance, infant causes interesting event in environment to occur (for example, infant kicks mattress, causing mobile over crib to move) and tries to re-create event; beginning of control of objects and events external to infant; as in previous stage, initial occurrence of interesting event is by chance, so need follows action.
Stage 4 (coordination of secondary circular reactions): 8 to 12 months	Infant uses two previously acquired schemes in coordination with each other to achieve a goal; first sign of need preceding action, or goal-directed behavior, is exhibited.
Stage 5 (tertiary circular reactions): 12 to 18 months	Infant discovers new means through active experimentation, develops new techniques to solve problems; goal-directed behavior is exhibited, but entire problem-solving process is conducted by overt trial and error; intelligence is still limited to child's actions on objects.
Stage 6 (mental combinations): 18 to 24 months	Infant shows first signs of symbolic functioning; infant is able to represent events in environment in terms of symbols (for example, language, imagery); problem solving can now be covert.

His hand or the skin surrounding the nipple was recognized as different from the nipple. Sucking at meal time had a nutritive purpose, and the infant was able to differentiate among these various objects and apply the scheme selectively.

In contrast to recogratory assimilation is *generalizing assimilation*, the "incorporation of increasingly varied objects into the reflex scheme" (Piaget, 1952, p. 34). That is, infants apply the scheme to most objects they encounter, showing little awareness for the uniqueness of the items to which the scheme is applied. In the case of Laurent's sucking scheme, Piaget observed him generalizing the scheme to include his hand, a quilt, and a woolen coverlet. Such generalization was most likely to occur, Piaget noted, when Laurent was not (very) hungry.

This brings us to the third type of assimilation, *functional*, or *reproductive, assimilation*. Piaget noted that Laurent used the sucking scheme even after his hunger had been assuaged. Why should infants exercise this scheme when they are not hungry, and why especially on objects that do not provide any chance of nourishment? Piaget proposed that the application of a scheme for no apparent reason was an example of functional assimilation. Under Piaget's assumption of intrinsic activity (see Chapter 2), it is the nature of schemes to be active. They are applied to objects in the world merely for the sake of exercise. Furthermore, if schemes are to develop, they must be used. According to Piaget, the "reflex is consolidated and strengthened by virtue of its own functioning" (1952, p. 32).

Stage 2: The First Acquired Adaptations and Primary Circular Reactions (1 to 4 Months)

During the first stage of the sensorimotor period, infants' intelligence is limited to inherited reflexes. In the second stage, reflexes are extended so that new patterns of behavior are acquired that were not part of the basic biological apparatus with which the child was born. However, these acquisitions are still based on innate reflexes and so do not reflect "new" behaviors, per se. What they do reflect is the accommodation of reflex schemes to the environment and, often, the coordination of such schemes. In other words, infants can modify their reflexes as a result of

the environment, reflecting what can be easily recognized as learning.

The basic mechanism for this change in behavior is the *circular reaction*, a concept first introduced by the American psychologist Baldwin (1895). Most simply stated, circular reactions are acquired, repetitive behaviors. Primary circular reactions are the first class of these patterns to be observed in development and the only ones that are based on hereditary reflexes. According to Piaget, the major purpose of primary circular reactions is to prolong "the functional use of the reflex . . . but with the acquisition of some element external to the heredity mechanism" (1952, p. 55). Piaget discussed these first circular reactions primarily with regard to sucking, vision, hearing, vocalizations, and grasping. For example, he detailed how Laurent, between 1 month, 1 day and 1 month, 21 days, acquired the ability to suck his thumb. The initial contact between Laurent's hand and his mouth was by chance. Once thumb or fingers were in his mouth, however, sucking occurred. Over repeated trials, Laurent attempted to re-create the experience, gradually coordinating his arm, hand, and finger movements with his mouth until he had established the ability to suck his thumb whenever (presumably) he pleased.

Although watching babies gaining proficiency in sucking their thumbs may be interesting for some people, what significance do such observations have for the development of intelligence? The significance is the advancement that this ability represents beyond the previous stage. In Stage 1, infants were primarily victims of their environment. They did actively assimilate objects to reflexive schemes, but the exercise of these reflexes was dependent on the chance occurrence of a stimulus that fit with a hereditary action pattern. In this second stage, infants show the first primitive signs of intentionality: they initiate a scheme that, although composed of reflexes, is itself not inherited. That is, once infants acquire the ability to suck their thumbs, that behavior is theirs to use whenever and wherever they please.

I refer to the intentionality displayed during this stage as primitive because these circular reactions pertain only to existing reflexes and, according to

Piaget, the initial occurrence of the circular reaction happens by chance. That is, babies do not start out by thinking: "Gee, I'd like to suck my thumb. I wonder how I should go about it?" Rather, in the process of random activity or activity directed toward a biological outcome (for example, nursing), reflexes are fortuitously activated. (Such chance occurrences as thumb sucking can even happen prenatally!) The exercise of a reflex is intrinsically rewarding, and the infant attempts to re-create the conditions that produced the reflex. After repeated exposure to similar situations and repeated attempts at reproducing the desired outcome, it is achieved and then exercised until it becomes well established. Sucking one's thumb, grasping one's rattle, or gazing at the mobile over one's crib are now behaviors that can be instigated at will. Furthermore, these schemes become broadened, so that an infant can soon suck the thumb on either hand, grab the railing on the crib, and look intently at other interesting objects in the room. There is a form of intentionality here, but only of the most limited kind. Infants are restricted to basic hereditary reflexes and to the fact that the first occurrence of these patterns happened by chance. Need does not precede the act, but rather vice versa.

Stage 3: Secondary Circular Reactions and Procedures Destined to Make Interesting Sights Last (4 to 8 Months)

As mentioned, a circular reaction is a repetitive behavior. Unlike the primary circular reactions characteristic of Stage 2, secondary circular reactions are not based on reflexes but represent the first acquired adaptations of new (that is, not reflexive) behaviors.

The establishment of secondary circular reactions is similar in form to the establishment of the earlier primary circular reactions. With no intention beforehand, babies cause something interesting to happen and attempt to re-create the interesting event. A major difference between primary and secondary circular reactions is that for the former, the interesting events are based on reflexes and thus are necessarily centered on the infant's body. With secondary circular reactions, in contrast, interesting events are

not child-centered but are found in the external world. This is especially true of visual events, although Piaget discussed secondary circular reactions for other schemes, particularly grasping and hearing.

Let me provide an observation of my own with respect to secondary circular reactions and infants' attempts to make interesting sights last. My daughter Heidi, at 4 months of age, was lying in her playpen. She did not seem particularly interested in any of the toys that surrounded her, although she was awake, alert, and active. Strung over her head was a "crib gym," a complex mobile with parts that spin when they are hit. I had spun the objects for her on several occasions, and when I had, Heidi seemed to like it. But today was to be different. While flailing her arms and legs, she hit the mobile, causing it to spin. She happened to be looking at the mobile, and its movement caught her attention. She suddenly stopped and stared intently at the moving object over her head. It ceased moving, and she began to shake her arms and legs, to squirm, and finally to cry. Again she hit the mobile, and again she froze and quieted, staring straight ahead at the wonderful event she had caused.

This observation is similar to those reported by Piaget of his own children (1952). My daughter did not start out to spin the mobile. Her hand made contact while, from the point of view of an adult observer, she was randomly moving her limbs. The result of her act was an interesting visual event. She had caused a change in an object she was looking at and tried to reproduce that outcome. Although she apparently realized, at some level, that she had been responsible for the change, babies do not have a well-developed notion of cause and effect. Thus, she presumably did not know whether it was the movement of her legs, the turn of her head, or her vocalizations that had made the difference. Through a trial-and-error process, however, she reduced her options concerning what exactly she was doing that made the interesting event occur, and she eventually gained control over the situation.

Infants in this stage greatly expand the number of behaviors with which they can cause things surrounding them to happen. Although, as with primary circular reactions, the initial interesting event occurs accidentally, once under children's control, the new behavior is theirs to use whenever and wherever they please. Babies have always had some control over their environment; just ask the parents of a 1-month-old. From the current perspective, however, it is not until the age of 3 or 4 months that infants begin to realize this, and there are important implications for future development. Once an infant learns to spin the mobile over her crib, that scheme generalizes to new situations. She can switch hands or adjust the strength of her stroke and produce slightly different outcomes. This is truly the beginning of intelligence: infants acting intentionally on their environments, attempting to exert control over their world.

Although infants may reliably emit a behavior that consistently produces a desired result, Piaget proposed that infants in Stage 3 are not aware of exactly what it is about their behavior that yields a particular outcome. They do not appreciate, for example, that it is the fact that their hand strikes the mobile that is responsible for its movement. Cause is related to their own global actions and not to the necessity of spatial contact. Infants who have learned to pull a cord to shake connected rattles, for instance, will also pull that same cord in an attempt to act upon disassociated objects 2 meters away or to act on sounds (Piaget, 1954). That is, infants at this stage will attempt to exert control over objects and events in their world without an awareness of the necessity of physical contact between agent and object. Piaget referred to this early notion of causality as *magical-phenomenalistic*. It is "phenomenalistic" because it requires only the contiguity of two events for cause to be inferred (that is, the events need only follow each other closely in time), and it is "magical" because it is centered on the action of the child "without consideration of spatial connection between cause and effect" (Piaget & Inhelder, 1969, p. 18).

Stage 4: Coordination of Secondary Circular Schemes and Their Application to New Situations (8 to 12 Months)

The intentionality observed during the stage of secondary circular reaction just discussed is limited in at least two respects. First, as mentioned previously, the initial relation between an infant's behavior and the environmental outcome occurs by chance. The "need" of hitting a mobile in order to watch it move, for example, arose from the fortuitous discovery of this phenomenon, and not vice versa. Second, the infant's need seems mainly to be that of repetition, that is, the need to activate a scheme. The goal of a secondary circular reaction appears to be its own exercise. A major change in intentionality is found in Stage 4, in that the need now precedes the act. That is, we have for the first time *goal-directed behavior* and the beginning of the differentiation between means and ends (that is, cause and effect).

This means/ends separation is first accomplished by the coordination of two previously acquired secondary schemes to obtain a specific goal. Previously, a secondary circular reaction was executed only for its own sake. Now, one circular reaction can be used in the service of another.

Piaget suggested that one of the simplest coordinations is that of removing an obstacle in order to retrieve a visible object. He provided a lengthy description of experiments in which he placed obstacles, such as his hand, between Laurent and some desired objects (Piaget, 1952). Laurent acquired the ability to brush aside his father's hand in order to obtain a desired goal. He was able to use one well-established scheme (striking) in order that another scheme be activated (reaching, grasping, and retrieving an object).

With respect to the concept of causality, Stage 4 children realize the necessity of physical contact between agent and objects. For example:

> *Observation 142.* . . . At 0;10 (30) [read 0 years, 10 months, 30 days] Jacqueline takes my hand, places it against a singing doll which she is unable to activate herself, and exerts pressure on my index finger to make me do what is necessary. This last observation reveals to what extent, to Jacqueline, my hand has become an independent source of action by contact [Piaget, 1954, p. 260].

Although this represents a dramatic improvement over the preceding stages, Piaget asserted that Stage 4 children regard external sources to be truly causal only when *they* act upon the agent. In the above example, it was Jacqueline's intervention that led to the causal link between her father's action and the desired outcome.

Stage 5: Tertiary Circular Reactions and Discovery of New Means through Active Experimentation (12 to 18 Months)

Tertiary circular reactions are the final member in Piaget's class of repetitive sensorimotor schemes. As in Stage 4, infants' reactions are characterized by clear means/ends differentiation: need precedes action. During Stage 5, however, infants are not restricted to applying previously acquired and consolidated schemes to achieve a goal. Rather, when faced with a problem, they can now make subtle alterations in their existing schemes that are directly related to obtaining a solution. This, Piaget stated, reflects a process of active experimentation.

Piaget (1952) gives the example of his daughter Jacqueline attempting to get a long stick through the bars of her playpen. The intent is there from the beginning, but it is only through a process of trial and error that the stick is successfully maneuvered between the bars and into the playpen. Piaget noted his daughter's surprise when some of her attempts failed and the gradual accommodations she made before mastering the problem.

Along with infants' new intellectual tools come increasing locomotive abilities. By 12 months of age most babies can get around well, be it on two limbs or four, and this combination of increased locomotor and cognitive skills results in a child who is likely to be into everything. Children of this age often show a peak in curiosity. They want to know what makes things tick and, more importantly, how they can make them tick. They are explorers and adventurers. "Is it possible to unravel the toilet paper, getting it all into the toilet without breaking the paper? How do I get into the bathroom sink? Isn't it interesting how by turning one knob I can make the music become so much louder?" Adults are often perplexed at why 15-month-olds find dog food and kitty litter so fascinating, why they are so interested in electric sockets and wastebaskets, and why they insist upon climbing out of their high chairs and manipulating and mouthing everything on the kitchen table.

Although children during this stage are wonderful problem solvers, their intelligence is still basically limited to physical actions on objects. They know objects by acting on them and cannot yet make mental comparisons or represent objects and events symbolically. These children solve problems by a trial-and-error process, with all their trials being available for public examination. So, for example, if a 15-month-old wants to see whether her brother's tricycle fits beneath the coffee table, she has to do it by physically attempting to place it under the table. It makes no difference that the tricycle rises a foot above the table. She cannot simply examine the two objects and discern that one is too big to fit under the other. She can learn this, however, by attempting it, although it may take several such tries before she concludes what, to an adult, is obvious.

By this stage most of the remnants of magical-phenomenalistic causality (Stage 3) have been replaced by an understanding that events in the world have causes independent of themselves and that spatial contact is necessary between agents and objects. For example, Stage 5 children place a ball on an incline and wait for it to roll (Piaget, 1954), and they realize that a swinging stick must hit an object before the object moves. Because there is no mental representation during this stage, however, causal inference cannot take place. That is, children must directly observe the agent acting on the object in order to understand any causal relationship.

Stage 6: Invention of New Means through Mental Combinations (18 to 24 Months)

Until this time, development in the sensorimotor period has been relatively continuous, with behavior patterns acquired at one stage being superimposed onto those of earlier stages. In contrast, the transition between Stages 5 and 6 is more dramatic and discontinuous. It is during this last sensorimotor stage that symbolic functioning is first seen. Children are showing the first glimmer of mental representation, of being able to think about objects without having to directly act upon them. With the advent of mental representation, the process of children's problem solving is no longer totally in the open. Trial-and-error procedures can occur covertly "in the head," producing what appears to be sudden comprehension or insight. An example of this change in problem solving is illustrated in the following observation by Piaget (1952):

Observation 182 repeated.—In the same way Jacqueline, at 1;8 (9) arrives at a closed door—with a blade of grass in each hand. She stretches out her right hand toward the knob but sees that she cannot turn it without letting go of the grass. She puts the grass on the floor, opens the door, picks up the grass again and enters. But when she wants to leave the room things become complicated. She puts the grass on the floor and grasps the doorknob. But then she perceives that in pulling the door toward her she will simultaneously chase away the grass which she placed between the door and the threshold. She therefore picks it up in order to put it outside the door's zone of movement.

This ensemble of operations, which in no way comprises remarkable invention, is nevertheless very characteristic of the intelligent acts founded upon representation or the awareness of relationships [p. 339].

It is around this time that children customarily start to put words together in sentences, an action that psycholinguists consider the beginning of language. Language is certainly an expression of the symbolic function, permitting children to conceptualize events past and future. However, Piaget contended that language is only one of several forms of symbols children use to represent their world and that it is the advent of the symbolic function that makes the symbolic use of language possible, not vice versa. In addition to language, the symbolic function includes the use of gestures, deferred imitation, symbolic play, and mental imagery. Deferred imitation is discussed in greater detail later in this chapter, and other aspects of the symbolic function will be discussed in Chapter 6.

With respect to causality, children in Stage 6 possess the rudiments of mental representation necessary to make simple causal inferences. An example from Piaget (1954) illustrates this point:

Observation 159. . . . At 1;1 (4) Laurent is seated in his carriage and I am on a chair beside him. While reading and without seeming to pay any attention to him, I put my foot under the carriage and move it slowly. Without hesitation Laurent leans over the

edge and looks for the cause in the direction of the wheels. As soon as he perceives the position of my foot he is satisfied and smiles [p. 269].

These varied, mentalistic abilities arise alongside the more action-based forms of intelligence during the latter part of the second year. It is during this stage that the cognitions of the sensorimotor period begin to be internalized as representational thought, setting the stage for a revolutionary change in the nature of human intelligence.

Non-Piagetian Research into the Stages of Sensorimotor Intelligence

There has been no lack of research into or alternate theories of the development of intelligence during the sensorimotor period. One of the largest research projects to provide a test of Piaget's theory of infant development is that of Uzgiris and Hunt (1975). Based on the observations of Piaget (1952, 1954, 1962), Uzgiris and Hunt developed a test of sensorimotor intelligence that assessed the development of circular reactions, object permanence, imitation, space, and causality. One major contribution of this work was their demonstration of interobserver reliability. A major complaint with Piaget's observations was that they had been highly subjective. Uzgiris and Hunt developed items that could be scored reliably by independent examiners. The average agreement among different examiners' evaluations of infants' performance on this scale was an impressive 96%.

In addition to demonstrating that Piagetian tasks could be standardized, the sequence of sensorimotor accomplishments that Uzgiris and Hunt found in their cross-sectional sample was much as Piaget had described. There have been a number of other, smaller-scale studies investigating the sequential nature of sensorimotor accomplishments, and most of these studies confirm the basic Piagetian stage sequences (Corman & Escalona, 1969; Kopp, Sigman, & Parmelee, 1974; Uzgiris, 1973). In addition, research using results from infant psychometric tests has also provided support for Piaget's developmental progression (McCall, Eichorn, & Hogarty, 1977). The consistency of the research findings led Uzgiris

(1983) to report that the "available literature on infant functioning during the sensorimotor period demonstrates that an orderly sequence of achievements is manifested in the formation of a number of competencies. The regularity of these sequences and their high correlation with chronological age are among the most consistently reported findings" (p. 182). Note that the similarity of the observations does not make Piaget's theory *right*. There may be a number of explanations for the developmental trends observed by these researchers. However, such consistency of findings does suggest that we are on the right track concerning what phenomena are important.

☐ Imitation

Piaget's View of Imitation in the Sensorimotor Period

Imitation refers to a person matching his or her behavior to that of a model. True imitation is not reflexive but is voluntary and selective, involving the modification of one's own behavior in accordance with that of a model. In fact, Piaget stated that imitation is the purest example of the predominance of accommodation over assimilation, with people changing their schemes in response to cues from the environment. Piaget (1962) did not view imitation as a unique cognitive phenomenon but, rather, proposed that imitation is primarily a function of the development of general intellectual abilities during the sensorimotor period. A brief description of Piaget's view of imitation at each sensorimotor stage is provided in Table 5-2.

In Stage 1 (birth to 1 month), infants are limited to interpreting the world in terms of their inherited reflexes. During this first stage, some imitation-like behavior can be seen, but it is reflexive in nature and not true imitation. For example, a baby may begin crying when he or she hears the cries of other babies. Although this response could reflect merely an annoyance at being disturbed by the aversive wailing of nursery mates, Piaget suggested that infants may confuse the cries of others with their own, thus eliciting crying in a reflexive manner.

During Stages 2 and 3 (1 to 8 months), sounds that infants can already make are repeated for their own sake (primary circular reactions), and such reactions can be prolonged by the presence of a model displaying the same behavior as the infant. In these cases, the baby initiates a behavior that is mimicked by the adult, which in turn activates the baby to continue that behavior. Piaget's (1962) description of such interaction with his daughter will help illustrate this phenomenon:

> OBS. 4. . . . At 0;3 (5) I noted a differentiation in the sounds of her laughter. I imitated them. She reacted by reproducing them quite clearly, but only when she had already uttered them immediately before [p. 10].

Piaget referred to this behavior as *mutual imitation*, with the infant imitating the adult who is imitating her. The imitation is exact, but only to the extent that the adult imitated the infant exactly. This, again, is not true imitation, for infants never utter new sounds through imitation. That is, nothing new is acquired by the imitative-like behaviors observed here, with this pre-imitation representing primarily the assimilation of previously acquired circular reactions.

Piaget first observed true imitation in Stage 4 (8 to 12 months). Children are now able to imitate behaviors for which they receive no perceptual feedback, such as facial gestures. Infants can see the movements of their own fingers or hear their own voices when they attempt to imitate a hand gesture or a sound produced by another person, but they cannot see themselves imitate an adult's grimace or pout. Piaget referred to these unseen actions as *invisible gestures*. Infants in this stage are also now able to acquire new behaviors by imitation. Before this stage, infants' matching was limited to schemes they had previously acquired. During Stage 4, infants can learn new patterns of responding by actively and intentionally imitating a model. Accommodation begins to predominate over assimilation. Although new behaviors are learned through imitation, the model's behavior must be very similar to what a child can already produce if it is to give rise to imitation.

Patterns that are too discrepant from a child's current schemes are not good candidates for imitation.

The process of true imitation that is begun during Stage 4 continues in Stage 5 (12 to 18 months). Piaget contended that imitation becomes more systematic and exact at this time. It becomes more deliberate and is more accommodative to the model than at previous stages. Nevertheless, the differences between imitation in Stage 4 and in Stage 5 are ones of degree rather than kind.

In both Stage 4 and Stage 5, children are limited to imitating a model in the model's presence. They are unable to observe a model and delay imitation for any length of time. Delayed, or *deferred*, imitation is the hallmark of Piaget's sixth sensorimotor stage (18 to 24 months). It is with the advent of mental representation that children can observe a model and mentally code the behavior in terms of images or "suggestions of actions" (Piaget, 1962, p. 62). With mental representation, events can be coded symbolically and retrieved at a later time. An interesting example of deferred imitation is provided by Piaget (1962):

OBS. 52. At 1;4 (3) J. (Jacqueline) had a visit from a little boy of 1;6, whom she used to see from time to time, and who, in the course of the afternoon, got into a terrible temper. He screamed as he tried to get

out of a play-pen and pushed it backwards, stamping his feet. J. stood watching him in amazement, never having witnessed such a scene before. The next day, she herself screamed in her play-pen and tried to move it, stamping her foot lightly several times in succession. The imitation of the whole scene was most striking. Had it been immediate, it would naturally not have involved representation, but coming as it did after an interval of more than twelve hours, it must have involved some representative or pre-representative element [p. 63].

In addition to being able to defer imitation, the Stage 6 child can mentally practice a behavior before actually imitating it. The trial-and-error process involved in the Stage 5 child's imitation of a model can now be accomplished covertly. Accordingly, a Stage 6 child's first public attempt at imitation is likely to be more accurate than that of a Stage 5 child, primarily because the trial-and-error process of the latter child is all overt.

Non-Piagetian Research into Imitation in the Sensorimotor Period

Unlike other aspects of Piaget's theory, his work on imitation in infancy has, until recently, provoked little controversy. Piaget's observations and theory of

TABLE 5-2   Imitation at Each Stage of Piaget's Sensorimotor Period

Stage	Approximate age	Major characteristics
Stage 1	birth to 1 month	Infant is limited to inherited reflexes, with no true imitation.
Stage 2	1 to 4 months	Sounds and gestures that infant already possesses can be prolonged by adult displaying same behavior as infant; infant must be currently engaging in behavior for imitation to occur.
Stage 3	4 to 8 months	Number of behaviors infant can copy increases; imitation is still limited to behaviors child already possesses; infant need not be engaging in behavior for it to be copied; infant cannot imitate "invisible" gestures (for example, facial expressions).
Stage 4	8 to 12 months	First true imitation: infant can acquire new behaviors by imitation and can copy facial (that is, invisible) gestures; accommodation begins to predominate over assimilation.
Stage 5	12 to 18 months	Imitation becomes more deliberate and systematic, with greater accommodation to model; Stage 5 is continuation of true imitation first seen in Stage 4.
Stage 6	18 to 24 months	Child is able to use mental representation to code model's behavior, permitting deferred imitation (that is, delaying imitation of model for hours after model was observed).

infant imitation were basically consistent with the findings of his predecessors (Baldwin, 1895; Guillaume, 1927/1971) and with the results from psychometric tests of infant intelligence (Bayley, 1969). Beginning in the 1970s, however, research interest in the origins of imitation increased, and in the process, Piaget's observations, which had remained essentially unchallenged for nearly three decades, were put to empirical test.

Assessing Piaget's Sequence of Imitation

Uzgiris and Hunt (1975) were the first to systematically investigate Piaget's developmental progression of infant imitative abilities. Test items were selected based on Piaget's (1962) observations, and they included tasks from the first months of life (Stage 1) through imitation at Stages 4 and 5 (for example, imitation of invisible gestures). Results from this cross-sectional study were very consistent with those reported by Piaget (1962), implying a gradual change in imitative abilities that corresponds to changes in other aspects of infants' cognitive functioning.

Other studies, looking at smaller age ranges, began to appear in the literature during the mid-1970s, with most generally confirming Piaget's observations of his own three children. For example, babies do not mimic a behavior perfectly the first time they observe it but, over time, gradually acquire individual components of that behavior. For instance, Kaye and Marcus (1981) described how a longitudinal sample of infants between the ages of 6 and 12 months learned to imitate hand clapping. Most infants demonstrated a series of partial imitations before their first successful imitation (which occurred, on average, by 11 months). First in the sequence was touching the experimenter's hand, followed by touching their own hand and with their pulling the experimenter's hands together in a clapping motion. Only after going through this progression did infants imitate hand clapping.

What are interesting about the Kaye and Marcus findings are the systematic responses that infants made to the experimenter's hand-clapping gesture. Kaye and Marcus suggest that infants assimilate the model's behavior to their existing schemes and "imitate" only those aspects of the behavior that fit with these schemes (or those that require only small accommodations to the existing schemes). Thus, failure to observe imitation in infants may not be due to infants' inability to imitate but to the fact that they are assimilating the observed behavior to different schemes from those intended by the model. For example, Kaye and Marcus reported that several infants clapped their hands for the first time after watching the experimenter demonstrate another topographically similar behavior, touching one's ear (both involve extension of the arm and hand before execution). These observations suggest that we cannot always guess what an infant is thinking. A behavior intended to elicit one response may be construed very differently by the child and result in "imitation" of another, previously modeled behavior.

Other studies have indicated, consistent with Piaget's findings, that imitation of novel acts is not reliably observed until approximately 7 to 8 months (Abravanel, Levan-Goldschmidt, & Stevenson, 1976; Killen & Uzgiris, 1981; Paraskevopoulous & Hunt, 1971). Imitation has been found to take another qualitative step forward somewhere around 12 to 13 months, a time corresponding to Piaget's Stage 5. For example, McCall, Parke, and Kavanaugh (1977) reported that infants at this age are for the first time able to imitate a coordinated sequence of actions. For example, an experimenter picks up a string attached to a metal cup and, with his other hand, strikes the cup three times with a rod. This action requires the coordination of two sets of behaviors and is contrasted with the imitation of simple behaviors such as lifting the cup or striking it while it remains on the table (see also Abravanel & Gingold, 1985; McCabe & Uzgiris, 1983).

McCall, Parke, and Kavanaugh (1977) were also the first to empirically demonstrate deferred imitation (for example, imitating a behavior after a 24-hour period), which occurred in their sample between 18 and 24 months of age. This corresponds well with Piaget's observation that deferred imitation is not seen until the advent of symbolic relations. More recently, Meltzoff (1985) has replicated the deferred imitation effect with 2-year-old children and also reported successful deferred imitation over a 24-hour period for a sample of 14-month-old toddlers. Results from another study by Abravanel and Gingold (1985) provide additional evidence that deferred imitation may be found earlier than had been previously believed. In their study, 12-month-old infants displayed imitation of simple behaviors (for example, removing one object from inside another) following a 10-minute delay. However, these infants were no more likely to reproduce the modeled actions than were control subjects (who had not observed a model) when more complex behaviors were illustrated (for example, arranging three blocks in a particular order or inserting a stick in a cylinder to remove an object).

Although deferred imitation was found in both the Meltzoff (1985) and Abravanel and Gingold (1985) studies at ages much younger than previously reported, it should be noted that the absolute percentage of 12- and 14-month-olds showing deferred imitation was low (45% of 14-month-olds in the Meltzoff study and 33% of 12-month-olds in the Abravanel & Gingold study), with higher levels of deferred imitation being observed for older children in these experiments (70% of 24-month-olds in the Meltzoff study and 80% of 18-month-olds in the Abravanel & Gingold study). Thus, I concur with the interpretation of Abravanel and Gingold (1985), who suggested that imitative abilities increase over the 12- to 18-month period and are related to the extent to which toddlers can encode action schemes for later retrieval.

All in all, there has been relatively little controversy over Piaget's account of the development of imitation from the latter half of the first year on. Although alternative interpretations of findings have been presented, most theorists have not strayed far from the classic line (Uzgiris, 1984). The picture is much different, however, concerning imitation during the first 6 months of life. As you will recall, Piaget stated that there is no true imitation until the fourth sensorimotor stage (approximately 8 months). The matching behavior that is observed earlier is primarily reflexive, or at best mutual imitation: infants imitating adults who are imitating them. Furthermore, when real imitation is first observed in

development, it is of behaviors for which infants have feedback about their own actions, for example, sounds and hand gestures. Imitation of invisible gestures such as facial expressions is not achieved, according to Piaget, until between 8 and 12 months.

Imitation in Early Infancy

There seems to be little argument that many of the phenomena Piaget described actually exist in early infancy. Recent research has suggested, however, that there may be more imitation going on during the first 6 months of life than Piaget proposed.

The controversy began with the publication in 1977 of a paper by Meltzoff and Moore demonstrating what they contended was imitation of tongue protrusions and mouth openings by infants ranging in age from 6 to 21 days. Examples of the facial gestures modeled in this experiment and responses by infants are shown in the accompanying photo. The tongue protrusions and mouth openings that infants made in response to an adult model were counted from video recordings and were contrasted with the number of each gesture made during baseline periods (that is, when no gestures were modeled). Meltzoff and Moore reported that infants made significantly more tongue protrusions in re-

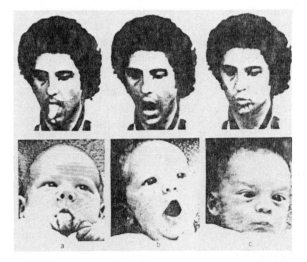

PHOTO 5-1 Photographs of 2- to 3-week-old infants imitating (a) tongue protrusion, (b) mouth opening, and (c) lip protrusion demonstrated by an adult experimenter (Meltzoff and Moore, 1977)

sponse to the tongue model than to the open-mouth model or during baseline. Similarly, infants opened their mouths significantly more often to the open-mouth model than to the tongue model or during baseline. Meltzoff and Moore interpreted these results as clear evidence of selective imitation of invisible gestures during the first month of life.

Following Meltzoff and Moore's initial findings, other researchers reported apparent imitation of tongue protrusion in infants between the ages of 4 and 6 weeks (Abravanel & Sigafoos, 1984; Fontaine, 1984; Jacobson, 1979). Furthermore, Meltzoff and Moore (1983), Field and her colleagues (Field, Woodson, Greenberg, & Cohen, 1982; Field, Woodson, Cohen, Greenberg, Garcia, & Collins, 1983), and Vinter (1986) have since demonstrated imitation of facial gestures in newborns. However, this early matching phenomenon is not as robust as the above list of studies may lead one to believe, for several experimenters have failed to replicate early imitation using procedures similar to those used by Meltzoff and Moore (Hayes & Watson, 1981; Koepke, Hamm, Legerstee, & Russell, 1983; Lewis & Sullivan, 1985; McKenzie & Over, 1983).

Despite the controversy, most researchers agree that there is something interesting going on in early infancy that has some imitation-like characteristics. Even if we are willing to describe these phenomena as early forms of imitation, however, we are faced with the somewhat incongruous finding that imitation of facial gestures actually *declines* over the first year of life. For the most studied facial gesture, tongue protrusion, every investigator who has examined infants of different ages reports a peak in imitation sometime during the first 2 months followed by a decline within weeks to chance values (Abravanel & Sigafoos, 1984; Fontaine, 1984; Gardner & Gardner, 1970; Jacobson, 1979; Maratos, 1973). This is indeed perplexing, in that we have what appears to be a sophisticated cognitive phenomenon that actually decreases in frequency over a very brief period of time.

How can neonatal imitation be explained? Meltzoff and Moore (1977, 1983) have suggested three possible alternatives for modeling effects during early infancy. Imitative-like responses of young infants could be attributed to (1) learning; (2) selective imitation, guided by the integration of information from one sensory modality (vision) with information from another (proprioception derived from self-initiated movements); and (3) an innate releasing mechanism, where reflex-like responses are elicited to a specific set of stimuli.

Concerning the first alternative, Meltzoff and Moore (1977, 1983, 1985) and others (Field et al., 1982, 1983; Jacobson, 1979) suggest that learning is an unlikely candidate to explain early imitation. The most compelling reason for rejecting a learning or reinforcement interpretation is that infants only hours old will match certain facial expressions to those of an adult (Field et al., 1982, 1983; Meltzoff & Moore, 1983; Vinter, 1986). It is unlikely that such young infants would have had sufficient experience to "learn" these responses.

The second interpretation is the one favored by Meltzoff and Moore. They propose that the matching behavior observed in the early weeks of life is true imitation. Newborns are able to coordinate information from two senses. They can visually observe a stimulus, store an abstract representation of that stimulus, and compare it shortly thereafter with a proprioceptive representation (that is, their own movements). This position holds that newborns possess the ability to integrate information from two senses (that is, they possess intermodal integration). Meltzoff and Moore (1983, 1985) refer to this behavior as *active intermodal mapping*. If one accepts this interpretation, it advances the ability to coordinate two sensory modalities to a period many months earlier than that suggested by Piaget and others (Birch & Lefford, 1963). Such an interpretation is not without some empirical support. As discussed in Chapter 4, for example, research by Rose, Gottfried, and Bridger (1981) has demonstrated tactual/visual transfer of information in 6-month-olds, and Meltzoff and Borton (1979) reported visual/tactual integration in infants less than 1 month old. In the latter study, infants looked significantly longer at a pacifier they had orally (but not visually) inspected seconds earlier, indicative of recognition by intermodal matching.

Yet, if the imitation observed in very young infants is selective and is accomplished via active intermodal mapping, why does it seemingly disappear only months after its appearance? The third alternative, that neonatal matching behavior is attributed to innate releasing mechanisms, attempts to account for the decline in imitation over the first 6 months (Abravanel & Sigafoos, 1984; Jacobson, 1979; Kaye, 1982). Releasing mechanisms, or fixed-action patterns, refer to inherited sets of behaviors elicited to specific sets of stimuli without the need of prior environmental experience (Lorenz, 1973; Tinbergen, 1951).

The best evidence for this position comes from an experiment by Jacobson (1979). Jacobson tested a sample of 24 infants at 6, 10, and 14 weeks. The incidence of tongue protrusions was measured at each session to each of five stimuli: (1) tongue protrusion, (2) opening and closing hand movements, (3) a closed felt-tip pen moved toward the infants' faces, (4) a small white ball moved toward the infants' faces, and (5) a plastic ring attached to a string raised up and down in front of the infants. (Imitation of hand movements was also assessed, but it will not be discussed here.) Following the testing session at 6 weeks of age, half of the infants were assigned to an experimental group, and their parents were asked to practice tongue protrusions with their babies several times each day. Parents of infants in the control group were asked not to practice tongue protrusions between laboratory visits.

The results of Jacobson's study are shown in Table 5-3. At 6 weeks, there was no statistical difference in the number of tongue protrusions babies made to the tongue, the pen, or the ball, although each of these produced a greater number of tongue protrusions than the hand or the ring. Also, for infants in the control group, the incidence of tongue protrusions to all stimuli decreased over the next two testing sessions, so that by 14 weeks, there was no difference in the number of tongue protrusions produced among the five stimuli. In contrast, for the experimental infants, whose mothers practiced tongue protrusions at home with them, the decline was less steep, and these babies still showed a selective response of tongue protrusions to the tongue model at 14 weeks.

Jacobson maintained that the fact that several different stimuli elicited tongue protrusions equally well, at least at 6 weeks, argues against selective imitation and for the interpretation that the matching behavior seen for these young babies represents an innate releasing mechanism. Also, the decline of matching responses over time for the control group and the maintenance of tongue protrusion for the experimental group is a pattern similar to the developmental course of other neonatal reflexes. For example, a number of reflexes present at birth disappear over the course of the first year of life, including rooting (moving the head toward stimulation in response to touching of the baby's cheek), Moro (extension of the arms followed by return to the chest in response to a loss of support or loud noise), sucking, and swimming (see LaBarba, 1981). Furthermore, Zelazo, Zelazo, and Kolb (1972) have demonstrated that exercising of neonates' stepping reflex (stepping-like movements of the legs when the infant is lifted in an upright position) results in infants who walk at an earlier age than those who do not receive such exercise. The similar developmental course observed for imitation during the first months of life and for the above neonatal reflexes (both under normal and "exercised" conditions) is consistent with the interpretation that what matching behavior is observed in the early weeks of life is not deliberate imitation but, rather, complex reflex

TABLE 5-3 Mean Number of Long Tongue Protrusions per Minute as a Function of Age, Stimulus, and Condition (N = 24) (Jacobson, 1979)

Stimulus	6 weeks	10 weeks	14 weeks
Experimentals			
Tongue	4.87	4.42	3.47
Ball	3.64	2.32	0.40
Pen	3.89	3.39	0.95
Hand	2.88	1.62	1.28
Ring	1.16	3.18	0.88
Controls			
Tongue	4.09	3.96	1.81
Ball	3.08	2.02	1.10
Pen	3.71	3.25	2.54
Hand	2.01	2.65	0.77
Ring	2.23	1.49	1.34
M	3.16	2.83	1.45

patterns made to specific sets of stimuli that disappear over time and are unrelated to the imitation observed later in infancy.

The above position is at odds not only with that of Meltzoff and Moore but also with Piagetian theory. Piaget's epigenetic approach holds that nothing comes from nothing, that every structure has its genesis in earlier structures. A corollary to this view is that every form of early intelligence serves as preparation for later forms of intelligence. Thus, early reflexes, although they may eventually drop out of the child's repertoire, serve as a basis for later, more advanced cognitive functioning. This is clearly seen in Piaget's description of imitative-like responses during the first three sensorimotor stages. The interpretation of early imitation as a fixed action pattern is counter to Piaget's view, in that this reflexive matching behavior, which has the appearance of a legitimate cognitive function, need not lead to more advanced forms of imitation. Rather, the behavior disappears without specifically preparing the child for subsequent intellectual accomplishments.

What function may neonatal imitation play, then, if it is not preparation for later cognitive development? One interpretation is that such responses are phylogenetic vestiges and have no function in human development or survival. Another interpretation, suggested by Bjorklund (1987b), is that such responses may play a specific role in survival for the infant at that time, and that time only, and that they disappear when they are no longer needed. Oppenheim (1981) has referred to such phenomena as *transient ontogenetic adaptations*. He argues that the young organism lives in a very different world from the adult, requiring different behavioral or neurological organization to cope with life. Such organization may not be the basis for later development but may rather be present only for survival at that time and in that specific environment. With respect to neonatal imitation, Jacobson (1979) suggests that tongue protrusions may be functional in early nursing. Bjorklund (1987b) suggests that the apparent imitation by young infants may play a role in early social development. The matching of adult facial gestures by the infant may help to maintain social interaction between the two, with these reflexes

declining when infants are able to "intentionally" direct their gaze and control their head and mouth movements to social stimulation, somewhere between the second and fourth months of life (Cairns, 1979).

It must be noted that although the innate releasing mechanism is the interpretation favored here, the debate is far from settled. For example, Meltzoff and Moore (1983, 1985) argue against this position, writing that infants' imitative responses are not strongly stereotyped, as would be expected if they were governed by innate releasing mechanisms. Also, they note that infants have been shown to imitate a large number of different gestures and that it is not reasonable to propose a different reflex for each gesture. The book is by no means closed on early infant imitation. Research over the past decade has sparked a controversy that goes beyond the question "Do babies imitate?" The presence of matching behavior during the early weeks of infancy is causing us to re-examine many of our basic beliefs about the early nature and origins of intellectual life, and we can expect debate on these issues to continue for years to come.

☐ Object Permanence

If a tree falls in the middle of the forest and no one is there to witness it, is there any noise? This perennial philosophical question would be answered very easily by young infants, presuming, of course, that they could communicate their answer to us. Their answer would be no, for there can be no noise unless someone is there to perceive it. But the young infant would go on to say that there is also no tree and no forest. Nothing exists unless it is directly perceived, or, more precisely, unless it is personally perceived by them.

This hypothetical philosophical discussion illustrates Piaget's concept of *object permanence* or, more appropriately, the lack of object permanence. Object permanence refers to the knowledge that objects have an existence in time and space independent of one's perception or action on those objects. For infants who lack object permanence, out of sight is literally out of mind. Object permanence is obviously a cognitive skill necessary for normal intellectual functioning in all human cultures, and this has been the most investigated cognitive content of Piaget's infancy theory. Understandably, Piaget discussed the development of object permanence in the context of his broader theory of sensorimotor intelligence (Piaget, 1954). A brief description of his view of object permanence at each sensorimotor stage is provided in Table 5-4.

Piaget's Description of the Development of Object Permanence

During the first two stages of the sensorimotor period (from birth to approximately 4 months), Piaget stated that objects are understood only as extensions of infants' actions. Objects have no reality for babies independent of their perceptions of or actions upon them. For example, a 2- or 3-month-old follows his mother with his eyes, but when she leaves his visual field, he continues to gaze at the point where he lost sight of her, not anticipating her re-appearance at another location.

The first semblance of object permanence appears during the third sensorimotor stage (approximately 4 to 8 months). Infants now attempt to retrieve objects that "disappear," although only if the object is still partially visible. For example, babies at this stage fetch a toy that has been partially covered by a cloth, realizing, apparently, that the entire toy exists under the cloth even though they can see only a

portion of it. They do not search, however, for a toy that is completely hidden, even if the hiding occurred right before their eyes. An exception to this behavior seems to be that, late in this stage, infants search for a completely hidden object if they are moving in that direction when the object is hidden. So, for example, a 6-month-old infant playing with a favorite toy does not attempt to retrieve that toy when her father places it under the blanket while she is watching. She does retrieve it, however, if she is reaching for the toy in front of her as Dad places a blanket over it.

By Stage 4 (approximately 8 to 12 months), infants are able to retrieve a completely hidden object. To do this, they must be able to use one scheme (removing an obstacle) in the service of another (retrieving a desired object), which, according to Piaget, is the major cognitive accomplishment of this stage. However, object permanence is not yet complete, for if an object is hidden in one location and then later moved to a second, all while the child is watching, the infant searches at the first location and often acts quite surprised not to find the desired object. The following excerpt from Piaget (1954) illustrates this behavior:

OBS. 42. At 0;10 (9) Lucienne is seated on a sofa and plays with a plush duck. I put it on her lap and place a small red cushion on top of the duck (this is position A); Lucienne immediately raises the cushion and takes hold of the duck. I then place the duck next to her on the sofa in B, and cover it with another cushion, a yellow one. Lucienne has

TABLE 5-4   Object Permanence at Each Stage of Piaget's Sensorimotor Period

Stage	Approximate age	Major characteristics
Stages 1 and 2	birth to 4 months	No object permanence.
Stage 3	4 to 8 months	Infant will retrieve a partially hidden object; infant will search for a completely hidden object only if moving in direction of object when it is hidden.
Stage 4	8 to 12 months	Infant will search for a completely hidden object; if object is hidden under a series of covers, infant will search at first, not final, location.
Stage 5	12 to 18 months	Infant will search at last place an object was hidden; infant cannot solve invisible displacements, in which hiding is carried out so that infant cannot see it.
Stage 6	18 to 24 months	Infant possesses mental representation and can solve invisible displacements.

watched all my moves, but as soon as the duck is hidden she returns to the little cushion A on her lap, raises it and searches. An expression of disappointment; she turns it over in every direction and gives up [p. 52].

Let me provide an observation of my own for what has been termed the "A not B" (A$\overline{\text{B}}$) object permanence task. At approximately 10 months Heidi was seated in her high chair, having just completed lunch. She was banging her spoon on the tray of the chair when it fell to the floor to her right. She leaned to the right, saw the spoon on the floor, and vocalized to me, and I retrieved it for her. She began playing with the spoon again, and it fell to the right a second time. She again leaned to the right, saw the spoon on the floor, and vocalized until I returned it to her. Again, she played with the spoon, and again it fell to the floor, but this time to her *left*. After hearing the clang of the spoon hitting the floor, Heidi leaned to the *right* to search for the spoon, and she continued her search for several seconds before looking at me with a puzzled expression. Heidi had been watching the spoon at the time it fell. Thus, when it fell the third time, she had both visual and auditory cues to tell her where it must be. But, like Piaget's daughter Lucienne, she searched where she had found the vanished object before. She trusted her own past actions with the fallen spoon more than her perceptions. At this age children still understand objects by their actions on them, in these cases by their prior actions.

In Stage 5 (approximately 12 to 18 months) infants can solve problems like the one described above. What they cannot yet do, however, is solve what Piaget called *invisible displacements*. In invisible displacements an object is hidden in one container and then hidden under another container out of the vision of the observer. An example from Piaget (1954) will help clarify this task:

OBS. 55. At 1;6 (8) Jacqueline is sitting on a green rug playing with a potato which interests her very much (it is a new object for her). She says "po-terre" [*pomme de terre*] and amuses herself by putting it into an empty box and taking it out again. For several days she has been enthusiastic about this game.

I. I then take the potato and put it in the box while Jacqueline watches. Then I place the box under the rug and turn it upside down, thus leaving the object hidden by the rug without letting the child see my maneuver, and I bring out the empty box. I say to Jacqueline, who has not stopped looking at the rug and who has realized that I was doing something under it: "Give papa the potato." She searches for the object in the box, looks at me, again looks at the box minutely, looks at the rug, etc., but it does not occur to her to raise the rug in order to find the potato underneath.

During the five subsequent attempts the reaction is uniformly negative. I begin again, however, each time putting the object in the box as the child watches, putting the box under the rug, and bringing it out empty. Each time Jacqueline looks in the box, then looks at everything around her including the rug, but does not search under it [p. 68].

In order to solve invisible displacement problems, according to Piaget, children must be able to mentally represent objects, something that is not found until the last sensorimotor stage, beginning around 18 months.

Non-Piagetian Research into the Development of Object Permanence

There seems to be little doubt that Piaget's observations concerning the development of object permanence are accurate. Several projects assessing infants over a broad age range have replicated Piaget's basic findings, confirming the stage sequence of object permanence (Corman & Escalona, 1969; Kramer, Hill, & Cohen, 1975; Uzgiris & Hunt, 1975).

Although Piaget's data base seems to be sound, there has been controversy over the interpretation of the results and over whether the tasks Piaget used adequately assess what young infants are actually capable of doing. Bower (1982) has provided evidence of rudimentary object permanence in the first months of life, for example, and other researchers have suggested that infants' failures to demonstrate object permanence may be due to deficits of motor control, memory, or attention and not to an inability to conceptualize objects, per se. That is, infants may have the *competence* to solve object permanence problems but fail to *perform* them successfully because of deficits in related skills.

Object Permanence during the Early Months of Life

T. G. R. Bower (1982) has reviewed evidence accumulated through the 1970s indicating that infants in the first 2 months of life possess a primitive form of object permanency. For example, Bower (1971) showed an object to 20-, 40-, 80-, and 100-day-old infants and placed a screen in front of the object while the babies were watching. The screen covered the object for an interval ranging from 1.5 to 15 seconds. On half of the trials the object was still there when the screen was removed. For the other half of the trials the object was gone. Bower reasoned that if infants have some notion of the permanence of objects, they should expect to see the object when the screen is removed and be surprised when it is not there (as measured by a change in heart rate). In contrast, if babies have no sense of objects as being permanent in time and space, they should not be startled by its disappearance and, in fact, may even be startled when it is there. Bower reported that at the shortest delay (1.5 seconds) all groups of infants displayed an increase in heart rate when the object was missing. Even the youngest babies expected to see the object, and they were surprised when it was not there. At the longest delay (15 seconds) only the oldest infants showed a startle response. In fact, the 20-day-old infants were surprised at the 15-second interval when the object *reappeared*. These results suggest that memory is an important variable in demonstrating object permanence. Infants cannot be expected to act as if a vanished object still exists if they cannot remember the object in the first place.

Bower and his colleagues have done other research consistent with the position that infants possess some form of object permanence at ages much younger than proposed by Piaget. For example, Bower, Broughton, and Moore (1971) observed 8-week-old infants as they followed (visually) a moving object behind a screen. They reported that the infants continued to track the object as if anticipating its reappearance on the other side of the screen, a finding they interpreted as reflecting object permanence. However, subsequent research by Bower and Paterson (1972) cast some doubt on this interpretation. They demonstrated that infants at this age make perseverative eye movements, continuing to move their eyes in the direction that the object is heading even when the object stops in full view of them.

Bower's research is provocative and illustrates the importance of using a variety of tasks and measures when assessing cognition in young infants. For the most part, however, Bower's findings concerning the early advent of object permanence stand alone in the research literature, and more work must be done replicating and extending his findings before any definitive statements can be made.

Manual Search Skills

One skill obviously necessary for completion of most Piagetian object permanence tasks is the ability to search by hand. In order to retrieve an object from under a cover, the infant must be able to reach out and remove that cover. Bower and Wishart (1972) developed a simple procedure to test this motor-skill hypothesis. Five-month-olds were given a Stage 4 object permanence task of retrieving an object after it had been completely covered by an opaque cloth. The infants were given a second task in which an object was covered by a *transparent* cloth, so that the "hidden" object was fully visible after it was covered. If infants' failure to perform Stage 4 object permanence tasks is due to a motor deficit, they should be unable to solve either problem. However, Bower and Wishart found that infants retrieved the object covered by the transparent cloth more often than the object covered by the opaque cloth, indicating that the difference in object permanence performance between infants in Stage 3 (4 to 8 months) and Stage 4 (8 to 12 months) is probably not attributable to differences in motor skills. This does not prove that Piaget was right, for other task variables might influence task performance, but it does seem to make less probable one important alternative explanation.

Memory Deficits

A second skill that has received much research attention is memory. At the least, infants must possess a memory of an object before they can show any evidence of the permanence of that object. Bower (1982) suggested that one reason for very young infants' failures at object permanence tasks is their poor memories. Bower believes that infants during the first 2 months of life have some notion of the constancy of objects but "forget" them shortly after they are hidden. Out of sight may be out of mind, but it is because of poor memory and not because of a lack of object permanence.

Other researchers have looked at memory as a factor in older infants' performance on object permanence tasks. For instance, Gratch and his colleagues presented infants between the ages of 7½ and 10½ months a standard $A\overline{B}$ object permanence task, in which an object was hidden at a second location (B) after being retrieved successfully several times at a previous location (A) (Gratch, Appel, Evans, LeCompte, & Wright, 1974). All hidings were done in plain view of the infants. What differed in this experiment was the delay between hiding the object and permitting the infants to search. Delays of 0, 1, 3, or 7 seconds were imposed on the infants. For the 0 delay condition, 11 of 12 infants successfully retrieved the object at the new location (B). At each of the other three delays, however, a majority of the infants searched at the incorrect A location, with no differences among the 1-, 3-, and 7-second delay intervals. These results suggest that even after a very brief delay infants forget where an object is hidden and, lacking an accurate memory for the location of the object, make perseverative responses (that is, make the same response they made previously). Similar findings were reported by Harris (1973) for 10-month-old infants.

The role of memory in $A\overline{B}$ object permanence tasks was also assessed in a longitudinal study by Diamond (1985). Diamond tested 25 infants in the $A\overline{B}$ task beginning at about 7 months and continuing until 12 months of age. She reported that the delay between hiding and searching that was necessary to produce the $A\overline{B}$ error increased with age at a rate of about 2 seconds per month. That is, 7½-month-old infants would search for the hidden object at the erroneous A position following only a 2-second delay. By 12 months of age infants made the error only if approximately 10 seconds transpired between the hiding of the object and the beginning of the search. Diamond's results are graphically displayed in Figure 5-1. Such findings clearly implicate changes in infants' memories as an important factor in the development of object permanence during this period.

Related research by Bjork and Cummings (1984) provides additional evidence that infants' performance on $A\overline{B}$ tasks has a substantial memory component. Bjork and Cummings pointed out that in most previous $A\overline{B}$ tasks, only two options had been provided to infants: the initial location, A, and the second location, B. In their study, infants ranging in age from 8 to 12 months were given a task consisting of five possible locations. The hidden object was initially placed at location A (far right); after several successful retrievals it was placed at location B (far left) while the infants were watching. Other infants were given the standard two-choice $A\overline{B}$ task. Overall, the number of correct responses on the B trials was comparable between the two- and five-choice problems. For the five-choice problem, however, the majority of search errors (46 of 49 across two experiments) were *not* perseverative (that is, not at location A). Rather, most of the errors were at locations closest to the correct location, B. Bjork and Cummings argue that these results indicate memory as a major factor in infants' performance on object permanence tasks. It is not that 9-month-olds understand objects only by their prior actions on them. If that were so, most of the errors on the five-choice problem would have been perseverative (that is, location A). The fact that they were not indicates that the infants knew the object was hidden somewhere else but could not remember exactly where. Similar results have since been reported by Horobin and Acredolo (1986) and Sophian (1985).

Attentional Deficits

Related to the memory interpretation is the possibility of differences in attention to the hiding of objects. Infants cannot be expected to remember

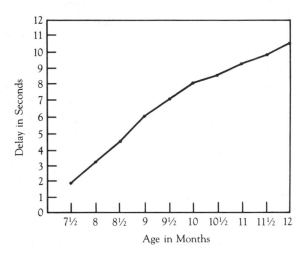

FIGURE 5-1 The delay between hiding of an object and infants' searching for it at which the infants made the $A\overline{B}$ error, by age (adapted from Diamond, 1985)

and then retrieve a hidden object if they have not attended to where it was hidden. Gratch and his colleagues (1974) reported age trends in infants' visual attention to objects when they were hidden at location B in $A\overline{B}$ object permanence tasks. Younger infants were more likely to gaze at location A, even while the object was being hidden at location B. Infants who showed this pattern of visual attention almost always searched incorrectly at location A during the B trials.

Horobin and Acredolo (1986) extended the results of Gratch and his colleagues using a multiple-choice object-permanence problem ($A\overline{B}$) similar to that used by Bjork and Cummings (1984). Horobin and Acredolo suggested that one reason for infants' performance on the five-choice problem of Bjork and Cummings was that the A and B alternatives were farther apart and thus more distinct than on the two-choice problem. Infants ranging in age from 8 to 10 months were given three $A\overline{B}$ object permanence tasks to solve. One task involved six alternatives, with the A and B locations (both end points) being separated by 18 inches. The remaining two tasks involved only two choices, but in the close pair the A and B alternatives were 6 inches apart, and in the far pair they were 18 inches apart. Correct respond-

ing on the B trials was 57% for the close-pair problem and 51% for the six-choice problem. As in Bjork and Cummings's study, the majority of errors on the six-choice problem were not perseverative, but, rather, were at locations near B. In contrast to these two conditions, correct performance on the far-pair problem was 89%.

Horobin and Acredolo also obtained measures of visual attention on these tests. They reported, much as had Gratch and his associates (1974), that if infants gazed at A when the object was being hidden at B, they were likely to make perseverative errors (that is, choose A). Infants were more likely to gaze at A during B trials in the close-pair task than in the far-pair or six-choice tasks. The reduced distance between locations A and B for the close pair presumably made it difficult for the infants to discriminate between the two alternatives. In other words, one reason for infants' failures to solve $A\overline{B}$ problems is that they are inappropriately attentive to the various alternatives. These findings do not contradict the results of Bjork and Cummings (1984), who asserted that the major reason for infants' failures on this task was one of memory; rather, they extend them, including attention as a factor that must be considered in evaluating children's performance on object permanence tasks.

And there is more. Performance on object permanence tasks has been found to vary as a function of infants' familiarity with the hidden objects (Jackson, Campos, & Fischer, 1978), the type of covering used in hiding an object (Rader, Spiro, & Firestone, 1979), and whether the object is hidden under a cloth, behind a screen, or inside a cup (Danst, Brooks, & Doxsey, 1983). In short, from this research it appears clear that Piaget's competence interpretation with regard to object permanence was overstated (see Bremner, 1985). Nonetheless, the phenomenon that Piaget described nearly half a century ago is alive and well today, although we are not so certain as we would like to be about what exactly it is that underlies children's performance on these tasks. (For more extensive reviews of the development of object permanence, see Brainerd, 1978a; Gratch, 1975; and Harris, 1975.)

☐ Summary

Piaget described the intelligence of human infants as *sensorimotor* in nature, in that infants through the first 2 years of life understand the world mostly in terms of their actions upon it. Piaget divided the sensorimotor period into six stages (see Table 5-1). During the earliest stages, cognition is limited to inherited reflexes (Stage 1) and simple extensions of these reflexes (Stage 2). Infants are capable of developing new (that is, not reflexive) behaviors during Stages 3 through 5 and are capable of mentally representing environmental events by Stage 6. When new adaptations are first acquired (Stages 2 and 3), the action itself precedes the need (that is, there is no intentionality before the fact). *Goal-directed behavior* is first seen in Stage 4, when two previously acquired schemes are coordinated with each other to obtain a specific goal. It is not until Stage 5 that new behaviors are developed to achieve a particular end. Infants' problem solving and their understanding of relationships through Stage 5 are limited to their overt actions on objects. With the advent of symbolic function during the final stage of the sensorimotor period, children are able to represent events symbolically, and this stage represents a transition to the mental-representational abilities of the preoperational period. Piaget's observations and the sequential nature of development over the first 2 years of life have generally been confirmed by researchers using both Piagetian and non-Piagetian tasks.

Piaget believed that imitation and object permanence each developed as a function of infants' overall cognitive development. He believed that "true" imitation involves the learning of new behaviors and that this behavior is not observed until Stage 4 (see Table 5-2). However, pre-imitative behaviors can be observed during Stages 1 through 3 and include *mutual imitation*, or infants imitating adults who are imitating them. Piaget contended that imitation of *invisible gestures* (for example, facial gestures) is not possible until Stage 4 and that *deferred imitation* is not seen until children possess symbolic functioning (Stage 6).

Generally, Piaget's observations concerning imitation from approximately 6 months on have been confirmed. Over the last decade, however, substantial controversy has arisen concerning imitation during the first several months of life, with a number of researchers observing imitation of facial expressions in very young infants. Some researchers have proposed that this imitation reflects the coordination of information from two sensory modalities, suggesting that intermodal integration is innate. Others have suggested that such matching behavior is reflexive, quickly dropping out of infants' cognitive repertoires, and is not a precursor of the "true" imitation seen later in infancy. Regardless of the interpretation, the phenomenon of neonatal imitation requires a re-examination of Piaget's infancy theory and the nature of early infant intelligence in general.

A major accomplishment of the sensorimotor period is the development of *object permanence*, the knowledge that an object has an existence independent of one's perceptions of or actions on that object. Piaget stated that infants have no notion of objects as being permanent in time and space during the first two sensorimotor stages (see Table 5-4). Infants' understanding of objects as independent entities develops gradually over the next three stages, although even Stage 5 children know objects only by their actions on them. It is not until Stage 6 and the beginnings of mental representation that objects can be conceived as having an existence that is truly independent of the child. Although Piaget's stage sequence of the development of object permanence has generally been replicated, controversy exists concerning the extent to which performance on object permanence tasks reflects competence (Piaget's position) or performance. Specifically, deficits in memory and attentional skills have been shown to influence infants' performance on object permanence tasks.

6

Thinking in Symbols

Transitions in Symbolic Representation

☐ From Sensorimotor to Symbolic Representation   ☐ From Literal to Conceptual Representation
☐ From Action-Based to Conceptual Representation
☐ From Conceptual to Abstract Representation

Some Phenomena That Vary as a Function of Children's Use of Symbols

☐ Classification   ☐ The Appearance/Reality Distinction
☐ Children's Number and Arithmetic Concepts

Children's Development of Representational Abilities

Summary

The transition from the curious, hands-on-everything toddler to the contemplative, speaking child is a remarkable one indeed. Sensorimotor infants possess some impressive problem-solving skills, but their thinking is still basically limited to overt actions on objects. In contrast, the 2- or 3-year-old, using symbols via language and imagery, is a totally different kind of thinker. Children at this age can retrieve events from the past and use them to plan for the future. They can make mental comparisons between objects that are not immediately within their perception and can mentally "try out" a behavior before actually executing it. In comparing the intellectual abilities of a 12-month-old infant, a 3-year-old child, and a 21-year-old adult, most would agree that the 3-year-old and the 21-year-old are more alike, cognitively speaking, despite their vast age difference. The possession of symbols transforms the intellect, and although children's thinking goes through other significant changes over the next dozen or so years, they remain symbol users.

Other qualitative changes in modes of *representation* take place throughout development, most notably at adolescence when "abstract," or "hypothetical," representation becomes possible. Some theorists postulate another change in mode of representation between the preschool and early school years. Typically, changes at this time reflect a shift from representations of literal (that is, perceptual) stimulus features to representations of more conceptual features. Related to this shift is a change from action-based or functional representations of objects and events to conceptually or categorically based representations. In all cases, the modes of representation beyond infancy are symbolic, in that they involve a mentalistic representation of events and do not depend on the physical presence of a stimulus before that stimulus can be thought about. What differs is the quality of the symbol and the degree to which it can be mentally manipulated.

☐ Transitions in Symbolic Representation

From Sensorimotor to Symbolic Representation

There seems to be little argument that infants represent information differently than older children do.

In Chapter 5 Piaget's account of *sensorimotor* development was examined in some detail. In brief, infants during their first 18 months or so are hypothesized to represent objects and events by means of self-produced action (including perceptual "action"). They cannot mentally "try out" a behavior before executing it and cannot make mental contrasts between stimuli. In a similar vein, Jerome Bruner (1966) described representation during the first 2 years as *enactive*, deriving from the action of the child, most notably from the sensory feedback accompanying movement. It is not until 18 to 24 months that symbolic representation becomes possible. Most contemporary theorists concur with Piaget's and Bruner's descriptions of action-based representation in infancy, with symbolic functioning appearing during the latter part of the second year of life (Case, 1985; Fischer, 1980; Halford, 1982).

Expressions of the Symbolic Function

According to Piaget, the symbolic (or, more properly, the *semiotic*) function has its origins in sensorimotor operations. This view is consistent with Piaget's epigenetic position (see Chapter 2), which posits that every form of cognition has its beginnings in earlier, more primitive functioning. The symbolic function is expressed via a variety of mechanisms, including deferred imitation (discussed in detail in Chapter 5), language, symbolic play, and mental imagery.

Language is the most obvious form of the symbolic function. Although most children start uttering individual words by 10 to 12 months, it is not until 18 months or so that they put two words together into sentences. Piaget recognized language as a useful means by which people express their knowledge. But he was firm in his belief that we use language because we are symbolic, and not vice versa. In other words, language is a symptom of the symbolic function and not its cause. More will be said of Piaget's views of the relationship between language and thought in Chapter 7.

Symbolic play is basically the game of pretending. Examples of symbolic play can be obtained from most parents of 2-year-olds. The 18-month-old who holds his mother's shoe to his ear and says "Hello" or the 2-year-old who feeds her doll imaginary cereal and scolds her for playing with her food, for example, are endearing to adults and reflect a child's increasingly sophisticated cognitive system. For Piaget, play is the purest example of assimilation predominating over accommodation, with children not adapting to the external world but transforming reality to their cognitive schemes.

Imagery refers to the internal representation of an external event. Although it is most easily thought of in terms of vision, Piaget used imagery to refer to the mental representations of information from any sensory modality (for example, hearing or kinesthesia). According to Piaget, mental images are the result of internalized imitation. Imagery is not merely an exact copy of the perception of an object but is an active re-creation of a perception. I have more to say about Piaget's conception of imagery later in the chapter.

Is There Symbolic Functioning in the First Year?

Some debate has arisen over when symbolic representation first appears. For example, several researchers (Ashmead & Perlmutter, 1980; Kessen & Nelson, 1978) have reported evidence of young toddlers' ability to recall events or objects from the past, given certain cues, months earlier than Piaget and others have suggested. Examples of memory that are based on symbolic representation are found in a diary study of infants between the ages of 7 and 11 months (Ashmead & Perlmutter, 1980). Evidence of memory was found for infants of all ages, with many of the episodes reflecting recall of the location of an object or person. An impressive example of recall by an 11-month-old infant is found in the following observation:

> Louise had been playing with a small doll bottle. She let it go on the floor and it rolled partially under the refrigerator. She went in her room and was playing for fifteen to twenty minutes when she found her doll and went back to where she had left her bottle, picked it up, and went back to her room [p. 8].

Louise's behavior clearly reflects recall and thus, presumably, symbolic representation. However, the recall was also clearly prompted by a cue closely associated with the remembered stimulus. There is an obvious reliance on tangible objects in the environment to trigger the memory. Similarly, recent evidence that deferred imitation is observed in 12- to 14-month-old infants also suggests that some symbolic ability is within the competence of infants at an earlier age than had been previously proposed (Abravanel & Gingold, 1985; Meltzoff, 1985; see Chapter 5). However, these demonstrations of symbol use do not appear to involve the formation of relations between symbolic entities independent of action, and thus they can be considered as precursors to the more sophisticated symbol use of the 2- and 3-year-old.

From Literal to Conceptual Representation

Although symbolic, the mental representations of young children do not have the quality that the representations of older children have. Piaget believed that preoperational children (ages 2 to 7 years) are highly attentive to the absolute properties of stimuli (perceptual centration), often ignoring relations between objects or events. In other words, preschoolers' thinking is *stimulus bound*, with their attention and, thus, decision making confined to the *literal*, perceptual properties of the objects they are thinking about.

Thinking in Images

Reproductive versus Anticipatory Images   Piaget asserted that one expression of the symbolic function was imagery but that the nature of imagery changed between the preoperational and concrete operational periods. He described two types of images: *reproductive* and *anticipatory*. Reproductive images are limited to evoking previously experienced sights and involve relatively static representations of objects. Anticipatory images allow the individual to envision transformations of an image, even if one has never experienced such transformations in the past. For instance, imagine your car rotated upward 90 degrees and suspended by its bumper from the branch of a tree. It is to be hoped that this is an image of an event you have never actually experienced, but it is one most adults can generate without much difficulty. Piaget contended that anticipatory images are not found until the concrete operational period, beginning around 7 years of age, with pre-school children's use of images being limited to the reproductive type.

Ikonic versus Language-Based Representation
Consistent with Piaget's emphasis on preoperational children's limited use of imagery is Bruner's (1966) theory. Bruner described preschool children's representations as *ikonic*. Basically, ikonic (or iconic) representation is representation by means of images. Bruner contrasted the literal, stimulus-bound thinking of the ikonic preschooler with the more abstract, language-based thinking of the school-age child. For Bruner, language is not used simply for communication but also provides a means for manipulating symbols. The power of language as a conceptual tool emerges around the age of 7 or 8, with formal schooling playing a significant role in the extent to which language is used to guide thought. Other researchers, most notably Kosslyn (1978, 1981), have observed age changes from imaginal to verbal representation around this time, although Kosslyn (like Piaget) believes that older children and adults can use images effectively as tools for thought in addition to language.

Developmental Differences in Word Perception
In a related area of study, there is evidence of a developmental shift in word perception from an encoding of physical or perceptual properties of words (for example, their acoustic or graphic features) to an emphasis on encoding semantic word properties (that is, meaning). This shift is illustrated by recognition memory experiments in which children are given sets of target words to remember and later shown or read a list of words and asked to select from the list the words that were presented earlier. Included on this list are the target words as well as words that were not presented previously, called foil or confuser words (see Table 6-1). Using variants of this paradigm, researchers have found that young children are more likely to say they have seen or heard a word before, when in fact they have not, for words that are *graphically* or *acoustically* similar to the actual stimulus word (to say, for example, that *log*

was presented earlier when the actual target word was *dog*). In contrast, older children are more likely to make such confusion errors for words that are conceptually related to the targets (to say, for example, that *cat* was presented earlier when the actual stimulus word was *dog*). Presumably, younger children pay more attention to the perceptual properties of the words when encoding them, whereas older children give more emphasis to conceptual word features, accounting for the pattern of errors (Bach & Underwood, 1970; Felzen & Anisfeld, 1970).

Eleanor Gibson (1971) proposed a model of word identification to account for these data. In her theory, words are represented in terms of syntactic, acoustic, graphic (when written), and semantic features. Meaning is achieved by analyzing word features, with features arranged in a hierarchy and processed serially. The order in which word features are processed varies developmentally. Young children typically give acoustic and graphic word features higher processing priority than semantic features, whereas the reverse is true for older children and adults. That is, young children attend primarily to literal, perceptual word features (the sound a word makes and its graphic representation), whereas older children are more attentive to a word's meaning.

If young children are biased toward encoding events in terms of perceptual features, might they not perform better on learning and memory tasks when they are specifically oriented to perceptual rather than semantic features? This question was

TABLE 6-1 Example of Stimuli Used in Recognition Memory Experiments

Target items	Foil (confuser) items		
	Conceptually related	Acoustically related	Unrelated (controls)
dog	cat	fog	book
coat	shirt	boat	hammer
peach	pear	beach	pen
boy	girl	toy	arm
chair	table	fair	dime
red	orange	dead	clock
gun	rifle	sun	snow

investigated in a study by Geis and Hall (1976). Children in grades one, three, and five were asked to judge whether certain statements about words were true. The questions oriented the children to one of three features of the words: acoustic (for example, "ARMS: Does it sound like larms?"); graphic (for example, "ARMS: Is it in big letters?"); or semantic (for example, "ARMS: Are they part of your body?"). For half of the questions the answer was yes, and for the other half, no (for example, "ARMS: Does it sound like leel?"). Following the questions the children were unexpectedly asked to remember all the target words that they had been presented.

If children's preferred mode of encoding influences their memory performance, one would expect the first-graders to remember more words for which they received acoustic or graphic orienting and the fifth-graders to remember best the semantically oriented words. However, those were not the results. Children of all ages remembered best when they had been oriented to the semantic properties of words, as is the case with adults (Craik & Lockhart, 1972). Geis and Hall interpreted these findings as support for a *levels-of-processing model* proposed by Craik and Lockhart (1972). Making decisions about the physical or perceptual features of words involves only "shallow" processing, in that it does not require an analysis of word meaning. Thus, retention following perceptual orienting is less than retention following semantic orienting, which involves processing at a "deeper" level of analysis. Apparently the same holds true for children, even children whose preferred mode of representation is perceptual (see also Ghatala, Carbonari, & Bobele, 1980; Perlmutter, Schork, & Lewis, 1982).

From Action-Based to Conceptual Representation

The transition from sensorimotor to symbolic representation discussed earlier represents a drastic discontinuity, in that aspects of sensorimotor functioning are not necessarily observed in the use of these symbols. As you may recall, however, Piaget held that the symbolic function was an outgrowth of sensorimotor functioning, with mental representation being the result of the internalization of action

schemes. Accordingly, young children's early concepts and mental representations should be based on overt activity, either the child's or activity inherent in the object that is being represented.

In Bruner's (1966) theory, already discussed briefly, enactive representation characterizes the sensorimotor child but does not disappear when ikonic and later language-based representations dominate children's thinking. In fact, Bruner noted that there is a "strong component of manipulation as a necessary aid to imagery" (p. 21) during the early stages of ikonic representation. Furthermore, he and his colleagues speculated that enactive representation, in combination with the use of language, can facilitate the transition from ikonic to symbolic representation in certain situations. In one experiment (Sonstroem, 1966), first-grade children, who were classified as nonconservers of solids, were given conservation training. The training consisted of a series of trials in which a ball of clay was transformed into a "sausage." For some children the training involved the active manipulation of the clay. They rolled one ball of clay into a sausage and were asked to compare it with an unchanged ball of clay (manipulation condition). Other children simply observed an experimenter modifying the ball of clay but were provided with specific descriptions of the changes in the clay. For instance, they were told explicitly that although the sausage was the longer, the ball was the fatter. Differences in the length and fatness of the sausage and ball of clay were emphasized continually to the children (labeling condition). Children in a third condition manipulated the clay *and* were provided specific labels (manipulation with labeling). Finally, children in a control group merely observed an experimenter making changes in the clay and received neither manipulation nor labeling training. When the children were subsequently tested for conservation, neither the manipulation alone nor the labeling alone resulted in significant improvements in conservation judgments. However, substantial improvements were noted for children who received *both* the manipulation and labeling training. Sixteen of 21 subjects in this condition demonstrated conservation on the posttest, compared with only 5 of 20 children in the control group. Sonstroem proposed that it is through the combined effects of doing and saying (physically acting on the clay and verbalizing the results) that children are able to overcome the potent visual illusion of the conservation task.

More recently, this shift from *action-based* to *conceptual* representation has been examined with respect to the development of word and language concepts. Katherine Nelson and her colleagues have been primarily responsible for stimulating recent research into this topic (Nelson, 1974, 1983, 1986; Nelson, Fivush, Hudson, & Lucariello, 1983). Nelson (1973) speculated that children's earliest words have their origins in action-based or functional properties. To investigate this hypothesis, she examined the first 50 words that a group of children spoke. She reported that a majority of these words represented small objects that children could manipulate themselves (for example, *shoe, bottle, ball*) or large objects that "act" themselves (for example, *dog, cat, car, clock*). Mentioned surprisingly seldom were large though familiar objects that just "sit there" (for example, *table, bed, tree*). In other words, children's early words tended to represent objects with which they had directly interacted or objects that did things, suggesting to Nelson a *functional core* as the basis for early word concepts.

Support for Nelson's position comes from a study by Heidenheimer (1978). Heidenheimer used a recognition memory task to ascertain the features that 4- and 5-year-old children attend to when attempting to remember words. Children were read a set of words and asked to remember them. They were later read another list of words and asked to determine whether they had heard each word on the previous list. Table 6-2 shows the target and confuser words Heidenheimer used in her experiment. As can be seen, some of the confuser words were related to the original target words on the basis of action (for example, *eat* for *apple*), and others on the basis of similar category membership (for example, *orange* for *apple*). The critical comparisons for our purposes are for the action and coordinate confusers. If young children represented the original stimulus words primarily in terms of action features, any memory errors should be for words reflecting such action. If they represented the original stimulus words in terms of

common category features, however, memory errors should be for items sharing these features. Heidenheimer reported an age difference in the percentage of errors children made to the action and coordinate confusers. Four-year-olds made more "false alarm" errors (saying they had heard a word earlier when in fact they had not) to the action words (17%) than to the coordinate words (4%), whereas the reverse was true for the 5-year-olds (3% for the action words and 11% for the coordinate words). These findings provide support for Nelson's argument of the importance of action encoding in the word concepts of young children.

Nelson and her colleagues have also suggested that children's early language concepts are based on functional relations among words rather than on conceptual relations (Nelson, 1983, 1986; Nelson et al., 1983). More specifically, she proposed that children's early language categories are *schematically organized*, in that they are based on relations typifying real-world scenes, stories, and events (for example, what is involved in having breakfast or objects and events associated with going to the park) rather than more abstract categories (for example, TOOLS, ANIMALS, VEHICLES). I will reserve a discussion of this research until Chapter 7, in which the development of children's language concepts will be examined in some detail.

From Conceptual to Abstract Representation

Piaget's views on the change in representation occurring with formal operations were discussed in Chapter 2. To reiterate, Piaget proposed that it is the

TABLE 6-2 Stimuli Used in a Recognition Memory Experiment by Heidenheimer (Heidenheimer, 1978)

Critical stimulus	Action word	Coordinate word	Superordinate word	Control word
Apple	Eat	Orange	Fruit	Shampoo
Hammer	Hit	Axe	Tool	Nickel
Wasp	Sting	Beetle	Insect	Gun
Blocks	Build	Legos	Toys	Cloud
Couch	Sit	Chair	Furniture	Street
Dog	Bark	Cat	Animal	Match
Shirt	Wear	Jacket	Clothes	Broom
Flower	Grow	Tree	Plants	Ocean

advent of *hypothetico-deductive reasoning* that allows children to ponder events that they have not directly experienced and to think "abstractly." According to Piaget, hypothetico-deductive reasoning allows the child to acquire a new form of knowledge. Piaget (1971) proposed that knowledge comes in three types. First, there is instinctive knowledge, or knowledge structured by hereditary mechanisms. Included in this restricted category are certain perceptual phenomena such as color perception, three-dimensional vision, and possibly some of the Gestalt principles. A second, very broad category includes knowledge acquired through physical experience of every type. Both of these forms of knowledge are available to the preadolescent child. It is the third form of knowledge, *logico-mathematical*, that is not found until early adolescence and is the result of children's ability to reason hypothetically. Logico-mathematical knowledge refers to knowledge that is independent of experience, and Piaget proposed that this form of knowledge is as extensive as the type derived directly from experience. Logico-mathematical knowledge is generated by the individual and is the result of mental coordinations of actions on objects or of actions on cognitive operations. It is the type of knowledge used in mathematics and in theory construction.

Many contemporary theorists concur with Piaget that a change in representation occurs between late childhood and adolescence and that this change results in the child being able to make mental evaluations on the basis of abstract qualities of objects and events. For example, Fischer (1980) proposed an abstract tier beginning around age 10, in which a person can "abstract an intangible attribute that characterizes broad categories of objects, events, or people" (pp. 494–495). In Halford's (1982) theory, Level 3 cognitive systems, acquired shortly after 11 years, allow children to coordinate symbolic and environmental elements in sets of three, which in turn allows them to successfully make and test hypotheses and to reason inferentially. Similarly, Case (1985) proposed a stage of vectorial (abstract-dimensional) operations, beginning around 11 years, in which children can coordinate sets of abstract operations. Although these theories conceptualize the changes in thinking that occur in early adolescence

generally in information processing terms, they are in basic agreement with the Piagetian position that a qualitatively different form of representation characterizes the thought of teenagers and serves as the basis for adult thinking.

☐ Some Phenomena That Vary as a Function of Children's Use of Symbols

Most forms of thought beyond infancy involve symbolic functioning to one degree or another. Thus, any list of cognitive contents that require the use of symbols would essentially mirror a list of topics that can be subsumed under the heading *cognition*. Yet, it seems worthwhile to describe the development of some important and interesting cognitive contents that, according to some theorists, change as a function of children's use of symbols. The short but diverse list discussed in this chapter includes classification, the appearance/reality distinction, and children's number and arithmetic concepts. Other potentially "classic" topics that have been related to children's use of symbols are discussed elsewhere in this book, notably, conservation and transitive inferences in Chapter 2 and the development of perspective taking and humor in Chapter 9.

Classification

Classification refers to the grouping of objects on the basis of some set of characteristics. In many classification experiments, children are given a set of objects, pictures, or words and asked to group them so that items that are alike or go together in some way are grouped together. Following classification, children are usually asked to justify their groupings. By examining the composition of and justifications for children's groupings, one can infer how children represent sets of items and the type of relations they use for categorizing diverse stimuli.

Styles of Classification

Four Phases of Classification Although there is a variety of ways of describing age-related changes in classification, four general phases in classification can be identified. These are summarized as follows:

1. *Idiosyncratic* (also called fiat equivalence, random). Items are grouped, usually in pairs, with groupings not based on any apparent physical or semantic properties of stimuli. Idiosyncratic justifications typify the groupings of 2- and 3-year-old children. Examples:
   a. "Horse and pants go together because that's a horse and those are pants."
   b. "Cat and chair go together because a cat meows and you sit in a chair."
   c. "Boy and hammer go together because they're alike."
   d. "Shovel and dog go together because I like shovels and I like dogs."
2. *Perceptual* (also called graphic collections). Items are grouped together on the basis of common perceptual characteristics. Perceptual justifications are found mainly in the groupings of 3- and 4-year-old children but are also found in the classifications of older children. Examples:
   a. "Pie and hat go together because they're both round."
   b. "Cat and squirrel go together because they both have long tails."
   c. "Rabbit and milk go together because they're both white."
   d. "Train and ship go together because they're both big."
3. *Complementary* (also called functional, schematic, thematic). Items are grouped on the basis of real or potential interactions as in real-world scenes or stories. Complementary justifications increase in incidence over the preschool years and typically are replaced by conceptual justifications some time between the ages of 6 and 9 years. However, complementary justifications persist into adulthood and are not totally replaced by conceptual classification (see the cartoon). Examples:
   a. "Cowboy, horse, and pants go together because a cowboy needs pants to ride a horse."
   b. "Cat and milk go together because a cat drinks milk."
   c. "Sailor, hat, and ship go together because a sailor wears a hat and works on a ship."
   d. "Hamburger, knife, napkin, and menu go together because when you're at a restaurant,
   you get a menu and order a hamburger and use a knife and napkin when you eat."
4. *Conceptual* (also called similarity, taxonomic, nominal, categorical). Items are grouped on the basis of inherent similarity such as being a member of a category or having similar functions. Conceptual justifications can be found in the classifications of preschool children, but they increase in frequency between the ages of 6 and 10 years. The use of conceptual classification seems to be related to formal schooling. Examples:
   a. "Coat and shirt go together because you wear them."
   b. "Shovel, hammer, saw, and screwdriver go together because they're all tools."
   c. "The man, woman, boy, and baby go together because they all belong to a family."
   d. "Baseball, jacks, and tag go together because they're all games."

The earliest phase, typifying most 2- and some 3-year-olds, I have labeled *idiosyncratic*. Children group items together, usually in pairs, and either fail to provide a reason for their groupings or provide one that is independent of any physical or conceptual characteristics of the stimuli (Denney & Acito, 1974; Inhelder & Piaget, 1964; Vygotsky, 1962). For example, a child may sort pictures of a dog and an apple together and, when asked why he made such a grouping, answer "Because a dog barks and you can eat an apple." Alternatively, the child may simply label each object or state that "I like dogs, and I like apples." This latter explanation may seem to reflect a grouping on the basis of likes and dislikes, but such a child will probably give the same justification for all pairings.

In a second phase, labeled here *perceptual*, children group items on the basis of perceptual characteristics. For example, *table* and *chair* go together because they both have four legs, or *elephant* and *car* go together because they are both big, or *frog* and *tree* go together because they are both green.

Slightly older children tend to form their groupings on the basis of *complementary* relations. N. Denney (1974) has described groupings based on complementary relations as those "composed of items that are different but share some interrelation-

© 1984 King Features Syndicate, Inc. World rights reserved. Reprinted with special permission.

Complementary classification persists into adulthood.

ship either in the subject's past experiences or in the experimental situation" (p. 41). For example, *dog* and *apple* go together because dogs can eat apples, or *barn*, *tractor*, and *farmer* go together because a farmer can drive the tractor into the barn.

Finally, children group items on the basis of *conceptual* relations. I use this term to mean groupings based on similar category membership (for example, ANIMALS, FURNITURE, CLOTHING) or shared function (for example, both *birds* and *airplanes* fly).

Evidence for these transitions in classification style has been reported in the research literature since the 1940s (Anglin, 1970; Melkman & Deutsch, 1977; Sigel, 1953; Thompson, 1941). Results consistent with the above findings have also been obtained from a number of nonsorting studies, including word associations (Emerson & Gekowski, 1976), recognition memory (Scott, Serchuk, & Mundy, 1982), cued recall (Ackerman, 1986), children's specification of relations existing among a series of items (Anglin, 1970; Olver & Hornsby, 1966) and word definitions (see N. Denney, 1974).

It should be noted that this developmental trend in classification does not have the characteristic of stages. Although a preference for conceptual classification is usually observed in children 8 or 9 years of age, for example, complementary classification does not disappear. Complementary schemes continue to be used by older children and adults when the stimuli and task demands call for them (Greenfield & Scott, 1986; Rabinowitz & Mandler, 1983). Thus, subjects over a broad age range have available to them a variety of relations by which to classify objects. What changes in development seems to be the tendency for various forms of relations to be used, with conceptual relations being used in a wider range of contexts with increasing age.

The use of alternative classification styles is not limited to older children and adults. Although one would not expect many conceptually based groupings in the sortings of 3-year-olds, children at least as young as 4 and 5 years use a variety of these classification schemes. Let me provide an example of a not too atypical 5-year-old, who used an interesting mixture of styles in a single sorting task. The child was given 16 black-and-white line drawings of familiar objects that could, from an adult's perspective, be grouped into four categories (ANIMALS, CLOTHES, FOOD, and TOOLS). He was told to put the drawings into groups so that "pictures that are alike or go together in some way are grouped together." He spontaneously provided justifications for his groupings as he sorted. This child grouped all items into pairs, although this was not a requirement of the task. His first pair was *corn* and *banana*, and they went together, he said, because they are both yellow (perceptual). *Horse* and *pants* go together because a cowboy needs pants to ride a horse (complementary); *saw* and *shovel* go together because they both have sharp points (perceptual); *coat* and *shirt* go together because you wear them (conceptual); *pie* and *hat* go together because they're both round (per-

ceptual); *hammer* and *saw* go together because they're both tools (conceptual); and *rabbit* and *milk* go together because they're both white (perceptual). This child had more perceptual justifications than is usual for a 5-year-old, but his mixture of justifications is typical for children of this age.

An example from another 5-year-old reflects the mixture of classification styles for children of this age, as well as their creativity and lack of planning. This child's first group consisted of the items *shovel, saw, screwdriver,* and *hammer,* and her justification was that they are all tools (conceptual). Next, she placed *cat* and *milk* together and said that a cat drinks milk (complementary); *horse* and *corn* go together because a horse eats corn (complementary); *hat* and *coat* go together because you wear them (conceptual); and *squirrel* and *banana* go together because a squirrel *might* eat a banana. The child was then left with three pictures, and, rather than not including them in any group or rethinking some of her earlier categories, she paused and then placed *pants, shirt,* and *pie* together and said, "Well, you've got to get dressed to eat dessert." This last example shows children's tendencies to follow instructions to "make groups" even if it means being inventive. It also reflects young children's lack of planning. This child did not look at all the pictures first and then decide the best categorization plan. Rather, she noticed salient relations among items and formed her groups on an item-by-item basis. Older children, with more foresight, would not be left with *squirrel* and *banana* or *shirt, pants,* and *pie.*

Classification Preferences   The diversity of classification judgments made by the same child indicates that these styles reflect, for the most part, preferences on part of the child. For example, children alter their sorting style as a function of changes in procedures or instructions (see Flavell, 1970b; Markman, Cox, & Marchida, 1981). A clear example of the preference basis of children's classification styles is found in a study by Smiley and Brown (1979). Subjects were to choose which of two pictures "goes best" with a standard picture. One of the alternatives was related to the standard on the basis of complementary relations (for example, for *needle,*

THREAD), whereas the other alternative was related on the basis of conceptual relations (for example, for *needle*, PIN). The majority of the selections of preschool and first-grade children reflected complementary relations. In contrast, fifth-grade and college students showed a marked preference for the conceptual relations. In a second experiment, kindergarten children were successfully trained to make selections based on conceptual relations. One day after training, however, the children were tested again, and their bias for complementary classification returned. Thus, young children can easily be trained to use conceptual relations, but they revert to their preferred mode when given the opportunity to do so.

A Cross-Cultural Look at Classification Denney (1974) speculated that the shift from complementary to conceptual classification (complementary to similarity in her terms) is primarily a function of formal schooling. Evidence for this hypothesis is found in research examining the thinking of people from nontechnological cultures, where the shift from complementary to conceptual classification, as defined here, is typically not found (Cole & Scribner, 1977). The Soviet psychologist A. R. Luria (1976) studied the thinking styles of people from a remote area of the country in the 1930s. Following are excerpts from Luria's study that reflect complementary classification similar to that shown by 5- and 6-year-olds from technologically advanced cultures. In these examples, the subject was shown four pictures and was to choose the one that was different. This is known as an oddity problem.

> *Subject:* Rakmat, age thirty-nine, illiterate peasant from an outlying district; . . . He is shown drawings of the following: *hammer-saw-log-hatchet.*
>
> "They're all alike. I think all of them have to be here. See, if you're going to saw, you need a saw, and if you have to split something you need a hatchet. So they're *all* needed here."
>
> We tried to explain the task by another, simpler example: "Look, here you have three adults and one child. Now clearly the child doesn't belong in this group."
>
> "Oh, but the boy must stay with the others! All three of them are working, you see, and if they

have to keep running out to fetch things, they'll never get the job done, but the boy can do the running for them. . . . The boy will learn; that'll be better, then they'll be able to work well together" [p. 55].
> Subject is then shown drawing of: *bird-rifle-dagger-bullet.*
>
> "The swallow doesn't fit here. . . . No . . . this is a rifle. It's loaded with a bullet and kills the swallow. Then you have to cut the bird up with the dagger, since there's no other way to do it. . . . What I said about the swallow before is wrong! All these things go together" [pp. 56–57].

The classification responses of this uneducated adult are reminiscent of the thinking of 5-year-olds described above. However, one must be cautious not to make value judgments concerning the thinking of people from nontechnological cultures. The thinking of the people described in Luria's study was well suited for their environment, and, in some ways, may be more advanced than our own. The demands of their world are different, requiring a different cognitive system. They do not have to worry about a monetary system of checks, automatic tellers, and credit cards, whereas we do. Human cognitive abilities are flexible. In fact, Luria noted that the thinking of these people became more conceptual as a result of formal education, reflecting the plasticity of human intelligence, even in adults.

Classification and Symbolic Functioning The findings from the classification literature are generally consistent with the developmental trend in symbol use discussed earlier. Children's earliest classifications are based on the physical characteristics of the stimuli (literal representation). Their first meaning-based groupings are typically complementary, using real-world relations and potential interactions among items as the basis for classification (action-based representation). Conceptual classification, based on taxonomic relations and functional similarity, reflects conceptual representation, with the use of conceptual thinking being influenced by environmental demands. It should also be noted, however, that developmental changes in classification do not seem to be stage-like in nature. Even young children occasionally use conceptual criteria in sorting and can be trained to do so consistently with only brief instruction. Yet, the durability of such training is typically short-lived, with children reverting to their preferred mode when given the opportunity (Smiley & Brown, 1979).

Piaget's Perspective on Classification

Piagetian Stages of Classification   Not surprisingly, Piaget had something to say about the development of classification, viewing changes in classification in terms of his broader developmental theory. In experiments conducted by Inhelder and Piaget (1964), children were given sets of geometric forms varying on at least two dimensions (for example, shape and color) and asked to "put together things that are alike" or to "put them so that they're all the same" (p. 21). Inhelder and Piaget described three stages in classification. In the first stage, called *graphic collections*, children make pictures of the objects. For example, a child may arrange the forms in a row and call it a snake or may build a house. In other situations, children may relate two objects on the basis of a single feature (for example, blue triangle, red triangle), but switch criteria for subsequent selections (for example, blue triangle, red triangle, red square). In other words, pairs of objects are related, but children follow no overall plan in grouping the set of items, making decisions on an item-by-item basis. According to Inhelder and Piaget, graphic collections typify the classifications of children 5 years of age and younger.

The second stage in Inhelder and Piaget's model is that of *nongraphic collections*. Now children can group a set of items on the basis of a single dimension. So, for example, a 7-year-old can group a set of blocks on the basis of color (all the reds in one pile, the blues in another) or on the basis of shape (all the triangles in one pile, all the squares in another). But these children, asserted Inhelder and Piaget, do not have a hierarchical classification system based on logical operations. For one thing, they can classify a set of stimuli on the basis of a single dimension only. They cannot classify objects simultaneously on two dimensions (size and shape, for instance). Figure 6-1 illustrates a *multiple classification* problem. To com-

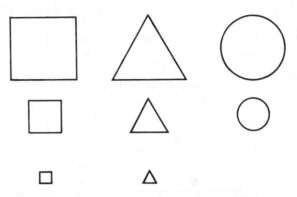

FIGURE 6-1   An example of a multiple classification problem. Subjects must choose an object that completes the pattern.

plete the matrix, a child must select a stimulus that appropriately completes the series both across the row and down the column (here, a small circle). Multiple classification is mastered by children around 7 or 8 years of age.

True hierarchical classification is achieved in the third stage, that of *class inclusion*. Class inclusion refers to the knowledge that a class must always be smaller than any more inclusive class in which it is contained. In a typical class-inclusion problem, children are given several examples from two subordinate categories of a single superordinate category (for example, seven pictures of dogs and three pictures of cats). They are then asked whether there are more dogs or more animals. In other words, they are asked to make a comparison between a subordinate set (dogs) and its superordinate set (animals). Although preschool children can easily make correct numerical judgments between two subordinate sets (for example, dogs versus cats), correct responses on class-inclusion problems using Inhelder and Piaget's procedures are not found reliably until late childhood or early adolescence (see Winer, 1980).

The bulk of research examining Inhelder and Piaget's classification theory has concerned the development of class inclusion. However, research into children's graphic and nongraphic collections has not been totally ignored. Several researchers have noted that preschool children do indeed construct graphic collections when presented with a series of items and that the frequency of these groupings decreases with age (Annett, 1959; Lovell, Mitchell, & Everett, 1962). However, graphic collections never dominate children's groupings. Rather, even preschool-age children form discrete groups of objects (that is, form nongraphic collections).

The Development of Class Inclusion With respect to class inclusion, Inhelder and Piaget's description of its development has generally been replicated using variants of their original tasks (Winer, 1980). As with other aspects of Piaget's theory, however, there has been considerable controversy concerning the nature of the task itself and young children's class-inclusion abilities. For example, the questions posed to children in class-inclusion problems have been criticized as being a bit bizarre. Why would any well-meaning adult ask a child if there are more *dogs* or more *animals*? It is an unusual question and can easily be misinterpreted by children. Research by Brainerd and Kaszor (1974) indicated, however, that children who had failed class-inclusion problems rarely misinterpreted the questions. Moreover, there was no relation between children's abilities to recall the class-inclusion questions and their performance on the task.

Children's difficulty in dealing with subordinate and superordinate concepts can be seen in other situations in which potentially confusing questions are not a problem. For instance, my daughter Heidi at 6 years of age called me at work one day to talk.

"Is Julie visiting you today?" I asked.

"Which Julie?" Heidi asked. "Julie my friend or Julie my cousin?"

"Julie your friend," I said.

"No," she replied.

"Then your cousin's there?"

"No, she's not here either."

When I initially posed the question, she was not able to respond because I did not specify which Julie. She could field a question about Julie her friend or Julie her cousin, but I had to make up my mind which one I wanted to know about. She could not deal with the larger set of Julies, in general.

There has been much debate among psychologists concerning how children go about solving class-inclusion problems and when they can comprehend

class-inclusion relations. One interesting study by McCabe and her colleagues found qualitative differences in how children of different ages solved these problems (McCabe, Siegel, Spence, & Wilkinson, 1982). The researchers gave standard class-inclusion problems to children ranging in age from 3 to 8 years. They reported that the 7- and 8-year-olds performed the best, followed by the 3- and 4-year-olds, with the 5- and 6-year-old children performing the worst! This somewhat anomalous finding was explained in terms of how children of different ages had approached the task. The 3- and 4-year-olds failed to discern any rule governing task performance and so responded randomly. As a result, they were correct on about 50% of the trials. In contrast, the 5- and 6-year-olds had figured out a rule for solving the task and followed the rule consistently. As it happened, however, the rule (pick the larger of the two subordinate sets) produced consistently wrong answers. The oldest children also had a rule for guiding their problem solving, and, for most of the children, the rule yielded correct solutions.

As with much of Piaget's work, there is evidence that children much younger than hypothesized by Piaget can solve class-inclusion problems when they are trained or when the task is simplified. Even 3- and 4-year-olds have been shown to solve class-inclusion problems after being trained and to generalize this training to similar problems (Brainerd, 1974; Siegel, McCabe, Brand, & Mathews, 1978; Waxman & Gelman, 1986). Other researchers have modified the class-inclusion task considerably and have reported that preschoolers, without the need of specific training, illustrate knowledge of class inclusion (Markman & Seibert, 1976; Smith, 1979; Steinberg & Anderson, 1975). For instance, Smith (1979) gave nursery school, kindergarten, and first-grade children a series of questions concerning their knowledge of superordinate relations. Some questions assessed the children's knowledge of subordinate and superordinate relations (for example, "Are all dogs animals?" or "Are all animals dogs?"), and other questions required inferences based on class-inclusion relations (for example, "A pug is a kind of dog. Does a pug have to be an animal?" or "A pug is a kind of animal. Does a pug have to be a kind of dog?"). Based on the children's answers to these and other questions, Smith concluded that young children do indeed represent class-inclusion relations; their difficulties lie not so much in their representations of knowledge as in their inability to activate that knowledge to solve problems.

Factors Influencing Children's Class-Inclusion Performance In addition to greatly modifying the nature of the class-inclusion task, researchers have influenced children's performance on more standard class-inclusion problems by introducing factors that affect (1) their knowledge of the number of items in the subordinate or superordinate sets and (2) their familiarity with the concepts used on the tasks.

With respect to influencing children's knowledge of the number of items that constitute the various sets, several researchers have shown that young children's performance on class-inclusion tasks can be enhanced simply by enumerating the items in each subclass (Brainerd & Kaszor, 1974; Winer, 1974). For example, Winer (1974) modified the standard class-inclusion instructions by telling children how many instances there were of each subset. Some children were told: "Here are six dogs and two cats. Are there more dogs or animals?" This version was contrasted with the standard procedure in which children are shown the pictures of the six dogs and two cats and merely asked, "Are there more dogs or more animals?" This simple change in procedure ensures that children encode the number of items in the subordinate sets. They then are able to compare the number of items in a superordinate set with a previously encoded number of items in the subordinate set. Winer reported that children given the modified instructions solved a greater number of class-inclusion problems correctly than did children given the standard instructions. Perhaps what is most surprising about these findings is that young children apparently do not count the number of items in the subordinate and superordinate sets spontaneously.

Other techniques that have increased children's likelihood of recognizing the difference in size between the superordinate and subordinate sets involve making the superordinate set visually salient (Tatarsky, 1974; Wilkinson, 1976). For example, Tatarsky (1974) presented children from kindergarten through the third grade with sets of painted blocks. In a standard class-inclusion task using blocks, children were shown, for instance, 12 wooden blocks, 8 of them painted red and 4 blue. They were then asked whether there were more wooden blocks or more red blocks. In one condition of this experiment, Tatarsky painted only *half* of each block. For example, some of the blocks were painted red on their top halves but left unpainted on their bottom halves. Others were half blue and half unpainted. In this way, the salience of the "woodenness" of the blocks was enhanced, in that the bottom half of each of the blocks was clearly wooden. When asked whether there were more wooden blocks or more blue blocks, the children performed significantly better than they had when the standard Piagetian procedure was used.

Other researchers have shown that children's familiarity with the concepts used on class-inclusion tasks influences their performance. For example, several researchers have presented children with standard class-inclusion problems but have varied the *typicality* of the subordinate categories used (Carson & Abrahamson, 1976; Lane & Hodkin, 1985). Category typicality refers to differences in how representative various items are of their superordinate category (Rosch, 1975). Both adults (Rosch, 1975; Uyeda & Mandler, 1980) and children (Bjorklund, Thompson, & Ornstein, 1983) evaluate some members of natural language categories as being "better" examples of those categories than other members. For instance, *shirt, dress, pants,* and *coat* are all typical exemplars of the category CLOTHING. In contrast, *shoes, belt, socks,* and *scarf* are all atypical members of the same category, despite the fact that people are just as familiar with the latter items as with the former. In general, both adults and children process category-typical information differently than they do category-atypical information (see Bjorklund, 1985). More will be said about category typicality in Chapter 7.

With respect to class inclusion, both Carson and Abrahamson (1976) and Lane and Hodkin (1985) reported better performance when category-typical items were used as exemplars. For example, children were more likely to answer class-inclusion problems correctly when presented with pictures of robins and blue jays (both typical examples of BIRDS) than when presented with pictures of chickens and ducks (both atypical examples). In other words, the children's knowledge of category relations influenced their class-inclusion decisions, indicating that children's abilities to deal simultaneously with subordinate and superordinate relations is not absolute but varies as a function of their knowledge of the category relations used in the task.

Another reason why young children have difficulty dealing with class-inclusion problems may be that the categories usually used in these tasks do not correspond to their underlying cognitive representations. Categories used in the research cited above are hierarchical in nature, with items within a category being related to one another on the basis of inclusion relations. If a collie is a dog and a dog is an animal, then a collie must be an animal. Not all categories of objects are typified by class-inclusion relations, however. Markman (1983, 1984) has defined *collections* as groups of items related on the basis of part/whole relations. For instance, a child is part of a family, a tree is part of a forest, and a soldier is part of an army. Collections are also arranged in hierarchies, but Markman has proposed that the part/whole relations of collections are easier for children to deal with than are class-inclusion relations.

Evidence of young children's greater facility with collections than with classes on a class-inclusion problem was presented by Markman and Seibert (1976). In their experiments, children were asked standard class-inclusion questions; for some children, however, class terms were used, whereas for others collective terms were employed. For example, some children were asked, "If there are ten kindergarten boys and five kindergarten girls, who would have a bigger party, someone who invited the boys or someone who invited the children?" This question is phrased according to class-inclusion relations (*boys* and *girls*, both included in the category CHILDREN). For other children, the question was rephrased so that they were asked about boys and girls in a kindergarten class (*class* being a collective term). Markman

and Seibert reported significantly higher levels of performance when the questions involved collective as opposed to class relations. Markman and her colleagues subsequently presented evidence that young children prefer collections to classes when they are free to impose their own organization on a set of items and that they spontaneously interpret relations among items in terms of collections (Callanan & Markman, 1982; Markman, Horton, & McLanahan, 1980). Accordingly, Markman asserts that we may be underestimating children's actual cognitive abilities by using concepts that do not correspond to their underlying cognitive representations.

Adults' Class-Inclusion Reasoning On the other side of the coin, however, is evidence that even adults fail to use inclusion relations under some circumstances. For example, Tversky and Kahneman (1983) presented college students with passages describing people, including the following: "Linda is 31 years old, single, outspoken and very bright. She majored in philosophy. As a student, she was deeply concerned with issues of discrimination and social justice, and also participated in anti-nuclear demonstrations" (p. 297). The subjects were then given a set of eight occupations and avocations associated with Linda, including (1) Linda is active in the feminist movement, (2) Linda is a bank teller, and (3) Linda is a bank teller and is active in the feminist movement. The students were to rank the eight statements associated with Linda by "the degree to which Linda resembles the typical member of the class." Not surprisingly, the statement given the highest probability was the one stating that Linda was an active feminist. However, 85% of the subjects rated the statement that Linda was a bank teller *and* a feminist as more probable than the statement that Linda was a bank teller. Following class-inclusion reasoning, the class BANK TELLER is more inclusive than the class BANK TELLER AND FEMINIST. Nonetheless, college students rated the latter as more likely than the former. Tversky and Kahneman proposed that adding *feminist* to *bank teller* produced a statement that more resembled the description of Linda than *bank teller* alone, making the conjunctive statement (*feminist* and *teller*) seem (erroneously) more probable than the unrepresentative statement (*teller*).

Research from a variety of perspectives indicates that even young children possess basic categorical and inclusion relations. Their knowledge of conceptual category relations is restricted, however, in that they often display categorical sophistication only under optimal instructional and procedural conditions. There are developmental differences in children's knowledge and use of such concepts, with the number of situations in which they will demonstrate conceptual knowledge expanding with age. As the Tversky and Kahneman results indicate, however, even adults sometimes fail to use inclusion reasoning when it would be appropriate to do so.

The Appearance/Reality Distinction

Adults know very well that things are not always what they appear to be. We realize that the appearance of an object does not necessarily correspond to its reality. This is not a knowledge we were born with but one that has a gradual developmental history. One form of this appearance/reality distinction can be seen in conservation. When water is poured from a short, stout glass into a tall, skinny one, the amount of water really appears to have increased. We know, of course, that in reality the amount of water is the same. We also know that children much younger than 7 years of age are not cognizant of this fact.

As we have seen, conservation refers to the knowledge that *quantitative* relations between objects remain the same despite irrelevant perceptual transformations. A more basic form of the appearance/reality distinction concerns the knowledge that *qualitative* relations between objects remain the same despite some perceptual transformation. Quantitative properties refer to amount, as in number, length, weight, or volume. In comparison, qualitative properties refer to characteristics of type or form. For example, children would demonstrate qualitative constancy if they realized that their parents' car remained the same despite being painted. Piaget (1968) referred to such knowledge as reflecting *identity*. Identity and conservation are similar in

that both involve a form of cognitive constancy, a realization that an entity remains unchanged despite changes in appearance. However, Piaget asserted that constancies involving qualitative properties do not require reversibility but merely a dissociation of the permanent and variable properties of an object. As such, qualitative constancies are developed during the preschool years. In fact, Piaget (1968) contended that object permanence is the first qualitative identity, being achieved between 18 and 24 months of age.

A pioneering study of qualitative identity was published by De Vries in 1969. In her study, children 3 to 6 years of age were familiarized with a trained cat named Maynard. In one condition, after the children petted Maynard, he was fitted with a realistic dog mask. Although the children did not actually see the mask being placed on Maynard, the cat's body and tail remained in full view of the children during the transformation. They were then asked questions concerning the identity of the animal. "What kind of animal is it now? Would this animal eat dog food or cat food? Does it bark or meow?" In general, 3-year-olds frequently believed that the mask had actually changed the identity of the animal, whereas most 5- and 6-year-olds believed that changes in the appearance of the animal had not altered its identity. De Vries referred to this type of qualitative constancy as *generic identity*.

In addition to her research into changing the appearance of animals, De Vries also interviewed children on their beliefs about people wearing masks and about the constancy of gender as a result of certain irrelevant changes (for example, boys wearing dresses). Again, she reported that 3-year-olds tended to believe that changes of appearance result in a change in identity. This belief of young children can account for their sometimes puzzling responses to costumes, worn both by others and by themselves. For example, it is not uncommon at Halloween for 2- and 3-year-old children to be excited about wearing a costume, only to become distressed when the mask is placed over their faces or when they look at themselves in the mirror. Wearing Darth Vader's cape and carrying his light saber are one thing, but wearing the mask is another story. Not all transformations of personal identity are so upsetting, however, as is evidenced by the number of scraped elbows and knees on children who wear their Superman "underroos," tie a cape around their neck, and jump from tables, fences, and windows, convinced that they can fly. These children's behaviors are consistent with the belief that a significant change in appearance results in a change in identity.

Let me provide an anecdote to illustrate young children's thinking about how appearance can influence reality and their application of this thinking to solve problems. Three-year-old Nicky sometimes spent the night with his grandparents, who would take him to preschool the following morning. Nicky especially liked to ride with his grandfather because he drove a somewht battered, stick-shift Chevy, which Nicky called "Papa's car." Nicky's grandmother, however, drove only cars with automatic transmission, and thus she was unable to take Nicky to school in Papa's car. One morning when Grandma was about to drive Nicky to school, he said, "Grandma, dress up like a man this morning. Put on Papa's shirt and wear his hat." When asked why he wanted her to do that, he responded, "Then you can take me to school in Papa's car." Nicky had a problem and attempted to solve it by transforming his grandmother, temporarily, into a man, which would thus give her the ability to drive a stick-shift car. More will be said concerning children's belief in the constancy of gender as a function of behavior or dress in Chapter 9, on social cognition.

In related research, Flavell and his colleagues have extensively investigated young children's knowledge about the distinction between appearance and reality (Flavell, Flavell, & Green, 1983; Flavell, Green, & Flavell, 1986; Flavell, Zhang, Zou, Dong, & Qi, 1983; Taylor & Flavell, 1984). In some experiments children were presented with a realistic looking fake rock made of sponge or watched as white milk was poured into a red glass. The children were then asked two questions. The first concerned what the objects looked like, "how they look to your eyes right now." The second concerned the actual identity of the objects, "how they really and truly are." Somewhat surprisingly, Flavell reported that most 3-year-olds could not solve these seemingly simple problems. Their errors tended to be one of two types: *phenomenism errors* and *intellectual realism errors*. Phenomenism errors typically occurred when appearance/reality tests involving color were used. Children stated, for example, that the milk looked red and "really and truly" was red. In contrast, intellectual realism errors were more likely to occur on tasks involving objects that looked like something they were not. For example, children would say that the fake rock was indeed a sponge and *looked like* a sponge. In general, when children erred, they did so by giving the same answer to both questions.

Before assuming that 3-year-olds cannot solve appearance/reality tasks, Flavell and his colleagues (1986) simplified their problems. Children were acquainted with an experimenter, for example, and watched as she put on a soft plastic mask; then they were asked who the person in the mask "really and truly" was. For other tasks, they were asked questions about objects that had uncharacteristic sounds or smells (for example, socks that smelled like peanut butter). The 3-year-olds' performance on these simplified tasks was surprisingly poor, and in a subsequent study explicit training in making the appearance/reality distinction did little to improve their performance. Given these findings, the researchers concluded that 3-year-olds "truly did not understand [the appearance/reality distinction], even minimally" (p. 23).

By 5 or 6 years of age children correctly answered the simple appearance/reality questions that gave so much trouble to 3-year-olds. However, 6-year-olds' knowledge of the distinction between appearance and reality was not complete. When shown two objects, for example, one that unambiguously looked to be what it was (for example, a candy bar in a candy wrapper) and another that looked to be something it was not (for example, a magnet that looked like a piece of chocolate), first-grade children had difficulty selecting the one whose reality differed from its appearance. By 11 or 12 years of age, children had developed a rich knowledge of the distinction between appearance and reality, realizing that things are not always what, on first impression, they appear to be (Flavell et al., 1986).

Flavell and his colleagues (1986) speculated about the factors that may mediate children's development of the appearance/reality distinction. One likely candidate is *dual encoding*. Three-year-olds' inability to differentiate between the appearance of an object and its actual identity may stem, in part, from their difficulty in representing an object in more than one form at a time. That is, young children may focus on one aspect of a stimulus (its appearance or its actual identity) and give the same answer, based on either appearance or reality, regardless of the question asked. Thus, on the one hand, if the change in color is more salient to a child (phenomenism error), the object *looks* red and *is* red. If, on the other hand, the identity of the object is more salient, it *is* a sponge and *looks like* a sponge. Young children cannot act on multiple representations of an object simultaneously. With increasing age they become more adept at dual encoding, but it is not until later childhood or early adolescence that they can "think about notions of 'looks like,' 'really and truly,' 'looks different from the way it really and truly is,' and so on in the abstract, metaconceptual way that older subjects can" (Flavell et al., 1986, p. 59).

Children's Number and Arithmetic Concepts

Although the quintessential symbols of human cognition are probably found in language (see Chapter 7), a good case can be made for the primacy of number. Our tendency to quantify objects and events in our world is ubiquitous. The bulk of the technological advancements made over the past three centuries, and particularly in this century, can be attributed to our species' quantitative skills. Thinking in numbers (and subsequently in terms of mathematical relations) is not innate but, like other aspects of cognition, has a developmental history. In this section I review aspects of children's earliest concepts of number and then take a brief look at the development of basic arithmetic skills.

Children's Number Concepts

Children seem very early to have some sense of what numbers mean, but adults watching a 2- or 3-year-old use numbers may wonder exactly what that sense

is. The 18-month-old may respond with a loud and definitive "Two!" when asked how many cookies he wants, and the 3-year-old may point at her dolls, saying "One, two, three, seven, nine, twelve-teen, three-teen, seventeen." Each is displaying some knowledge of number, yet neither is using numbers with the same consistency and meaning that a 7- or 8-year-old child uses them. Primitive notions of number (or at least quantity) can be found very early in development: newborns can discriminate between arrays differing in only one element (Antell & Keating, 1983). Yet a full understanding of the number concept is not obvious until the early school years, and possibly beyond.

Conservation of Number   Piaget (1965a) believed that the concept of number is reflected in conservation. Conservation-of-number tasks follow the same basic procedures as all of Piaget's conservation problems. Children are first shown a set of items, black jelly beans, for instance. The children are then asked to take white jelly beans from a container so that there are an equal number of black and white beans. Once the appropriate number of white beans has been selected (with assistance from the experimenter, if necessary), the beans are arranged in two rows, one black and one white (see Figure 6-2). The experimenter then spreads out the white jelly beans so that the line of white beans extends beyond the line of black beans. This is all done while the children are watching. They are then asked if the two rows still have the same number of jelly beans. If they answer no, they are asked which row has more, and why.

As with conservation in general, Piaget proposed three stages in the acquisition of the operational conservation of number. In Stage 1, children are unable to consistently establish a one-to-one correspondence between the two sets of items. So, for example, Stage 1 children select too few or too many white jelly beans or fail to arrange them in a one-to-one relationship with the black beans. When two equal sets of beans are established and one is modified (example 3, Figure 6-2), children say that the longer, less dense row now has more beans in it, being unable to ignore the perceptual differences

"Select from the jar the same number of white jelly beans as there are black jelly beans."

"Are there the same number of black jelly beans as there are white jelly beans?"

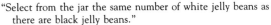

The row of white jelly beans is extended while the child watches.

"Are there the same number of white jelly beans as there are black jelly beans now? Which has more? Why?"

FIGURE 6-2   A conservation-of-number task

between the two rows. During Stage 2 children can establish an "intuitive one-to-one correspondence" (Piaget, 1965a) between the items in the two sets, but judgments of equivalence between the sets do not last long. Once the beans in one row are extended, the children say that there are more in the longer row. It is only the Stage 3 child (concrete operations) who realizes that the number of beans does not change when one of the rows is elongated but that changes in spatial extension of elements are compensated for by equivalent changes in the density of the elements.

Non-Piagetian research, using variants of Piaget's original task, has generally replicated his observations, illustrating that (1) children are able to form a one-to-one correspondence before they can conserve; (2) young children make their evaluations on the basis of relative length, independent of other factors; (3) slightly older children sometimes consider density but do not coordinate the dimensions of length and density, thus failing to conserve in many situations; and (4) it is not until 7 or 8 years of age

that children consistently pass conservation-of-number tasks (Brainerd, 1977b; Pufall, Shaw, & Syrdal-Lasky, 1973).

Young Children's Knowledge of Number

Although most children do not display conservation of number before 7 years of age, anyone who has been around preschoolers for any length of time knows that they obviously have some concept of number. They count (not always accurately) and can certainly differentiate between sets of various sizes (Gelman, 1972). Gelman and her colleagues have tried to emphasize what knowledge of numbers preschool children possess rather than stressing what they do not know. They have concluded that young children have a rather sophisticated, though limited, knowledge of numbers.

Gelman (1972) developed the "magic task" to assess young children's number concepts. In the magic task, children are presented with two arrays of items, one of which is described as the "winner" and the other the "loser." The critical difference between the two arrays is in the number of elements (for example, one array consists of two mice and the second array consists of three mice). After several trials in which the children correctly identify the winning and losing sets, the winning set is surreptitiously altered by adding or subtracting an element. The children's responses to the "magical" change in the arrays are then assessed, in an attempt to ascertain whether they were cognizant of the significance of number in differentiating the winning from the losing array.

Gelman reported that changes in number were identified by nearly all of her subjects, who ranged in age from 3 to 5½ years. In contrast, changes in the placement of the elements (for example, increasing the separation between them) were not regarded by the children as being important in determining the "winner." Also, many children spontaneously commented that one item had been added or deleted from the winning array, indicating that young children not only possess a rudimentary concept of number but also have an implicit understanding of addition and subtraction. These findings indicate that children who fail to conserve number on traditional Piagetian tasks nonetheless display a knowledge of number invariance under conditions involving relatively small sets.

Given that children have some concept of number prior to their ability to conserve, how does the number concept develop? One popular non-Piagetian candidate for the precursor of number conservation is counting. Gelman and Gallistel (1978) have extensively investigated children's early counting and have proposed five principles of counting:

1. *The one-one principle:* Each item in an array is associated with one and only one number name (such as *two*).
2. *The stable-order principle:* Number names must be in a stable, repeatable order.
3. *The cardinal principle:* The final number in a series represents the quantity of the set.
4. *The abstraction principle:* The first three principles can be applied to *any* array or collection of entities, physical (for example, chairs, jelly beans) or nonphysical (for example, minds in a room, ideas).
5. *The order-irrelevant principle:* The order in which things are counted is irrelevant.

Gelman and Gallistel referred to the first three principles as the "how-to" principles of counting and proposed that children as young as 2½ years of age demonstrate knowledge of them under some circumstances. For example, in a counting experiment where 3-, 4-, and 5-year-old children were asked to discern the number of objects in a series of arrays, all the groups of children used the one-to-one rule (that is, one unique number name per object), although performance deteriorated for the youngest children for arrays of six or greater. Gelman and Gallistel also reported that children who counted items in arrays used the stable-order principle, with more than 90% of the 4- and 5-year-olds and 80% of the 3-year-olds using the same list of number words in the same order on all of their trials. The children sometimes used an idiosyncratic list of number words (for example, "One, two, six"), but they used this list consistently across arrays of varying size.

More recent research has shown that preschoolers seem to know the cardinal principle. Fuson and her colleagues demonstrated that, after counting arrays of objects ranging in size from 2 to 19, 3- and 4-year-old children generally gave the last counting word they had spoken in response to the question "How many things are there?" (Fuson, Pergament, Lyons, & Hall, 1985). This was true even for children who counted incorrectly, implying that accurate counting is not a requirement for attainment of the cardinal rule (see also Gelman, Meck, & Merkin, 1986).

In a related study, Briars and Siegler (1984) investigated children's knowledge of the counting principles. They asserted that children must induce which features of counting are critical and which are merely optional in enumerating an array, and they speculated that some children may believe that more is required for successful counting than is actually the case. In their experiment, 3-, 4-, and 5-year-old children watched a puppet counting and were asked to determine whether the puppet had counted properly. The puppet demonstrated (sometimes accurately and sometimes inaccurately) five features of counting, one of which was necessary for counting and four of which were optional. The necessary feature was that of *word/object correspondence*, which encompasses the first two principles of Gelman and Gallistel (one-one correspondence and stable order). The four optional features were that (1) adjacent objects were counted consecutively, (2) counting started from the end rather than the middle, (3) counting progressed from left to right, and (4) each object in an array was pointed to exactly once. Children's knowledge that word/object correspondence was critical in counting increased with age (30%, 90%, and 100% for the 3-, 4-, and 5-year-olds, respectively). However, 60% of the 5-year-olds viewed other features, such as beginning to count at an end rather than in the middle and pointing to each object only once, as also being essential features of counting. In other words, young children learn the critical features of counting by 4 years of age but infer, from watching others, additional features that are characteristic of but not necessary for proper counting.

The relation between children's counting and conservation of number has been explored in several experiments. For instance, Fuson, Secada, and Hall (1983) reported significantly higher levels of number conservation (69%) by 4- and 5-year-old children who were required to count the elements in both sets before judging which set, if either, was larger than by children given a standard conservation-of-number task (14%).

In a related experiment, Saxe (1979) administered a series of counting and conservation tasks to 4-, 5-, and 6-year-old children. On the counting tasks the children were required to assess the equivalence of two rows of dots differing in length and, later, to select the same number of beads from a container as there were dots on a card. In each case, the task was constructed so that counting was necessary to yield the correct answer. The conservation tasks were similar to those used by Piaget, with beads in one row compressed on one trial and elongated on another. Saxe classified each child as conserving or not conserving on the conservation-of-number tasks and as prequantitative or quantitative on the counting tasks. The children were classified as prequantitative if they counted items in the arrays but did not use the results of counting to solve the problem. They were classified as quantitative counters if they used counting to aid their performance, although they may not have used exactly the same number words or order as adults conventionally do. The classification of children with respect to counting and conservation-of-number skills in Saxe's experiment is presented in Table 6-3. As can be seen, no child who was classified as prequantitative with re-

TABLE 6-3 Number of Children Classified Jointly According to Understanding of Number Concept (Conservers versus Nonconservers) and Counting Ability (Prequantitative versus Quantitative) (adapted from Saxe, 1979)

Counting ability	Number concept	
	Nonconservers	Conservers
Prequantitative	12	0
Quantitative	22	20

spect to counting was also classified as a conserver. In contrast, 22 children displayed sophisticated counting skills but were still unable to conserve. These findings are consistent with the view that quantitative counting skills are a necessary but not sufficient condition for the attainment of conservation of number.

In summary, young children do possess a limited knowledge of numbers and relations among numbers, but they are restricted to dealing with small quantities. As children's knowledge of numbers expands, they refine their number concept, discriminating between what is necessary and what is optional in dealing with numbers; and importantly, their ability to deal with large quantities increases and their belief in the invariance of number is applied more consistently across a wider range of tasks.

Children's Arithmetic Concepts

It is clear that young children have some concept of number. They can count and can determine which of two quantities is the larger. But when can children perform tasks of basic arithmetic such as addition and subtraction? These skills are not formally taught until the first grade in many schools, and from a Piagetian perspective they require concrete operational ability.

Piaget's Perspective on Children's Early Arithmetic Piaget's (1965a) work on early arithmetic was less extensive than his work on children's number concept. He proposed that addition and subtraction require inversion reversibility, something that is not achieved (according to Piaget) until about 7 years of age. For example, if $5 + 3 = 8$, then, by the logical rule of inversion, $8 - 3 = 5$.

In one experiment by Piaget (1965a), children were shown an array of eight objects. The array was then modified, so, for example, it was divided into two equal sets of four objects and was then divided a second time into unequal sets (seven and one, for instance). Do children recognize the equivalence of these two groupings? In other words, do they know that $4 + 4 = 7 + 1$? As with conservation of number, Piaget reported three stages in children's early arithmetic abilities. In Stage 1, characterizing 5- and 6-year-olds, the children typically relied on the spatial arrangement of objects, erroneously asserting that there were different numbers of elements in the two combinations. In Stage 2, the children could correctly solve the task, but only after counting the objects or establishing a spatial one-to-one correspondence between the items. The Stage 3 children (7-year-olds) solved the problem without resorting to physical counting techniques. Without this understanding, according to Piaget, children cannot have a true understanding of addition, although they can be taught to memorize certain formulas (for example, 2 + 3 = 5; but will they know what 3 + 2 equals?).

More recent research has questioned some of Piaget's interpretations and has demonstrated that even preschool children are able to handle simple addition and subtraction problems. For example, given the problem of 3 + 2 = ?, a 4- or 5-year-old is likely to count to three, using objects or his fingers, and then add two more objects or fingers, saying "four, five." By 6 years of age, children may start with the cardinal value of the first number ("three") and continue counting from there ("four, five"). Preschoolers use a variety of such rules to arrive at correct answers to simple addition and subtraction problems. These rules, however, almost always involve forward counting by ones of concrete objects, including fingers (Carpenter & Moser, 1982; Ginsburg, 1977). Such addition and subtraction by counting can be successful for unpracticed combinations such as 14 + 1 = ? and 15 − 1 = ?, which is in violation of Piaget's tenet that true addition cannot be achieved by simple counting (Starkey & Gelman, 1982).

The Development of Mental Arithmetic
Sometime during the early school years, children's solutions to simple arithmetic problems become covert. They no longer rely on counting objects or their fingers but perform the calculations "in their heads." At this point, knowing precisely what children are doing becomes more difficult, because the only evidence of the mental processes underlying performance is the answers they give.

One popular technique for evaluating mental processes is to use the amount of time it takes for children to solve problems to infer the underlying operations. One model that describes relatively well the simple addition of grade school children has been termed *min* (Groen & Parkman, 1972; Groen & Resnick, 1977). In the min model, a mental counter is set for the first addend (in the problem 5 + 3 = ?, the counter would be set at 5). The counter is then increased by increments of one until enough have been added (here, 3). Children's reaction times to solve problems vary as a function of the second, smaller addend. Thus, arriving at an answer for 5 + 4 takes longer than arriving at an answer for 5 + 2 because the mental counter must tick off four times for the former problem but only two times for the latter. In other words, reaction times are proportional to the smaller, or *minimum*, number being added.

Children's arithmetic becomes more complex over the school years, however, and so must models for describing their problem solving. One model that has been successful in describing changes in elementary school children's arithmetic has been proposed by Ashcraft and his colleagues (Ashcraft, 1982, 1983; Ashcraft & Fierman, 1982; Hamann & Ashcraft, 1985). Ashcraft proposed a shift in arithmetic problem solving from the counting-based procedures used by first-graders to *retrieval of arithmetic facts* by older children and adults. When adults are given the problem 7 + 5 = ?, for example, they need not start at seven and mentally increase this by five to arrive at the answer. Rather, the knowledge that 7 + 5 = 12 resides in memory, and this fact can be retrieved just as can any other fact in the memory. A listing of some basic arithmetic facts is shown in Figure 6-3 (from Brainerd, 1983). To test this hypothesis, Ashcraft and Fierman (1982) presented children in grades three, four, and six with addition problems of varying difficulty. The children were to determine whether each problem was true or false as quickly as possible (for example, 5 + 3 = 8 or 9 + 7 = 15). Analyses of the children's reaction times revealed

	1	2	3	4	5	6	7...
1	2	3	4	5	6	7	8
2	3	4	5	6	7	8	9
3	4	5	6	7	8	9	10
4	5	6	7	8	9	10	11
5	6	7	8	9	10	11	12
6	7	8	9	10	11	12	13
7	8	9	10	11	12	13	14
:							

FIGURE 6-3 A table of arithmetic facts for mental arithmetic problems solved by the fact-retrieval method. If the problem is of the form 4 + 3 = ? the child simultaneously enters the table at the column corresponding to 4 and the row corresponding to 3. The problem is solved by scanning down the column and across the row until the two operations intersect at a given cell (adapted from Brainerd, 1983).

that most fourth- and sixth-graders were solving the problems by retrieving arithmetic facts from memory, just as adults solve such problems. The third-grade data, however, reflected a transitional age, with about half of the children solving the problems by counting procedures similar to those used by younger children (such as that described by the min model), with the remainder solving problems by fact retrieval.

This shift in development from procedural to retrieval-based techniques for solving simple arithmetic problems reflects changes in the efficiency of information processing. With age, children solve problems faster. This increased speed can be attributed to processes becoming more automatic, requiring less of one's limited mental capacity for successful execution. First-graders' use of counting strategies is highly conscious and laborious in contrast to the fact retrieval of older children. However, even 5- and 6-year-olds apparently store and retrieve some arithmetic facts. For small whole-number problems (for example, 2 + 2 = ?), young children's performance is relatively rapid, indicating fact retrieval (Hamann & Ashcraft, 1985; Siegler & Shrager, 1984). With age and experience, more arithmetic facts become stored and can be retrieved with increasing ease, without the need of laborious counting procedures.

Arithmetic becomes more complex, of course, and as it does, children must rely again on procedural knowledge. When subtraction involves "borrowing" (as in 92 − 59 = ?) or addition involves "carrying" (as in 92 + 59 = ?), procedures are at first slow and difficult; but with practice they become more efficient. In general, based on the work of Ashcraft and others, the development of arithmetic competence can be described as involving an increase in the efficiency of both procedural knowledge and, most importantly, information retrieval (see also Kaye, 1986; Resnick, 1983). Older children know more facts, can retrieve those facts more easily, and, when necessary, can use arithmetic procedures more efficiently than younger children.

Recently, Siegler (1987; Siegler & Shrager, 1984) has questioned the generality of the information processing models of children's arithmetic thinking. From the work of Ashcraft and others, it would appear that most children of a given age use a single approach to solving arithmetic problems (the exception being children in transition stages) and that a given child uses the same technique for solving most problems of a given type. Siegler doubts both conclusions and evaluated them in a recent study. Siegler (1987) assessed the techniques used by kindergarten, first-, and second-graders in solving a variety of addition problems. The children's reaction times to solve the problems were obtained from a video recording of the sessions. Following completion of each problem, the children were asked what they had done to "figure out the answer to that problem." The problems were selected so that different patterns of reaction times among the problems were predicted by various models (for example, the min model, the fact-retrieval model, and a counting model). Rather than analyzing performance collapsed over all trials, Siegler conducted separate analyses for different strategies.

Based on analyses of reaction times, errors, and verbal reports, Siegler discerned five general approaches to solving the addition problems. Two of these were the min strategy and the fact-retrieval technique, as discussed previously. A third involved counting all elements, with children starting at "one" and continuing until the sum of the numbers was reached. A fourth strategy was labeled *decomposition*, with children transforming the original problem into two or more simpler problems. If the problem were $13 + 3 = ?$, for example, a child might say, "13 is 10 and 3; 3 and 3 are 6; 10 and 6 are 16; so the answer is 16." A fifth strategy was guessing. Most children used a variety of these strategies on the problems, with 62% reporting using three or more across the various problems. The min strategy was used most frequently, but even it was used on no more than 40% of the trials at any age. The older children were more likely to use the fact-retrieval and decomposition strategies than were the kindergarten children.

In general, children showed little homogeneity of strategy use in these addition problems. Similar findings were reported by Siegler and Shrager (1984) for 4- and 5-year-olds. In their study, the use of strategies varied as a function of the difficulty of the problem. The harder the problem, the more likely the children were to use overt strategies such as counting on their fingers, as opposed to covert strategies such as fact retrieval.

The findings of Siegler call into question the generality of the interpretation derived from the work of Ashcraft and others. We must keep in mind that there are a variety of ways of approaching any problem and that, depending on the age of the child and the perceived difficulty of the problem, different strategies will be chosen. Processing still becomes more efficient with age, as procedures for solving problems and retrieving relevant facts require less expenditure of mental effort. Yet, strategy use in solving arithmetic problems does not vary only with development; there are also substantial differences among individuals of a given age and within the same individual over different problems.

☐ Children's Development of Representational Abilities

In Chapter 1, I wrote that one issue central to cognitive development is that of representation. In this chapter, changes in children's cognitions as a function of their use of symbols have been investigated. What conclusions, if any, can we make? Are there stage-like changes in children's ability to use symbols, much as postulated by Piaget, or do children become increasingly adept at using a single symbol system that does not really change from the second year onward?

From my interpretation of the cognitive developmental literature, the truth lies somewhere between these two positions. Young children are often able to switch between forms of symbols, thinking like a typical 3-year-old at one time and a typical 8-year-old at another. Children use a variety of criteria, from perceptual to conceptual, in forming classifications of objects. Furthermore, children who spontaneously classify information according to one criterion (complementary, for example) can easily be trained to classify similar information according to a more advanced criterion (conceptual, for example) (Smiley & Brown, 1979). In other situations, children seem to have the symbolic knowledge necessary to handle simplified problems (number concept, for example) and fail only when the problems become overly complex (Gelman & Gallistel, 1978). Similarly, a multitude of studies have demonstrated that young children can be trained to solve problems presumably requiring the manipulation of symbols, manipulations that are beyond what they do spontaneously (see Chapters 2 and 3). Such evidence would suggest that children's ability to use symbols develops gradually. There is no abrupt change in the symbolization process (beyond the advent of the symbolic function) but merely an expansion of the number of situations in which symbols can be used successfully. Given the proper stimuli, context, and instructions, even very young children display a reasonably sophisticated use of symbols.

Yet, there is other evidence to the contrary. The failure of Flavell and his colleagues (1986) to train

3-year-olds to distinguish between appearance and reality is in marked contrast to the success of other researchers in training children only slightly older to perform much more sophisticated tasks (Gelman, 1969). The stage-like nature of children's symbolic functioning is familiar to anyone who has tried to explain a joke that is conceptually over the head of a child (see Chapter 9). Even after a full explanation the child still does not get it. Attempting to teach mental addition and subtraction to a child who is just not ready to internalize arithmetic procedures can be frustrating to someone who believes that all the child has to do is try harder. It does not seem to work that way.

How, then, can children's development of mental representational abilities, their use of mental symbols, best be conceptualized? Here, I favor variants of contemporary information processing models as advocated by Case (1985) and Fischer (1980). In both Case's and Fischer's theories, there is an optimal level of information processing ability that a child cannot exceed. This level increases with age and is heavily affected by maturational factors. There are also real stage-like changes in children's abilities to use symbols. Case, like Piaget, proposed that there are four such stages over childhood, whereas Fischer proposed only three, which he called tiers (see Chapter 2). Within each stage or tier, however, increases in information processing capacity allow children to handle more information more efficiently.

In Fischer's theory, for example, children in a given tier can handle certain types of representation: sensorimotor, representational, and abstract. Within each tier, however, there are four levels, with the highest skill level of one tier (for example, sensorimotor, Level 4) corresponding to the first level of the next tier (for example, representational, Level 1). Development proceeds by the coordination of skills, as is graphically illustrated in Figure 6-4. Within any tier, a Level 1 skill allows the child to control variations in only one set of behaviors: one action, one representation, or one abstraction; this is represented by a single point in Figure 6-4. At the representational Level 1, for example, children can control a single representation, such as representing

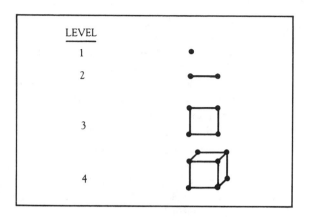

FIGURE 6-4 A schematic representation of the cycle of four levels in Fischer's theory (Fischer, 1980)

simple properties of objects, people, and events independent of their own actions, but they cannot coordinate two or more of these representations. At Level 2, two representations become coordinated. This may correspond to the dual coding Flavell and his colleagues proposed was necessary for children to solve appearance/reality problems. Fischer calls the coordination of two skills a *mapping*, and this is represented by the two connected points in Figure 6-4. At Level 3, two (or more) mappings are integrated to produce what Fischer has termed a *system*, illustrated by the four connected points in Figure 6-4. Such coordination seems to be necessary for solving most conservation problems. Level 4 represents the culmination of one tier and the beginning of the next and is represented by the box in Figure 6-4. At this level two or more systems are coordinated, yielding what Fischer calls a *system of systems*. Fischer proposes that the combination of systems produces a new type of set, the most basic of the next tier, in this case the abstract tier.

From this viewpoint, children's abilities to handle symbolic information increase both quantitatively and qualitatively. Within a stage or tier, differences in information processing capacity, as reflected by how many different skills or schemes can be coordinated at once, allow children to deal with symbols more effectively. Age-related changes in knowledge and familiarity with the task demands also affect how children use symbols. In addition, some symbols, although available to a child, may be more difficult to use than others. Although young children can be trained to use a conceptual classification style, for example, they quickly revert to their preferred complementary style when given the opportunity (Smiley & Brown, 1979). One speculation about why this may be so concerns young children's facility with conceptual relations. They can identify such relations and use them to solve problems, but they are more comfortable with complementary relations. This may be because complementary relations require less in the way of mental effort to activate than do conceptual relations. Complementary relations are a mentally "easier" symbol system to deal with and they will be preferred unless external pressure is applied to abandon them in favor of another system (Bjorklund, 1985).

In sum, I believe that children have some flexibility in their use of symbols. But that flexibility is not infinite. Some children may not be able to hold enough information in mind at once to deal with problems requiring the comparison of symbols (Brainerd, 1983) or may not be able to divorce themselves from the physical context to "think" about an object in more abstract terms (Bruner, 1966). The issue of the development of children's representational abilities is an old one, and one for which we still do not have a definitive answer.

☐ Summary

The use of symbols to represent knowledge reflects the transition from the thinking of infancy to that of early childhood. *Representation* refers to the way in which objects, events, and experiences are encoded or represented in the mind. Developmental shifts in the primary mode of representation have been hypothesized. Children's earliest representations have been called *sensorimotor*, in that objects and events are known in terms of action associated with those objects (either activity inherent in the object itself or the child's action on the object). Sensorimotor, or, in Bruner's terms, *enactive*, representation is replaced by mentalistic, symbolic representation sometime around 18 to 24 months of age. The nature of children's symbolic representation varies developmentally, with preschool children being especially attentive to *literal* or *ikonic* stimulus features, whereas older children are more likely to be attentive to *conceptual* stimulus characteristics. Young children's representations have also been hypothesized to be *action-based*, with the function of an object contributing significantly to that object's meaning. Most theorists agree that representation takes another qualitative turn around adolescence, with children able to think *hypothetically* and to abstract intangible qualities of objects and events.

Several phenomena that vary as a function of children's use of symbols include *classification*, the *appearance/reality distinction*, and children's *number and arithmetic concepts*. In classification experiments, children sort sets of objects so that items that are alike or go together in some way are grouped together. Four different phases in children's classification can be identified: (1) *idiosyncratic*, in which children's justifications for their classifications are independent of any physical or semantic characteristic of the stimuli; (2) *perceptual*, in which items are grouped on the basis of some perceptual similarity; (3) *complementary*, in which items are grouped on the basis of real or potential interactions among objects; and (4) *conceptual*, in which items are grouped on the basis of category membership or common function. These classification phases do not have the quality of stages, in that children may display several classification styles simultaneously. Furthermore, children can easily be trained to use a more advanced style than they use spontaneously, and even adults frequently use complementary schemes under certain situations.

Piaget's concept *class inclusion* refers to the knowledge that any subordinate category (DOGS, for example) can be no larger than its superordinate category (ANIMALS, for example). Children typically do not solve class-inclusion problems until late in childhood, although non-Piagetian research has questioned this conclusion. Children's class-inclusion performance is influenced by variations in the tasks, factors that affect their knowledge of the number of items in the subordinate or superordinate sets, and factors that affect their familiarity with the concepts used on the tasks.

Young children have a difficult time distinguishing between an object's appearance and its actual identity. For example, research by De Vries indicated that most 3-year-olds believed that a cat wearing a dog mask actually became a dog. More recent work by Flavell and his colleagues confirms young children's difficulty in differentiating between appearance and reality, and they speculated that children must be able to engage in *dual encoding* before this distinction can be made.

Children's concept of number has generally been studied in terms of *conservation of number*, following Piaget. Children cannot conserve number until approximately 6 or 7 years of age. However, recent research indicates that children as young as 2 have some notion of number. Some researchers have focused on counting as a precursor to conservation of number. It appears that children gradually acquire a knowledge of counting over the preschool years and that this knowledge precedes that necessary for conservation of number.

Research on children's arithmetic ability has concentrated primarily on the strategies they use to solve simple problems. Using reaction times, researchers such as Ashcraft have proposed that children first apply effort-consuming procedures and later retrieve addition and subtraction facts from their memory. Siegler has proposed that children actually use a variety of strategies, making it inappropriate to classify children as users of a single approach to solving arithmetic problems.

Children's development of mental symbols appears to be both qualitative and quantitative in nature. There is an absolute level of symbolic functioning beyond which children cannot operate. At any time, however, children have available to them a wide range of symbolic skills, although they display their most sophisticated functioning only under optimal conditions.

7

Language and Thought

Language Acquisition

☐ Precursors to Language   ☐ From Words to Sentences

The Development of Communication Skills

☐ Communication and Egocentrism
☐ Metacommunication   ☐ Preschoolers' Communication Competence

Language and Thought

☐ The Self-Regulatory Function of Language   ☐ The Development of Inner Speech

The Development of Semantic Memory

☐ The Development of Word Meaning   ☐ The Development of Natural Language Categories
☐ How Does Semantic Memory Develop?

Summary

The quintessential symbol system for human thought is language. It is through language that we communicate to one another about the past, present, and future, and we often use language to direct our own behavior as well as the behavior of others. However, language serves not only as a means for communicating and instigating action but also, in many situations, constitutes the content of thought itself. We use language to categorize objects, events, people, and ideas in a way that other speakers of our language can understand. Writers, poets, and orators often cherish words, carefully combining them to connote complex emotions, images, and ideas. Many psychologists also revere words, believing that how meaning is represented in the form of words and how these words (or the concepts underlying words) are interrelated determine important aspects of our thinking.

The major focus of this chapter is the relationship between language and developmental cognition. Before delving into issues relating to language and thought, however, I will examine children's acquisition of language. The coverage of language acquisition is intentionally cursory, and it is provided only to give you a flavor of the research into how children learn to speak. If you are interested in the topic, several reviews examine language development in greater detail (Clark & Clark, 1977; Dale, 1976; de Villiers & de Villiers, 1978, 1979; Kuczaj, 1982; Maratsos, 1983; Owens, 1984). In the remainder of the chapter I will take up the development of children's communication skills, the developmental relationship between speech and thought, and the development of semantic memory.

☐ Language Acquisition

Precursors to Language

Children typically do not say their first words until approximately 10 to 12 months of age, but these words are preceded by a history of vocalization. Babies' first utterances are cries. At first cries are undifferentiated (to the untrained ear), but by the end of the first month they vary as a function of what

the infant wishes to communicate, and a mother can typically discriminate among her baby's different cries. By 2 months, infants have developed the musculature to produce certain sounds basic to language. These sounds include some vowels, such as those found in the words *cook, hall,* and *off,* and consonants similar to *s, k,* and *g* (Stark, 1978).

With increased control of the tongue and mouth, a baby progresses to babbling. Babbling involves the prolonged production of a wide variety of speech sounds. Infants appear to be experimenting with sounds during this time. Babbling seems to be predestined by biology. Even deaf babies begin to babble around 4 months of age, and the babbles of French, American, and Chinese babies are indistinguishable at 5 months (Nakazima, 1962). The babbling sounds become differentiated beginning at about 6 months. The strings of sounds become longer, with infants often repeating the same sounds over and over. By 10 months, the babbles of Chinese children, for example, can be differentiated from those of a child from an English-speaking home. Infants' vocalizations are taking on many of the characteristics of the language that surrounds them.

By the end of the first year, children are putting their babbles together in ways that resemble sentences. They produce a gibberish that often has the qualities of statements or questions. Around this same time, children produce sounds that have meaning for them. These sounds serve as their first "words." So, for example, an infant may refer to her blanket as *baboo* and her bottle as *fafa*. These are not terms learned from adult language but are infants' own constructions, which they use consistently and which are understood, after a while, by their parents. At about this same time children acquire their first "real" words, words with a meaning agreed upon by speakers of the language.

As was noted in Chapter 5, babies seem particularly prepared to perceive language. To reiterate, infants can discriminate (and prefer) their mothers' voices as early as 3 days of age; by 2 months they can perceive the difference between phonemes such as *bah* and *pah,* although some of these discriminations are lost over the first 6 months if those sounds are not found in adults' speech of their culture. Babies can discriminate polysyllabic sequences most easily when they are spoken in motherese, the highly intonated style of speech that mothers frequently use in talking to babies. All in all, human infants seem well equipped with a potent biological preparedness for learning to produce and understand language.

From Words to Sentences

As noted, children typically say their first words by 10 or 12 months, and over the next half-dozen months or so, they substantially increase the number of words they use. Children of this age can understand more language than they can speak, but *productive* language (what they actually produce, or say) is limited to single words at a time. Yet, children's one-word utterances carry more meaning than might be expected from their brevity, and the term *holophrastic speech* has been used to describe the notion that toddlers' words sometimes serve as entire sentences. Gestures, emphasis, and the context in which the word is uttered can provide a richness of meaning to a single word. For example, a 15-month-old shouting "juice" while raising an empty glass before the eyes of her father seems to be expressing "I want more juice." The same word spoken with a rising intonation while pointing to an unfamiliar container can be inferred to mean "Is that juice?" Such interpretations must be made cautiously, of course, for we can easily read into a child's single word what we believe the child "should" be thinking. However, children's single words during the teen months do serve as more than just labels; exactly how much more is difficult to say.

Beginning around 18 months, children start to string words together into two-word sentences. Their constructions are not random but seem to follow some set of guidelines, or a *grammar*. A grammar is a theory of how one's language is structured. Basically, children must learn how to combine words so that another speaker of their language will be able to understand them.

Children's two- and, later, three-word sentences are also economical, in that they omit all the "little" words that make language easy to understand but that are not absolutely necessary for comprehension.

For example, the sentences "I ride bike" or "Jimmy, me go store?" are easily understood, given the proper context, as "I can ride the bike" and "May Jimmy and I go to the store?" despite their truncated form. What remains are the concrete and high-information terms, allowing a child to convey much meaning in a very few words. This economical form of speech has been referred to as *telegraphic*, in that it is accomplished much as a telegram is written, with high-content words only, omitting all the ifs, ands, and buts (Brown & Fraser, 1964).

In acquiring the structure, or *syntax*, of language, children learn rules. There is little argument among developmental psycholinguists that language development entails the acquisition of rules. What is controversial, however, is the nature of these rules and how they are acquired. Over the past two decades many developmental psycholinguists have concentrated on describing the acquisition of grammatical rules in children's language, and it seems that the more we know, the more we realize how much we do not know. In a paper reviewing current issues on the topic Maratsos (1983) said that "a review written at this point in time about the state of grammatical acquisition as a field cannot objectively present a certain and unified picture. Things are unsettled" (p. 708). Debate continues over what grammars best describe children's language. I do not attempt to examine the controversies concerning the child's acquisition of syntax here but merely provide a brief description of some of the rules children acquire in learning their mother tongue.

Some of the most easily observable rules involve *inflections*. Many languages, including English, make heavy use of inflections, prefixes or suffixes added to words to convey meaning such as the *-ed, -ing,* and *-s* added at the end of words in English to express the past tense, present progressive, and plural. Typically between 2 and 3 years of age, children begin to use inflections. There is a tendency to *overregularize*, however, using inflections on words for which the inflection is incorrect. For example, children may learn to add *-ed* to the end of words in order to make them past tense. Once they have acquired this knowledge, they apply it incorrectly even to words they had previously used properly, such as "*goed*," (or "wented"), "drinked," and "runned." Children who have been using the terms *feet, mice,* and *cups of sugar* may suddenly and consistently switch to "foots" or "feets," "mouses" or "mices," and "cup of sugars." They have learned a rule for regular words and generalize it to irregular words. Apparently, having a history of being understood is not so potent a motivator for using a certain form of language as is the acquisition of a rule and its generalization to all situations where it might apply. Similar patterns of inflection development have been observed for a wide variety of languages, indicating that children all around the world approach the problem of language acquisition similarly (see Slobin, 1970).

Changes in children's language that seemingly involve the acquisition of rules can be found in children's use of questions and negatives. In learning to pose questions, for example, children do not produce the adult form on their first try. The earliest questions involve only changes in intonation. The statement of fact "Daddy go," expressed with a falling or flat intonation, is changed into a question simply by enunciating the phrase with a rising intonation ("Daddy go?"). Later, *wh* words (*who, which, when,* and particularly *what* and *where*) are placed before an active sentence, as in "Where we go?" or "Who you are?" It is not until after 3 years of age that most children invert the auxiliary verb (*be, can, do, have*), displaying the rule necessary to produce proper questions such as "Where are we going?" "Who are you?" and "Can you come?" (Klima & Bellugi, 1966).

Negatives develop similarly. Children's first negatives consist of single words (*no, allgone*), negating an action or suggestion of another. Later, *no* or *not* is placed before a declarative sentence, negating the entire idea ("No daddy go," "Not big boy"). In a related usage, 2-year-old children sometimes make a statement such as "more milk" while vigorously shaking their heads no. Finally, children acquire the rule of placing the negative element between the subject and predicate ("I don't want to go," "Gramma not make bed"). Auxiliaries such as *can, do, does,* and *will* as well as their negative forms (*can't, doesn't, isn't*) develop gradually over the third and fourth years (Bellugi, 1967).

The Development of Communication Skills

As children's language becomes more complex, their ability to communicate their needs, wants, and ideas through speech increases. Vocal communication is nothing new for the toddler; from the first months of life, infants have used cries and coos to communicate with adults and to modify the behavior of their parents. With the advent of language, children's communicative power increases substantially. They can express complex ideas, specifying in words, for example, exactly what they would like to eat or what shirt they would like to wear. They can also comprehend adult speech and, through language alone, understand that they must return their toys to their room and stop feeding candy to the dog.

There is more to effective verbal communication than just words, however. A responsive listener provides a speaker with nonverbal cues such as nods, gazes, and smiles and says "yes" and "uh-huh" at appropriate times to make it clear that the message is being understood. These skills also increase with age, but even 2-year-olds use many of these tactics when listening to an adult (Miller, Lechner, & Rugs, 1985). Despite the seeming communicative sophistication of many preschoolers, effective communication between adult and child, or between child and child, is variable. Many messages within the grammatical competence of a child are simply not understood. Also, young children often have difficulty in conveying exactly the right message and are frequently unaware that their message was inadequate.

Communication and Egocentrism

For years, research and theory in communicative development followed the interpretation of Piaget (Flavell, Botkin, Fry, Wright, & Jarvis, 1968; Glucksberg, Krauss, & Weisberg, 1966). Piaget (1955) proposed that young children's speech is *egocentric* and *presocial.* In social situations, they attempt to communicate with others, but their egocentric view of the world often results in speech that does not get the message across to a listener. This failure often does not bother preschool children, however, for in many cases they are unaware that the message is not being comprehended. Such egocentric speech can be observed in young children in a variety of contexts. Listen to the phone conversation of a 4-year-old. When the voice on the other end of the receiver asked Kelly, "What are you wearing today?" Kelly responded, "This" while looking down and pointing at her dress. The conversation of two 5-year-old boys playing together in a sandbox can be interesting. "I drive my truck over here, and then I drive beside your plane and I fill it up with stuff," says one child. In the meantime, the other is saying, "My plane's coming in for a landing. I drop bombs on your truck and crash into it. Boom!" Such a "conversation" would not be taking place if each child were alone. However, what one child says has little to do with the comments of the other. The two boys are talking "with" each other but not necessarily "to" each other. Piaget labeled such egocentric exchanges *collective monologues*.

Subsequent research has confirmed Piaget's observation of the poor communication abilities of young children in more structured experimental tasks than the ones he used (Beal & Flavell, 1982; Flavell, Speer, Green, & August, 1981; Glucksberg et al., 1966; Sonnenschein, 1986). In a pioneering study by Glucksberg and his colleagues (1966), 4- and 5-year-olds were placed on opposite sides of a table so that they could not see one another. Visible to each child was an array of abstract forms (see Figure 7-1). The task of one child was to communicate to the other which form to choose. Although the children were apparently highly motivated to do the task, they rarely performed well. Rather, the speaker frequently gave incomplete instructions (for example, "Pick the red one" when there were several red objects) and used idiosyncratic descriptions of objects (for example, "Pick the one that looks like Mommy's shirt"), leaving the listener with little pertinent information for making a decision.

Metacommunication

More recent research by Flavell and his associates (Beal & Flavell, 1982; Flavell et al., 1981) indicates that children 5 years of age and younger seem to

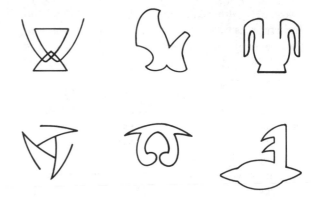

FIGURE 7-1 Examples of abstract stimuli used in a communication task. Children are to tell another child which abstract form to select by means of language alone (Glucksberg, Krauss, and Weisberg, 1966).

recognize an inadequate or ambiguous message but seldom act on their uncertainty, behaving as if the message had been understood loud and clear. When kindergarten children were provided with ambiguous instructions for making a block building, for instance, they often looked puzzled and hesitated in selecting the appropriate block. Yet, when their building was completed, these children said that it was just like the model (which it was not) and that the instructions had been adequate for reproducing the model (which they had not). Beal and Flavell (1982) found that children's difficulties on these tasks were not related to an inability to attend to or remember their uncertainty about the messages. Rather, their problems were a result of *metacognitive* deficits; they had "a poor understanding of message quality and its role in determining the success or failure of a communication" (p. 48).

Another metacognitive (or, more specifically, *metacommunication*) skill involves children's abilities to monitor their own speech. Are children aware of what they are saying and of the fact that they may not always be providing the listener with adequate information to be properly understood? Again, young children tend to display deficits in this area of metacommunication (for reviews see Shatz, 1983; Whitehurst & Sonnenschein, 1985). Young children's speech includes a greater incidence of omissions and ambiguities than does the speech of older children and requires greater contextual support to be comprehended.

One way of assessing children's self-monitoring abilities is to examine the frequency with which they correct their speech by repeating, by including new information, by telling the listener to forget the last thing that was said until later, and so forth. Evans (1985) studied such *verbal repairs* in the speech of kindergarten and second-grade children during classroom "show and tell" sessions. Evans reported that the incidence of verbal repairs was significantly greater for the second-grade children than for the kindergarteners, occurring for 19% of all the utterances for the older children compared with only 7% for the younger. Following is an example of a story by a second-grade girl that includes several verbal repairs:

> We went to—uh me and Don went to Aunt Judy's. And . . . and uh my brother came down on Fri— Friday night, Uh there was a acc—came on the train, And there was an accident. And they thought uh . . . that uh . . . the—there was an accident with a—a van, And they thought—there was pig's blood in it, And they thought there was somebody hurt. But it was the pig [p. 370].

Evans proposed that the high incidence of self-repairs for the second-grade children relative to the kindergarteners reflected an increased ability on the part of the older children to monitor their speech. Evans suggested that as communication skills increase from this point through childhood, the ability to plan and organize one's thoughts improves, resulting in a reduction of verbal repairs into adolescence (Sabin, Clemmer, O'Connell, & Kowal, 1979). Thus, the incidence of verbal repairs is low in young children's speech because of poor self-monitoring skills, increases during middle childhood as children become increasingly aware of the effectiveness of their speech in conveying a message, and then decreases as other skills such as planning improve.

Preschoolers' Communication Competence

Despite the ample evidence of young children's poor communication skills, preschoolers' language is not as egocentric as Piaget and other early researchers believed. In the study of speech repairs by Evans (1985) just cited, for instance, many 5-year-olds displayed at least limited self-monitoring abilities. Young children's metacommunication skills may be poor in comparison with those of older children, but they are not nonexistent. In fact, a number of researchers have reported clearly nonegocentric use of language in the communication attempts of young children. Shatz and Gelman (1973) observed the speech of 4-year-old children when they talked to adults, to other 4-year-olds, or to 2-year-olds. They found that these children modified their speech to the 2-year-olds, using different tones of voice and shorter sentences, much as adults do.

In more recent research, Revelle, Wellman, and Karabenick (1985) proposed that one reason that young children's metacognitive abilities seem so poor is that the subjects are typically assessed in unfamiliar experimental settings, yielding an underestimation of their actual skills. The researchers used a quasi-naturalistic method to assess comprehension monitoring (the degree to which an adult's message is comprehended by children 2½ to 4½ years of age). The children interacted with an adult in two play settings: one in a sandbox and the other as they were preparing for a tea party. During the course of the session, the adult requested that the child get several objects. Some of the messages were ambiguous (for example, "Bring me the cup," when there were four cups), were unintelligible, or were impossible to comply with (for example, "Bring me your mother's shoes"). Children's responses to the problem questions were noted and used as a reflection of their comprehension monitoring abilities. Unlike previous experimenters who found very little evidence of comprehension monitoring in preschool children (for a review see Markman, 1981), Revelle and her colleagues reported that even 3-year-olds discriminated between requests that posed certain types of problems and requests that did not and that these children made appropriate responses for resolving the problems. The 4-year-olds were more effective still, displaying appropriate comprehension monitoring even for the most difficult problems.

The findings of Revelle and her associates (1985) and of Shatz and Gelman (1973), among others, suggest that young children have substantial meta-communication skills. As with many newly acquired skills, however, communication abilities seem to develop first in highly specific, familiar situations and are easily disrupted. With age, children display their communicative skills in increasingly diverse contexts, generalizing what they know to new and unfamiliar settings.

☐ Language and Thought

When most people think about "thinking," they usually do so in terms of language. For many people, thought without language is unthinkable. Language, of course, is not our only means of symbolic representation, but few would dispute that much, if not most, of cognition is language-based. Language is a rich, uniquely human system of symbols that allows us to express novel ideas and to communicate past events to others and to plan future events. Given the extent to which language dominates our perception of a person's intelligence, it is hard to argue that language is not a potent tool for human thinking. Theorists such as Jerome Bruner argued that it is the ability to use language as a conceptual tool that transforms a child's thinking during early childhood. Along these same lines, the Soviet psychologists A. R. Luria (1961) and Lev Vygotsky (1934/1962) have proposed that language serves to direct much of children's intelligent behavior, with the relationship between language and thought changing developmentally.

The Self-Regulatory Function of Language

Luria (1961) proposed three stages in the ability of language to regulate behavior. In the first stage, occurring between approximately 18 months and 3 years, the language of others can initiate motor action, but language does not function to inhibit an ongoing activity. For example, giving a 2-year-old a rubber ball and saying "Squeeze" may result in the child's squeezing the ball, but simple statements such as "Stop" or "That's enough" will not be sufficient to inhibit the motor action. (Exceptions to this would

be toddlers' well-learned reactions to parental commands such as "No!" or "Don't touch that!") In the second stage, occurring from approximately 3 to 4½ years of age, speech has an *impulsive* role in regulating behavior, in that children respond not to the conceptual message of a language command but to its physical characteristics. A 3-year-old told to press a ball twice in response to a light, for example, will customarily press many times, being unable to inhibit excitation from tactual sources. But if the child is instructed to say "Go! Go!" to a flash of light and to accompany her verbalizations with two presses, she will easily learn the task. Finally, in Stage 3, from approximately 4½ to 5½ years of age, children are able to use the meaning of speech to regulate their behavior. According to Luria (1961), *"the regulatory function is steadily transferred from the impulsive side of speech to the analytic system of elective significative connections which are produced by speech"* (p. 92).

Western scientists' attempts at replicating the findings of Luria and his colleagues have had mixed results. Wozniak (1972) and Fuson (1979) each state that most American research designed to assess the Soviet position has suffered from inadequate methodology, has been conceived too narrowly, or has misinterpreted the Soviet approach. In many cases these difficulties are understandable, for available reports of the research of Luria and others are ambiguous with respect to their methods. However, the results of several recent, well-designed American studies have provided support for Luria's position (Saltz, Campbell, & Skotko, 1983; Tinsley & Waters, 1982). In the study by Saltz and his colleagues (1983), it was hypothesized, following Luria, that young children should have increasing difficulty inhibiting motor action as the intensity of the verbal command increases. The louder the command, the greater the tendency to make impulsive responses. Preschool children were given a set of positive instructions to follow (for example, "Clap your hands") and a set of negative instructions (for example, "Don't touch your toes"). The instructions were given in one of three different intensities, ranging from soft, which was slightly below normal speaking intensity, to loud, which was a shout. For the younger children (average age 4 years 1 month), the

DENNIS THE MENACE® used by permission of Hank Ketcham and © by North America Syndicate.

"I'M GONNA HAVE TO STOP THINKIN' OUT LOUD."

Young children often have a difficult time keeping their thoughts to themselves.

number of impulsive errors (that is, responding when instructed not to respond) increased with the intensity of the command. The reverse was true for older children (average age 5 years 6 months), with the loudest commands producing the fewest impulsive errors. These results are consistent with Luria's position that children under 5 years of age respond to the physical energy of spoken words, with word meaning playing a lesser role in the inhibition of an ongoing activity.

The Development of Inner Speech

Luria's work represents extensions of a theory originally proposed by Vygotsky (1962). He believed that thought and speech have different roots in development, with the two initially being independent; that is, thought is prelinguistic, and speech is preintellectual. In development, however, thought and speech merge, with thought becoming verbal and speech rational. It is this developmental relationship be-

tween language and thought, particularly during the stages where the two cross, that has attracted the interest of psychologists.

Vygotsky was particularly interested in the role of *egocentric speech* in affecting children's thought. Egocentric speech, or *private speech*, as it is commonly referred to, can be thought of as speech-for-self. It is overt language that is carried out with apparent satisfaction even though it does not function to communicate. Private speech can be observed both when children are alone and in social settings.

Vygotsky believed that private speech plays a specific role in affecting children's thought and problem solving. Language can serve to guide children's behavior (and thus their thought), but young children cannot yet use language covertly, "in their heads." In order to benefit from the self-regulatory function of language, young children must essentially talk to themselves, using their speech to guide thought and behavior. With development, the self-regulatory function of language changes so that children can direct their behavior using *inner speech*. In other words, private speech serves as a cognitive self-guidance system and then goes "underground" as covert verbal thought.

In contrast to Vygotsky's viewpoint on the role of private speech in cognitive development is that of Piaget (1955), discussed earlier with respect to communication. Piaget believed that the egocentric speech of preschoolers reflects their general egocentric perspective of the world. As children become increasingly able to decenter their cognition and perception and see the point of view of another, private speech decreases. In other words, for Piaget, private speech plays no functional role in cognitive development but is merely symptomatic of ongoing mental activity.

One early study contrasting the positions of Vygotsky and Piaget was conducted by Kohlberg, Yaeger, and Hjertholm (1968). They proposed that private speech can be classified according to its function and that it has different functions at different ages. The earliest form of private speech serves only as self-stimulation and word play. This is followed by children's speech describing their action but not directing their behavior. In a third stage, overt speech serves to direct problem solving, with this self-regulatory function of speech evolving into inaudible mutterings as speech goes "underground" as covert verbal thought.

In a series of experiments assessing children's private speech while solving problems, Kohlberg and his colleagues reported that the incidence of word play and simple descriptions decreased with age, whereas private speech used to guide performance increased over the preschool years, peaking between the ages of 6 and 7 and declining thereafter. This trend was accompanied by an increase in inaudible mutterings with age, peaking between 8 and 10 years. The researchers interpreted their findings as supporting Vygotsky's position, with the self-guidance function of private speech varying with age and eventually giving way to covert, "inner" speech. Furthermore, they reported that the incidence of private speech to guide task performance peaked earlier for brighter children, suggesting that intellectually more advanced children go through this sequence sooner than other children.

Confirmation of the findings of Kohlberg and his colleagues has come from a naturalistic study by Berk (1986). Berk observed first- and third-grade children during daily math periods over four months. Various forms of private speech were recorded (for example, task irrelevant, self-stimulating speech; task-relevant, externalized speech; and task-relevant, external manifestations of inner speech), as well as other aspects of their overt behavior (movement, pointing to objects to help them add) and measures of their task performance (daily math papers and achievement and IQ tests). Berk reported high levels of private speech in this sample of children, with the type of private speech changing with age, in agreement with the developmental sequence of Kohlberg and his associates (1968). Most of the children's task-relevant externalized speech was used to guide their problem solving, with third-graders using more internalized forms of speech to facilitate their performance (for example, inaudible mutterings, lip and tongue movements). The total amount of private speech was positively related to intelligence at grade one but not at grade three, again confirming Kohlberg's findings that brighter children begin to

use private speech to guide their problem solving earlier than less bright children and also stop sooner, as thought goes "underground" as inner speech. In general, the findings of Kohlberg and his colleagues (1968) and Berk (1986) provide some of the strongest evidence for Vygotsky's theory of the developmental relationship between language and thought.

Research aimed at modifying children's inefficient problem-solving strategies has also provided support for Vygotsky's viewpoint. For example, Meichenbaum and Goodman (1971) found that school children who responded quickly and inaccurately on visual match-to-sample problems (for example, finding which of six pictures exactly matches a standard picture) could be trained to improve their performance by talking to themselves. Meichenbaum and Goodman trained children to verbally guide their problem-solving behavior by instructing these impulsive children to tell themselves to check each alternative and not to make a response until all possibilities had been examined. The children initially talked to themselves out loud, then in whispers, and finally covertly.

Although not all subsequent research has provided strong support for Vygotsky's theory, most recent research suggests that he was closer to the truth than was Piaget. For example, Berk and Garvin (1984), working with low-income Appalachian children, presented data similar to those reported by Kohlberg and his colleagues, suggesting that most private speech has a cognitive self-guidance function. A similar interpretation was provided by Frauenglass and Diaz (1985), who also presented evidence that overt private speech is replaced by whispers and muttering, suggesting that it goes "underground" as inner speech. Finally, research by Behrend, Rosengren, and Perlmutter (in press) indicates that private speech among preschoolers is most likely to be found on tasks of intermediate difficulty and that it is for these tasks that talking to oneself is most likely to improve performance. That is, the incidence and effectiveness of private speech varies not only with age but also with task difficulty. In general, although some discrepancies with Vygotsky's theory have been reported, the conclusion of the existing research seems to be that there is indeed a developmental relationship between language and thought, much along the lines that Vygotsky and his colleagues hypothesized.

☐ The Development of Semantic Memory

Language serves to communicate ideas, but the stuff that ideas are made of is words and the concepts that underlie words. Words themselves are arbitrary vocal signals, but speakers of a language have agreed that certain words have specified meanings (some more specified than others), and we use these shared meanings to communicate. How is it that children acquire word meaning, that they come to use words in basically the same way as adults do? In this section I examine the development of language concepts, the process by which children acquire the meaning of individual words and broader language category terms. The representation of such knowledge has been referred to as *semantic memory*, the long-term repository of language terms, their definitions, and their interrelations with other entries in memory.

The Development of Word Meaning

Children typically speak their first words around 10 or 12 months, as we have seen, with the number of words in their vocabularies increasing gradually over the next several months and then growing rapidly beginning about the age of 2. By the time children enter the first grade, they have between 8000 and 14,000 words in their productive vocabularies (Carey, 1977). Children's first words are usually nouns, typically including important people in their lives such as *Mommy* and *Daddy*, and objects with which they frequently interact such as *milk, juice,* and *cookie*. Animals are frequently included in children's ear'y words, even for city slickers, whose parents point out animals from picture books (de Villiers & de Villiers, 1979).

Overextensions and Underextensions

Children's early words often do not have exactly the same meaning as the comparable adult words. One frequently observed phenomenon in children's early speech is *overextension*, in which the child extends the meaning of a word over a broader range of referents than the word actually covers. For example, a child may use the word *doggy* to refer to all four-legged animals, including cats, horses, cows, and elephants. Not yet having language terms for these other concepts, children generalize the word meaning to describe objects that are perceptually similar to the original referent (Clark, 1973) or that have a similar function (Nelson, 1973). Clark (1973) proposed that words can be described as having a set of semantic features and that children gradually acquire the complete set of features that defines a concept. For instance, the concept *bird* may include the features *animal, flies, has feathers,* and *has a beak* and may specify a certain size and shape. Clark proposed that children gradually acquire the adult features for a term, restricting as they do the number of referents to which the word can apply (that is, minimizing overextensions).

Children do not always overextend words. They sometimes use them correctly from the beginning and at other times *underextend* them. For instance, a child may apply the term *dog* only to his own pet or only to dogs he sees in his yard. Such a child has at least one too many features for the term, limiting the situations in which the word is used. It seems that in the course of development, children must acquire features for many words, making their definition of a word more specific. In many cases, however, they must also rid themselves of inappropriate features that they have acquired, expanding the range of circumstances in which they can use a term properly (see Clark, 1983, for a review).

The Development of Semantic Features

Representations of words are more than just the sum of their features. Most feature-list theories of adult semantic memory hold that features are differentially weighted, with some being more important for the definition of a word than others (McNamara & Sternberg, 1983; Rosch & Mervis, 1975; Smith, Shoben, & Rips, 1974). Thus, in development, children must learn to use features in the way adults do. As discussed in Chapter 6, when children encode an event they often emphasize different word features than adults. Following Nelson's (1974) theory of a functional core, for instance, children may emphasize functional rather than categorical word properties, and children just learning to read may be unduly attentive to physical word features, such as the sound a word makes or its graphic characteristics (Gibson, 1971).

More recently, researchers have suggested that children may underestimate the *defining features* of words, features that provide necessary and sufficient conditions for defining a word, and may give undue emphasis to *characteristic features*, attributes that are only generally true of a concept. For example, the feature *has water on all four sides* would be a defining feature for the concept *island*. In contrast, *tropical* would be a characteristic feature of *island* because it typifies some but not all islands. Keil and Batterman (1984) suggested that young children actually give greater emphasis to characteristic than to defining features in defining words. In their experiment, children in kindergarten and the second and fourth grades were presented with passages and were to determine whether each passage accurately described the concept in question. Some passages contained several characteristic features of the concept but no defining features (+ characteristic/ − defining), whereas others contained no characteristic features but at least one defining feature (− characteristic/ + defining). An example of these two types of passages for the concept *island* is given by Keil and Batterman (1984):

+ characteristic/ − defining: There is this place that sticks out of the land like a finger. Coconut trees and palm trees grow there, and girls sometimes wear flowers in their hair because it's so warm all the time. There is water on all sides except one. Could that be an island?

− characteristic/ + defining: On this piece of land, there are apartment buildings, snow, and no green things growing. This piece of land is surrounded by water on all sides. Could that be an island?

Keil and Batterman reported that the kindergarteners but not the second- and fourth-grade children often said that the passages with the defining features

but no characteristic features were *not* appropriate examples of the concept. In contrast, these young children readily said that passages with characteristic but no defining features were, in fact, examples of the category. Thus, 5-year-olds were likely to say that a smelly, mean old man with a gun in his pocket who took one's television set was a robber, even though their parents did not want the set anymore and had told the man he could have it. However, a friendly, cheerful woman who gave the children a hug was not declared to be a robber, even though she removed their toilet bowl and took it without permission. Keil and Batterman interpreted these results as indicating that young children do not realize that some features are more important than others and that their judgments of whether an item is an example of a concept or not are based on the total number of features (particularly characteristic) that are associated with it.

In related research, Schwanenflugel, Guth, and Bjorklund (1986) asked kindergarten, second-, and fourth-grade children to rate the importance of features in defining words. The features had previously been rated in terms of importance by college students and were classified as being high, medium, or low in importance. Table 7-1 provides examples of these three types of features for the words *cheese* and *sailor*. The ratings of the children and of the college students are shown in Figure 7-2. As can be seen, the kindergarten and second-grade children were less able to differentiate among the importance of the three classes of features than were the fourth-graders and adults. Although no shift from characteristic to defining features was observed in this experiment, as in the Keil and Batterman study, the results indicate that children give different weights to semantic word features than do adults, with this difference diminishing with age.

The Development of Natural Language Categories

Words such as *island, robber, cheese,* and *sailor* all refer to more than a single referent. Islands and cheese come in a variety of types, robbers specialize in the things they steal, and sailors may be particular about the type of ship they sail or differ in their ranks and duties. These words are natural language categories, comprising items that are related and can be referred to by a single language term. So, for example, COLLIE is a language category term that includes all creatures of a particular canine breed. A more inclusive category is DOG, which includes all collies but also many other breeds that are not collies. From here our language provides us with terms of increasing inclusiveness, from PETS or CANINES to ANIMALS. If one wanted to get technical about it, one could list the biological species, genus, family, class, and so on of which Fido is a member, with each step up the ladder being more inclusive than the one preceding it. Such language categories are obviously very important in communicating and classifying information. However, their development requires more than just learning the term; what children must learn is what characteristics an object must have to qualify for membership in a language category and when to use the term.

Two- and 3-year-old children obviously have some understanding of broad, superordinate category terms such as ANIMAL, CLOTHES, or FOOD. They use these words occasionally (for example, "Dresses are girls' clothes, not boys'"), and they seem to comprehend their meaning when used by an adult (for example, "Stop playing with your food!"). Yet, there are many superordinate category terms that young children typically do not use (most 3-year-olds do

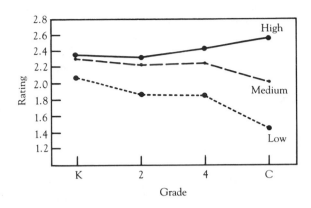

FIGURE 7-2   Mean ratings for concept attributes of high, medium, and low importance for kindergarten, second-grade, fourth-grade, and college subjects. Subjects rated various features for defining that word (Schwanenflugel, Guth, and Bjorklund, 1986).

not speak of "vehicles," "weapons," or "tools"), and we must be careful not to attribute adult meaning to children's language categories. Young children may speak of "food," "clothes," and "animals," but they may not give these words the same meaning that adults do.

Basic-Level Categories

Rosch, Mervis, and their colleagues (Mervis & Crisafi, 1982; Rosch, Mervis, Gray, Johnson, & Boyes-Braem, 1976) proposed that young children's early categories are not at the superordinate level but

TABLE 7-1   Examples of Word Concepts Used in Experiment in Which Children Rated How Important Each Attribute Was in Defining the Associated Word Concept (Schwanenflugel, Guth, and Bjorklund, 1986)

	Concept	
Attribute importance	Cheese	Sailor
High	Made with milk Is healthy	Found on ships Likes the ocean
Medium	Is good Melts	Wears a uniform Travels
Low	Found near mice Found on crackers	Has a hat Has a tattoo
Superordinate	Is food	Is a person
Distractor	Is black	Works in a hospital

rather include objects that have similar overall configurations (for example, CARS and CHAIRS but not VEHICLES and FURNITURE). As we saw in Chapter 4, infants can form primitive concepts for sets of objects that are perceptually similar (see Cohen & Younger, 1983; Reznick & Kagan, 1983). Rosch and her colleagues (1976) referred to such groupings as *basic-level categories*. In a series of experiments, they demonstrated that 3- and 4-year-old children were easily able to categorize sets of objects at the basic level, whereas few could organize items according to more superordinate categories. The children were shown sets of three pictures and asked to point to the two pictures "that are alike, that are the same kind of thing." In some triads, two of the pictures were examples from the same basic-level category (for example, two different types of cats or types of cars). In other triads, the pictures were from different basic-level categories but from the same superordinate category (for example, a car and a train—both vehicles—or a cat and a dog—both animals). Both the 3- and 4-year-old children had no difficulty identifying the category membership of objects from the same basic-level categories. The 4-year-olds also performed well when matches were based on superordinate category relations; in contrast, the 3-year-olds' performance was at chance values for these latter problems. A similar developmental trend was observed in a more demanding sorting task, where children were to group pictures that went together or were alike in some way. Kindergarten and first-grade children easily grouped items according to basic-level categories. But only half of these children were able to sort items on the basis of superordinate category membership.

The Development of Category Prototypes

Other researchers have suggested that children acquire sets of features that characterize specific members of a category and gradually integrate these features to develop a higher-level, taxonomic concept. For instance, Anglin (1977) proposed that children abstract the general features of a category and form a *prototype*. A prototype is a mentalistic representation reflecting the most typical or best examples of that category. It involves abstracting

features that are possessed by most or all members of the category and ignoring features that are idiosyncratic to specific members and do not characterize the category as a whole. For example, one's prototype for DOG probably includes four legs, hair, a tail, a certain shaped head, and a certain size. Your Chihuahua may be your favorite dog, but with its tiny size and lack of body hair it is unlikely that it resembles your prototype for DOG.

Anglin suggested that children's prototypes develop from their experiences with specific members of the category. In defining a category, Anglin suggested, young children often rely on visual imagery and their recollection of specific experiences with particular instances of the category. For instance, Sharon, at 4 years 7 months, described a dog as something that has "soggy ears that go, that hang down"; that "goes 'ruff'"; and that "chases cats" (p. 205). Her definition of DOG is based on specific experiences with them. Eventually, as children's experiences with the real world increase, their knowledge becomes broader and their categories more closely resemble those of adults. Keil and Batterman (1984) also proposed that children's early categories are based on specific exemplars. They suggested that when people are unfamiliar with a category, they use an exemplar-based representation and only later switch to a more analytic category consisting of sets of defining features. Such a process not only describes children's acquisition of categories but also should describe the acquisition process for adults who are learning new categories (see Chi, Feltovich, & Glaser, 1981).

Category Typicality

Related to the notion of category prototypes is that of *category typicality*, which was introduced briefly in the preceding chapter with respect to children's class-inclusion performance (Carson & Abrahamson, 1976). Eleanor Rosch and her colleagues (Mervis & Rosch, 1981; Rosch, 1973, 1975), among others (Smith et al., 1974), popularized the idea that natural categories cannot be viewed as having a set of features that absolutely determines category membership. Rather, natural categories can be viewed as having a core meaning, or prototype, with some items being more representative of the prototype than others. Items that are highly typical of a category have more features in common with the category prototype than do less typical items. For example, both *socks* and *shirt* are appropriate examples of the category CLOTHING, but most adults would say that *shirt* is more typical of their idea of clothing than *socks*. In other words, not all category members are created equal, with some items being more representative of our idea of a category than others. Adults show high intersubject agreement in their ratings of items in terms of typicality (Rosch, 1975; Uyeda & Mandler, 1980), and differences in the typicality of category items influence adults' performance on a variety of cognitive tasks (Keller & Kellas, 1978; Rosch, 1973; Smith et al., 1974). The questions of importance here are how children achieve an adult understanding of natural language categories and what role category typicality may play in this development.

Several researchers have investigated the development of children's natural language categories using the notion of category typicality. For example, in experiments where children are asked to select from a set of pictures or words all the examples of a specified category (for example, "Pick out all the pictures of CLOTHES—things you can wear"), young children usually choose most of the items that adults judge to be highly typical of the category (for example, *shirt* and *pants*), but they often fail to include many items that adults judge to be less typical of the category (for example, *gloves*, *hat*, and *tie*) (Anglin, 1977; Rosch, 1973; Saltz, Soller, & Sigel, 1972; White, 1982).

In a study by Bjorklund, Thompson, and Ornstein (1983), children's category selections were supplemented with judgments of typicality. Kindergarten, third-, and sixth-grade children were read lists of words from 12 natural language categories and were to decide whether each word was a member of a designated category. The children were again presented each word they had selected and asked to rate it on a three-point scale in terms of typicality, or "goodness of example." They were to pretend that there was a person from outer space who knew nothing of the category under question. Their job was to

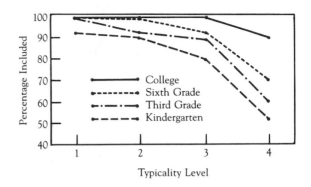

FIGURE 7-3 Percentage of appropriate category items included by grade as a function of level of adult-judged typicality (Level 1 = most typical; Level 4 = least typical). Subjects were given a category name (for example, FRUIT) and asked to select from a set of items those that were appropriate members of that category and then to rate each item in terms of how typical it was of its category (Bjorklund, Thompson, and Ornstein, 1983).

teach him the meaning of the category by rating each word in terms of typicality. "Very good" examples were those that would help the spaceman understand the category a lot; "OK" examples were those that would help him some but not as much as the "very good" examples; and "poor" examples were those that were category members but would not help the spaceman understand the meaning of the category very well. A group of college students was given a similar rating task.

Figure 7-3 presents the percentage of appropriate category items included as a function of grade and level of adult-judged typicality (Level 1 was most typical, and Level 4 was least typical). As can be seen, there were few age differences in the percentage of items included as appropriate category members for the more highly typical items (Levels 1 and 2). But there were considerable age differences for the items the college students judged to be less typical (Levels 3 and 4). In general, children were reluctant to include many adult-judged atypical items as appropriate category exemplars. The researchers also reported a significant correspondence between the children's typicality ratings and those of the college students. That is, many items that the adults viewed as typical (or atypical) were similarly viewed by the children. Despite this correspondence, however, the ratings became progressively more adult-like with age. The correlations between the ratings of the college students and children (a measure of how adult-like the children's ratings were) increased with age (average correlations between the ratings of children and college students were .72, .84, and .92 for kindergarten, third-, and sixth-graders, respectively). Thus, not only were *quantitative* age differences found in the number of items the children considered to be appropriate category examples, but there were also *qualitative* differences in the nature of children's category prototypes, reflected by developmental differences in typicality judgments.

Other researchers, using a variety of cognitive tasks, have reported developmental differences in the semantic representation of category-typical and -atypical items (Ackerman, 1986; Duncan & Kellas, 1978; Keller, 1982; Whitney & Kunen, 1983). In general, these researchers assert that age differences in how children process category information are due to the fact that, with age, children reorganize their semantic concepts, realizing that some features are more important than others in defining items (see Bjorklund, 1985, for a review). Thus, although children's natural language categories can be described in terms of prototypes much as adults' categories can, the nature of the prototypes changes. Children include fewer items as appropriate category members, with more typical exemplars being incorporated into children's category structures before less typical items (Rosch, 1973). Furthermore, children's prototypes seem to be structured slightly differently from those of adults, with children emphasizing different features in defining natural language categories. Differences are most apparent during the preschool years and are greatly minimized (although not eliminated) by the time a child is 10 or 11 years of age (Bjorklund et al., 1983; Whitney & Kunen, 1983).

The Development of Scripts

Recently, Katherine Nelson and her colleagues have suggested that children's early language categories should be based on functional relations among words rather than taxonomic relations (Nelson, 1983, 1986; Nelson, Fivush, Hudson, & Lucariello, 1983; see also Mandler, 1983). More specifically, Nelson

has suggested that children's early language categories are *schematically organized*, in that they are based on relations typifying real-world scenes, stories, and events (for example, what is involved in eating at a restaurant; objects and events dealing with sailing a ship) rather than more abstract conceptual categories (for example, FRUITS, VEGETABLES, VEHICLES). Children's representations can be expressed in terms of *scripts* (Schank & Abelson, 1977). Scripts are a form of schematic organization, with real-world events "organized in terms of temporal and causal relations between component acts" (Nelson, 1983, p. 55). For example, a breakfast script may include setting the table, eating breakfast, and washing the dishes.

Nelson and her colleagues have argued that superordinate language categories such as FOOD, ANIMALS, and CLOTHES have their origins in earlier acquired, schematically based scripts (Lucariello & Nelson, 1985; Nelson, 1983). Certain items are more likely to be found in specific scripts than other items. So, for instance, a breakfast script is likely to include eating toast, cereal, or pancakes and drinking orange juice, milk, or cocoa. Much less likely to be found in a breakfast script would be French fries, ice cream, beer, or macaroni and cheese. Thus, in a particular script, several different items can be included, each of which would satisfy the conditions of the script. *Slot fillers* refer to items that could successfully complete the script (for example, juice and cocoa). Nelson has suggested that it is from these slot-filler categories that context-free, superordinate taxonomies develop.

This hypothesis was tested in a memory experiment by Lucariello and Nelson (1985). Children's recall of sets of words was compared using lists consisting of items from different superordinate categories (ANIMALS, FOOD, CLOTHES) and lists consisting of items from script-derived categories, or slot-filler categories (ZOO ANIMALS, LUNCH FOOD, CLOTHES YOU PUT ON IN THE MORNING). Children remembered significantly more items from the slot-filler than from the superordinate categories. Based on these findings, Lucariello and Nelson asserted that slot-filler categories have a more cohesive structure than superordinate categories and that these schematically based groupings may serve as the beginning for broader, context-free natural language categories.

Support for the schematic nature of children's semantic memory comes from research demonstrating that young children are able to use the schematic organization to help them remember stories or events (Hudson & Fivush, 1983; Hudson & Nelson, 1983, 1986; Mandler, 1978; Stein & Glenn, 1979). At other times, however, events that fit easily into a previously established script are difficult to retrieve because they are so similar to related events. For instance, Hudson and Nelson (1986) asked 3-, 5-, and 7-year-old children to tell about "what happens" generally at snack and dinner times and to recall "what happened yesterday" at snack and dinner. The children had a difficult time recalling what had happened the day before, although their knowledge of what happens generally was quite good. From these and other results, Nelson and her colleagues speculated that memories for familiar occurrences fuse with one another, making the retrieval of any specific event difficult (Fivush, Hudson, & Nelson, 1984; Nelson & Ross, 1980). Thus, our past knowledge provides a context in which we can place events, facilitating our recall of general information; but the same well-established knowledge base makes it difficult to separate one specific episode from others similar to it.

How Does Semantic Memory Develop?

Children's word and category definitions exist in semantic memory, the long-term store where representations of language terms and their relations with one another are hypothesized to reside. Semantic memory can be described as a system of interconnecting nodes (Anderson, 1976; Collins & Loftus, 1975; see Figure 3-2), with each item connected to other items in semantic memory and also having associated with it a set of features (for *dog*, for example, the features might include *small, barks, chases cats*). In order for an item in semantic memory to be brought into consciousness, it must be activated, which requires a certain amount of mental effort. This process need not be deliberate. When someone speaks to us or when we see an example of a familiar concept, pertinent information in semantic memory is activated. Because items in semantic memory are connected to other items, the activation of one item may spread to others in the system. Accordingly, individual differences in how we process language information are related to the contents of semantic memory, the number and nature of the links among semantic entries, and the ease with which items can be activated (that is, the amount of mental effort required for an item to be activated and entered into short-term store).

Given this simplified model of semantic memory, what changes in development? The most obvious age-related change surely is the absolute number of entries in semantic memory, with vocabulary growth increasing steadily throughout childhood (McCarthy, 1954). The remaining factors all influence the ease with which items in semantic memory can be activated and introduced into consciousness (see Bjorklund, 1987a).

The factor that is probably most responsible for developmental differences in ease of activation is the frequency of occurrence of a particular item. After there is repeated exposure to an item and frequent activation of it, its threshold for becoming activated is reduced in certain contexts. Similarly, the more frequently an item is encountered and activated in a variety of contexts, the more features are likely to become associated with it. Accordingly, such elaboratively encoded items can be activated by a greater number of both internal and external cues than can items having a smaller set of features associated with them. Support for this contention comes from the results of memory experiments by several researchers, who report age differences in the number of semantic features that children use to encode words (Ackerman, 1984; Ceci & Howe, 1978; see the discussion of age differences in encoding for memory in Chapter 8). Likewise, with increased exposure to an item, more links with other entries in semantic memory are established, and there are more chances that that item will be activated given the activation of other items.

In addition to the number of features or links associated with items, the strength of those links also changes developmentally. Strength of relationship refers to the amount of mental effort that is required to activate one concept given the prior activation of another concept (for example, the activation of the concept *cat* given the previous activation of the concept *dog*). Strength of relations among items in semantic memory varies with frequency of exposure, but other factors also influence it. Research evidence has been presented in this and the preceding chapter illustrating that children give differential weight to some features and that these weights change with age. For example, young children apparently give more emphasis to functional or schematic word features (Nelson, 1973) and to acoustic or graphic word features (Gibson, 1971) than they do to categorical features. Similarly, young children give less emphasis to defining word features and more to characteristic word features than do older children or adults (Keil & Batterman, 1984). A similar developmental shift, not discussed previously, occurs with respect to associative (for example, dog/bone) versus categorical (for example, dog/lion) relations. Associative relations, based on the frequency of co-occurrence of items, are processed more readily by young children than are categorical relations (Bjorklund & de Marchena, 1984; McCauley, Weil, & Sperber, 1976). Which items become activated and how quickly will thus be a function of which features are given the most emphasis, and this varies as a function of development.

The development of semantic memory seems to be characterized by both quantitative (number of items, strength of relations) and qualitative (which features are weighted most heavily) changes. Children's knowledge of the words and concepts of their language is influenced substantially by the speech and experiences to which they are exposed, but it is also influenced by underlying changes in representational skills (see Chapter 6). It seems unquestionable that the words and concepts we possess influence our thought processes. It also seems clear, however, that there are changes in cognitive functioning that affect how we construct language concepts and how we use language terms to represent our experiences.

☐ Summary

Children begin speaking their first words around 10 to 12 months of age. However, they have a history of vocal communication, including cries, coos, babbles, and pseudowords. Children's one-word utterances have been described as *holophrastic*, in that they convey substantial meaning in a single word. Children begin to put words together into two-word sentences by approximately 18 months. They acquire rules concerning how to convey specific meanings (for example, past tense, plurals, questions, negatives), and there is much debate over the nature of these rules and how they are acquired.

Children's verbal communication has received much attention, with initial research being based on Piaget's view of young children as egocentric and unable to consider the perspective of another. Research has to a large extent confirmed Piaget's position, with preschool children displaying poor communication abilities. Flavell and his colleagues have shown that young children have poor *metacommunication* skills, being generally unaware of factors that influence the comprehension of messages. Despite these shortcomings, other researchers have shown that young children's language is not as egocentric as Piaget contended and that the roots of metacognitive competence can be found in 2- and 3-year-old children. In general, children's communicative and metacommunicative skills increase with age, with children displaying communication competence first in highly familiar situations and only later generalizing them to less familiar settings.

Research into the developmental relationship between language and thought has concentrated on the self-regulatory role of speech. The Soviet psychologists *Luria* and *Vygotsky* have proposed that language serves to direct much intelligent behavior in children. Luria proposed that speech cannot serve to inhibit the motor action of young children, with slightly older children's responses to speech being *impulsive*, in that they respond to the physical and not the conceptual features of language in directing their behavior. By 5 years of age, children are able to use the conceptual features of speech (that is, its meaning) to guide their behavior. Vygotsky proposed that *egocentric*, or *private*, speech has a special role in guiding children's thinking and behavior. Young children's private speech serves as a cognitive self-guidance system and is eventually replaced by covert verbal thought. Although Western research on these topics has not been uniform, recent work provides general support for the Soviet psychologists' position.

Children's early words have slightly different meanings from those of the comparable words used by adults. This difference is illustrated by children's tendency to *overextend* the meaning of words, applying a label to a broader range of referents than the words denote (for example, calling a horse a "doggy"). Children also *underextend* words, inappropriately restricting their meaning (for example, using the term *doggy* to refer only to one's own pet). In acquiring word meaning, children must learn to give differential weight or influence to word features. Research by Keil and Batterman (1974) suggested that children give inappropriate emphasis to *characteristic features* and only gradually give appropriate emphasis to *defining features*.

Natural language categories comprise items that are related on the basis of some sets of features and can be referred to by a single language term (for example, DOGS, PETS, ANIMALS). Children tend to be able to categorize items at the level of *basic objects* first (for example, CARS, CHAIRS, DOGS) and only later on

the basis of more superordinate categories (for example, VEHICLES, FURNITURE, ANIMALS). One factor influencing the formation of superordinate natural language categories is that of *category typicality*. Some items are more representative of the category *prototype* than others. Children tend to learn the category membership of more typical items before that of less typical items, and their judgments of category typicality vary with age. Aspects of children's semantic memories seem to be *schematically* organized, with Nelson proposing that broad-based superordinates (such as FOOD) have their basis in context-specific, script-related categories (such as THINGS YOU EAT AT BREAKFAST).

It has been proposed that developmental differences in semantic memory can be attributed to the number of entries in long-term store and to the ease with which items in semantic memory can be activated. The frequency of occurrence of an item influences the ease with which it can be activated and the number of features and links associated with it. Developmental differences also occur with respect to the strength of relations among items (that is, how much mental effort is required for an item to be activated). Strength of relations among items is influenced by frequency of exposure but also by the weight that children of different ages give to different word features. In sum, the development of semantic memory involves both quantitative and qualitative changes.

8

Memory

The Structure of Memory

The Development of Memory in Children

☐ Memory Development in Infancy ☐ Recognition ☐ Recall ☐ Constructive Memory

The Development of Memory Strategies

☐ Rehearsal ☐ Organization ☐ Retrieval ☐ Other Strategies

Factors That Influence Children's Use of Memory Strategies

☐ Encoding ☐ Knowledge Base ☐ Efficiency of Cognitive Processing ☐ Metamemory

Summary

Note

A 4-month-old looks longer at a new picture than at one he has seen repeatedly; a 13-month-old retrieves a favorite toy hidden seconds earlier behind one of several pillows; a 7-year-old lists for her mother the names of all her classmates in preparing to send Valentine's Day cards; and a high school sophomore attempts to remember everything his father asked him to get at the corner store. Each of these diverse activities has at least one common component: memory. The 4-month-old can recognize a new stimulus only if he has some notion that it is different from a previous, unseen stimulus, and the 13-month-old must remember under which of several different pillows her favorite toy was placed. The memory requirements for the two older children are more demanding, but all involve retrieving from memory some previously stored information.

Memory is not a unitary phenomenon. Information must be encoded and possibly categorized with other information known to the individual. What knowledge already resides in memory influences the ease with which new information is stored and later retrieved. Furthermore, few acts of cognition do not involve memory. Classification, problem solving, and decision making all require the retrieval of previously stored information.

To make matters even more complex, memory can refer to the contents of one's mind (one's memories) or to the process of bringing that information to consciousness. Researchers have divided the contents of memory into two general types: *semantic* and *episodic* (Tulving, 1972). Semantic memory refers to the long-term repository of language terms, their definitions, and their relations to one another (see Chapter 7). Episodic memory refers to memories for events or episodes. For example, the definition for the word *avuncular* is part of my semantic memory; but my recollections of the events surrounding my learning the word (preparing for the Graduate Record Exam) are part of my episodic memory.[1]

Concerning the *process* of remembering, researchers have specified different operations by which information in our minds can be retrieved. The most basic form of retrieval is *recognition*, in which a stimulus is presented to a person and he or she must merely signify whether that stimulus is new

(not experienced previously) or old. More demanding in terms of self-activation is *recall*, in which some information not currently perceived must be retrieved from memory. Retrieval may be prompted by a specific environmental context or cue (cued recall), or the reminder may be general or be internally generated (free recall). Examples of cued recall include a 6-year-old remembering to bring her baton to school by leaving it by the door in the morning and an 8-year-old recalling by specified categories all the pictures recently presented to him (for example, "Remember all the pictures of *animals* that I just showed you"). Examples of free recall include retelling a story and remembering the items on a grocery list. An important developmental consideration in retrieving information in memory is the degree to which children will use information they have available to them. In general, recall (especially free recall) requires more in the way of self-initiation and the application of prior knowledge than recognition does. However, recognition is not purely automatic, and developmental differences in children's application of what they know to the task at hand have also been reported for this form of memory.

In this chapter, research and theory dealing with the development of memory in children are examined. In the initial section, the structure of memory is reviewed, following the information processing model of memory discussed in Chapter 5. Next, patterns of memory development from infancy through adolescence are reviewed. Children's use of memory strategies is then examined, followed by an assessment of some of the factors that influence memory development.

☐ The Structure of Memory

Although the memory system can be conceptualized in a number of ways, one convenient framework for developmental researchers has been the multistore model as exemplified by the work of Atkinson and Shiffrin (1968). Basically, this model holds that memory can be divided into a series of three stores: the sensory register, the short-term store, and the long-term store (see Chapter 3 and Figure 3-1). To reiterate my earlier discussion, the sensory register holds relatively large amounts of information but only for milliseconds. There appears to be little in the way of developmental differences in the capacity of the sensory register, although differences are found in terms of procedures for getting information from the register to the more durable short-term store (Sheingold, 1973).

The short-term store holds less information (7 ± 2 items for adults) but for longer periods of time (seconds). It is while information is in the short-term store that strategies can be applied for getting the information through the memory system. Reliable age differences have been reported for the short-term store (assessed by tests of memory span). Although some theorists have proposed that these differences can be attributed to maturation (Pascual-Leone, 1970), others have proposed that differences are more likely to stem from developmental changes in the efficiency with which information can be processed (Case, 1985; Dempster, 1981). Efficiency of processing (as assessed in terms of speed of processing) is affected both by maturation and by the degree of knowledge that children have for the information to be remembered (Chi, 1977; Dempster, 1985).

The long-term store is permanent and apparently infinite in capacity. We do not have to evict one piece of information from our long-term store to make room for something new. Both episodic and semantic memories are parts of the long-term store, as is our knowledge of procedures (strategies) for operating on information (Tulving, 1985). However, just because information is in long-term storage does not mean that we can retrieve it whenever we wish. Information is forgotten and, in some cases, transformed so that what we remember may not coincide exactly with what we originally experienced.

☐ The Development of Memory in Children

Most research in memory development has been concerned with the retrieval of information from the long-term store. Whether a 6-month-old infant is recognizing its mother's face or a 12-year-old is recounting the details of the American Revolution, retrieving information from the long-term store is called for. The remainder of this chapter deals primarily with retrieval of information from long-term memory. As will be seen, many factors influence age differences in memory performance, with these factors interacting to yield patterns in memory development.

Memory Development in Infancy

Babies obviously remember things. The questions of interest are when and under what conditions infants demonstrate memory and how long these memories last. Research examining infants' search behavior, as reflected by object permanence tasks, indicates age changes in memory over the first year (Diamond, 1985; Sophian, 1980). The research of Diamond (1985), discussed in Chapter 5, provided evidence of increased memory abilities for infants between the ages of 7 and 12 months. After the infant has successfully retrieved a hidden object at one location (A), the object is hidden at a second location (B). When searching for the object, infants younger than 12 months typically look first at position A. Diamond varied the delay between hiding the object at location B and permitting the babies to search for it. For 7-month-olds, a 2-second delay was sufficient to produce the $A\overline{B}$ error (searching incorrectly at position A). The amount of delay necessary to yield this error increased with each successive month, so that by 12 months, errors occurred (usually) only after a 10-second delay. These data clearly indicate age-related improvements in memory over this 6-month period (see Chapter 5).

The bulk of research assessing infant memory has used variants of the habituation/dishabituation paradigm discussed in Chapter 6. To review, infants' attention to a stimulus declines as a result of repeated presentation of that stimulus (habituation) but returns to its previously high levels when a new stimulus is presented (dishabituation). Such a finding not only indicates that infants can discriminate between the two stimuli but also implicates memory, in that the discrimination is being made between one stimulus that is physically present and another that is present only in memory. In a related procedure, infants are familiarized with a stimulus and later shown two stimuli: the original, familiarized stimulus and a novel one. As in the habituation/dishabituation paradigm, preference for the novel stimulus is taken as evidence of memory for the original.

Using these *preference for novelty* paradigms, memory for visual stimuli has been found for newborns. In an experiment by Friedman (1972), infants 1 to 3 days old were habituated to one visual pattern and then, immediately after habituation, shown a novel pattern. These neonates displayed the classic increase in responding to the new stimulus, indicative of memory (be it ever so brief). One word of caution about Friedman's results is in order, however. Of 90 newborns initially tested, 50 were excluded for reasons such as crying and falling asleep. Of the 40 remaining, only 29 displayed dishabituation. Thus, only 32% of the original sample demonstrated the habituation/dishabituation phenomenon. This result questions the generalizability of Friedman's findings, and not all subsequent research has found dishabituation in samples of very young infants (Cohen & Gelber, 1975). What Friedman's results indicate is that memory is within the capability of many human newborns, although the possibility exists that the majority of infants do not possess such memory until several weeks after birth.

Perhaps the most influential work demonstrating memory in infants by using the preference for novelty paradigm is that of Fagan (1973, 1974). One study showed that 5- and 6-month-old babies formed visual memories following brief exposures (5 to 10 seconds), and that these memories lasted for up to 2 weeks (Fagan, 1974).

More recent work by Rovee-Collier and her colleagues has used conditioning techniques, demonstrating retention over relatively long periods for very young infants (Rovee-Collier & Fagen, 1981). In their procedure, a ribbon is tied to an infant's ankle and connected to a mobile that is suspended over the crib. Infants quickly learn that when they kick their feet, the mobile moves, and they soon make repeated kicks, controlling the movement of the mobile overhead. In a typical experiment, for

the first 3 minutes the ribbon is not connected to the mobile, so that kicks do not cause it to move (baseline nonreinforcement period). This period is followed by a 9-minute reinforcement period in which the ribbon and mobile are connected, and infants quickly learn to kick to make the mobile move. What will happen when the infants are hooked up to the apparatus hours or days later? Will they resume kicking (even when the ribbon is not connected to the mobile), or will their level of kicks be comparable to that observed during the 3-minute baseline? If the kicking rate is high on these delayed trials, it reflects memory; if it is low, it reflects forgetting. This was the procedure used in a study of memory in 3-month-olds by Sullivan, Rovee-Collier, and Tynes (1979). They varied the delayed-memory test between 48 hours and 336 hours (2 weeks). The researchers reported no forgetting by these young infants for a period of up to 8 days, and some babies displayed memory for the full 2-week interval. In related work, retention of conditioned responses over a 2-week period was obtained for infants as young as 8 weeks, although evidence of memory was obtained only under optimal conditions (distributing training over several sessions) (Vander Linde, Morrongiello, & Rovee-Collier, 1985). These results indicate that young infants can remember events over long intervals, although these skills do improve over the first several months of life.

Recognition

In recognition, as we have seen, a stimulus is presented, and the subjects must decide whether they have experienced that stimulus before. In the preference for novelty paradigm used with infants, babies display recognition by attending more to a previously unseen stimulus than to a familiar one (they recognize it as different from something they have seen before). With older children, most recognition procedures involve the presentation of a set of stimuli (for example, pictures or words), with the children later being presented with a larger set of items, some of which had been presented earlier (old items) and some of which had not (new items). The task is to determine which items are old and which are new.

Adults' recognition is exceptional. Shepard (1967) reported that adults recognized more than 90% of 600 photos after a 1-week delay. Research with children by Brown and Scott (1971) has shown similarly high levels of performance for 3- to 5-year-old children. Children shown 100 pictures displayed remarkably high levels of recognition over delays ranging from 1 to 28 days. Performance did decrease over time, but overall the findings were comparable to those reported for adults. Daehler and Bukatko (1977) reported similarly high levels of recognition (using a preference for novelty paradigm) for 1½- to 3½-year-old children for sets of 50 pictures.

The high levels of recognition performance by young children have caused some to assert that this ability changes little with development (see Perlmutter & Lange, 1978). Other researchers have argued differently, however, demonstrating age-related increases in recognition when the task requirements are more demanding (Dirks & Neisser, 1977; Mandler & Stein, 1974; Stein & Mandler, 1975). For example, Dirks and Neisser (1977) showed children in grades one, three, and six and adults crowded arrays of toys and then added, deleted, or moved objects. The subjects were to determine what changes had been made in the arrays. Developmental differences in performance were noted for each type of change, causing the researchers to propose that recognition ability improves substantially over the school years.

Other researchers have reported that age differences emerge on recognition tasks only under certain conditions. For example, Mandler and Robinson (1978) showed pictures to children in grades one, three, and five and later showed them variants of those pictures, some of which were identical to the originals and others of which had been changed in some way. Half of the children at each grade level were shown *organized scenes*, in which sets of objects were placed in juxtaposition to one another so that they formed a coherent picture, such as a living room. The remaining children were shown the same sets of objects but with no coherent arrangement to them (*unorganized scenes*). Examples of an organized and an unorganized scene are shown in Figure 8-1.

FIGURE 8-1   An organized and an unorganized scene (Mandler and Robinson, 1978)

The results of the Mandler and Robinson study are presented in Figure 8-2. No age differences were found for the unorganized scenes, with performance being generally poor. However, performance increased with age for the organized scenes. Thus, older children were more likely than younger ones to use what they knew about the world (how living rooms are organized, for example) to guide their recognition. Yet, when no organization was imposed by the picture (the unorganized scene), the youngest children did as well as the oldest. This pattern of data reflects young children's relatively good recognition abilities in some situations (for rote remembering, they are as good as older children) and their relatively poor abilities in others (when they can apply what they already know to the task at hand, they are much worse than older children).

Another recognition study examined a slightly different aspect of children's applying what they know to a memory problem (Hock, Romanski, Galie, & Williams, 1978). Hock and his colleagues also investigated the recognition of scenes, but they were interested in how novelty influences memory. They constructed simple scenes, some that depicted familiar arrangements of objects and others that depicted novel but possible arrangements of the same objects. Examples of a familiar and a novel scene are shown in Figure 8-3. In an initial experiment, adults displayed superior performance for the novel scenes. The researchers then presented novel and familiar

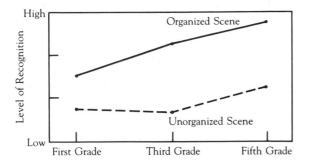

FIGURE 8-2 Children's recognition performance for organized and unorganized scenes (adapted from Mandler and Robinson, 1978)

scenes to a group of 8- to 10-year-old children. Approximately half of these children had been classified as conservers based on Piaget's conservation-of-liquid task, and the remainder as nonconservers. The conservers showed the same pattern as the adults, having higher recognition scores for the novel scenes than for the familiar ones. In contrast, the nonconservers' recognition was comparable for the familiar and novel pictures. Hock and his associates speculated that the conservers had used their real-world knowledge to form a representation (or schema) of the novel scenes that was difficult to forget (as do adults). The nonconservers were not able to do this. That is, although the nonconservers presumably had the same knowledge of the objects as did the conservers (the two groups had been matched for age), they did not apply this knowledge to guide task performance. As a result, recognition performance suffered for the novel scenes.

In sum, recognition does improve with age, but the basic ability to recognize information is found very early. Age differences are most apt to be observed when the information to be remembered is complex, possibly resulting in inadequate encoding of the critical information (Dirks & Neisser, 1977), and when children can apply their world knowledge to assist them in the recognition process (Hock et al., 1978; Mandler & Robinson, 1978). In the latter case, age differences may account for older children's greater world knowledge and their tendency to apply what they know to the task at hand.

Recall

Unlike recognition, recall does not involve the presentation of a target stimulus. Rather than matching a memory representation to a currently perceived object or event, one must retrieve a representation "from memory," without the benefit of having the original stimulus as a referent. The prompts for recall vary, however. Earlier in the chapter, I differentiated between *cued recall* and *free recall*. In the former, a specific external cue is provided that is in some way related to the target information. In free recall, the prompts are much less specific. Rather, they are either internally generated ("Let me see if I can remember all my cousins on my father's side of the family," or "What was that guy's name who did all those studies of conservation?") or are prompted by a general request ("Remember all the presidents of the United States" or "Tell me what happened at school today"). The less explicit the retrieval context, the greater the demands on the individual to activate his or her knowledge to recall information.

Variants of cued recall are even found in infants. Babies conditioned to kick in a certain situation recall those behaviors when placed in the conditioning context, and infants who search for and find a toy

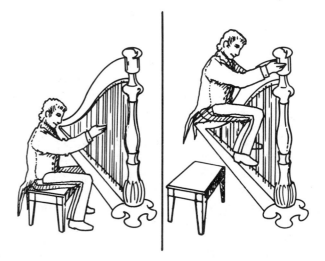

FIGURE 8-3 A familiar and a novel scene (thanks to Howard Hock)

in one of several locations are recalling where the object was hidden (although they may merely recognize the location). In general, the ability to recall information increases developmentally, with children requiring fewer prompts to mediate successful memory performance as they get older (Bjorklund & Muir, 1988).

Research with children has used many of the procedures used in studies of adult memory. In a typical free-recall experiment, children are presented with a list of items at a relatively slow rate (for example, one item every 5 seconds) and then are asked to remember as many of the items as they can in any order they wish. The items may be unrelated to one another or be members of familiar categories (for example, different instances of the categories ANIMALS, CLOTHING, and FRUITS).

A general finding is that for both related and unrelated materials, the amount recalled increases with age, although *patterns* of recall also vary developmentally (Cole, Frankel, & Sharp, 1971). For example, there are developmental differences in *serial position* effects. Serial position effects refer to differences in the average amount recalled as a function of where on the list an item was presented. For adults who are given lists of unrelated items to recall, items presented toward the end of the list (the last three or four) are usually recalled very well. This phenomenon is referred to as a *recency effect*. Adults also show better recall for the first several items presented, displaying a *primacy effect*. The result is a bow-shaped curve, with levels of recall being greatest on either end and lowest in the middle. The usual interpretation of this curve is that the most recently presented items are still in a subject's short-term store, making their retrieval relatively easy. The high levels of recall for the primacy items are attributed to the use of *strategies*. These items have particular saliency because of their early position in the list, and subjects have more opportunity to apply memory strategies to them than they do to items in the middle of the list.

This pattern changes, however, when children are tested. Figure 8-4 shows idealized serial position curves for three age groups of children (6, 9, and 14 years). All groups display substantial recency effects,

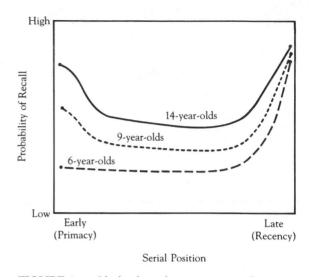

FIGURE 8-4   Idealized serial-position curves for 6-, 9-, and 14-year-old children

with differences most apparent for the primacy and middle portions of the curves. Adolescents show the adult pattern, with the youngest children's recall not being differentiated across the early and middle serial positions (Cole et al., 1971; Ornstein, Naus, & Liberty, 1975). These data seem to indicate that there are minimal age differences in the capacity of the short-term store (as reflected by the comparable recency effects across age); rather, age differences are in terms of the use of memory strategies, or *mnemonics*, as reflected by the age differences for the early and middle serial positions. The role of memory strategies, particularly as they relate to recall, is examined later in the chapter.

Constructive Memory

Much of the remembering we do is not for specific sets of items but, rather, for more complex stories and events. Although actors may learn verbatim long sequences of prose and dialogue, when we retell the happenings of the day or of a particular conversation, we are rarely exact. We recall the gist of the message, and in the process we transform what was actually said or done. That is, our memory is *constructive*; we interpret our experiences as a function of what we already know about the world, and our

FIGURE 8-5 Children's drawings representing (a) immature, (b) transitional, and (c) mature concepts of verticality (Liben, 1981)

memory for events is colored by previous knowledge (Bartlett, 1932).

Piagetian Research on Reconstructive Memory

Piaget believed that cognition is an act of construction, that children construct reality as a function of what is in the external world and their current cognitive structures (see Chapter 2). He viewed memory in a similar way, and this perspective is illustrated in a series of experiments by Piaget and Inhelder (1973). They reported that the stage of development of a child affects the retention of "operationally relevant" stimuli. For example, concrete operational children reconstruct seriated arrays (▪ ▪ ▪ ▪ ▪) more accurately than preoperational children. In fact, Piaget and Inhelder reported that the performance of some preschool children who were shown seriated arrays was better 8 months later than it had been just 1 week after they saw the original stimulus! They proposed that children's memories become reorganized over time, consistent with the reorganization of mental schemes from the preoperational to the concrete operational period. More recent research has seriously questioned that there is actually improvement in memory over time (Maurer et al., 1979). However, an alternate but related interpretation that has received research support is that the preoperational and concrete operational children encode the stimuli differently, giving them slightly different memory representations to remember.

A study by Liben (1981) illustrates this position nicely. Children in grades one through five drew pictures of houses and trees on a hill, and their

drawings were rated in terms of the concept of verticality. Figure 8-5 presents drawings reflecting immature (preoperative), transitional, and mature (operative) concepts of verticality. As can be seen, immature children draw objects so that they are perpendicular to the hill, whereas mature children draw objects so that they are perpendicular to the horizon. After being classified as immature, transitional, or mature, children were shown two drawings of a tree growing on a hill, one depicting an operationally advanced concept of verticality (the tree is perpendicular to the horizon, as in the mature drawing in Figure 8-5) and another depicting an operationally primitive concept of verticality (the tree is perpendicular to the hill, as in the immature drawing in Figure 8-5). The children were given a sheet of paper and asked to copy the picture. They were also asked to reconstruct the picture from memory, with the delay between seeing the picture and reconstructing it being immediate in one experiment, 1 week in a second, and 5 months in a third.

The results of most interest for us concern the advanced stimulus (straight tree). With respect to memory, the mature children reconstructed the stimulus more accurately than the less mature children for all three memory delays (mature > transitional > immature). What is especially interesting here, however, is that the results for *copying* mirrored those reported for recall. The children with the mature verticality concept copied the advanced stimulus more accurately than the transitional children, who were better than the children with the immature concept. In fact, there was virtually no difference between how the immature children drew the advanced stimulus when they were reconstructing it from memory (in some cases over 5 months) and how they drew it when they were copying it. In other words, the children with the immature concept of verticality distorted the advanced stimulus at encoding, making it conform to their preoperational level (that is, they copied it as being tipped). In reconstructing the image, they drew it as they had seen it. Thus, their memory was relatively accurate. What was inaccurate was their perception (encoding) of the stimulus.

Memory and Inferences

When we recall a story or conversation, we rarely do so verbatim. Rather, we recall the gist of the message, often modifying some of the actual content, and infer that certain things occurred even if they were not explicitly stated. In other words, we reconstruct the story or conversation, filling in the missing or assumed parts. Construction requires inference. Take, for example, the following sentence:

Jimmy banged on the keys, making a noise that certainly didn't sound like music.

In remembering this sentence, a person may recall that "Jimmy banged on the piano, making an awful noise." The listener infers that Jimmy was banging on a piano and, when later asked, may be very confident that the word *piano* was indeed in the original sentence. Adults make these types of inferences constantly, applying what they know to interpret what they experience, making the necessary inferences along the way (Bransford & Franks, 1971). What about children?

Paris and his colleagues, among others, have investigated extensively children's abilities to make inferences from sets of sentences and stories, and they provide an unequivocal yes to the question (see Paris, 1978; Paris & Lindauer, 1977). Children make inferences much as adults do, imposing their own structure on stories and events. The ability to make inferences does improve with age, however, as reflected by experiments by Paris and Lindauer (1976). In one experiment, sentences were read to 7-, 9-, and 11-year-old children in which a specific instru-

ment was either stated or implied. For example, "The workman dug a hole in the ground [with a shovel]." In a subsequent test of recall, it was shown that the older children benefited from the naming of the instrument as a retrieval cue whether it had been explicitly stated in the target statement or not. For the younger children, however, only when the instrument had been explicitly named did presenting it as a retrieval cue improve recall. An additional experiment succeeded in removing these differences by asking children to act out each sentence, thereby elucidating the implicitly or explicitly stated instrument. This request seemed to force the children to actively construct the implied relationship in their memory structures. This procedure not only eliminated the differential effectiveness of implicit and explicit cues but also resulted in a higher level of recall overall, attesting "to the functional value of inferential, constructive processes for access to memory" (Paris & Lindauer, 1977, p. 45).

Although the development of inferential processing parallels general cognitive development, it is also highly dependent on one's knowledge base. This fact was well illustrated in a study by Brown, Smiley, Day, Townsend, and Lawton (1977). They presented children in grades two through seven with a story about the fictitious Targa people and then assessed the degree to which the children incorrectly "remembered" (inferred) additional information that had not been presented. They found that children inferred a considerable number of details based on the information provided. For example, the phrase *the weather was bad* was recalled quite differently (to mean it was either hot or cold) depending on whether the children had been told that the Targa were desert Indians or Eskimos. The frequency of these intrusions, furthermore, increased from 51% to 79% for second- and seventh-graders, respectively. It seems that with increasing age, children elaborate upon newly acquired information according to their relevant knowledge in such a way as to make it more coherent and understandable.

Recollections from Early Childhood and Infancy

The longer the delay between experiencing an event and recalling it, the greater the distortion is apt to be. Memories from our childhood are good examples. Few of us have verifiable memories from our infancy, and many of the memories we do have are reconstructions, often based on events that transpired years after the event we are "recalling." I, for example, have a memory of being an infant (about 6 months) and having the croup (something like bronchitis). My memory of this event is vivid. I can feel the congestion in my chest, hear the vaporizer whir, smell the Vicks VapoRub, and see the living room of my grandparents' house while looking through the bars of my crib. My mistake was relating this memory to my mother. She listened carefully and then told me that I had never had the croup; it was my younger brother, Dick, who had the croup as an infant. I was about 4 years old at the time.

One interesting phenomenon concerning recalling our past is our seeming inability to remember much before the age of 4 (Cowan & Davidson, 1984; Sheingold & Tenney, 1982). Several possible explanations have been proposed to explain this *infantile amnesia*, including the possibility that information is not stored for long-term retention before about 2 years of age and the possibility that information is encoded differently by infants and toddlers than by older children and adults (see White & Pillemer, 1979; Spear, 1984; see also a recent study by Myers, Clifton, & Clarkson, 1987). The first possibility seems unlikely. For example, Nelson and Ross (1980) have shown that 2-year-olds can remember information for as long as a year, even if the event happened only once. The alternative interpretation, that information is encoded differently during the early and later years of life, is consistent with observations made by Piaget and others that the nature of representation changes from infancy to early childhood (Bruner, 1966; Case, 1985) and then again (although less drastically) somewhere between the ages of 5 and 7 years (White, 1965). The minds that resided in our heads when we were infants are no longer there, replaced by minds that process symbols, especially verbal ones. According to this viewpoint, it is unlikely that we would be able to locate early events in memory, and were we to retrieve a memory we had encoded as an infant, we would probably not be able to understand it.

☐ The Development of Memory Strategies

Children's use of memory *strategies* has been the focus of most of the researchers studying memory development over the past 20 years. Although *memory strategies* are defined slightly differently by different people, they generally refer to deliberate plans adopted to enhance performance and subject to conscious evaluation (Brown, 1975; Naus & Ornstein, 1983; Pressley, Forest-Pressley, Elliot-Faust, & Miller, 1985). Three of the most investigated memory strategies in developmental psychology are *rehearsal*, in which a child repeats the target information; *organization*, in which the child combines different items into categories, themes, or other units; and *retrieval*, the process of accessing information and entering it into consciousness. The development of these and related strategies is examined briefly in the following sections.

Rehearsal

The study most responsible for the present interest in memory development was published in 1966 by John Flavell and his colleagues (Flavell, Beach, & Chinsky, 1966). Children in kindergarten and the second and fifth grades were shown a set of pictures that they were asked to remember. Following the presentation, there was a 15-second delay during which the children could prepare for the recall test. An experimenter, who was trained to identify lip movements corresponding to the words the children were trying to remember, watched the subjects' mouths. Flavell and his associates reported age-related increases in recall with corresponding increases in the amount of rehearsal. Eighty-five percent of the fifth-graders displayed evidence of some spontaneous rehearsal, whereas only 10% of the kindergarten children did so. Furthermore, within a grade level, children who had rehearsed more recalled more, on average, than children who had rehearsed less. These findings led the researchers to conclude that rehearsal is a powerful mnemonic that increases with age, with the frequency of rehearsal (the absolute number of times one rehearses) determining memory performance.

Later research by Ornstein, Naus, and Liberty (1975) questioned Flavell's frequency interpretation. These researchers used an *overt rehearsal procedure* with children in grades three, six, and eight. In this procedure, children are presented with a series of words to recall, with several seconds between each successive word. During this interval, the children are told they must repeat the most recently presented word at least once, and, if they wish, they may practice any other words they like. Thus, rehearsal is made obligatory (they must "rehearse" at least one word once during each interval), and the experimenters are able to determine exactly what it is the children are doing. Using this procedure, the researchers found *no* differences in the frequency of rehearsal across the three grade levels. Despite this equivalence in quantity of rehearsal, age differences in recall persisted, a perplexing finding given the interpretation of the earlier study by Flavell and his colleagues. However, Ornstein and his associates reported differences in the quality, or *style*, of rehearsal. Typical rehearsal protocols for a third- and an eighth-grade child are shown in Table 8-1. As can be seen, the number of words actually rehearsed is similar for the two children. But the style of rehearsing is very different. The younger child includes only one or, at best, two unique words per rehearsal set. (A *rehearsal set* refers to the words repeated during the interstimulus interval.) The researchers referred to this method as a *passive* rehearsal style. In contrast, the older child includes several different words per rehearsal set, a style labeled *active* or *cumulative*. The child repeats the most recently presented word and then rehearses it with as many other different words as possible. From these and other data, Orn-

stein and his colleagues asserted that the important developmental changes are in terms of style rather than frequency of rehearsal (see also Cuvo, 1975; Kellas, McCauley, & McFarland, 1975).

A causal relationship between differences in the frequency and style of rehearsal and age differences in memory performance has been demonstrated in training studies. Preteenage children trained to use an active rehearsal strategy display elevated levels of recall, especially for the primacy portion of the serial position curve (Keeney, Cannizzo, & Flavell, 1967; Kingsley & Hagen, 1969; Ornstein, Naus, & Stone, 1977). Thus, young children can be trained to use a rehearsal strategy, resulting in increases in memory performance (although age differences are rarely eliminated). What differs in development is children's inclination to implement a strategy, not their ability to use it. This general pattern is not unique to rehearsal but, as will be seen, typifies other strategies as well. Flavell (1970a) referred to this phenomenon as a *production deficiency* (see Chapter 3). Children have available to them techniques to facilitate their performance but fail to produce that strategy when it would be beneficial to do so.

Organization

One reason that active rehearsal benefits memory may be that conceptual relations are noticed among items that are rehearsed together (Ornstein & Naus, 1978). Organization in memory refers to the structure discovered or imposed upon a set of items that is used to guide subsequent performance. In attempting to remember what groceries one must buy at the store, for example, we benefit by organizing the

TABLE 8-1 Typical Rehearsal Protocols for an Eighth- and a Third-Grade Child (Ornstein, Naus, and Liberty, 1975)

	Rehearsal sets	
Word presented	*Eighth-grade subject*	*Third-grade subject*
1. Yard	Yard, yard, yard	Yard, yard, yard, yard, yard
2. Cat	Cat, yard, yard, cat	Cat, cat, cat, cat, yard
3. Man	Man, cat, yard, man, yard, cat	Man, man, man, man, man
4. Desk	Desk, man, yard, cat, man, desk, cat, yard	Desk, desk, desk, desk

information by categories (dairy products, meats, vegetables) or meals (food necessary for pot roast, food necessary for Saturday's barbecue).

In a typical study of organization and recall, subjects are given a list of items that can be divided into categories (several instances of FURNITURE, TOOLS, and OCCUPATIONS, for example), with the items being presented randomly. When the subjects recall the items, will they remember different ones from the same category together, even though they were not originally presented together? Recalling items from the same category together has been referred to as *clustering*, and adults who display high levels of clustering in their recall typically remember more than adults displaying lower levels of clustering (Bower, 1970; Mandler, 1967). Developmentally, levels of recall and clustering usually increase with age, with preschool children's clustering often being at chance levels (Arlin & Brody, 1976; Furth & Milgram, 1973).

Organization in memory can be measured more directly by giving children the opportunity to sort items into groups before recall. For example, Salatas and Flavell (1976) presented first-graders with a set of 16 pictures, 4 each from four different categories (for example, ANIMALS, CLOTHES, TOYS, and TOOLS). The experimenter named each picture, identified the categories, and placed the pictures randomly on a table in front of the children. The children were told that they would be asked to remember the pictures later on and that they should put them together in a way that would help them recall the pictures. Following a 90-second study period, the children were asked to remember as many of the pictures as they could. Although the instructions would seem to bias children to organize the items for recall, only 13 of 48 children (27%) organized the pictures according to categories to a significant degree. Other studies, requiring children to sort items before recall with instructions similar to those used by Salatas and Flavell ("Make groups that will help you remember"), report that children as old as 8 years often fail to organize items on the basis of meaning, placing items into groups randomly. Older children are more likely to group items on the basis of meaning and, as a result, realize higher levels of recall (Best & Ornstein, 1986; Bjorklund, Ornstein, & Haig, 1977; Corsale & Ornstein, 1980). Yet, when the instructions are modified, stressing to children that they should make their groups on the basis of *meaning*, even preschoolers comply and demonstrate enhanced levels of memory performance (Corsale & Ornstein, 1980; Lange & Jackson, 1974; Sodian, Schneider, & Perlmutter, 1986).

Other experiments, more explicitly training children to use an organizational strategy, have also yielded positive results. Young children, under certain instructional conditions, use an organizational strategy and display elevated levels of memory performance (Bjorklund et al., 1977; Black & Rollins, 1982; Cox & Waters, 1986; Moely, Olson, Halwes, & Flavell, 1969). In other words, young children are capable of organizing information for recall, but they generally fail to do so spontaneously. As with rehearsal, training children to use an organizational strategy rarely eliminates age differences, and, under most conditions, young children fail to generalize the strategy to new situations or new sets of materials (Bjorklund et al., 1977; Cox & Waters, 1986).

Retrieval

Once information has entered the memory system, something must be done to get it out. For recognition, the task is usually easy, with the original stimulus prompting the retrieval of the memory representation. For recall and constructive memory, however, it is not so simple. In fact, Howe, Brainerd, and Kingma (1985) assert that age differences in retrieval ability account for a greater proportion of the developmental difference in memory performance than age differences in storage ability (see also Morrison & Lord, 1982).

Young children's retrieval deficits apparently have to do with their need to have the original encoding environment reinstated. For example, in research by Ackerman (1985a; 1985b), children were given a set of cues associated with a target word at the time of presentation (for example, the cues *rose* and *tulip* for the target *lily*). Then they were re-presented with some or all of these cues at the time of retrieval or possibly with an *extralist cue* that is associated with the target but was not paired with it at the time of presentation (for example, *flower* for *lily*). Children were to recall the target words associated with the cue words. Ackerman reported that 7-year-olds needed more of the original encoding environment reinstated to yield correct recall than did older children or adults. In other words, young children can get at the information, but they require more explicit reminders than older children before retrieval is successful.

An excellent study for demonstrating age differences in retrieval was done by Kobasigawa (1974) (see Chapter 3). To reiterate, 6- and 8-year-old children's recall was relatively poor under free recall conditions or when retrieval cues were available for their use but the children were not required to use them. The children's recall was greatly improved, however, in a directed-cue condition, in which they were given the cues, one at a time, and told to recall all items that had earlier been associated with each cue (for example, "Here's the picture of the zoo. Six pictures went with the zoo. Remember as many of them as you can"). This pattern of results reflects that these young children had gotten information into their memory systems. Their problem was in getting it out. Other studies using similar procedures have also reported substantial reductions in younger children's recall deficits under directed-cue conditions (Eysenck & Baron, 1974; Kee & Bell, 1981; Williams & Goulet, 1975). Similar results have been found when children are to recall information from stories. Young children benefit more from the imposition of retrieval cues than older children, presumably because older children spontaneously generate retrieval plans while hearing the stories, making the cues provided by the experimenter superfluous (Mistry & Lange, 1985; Schmidt & Schmidt, 1986). In general, research has confirmed age differences in the efficient use of retrieval cues and in children's knowledge of their effectiveness (Beal, 1985; Fabricius & Wellman, 1983), with young children being able to implement retrieval strategies when properly instructed.

Other Strategies

Related to organization is the strategy of *elaboration*. Elaboration involves associating two or more items

by creating a representation of them. If I needed to remember to buy a carton of milk on my way home from work, for example, I could generate an image of a cow sitting on the hood of my car or form a verbal elaboration, so that when I saw my car I would think of *carton*. In both cases, the sight of my car should elicit for me the thought of milk. Most research examining elaboration has used paired-associate procedures, in which children are given pairs of words and learn to recall one word when given its mate. Children tend not to use elaboration spontaneously until adolescence (Pressley & Levin, 1977; Rohwer, Raines, Eoff, & Wagner, 1977), although as with other mnemonics, young children can be trained to use it (Pressley, 1982).

Rehearsal, organization, retrieval plans, and elaboration are all relatively complex and demanding memory strategies and are not used spontaneously by children to any substantial degree until late childhood or early adolescence. Other memory-facilitating procedures, however, are used even by preschool children, although they may not be so effective in influencing memory behavior as the aforementioned mnemonics (Bjorklund & Muir, 1988; Wellman, 1988). One very simple strategy involves just *trying hard*. Preschoolers believe that one of the best things they can do to facilitate memory is to concentrate (Wellman, 1988; Wellman, Collins, & Glieberman, 1981). A more sophisticated and effective strategy used by 3- and 4-year-olds involves selectively attending to the items to be remembered (Baker-Ward, Ornstein, & Holden, 1984; Yussen, 1974), including frequently re-attending to the stimuli, which reflects a form of visual rehearsal (Wellman, Ritter, & Flavell, 1975).

Other early strategies include spontaneously labeling items presented for recall, a technique that is not very effective (Baker-Ward et al., 1984), and using external memory cues. An example of the latter is found in the work of Heisel and Ritter (1981). Children were asked to hide an object in one of 196 containers, arranged in a 14 x 14 grid, so that they could remember the location. Children 5 years of age and older chose distinctive positions for hiding the items (for example, the corners), demonstrating a memory strategy. Three-year-olds did not use such techniques, although some of them did use the strategy of attempting to hide the objects in the same location on all trials. Because the locations were not distinctive, this strategy did not facilitate memory performance, but it does reflect the intent to do something "special" in an attempt to aid memory.

Assessing memory strategies in naturalistic settings (for example, children's homes), DeLoache, Brown, and their colleagues have reported memory strategies for children as young as 18 months (DeLoache, 1986; DeLoache & Brown, 1983; DeLoache, Cassidy, & Brown, 1985). The procedure involves a hide-and-seek game, in which a toy (Big Bird, for example) is hidden in one of several locations in a child's home. Following delays of several minutes, the child is asked to retrieve the toy. DeLoache and Brown report that young children engage in mnemonic behavior during the delay periods, including looking or pointing at the hiding location and repeating the name of the toy.

Following the findings of DeLoache, Brown and others, it seems clear that preschool children engage in some planning related to memory (Wellman, Fabricius, & Sophian, 1985). These strategies lack the effectiveness of the procedures used by older children and often may not aid memory performance at all. However, Wellman (1988) asserts that preschoolers' strategies are every bit as goal-directed and influential to memory performance as are the strategies of older children and that they are used in a wide range of situations. Recent findings support Wellman's interpretation, although we must be careful not to attribute too much in the way of strategic competence to the preschool child, for memory-related skills are clearly more effective and more easily observed in older children.

☐ Factors That Influence Children's Use of Memory Strategies

Although even young children apparently engage in some form of strategic activity, the sophistication and effectiveness of children's memory strategies increase with age, as does their tendency to use them spontaneously in appropriate situations. Many factors influence children's strategic functioning, and

some of them are examined in this section: encoding, knowledge base, efficiency of cognitive processing, and metamemory. As you will see, these factors are interactive and can affect both strategic and nonstrategic aspects of children's memory. No single factor can be pointed to as the principal cause of strategy development. Depending on the strategy in question and the age of the child, some factors may be more critical than others, but, in general, an understanding of memory development requires an understanding of the many interrelated cognitive changes that occur over development.

Encoding

What one remembers is a function of how one *encoded*, or represented, the information. In encoding individual words, young children use fewer features to represent the words than older children (Ackerman, 1984; Ceci, 1980; Ceci & Howe, 1978). For example, in research by Ceci (1980), 4-, 6-, and 9-year-olds were given intensive semantic training for sets of words that they were later asked to remember. The children were told about common characteristics of animals (for example, diet and habitat). The greater the number of features they were given for the items, the greater was their subsequent recall. However, the younger children were more reliant on the externally provided information than the older ones, which suggests that older children spontaneously encode words with more features, resulting in elevated levels of memory performance.

Making comparisons among features when items are presented also varies with development and can affect the strategy of organization (Brainerd, Kingma, & Howe, 1986). Brainerd and his colleagues reported that although second- and sixth-grade children apparently encoded categorical features of words (for example, ANIMAL for the word *horse*), there was little spread of activation to other similarly encoded items at the time of presentation by either age group. This result is counter to findings for adults. In other words, the children encoded the individual items by category features but failed to identify categorical relations among the items.

Such "item-by-item encoding" limits children's ability to use an organizational strategy. For example, it is well established that when information is organized at the time of learning, it will be retained for a longer period than unorganized information (Bartlett, 1932; Posner & Keele, 1970). Using this logic, Bjorklund and Hock (1982) tested the recall of 9- and 14-year-old children on sets of categorically related items under two conditions: immediately after presentation and after a 4-minute period in which the children were engaged in another task. In a series of experiments, Bjorklund and Hock demonstrated that the 9-year-olds had not organized the items at input and, as a result, suffered a greater decrement in recall after a delay than did the older children. When biased to organize the items at input and provided with the proper prompts at the time of retrieval, the young children recalled at a level comparable to that of the 14-year-olds. These findings indicate, however, that preadolescent children typically do not encode categorical information in a way conducive to the use of an organizational strategy.

Knowledge Base

In recent years, several investigators have postulated that, to a large extent, age differences in what children know, or their *knowledge base*, are responsible for corresponding differences in memory performance (Bjorklund, 1985, 1987a; Chi, 1978, 1985; Ornstein, Baker-Ward, & Naus, 1988; Ornstein & Naus, 1985). Some data pertinent to this issue were presented in Chapter 3 (Bjorklund & Zeman, 1982; Case et al., 1982; Chi, 1977). Basically, when children are very knowledgeable about a particular domain, they process information from that domain rapidly and display enhanced levels of memory performance (recall Chi's chess-expert children). A similar interpretation was proposed for age differences in recognition, with older children knowing more about relations among objects in scenes and using this increased knowledge to guide memory performance (Mandler & Robinson, 1978).

With respect to recall, Bjorklund (1987a) has proposed that age differences in knowledge base can affect memory in one of three general ways: (1) by increasing the accessibility of specific items (item-specific effects); (2) by the relatively effortless activation of relations among sets of items (nonstrategic

organization); and (3) by facilitating the use of deliberate strategies. Research examining each of these alternatives is reviewed briefly below.

Item-Specific Effects

Item-specific effects are most easily observed when children are asked to recall sets of unrelated items (for example, *apple, army, clock, day, dress, flower, hammer, snow*). Recall typically improves with age, but there are no corresponding improvements in organization (Laurence, 1966; Ornstein, Hale, & Morgan, 1977). One interpretation of these findings is that individual items are more richly represented in the semantic memories of older children than in those of younger children, resulting in greater ease of retrieval. This interpretation is bolstered by studies using lists of unrelated items that are chosen because of their *meaningfulness* for children of different ages. In these studies, groups of children first evaluate words in terms of how meaningful each one is to them. From these ratings, recall lists are constructed that are balanced in terms of meaningfulness over several ages, thus eliminating age differences in knowledge for the information to be remembered. Under these conditions, age differences for short lists of words are eliminated (Chechile & Richman, 1982; Ghatala, 1984; Richman, Nida, & Pittman, 1976).

Item-specific effects are not limited to the retention of unrelated information but can also be found for sets of related materials. For example, Perlmutter and Myers (1979) reported increases in children's recall from the ages of 2 to 4 years for categorically related items without commensurate improvements in measures of organization. They attributed these memory gains to growth in semantic knowledge, with older children representing individual items with more features than younger children do.

Nonstrategic Organization

Concerning nonstrategic organization, Bjorklund has suggested that much of the improvement seen in children's recall of categorically related material over the school years can be attributed to age-related increases in the relatively automatic (effortless) activation of semantic memory relations (Bjorklund, 1985, 1987a). For instance, highly associated words (for example, *dog* and *cat*, *mouse* and *cheese*, *hand* and *glove*) are processed faster and are more likely to be sorted together by 5- and 6-year-old children than are nonassociated words that are categorically related (for example, *dog* and *lion*, *cheese* and *milk*, *hand* and *head*). Older children show efficient processing for both highly associated and nonassociated categorically related words (Bjorklund & de Marchena, 1984; McCauley, Weil, & Sperber, 1976). When highly associated words are used on memory tests, levels of recall and clustering are high for both younger and older children. When associative strength is low among categorically related words, however, only older children show elevated memory performance (Bjorklund & Jacobs, 1985; Frankel & Rollins, 1985; Lange, 1973; Schneider, 1986). One reason proposed for this effect is that semantic relations between high associates are activated with relatively little expenditure of mental effort, resulting in retrieval that appears organized (all the high associates are recalled together) but does not require the use of a deliberate strategy.

In other studies, age differences in recall have been eliminated or greatly reduced when children have detailed knowledge about the information they are asked to remember (Bjorklund & Zeman, 1982; Chi, 1985; Lindberg, 1980). For example, in a study by Bjorklund and Zeman (1982), discussed in Chapter 3, children in grades one, three, and five were asked to recall the names of their classmates. Age differences in *class recall* were small and were significantly less than age differences found for lists of categorically related words. Furthermore, children's recall of their classmates' names was not random but typically was highly organized (in terms of seating arrangement, reading groups, sex, and so on). Yet, when queried about their use of strategies, most of the children in all grades were unaware of using any special technique to remember the names. Bjorklund and Zeman proposed that the classmates' names represented a well-established knowledge base, with relations among names being activated with relatively little effort. Thus, a strategy was not necessary for successful retrieval. In other words, although the outcome of the children's recall looked to be strategic (highly organized retrieval), the processes underlying their performance were not but, rather,

represented the relatively automatic activation and retrieval of relations among items in memory.

Facilitating Strategies

Another interpretation for the Bjorklund and Zeman findings is that the elaborated knowledge base that the children had for their classmates' names allowed them to use memory strategies efficiently. In fact, Bjorklund and Zeman proposed this possibility for the older children, who might have identified categorical relations in their recall while retrieving names on the basis of the relatively automatic activation of semantic memory relations and then have continued to use this fortuitously discovered strategy for the remainder of their recall ("Hey, all those kids sit in the same row. I think I'll remember the rest of the kids by where they sit"). Ornstein, Naus, and their colleagues have championed this position, proposing that an elaborated knowledge base for sets of items allows the effective use of mnemonics (Naus & Ornstein, 1983; Ornstein et al., 1988; Ornstein & Naus, 1985; see also Rabinowitz & Chi, 1987).

Support for the position that an elaborated knowledge base facilitates strategy use comes from a rehearsal experiment by Zember and Naus (1985). These researchers, using the overt rehearsal procedure used by Ornstein and his colleagues (1975), asked third- and sixth-grade children to rehearse out loud sets of words in preparation for a memory test. They varied the children's familiarity with the list items, having a standard list (for example, *fern, astronaut, taco*), an easy list (for example, *shoe, doll, milk*), and a difficult list (for example, *limpet, galleon, rapier*). For the standard list, they found typical developmental differences in levels of recall and style of rehearsal. However, grade differences in both levels of recall and rehearsal style were eliminated when the third-graders were given the easy list and the sixth-graders were given the difficult list, clearly indicating that differences in the meaningfulness of the words to be remembered can influence the use of memory strategies.

Efficiency of Cognitive Processing

The effects that differences in knowledge base have on children's memory probably stem from differences in the efficiency with which children expend their limited cognitive resources, as in Case's (1985) theory. Items that have many features associated with them probably require less in the way of mental effort to be activated than less elaborately represented items, and memory strategies are likely to be employed only when children have sufficient mental resources available to them after executing other task-related operations (such as identifying individual items). When extensive mental effort is required to process relatively unfamiliar information, strategies, when used at all, are used inefficiently (Bjorklund, 1987a).

Research has illustrated the developmental relationship between *efficiency of cognitive processing* and memory performance (Guttentag, 1984). Guttentag trained children in grades two, three, and six to use a cumulative (active) rehearsal strategy. While the children were rehearsing the items, they were also required to tap their index fingers as fast as possible. The tapping rate during rehearsal was compared with the rate during a baseline period, when the children were only tapping. The degree to which the tapping rate was slowed during rehearsal is an indication of the amount of mental interference the children experienced because of the rehearsal task. In other words, the greater the reduction in tapping rate, the more mental effort was required for the children to execute the rehearsal task. In a series of three experiments, Guttentag reported that (1) when the younger children performed the rehearsal task as well as the older children, there was more interference for the younger subjects and (2) when interference was equivalent between the younger and older children, levels of recall and styles of rehearsal were more advanced for the older children. That is, the younger children required relatively more mental effort to use a memory strategy, and, in other situations, failed to realize the benefits of the strategy instructions although expending comparable amounts of mental effort. Similar findings have been reported for the strategy of organization (Bjorklund & Harnishfeger, 1987), with third-grade children showing fewer benefits of a memory strategy than seventh-graders despite displaying equal amounts of mental effort. Similar interpretations have been made by DeMarie-

Dreblow and Miller (in press) in a study using a selective attention strategy with children in grades two, three, and four, and by Rohwer and Litrowink (1983) in a study assessing training and transfer effects of an elaboration strategy by adolescents. In other words, memory strategies require effort. Young children process information less efficiently than older children, making them less likely to use a strategy spontaneously and less likely to benefit from the imposition of a strategy.

Metamemory

Metamemory refers to a knowledge of the workings of one's memory. If you were asked to recall your previous telephone number, for example, you would know that the information was there and that it was worth searching your memory for it. If I were to ask you for the telephone number of Jimmy Carter, however, you would not bother to try to find it in the recesses of your mind. It is not there and never was, making any attempt at retrieving it ridiculous. This is an example of metamemory, knowing what you know, what you might know, and what you definitely do not know. Kail (1984) described the process of remembering as occurring in a three-part sequence: diagnosis (deciding what needs to be done), treatment (executing the appropriate operations to do the job), and monitoring (checking how things are progressing). The use of strategies, discussed in earlier sections, falls within the realm of treatment. Diagnosis and monitoring are in the realm of metamemory. In general, the conclusion of research conducted over the past two decades is that metamemory knowledge increases with age, mirroring the increases typically reported for actual memory behavior (for reviews see Brown, Bransford, Ferrara, & Campione, 1983; Cavanaugh & Perlmutter, 1982; Flavell & Wellman, 1977; Schneider, 1985; Wellman, 1983).

How do we know what children know about their memories? One straightforward way of finding out is simply to ask them. This is essentially what was done in an interview study by Kreutzer, Leonard, and Flavell (1975). They asked children in kindergarten and the first, third, and fifth grades a series of questions about memory. For example, the children were asked if they ever forget things, if it would be easier to remember a phone number immediately after being told the number or after getting a drink of water, and if learning pairs of opposites (for example, boy/girl) would be easier or harder than learning pairs of unrelated words (for example, Mary/walk). Some kindergarten children asserted that they never forgot things, and fewer than 50% believed that phoning the friend immediately would yield more accurate recall. About half of the kindergarten and first-grade children believed that the arbitrary pairs would be easier to learn than the opposites or as easy.

Young children's problems in evaluating task difficulty are illustrated in other situations also. For example, there are age-related improvements in making estimates of memory span (Flavell et al., 1970; Yussen & Levy, 1975). There are similar improvements in knowing that it is easier to remember the gist of a story than to recall it verbatim (Kreutzer et al., 1975; Myers & Paris, 1978); that more study time should be apportioned to previously missed items than to previously recalled items (Masur, McIntyre, & Flavell, 1973); that the length of delay before testing should affect the amount of time one spends studying the target items (Rogoff, Newcombe, & Kagan, 1974); and that sets of categorized items are easier to recall than sets of noncategorized items (Moynahan, 1973).

In many situations, however, young children display metamnemonic competence. Even 3- and 4-year-olds realize that remembering many items is more difficult than remembering just a few (Yussen & Bird, 1979), and 4-year-olds pay more attention to the information to be remembered when they are given instructions to remember than when they are not (Acredolo, Pick, & Olsen, 1975; Baker-Ward et al., 1984; Yussen, 1974). One group of researchers reported that kindergarten and first-grade children understood reasonably well that re-learning something is faster than learning that same information for the first time and that the longer one studies something, the better one is likely to remember it (Kreutzer et al., 1975). When asked what they normally do to remember a phone number, even a majority of the kindergarten children mentioned

writing it down, illustrating that they were aware of external devices for remembering information.

Children also show greater metamnemonic competence when they are in familiar surroundings. For instance, Ceci and Bronfenbrenner (1985) required 10- and 14-year-old children to perform a task in the near future (for example, take the cupcakes out of the oven) and observed their *strategic time monitoring*, the frequency with which they checked a clock during a waiting period. The children showed less strategic time monitoring when tested in a laboratory than in their homes, indicating to the authors that children may display greater metamemory competence in real-world versus contrived, laboratory settings (see also Wellman & Sommerville, 1980). Children may also have the metamemory knowledge but be unable to articulate it. For example, research by Weaver and Cunningham (1985) replicated preschool children's poor prediction of their memory spans when asked how many words they thought they could remember. Predictions were more accurate, however, when the children listened to a tape recording of words, stopping the tape when they had heard as many words as they thought they could recall.

One important aspect of metamemory knowledge concerns the role of strategies in facilitating memory performance. Young children are often unaware of strategies such as organization and rehearsal, or at least they are not conscious that these and related techniques may be useful when they are given a specific memory task (Justice, 1985; Kreutzer et al., 1975). Furthermore, young children who have been taught a strategy are often unaware that using it facilitated their memory performance. This is illustrated in an experiment by Ringel and Springer (1980). They trained first-, third-, and fifth-grade children to use an organizational strategy. The children were given pictures and instructed to sort them into groups on the basis of meaning and to use the groupings to help them remember the pictures. Each group of children showed improved memory performance as a result of training (relative to an earlier baseline phase). The children were then given a third memory task to assess transfer of training. After completing training but before beginning the transfer list, some of the children were provided with explicit feedback concerning their improved performance on the task, whereas others were not. The fifth-grade children transferred the organizational strategy to the new task under all conditions, whereas there was no evidence of significant transfer for any group of first-graders. For the third-grade children, however, feedback made a difference. Those third-graders who had received feedback concerning their memory performance transferred the organizational strategy to a new set of pictures. Third-graders receiving no feedback did not but, for the most part, reverted to a nonorganizational style characteristic of their pretraining behavior. In other words, knowing how well they were doing influenced the third-graders' generalization of a strategy. The older children, apparently being better able to assess their own progress, did not require such feedback to transfer the strategy, and the younger children either were unable to transfer the strategy or at best needed more intensive instructions before generalization would take place. Other researchers have emphasized the role of metamemory in the effectiveness of strategy use and transfer, demonstrating that training in memory monitoring or other aspects of metamemory is responsible for the effectiveness and maintenance of strategy training (Ghatala, Levin, Pressley, & Goodwin, 1986; Leal, Crays, & Moely, 1985; Lodico, Ghatala, Levin, Pressley, & Bell, 1983; Paris, Newman, & McVey, 1982).

Given the impressive findings of the training studies, it seems reasonable that improvements in metamemory knowledge must be causally related to improvements in memory behavior, or metamemory knowledge → memory behavior. Yet, an argument can be made that metamemory knowledge grows out of memory behavior, or memory behavior → metamemory knowledge. That is, children perform memory strategies effectively and, as a result, acquire knowledge about strategies. Pressley and his colleagues referred to this position as the laissez-faire approach (Pressley, Borkowski, & O'Sullivan, 1984).

Research aimed at elucidating the relationship between metamemory knowledge and memory behavior in development was conducted by Cavanaugh and Borkowski (1980). They administered extensive memory and metamemory interviews to children in kindergarten and the first, third, and fifth grades. They reported that both metamemory knowledge and memory behavior increased with age but that, within a grade level, there was little significant relationship between the two factors. That is, knowing a child's level of metamemory knowledge did not predict well his or her level of memory performance when age was held constant.

Following the publication of Cavanaugh and Borkowski's paper, two reviews appeared in the literature, one confirming the lack of relationship between metamemory and memory (Cavanaugh & Perlmutter, 1982) and another asserting just the opposite: that, in general, good metamemory knowledge leads to good memory behavior (Wellman, 1983). More recently, Schneider (1985) concluded that both positions have some truth to them. Studies looking at metamemory/memory relations in categorization and elaboration tasks do not yield strong connections between the two factors for children under 10 years of age. The metamemory/memory relationship is stronger for tasks assessing memory monitoring, especially when the tasks are not overly demanding. In related work, Cantor, Andreassen, and Waters (1985) report that, within the same set of data, the relation between metamemory and memory depends on what questions are asked. When children are asked general questions about their memory performance, there is little relationship between metamemory knowledge and memory behavior. The strength of the relationship increases, however, when children are asked more specific questions concerning the reasons for making particular responses. In other research, Rushton, Brainerd, and Pressley (1983) illustrated that the correlations between metamemory knowledge and memory behavior are enhanced when multiple measures of metamemory are used in an aggregate (combined) measure, rather than computing correlations between single measures of metamemory knowledge and memory behavior. They argue that error is associated with the measurement of metamemory and that a more accurate picture is obtained when an aggregate measure, derived from several different indices of metamemory, is used. Basically, they contend that the relationship between metamemory knowledge and memory behavior is relatively strong when an appropriate (aggregate) measure of metamemory is used and is relatively weak when an inappropriate (single-task) measure is used.

In general, Schneider (1985) favors a bidirectional hypothesis with respect to the relationship between metamemory knowledge and memory behavior, as advocated by Flavell (1978b) and Brown (1978). Metamemory knowledge can result in improved memory performance, which, in turn, results in enhanced metamemory knowledge. Metamemory is obviously an important component in children's memory development. However, research findings suggest that metamemory competence is as much a consequence as it is a cause of competent memory behavior, the two being intimately entwined, with this relationship varying as a function of age and task variables.

☐ Summary

Memory is multifaceted, involving a host of other cognitive operations, and it is involved in all other complex forms of thinking. Memory can refer to the process of bringing information to consciousness or to the contents of memory. In the latter case, psychologists have differentiated between *semantic memory*, knowledge of language terms and rules for operating on information, and *episodic memory*, memories for episodes or events.

Infants display memory in habituation/dishabituation and preference-for-novelty paradigms shortly after birth. Conditioning techniques have been used to demonstrate memory in infants as young as 3 months for periods up to 2 weeks. Evidence of memory in infants has also been shown in search paradigms and is believed responsible for age changes in object permanence.

Recognition is generally good in young children and is the type of memory assessed in habituation/dishabituation and preference-for-novelty tasks. Age changes in recognition are found, however, when the task demands become difficult or when children can apply their world knowledge to assist them in the recognition process. More substantial age differences are found for *recall*. Levels of recall improve with age for sets of related and unrelated items and when children are to recall events or stories by reconstruction. With respect to *constructive* memory, young children make inferences as older children and adults do, and their recall is facilitated when information is schematically organized. Recall of events from infancy and young childhood is particularly difficult for people of all ages, possibly because information is represented differently by infants and toddlers than by older children and adults.

The development of memory *strategies* has been found to be of critical importance to age changes in children's memory. In general, the use of strategies such as *rehearsal, organization, retrieval*, and *elaboration* increases with age. Young children who do not use a strategy spontaneously can be trained to use one with corresponding improvements in memory performance. However, levels of performance are typically less than those shown by older children who use the strategy spontaneously, and children often do not transfer the strategy to new sets of materials. Preschool children use low-level memory strategies that seem to be the precursors of the more sophisticated and effective strategies used by older children.

A number of factors influence developmental differences in children's use of strategies and memory performance, including encoding, knowledge base, efficiency of cognitive processing, and metamemory. Age differences in *encoding* are reflected by younger children using fewer semantic features to encode items than older children and being less likely to make comparisons among features. There are also qualitative differences in children's encoding, as reflected by tasks that use operatively relevant stimuli. Age differences in *knowledge base* have been shown to affect children's use of strategies and their memory performance when strategies are not involved. When information is elaborately represented in children's memories, there is greater *efficiency of cognitive processing*, making the acquisition and retrieval of information easier. Finally, age differences in *meta-memory*, what children know about the workings of their own memories, have been reported. Although even preschool children reveal metamemory knowledge in some situations, it increases throughout childhood. The effectiveness of memory training and its transfer are greater when the training involves a metamemory component. Research into the developmental relationship between metamemory knowledge and memory behavior has yielded mixed results, with the two apparently developing simultaneously and interactively.

□ **Note**

1. **avuncular:** Of, pertaining to or resembling an uncle (*The American Heritage Dictionary of the English Language*).

9

Social Cognition

Taking the Perspective of Another

Social Information Processing

Children's Humor
□ Humor and Mental Effort □ Humor and Cognitive Development

Cognitive Bases of Gender Identity
□ Kohlberg's Theory of Gender Identification and the Concept of Gender Constancy
□ Gender Schemas □ Children's Theories of Gender

Cognitive Bases of Early Social Functioning
□ The Nature of Mother/Infant Attachment
□ Perceptual and Cognitive Bases of Attachment □ Mental Models of Attachment
□ Can Individual Differences in Quality of Attachment Be Responsible for Individual Differences
in Cognitive Competence?

Summary

As a cognitive psychologist, I tend to believe that most aspects of human behavior are a function, to some significant degree, of one's cognitions. I find this especially easy to believe of the social behavior of children. A child can be only as social as his or her level of cognitive functioning will permit. One cannot expect a child to behave in a socially appropriate way if that child cannot understand the social relations among individuals and the ramifications of behaving in one way as opposed to another. Social cognition refers to cognition about social relations and social phenomena. Nonsocial cognition deals with words, numbers, maps, images, and inanimate objects in general. Such "hard," or "cold," cognition can be contrasted with the "soft," or "warm," cognition that involves thinking about people and their relations with one another.

Much of a child's day-to-day activities involve interactions with people. These interactions require thought. Children must make evaluations of social situations and must understand their relationships with other people in a particular context. This requires an appreciation of who they are as social beings and who their fellow interactants are. It involves anticipating the thoughts and feelings of others and the execution of social "strategies." These strategies may be aimed at facilitating the formation of relations, such as mother/infant attachment or playground friendships, or the successful completion of some cooperative task, such as playing jump rope or baseball.

Children's thinking concerning important social phenomena has been studied for nearly as long as has children's "cold" cognition. For example, Piaget's classic studies of children's understanding of rules in social games such as marbles and their moral judgments of hypothetical situations would qualify as studies of social cognition (Piaget, 1932/1965b). Despite a long history of research on issues pertinent to social cognition, social cognition as an integrated field of study can probably be traced to the 1968 book by John Flavell and his colleagues concerning the development of role taking and communication skills (Flavell, Botkin, Fry, Wright, & Jarvis, 1968). From this time, research in both the adult and devel-

opmental literatures has exploded, making social cognition one of the "hot" areas of psychological inquiry in the 1980s (for reviews see Butterworth & Light, 1982; Flavell & Ross, 1981; Higgins, Ruble, & Hartup, 1983; Lamb & Sherrod, 1981; Shantz, 1975, 1983; Wegner & Vallacher, 1977).

There are few "narrow" topics in cognitive development. Research into memory, perception, and language involves many subtopics, with numerous facets to each. The topics subsumed under the rubric of social cognition, however, are even greater. Any "thinking" involved in any social setting or about any social phenomenon is a potential area of inquiry. I will not attempt to provide a representative review of the topics in developmental social cognition. Rather, I have selected five topics to review in relative detail, hoping to provide you with a flavor of developmental social cognition, how the research is done, and how it is related to nonsocial cognitive development. In the sections to follow, I review research in children's perspective taking, a relatively recent model of social information processing by Kenneth Dodge, children's humor, the cognitive bases of gender identification, and the cognitive bases of early social functioning. I conclude this last section with an examination of the effects that social factors (quality of mother/infant attachment) may have on individual differences in cognitive abilities, reversing somewhat the arguments made in the rest of the chapter. This section also serves as a preliminary introduction to the study of individual differences in children's thinking, which will be the topic of the remaining chapters of the book.

☐ Taking the Perspective of Another

Being social requires interacting with other people, and successful interaction requires understanding the perspectives of others. We have all dealt with people who seem to believe that anything that is of interest to them must be of interest to us, while giving us strange looks when we tell them something of particular concern to us, as they ask why anyone would be interested in *that*. Such people have a difficult time taking the viewpoint of another—they cannot easily put themselves in someone else's shoes—and thus are difficult to communicate with and unpleasant to interact with in a social setting. Although we could all provide long lists of such egocentric adults, the issue here is not of individual differences but of developmental function. In development, children are increasingly able to take the perspective of another, making them increasingly successful at social interactions.

The topic of developmental differences in perspective taking should be familiar, for it has been discussed in several contexts in this book previously. Piaget proposed that children much younger than 7 or 8 years of age are egocentric, in that they see the world from their own perspective and have a difficult time understanding that other people may have points of view different from their own. According to Piaget, this egocentric attitude permeates children's entire cognitive lives, including their understanding of social relations.

To reiterate briefly our previous discussion (see Chapters 2 and 7), preschool children's visual perspectives and communicative skills are more self-centered than those of older children. However, perspective-taking abilities in both vision and communication develop gradually over the preschool and school years and do not show abrupt changes around the age of 7, as Piaget hypothesized. So, for example, children as young as 18 months point out interesting objects to their parents, apparently being aware that they are seeing something that their parents are not (Rheingold, Hay, & West, 1976). Four-year-olds adapt their speech as a function of whom they are speaking to, realizing that people of different ages require that they use different tones of voice, different words, and different sentence structures to be properly understood (Shatz & Gelman, 1973). Yet, when the tasks get more complex, children's performance deteriorates, illustrating their egocentric perspective. For example, 4- and 6-year-olds, asked to describe complex geometric forms to another child, use idiosyncratic terms, making any selections by the other child not much easier than if he or she had never received the egocentric communication in the first place (Glucksberg, Krauss, & Weisberg, 1966); and 7-year-olds seated at a three-dimensional display who are asked to describe what a doll placed at some point around the display is "seeing" provide descriptions of what *they* see at that time (Piaget & Inhelder, 1967).

As can be seen, perspective-taking abilities develop gradually over early childhood, with the range of situations in which children can accurately take the perspective of another increasing with age. Sometimes, the same child displays aspects of both egocentric and nonegocentric perspectives in the same behavior. For example, 3-year-old Joey saw his mother crying, upset about something that he did not quite understand. Joey ran and got his teddy bear and gave it to his mother, telling her that she could hold it for a while until she felt better. Joey was showing empathy for his mother, illustrating that he could recognize an emotion in someone else. This clearly requires a nonegocentric perspective of the world. However, Joey's solution to his mother's problem was to give her his teddy bear. It made him feel better when he cried, so surely it would relieve his mother's distress. Although the teddy bear may actually cheer his mother up, it will not be for the reason that Joey inferred. His limited knowledge of adult concerns and his own history with feelings of sadness resulted in an egocentric solution, despite the fact that he was nonegocentric enough to identify a familiar emotion in another person.

One neo-Piagetian theory that deals specifically with developmental differences in children's ability to take the perspective (or role) of another is that of Selman (1976). Selman presented children ranging from preschool-age to adolescence with various dilemmas. One story dealt with a little girl named Holly, who was the best tree climber in the whole neighborhood. Worried about her safety, however, her father made Holly promise not to climb trees anymore. Later, a friend asked Holly to climb a tree to rescue a kitten that was stuck in the branches. Holly was the only person in the neighborhood who could climb well enough to save the kitten. Yet, she had promised her father not to climb trees. After hearing this story, the children were asked what

Holly should do, and why. From their answers to these and other dilemmas, Selman was able to infer their perspective-taking ability.

Selman proposed five levels of perspective taking in children. During the earliest stage (Stage 0: approximate ages 4 to 6 years) children know that other people are different from them and that they have thoughts and feelings. As Piaget had suggested, however, Selman concluded that Stage 0 children believe that other people's thoughts and feelings are nearly identical to their own. In the story about Holly, for example, a child may say that Holly's father would be pleased if Holly saved the kitten. Holly sees the importance of it, so surely her father would, too. At this stage, children understand the thoughts and emotions of others by projecting their own past experiences onto others. "A teddy bear makes me happy when I'm sad, so it will also make Mom happy." Selman referred to this period as the stage of *egocentric role taking*.

Stage 1, that of *social information role taking*, covers children from the ages of about 6 to 8 years. During this stage, children realize that two different people can have different perspectives of things that can lead them to different actions. What motivates one person to one action may not motivate another in the same way. Despite this ability, children have great difficulty keeping both viewpoints in mind at once, and they are likely to focus on one perspective at the expense of another. In the story about Holly, children may concentrate on her promise to her father or on the importance of saving the kitten. They are capable of noticing the conflict, but it is not salient to them. Children at this stage begin to think of the intention behind actions and realize that other people also take intent into consideration when behaving or when evaluating someone else's behavior.

In the next stage (Stage 2: *self-reflective role taking*), characterizing children from the ages of about 8 to 10 years, children begin to realize that other people can evaluate *their* actions. They understand that their own perspective is not the only valid one, and they can begin to evaluate themselves in terms of how others view them. However, children of this age cannot simultaneously coordinate their own per-

spective and that of another. A child in Stage 2 may know her own desires and those of her brother but be unable to coordinate the two to yield a successful compromise.

In Stage 3 (*mutual role taking*: approximately 10 to 12 years) children are able to take two points of view simultaneously. They realize, furthermore, that other people can take their perspective. In the story about Holly, Stage 3 children realize that Holly's father might not agree with her about her climbing the tree to rescue the kitten; however, they believe that Holly's father would be able to understand if she did save the kitten. Her motives could be expressed and could be understood by her father.

In the final stage, that of *social and conventional system role taking* (Stage 4: 12 to 15 years and older), the adolescent is able to take a detached view of a dyadic relationship and view it from the perspective of a third person. This third person could be a peer, a parent or teacher, or society. Children begin to compare their own views with those of society at large, and they realize that the social system in which they operate is a product of the shared views of the members of society.

Selman's theory has generally received support from the research literature (Gove & Keating, 1979; Selman, Schorin, Stone, & Phelps, 1983; Urberg & Docherty, 1976). Children's perspective-taking ability improves gradually with age, and as it does, their ability to successfully interact with others and to take a broader view of their worlds likewise improves.

☐ Social Information Processing

Recent theories of social cognition have adopted many of the tenets of information processing. Social information must be encoded, compared with other pertinent information, and retrieved so that social interactions run smoothly. The more skillfully social information is processed, the more socially competent a child is seen to be. Kenneth Dodge and his colleagues have postulated a theory that describes the mental processes involved in evaluating social information (Dodge, 1986; Dodge, Pettit, McClas-

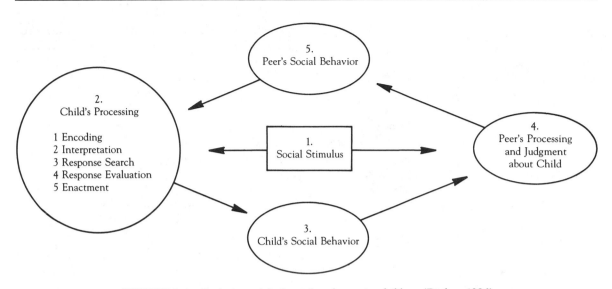

FIGURE 9-1 Dodge's model of social exchange in children (Dodge, 1986)

key, & Brown, 1986; see also Rubin & Krasnor, 1986). Dodge's model of social exchange in children is shown in Figure 9-1.

As can be seen from the model, there are five major units of social interaction. The first is the social stimulus, or cue. This is the information that a child must process. For example, a shove by another child, a smile, a scowl, a pout, and an invitation to join a game are all social signals that must be interpreted. The second unit of the model is a child's social information processing of these cues. A child must make sense of the social cues and decide how to respond. More will be said of this unit shortly. Once a child evaluates the information, he or she must emit some social behavior. Does the 6-year-old enter the play group by jumping in the middle of an ongoing game, ask if she can play, too, or just stand to the side, waiting to be asked? This behavior serves as a social stimulus for a child's peers, who make some judgment of the child.

Of major concern here is the part of Dodge's theory dealing with social information processing. How do children make sense of social information to select a proper social response? Dodge postulated five sequential steps of information processing that are necessary for competent social functioning:

Step 1: encoding. The child must first encode the social stimulus. This requires that the child be properly attentive and adequately perceive the social signal. The child must know what cues are important to encode. For a child entering an already established group, for example, whether he is greeted by a smile or a frown is an important social cue. Less critical are things such as what the other children are wearing or that Kevin needs a haircut.

Step 2: interpretation. Once encoded, the social information must be interpreted. What does this information mean? To determine meaning, children must compare this information with what they already know. What does it mean if the child is greeted by smiles? This will depend on what this child knows about the smiles of others in similar situations. "When I approach a group of kids I know who are already playing a game, smiles are usually a sign of welcome. But when Marvin smiles at me, it usually means he's going to trip me the first chance he gets." Children develop rules for interpreting social signals. These rules are probably not conscious and are executed in a matter of microseconds.

Step 3: response search. Once an interpretation has been made, children must decide what their next move is. They must generate a variety of response alternatives. Do they join the group? If so, by what means? Do they approach the playground bully, walk around him, think of something clever to say, or run away? With age, children have a greater number of more sophisticated options from which to choose, which should contribute greatly to behaving in a socially competent fashion.

Step 4: response evaluation. Once responses have been generated, they must be evaluated. Does it make sense to approach the bully, hitting him before he hits me, or might one of the other options be wiser? To what extent can children anticipate the consequences of their behavior, selecting the response alternative that will be most successful in the current situation?

Step 5: enactment. Finally, the child must execute the chosen response.

Dodge proposed that these steps are executed in order. However, steps of processing can be skipped. When they are, it is likely that socially *incompetent* behavior will result. The first response a child comes up with may not be the ideal response for the situation. If this response is not evaluated and found wanting, the resulting behavior will probably not ingratiate the child to her peers. Similarly, a child may make a decision based on misinterpreted information. The quiet manner of a peer while studying may have been interpreted as an invitation to horse around, or the smile of the well-known bully may have been construed erroneously as a peace offering. Also, as mentioned above, the wrong information may be encoded. The cues may be there, but they may have been ignored or missed because the child was attentive to other more salient environmental or internal cues.

Dodge and his colleagues tested this model with respect to the social skill of peer-group entry, that is, children's entering of an established group of other children (Dodge et al., 1986). Children in kindergarten and the first and second grades were shown videotapes of two children playing a game and were asked a series of questions related to peer-group entry. Questions were selected so that each of the five aspects of Dodge's model of social information processing could be evaluated. After viewing the video, for example, the children were asked to imagine that they wanted to join the group. They were then asked how much the child on the left and then the child on

the right would like to play with them. Answers to these questions reflect children's interpretation of social cues, step 2 (interpretation) of the model. The children were then asked the reasons for their decisions. Answers to this question assess children's use of specific cues from the videotapes in making their decisions, step 1 (encoding) of the model. The children were then asked to think of as many ways as possible to join the group, step 3 (response search) of the model. After this, the children viewed five scenarios consisting of the original video of two children playing followed by the arrival of a third child who attempted to join the group. The new arrival displayed one of five strategies for joining the group (competent, aggressive, self-centered, passive, or authority intervention). The children were asked a series of questions concerning the potential effectiveness of each of the five strategies. This assesses step 4 (response evaluation) of the model. Finally, the children were asked to pretend that they wished to play with the experimenter and were told to "show me how you would ask me if you could play with me." This corresponds to step 5 (enactment) of the model.

In a separate session, conducted one to two weeks later, each child was brought into a room in which two other children were already playing and was told to play with these children. Based on videotapes of these sessions and interviews with the children, each child's actual peer-group entry was evaluated.

The most important aspect of the results of this study concerns the prediction of children's peer-group entry (their actual social behavior) as a function of their skills at social information processing. In general, children who scored higher on the assessment of social information processing were rated as more successful at actual peer-group entry.

> Children who utilized presented cues (step 1), who generated competent and nonaggressive strategies in response to a hypothetical entry situation (response search step 3), who evaluated incompetent responses negatively (response evaluation step 4), and who demonstrated high skill in enactment of responses (step 5) were relatively likely to perform competently and successfully in actual group entry [Dodge et al., 1986, p. 24].

Furthermore, Dodge and his colleagues reported that these skills were relatively independent of one another, suggesting that each contributes something unique to social judgment and behavior rather than reflecting different aspects of a single social intelligence. The researchers replicated the results of this study in a second experiment and extended the findings to children's responses to aggressive provocations.

The work of Dodge and his colleagues clearly points to the cognitive basis of social behavior. Complex social situations must be evaluated and thought about just as strictly intellectual situations must be contemplated. Theories of nonsocial information processing have specified routines, such as encoding and retrieval, and structures, such as the short-term store and semantic memory, with relative precision. Although there is still much debate concerning the particulars of nonsocial information processing, there is also much consensus. The field of social information processing is less advanced. How can one specify the features of a social stimulus? How is social information represented in long-term memory? How is it retrieved? Can the concepts of the short-term store, schemas, and strategies, so useful for explaining nonsocial cognition, be successfully applied to social cognition? Social information processing is in its infancy. However, the work of Dodge and others (Rubin & Krasnor, 1986) represents an exciting beginning to research that will surely lead to a better understanding of the development of children's social lives.

☐ Children's Humor

Developmental differences in the appreciation of humor have been hypothesized to be a function of children's level of cognitive development, specifically, their ability to deal with symbols. Most developmental researchers have proposed that humor is reflected in the child's ability to perceive *incongruity*, noticing (or creating) a discrepancy between what is usual or expected and what is experienced (McGhee, 1979; Pien & Rothbart, 1980; Shultz & Robillard, 1980). Of course, incongruity can be de-

fined only in terms of what a child already knows, both in terms of world knowledge and in terms of general cognitive capabilities. As such, what is incongruous, and thus funny, to a 2-year-old (for example, calling the family cat "doggie"), will be perceived as babyish and just plain stupid to an older child. Likewise, because of older children's greater knowledge base and increased abilities to process information, things they find funny (such as knock-knock jokes) will go over the heads of most preschool children.

Humor and Mental Effort

According to McGhee (1974, 1976), incongruity is most likely to be perceived as humorous when the discrepancy is of some intermediate magnitude (compare with Kagan's (1971) discrepancy principle, discussed in Chapter 4). In other words, there is an inverted-U relationship between magnitude of cognitive incongruity and appreciation of humor. McGhee proposes that children (and adults, for that matter) gain the greatest satisfaction in resolving problems of some moderate degree of difficulty. Creating or comprehending humor is perceived as being an intellectual challenge, with "pleasure in mastery" being intrinsically rewarding (see White, 1959). The funniest jokes, for both adults and children, are those that take a little mental effort to figure out. Too easy, and they are boring; too difficult, and they are not worth the effort.

McGhee (1976) tested this theory by assessing children's appreciation of jokes as a function of their level of cognitive development. In one experiment, McGhee tested children in grades one, two, and five and college students. Within the first and second grades, half of the children were classified as conservers on conservation-of-weight tasks, and half were classified as nonconservers. All of the fifth-grade and college students were conservers. The subjects were read jokes requiring a knowledge of conservation for their appreciation. After reading each joke, the experimenter asked the child to rate the joke on a five-point scale in terms of how funny it was. An example of the jokes used in this study is as follows:

Mr. Jones went into a restaurant and ordered a whole pizza for dinner. When the waiter asked if he wanted it cut into six or eight pieces, Mr. Jones said: "Oh, you'd better make it six. I could never eat eight!"

McGhee evaluated the children's appreciation of the jokes as a function of their level of cognitive development (that is, conservers or nonconservers) and grade level. The children who found the jokes most funny were the first- and second-grade conservers. Nonconservers generally did not find the humor in the jokes, nor did the older children, though for different reasons. For the nonconservers, there was nothing to laugh about. The response given by Mr. Jones in the joke mentioned above is one they might have given. In contrast, the joke was trivial for the fifth-graders, taking little in the way of mental effort. Only for the young conservers was the joke funny. These children had only recently mastered conservation, making the challenge of interpreting the joke greatest for them.

Humor and Cognitive Development

According to McGhee (1979), incongruity alone is not enough for humor. Of course, a playful attitude and atmosphere will increase the likelihood of any incongruous event being perceived as funny. The same incongruous episode may be viewed as interesting or even fearful in one situation and humorous in another as a function of the cues available in the environment. Most critical for humor, according to McGhee, is the ability to represent objects and events symbolically. McGhee proposed that humor requires comparing some event with a similar event in memory, and he believes that children do not develop this ability sufficiently well until sometime between their first and second birthdays. He sees humor as a type of intellectual play that requires symbols. Symbols allow children to engage in fantasy and make-believe, and these "pretend" activities serve as an introduction to the world of humor. Preschoolers play with make-believe friends and slay make-believe monsters right out in the open. Make-believe, of course, is not always humorous, but it

allows children to craft incongruous and thus funny situations that do not exist in reality, such as pretending that their dog is a horse or that their playmate has purple hair.

McGhee proposed four stages of humor development, beginning when the capacity for fantasy and make-believe develops, sometime late in the second year. In Stage 1, typifying children between 18 and 24 months, children substitute one object for another in a playful game of pretending. For example, Piaget (1962) observed his daughter Jacqueline at 15 months clutching a cloth that vaguely resembled her pillow. She held it in her hand, sucked her thumb, and lay down, closing her eyes. But while she was pretending to sleep, she was laughing hard. To this toddler, pretending the cloth was her pillow was funny.

Children's first verbal jokes occur in Stage 2. The simplest of these jokes involve calling something by its wrong name. A 2-year-old finds great mirth in calling the family dog a cow, in labeling a hamburger macaroni and cheese, or in pointing to her eye and calling it a nose. Such humor may not seem all that sophisticated, but it requires greater abstraction than the object-dependent humor of Stage 1. Children no longer need a physical prop to make a joke. The word is enough.

Soon, however, children's humor becomes more complex, usually beginning around age 3. Now, it is not enough merely to call a dog a cat. Because of 3-year-olds' increasing knowledge of things in their environment, distortions must be more drastic for something to be funny. So, for example, a cow that says "oink oink" and has a curlicue tail is funny, whether that cow is seen in a picture or is just imagined.

What is humorous to a Stage 3 child is often a function of how absurd something looks. Recall preschool children's attentiveness to perceptual or literal stimulus features (see Chapter 6). This overreliance on appearance affects children's humor. A picture of an elephant sitting in a tree is funny to a 3-year-old, as is a picture of a fish swimming inside a car filled with water. These pictures are funny to 3-year-olds not because they defy logic but just because they are unusual. The incongruity is visual, not logical.

Beginning around 6 or 7 years of age, children's humor makes a more drastic change and starts to resemble the humor of adults. According to McGhee, it is the ability to understand double meanings of words and sentences that is the hallmark of Stage 4 and much of adult humor. A sentence with a serious (and obvious) meaning taken one way can be funny if viewed differently. A favorite of my daughter Heidi at 6 years involved a woman mailing three socks to her son away in the army. Why did she mail three socks? Because he had written saying he had "grown another foot." Appreciation of the joke requires an understanding of the double meaning of "grown another foot." Most 7-year-olds have the ability to represent two meanings of a single word or phrase simultaneously, and from this time on, humor takes a distinctly adult form, although most adults are still likely to groan at jokes that have an 8-year-old rolling on the floor with laughter.

Fortunately, children's humor develops beyond the simple jokes described above as their knowledge bases and cognitive abilities increase over the elementary school years. Such changes are especially apparent in children's appreciation of verbal jokes and riddles, which has been studied extensively by Shultz and his colleagues (Shultz, 1972; Shultz & Horibe, 1974; Shultz & Pilon, 1973). In their experiments, children were told jokes and were asked to rate them on a five-point scale in terms of how funny they were. The children were later asked to explain the jokes and were asked whether they could have a second meaning. The extent to which the children smiled or laughed at the jokes was also measured.

Most jokes and riddles revolve around the discovery of ambiguities, although some ambiguities require more in the way of cognitive abilities to discover than others. The earliest ambiguities that children can appreciate involve two words that sound alike, termed *phonological ambiguity*, for example:

Waiter, what's this?
That's *bean* soup, ma'am.
I'm not interested in what it's *been*, I'm asking what it is now.

The joke centers on the different meanings of the similar sounding words *bean* and *been*. Many knock-knock jokes rely on this type of ambiguity for their humor. For example:

Knock, knock.
Who's there?
Freeze.
Freeze who?
Freeze the jolly good fellow!

Although 6- and 7-year-old children can appreciate the two meanings of two words that sound alike, their appreciation is limited by their attentiveness to literal (here acoustic) perceptual features.

Following close behind in appreciation are jokes based on the dual meaning of a single word, termed *lexical ambiguity*, for example:

Order! Order in the court!
Ham and cheese on rye, Your Honor.

Here the humor does not derive from a confusion of two different words but revolves around two different meanings of the same word. One more example of lexical ambiguity:

How do you keep a skunk from smelling?
Hold its nose.

Most of the verbal jokes and riddles of elementary school children are based on phonological or lexical ambiguity. There are more complex forms of jokes, of course, involving ambiguities not of a single word but of the entire structure of the sentence. For example:

I saw a man eating shark in the aquarium.
That's nothing. I saw a man eating herring in the restaurant.

or:

I would like to buy a pair of alligator shoes.
Certainly. What size does your alligator wear?

In these two cases the jokes do not hinge upon the interpretation of a single word but upon how the whole sentence is interpreted. Is it a shark who eats men, or a man who is eating shark; are the shoes made of alligator hide, or are the shoes made to fit your pet alligator's feet? The humor is based on two different syntactical relations among words within a sentence. Shultz referred to these jokes as being based on *surface-structure ambiguity*.

More complex yet are jokes based on *deep-structure ambiguity*. For example:

Call me a cab.
OK, you're a cab.

Deep-structure ambiguity results when two different underlying meanings (or deep structures) are projected onto a single sentence structure (or surface structure). Appreciation of the humor based on surface- and deep-structure ambiguities is not usually attained until 11 or 12 years of age, reflecting changes in representational abilities associated with the onset of adolescence.

Masten (1986) demonstrated that humor appreciation in early adolescence is related to intellectual functioning. She found that the ability to create and comprehend humor (in her study, Ziggy cartoons) was associated with greater social and academic competence and intelligence in 10- to 14-year-old children.

Shultz and Horibe (1974) further proposed that there are two steps in interpreting most jokes: first, an appreciation of the incongruity and second, an appreciation of the resolution of the joke. Shultz and Horibe presented jokes to children between the ages of 6 and 12 years. The original form of the jokes had incongruity and resolution, as in the "Order in the court" joke mentioned above. The response ("Ham and cheese on rye, Your Honor") is both incongruous and presents a resolution to the incongruity. Other forms of the jokes maintained the incongruity but eliminated the resolution. For example:

Silence! Silence in the court!
Ham and cheese on rye, Your Honor.

There is incongruity here. Ordering lunch to a judge's request for silence is not expected. But the joke loses its punch when the ambiguous word *order* is replaced by the nonambiguous word *silence*. The third form of the joke removed the incongruity. For example:

Order! Order in the court!
I only want the truth to be told, Your Honor.

There is no incongruity in this version and, thus, no chance of humor.

Children of all ages concurred that the form of the joke in which the incongruity was removed ("I only want the truth to be told, Your Honor") was not funny. However, the 6-year-olds tended to view both the original jokes and the forms with the resolution removed ("Silence in the court!") as equally funny. Older children found the original jokes funnier than those with the resolution removed, with this difference increasing with age. Shultz and Horibe proposed a two-step developmental process, with young children finding humor in pure incongruity and older children appreciating the resolution of the incongruity.

Later research by Pien and Rothbart (1976) showed that when simpler jokes were used, presented via cartoons, even 4-year-olds could resolve the incongruity and found the resolved jokes funnier than those having incongruity only. In one cartoon, for example, a child is holding a book upside down and is told so by an adult. The resolution is that the child stands on his head while continuing to hold the book upside down. The version with incongruity but no resolution has the child standing on his head but without the book. Four-year-olds found the former cartoon funnier than the latter, indicating that even preschoolers are able to find humor in the resolution of simple jokes.

Research has clearly demonstrated that a child's understanding and appreciation of humor vary as a function of his or her level of cognitive development. Other factors, of course, affect humor. Some topics (aggression, sex) are more likely to be the source of humor than others, and humor plays an important role in greasing the gears of social interaction. Yet, the core of humor is cognitive. Simple, visual jokes can be comprehended by 3-year-olds. But as the basis of jokes becomes more abstract and less dependent upon visual cues, it becomes increasingly difficult for children to identify and resolve the conflict. Children's abilities to represent events, both real and unreal, and to view multiple meanings of a single situation determine what they find funny.

☐ Cognitive Bases of Gender Identity

Being male or female is a matter of biology, plain and simple. But behaving in a fashion consistent with societal views of masculinity and femininity and identifying oneself with males or females encompasses more than biology. This process of incorporating the roles and values of one's sex is referred to as *gender identification*. Our identification of ourselves as male or female has implications far beyond reproduction. Unlike other demarcations of social standing such as age, occupation, or marital status, our gender is one characteristic that remains constant throughout development. All societies make distinctions between the sexes, although, outside of reproduction, there are few if any universal roles or behaviors delineating the sexes. What are universal are the significance that gender has in defining who an individual is in society and the striving of children around the world to acquire an appropriate gender role.

Children learn early that gender is important and then work at becoming the best boy or girl that they can be. Many factors contribute to children's gender identification. One important factor is their ability to understand gender as a concept and that gender remains stable over time and is consistent over situations. Whether a boy decides to identify with his father is related to what he understands about his gender, that of his father, and the continuity of his own gender over time. What children know about gender varies as a function of their level of cognitive development. They should not be expected to behave as if gender is important if they are not yet aware that differences among males and females exist and that their own gender is constant. In fact, it is not uncommon to find preschool children who have not yet made up their minds about their adult sexual status. Most little boys want to be daddies when they grow up, but some are leaving the question open.

Kohlberg's Theory of Gender Identification and the Concept of Gender Constancy

One of the first people to postulate a cognitive basis for gender identification was Lawrence Kohlberg (1966, 1969). He proposed that children's understanding of gender develops in the same way as their understanding of the physical world. According to Kohlberg, knowledge of gender follows Piaget's model of cognitive development, with children not having a mature notion of gender until the advent of concrete operations, beginning about 7 years of age.

During the preschool years, children must acquire several pieces of knowledge about gender. First, they must know that the world is made up of males and females and identify themselves as one or the other. Being able to discriminate between males and females is not a matter of knowledge of genitals, however. Rather, Kohlberg speculated that differences in the outward appearance and activities of men and women (and, to a lesser extent, boys and girls) are the determining factor in gender differentiation for young children.

The Development of Gender Constancy

Knowing the difference between the sexes is only the beginning of the cognitive process of gender identification, however. Kohlberg proposed that children must realize that gender is not merely a transitory phenomenon. *Gender constancy* refers to the belief that gender remains the same despite changes in physical appearance. One of the first studies to test this aspect of Kohlberg's theory was conducted by De Vries (1969) as part of a larger study of the appearance/reality distinction (see Chapter 6). De Vries reported that 3-year-olds believed that a person temporarily changes his or her sex when engaging in opposite-sex behavior or when wearing opposite-sex clothing. That is, boys who wear girls' clothes or play girls' games are, for the time being, girls. Some young children refuse to engage in cross-sex behavior. "I *can't* play hopscotch, because if I did I'd be a girl, and I just can't do it!" Others realize the transient nature of this change and do not mind the momentary switch. "If I played a boys' game, like football, I'd be a boy, at least for a little while. But that's OK, I like football."

There are few unambiguous sex roles in our society, although each of us could easily list characteristics of dress and behavior that generally differentiate males and females of various ages. Young children attempt to learn these "rules" and apply them to ascertain what is appropriate male and female behavior. An early "rule" that most children adopt is that how one dresses or behaves is critical in determining one's gender. The significance of dress in determining gender for young children is illustrated by an observation reported by Stone and Church (1973). A new family had moved into the neighborhood with a baby. When a 4-year-old girl was asked whether the baby was a boy or a girl, she responded, "I don't know. It's so hard to tell at that age, especially with their clothes off" (p. 297). Another demonstration of gender being determined by dress came from my daughter Heidi when she was about 3. She declared that I could not wear a pink shirt because if I did, I would be a girl. The major difference between boys and girls, she said, is that girls wear pink and boys do not. Always fashion conscious, she added that both boys and girls could wear blue and yellow. Pink, it seemed, is the critical color.

Following De Vries's study, a number of researchers investigated the development of gender constancy in greater detail (Eaton & Von Bargen, 1981; Ruble, Balaban, & Cooper, 1981; Slaby & Frey, 1975). In a study by Slaby and Frey (1975), children aged 2 to 5½ years were interviewed about their belief in the constancy of gender. In agreement with Kohlberg's theory, Slaby and Frey reported three components in the development of gender constancy: *gender identity*, *gender stability*, and *gender consistency*. They defined gender identity as the ability to identify oneself as male or female and to accurately identify the gender of others. Gender stability refers to the knowledge that gender remains stable over time. Thus, little boys at some point come to believe that they will become fathers when they grow up, and little girls believe that they will become mothers. The researchers asked questions, making it clear that the children were expressing not just a preference but a necessity. (Question to a boy, for example: "Could you ever be a mommy when you grow up?") Gender consistency refers to the knowledge that gender remains the same despite changes in behavior or dress: "If you wore boys' clothes, would you be a girl or a boy?" "If you played girls' games, would you be a boy or a girl?" These questions may seem trivial to an adult, but answers by pre-

school children can be quite revealing (for example, "I *can't* wear girls' clothes, 'cause then I'd be a girl!").

Slaby and Frey reported an age-related developmental sequence, with gender identity being acquired before gender stability and gender stability being acquired before gender consistency (that is, identity → stability → consistency). Other researchers have confirmed this three-stage sequence, with gender identity being achieved, on average, by 2½ years, gender stability by 4 or 5 years, and gender consistency by 6 or 7 years (Eaton & Von Bargen, 1981; Ruble et al., 1981). This sequence of development is not confined to North America or to industrialized countries but has also been found in traditional communities in Belize, Kenya, Nepal, and American Samoa (Munroe, Shimmin, & Munroe, 1984).

An interesting aside to this developmental pattern is that children are better able to answer gender constancy questions posed about themselves than they are those posed about other children. For example, Eaton and Von Bargen (1981) asked preschool children gender constancy questions pertaining to (1) themselves, (2) a same-sex child, and (3) an opposite-sex child. The children answered the questions relating to themselves at a more advanced level than they did the questions relating to a same-sex child; these latter questions were answered at a more advanced level than the questions relating to an opposite-sex child (see also Gouze & Nadelman, 1980; Marcus & Overton, 1978). In other words, young children become confident of the stability and consistency of their own gender before they do of the gender of other children, particularly children of the opposite sex.

One criticism of this and related work was that the tasks often confused the children. Questions posed to the children were hypothetical or related to dolls. In the latter case, placing boys' clothes on a girl doll may be viewed as changing the gender of the doll, because the actual defining features of gender (the genitals) are not visible. McConaghy (1979) proposed that young children would display greater evidence of gender constancy if they could see the doll's genitals during the task. In an experiment conducted in Sweden, McConaghy asked children between the ages of 3 and 10 years gender constancy questions pertaining to dolls. For one group of children, changes in the doll's dress (for example, putting girls' clothes on a boy doll) were done so that the doll's genitals remained visible. The genitals were not visible for a second group of children. McConaghy concluded that children's understanding of gender constancy and the genital basis of sex are independent, with the former developing first. Young children in both groups asserted that the doll's gender changed when it was wearing opposite-sex clothing. In other words, what the doll wore was more significant to these young children in determining its gender than the genitals themselves.

As with many other aspects of cognition in young children, however, performance can be helped or hindered by subtle changes in the task. For example, MacKain (1987) asked 3- and 4-year-olds gender constancy questions about children who were viewed on videotapes. Counter to other research with children of this age, two-thirds of the 3- and 4-year-olds answered all of the questions correctly. In other research, preschoolers and second-grade children were asked gender constancy questions in which a pictured child was either referred to by a proper name (*John* or *Jane*), a pronoun (*he* or *she*), or a neutral phrase (*this child*). Children at both grade levels answered most of the questions correctly when a proper name was used. Only the second-grade children continued to show constancy when pronouns were used to refer to the pictured children, but even they failed to show high levels of constancy when the neutral phrase was used (Beal & Lockhart, in press). Thus, seemingly subtle differences in how the gender constancy task is administered can result in dramatic changes in children's responses. These findings reflect the fact that beliefs about the constancy of gender are not well established until middle childhood. However, they also reflect the fact that even preschoolers sometimes believe that gender is constant over time and situations. The range of situations in which they believe this, however, is limited and expands with age.

Consequences of Gender Constancy for Gender Identification

Why should knowing that gender is constant over time and over situations affect children's gender identification? For one thing, it makes little sense to learn the behaviors and roles of one gender if you are not certain that your own gender will remain the same. This issue was addressed by Slaby and Frey (1975) in the gender constancy study discussed earlier.

One tenet of social learning theory is that gender roles are acquired primarily (though not exclusively) through observational learning (Bandura, 1977; Mischel, 1970). Children watch adults and other children and incorporate into their own behavior that which is deemed sex-appropriate. Following this logic, young children should selectively attend to members of their own sex. Although this theory makes intuitive sense, research findings through the 1960s were mixed, with many studies failing to find any selective attention by children to same-sex models (Maccoby & Jacklin, 1974). Slaby and Frey reasoned that children's level of gender constancy may influence their attention to a same-sex model. Children who are unaware that gender is stable over time and consistent over situations may not be motivated to attend to a same-sex model any more than to an opposite-sex model.

In their study, preschool children were administered a test of gender constancy as described previously. Based on responses to the gender identity, stability, and consistency scales, the children were classified into one of four groups. Children in the first group had failed to answer correctly a sufficient number of questions of any type ($-\ -\ -$). The average age of these children was 34 months. Children in a second group had answered the gender identity questions correctly but had failed the gender stability and consistency questions ($+\ -\ -$). The average age of this group was 47 months. Children in the third group had answered the identity and stability questions correctly but not the consistency questions ($+\ +\ -$), whereas children in the last group had been able to answer all three sets of questions ($+\ +\ +$). The average age of the children in these last two groups was 53 and 55 months, respectively.

In a second session, the children were shown a 5½-minute silent video depicting a man and a woman engaging in simple, separate activities. The man was on one side of the screen, and the woman on the other. As children watched the film, an observer recorded the amount of time they spent attending to the male and female models. Initial analyses indicated that the children's stage of gender constancy was related to the amount of time they spent looking at the same-sex model, with more advanced children attending more to the same-sex model. Other tests compared the looking times of the children classified as low in gender constancy (− − − and + − −) with those of the high-gender-constancy children (+ + − and + + +). The high-gender-constancy children spent more time looking at the same-sex model than did the low-gender-constancy children, with this effect being stronger in boys than in girls. That is, the high-gender-constancy boys looked at the male model longer than did the other boys (108.2 seconds versus 63.0 seconds), and the high-gender-constancy girls looked more at the female model than did the other girls (86.8 seconds versus 63.8 seconds). Selective attention to same-sex models was found, but only for children who realized that gender was stable over time.

High-gender-constancy children are not only more attentive to same-sex adults but also more influenced by the behaviors of same-sex children. One study, for example, assessed the effects of televised sex-stereotyped commercials on children's behavior (Ruble et al., 1981). Children between the ages of 4 and 6 years were administered a gender constancy questionnaire and were divided into high- and low-gender-constancy groups, following the procedures used by Slaby and Frey (1975). Each child (one at a time) viewed a 5-minute Bugs Bunny cartoon, complete with a 1-minute commercial. The commercial depicted a child playing with a toy movie viewer chosen because it was sex-neutral. Half of the children saw the commercial with a same-sex child playing with the toy (for example, a boy watching a boy playing with the viewer). The remaining children saw an opposite-sex child playing with the toy. Approximately half of the children in each of these groups (same-sex versus opposite-sex viewing) were classified as high-gender-constancy and half as low. After the cartoon, each child was brought into another room. The experimenter explained that she had to leave for a few minutes but that the children could play with any of several toys in the room. One

of the toys was the movie viewer that had been seen in the commercial.

Of interest here is the amount of time high-gender and low-gender children played with the movie viewer as a function of which commercial they had seen (same-sex versus opposite-sex child). The results of this study are shown in Figure 9-2. As can be seen, there was little difference between the high- and low-gender-constancy children when viewing a same-sex model. Differences were dramatic, however, when the children had viewed an opposite-sex model playing with the toy. The low-gender-constancy children showed no differentiation. They actually played with the movie viewer slightly more when they had seen an opposite-sex child in the commercial. Not so for the high-gender-constancy children. These children knew that gender remains constant over time and that there are certain things that boys do and other different things that girls do. When these young children thought that a toy was appropriate for an opposite-sex child (as reflected by the commercial), they avoided it. The important point here is that this distinction is not made until children have acquired the cognitive sophistication to know that gender is a stable characteristic.

The results of this study indicate that other children serve as potent models with respect to sex-appropriate behavior. Once a child starts mingling with peers, what other children do determines to a large extent what is viewed as appropriate male and female behavior, often independent of the wishes of that child's parents. For example, friends of mine refused to buy guns for their 3-year-old son and restricted the amount of aggressive programs he watched on television. Nevertheless, the boy learned from his preschool peers that gun play is boys' stuff: he ran around the house pointing sticks, spoons, or fingers at people and saying "bang," despite constant reprimands from his parents. He had learned from other 3-year-olds one special thing that boys do and, over his parents' objections, was making it something that *he* did as well.

Gender Constancy, Sex-Stereotypic Behavior, and Intelligence

From a cognitive developmental viewpoint, gender is a concept that children acquire sometime by the

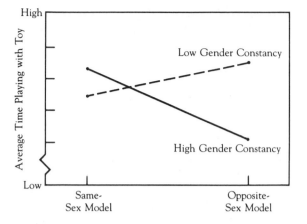

FIGURE 9-2 Average amount of time spent playing with a toy as a function of stage of gender constancy (high versus low) and sex of model in the commercial (same-sex versus opposite-sex) (adapted from Ruble et al., 1981)

early school years. Accordingly, bright children should acquire the concept of gender (that is, what gender-appropriate behavior is) earlier than others. Several researchers have examined this possibility. For example, in a study by Gouze and Nadelman (1980), children between the ages of 3½ and 7 years were given versions of Slaby and Frey's gender constancy task described previously. Children were also administered the vocabulary subtest from the Wechsler Preschool and Primary Scale of Intelligence (WPPSI) (see Chapter 10). This subtest is highly correlated with the WPPSI full-scale IQ test (Wechsler, 1967). There were positive correlations between gender constancy scores and scores on the vocabulary test, suggesting that, for children within this age range, more intelligent children acquire notions of gender constancy before less intelligent ones.

Perhaps a question of greater interest concerns the relationship between levels of cognitive development and sex-stereotypic behavior. Children who are more advanced with respect to gender constancy should be more aware of the different behaviors, roles, and expectations between the sexes. This possibility was assessed in a study of 2- and 3-year-old children by Kuhn, Nash, and Brucken (1978). The children were asked a series of questions concerning their knowledge of sex stereotypes (such as that girls

play with dolls and boys are strong). Children were later administered a gender constancy test. The researchers reported a significant correlation (.85; 1.0 is perfect) between children's knowledge of sex stereotypes and their scores on the gender constancy test. In other words, children who realized that gender is stable over age and consistent over situations were more cognizant of cultural stereotypes of appropriate male and female behaviors and traits than less advanced children.

Following these results, if knowledge of gender roles varies as a function of one's level of cognitive development, brighter children should behave in a sex-stereotyped way earlier than do average or below-average children. This possibility was investigated by Connor and Serbin (1977), who observed 35 play activities of preschool children. Some of these activities had been evaluated by a sample of adults as being "traditionally masculine" (for example, playing with balls and trucks), others as being "traditionally female" (playing with dolls and kitchen utensils), and others as being neutral (playing with a blackboard and puzzles). The amount of time each child spent playing in each activity was recorded and children were assigned a score for sex-stereotypic activity. Boys who engaged mainly in masculine-rated activities, for example, would have high sex-stereotypic scores, whereas boys who engaged mainly in neutral or feminine-rated activities would have lower sex-stereotypic scores. Similar scores were computed for girls. In addition, the children were administered the vocabulary subtest of the WPPSI, described above. The results of this study indicated a strong relationship between preschool children's scores for sex-stereotypic activities and their scores on the vocabulary test. When controlling for the effect of age, the researchers found a correlation between sex-stereotypic play activities and vocabulary of .88 for boys and .81 for girls. In other words, preschool children who engaged in sex-stereotypic activities had higher vocabulary scores than less sex-stereotypic children. Smaller but still significant correlations have been reported between tests of intelligence and 3-year-olds' knowledge of adult sex stereotypes (Weinraub, et al., 1984). These results are consistent with the position that brighter preschool children learn the significance of gender before less bright children (Gouze & Nadelman, 1980) and behave accordingly.

There are many levels of gender identification, however, and even young children who have mastered only the rudiments of gender differences may behave in a more sex-typed fashion than less knowledgeable children. For example, Fagot, Leinbach, and Hagan (1986) assessed the relationship between the ability of young children to identify pictures of males and females and their adoption of sex-typed behaviors. Children between the ages of 21 and 40 months were shown pairs of pictures (one of a male and one of a female) and were asked to identify the boys and girls (or men and women). The children were also observed in their preschool classroom to obtain measures of sex-typed behaviors. Differences in aggression, interaction with same-sex peers, and play with sex-stereotyped toys (for example, blocks, trucks, and carpentry tools for boys) were measured. The researchers reasoned that 2- and 3-year-old children with greater knowledge of gender differences (as reflected by their ability to identify males and females) should show greater sex-typed behavior.

The results generally supported the researchers' hypothesis of a relationship between gender knowledge and sex-stereotypic behavior in young children. Children who could correctly apply gender labels to the pictures were more likely to play with same-sex peers, and girls who performed well on this task showed almost no aggression in the classroom. Aggression is more associated with males than with females, so that preschool girls who showed low levels of aggression were assumed to be displaying more sex-appropriate behavior than girls who showed more aggression.

Unlike the other measures of sex typing in this study, toy preference (that is, which toys the children played with during school) was not related to the ability to identify males and females. Rather, boys and girls generally displayed a preference for sex-typed toys regardless of their level of gender knowledge. This finding is similar to one reported by Perry, White, and Perry (1984), who found no relationship between young children's toy preferences and their knowledge of sex stereotypes with respect to toys. Rather, children (particularly boys) showed

a preference for same-sex toys before showing a knowledge of which toys are usually for girls and which are usually for boys. These results suggest that early toy and play preferences are *not* related to children's understanding of gender. Instead, these patterns may be due to biological differences in activity and interactional styles between the sexes or to differences in the type of toys and activities adults introduce to children. As noted earlier, however, the relationship between preference for same-sex activities and cognitive factors associated with gender knowledge is strong for older children (Connor & Serbin, 1976; Ruble et al., 1981; Slaby & Frey, 1975). And differences in the rudimentary ability to discriminate between males and females are related to some aspects of sex-typed behavior among 2- and 3-year-olds (Fagot et al., 1986).

Gender Schemas

Contemporary cognitive theories of gender identification since Kohlberg have been based on the tenets of information processing, particularly the concept of *schemas* (Bem, 1981; Martin & Halverson, 1981). A schema is a mentalistic structure consisting of a set of expectations and associations that guide processing with respect to a particular content (see Chapter 7). Gender schemas influence how children process information about gender and serve as a way for them to organize information about sex. According to Martin and Halverson (1981), schemas develop primarily from observation. Sex is a salient characteristic in children's worlds, relating both to themselves and to others. It is thus used to organize information in place of other more subtle characteristics of a person or event that may be used by older and more knowledgeable children.

Children use their developing gender schemas to evaluate the appropriateness of some behavior ("Is this OK for boys to do?"). When children can answer these questions positively, they attempt to acquire more information about the activity ("What are the rules of football? How do you throw a pass?"). Accordingly, children's schemas for gender-appropriate areas should be better developed than their schemas for gender-inappropriate areas. Nevertheless, children do learn what is appropriate for both sexes. One set of activities is coded as positive and is to be pursued (same-sex activities), whereas the other is coded as negative and is to be avoided (opposite-sex activities).

A developmental assessment of gender schemas and their relations to sex-stereotypic behavior was done by Serbin and Sprafkin (1986). Because sex is a highly salient dimension, Serbin and Sprafkin hypothesized that young children would use gender to classify people and activities to a greater extent than older children would. Older children, whose knowledge of sex roles is greater and their gender schemas thus more elaborated, were expected to be more flexible in their classifications, relying less on gender and more on other characteristics of behavior. To assess this hypothesis, 3- to 7-year-old children were administered a *gender classification task*. In this task, the children were shown photographs of adults engaging in some routine activities. For example, one picture was of a man stirring a pot. The children were then shown three other pictures and were asked to choose the one that "went best" with the standard. One picture was of a man reading (same sex, different activity). Children who chose this picture as going with the standard would be making a classification based on gender. A second picture was of a woman rolling dough (different sex, similar activity). Children choosing this picture would be making their classification on the basis of type of activity. A third picture was that of a woman sweeping (different sex, different activity). This was a control picture, and children who chose this alternative would presumably be responding randomly. The children were also administered tests of sex typing. For example, they were shown pictures of objects typically associated with males (hammer, shovel, baseball) and others typically associated with females (iron, needle and thread, baby bottle) and were asked who would use each object—boys, girls, or both. When children said that the object could be used by either boys or girls, they were later asked which sex would use it most. The extent to which children made sex-stereotypic responses was used as an indication of their knowledge of sex stereotypes.

Following the researchers' predictions, children's

classifications of activities on the basis of gender declined with age. Three-year-olds chose the same-sex/different-activity picture 57% of the time. This percentage decreased to 20% for the 7-year-olds. Furthermore, children's gender classifications were significantly related to their knowledge of sex roles. Children who knew more about sex roles tended to make *fewer* classifications on the basis of gender. In other words, as children's knowledge of sex roles expands, so do their gender schemas. The better established children's gender schemas are, the more flexible they become in interpreting gender differences, and the more tolerant they become of people engaging in cross-sex activities (Stoddart & Turiel, 1985). Thus, whereas a 4-year-old may be aghast that his sister's teenage boyfriend wears an earring, the 7-year-old codes it only as an exception to the rule and realizes that it does not alter the "maleness" of the person.

Children's Theories of Gender

It seems clear that cognitive differences among children contribute substantially to their developing identification with members of their own sex. Controversy does exist concerning what aspects of cognitive development are most important and how gender constancy or gender schemas influence children's sex roles and behaviors. But there is no question that children's understanding of the concept of gender is important for development.

Children realize early that gender is an important dimension and formulate theories concerning exactly what it is that differentiates the sexes. Many of these theories are wrong. For example, a 6-year-old boy noticing that my infant daughter had brown hair, just like his, asked if that meant "she will be a boy when she gets older." A 4-year-old eating at an Italian restaurant with his parents and another couple noticed that his father and the other gentleman had ordered pizza, whereas his mother had ordered lasagna. In the car on the way home, the child announced that he had figured it out: "Men eat pizza and women don't."

Children continually gain knowledge about what differentiates males and females in our society, and

© 1984, Cowles Syndicate, Inc. Reprinted with special permission.

Copyright 1984
The Register and Tribune
Syndicate, Inc.

"How old do babies hafta get to start bein'
boys and girls?"

Children formulate theories about the nature of gender.
Many of these theories are wrong.

with this knowledge they continually devise and test
theories about sex differences. Their early theories
are simplistic, based on the grossest of characteristics
(clothing, for example), and often not even tangen-
tially related to societal sex stereotypes. However,
much like the scientist delving into a new field of
inquiry, they discard old theories, try new ones, and
eventually acquire the meaning of gender that is
implicitly agreed upon by members of their society.

☐ Cognitive Bases of Early Social Functioning

Infants learn much during their first year of life.
Perhaps their most important lessons are about social
relations and social responding. Humans are a social
species, and we are born immature and helpless. We
need a supportive parent or two to assist us through
the early months and years until we can fend for
ourselves. This process requires social interaction.

We must discriminate between the animate and inanimate and learn to respond to other people in a
way that is likely to increase social contact. We must
learn to communicate with other people. As we have
seen, communication precedes the advent of language. Babies signal parents with their cries, coos,
and smiles, and they can initiate or terminate social
interaction with an adult simply by making eye
contact or by turning away. The importance of
such interaction to proper development cannot be
stressed too much. Although as a species we no
longer worry about saber-toothed tigers running off
with an infant or toddler who is too far from its
mother, the formation of a secure bond between
mother and infant has significant implications for
personality, social, and possibly even intellectual
development.

The Nature of Mother/Infant Attachment

Attachment refers to the close emotional bond between an infant and its caretaker, usually its mother.
Attachment has been a popular research topic for
much of this century. It is universally recognized as
an important process in development, and it has
been analyzed from a variety of perspectives, including psychoanalytic (Freud, 1938), ethological
(Bowlby, 1969), behavioral (Gewirtz, 1972), and
cognitive (Kagan, 1974). Attachment is not limited
to humans but can be found in most altricial species
of birds and mammals (that is, those whose young
are born very immature). For humans, Freud considered the attachment between an infant and
its mother to be the basis for all subsequent social
relations.

Attachment is typically measured by some combination of three factors: proximity behavior, distress
upon separation, and the extent to which the
mother (or attachment figure) can soothe a distressed infant. Proximity behavior is a useful measure
for species or individuals that can locomote well.
Ducklings or goslings, waddling one behind the
other after their mother, reflect the infants' attachment. Proximity behavior is less useful for humans,
who do not locomote until months after birth. Yet,
the extent to which an infant keeps its eyes on its

mother can be used in some situations as a measure of attachment, as can more conventional measures of proximity for crawling or walking infants.

Distress upon separation (sometimes referred to as separation anxiety) typically occurs when the infant and mother are in an unfamiliar situation and the mother leaves. Not surprisingly, the young of many species find such separation distressful and cry, wail, or peep, depending on their vocal abilities. In humans, such separation distress is not typically found until between 8 and 10 months (Schaffer & Emerson, 1964). Often, infants who months earlier would go cheerfully to the arms of a stranger in the grocery store become greatly agitated when they are left with a familiar baby-sitter. Such separation distress is highly variable, with some children showing little more than a whimper and others shrieking uncontrollably for hours. (One word for parents here based on reports of experienced baby-sitters and child-care workers: It is not atypical for infants and young children to wail and plead with their parents not to leave them, only to settle down and be quite content within minutes or sometimes seconds after having been "abandoned.")

The ability of a parent to calm a distressed infant has been one of the most used measures of attachment in humans. Ainsworth and her colleagues have developed a procedure in which mother and infant are placed in a small room. After a brief period, the mother leaves, usually causing the infant distress. What Ainsworth is primarily interested in is what happens upon the mother's return. To what extent will her presence reassure the infant, allowing it to settle down and to continue to play or explore the novel environment? Based on such a procedure, Ainsworth is able to classify infants with respect to how securely attached they are to their mothers (Ainsworth & Wittig, 1969).

Based on the behaviors just described, mother/infant attachment would appear to arise sometime during the second half of the first year. However, the roots of attachment are firmly planted in the early months of life. Social give-and-take between infant and parent is seen from birth. Parents are responsive to their infants' cries, coos, smiles, and movements, and infants, in return, respond to their parents'

attention. The interactions that occur during feeding or diaper changing serve as the basis for later social relationships. During the first 2 to 3 months, the onus for this social relationship is on the parents. Babies seem to be more comfortable in the role of follower shortly after birth. Yet, they are not socially incompetent even during these first months, and they behave in ways that increase the likelihood of social interaction between themselves and their parents. By 3 or 4 months their ability to understand physical relations and cause and effect changes (see Chapter 5), and so does their ability to understand social relations.

I wish to make two points based on the above observations. First, attachment has its origins during the early days and weeks of life; and second, the formation of attachment between parent and child does not stem solely from the loving attention of a devoted parent. The infant also plays an important role in this process, providing cues to adults and responding to their social overtures. Of interest here is the extent to which cognitive factors influence infants' behavior in this social interchange. How are infants' perceptual and cognitive systems prepared from birth to be responsive to social stimuli? How do changes in cognitive development affect corresponding changes in social development? To what extent can attachment be construed as behavior guided by some mental schema? Finally, how do individual differences in attachment influence individual differences in cognition? If cognitive factors can affect social development, might not the reverse also be possible?

Perceptual and Cognitive Bases of Attachment

Abilities and Biases in Early Infant Perception and Cognition

Infants are born into a social world, and it would make sense, from an evolutionary perspective, for them to be prepared to perceive and respond to social stimuli. Research findings over the past 20 years clearly point to this conclusion. Counter to beliefs prevalent through the first half of this century, all sensory systems are functioning to some extent at birth, and infants are not born as blank slates. Rather, there are things they prefer to look at, smell, and hear. Some of these biases seem to be built into the nervous system. Others may be the result of early (in some cases prenatal) experience and a remarkable learning ability on the part of the young organism. Many of these early preferences result in babies' being oriented to other humans. The things they prefer to look at, hear, and smell happen to be associated with people. Such preferences may bias infants toward human contact; they may also help support the behavior of adults who are interacting with them. Attending and caring for an infant is more rewarding when the infant is responsive to the adult's social gestures.

Much of the research into perception discussed in Chapter 4 is pertinent to social cognition. For example, research into infants' visual perception has found a number of physical stimulus characteristics that seem to attract the visual attention of young infants. From shortly after birth, infants are attentive to stimuli that move, have areas of high contrast, and consist of curved lines (Haith, 1966; Ruff & Birch, 1974; Salapatek & Kessen, 1966). Each of these characteristics can be found in the human face. The entire head moves, as do individual components of the face such as the mouth and eyes. There is much contrast to the face. Infants during the first month, who tend to fixate only on the external area of an object (Salapatek, 1975), can attend to the contour of the head or to the contrast between the forehead and hair. Slightly older infants can gaze at the contour provided by facial features such as the eyes, nose, and mouth. And the face is clearly a curvilinear stimulus. We speak of someone with "square" features as an exception, and even then, the face and head of such an individual are more round than they are square. Also, the lenses of infants' eyes do not focus well for the first 2 months of life, with objects being "in focus" only when they are a specific distance from their eyes. This distance is about 8 or 9 inches (Haynes, White, & Held, 1965), which is about the distance an infant's face is from its mother's during nursing. Thus, if babies are going to see something with relative clarity, that something is likely to be an important social stim-

ulus. These biologically "wired-in" dispositions prepare infants well for life in a social world. Infants are oriented toward stimuli that, in most cases, will prove to be critical for their survival.

Perceptual biases are found for other senses as well. For instance, infants are more sensitive to high-frequency tones than low-frequency ones, possibly explaining their apparent preference for the voices of women over those of men (Trehub, Schneider, & Endman, 1980). Furthermore, infants 1 to 3 days old have been shown to display a preference for their mothers' voices over those of other women (DeCasper & Fifer, 1980), with recent research indicating that this preference is probably due to prenatal conditioning (DeCasper & Spence, 1986). To reiterate briefly a study described in Chapter 4, pregnant women read aloud a story to their unborn children during the final 6 weeks of pregnancy. Infants assessed shortly after birth (by conditioning techniques) preferred the story they had heard in the womb to another story, strongly suggesting that infants can learn the characteristics of their mothers' voices prenatally. Within 2 weeks, infants also prefer the odors of their mothers to those of other women (Macfarlane, 1975).

Other aspects of cognition early in infancy appear to facilitate social interaction. For example, the recently discovered ability of newborns to imitate some facial expressions of adults (Meltzoff & Moore, 1983) may play a role in early social development. These matching responses of infants may serve to maintain face-to-face contact between the infant and an adult via reflexive mechanisms during the early months of life when infants cannot intentionally control their social responding (Bjorklund, 1987b). Imitative responses decrease to chance levels around 2 months (Fontaine, 1984), possibly because they are no longer needed to elicit and maintain social interaction. Other researchers have suggested that infants can discriminate between animate and inanimate objects by 2 months. For example, Brazelton, Koslowski, and Main (1974) have shown that young infants regulate behavioral exchanges through repeated cycles of attention and withdrawal of attention to a familiar caregiver, whereas they behave impassively toward an inanimate object (see also Trevarthen, 1977).

All of the research cited above suggests that infants' perceptual and cognitive abilities bias them toward human social contact and, thus, attachment. Four-month-old infants may not show the same attachment responses as do 9- or 10-month-old infants, but they can discriminate their mothers from other women and show different patterns of interaction with familiar adults than with unfamiliar ones. The changes that occur typically around 9 months to produce distress upon separation do not reflect a new relationship between mother and infant. Rather, a previously established relationship is being expressed differently.

Cognitive Changes over the First and Second Years and Changes in Attachment Behaviors

Although the basis of mother/infant interaction clearly begins in the first weeks of life, it is equally clear that attachment behavior changes during the latter part of the first year. Infants now show the classic separation distress and, by 12 months, use their mothers as a secure base from which to explore novel environments. Kagan (1974, 1976) has suggested that these changes are related to maturationally based changes in how children understand their worlds. During this period, major changes in cognition are taking place (see Chapter 5, on sensorimotor development). Infants acquire the rudiments of Piagetian object permanence, realizing that an object that is no longer in their immediate perception continues to exist. They are developing a more sophisticated notion of cause and effect, displaying true goal-directed behavior (Piaget, 1952). Kagan also pointed to research into aspects of children's emotional development. Beginning around 8 months, infants often become wary of strangers, "active" unfamiliar toys such as a jack-in-the-box, and the visual cliff (Scarr-Salapatek & Salapatek, 1970).

Kagan proposed that infants at this time are developing a new competence, which he called "activation of hypotheses." They are now able to generate representations of past events as well as future ones. These representations can then be compared with the current situation. What we have here is the beginning of mental representation. Infants late during the first year can recall objects and events and act on those representations (Ashmead & Perlmutter, 1980; see Chapter 6). According to Kagan, they can generate structures *about* events and not just structures *of* events. For the first time they have the mental apparatus to attempt to figure out how some discrepant information fits with their previous knowledge (such as the fact that a toy hidden under a cloth is still there even when covered).

Kagan hypothesized that these changes in cognitive abilities are responsible for the separation distress associated with mother/infant attachment during the latter part of the first year. Unlike 6-month-olds, the older infants are able to generate questions or representations concerning separation from their mothers. Unfortunately, they are not yet able to answer these questions. Distress, indicated by crying upon separation or inhibition of play when a stranger is present, typically increases from this time to about 18 to 20 months and then declines (Lester, Kotelchuck, Spelke, Sellers, & Klein, 1974). Associated with the peaking of separation distress is a timidity toward peers. Children between the ages of 18 and 21 months show a wariness of unfamiliar children (Kagan, Kearsley, & Zelazo, 1975; Shirley, 1933). These transitions in social interaction are associated with another well-established shift in cognitive functioning: the transition from sensorimotor to symbolic representation (see Chapter 6). Children are now able to provide preliminary answers to their questions. If their mother is not with them, they can make reasonable hypotheses concerning where she might be. Note that this ability does not necessarily mean the cessation of separation distress. Dropping your 3-year-old off at nursery school will probably result in a brief resumption of separation distress. This is a novel situation, and the child will probably not be able to resolve the discrepancy of being separated from you and left in unfamiliar surroundings. With greater familiarity with the situation and the experience of being left with others, the distress upon separation will disappear. (As a parent who went through this, however, I must admit that sometimes I think our children persist with these distress displays just to make us feel guilty.)

Mental Models of Attachment

Attachment is reflected by behavior. But like cognition, which is inferred from behavior but never seen, attachment is hypothesized to involve a psychological organization that resides within a person (Ainsworth, Blehar, Waters, & Wall, 1978; Bowlby, 1969). In other words, attachment behaviors reflect some enduring cognitive representations of feelings of security and social relations and mechanisms to foster closer proximity to one's attachment figure. Bretherton (1980, 1985) has constructed an *internal working model of attachment* consistent with the theories of Bowlby and others, which is graphically presented in Figure 9-3. As in any information processing model, information from the external world must be monitored and compared with information the individual already possesses. Children must evaluate the information ("Is this a potentially dangerous situation?"), determine the accessibility of their attachment figure (AF in Figure 9-3), integrate that information, generate a goal or plan, select an appropriate response, and then perform the desired behavior. All of this decision making is done in the context of what children know about themselves and about their attachment figures. This "knowledge" is represented by the box in the upper-right-hand corner of Figure 9-3, "Internal Working Model of the Social and Physical World." Children establish working models, or schemas, of their attachment figures and of themselves. These models are based on information from the environment and are constantly being revised as a result of experience (thus, "working" models). These mental models provide children with a set of expectations for themselves and for their mothers under certain situations. "What will Mother do when I cry? How will she respond if I start babbling and making eye contact? Will I feel I need her assistance if that strange animal comes over and licks the milk off my face?" Attachment, when seen from this viewpoint, develops not only as a function of the quality of social interaction between a mother (or father) and child but also as a

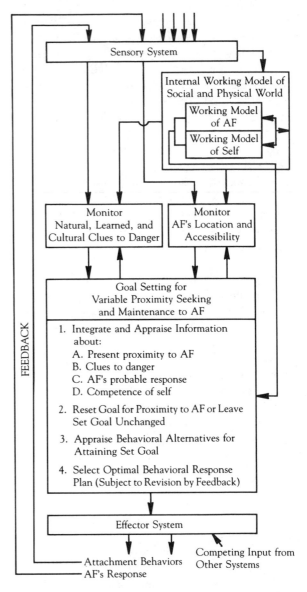

FIGURE 9-3 Model of the attachment system. AF is the attachment figure (from Bretherton, 1985).

function of the changing mental model the child carries in his or her head.

If attachment is conceived in terms of mental models, it would seem that the nature of attachment should change as children's abilities to represent information and relationships change. Furthermore, the use of specific attachment *behaviors* (for example, maintaining proximity, separation distress) could be supplemented with other "representational" responses, such as verbalizations about attachment figures or their pictures (Main, Kaplan, & Cassidy, 1985). For example, Robertson and Robertson (1971) reported the behaviors of a 2-year-old boy toward a photograph of himself and his mother over the course of a 10-day separation from his parents. During the early days of the separation, the boy hugged and kissed the photo, saying that he liked it. As the separation continued, the boy's behavior toward the photograph changed. He avoided the picture, insisting that it not be shown to him. These interactions were interpreted by Main and her colleagues as symbolic "reunions" with his mother. The child's behavior toward the photograph changed markedly over the separation period, although the "behavior" of the photo and of his mother toward the child were constant. What changed was the child's internal working model. The child restructured his model of the attachment relation even in the absence of his mother.

Recent research has used working models of attachment to assess attachment in older children (Bretherton & Ridgeway, 1987; Cassidy, 1987; Kaplan, 1987; Main et al., 1985; Oppenheim, 1987), adolescents (Kobak, 1987), and adults (Main, 1987; Main et al., 1985). In some experiments, children were shown a series of photographs of children undergoing separation from their parents (Klagsburn & Bowlby, 1976). Some pictures reflected nonstressful situations (for example, parents kissing their child good night), whereas others were designed to evoke more stress in a child (for example, parents leaving their child (1) on the first day of school, (2) for a weekend trip, and (3) for a 2-week trip). The children were asked what they thought a child their age would feel and do in situations depicted by the photographs. Their responses to these questions were evaluated in terms of emotional openness, the extent to which they expressed their feelings (the child in the photo would feel lonely, sad) and the extent to which they displayed distress during the task. In research with 6-year-olds, ratings of emotional openness were related to security of attachment with the mother at 1 year, measured in terms of behaviors of

infants toward their mothers following a brief separation (Kaplan, 1987; Main et al., 1985). The behaviors measured at the two testings are very dissimilar, yet there seems to be a single underlying structure connecting the two. This structure is the mental model children have for their attachment figure. Responses to situations will change over time as children's cognitive abilities change and as they venture out into the world more and more on their own. But there is a continuity of the internal working model of attachment. Early experiences are integrated into this model and influence the perception of later experiences. Thus, as the model changes, there is a continuity underlying development (see Chapter 1). The behaviors may vary considerably, but the mental model governing attachment-related behaviors traces its roots back to the earliest days of life.

Can Individual Differences in Quality of Attachment Be Responsible for Individual Differences in Cognitive Competence?

To this point, the cognitive basis of attachment has been explored. It seems clear from the literature that the development of a social phenomenon such as attachment can be greatly influenced by cognitive factors. Is it possible that the relationship might be reciprocal? Might a cognitive developmental phenomenon such as intelligence be influenced by social factors? This issue will be the primary focus of Chapter 11, which examines the role of experience in affecting individual differences in intelligence. It has long been believed that the experiences children have in the home greatly influence their intellectual functioning. These experiences are necessarily social in nature, in that most derive from parent/child interactions in the course of living in a family. What I wish to pursue here is a more specific question, namely, do individual differences in attachment lead to individual differences in cognition? Part of the reason for addressing this issue is to illustrate the difficulty of separating cognitive and social effects and phenomena.

Research into attachment over the last two decades has primarily followed the work and theory of

Mary Ainsworth (1967, 1979; Ainsworth et al., 1978). She believes that infants will become attached to their mothers or other attachment figures in all but the most extreme circumstances. However, the *quality* of attachment can vary considerably, and it is these individual differences in quality of attachment that are important for the social and emotional development of the child.

Ainsworth and her colleagues specified three major classifications of attachment: secure, avoidant, and resistant. The latter two classifications are sometimes lumped together as "insecurely attached," and no distinction will be made between them here. Quality of attachment is typically assessed by the *Strange Situation Test*, developed by Ainsworth and Wittig (1969). Briefly, the Strange Situation Test involves a mother (or father) and infant (usually between the ages of 12 and 18 months) entering a small room. The mother interests the infant in some toys and allows it to explore or play freely. This is followed by a series of 3-minute periods of comings and goings. First, an unfamiliar adult enters the room, talks to the mother, and interacts with the infant. Then the mother leaves the room, often resulting in a distressed infant. The behaviors that are important for attachment are those emitted by the baby when the mother returns. A securely attached infant often runs (or crawls) to its mother, greeting her warmly. The mother is able to soothe the child, so that the child will return to exploring the environment or even interacting with the stranger. An insecurely attached infant responds differently. It may refuse to look at its mother or show angry and resistant behavior. Or it may cling to its mother throughout the remainder of the session, never leaving her side to explore the room.

According to Ainsworth, securely attached infants get that way because of how their mothers interact with them. Mothers who are sensitive to their infants' signals of physical and social needs have babies who become securely attached. Mothers who respond contingently to their infants have infants who are able to predict reasonably well what to expect from them in various situations. These women are also warm and affectionate to their babies, leading to a secure attachment.

But what has this to do with cognitive development? Ainsworth's contention is that infants who are securely attached are more *independent* than insecurely attached infants and thus are more likely to leave their mothers' sides and explore the environment. Infants who are securely attached know that they are safe if their mothers are close by. If they do become frightened, they can quickly return, and their fears will be alleviated. This increased exploration, in turn, produces a more intelligent child. To summarize, Ainsworth and her colleagues proposed:

Mother's sensitivity to infant's signals → secure attachment → increased exploration → greater cognitive competence.

Intuitively, this pattern makes sense, but is it supported by research evidence? I know of no single study that adequately tests all aspects of the above progression. However, various components of the theory have been evaluated. For example, Egeland and Farber (1984) assessed patterns of mother/infant interaction and compared them with classification of attachment using the Strange Situation Test. Mothers of securely attached infants were more cooperative and sensitive to their infants than were mothers of insecurely attached babies. Mothers of securely attached infants were also more likely to have positive feelings about motherhood and were less likely to be tense and irritable. Other studies have shown a relationship between amount and quality of mother/infant interaction during the early months of infancy and later cognitive competence as measured by IQ or other standardized tests (Coates & Lewis, 1984; Cohen & Beckworth, 1979; Olson, Bates, & Bayles, 1984). More will be said of the relationship between quality of mother/infant interaction and later cognitive abilities in Chapter 11. A relationship has also been found between quality of attachment and exploration, with securely attached infants exploring novel environments more than insecurely attached infants (Ainsworth, Bell, & Stayton, 1971; Ainsworth et al., 1978; Hazen & Durrett, 1982).

Perhaps some of the most interesting research in this area has assessed children's intellectual and social competence during the preschool years as a function of their attachment classification during infancy. Research by Sroufe and his colleagues has followed a group of children from infancy through age 5. Infants were seen in the Strange Situation at 12 and 18 months and classified as securely or insecurely attached. These children were later observed in a variety of social and intellectual situations as preschoolers. The researchers reported that the children who were classified as being securely attached at 18 months showed better problem-solving behavior at age 2 than insecurely attached children (Matas, Arend, & Sroufe, 1978); were more socially competent, self-directed, and attentive at age 3½ (Erickson, Sroufe, & Egeland, 1985; Waters, Wippman, & Sroufe, 1979); and were more curious, flexible, persistent, and resourceful in problem situations and in better control of their impulses and feelings at age 5 (Arend, Gove, & Sroufe, 1979). In other research, 3-year-olds who had been classified as securely attached at 18 months showed increased effort during a competitive game with an adult (building a tower) following failure feedback (the adult's tower was bigger than the child's). In contrast, 3-year-olds who had been classified as insecurely attached at 18 months showed a corresponding decrease in effort as a result of failure feedback (Lutkenhaus, Grossmann, & Grossmann, 1985).

These results point to a relationship between quality of attachment and later cognitive competence. However, one must be cautious in interpreting this relationship. It is unlikely that being securely attached at 18 months *caused* children to be more intellectually advanced at age 5. Rather, securely attached 18-month-olds received greater support from their families to explore the environment and felt comfortable doing so. As the children grew older and their motor and cognitive skills became more advanced, they continued to receive support from their parents. That is, there was a *continuity* of parenting styles over time. Children who had sensitive and responsive parents at 6, 12, and 18 months usually had sensitive and responsive parents at 3 and 5 years (Arend et al., 1979).

This brings us to the question of whether quality of attachment is responsible for greater cognitive competence or whether the two (attachment and intelligence) are influenced by some common, third factor (parental sensitivity and responsiveness). There is no simple answer to this question. The relationship between social and cognitive factors is complex, and it is difficult to determine where social factors end and cognitive factors begin. It is clear that one's level of cognitive competence affects one's perception and understanding of social relations. As the research in this last section should also make clear, however, one's level of cognitive competence is influenced by social factors. The two are intricately entwined. There is a bidirectional effect between a child's intellectual abilities and his or her social environment. Both must be understood in order to appreciate the development of either.

☐ Summary

Social cognition refers to cognition about social relations and social phenomena. Many topics can be subsumed under the heading of social cognition, five of which are perspective taking, social information processing, children's humor, the cognitive bases of gender identification, and the cognitive bases of early social functioning.

One much-studied area of developmental social cognition is children's ability to take the perspective of another. Developmental differences in perspective taking have been studied with respect to vision, language, and role taking. Selman proposed a five-stage model, describing the perspective-taking abilities of children from about 4 years of age through adolescence. With age, children are increasingly able to take the perspective of another and are able to coordinate different perspectives.

Dodge proposed a model that adopts many of the tenets of contemporary information processing approaches to explain children's social functioning. Dodge proposed five sequential steps of information processing that are necessary for competent social behavior: (1) *encoding* of the social stimulus; (2) *interpretation* of the social information; (3) *response search*, in which children generate possible response alternatives; (4) *response evaluation*, in which children evaluate the potential effectiveness of the various alternatives; and (5) *enactment*, in which children execute the chosen response. Research by Dodge and his colleagues has shown a relationship between the efficacy of children's social information processing and their social behavior, suggesting that how children process social information plays a significant role in their social competence.

Children's humor develops through a series of stages, based on their level of cognitive development. Humor is based on the identification of *incongruity*, and incongruity is most likely to be perceived when the discrepancy is of some intermediate magnitude. McGhee proposed four stages of humor development. In Stage 1, 18- to 24-month-old children substitute one object for another in a game of pretending. In Stage 2, the first verbal jokes are made, with children calling objects by their wrong name. In Stage 3, humor is a function of how ridiculous something looks. In Stage 4, beginning around 6 or 7 years, children can understand double meanings of words, and their humor becomes more adult-like. Humor changes over the school years, with the type of verbal jokes children appreciate becoming more sophisticated into adolescence.

Children's knowledge of the constancy of gender was proposed by Kohlberg as important for a child's developing sense of gender identification. Research has shown a developmental progression of *gender constancy*, with children being able to *identify* males and females before they understand that gender is *stable* over time, followed by a realization that gender remains *consistent* over situations. Level of gender constancy has been associated with children's attention to same-sex models and their knowledge of sex stereotypes.

Gender schemas are mentalistic structures consisting of a set of associations and expectations related to gender. These schemas influence how children process information related to gender. As children's knowledge of gender expands, their schemas change, resulting in a more sophisticated use of gender in classifying people and behavior.

With respect to the cognitive bases of early social functioning, infants seem well prepared by biology to become attached to their mothers or other attachment figures. The perceptual and learning systems of infants bias them to attend to social stimuli, increasing the likelihood of parent/child interaction and, thus, attachment.

Changes in attachment behavior over time have been interpreted by some as reflecting changes in cognition. For example, Kagan proposed that the advent of separation distress in the latter part of the first year is due to infants being able to activate hypotheses concerning their mothers' disappearance but being unable to resolve the conflict. Other changes in distress behavior, seen between 18 and 22 months, are similarly associated with changes in mental representational abilities. Attachment can also be thought of in terms of *mental models*. Knowledge of one's attachment figure is represented by a schema, or *internal working model*, which changes as a result of experience.

Individual differences in quality of attachment have also been hypothesized to be responsible in part for individual differences in cognitive competence. Ainsworth proposed that mothers who are responsive to their infants' physical and social signals will have securely attached infants, who as a result will feel comfortable to explore their environment and, in turn, will develop greater cognitive skills. Research has shown that such a pattern probably exists. However, the results of such research are difficult to interpret because of the difficulty of distinguishing social from cognitive phenomena.

10

Individual Differences
in Intelligence

Approaches to the Study of Intelligence

☐ The Psychometric Approach ☐ Information Processing Approaches
☐ Piagetian Approaches ☐ Sternberg's Triarchic Theory

The Heritability of Intelligence

☐ The Concept of Heritability ☐ Elementary Cognitive Tasks and Intelligence
☐ Familial Studies of Intelligence ☐ Scarr and McCartney's Genotype → Environment Theory

Summary

"Look at the fingers of your right hand. No two are alike. That's the way *children* are." This homily, attributed to a retired elementary school teacher, reflects the individuality of children. In the remaining chapters of this book I deal with this uniqueness, assessing individual differences in children's thinking.

Up to this point, my focus has been on *developmental function*, the form that cognition takes in the species over time. Theories and research on developmental function are concerned with cognition in the typical child at any given age or stage and the general processes that influence transitions from lower levels of cognitive functioning to more advanced levels. As we have seen, much interest has been shown in developmental function. Comparable attention, however, has been given to the origins and stability of *individual differences* in children's thinking. At any given age, some children function better than others. Differences in rate of development are partly responsible. Johnny attains concrete operations 1 year ahead of Joey, but Joey will eventually catch up. Yet, within any given developmental level, some children solve most problems more efficiently than other children despite the qualitatively similar form of their cognitions. How can such differences be conceptualized? How and why do these individual differences come about? Are they stable over time? Are their origins found in biology or in the environment?

This brings us to the concept of *intelligence*. If you were to ask a psychologist her specialty and she stated "the study of intelligence," she would probably be referring to *individual differences* in how people process information, or think. The term *intelligence* itself need not be used solely to reflect the nature of individual differences in thought. As the term is used today, however, investigations of "intelligence" are almost always concerned with the magnitude, pattern, origins, or stability of individual differences in mental functioning.

Intelligence is an elusive concept. Generally, it refers to acting or thinking in ways that are goal-directed and adaptive (Sternberg & Slater, 1982). This definition covers a lot of ground, allowing much leeway for theorists to sculpture their own meanings of the concept while still being understood by others. Although what is viewed to be important in determining intelligence varies from theorist to theorist, there seems to be general agreement among professional researchers and laypeople alike about the common characteristics of intelligence. Based on interviews conducted both with the "man (and woman) on the street" and psychologists who study intelligence, Sternberg, Conway, Ketron, and Bernstein (1981) reported that people believe that intelligence involves three main sets of skills:

1. *Practical problem-solving ability:* These skills include getting to the heart of a problem, interpreting information accurately, seeing all aspects of a problem, and reasoning logically.
2. *Verbal ability:* These skills include speaking and writing clearly and articulately, dealing effectively with people, having detailed knowledge about a particular field, reading widely and with good comprehension, and having a good vocabulary.
3. *Social competence:* These skills include displaying curiosity, being sensitive to the needs and desires of others, being on time for appointments, having a social conscience, and making carefully considered and fair judgments.

Sternberg and his colleagues (1981) referred to such conceptions as *implicit* theories of intelligence and contrasted them with the *explicit* theories that psychologists and educators construct when generating their formal models and measures of mental functioning. In the greater part of this chapter, I examine some explicit theories of intelligence. In the later sections of the chapter, I discuss the issue of the heritability of intelligence. To what extent can differences in intelligence between people be attributed to inheritance? In the chapter to follow I will examine in greater detail the role of experience in shaping intelligence.

☐ Approaches to the Study of Intelligence
The Psychometric Approach
Factors of Intelligence
The major approach to the study of individual differences in intelligence since the turn of the century has been the *psychometric* (or differential) *approach*. Psychometric theories of intelligence have as their

basis a belief that intelligence can be described in terms of mental *factors* and that tests can be constructed that reveal individual differences in the factors that underlie mental performance. Factors are related mental skills that (typically) affect thinking in a wide range of situations. For example, a verbal factor may be tapped by tests assessing a variety of more specific verbal skills such as vocabulary and reading comprehension. An individual may possess a general facility with words and language concepts that influences his or her performance on most tasks involving the processing of language terms and concepts.

What constitutes a factor is determined by statistical tests known as *factor analyses*. In factor analysis, a large number of test items are administered to people, and the resulting data are examined to see which items fit together well. Tests may show, for example, that the pattern of individual differences among people is very similar on the following sets of items: vocabulary, reading comprehension, story completion, and verbal analogies. That is, people who score high on one of these tests usually score high on all of them, whereas people who score low on one usually score low on all of them. In contrast, performance on these test items may not correlate well with performance on items that involve rotating three-dimensional figures, solving maze problems, or quickly placing geometric forms in a form board, although these three sets may all correlate highly with one another. What do the first tests (vocabulary, reading comprehension, story completion, and verbal analogies) have in common? It is not difficult to conclude that all involve some aspect of verbal thinking, whereas the second set (3-D rotation, maze learning, and form-board performance) are all basically nonverbal and involve some form of spatial thinking. Accordingly, based on the results of the statistical analysis, an investigator can assume that two factors that account for individual differences among people are verbal ability and spatial thinking.

Patterns of performance are not always clear-cut, however. The extent to which sets of test items correlate with one another is a matter of degree. Only in textbooks do we find perfect data that can be interpreted in only one way. Thus, how one defines

mental factors is influenced not only by the data but also by one's theoretical and statistical perspective.

Determining the number and makeup of factors is a function of the items included on a test (you could not very well have a verbal component if no verbal items were included in your test) and the particular way one performs statistical analyses. Using variants of the same form of analysis, the number of factors that have been proposed to account for human intelligence has varied considerably. On the one hand, Spearman (1927) proposed that intelligence consists of only two kinds of factors. The most critical factor was viewed as a general one, labeled *g*, which influences performance on all intellectual tasks. The other type of factors were called *specific*, and they were not generalizable, with each specific factor being pertinent only to a single task. As such, these highly specified abilities are of little interest to psychologists trying to construct theories to explain individual differences among people. In other words, from Spearman's point of view, intelligence is viewed as existing on a single dimension and not as being some multifaceted phenomenon. People who behave intelligently in one situation should behave intelligently in other situations.

At the other extreme, Guilford's (1967, 1988) structure-of-the-intellect theory includes 180 unique intellectual factors organized along three dimensions. One dimension includes six forms of mental operations, a second, five contents on which the operations function, and a third, six possible products that result from applying a given operation to a particular content. Figure 10-1, on page 202, illustrates Guilford's model.

Between the extremes of Spearman and Guilford lie theories such as Thurstone's (1938), which includes seven "primary mental abilities":

1. *verbal comprehension*, which includes vocabulary and reading comprehension
2. *verbal fluency*, as measured by tests that require rapid production of words ("Tell me all names of animals that you can as quickly as you can")
3. *number*, as reflected by arithmetic word problems
4. *spatial visualization*, measured by the mental manipulation of symbols or geometric forms

CONTENT

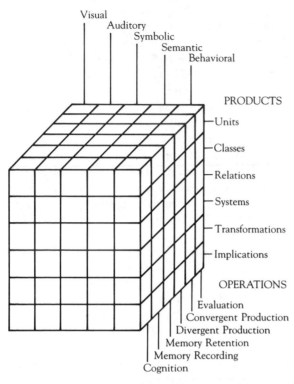

FIGURE 10-1 Guilford's structure-of-the-intellect model. Guilford specified 180 unique cognitive factors varying as a function of (1) the type of mental operation, (2) the type of content, and (3) the product that results from applying a given operation to a particular content (Guilford, 1988).

5. *memory*, evaluated by tests of recall for lists of words or of the ability to associate names with pictures of people
6. *reasoning*, as exemplified in analogies (for example, doctor is to hospital as teacher is to ———?)
7. *perceptual speed*, involving the rapid recognition of symbols, such as crossing out all the 3s that are embedded in a string of numbers

Also falling between the extremes is Cattell's (1963, 1971) theory, which recognizes both a general intellectual factor similar to Spearman's *g* and two second-order factors that he called *fluid* and *crystallized abilities*. Basically, fluid intelligence is proposed to be biologically determined and is reflected in tests of

memory span and most tests of spatial thinking. In contrast, crystallized intelligence is best reflected in tests of verbal comprehension or social relations, skills that are more highly dependent upon cultural context and experience.

Despite this plurality of theories, the diverse models are not as discrepant as they appear on first examination. In fact, whether there is only a single factor or many factors that make up intelligence is a matter of interpretation even within a given psychometric theory. Toward the end of his career, for example, Spearman acknowledged that group factors (such as verbal abilities) do exist along with a more general intellectual factor. Similarly, Thurstone conceded that his primary mental abilities typically do correlate with one another, suggesting a general factor of intelligence. Thus, despite their diversity, most psychometricians would agree that there is a general factor of intelligence but that there are also "lower-level" factors, reflective of more specific skills. Differences among the various theorists seem to concentrate on the extent to which intelligence can be described by *g* or by other sets of lower-level factors.

It is unquestionable that psychometric theories have had a significant impact on research and practice in psychology over the course of this century. For example, many of the achievement tests administered regularly in American schools are based on extensions of Thurstone's multifactor model; school curricula have been based on these theories, as exemplified by Meeker's (1969) application of Guilford's structure-of-the-intellect model; and researchers from a variety of theoretical perspectives continue to search for a general intellectual factor (Eysenck, 1982; Jensen, 1985) or to argue that the quest for *g* is fruitless (Borkowski & Maxwell, 1985; Detterman, 1982).

IQ Tests
Although mental testing has had a profound influence on psychologists' attempts to conceptualize the nature of intelligence, it has had its greatest impact in the form of *IQ tests*. Intelligence testing is so widespread in our society that it is virtually impossible for a child to graduate from high school without having been administered at least one IQ test and

over a dozen tests assessing more specific academic aptitudes. The significance of the IQ test to our culture was illustrated when *Science 84*, a popular publication of the American Academy for the Advancement of Science, listed the 20 scientific discoveries of the century that have most influenced modern life. On the list along with discoveries such as nuclear fission and DNA and technological innovations including the transistor and air flight was the IQ test.

IQ tests are less the result of psychometric theorizing than they are the instruments that produce the raw data for theory construction. IQ tests were developed at the turn of the century in France by Alfred Binet and Theodore Simon (1905, 1908). The original tests, and to a large extent even modern versions, were not based on theory. Rather, they were constructed to assess school-related abilities and to differentiate among those children who could benefit from standard school instruction and those who would require special education. It would be inappropriate, however, to classify IQ tests as atheoretical. As will be seen below, modern IQ tests are based on certain concepts of what intelligence "is." Nevertheless, pragmatic considerations of which items best differentiate children within a given age are critical in the construction of IQ tests, causing some to question their contribution to understanding the underlying mechanisms of intelligence (Sternberg, 1985).

There is an abundance of IQ-type tests available today. Many are pencil-and-paper tests that can be administered to a group. However, the standard tests by which most others are judged include the Stanford-Binet and the three intelligence scales developed by David Wechsler: the Wechsler Preschool and Primary Scale of Intelligence (WPPSI), the Wechsler Intelligence Scale for Children—Revised (WISC-R), and the Wechsler Adult Intelligence Scale—Revised (WAIS-R). These tests have been standardized on large samples and are individually administered by trained examiners using standardized procedures.

The Stanford-Binet was developed in 1916 by Lewis Terman, who made extensive revisions of Binet's original scale. The test has gone through revisions from time to time, the most recent one being in 1986 (Thorndike, Hagen, & Sattler, 1986). The current version consists of 15 subtests, organized in a three-level hierarchical model of the structure of intelligence. A general reasoning factor (*g*) is the most inclusive (see Table 10-1). The authors admit that the exact nature of this general ability is unclear but maintain that *g* reflects the type of intelligence that a person uses to solve problems that he or she has not been previously taught to solve.

There are three second-level factors: *crystallized abilities*, *fluid–analytic abilities*, and *short-term memory*. Crystallized abilities reflect cognitive skills used for solving verbal and quantitative problems. These abilities are greatly influenced by the environment, particularly school. Fluid/analytic abilities represent cognitive skills necessary for solving novel problems involving nonverbal stimuli, with the knowledge necessary to solve such problems being less influenced by academic experience. The short-term memory factor involves people's ability to retain newly perceived information for a brief time and to

TABLE 10-1   Three-Level Hierarchical Model of Stanford-Binet Intelligence Scale (adapted from Thorndike, Hagen, and Sattler, 1986)

g			
Crystallized abilities		Fluid–analytic abilities	Short-term memory
Verbal reasoning	Quantitative reasoning	Abstract/visual reasoning	
Vocabulary	Quantitative	Pattern analysis	Bead memory
Comprehension	Number series	Copying	Memory for sentences
Absurdities	Equation building	Matrices	Memory for digits
Verbal relations		Paper folding and cutting	Memory for objects

hold information retrieved from long-term store that is used in an ongoing task.

Three factors exist at the third level: *verbal reasoning, quantitative reasoning,* and *abstract/visual reasoning.* These factors are more specific and dependent on content than the first- or second-level factors.

The Wechsler scales have similarly been revised periodically since their inception in the 1940s. The three scales are similar in that each consists of a series of subtests that are organized according to two larger factors: verbal and performance abilities. Wechsler (1974) noted that the verbal/performance dichotomy reflects "two principal modes by which human abilities express themselves" (p. 9), while acknowledging that mental abilities could also be classified in other ways. A listing of the verbal and performance subtests for the WISC-R follows, along with a description of the type of questions posed in each subtest.

DESCRIPTION OF THE SUBTESTS OF THE WISC-R*

VERBAL IQ

Information: Children are asked questions assessing their general world knowledge, similar to the following: "How many pennies make a dime?" "What do the lungs do?" "What is the capital of Italy?"

Similarities: Children are read two words and are to tell how they are alike, or similar to the following: *pear–peach; inch–ounce; snow–sand.*

Arithmetic: Children are given arithmetic problems. The easiest involve counting and addition and subtraction using physical reminders. A child may be shown a picture of nine trees and asked to cover up all but five. More complex problems are read aloud, for example: "Joyce had six dolls and lost two. How many dolls did she have left?" "Three girls had 48 cookies. They divided them equally among themselves. How many cookies did each girl get?"

Vocabulary: Children are read words and are to tell what each word means.

*The examples provided here are *not* items from the WISC-R but are similar in form to items found on it.

Comprehension: Children are asked questions assessing their knowledge of societal conventions and of appropriate behavior in a variety of situations: "What are some reasons we need soldiers?" "What are you supposed to do if you find someone's watch in school?" "Why is it important to have speed limits on roads?"

Digit Span: Children are read digits at a rate of one per second and are to repeat them back in exact order. This is followed by a test in which children must repeat the numbers in the reverse order in which the examiner spoke them. This is an optional test.

PERFORMANCE IQ

Picture Completion: Children are shown black-and-white pictures and are to determine what important part of each picture is missing.

Picture Arrangement: Children are given a series of pictures in a mixed order and are to arrange them so that they tell a sensible story.

Block Design: Children are given nine cubes, colored red on two sides, white on two sides, and red/white on two sides. They are shown designs and are to reproduce them using the nine blocks. Bonus points are given for fast response times.

Object Assembly: Children have pieces of a familiar object presented to them in scrambled order. They are to put the pieces together to make the object. Bonus points are given for fast response times.

Coding: Children are shown a key of simple geometric figures (for instance, a triangle, square, and circle), with each being associated with other symbols (a cross, a vertical line, and so on). Children are to make the appropriate mark (cross, vertical line) below each of 45 randomly arranged figures without skipping any as quickly as possible. Bonus points are given for fast response times.

Mazes: Children are shown mazes drawn on paper and, with a pencil, are to draw their way out of the maze. This is an optional test.

A relatively new individually administered IQ test that is receiving attention in educational circles is the Kaufman Assessment Battery for Children (K-ABC) (Kaufman & Kaufman, 1983). This test evaluates intelligence in terms of a model of sequential and simultaneous information processing. Sequential processing is assessed on tasks involving the arrangement of stimuli in sequential, or serial, order. Simultaneous processing is assessed on tasks requiring the ability to integrate input simultaneously to solve a problem. Examples of sequential tests include number recall, which is similar to digit span, and hand movement, in which the child performs a series of hand movements in the same sequence as an examiner performed them. Examples of simultaneous tests include assembling several identical triangles into an abstract pattern to match a model and spatial memory, in which children must recall the placement of pictures on a page that was exposed only briefly. This recently developed and seemingly popular instrument has not escaped criticism (see Das, 1984a; Sternberg, 1984), and as of this writing, it is too early to assess the K-ABC's eventual contribution to the psychology of intelligence and mental testing. It will be discussed in greater detail in Chapter 13.

Basically, IQ tests are standardized on large samples of people, and items that differentiate among people of a given age are retained, whereas items that do not (those that are too easy or too difficult) are eliminated. For each age assessed, the number of test items the average child passes is determined. For example, the number of items passed by 50 percent of the 8-year-olds in the standardization sample would reflect the number of items an average 8-year-old should be able to pass.

Historically, the relationship between the number of items passed and the age of the child was expressed as a quotient of one's mental age to one's chronological age (thus the term *intelligence quotient*, or IQ). A child's mental age corresponds to the number of items he or she passes. If a child passes the number of items equal to the number passed by an average 12-year-old, the child's mental age is 12 years. The child's mental age is then divided by his or her chronological age, and the result is multiplied by 100. Thus, a 10-year-old child with a mental age of 10 years has an IQ of 100 (10/10 × 100). A 10-year-old with the mental age of 9.5 years has an IQ of 95

(9.5/10 × 100), and a 10-year-old with a mental age of 12 has an IQ of 120 (12/10 × 100).

The concept of mental age has received substantial criticism in recent years (see Wechsler, 1974), and neither the Wechsler scales nor the most recent version of the Stanford-Binet includes the concept of mental age. One criticism of the concept is that a 7-year-old with a mental age of 10 and a 10-year-old with the same mental age are not, in reality, of comparable intelligence. They may have the same mental age with respect to test performance, but they do not have the same kind of mind. Also a 5-year-old with a mental age of 6 has an IQ of 120; a 10-year-old with a comparable IQ has a mental age of 12. In the first case, the child's mental age is one year ahead of his chronological age; in the second case, it is a difference of two years.

These and other problems have led test developers to abandon the concept of mental age and develop instead a *deviation IQ*. Children's performance is compared with that of children of their own age and not with the performance of older or younger children. Thus, tests can be constructed so that the statistical characteristics of IQ are the same at each age level. Modern tests are constructed so that IQ scores are distributed according to a normal distribution with specified statistical properties. The distribution of IQ scores for the WISC-R (Wechsler, 1974) is shown in Figure 10-2. As can be seen,

FIGURE 10-2 Theoretical distribution of WISC-R scores. The test is constructed so that 50% of all people at a given age will have IQ scores of 100 and below and 50% will have scores of 100 and above.

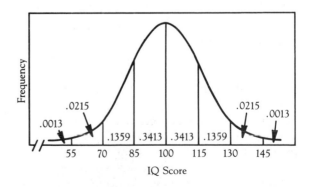

children with scores of 100 have IQs equal to or greater than 50 percent of the population. Children with scores of 115 have IQs equal to or greater than approximately 84 percent of the population. Thus, by knowing a child's IQ score, one knows where he or she stands with respect to "intelligence" relative to his or her agemates. Comparisons between ages are a bit more complicated.

The renouncement of the concept of mental age and the use of the deviation IQ allow a more accurate comparison among children of a specified age. However, the use of the deviation IQ to express intelligence makes developmental contrasts difficult. IQ tests are not constructed to be a mechanism for understanding the development of intelligence. By using the deviation IQ, in fact, we hold developmental differences constant, so that we can make comparisons among agemates in the same way for children of all ages. As I have noted above, this procedure has obvious advantages for making comparisons of children's intelligence. For the developmentalist, however, the difficulties arise when changes in intelligence over time are of interest.

IQ tests such as the Stanford-Binet and WISC-R provide not only an overall IQ score but also a pattern or profile of intellectual skills. Ideally, from the point of view of a clinician, there will be little variability in a child's score from subtest to subtest. Not all children's intellectual skills show such homogeneity, however, and different patterns of intellectual skills have been associated with exceptionalities in intellectual functioning. For example, Harvey and Seeley (1984) administered a series of psychometric tests in a correctional institution and found that 18% of the youths were classified as gifted. Further examination of these children's intellectual performance revealed that they excelled on tests assessing *fluid ability*, which has been defined by Cattel as being minimally affected by prior learning. The gifted inmates performed less well on tests assessing *crystallized intelligence*, which is more influenced by schooling and previous learning. Harvey and Seeley speculated that the classroom situation had worked against the use of fluid abilities for these children. They appeared bright to their teachers, displaying a thinking style characterized by a

nonverbal, quick perceptiveness; but they did not attain a level of academic achievement that would be predicted on the basis of their overall IQ. Harvey and Seeley suggested that some gifted children who have difficulty in the classroom (and outside) do so because of the particular pattern of their intellectual talents and that teachers should be sensitive to such differences. Heterogeneous intellectual profiles are, of course, not limited to gifted children, and Harvey and Seeley's suggestion to teachers to be sensitive to the particular intellectual patterns of students should be expanded to include all children.

There is nothing magic about the IQ test itself. It does not necessarily measure "innate" intelligence, nor does it necessarily reflect a constant value that will typify an individual throughout life. In fact, although IQ does correlate significantly with academic success and occupational status, many argue that it is limited in the type of mental functioning it measures and that to view an IQ score as an indication of a child's total intelligence is misleading.

Information Processing Approaches

One criticism of the psychometric approach, and IQ tests specifically, is that test construction is based primarily on pragmatic considerations—which items discriminate reliably among children—and not on theoretical considerations (Sternberg, 1985). The factors that constitute intelligence are determined by statistical analyses and not on the basis of any a priori model of intelligence. As I noted earlier, however, it would be unfair to say that IQ tests are atheoretical. The K–ABC and the most recent revision of the Stanford-Binet are clearly based on some underlying notions of the nature of intelligence. Nevertheless, pragmatic considerations of selecting items that discriminate among children of a given age are still of extreme importance in choosing which items will be included on the tests. Thus, although IQ tests may assess individual differences in intelligence well, they are less successful at providing insight into the nature of the intelligence that underlies test performance. Recent advances in information processing theory have been viewed by many as providing the theoretical and empirical basis for a more fully developed understanding of human intelligence.

Information processing approaches to thinking were discussed in some detail in Chapter 3. In a sense, the same mechanisms used to describe developmental function from an information processing perspective can be used to describe individual differences. Information processing approaches are not inherently developmental, so that developmental differences in children's thinking can be viewed as a special form of individual differences that vary reliably with age. Thus, for example, differences in how information is encoded, speed of processing, how easily information is categorized, and metacognition can all be sources of individual (as well as developmental) differences in thinking and intelligence.

When cognitive psychologists examine individual differences in children's thinking, contrasts are often made between groups known to vary on the basis of IQ (for example, mentally retarded and nonretarded children or gifted and nongifted children) or between children matched in terms of IQ who differ on the basis of some academic ability (for example, good and poor readers or learning-disabled and nondisabled children). In such studies, researchers attempt to discover the underlying processes responsible for group differences in IQ, task performance, or academic skill. No attempt will be made here to assess the origins of mental retardation, learning and reading disabilities, or giftedness. The etiologies and definitions of these intellectual exceptionalities are interesting and important but would require separate chapters (or books) to investigate properly. Rather, differences in cognitive processing between exceptional and normal children are examined to elucidate the nature of cognition in general and to discover educationally important differences in thinking among these groups of children.

Strategies

Information processing theories of development have stressed the role of strategies, or executive control processes, in affecting children's thinking. Basically, a strategy refers to some effortful mental operation aimed at facilitating the accomplishment of a goal. Just as developmental differences can be

explained in terms of children's tendency to use strategies and the efficiency of their strategies, so can individual differences among children of a given age be explained in terms of differential strategy use.

Research contrasting retarded and nonretarded children has indicated that the tendency to use memory and problem solving strategies is a major cognitive difference between the two groups. Strategies allow people to plan the course of their cognitive operations, to anticipate the consequences of their acts and the acts of others. Given this view of strategies, it is not surprising that many researchers have proposed that strategies are a central aspect of intelligence (Bray & Turner, 1986; Das, 1984b; Spitz & Borys, 1984). For example, Das (1984b) has written that "what qualifies as intelligence may be the ability to plan or structure one's behavior with an end in view. The more efficient and parsimonious the plan is, the more intelligent the resulting behavior" (p. 116). Researchers interested in cognitive functioning in mentally retarded people have investigated the use of strategies in a variety of tasks, attempting to elucidate the differences in information processing between retarded and nonretarded individuals.

A common finding on memory and learning tasks is that nonretarded children are more likely to use strategies to aid their performance than are mentally retarded children (Borkowski & Cavanaugh, 1979; Bray & Turner, 1986; Campione & Brown, 1984). For example, in memory studies where retarded and nonretarded children are given the opportunity to rehearse information before testing, retarded children are less likely to rehearse in preparation for recall than are nonretarded children of the same age. Similarly, when children are required to rehearse (as in the overt rehearsal procedure described in Chapter 8, see Ornstein, Naus, & Liberty, 1975), qualitative differences in rehearsal are found. Retarded children and adolescents are more likely to rehearse one or two unique items each time they rehearse than they are to rehearse several different items together (cumulative rehearsal). Such a simple "repetition" strategy is similar to that observed for younger nonretarded children (see Bray & Turner, 1986; Campione & Brown, 1977). In other words, retarded children show deficient rehearsal strategies, both in terms of the amount they rehearse and the style of rehearsal, which are directly related to their levels of recall. This strategy-deficit hypothesis is not limited to free recall and the strategy of rehearsal but has been proposed for a variety of problem-solving tasks and strategies (see Brooks, Sperber, & McCauley, 1984).

Retarded children, like young children, can be trained to use memory and learning strategies, with corresponding improvements in performance. Similarly, they are also likely to switch back to a nonstrategic style on subsequent tasks (Belmont, Ferretti, & Mitchell, 1982; Campione, Brown, Ferrara, Jones, & Steinberg, 1985). For example, Campione and his colleagues (1985) trained mildly retarded adolescents and nonretarded children (matched in mental age to the retardates) to solve matrix problems selected from the Raven Colored Progressive Matrices. Figure 10-3 presents two examples of these problems. To solve the matrices, children must select from six alternatives the one that best completes the matrix. For the first matrix, they must realize that the pattern has been rotated. The correct response for this problem is a circle with the filled quadrant oriented in the proper direction (about 5 o'clock). In the second example, the children must learn a subtraction strategy, realizing that the alternative on the far right is the same as the object on the far left with the smaller, inside object deleted. The correct response for this problem would be an empty diamond. Both the younger non-retarded children and the retarded adolescents learned how to solve the various matrix problems. When the children were presented with new problems, however, differences between the groups were found. The nonretarded children were able to transfer their newly learned strategies to other problems much more effectively than the retarded children. This was true both of problems similar to those on which they had been trained and of problems that were slightly novel. The researchers argued that their results point to an important difference in cognitive functioning between retarded and non-retarded children and provide support for the significance of transfer mechanisms to theories of intelligence.

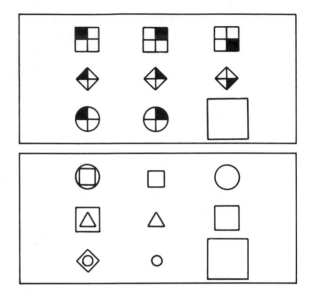

FIGURE 10-3 Examples of matrices used in a training study. Children must select an alternative that completes the pattern in each matrix (Campione, Brown, Ferrara, Jones, and Steinberg, 1985).

Similar deficits in strategy implementation have been hypothesized to explain the difference in task performance between good and poor readers or between learning-disabled and nondisabled children. For example, Ceci (1983, 1984) has shown that learning-disabled children perform simple cognitive tasks as well as nondisabled children when processing involves relatively automatic (that is, effortless) operations. Differences between the two groups become apparent only when deliberate, or *purposive* (that is, effortful and strategic), operations are required. In one study (Ceci, 1983), 4- and 10-year-old nondisabled (non-LD) children and 10-year-olds who had been classified as learning disabled (LD) were shown pictures of familiar items, which they were to name as quickly as possible. For half of all trials, a neutral prime preceded the picture (for example, "Here's something you know": *horse*). In the automatic condition, 20% of the remaining items were preceded by primes that were semantically related to the target picture (for example, "Here's an animal": *horse*), whereas 80% were preceded by primes unrelated to the target (for example, "Here's a fruit": *horse*). In the purposive-processing condition, the distribution was reversed, with 80% of the items being preceded by a semantically related prime and 20% by an unrelated prime. Ceci reasoned that in the purposive-processing condition, children could increase their speed of responding by intentionally activating the appropriate semantic category features when the prime was presented. Because 80% of the cues were related to the target, deliberately anticipating a target of a specified category should facilitate processing and, thus, speed of identification. This would not be the case in the automatic condition, where the primes were more often unrelated to the target. Thus, processing in this condition can be best done by the relatively automatic activation of "the corresponding pathways containing . . . [the stimulus'] representation in the central nervous system" (Ceci, 1983, p. 428).

Both the 4- and 10-year-old non-LD and LD children in this experiment demonstrated automatic semantic processing. In fact, the patterns of performance in the automatic condition did not vary among the three groups of children. However, age and group differences were noted for purposive processing. The 10-year-old non-LD children showed both a large advantage (relative to the neutral cues) when compatible primes preceded the target ("Here's an animal": *horse*) and a corresponding disadvantage when the cues were incompatible ("Here's a fruit": *horse*), implying that these children were deliberately processing the semantic information to aid their identification times. In contrast, both the 4-year-old non-LD and the 10-year-old LD children displayed only a small advantage with the compatible primes. There was no disadvantage for the incompatible primes. In other words, 10-year-old LD children were more similar to nondisabled 4-year-olds than they were to nondisabled children of their own age with respect to the intentional processing of semantic information. That is, under the conditions of Ceci's experiments, learning-disabled children were less likely than nondisabled children of their same age to implement the proper strategy or to execute the purposive process efficiently. However, no deficits were noted when processing required the relatively automatic activation of language terms.

A similar argument has been made to explain the memory deficits of learning-disabled and nondisabled children matched for IQ. LD children have been hypothesized to be less likely to use a memory strategy than are non-LD children, accounting for their overall lower levels of performance (Bauer, 1979, 1982; Worden, 1983). For example, Bauer (1979) gave 9- and 10-year-old LD and non-LD children a series of free recall tasks. An examination of recall as a function of serial position indicated no differences in performance for the last several items on the lists (recency effect). The recency effect is usually attributed to subjects' emptying the contents of their short-term store and does not involve a strategic component. In contrast, large differences were noted in the recall of items from the beginning of the recall list (primacy effect). The primacy effect has usually been interpreted as reflecting the use of strategies (see Chapter 8 for a more detailed discussion of the serial-position effect). In other words, the LD children differed from the nondisabled children in terms of strategy use but not in terms of nonstrategic functioning. This interpretation was bolstered by the results of two subsequent experiments in which Bauer observed lower levels of categorical clustering (an indication of the memory strategy of organization, see Chapter 8) for the LD children. Similar observations have been made for poor readers, who likewise show lower levels of memory performance than good readers of equal IQ (Dallago & Moely, 1980; Goldstein, Hasher, & Stein, 1983; Torgesen, 1977).

Knowledge Base
Recent research has emphasized that differences in what children know about any particular content area influence their processing of that information (Bjorklund, 1987a; Chi, 1985). Just as developmental differences can be explained, in part, by differences in knowledge base, so can individual differences. Concerning memory differences between good and poor readers, for example, some researchers have suggested that they are more likely to stem from differences in knowledge base than from differences in strategy use. The semantic memories of poor readers are not so well developed as the

semantic memories of good readers, resulting in the inefficient retrieval of word meaning from long-term store and, thus, less effective processing of verbal information (Bjorklund & Bernholtz, 1986; Vellutino & Scanlon, 1985). This possibility was illustrated in a study by Bjorklund and Bernholtz (1986). Good and poor junior high school readers (average age = 13 years), matched for IQ, were given a series of concept and memory tasks. In a first session, children were asked to select examples from specified natural language categories (for example, BIRDS, CLOTHES, TOOLS) and to rate each item in terms of how typical it was of its category. Category typicality was discussed in Chapter 7. In general, differences in judged typicality affect the performance of both children and adults in a variety of tasks, with children's judgments becoming more adult-like with age. Bjorklund and Bernholtz reported that the judgments of the 13-year-old poor readers resembled those of 9-year-olds (Bjorklund, Thompson, & Ornstein, 1983) and were less adult-like than were the ratings of the good readers. In other words, differences in the semantic memory organization of good and poor 13-year-old readers were found with respect to category typicality.

In later experiments, children were given sets of 12 typical and 12 atypical items to recall in any order they wished. In one experiment, the typicality of the items was based on norms generated by adults (adult-generated lists). In another experiment, the typicality of the items was based on each child's self-generated norms, obtained from the earlier session (self-generated lists). Significant differences in memory performance were observed only for the adult-generated lists. Recall was comparable between the good and poor readers when typical and atypical category items were selected based on each child's own judgments. Furthermore, measures of strategy use in these experiments (based on amount of clustering and latencies between the recall of words) indicated that the good readers were no more strategic than the poor readers. Rather, their superior memory performance could best be attributed to differences in knowledge base. These results do not mean that there are no strategic differences between good and poor readers. Rather, they indicate that differences in knowledge base contribute significantly to performance differences observed between these two groups of children and, in part, may be responsible for any apparent differences in "strategy use" that are noted.

In related research, Scott, Greenfield, and Sterental (1986) reported differences in knowledge for familiar words between groups of 6- to 8-year-old LD and non-LD students. Children were presented series of four pictures from a single superordinate category (for example, *banana, apple, strawberries, orange*—FRUIT). Twelve superordinate categories were studied in all. The children were asked a series of questions concerning how the items were alike and different from one another. LD and non-LD children differed considerably on the number of responses they provided to these questions, revealing a difference in knowledge for familiar superordinate categories. That is, as in the study by Bjorklund and Bernholtz (1986) of 13-year-old good and poor readers, a major difference between the LD and non-LD children was in terms of their knowledge base for familiar language concepts.

One study that demonstrates the importance of knowledge base in learning and memory is that of Schneider, Korkel, and Weinert (1987). German children in grades three, five, and seven were evaluated for their knowledge of soccer and were classified as soccer experts or soccer novices. The children were also administered a series of intelligence tests, and these results, along with their school grades in math and German, were used to classify them as successful or unsuccessful learners. The children were then presented a well-organized, narrative text about soccer and were later either asked questions about the story or asked to recall it. As would be expected, comprehension and memory performance were greater for the soccer experts than for the soccer novices. However, the researchers reported no difference in performance between the academically successful learners and the unsuccessful ones. That is, being a good learner did not result in better performance by either the expert or the novice children. Having a detailed knowledge of the subject was enough to yield high levels of memory performance. Similarly, having an impoverished knowledge of the subject was enough to yield low levels of perform- ance. The researchers concluded that "children's prior knowledge about text contents is a much more powerful predictor of their text comprehension and recall than their general intellectual ability or learn- ing skills" (Schneider et al., 1987, p. 16).

This situation is admittedly not typical. In most contexts, successful learners do, of course, perform better than unsuccessful learners. One important reason why this is so, however, is that successful learners generally know more about the things they are dealing with than unsuccessful learners. Success- ful learners acquire information more readily and thus have a more elaborated knowledge base on which to base future learning. The more children know, the more easily they are able to learn and remember new information.

Speed of Retrieval from Long-Term Memory
Older children retrieve information from long-term memory faster than younger children (see Whitney, 1986). Similar differences in speed of retrieval be- tween LD and non-LD children have already been noted (Ceci, 1983). In fact, it is possible that the differences in memory performance between LD and non-LD children and between good and poor readers attributed to strategy use or knowledge base may be mediated by differences in speed of retrieval. Some children may require more time to activate relevant concepts used on these memory and problem solving tasks than other children, which in turn requires greater expenditure of mental effort. The increased effort associated with the slower retrieval of language terms, for example, may be responsible, indirectly, for the less strategic approach of these children to the task and, thus, to their overall lower levels of performance.

In addition to distinguishing LD from non-LD children and good readers from poor ones, the effi- ciency of retrieval from long-term memory has been hypothesized to be an important component in indi- vidual differences in intelligence in the general pop- ulation. Most forms of intelligence require retrieving information in memory and acting on that informa- tion. Several researchers have reasoned that people who retrieve information quickly and efficiently will display an advantage on cognitive tasks, particularly verbal ones. Hunt and his colleagues provided sup- port for this position using a variety of experimental tasks. In one study, Hunt, Davidson, and Lansman (1981) asked adults to verify category statements such as "A dog is an animal." They found that the time needed to confirm such statements correlated significantly with verbal ability (see also Hunt, Lunneborg, & Lewis, 1975).

Similar procedures have been used with children, with mixed results. In general, speed of retrieval does increase with age (Bisanz, Danner, & Resnick, 1979; Ford & Keating, 1981). However, the relation be- tween speed of retrieval and verbal ability has been mixed. Some researchers have found faster retrieval speeds for highly verbal than for less verbal children (Keating & Bobbitt, 1979), whereas others have not (List, Keating, & Merriman, 1985).

Speed of retrieval seems to be related to the degree of knowledge a person has concerning the informa- tion to be processed. Information that is well inte- grated in semantic memory can be retrieved more quickly than less well-integrated information (Roth, 1983; Sperber, Davies, Merrill, & McCauley, 1982). For example, a study by Roth (1983) demonstrated that differences in response times between children and adults can be substantially reduced when deci- sions involve an area in which the children are experts. In his experiment, child chess experts pro- cessed some information about chess as quickly as adult chess experts and significantly faster than adult novices, clearly indicating a relationship between familiarity with the information to be processed and speed of processing. Differences among children within the same age level can similarly be attributed to differences in knowledge base. Children with well-elaborated semantic memories, for example, should process information faster than same-age children whose semantic memories contain fewer entries or connections among entries.

Age and developmental differences in speed of retrieval are reliable but often small (Gitomer & Pellegrino, 1985), and they point to important dif- ferences in intelligence at a microscopic level. Dif- ferences are often in terms of milliseconds, and it may be wondered what the significance of a 50-

millisecond (1/20th of a second) difference might be with respect to intelligence. Although such differences are small, they can be important indeed. Perhaps one of the most important cognitive skills for people in technological societies is reading. Small differences in rate of retrieving the meaning of a word or in integrating letters to form words can, over a very short time, result in substantial differences in reading rate and reading comprehension.

Metacognition

The rapid processing of words, numbers, and other symbols of thought is clearly important in intelligence. Yet, there are other more "macro" processes that vary among people and probably contribute to individual differences in intelligence. Strategies such as rehearsal have already been mentioned. A related phenomenon that has been postulated as being significant to individual differences in intelligence is *metacognition*, a person's understanding of his or her own cognitive abilities (Borkowski, 1985; Brown, 1978; Flavell, 1978b; Sternberg, 1985). Basically, the brighter individuals of any age are those who possess the executive functions to monitor their task performance and to apply the techniques they possess to solve a problem. Borkowski and his colleagues have suggested that differences in metacognition are a major cause of differences in strategy use and training effectiveness between retarded and nonretarded children (Borkowski, Reid, & Kurtz, 1984), between reflective and impulsive children (Borkowski, Peck, Reid, & Kurtz, 1983; see Chapter 13), and of differences in thinking between gifted and nongifted children (Borkowski & Peck, 1986).

In a study by Borkowski and Peck (1986), gifted and nongifted 7- and 8-year-olds were instructed to use an elaboration strategy or a simpler clustering strategy on a memory task. They were later tested for transfer of the strategy to other memory problems. Elaboration involves creating a relationship between two items, so that the presentation of one item will elicit the recall of the other. For example, if I wanted to remember the pair of words *banana–coat*, I might form an image of a bunch of bananas hanging in a closet where I usually find my coat. Or I might think that a banana peel covers a banana in a similar way

that a coat covers my body. Although forming such relations may seem like a lot of work, the memory performance of both children and adults is facilitated by the use of an elaboration strategy (see Pressley, 1982; Chapter 8). For the children who received the clustering instructions (for example, "Try to remember words from the same category together"), training was less explicit than it was for the children who were trained to use the elaboration strategy. Would both the gifted and nongifted children be able to benefit from the training, and would the extent of training affect the transfer of the strategy differently for the two groups of children?

Both the gifted and the nongifted children who were trained in the elaboration strategy learned it. Differences between the groups for this strategy became apparent during a generalization task, when the children were given different sets of problems to learn. The gifted children were more likely to generalize the strategy they had learned than were the nongifted children, with the extent of generalization being significantly related to scores on a battery of metamemory questions. For the clustering strategy, differences in training as well as transfer between the two groups of children were noted. The gifted children benefited more from the minimal training than did the nongifted children. This difference was extended to the transfer trials. In other words, differences between the gifted and nongifted children for training and transfer of a memory strategy were most pronounced for those in the clustering condition, where training instructions were only minimally emphasized. Gifted children required less explicit prompting before they would learn a strategy and generalized it to new situations. According to Borkowski and Peck (1986), because of their greater metamemory awareness, "gifted children realized the effectiveness of the strategy and applied it appropriately even without the aid of complete and explicit instructions" (p. 193).

Although the picture is obviously a complex one, cognitive models provide researchers with specific aspects of information processing to investigate the source of intellectual differences among people and experimental methods to facilitate the search. I expect that most advances in understanding human intelligence over the next several decades will involve theory and research that incorporate aspects of information processing approaches. Although my bias is certainly showing here, I believe that models that examine *developmental changes* in information processing are likely to lead the field in yielding important and exciting insights into individual differences in human intelligence.

Piagetian Approaches

Information processing approaches to individual differences in children's thinking have the advantage of reasonably well-developed theories and methods that can be applied to understanding intelligence. As with psychometric approaches, however, there is nothing inherently developmental about information processing theories. One theory that is developmental in its orientation is Piaget's. Although Piaget himself did not explicitly apply his theory to individual differences, others have, and some of this research is now examined briefly.

One way in which *Piagetian approaches* have addressed individual differences in intellectual functioning is to examine differences in *rate* of development (Bovet, 1976). Because of a nonsupportive social environment, for example, development may proceed slower than average. Conversely, an intellectually stimulating environment may produce accelerated development, moving a child through the stages at a faster-than-average rate. In a similar vein, mental retardation can be viewed as the result of never having progressed beyond a certain stage of development (preoperational, for example). From this perspective, factors that influence the rate of development or the transition from one stage to another are important determinants of individual differences in intelligence.

Several researchers have demonstrated that individual differences on Piagetian tasks (for example, conservation, seriation) are predictive of academic ability. For instance, performance on batteries of Piagetian tasks has been shown to predict early (first- and second-grade) academic skills as well as or even better than standardized IQ tests (Kaufman & Kaufman, 1972; Kingma, 1984; Lunzar, Dolan, &

Wilkinson, 1976). In related research, Byrd and Gholson (1985) reported that degree of operativity (evidenced by performance on a series of conservation, seriation, and classification tasks) was significantly related to the reading ability of second- and fourth-grade children. In fact, operativity was related to a variety of reading-related measures, including memory, metamemory, and metareading (knowledge about reading), although these other measures correlated only slightly with one another. These findings led Byrd and Gholson to conclude that developmental and individual differences in reading strategies are not mediated by memory skills or knowledge about memory strategies so much as they are by operative (that is, logical) abilities.

In other research, Keating (1975) reported significant differences in formal operational abilities between academically average and bright fifth- and seventh-grade children. However, Kuhn (1976), testing middle-class children from the first through the seventh grades, who were representative of a more normal range of academic abilities than Keating's sample, did not find a significant correspondence between Piagetian task performance and IQ for her older groups of children. All the children were administered a WISC and a series of Piagetian tasks. The Piagetian tasks for the younger children (first through third grade) included class inclusion, seriation, conservation of amount, and multiple classification. The older children were given three tests of formal operational ability (Inhelder & Piaget, 1958), including the pendulum problem that was discussed in Chapter 2. Kuhn reported a significant relation between scores on the battery of Piagetian tasks and IQ for 6- to 8-year-olds (correlation = .69) but not for children approaching formal operations (correlation = .22). Kuhn suggested that the environmental factors causing children to excel on IQ tests are not the same as those affecting the rate of progress through Piagetian stages. Such environmental influences increase over time, Kuhn proposed, resulting in reduced correspondence between Piagetian and psychometric tests with advancing age.

In related research, Humphreys and his colleagues have examined the relationship between a battery of Piagetian tasks, Wechsler verbal and performance

IQ tests, and academic ability for children of varying intellectual aptitudes (mentally retarded and normal children) and ages (6 to 18 years) (Humphreys, 1980; Humphreys & Parsons, 1979; Humphreys, Rich, & Davey, 1985). Humphreys and his colleagues administered 27 different Piagetian tasks to the children. The tasks ranged from those that assessed early concrete operational abilities to those that evaluated formal operational skills. Correlations between the children's performance on Piagetian tasks and on Wechsler verbal and performance IQ tests were in excess of .80. Comparable results were reported when a subset of only 13 Piagetian tasks was selected. Humphreys also reported significant correlations between sets of Piagetian tasks and measures of academic achievement (correlations in excess of .70), only slightly lower than those found with verbal IQ. Furthermore, correlations between performance on these tasks and a general intelligence factor (*g*) were also high for most tasks, indicating to Humphreys that the battery of Piagetian tasks measures the same aspect of general intelligence as do psychometric tests. In general, there was a great deal of overlap among the intelligence assessed by the Piagetian tasks, the Wechsler verbal and performance IQ scales, and measures of academic achievement. However, there were some differences between the tasks in terms of the intellectual skills they assessed. Humphreys was not able to specify the nature of these differences, but he asserted that, given the current data, each measure is a valid index of intelligence (Humphreys et al., 1985).

In comparison with the psychometric and information processing approaches, Piagetian researchers have done comparatively little work on individual differences in children's thinking. This is understandable given Piaget's emphasis on developmental function. What has been done, however, is encouraging. For example, Kuhn's (1976) data suggest that the relationship between Piagetian measures and psychometrically measured intelligence may vary as a function of developmental level, that is, that the nature of intelligence changes with age, influencing patterns of individual differences. And Humphreys's work demonstrates that statistical analyses typically used with psychometric data can be applied successfully to Piagetian tests of intelligence. Piaget's theory has been a favorite of many educators for years, and standardized variants of Piagetian tasks may be well received and utilized in the future.

Sternberg's Triarchic Theory

A recent theory of intelligence that has received substantial attention is Robert Sternberg's (1985) "triarchic" theory. The model includes three subtheories—the *contextual* subtheory, the *experiential* subtheory, and the *componential* subtheory—each of which will be examined briefly.

Contextual Subtheory

The contextual subtheory holds that intelligence must be viewed in the context in which it occurs. Intelligent behaviors for the middle-class American schoolchild may not be considered intelligent for the ghetto dropout or the unschooled Guatemalan farm boy. Sternberg defines intelligence as "mental activity directed toward purposive adaptation to, and selection and shaping of, real-world environments relevant to one's life" (p. 45). By defining intelligence in terms of real-world environments, he stresses the importance of the external as well as the internal world to intelligence. Such a definition also avoids the circularity of theories that basically define intelligence in terms of a score on an IQ test.

From this definition, Sternberg proposes three processes of intelligence: *adaptation*, *selection*, and *shaping*. Adaptation refers to adjusting one's behavior to achieve a good fit with one's environment. When adaptation is not possible or not desirable, a person may *select* an alternative environment in which he or she can adapt well. Failing to adapt to the whims of a new supervisor, for example, a person may choose to quit her job and select another. Or a child may find it difficult to get along with children in the neighborhood and instead become friendly with other children from school who do not live as close by. (This may require some adaptation on the part of the child's parents, such as providing transportation across town or permitting sleep-over parties.) If for some reason a new environment cannot be selected, however, a person may attempt to *shape* the environment. The employee may try to convince her supervisor to change his ways or may go over his head to bring changes from above. The child may try to alter the behavior of his neighborhood peers by placating them with his mother's cookies or by inviting one child at a time over to play instead of inviting the entire group.

Although these three processes typify intelligence universally, what is required for adaptation, selection, and shaping will vary among different groups of people, so that a single set of behaviors cannot be specified as "intelligent" for all individuals. Also, what is deemed to be intelligent at one point in life may not be so judged at a later time. For example, because children have less freedom than adults to select new environments and are often powerless to significantly shape certain aspects of these environments, adapting to their uncomfortable surroundings may be the most intelligent option they have. Thus, whereas the school-phobic adult will select nonacademic environments, the 10-year-old child typically cannot, making adaptation the most intelligent choice.

Basically, the contextual subtheory is one of cultural relativism. Intellectual skills that are critical for survival in one culture may not be so important in another. Likewise, important intellectual skills within a culture may undergo some change from one generation to another. For example, arithmetic computation has been an unquestionably vital skill for people from technological societies. The significance of arithmetic to intelligence was noted by Wechsler in the construction of the WISC-R and WAIS-R. Each has an arithmetic subtest. Yet, with the widespread use of calculators, being able to add and subtract numbers quickly and accurately becomes a little less critical to everyday functioning. Although I would not care to say that arithmetic computation will become unimportant, in the generations ahead it will probably be viewed as much less critical to intelligence than it is today and, certainly, than it was a generation ago.

Sternberg is not the only person to propose a theory of intelligence that is culturally relative (see, for example, Laboratory of Comparative Human Cognition, 1983; Neisser, 1979). Such theories have

rightly been criticized, however, for preventing any general conclusions about the universal nature of human intellectual functioning. Everything is relative, and thus intelligence can be studied only from the perspective of a particular culture or subculture. Sternberg avoids this problem by combining his contextual subtheory with the experiential and componential subtheories, which propose aspects of intelligence that are universal.

Experiential Subtheory

The experiential subtheory is concerned with how prior knowledge influences performance on certain cognitive tasks. More specifically, the subtheory examines the ability to deal with *novelty* and the degree to which processing is *automatized* (that is, made to involve relatively little mental effort). Both skills are highly dependent upon experience. A stimulus is novel only to the extent that it differs in some way from what is already familiar (Rheingold, 1985). Similarly, newly acquired processing skills are rarely executed effortlessly but require substantial expenditure of one's limited mental effort for their deployment. Only when a skill has been exercised frequently does it become automatized (Shiffrin & Schneider, 1977). Sternberg proposes that how people respond to novelty and the ease with which they can automatize information processing are important and universal aspects of intelligence.

The importance of such skills is apparent in any occupation. Good scientists must be able to quickly apprehend the relevant factors that are influencing whatever phenomenon they are concerned with. If scientists are to make major contributions to their field, however, they must also be able to devise clever ways of testing their hypotheses and to appreciate the significance of an unexpected result. These factors are important not only in the ivory tower but also in more worldly occupations. This importance was made apparent to me by an electrician who installed three ceiling fans in my home after two other electricians had failed. He quickly discerned what approach to take, and, after 9 hours of running into more obstacles than I knew existed in my walls and above my ceilings, he finished the task. After I expressed my appreciation for a job well done, the electrician commented: "Any yahoo can lay wire in a straight line. It only takes brains when things don't go as you planned."

The experiential subtheory suggests what tasks are good indicators of intelligence—namely, those that involve dealing with novelty or automatic processing for their successful completion. Many of the laboratory tasks of modern cognitive psychology are good candidates for assessing intelligence, because they stress speed of responding, which is a good indicator of the extent to which processing has become automatized. For example, simple letter-identification tasks, in which subjects must respond as rapidly as possible, signaling the presence of a specified letter, measure the degree to which processing for this over-learned code (the alphabet) is automatized. Similarly, word- and category-identification tasks also test automatic processing. More complex laboratory tasks such as solving analogies or syllogisms probably assess aspects of both automatic processing and response to novelty. Similarly, many items on psychometric batteries test the same processes as do lab tasks, and, Sternberg asserts, are probably better estimators of intelligence. That is because these items are usually more difficult than the lab tasks, involving, on the average, greater degrees of novelty. Examples of psychometric test items that would fit Sternberg's experiential subtheory include picture arrangement ("Put these pictures together so that they make a story"), similarities ("How are television and education alike?"), and comprehension ("Why might it be important that Supreme Court judges be appointed and not elected?").

Componential Subtheory

The componential subtheory is Sternberg's information-processing model of cognition and has already been discussed in some detail in Chapter 3. Briefly, Sternberg proposed three general types of information processing components: *metacomponents, performance components*, and *knowledge-acquisition components*. Metacomponents refer to metacognitive abilities and involve the monitoring of task performance and the allocation of attentional resources. Performance components include encoding, mental comparison, and retrieval of information. And knowledge-acquisition components are the processes involved in gaining new knowledge and selectively acting upon recently encoded information and information in one's long-term store. These three components interact so that deficits in any one component can result in deficits in any of the other components (see Chapter 3). Individual differences in any of these components reflect differences in how people process information and, thus, important differences in intelligence.

Following Sternberg's componential subtheory, why should intelligence increase with age? The major reason is a growth in knowledge base. The knowledge-acquisition components provide a mechanism for a steadily increasing knowledge base. As knowledge base increases, more sophisticated forms of knowledge acquisition are possible, which, in turn, serve to further increase knowledge base. The components lead to increases in knowledge, which lead to more effective use of the components, and so on. Similarly, feedback from the knowledge-acquisition and performance components to the metacomponents can result in improved metacognition. The metacomponents can learn from their own mistakes, which leads to increased self-monitoring, which, in turn, results in the increased efficacy of the metacomponents. Again, feedback loops among the components lead to increased efficiency and, thus, a smarter individual. In general, the mechanisms that explain how intelligence develops in children are basically the same mechanisms that explain how an adult becomes more effective at a particular task with increased experience.

Triarchic Theory and Gifted Children

Sternberg and his colleagues have recently tested aspects of his triarchic theory with gifted children (Davidson & Sternberg, 1984; Marr & Sternberg, 1986). For example, Davidson and Sternberg (1984) compared gifted (IQ = 140+) and nongifted fourth-, fifth-, and sixth-graders on a number of insight problems. Insight problems require one to find a novel and nonobvious solution to a problem that, at first impression, may or may not seem difficult. The following is a typical example of an insight problem:

Water lilies double in area every 24 hours. At the beginning of summer, there was one water lily on the lake. It took 60 days for the lake to become completely covered. How many days did it take for the lake to become half covered [Marr & Sternberg, 1986, p. 58]?

The answer is 59 days. The solution is actually very simple, although, on the surface, it may not appear so. According to Sternberg, insight problems assess a person's ability to deal with novelty and thus are good measures of intelligence.

In a first experiment, Davidson and Sternberg gave children insight problems to solve with irrelevant information. For instance: "A farmer buys 100 animals for $100. Cows are $10 each, sheep are $3 each, and pigs are 50 cents each. How much did he pay for five cows?" Subjects sometimes received cues intended to help them solve the problems (for example, relevant parts of the problem would be underlined, such as "Cows are $10 each" in the above example). In other experiments, children were given more explicit hints on how to solve problems or were given instructions in solving some problems and later asked to solve similar problems. In general, gifted children performed better on these tasks than

nongifted children. Their advantage, however, was more pronounced in some situations than others. For example, nongifted children required more prompting to solve most problems. Overall, the gifted children encoded, combined, and compared information more selectively than the nongifted students.

Marr and Sternberg (1986) similarly demonstrated cognitive advantages for gifted sixth-, seventh-, and eighth-graders. They presented children with verbal analogy problems. Each analogy was paired with a precue statement. The statements consisted of information that was either novel or familiar to the student and that was either relevant or irrelevant to the analogy problem. Table 10-2 presents the four types of problems used by Marr and Sternberg to determine differences between gifted and nongifted children's use of the precue information. Would both groups of children make use of the precue information, or would the information accompanying the analogy affect the gifted and nongifted children differently? The results indicated that the gifted children gave less time to irrelevant novel information than did the nongifted children. The nongifted children devoted the same amount of attention to the

TABLE 10-2   Examples of Items from the Four Novelty/Relevance Conditions of an Experiment with Gifted and Nongifted Children (Marr and Sternberg, 1986)

Item category	Precue	Analogy		
Novel relevant	Radishes are candies	Pretzel is to salty as radish is to		
		crunchy	*sweet
		bitter	tasty
Novel irrelevant	Lemons are animals	Lime is to green as lemon is to		
		hard	red
		*yellow	round
Familiar relevant	Pistols are weapons	Dagger is to knife as pistol is to		
		outlaw	*gun
		holster	steel
Familiar irrelevant	Zebras are wildlife	Leopard is to spot as zebra is to		
		*stripe	hoof
		tail	mark

*Indicates keyed response

novel information regardless of whether it was relevant to the analogy they were to solve. In other words, the intellectually gifted middle-school children were more sensitive to relevant novel information than were their nongifted peers.

Sternberg's theory is an attempt to go beyond earlier, single theories. The contextual subtheory points out the relativity of intelligence by emphasizing the importance of specifying *what* constitutes intelligent behavior. Alone, such a theory is incomplete, for it is almost impossible to make comparisons among people with different experiences. However, the experiential subtheory specifies what tasks are most likely to assess intelligence (those with a degree of novelty and those involving automatic processing), and the componential subtheory provides the universal mental mechanisms by which knowledge is acquired and manipulated. Together, the three subtheories provide a framework for understanding intelligence and its development that, in many ways, is more inclusive than earlier theories. The componential subtheory has already received substantial research attention (see Sternberg, 1985), and developmental and individual differences in automaticity have been the focus of recent research by other investigators (Bjorklund, 1987a; Case, 1985). Also, as will be seen in Chapter 12, individual differences in how children respond to novelty is proving to be an important factor in predicting the stability of individual differences in intelligence from infancy to childhood (see also Berg & Sternberg, 1985). In sum, I believe that Sternberg's triarchic theory, or other multifaceted theories like it, will lead research into the nature of human intelligence into the next century.

☐ The Heritability of Intelligence

A central issue in the study of intelligence has been the extent to which individual differences are a function of genetic or environmental factors. This nature/nurture controversy goes back to Sir Francis Galton, a cousin of Charles Darwin, who asserted that intelligence is mainly inherited, with environ-

ment playing only a minor role in its expression. Proponents of the nurture side have an equally prestigious heritage, however, with Alfred Binet believing that intelligence is mainly the product of culture and education.

The role that experience has in establishing, maintaining, and modifying intellectual competence will be examined in detail in Chapter 11. In the remainder of this chapter, the role of genetics in influencing intelligence is explored in studies that (1) assessed the relationship between low-level (thus presumably innate) cognitive abilities and IQ; and (2) compared the IQs of people as a function of genetic relationship (for example, identical twins, siblings, and unrelated individuals). Although environmental effects can be assessed in such studies, they are only global. For example, adoptive siblings are assumed to share the same environment but to have different genes, whereas monozygotic twins separated early in life are proposed to have identical genetic endowments but different environments. Despite the nonspecific way in which environments are usually defined in these investigations, such studies, particularly in combination with investigations providing detailed analyses of children's surroundings, yield important insights into the nature of individual differences in intelligence.

The Concept of Heritability

Some explanation concerning what is meant by the term *heritability* is appropriate here. Heritability refers to the extent to which differences in any trait within a population are attributed to inheritance. Heritability is expressed as a statistic that ranges from 0 (none of the differences in a trait is attributed to inheritance) to 1.0 (100% of the differences in a trait are attributed to inheritance). It reflects the proportion of variance in an observed trait that is due to genetic variability.

Heritability is a population statistic, in that it describes average differences among people within a population. It does not refer to "how much" of any one person's intelligence (or height or personality characteristics) can be attributed to genetic factors, only what percentage of the difference in a trait within a specific population can be attributed to inheritance, on average.

For the purpose of illustration, assume that individual differences in height are due to only two factors: inheritance and diet. On the mythical island Louie-Louie, every person receives 100% of his or her nutritional needs (no one receives more). The average height of men on Louie-Louie is 6 feet. If you were to meet two men from this island, one being 6 feet 1 inch tall and the other being 5 feet 11 inches tall, 100% of the 2-inch difference in their height would be attributed to inheritance. Heritability would be 1.0. The reason is that their environments (diets in this case) are homogeneous: no differences in environments exist. Thus, any difference in height between people must be attributed to inheritance.

What would happen if a famine hit the island, changing the diet of the people and thus the average height (from 6 feet to 5 feet 10 inches, say)? If the change were uniform (for example, everyone getting 75% of his or her nutritional needs) the heritability would still be 1.0. Although the environment changed drastically, it changed equally for everyone. Thus, because the people's environments remained homogeneous, 100% of the differences in height would still be attributed to inheritance. If the effects of the famine were not uniform, however, the picture would change. If some people still received 100% of their nutritional needs, others 75%, and others only 50%, when you met two men from Louie-Louie who differed by 2 inches in height you would know that, on average, some proportion of this difference must be attributed to differences in diet. That is, heritability has changed to something less than 1.0. The more heterogeneous the environments are, the lower heritability will be. Heritability is thus relative, varying with the environmental conditions in which people within the population live.

The concept of heritability is the same regardless of whether one is studying height or intelligence. One difference between concepts such as height and intelligence, however, is that of measurement. When one expresses height in terms of inches or meters, one is relatively confident that the measure accurately reflects the underlying concept. There is less confidence with intelligence. In most studies

examining the heritability of intelligence, IQ or other psychometric tests are used to measure intelligence. Thus, the findings of these studies more accurately pertain to the heritability of IQ, with IQ being one (popular) index of intelligence.

Elementary Cognitive Tasks and Intelligence

Elementary cognitive tasks (ECTs) are simple laboratory tests designed to measure subjects' response times to make presumably simple decisions. These include short-term memory scanning, retrieval of familiar words from long-term store, and simple categorization tasks (Jensen, 1985). Some of these tasks were described above in discussing information processing approaches to individual differences (Hunt et al., 1981). These "low-level" processes are presumed to be closely related to physiological functioning and thus primarily under the influence of endogenous (and inherited) factors.

Arthur Jensen and his colleagues, among others, have presented evidence that response times for several ECTs are significantly related to *g*-factor scores obtained from conventional psychometric tests (Carlson, Jensen, & Widaman, 1983; Jensen, 1981, 1985; Nettelbeck & Kirby, 1983; Vernon, 1983). As I noted earlier in this chapter, significant relations have been found between efficiency of retrieval from long-term memory store and verbal ability for both adults (Hunt et al., 1981) and children (Keating & Bobbitt, 1978). Following Jensen's argument, variations in these basic cognitive processes are probably inherited and are the basis for individual differences in intelligence. To bolster this contention, several researchers have demonstrated significant relationships between aspects of evoked brain potentials measured via EEG apparatus and psychometrically measured intelligence (Eysenck, 1982; Hendrickson & Hendrickson, 1980).

One study that attempted to assess the genetic basis of ECTs was done by McCue, Bouchard, Lykken, and Feuer (1984). They administered a series of cognitive tasks to monozygotic (that is, genetically identical) twins who had been reared apart. These adult subjects were also administered a battery of psychometric tests, including the WAIS-R.

Among the cognitive tasks were the Posner letter identification (Posner, Boies, Eichelman, & Taylor, 1969) and the Sternberg memory search (Sternberg, 1969). In the letter-identification task, subjects are shown pairs of letters and are to determine as rapidly as possible whether the letters are the same or different. In the *physical-identity* condition, the subjects must respond "same" only if the two letters are physically the same (for example, A and A or *a* and *a*, but not A and *a*). In the *name-identity* condition, the subjects must respond "same" if the letters have the same name (that is, both "A" and "a" have the same name). The difference in response times between the name identity and physical identity conditions has been proposed to reflect the time needed to retrieve the name of the letter from memory (Hunt, 1978). In the Sternberg memory search task, subjects memorize a set of either one, three, or five digits (selected from among 0 to 9). The subjects are then given a single probe digit and are simply to respond whether the probe was in the original set. The amount of time necessary to make a correct decision increases linearly with the number of digits in the memory set. Individual differences in response times on this task reflect differences in the speed with which active memory is scanned.

As in other research, correlations between response times on the information processing tasks and psychometrically measured intelligence were significant, although only of moderate magnitude (correlation between WAIS-R score and overall speed of response = − .31). However, factor analysis of the data revealed a general speed component for the information processing tasks that was strongly related to psychometric estimates of *g*. Furthermore, speed of responding had a strong genetic basis (McCue et al., 1984). The correlation between the component scores for overall speed of processing for the monozygotic twins was .46. This is in contrast to a correlation of − .14 for a smaller set of dizygotic (nonidentical) twins who were also reared apart. The researchers cautioned against interpreting the findings of the dizygotic twins because of the small sample size (number of pairs per test ranged from 11 to 13 for the dizygotic twins; number of pairs of the monozygotic twins per test ranged from 29 to

31). Nevertheless, the findings clearly reflect a strong genetic basis for overall speed of processing on experimental cognitive tasks, with this speed component being strongly related to a general intellectual factor.

Although these findings are intriguing and applauded by many, not all researchers are ready to accept them as conclusive or as representative of functioning on higher-level cognitive tasks. For example, Borkowski and Maxwell (1985) argue that other important cognitive skills are ignored in this research, such as strategic and metacognitive processes. Also, it is well established that response times on simple cognitive tasks can vary greatly as a function of a person's knowledge base. Response times are fast when decisions are made concerning very familiar information but slow when dealing with less familiar information (Case, Kurland, & Goldberg, 1982; Chi, 1977). It may be that differences in knowledge base are indirectly responsible for many of the group and individual differences observed in some of these experiments, and such differences may well be more a function of education and general experience than they are of genetics. As with most of the issues surrounding intelligence, the controversy continues, and future research awaits clarification of these provocative ideas.

Familial Studies of Intelligence

The preponderance of research examining the heritability of intelligence has dealt with comparisons of IQ scores among people of varying genetic relationships. If one holds a genetic theory of intelligence, the greater the genetic similarity between two groups of individuals, the higher the correlations of their IQs should be.

Correlations measure the degree to which two factors vary. Correlations range from 1.0 (a perfect positive relation) to − 1.0 (a perfect negative relation), with 0 being chance. In *familial studies of intelligence*, the IQs of people of a known genetic relationship are correlated. For example, the IQs of sets of monozygotic twins would be obtained, with the score of each twin paired with his or her mate's. These scores can be contrasted with the IQs of randomly chosen, genetically unrelated people. In the latter case, the IQ of one person is paired at random with the IQ of another, and the correlation is computed. In the former case, a high correlation is expected, because the twins are genetically identical and grew up in the same home at the same time. In fact, the strong genetic position would predict a correlation of 1.0 even for monozygotic twins reared apart. In the case of the unrelated people, the correlation should be 0; knowing the IQ of one "unrelated" person would not help predict the IQ of another such person.

Familial studies of intelligence have been conducted since the early part of this century. However, evidence of falsification of data by Sir Cyril Burt, a prominent British psychologist and important contributor to this literature, caused many to question the reliability of the early findings. Recently, Bouchard and McCue (1981) reviewed 111 familial studies of intelligence, eliminating the studies by Burt and others that did not meet their methodological and statistical criteria. Plomin and DeFries (1980) have similarly reviewed the more recent familial studies, and a summary of some of the average correlations from these two investigations is given in Table 10-3.

Generally, the correlations increase as genetic similarity increases, implying a significant role for genetics in patterns of individual differences in intel-

ligence. However, Plomin and DeFries (1980) state that when only the newer studies are considered, the heritability estimates are lower than the older (pre-1963) data indicated. As I mentioned above, heritability is expressed as the percentage of differences in a trait (here, intelligence) that can be attributed to genetics. It is a population statistic and does not indicate "how much" of any individual's intelligence was derived from nature as opposed to nurture. Plomin and DeFries propose that, based on the new data, the heritability of intelligence is approximately .50, meaning that, on average, 50% of the difference in intelligence between people in a population can be attributed to genetics. This is in comparison to the 70% estimates based on the earlier familial studies of intelligence (Erlenmeyer-Kimling & Jarvik, 1963). Both Bouchard and McCue (1981) and Plomin and DeFries (1980) point out that this figure leaves substantial room for the effects of environment on intelligence. But both also state that no other factor, including environment, contributes as much to determining individual differences in intelligence as does genetics.

The combined impact of environment and genetics on intelligence is illustrated in the Transracial Adoption Study of Scarr and Weinberg (1976, 1983). Black children, born primarily of parents from lower-income homes, were adopted by white, primarily upper-middle-class parents. The average

TABLE 10-3   Average Correlations of Familial Studies of Intelligence (Bouchard and McCue, 1981; Plomin and DeFries, 1980)

	Bouchard and McCue (1981)	Plomin and DeFries (1980)
Monozygotic twins reared together	.86	.87
Monozygotic twins reared apart	.72	—
Dizygotic twins reared together	.60	.62
Siblings reared together	.47	.34
Siblings reared apart	.24	—
Parent and child living together	.42	.35
Parent and child separated by adoption	.22	.31
Unrelated children reared together	.32*	.25
Adoptive parent and adoptive child	.19	.15

*Average of adoptive/natural (correlation = .29) and adoptive/adoptive (correlation = .34) pairings

IQ of the adopted children was 110, 20 points higher than the average IQ of comparable children being reared in the local black community. This effect demonstrates a potent influence of environment on IQ. However, the correlation between the children's IQs and their biological mothers' education level (IQ scores were not available for the biological mothers) was significantly higher (.43) than a similar correlation with the children's adoptive parents' educational level (.29). These results replicate the findings of an earlier adoption study reported by Skodak and Skeels (1945).

The findings of this study appear paradoxical at first. How can the level of the adopted children's IQ be more similar to that of their adopted parents, yet the correlation of their IQs be higher with the education level of their biological mothers? To help understand this difference, keep in mind that correlations in this type of research reflect the degree that knowing a parent's IQ (or equivalent) score will predict where a child's IQ will fall relative to other children in his or her particular group. Correlations are independent of level of IQ. That is, correlations predict rank order and not level of IQ. In fact, the 20-point IQ difference between the children and their biological mothers could, theoretically, have been accompanied by a perfect correlation (1.0). In such a hypothetical situation, the child with the highest IQ of all the children (135, let's say) would have the biological mother with the highest IQ of all the mothers (105, let's say), the child with the next highest IQ (125) would have the biological mother with the next highest IQ (100), and so on until the child with the lowest IQ (85), who would have the biological mother with the lowest IQ (60). The correlation would be perfect, yet there would be, on average, a 20-IQ-point difference between the children and their biological mothers.

In the Scarr and Weinberg study, the adopted children had all been placed in intellectually stimulating home environments and had received similar treatment at the hands of their academically accelerating adoptive parents. It was such stimulation that was responsible for their relatively high levels of IQ in comparison with their biological mothers. Furthermore, given the similar patterns of experience that these children had, individual differences

among the children are best predicted by genetics. When environmental conditions are relatively homogeneous, as they presumably were for the adopted children in the Scarr and Weinberg study, the best predictor of individual differences in intelligence will be genetics. Prediction here refers to knowing a child's relative rank in a specified group of children (that is, where the child stands compared with his or her peers) and not to the actual level of IQ. When environments vary considerably (that is, are heterogeneous), differences in environment will play a more substantial role in affecting individual differences in intelligence (see Chapter 11). Thus, had the environments of the adopted families been more varied, chances are the correlations between the IQs of the children and their adoptive parents would have been greater. In other words, the heritability of intelligence is not constant but varies as a function of the similarity of environments among the people under study.

Obviously, intelligence is influenced by both genetic and environmental factors. How the two factors interact to yield a particular level of intelligence is the question most psychologists are asking themselves. Eysenck (1985), a proponent of the genetic basis of intelligence, presented a simple way of conceptualizing the relationship between genetics, environment, and IQ, and this is shown in Figure 10-4. Intelligence A represents innate mental capacity built into the nervous system. Intelligence B represents "social intelligence," or the acquired ability to use one's innate intelligence (Intelligence A) in social situations. Thus, Intelligence B includes Intelligence A but also includes the effects of culture, education, motivation, and personality. IQ tests, contends Eysenck, include all aspects of Intelligence A and some aspects of Intelligence B. Thus, from Eysenck's perspective, IQ assesses mainly the innate contributors to intelligence but also includes some aspects of environmentally determined intelligence.

Scarr and McCartney's
Genotype → Environment Theory

Most of the research just discussed is based on the implicit assumption that genetics has a certain influence on intelligence. However, few studies have

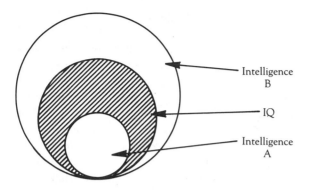

FIGURE 10-4   Hypothetical relation between types of intelligence, following Eysenck. Intelligence A embodies innate intelligence; intelligence B embodies social intelligence (Eysenck, 1985).

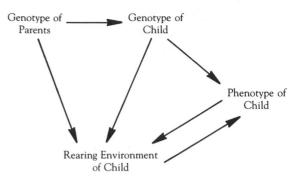

FIGURE 10-5   Scarr and McCartney's model of behavioral development (adapted from Scarr and McCartney, 1983)

addressed exactly how it is that genes affect intelligence or how the pattern of influence might vary with age. Sandra Scarr and Kathleen McCartney (1983) proposed a theory that attempts to do just those things. Basically, their proposal is that one's genotype (genetic constitution) influences which environments one encounters and the type of experiences one has. Their basic contention is that *genes drive experience*. One's genetic makeup determines how one organizes one's world. Thus, environment does play a significant role in shaping intellect, but it is a person's inherited characteristics that will determine, to a large extent, what those experiences are and how they are perceived.

Figure 10-5 presents a schematic of Scarr and McCartney's model of behavioral development. A child's phenotype (his or her observed characteristics) is influenced both by the child's genotype and by his or her rearing environment. The child's genotype is determined by the genotype of his or her parents. The parents' genotype also influences the environment. Parents' genetic characteristics affect the types of environments they feel most comfortable in. In this model, however, the *child's* genotype has an impact on the environment, which, as I said, affects the child's development. Thus, characteristics of the child, as well as the traditional characteristics of the rearing environment and genetic contributions of the parents, influence the course of development.

Scarr and McCartney posit three *genotype → environment* effects, that vary in influence over development. They are *passive*, *evocative*, and *active*. For passive effects, genetically related parents provide the rearing environment for the child. Accordingly, when biological parents rear a child, the effects of genetics and environment cannot be separated, because the people who provide the genetic constitution for a child also provide the environment. The influence of passive effects is proposed to decline with age.

Evocative effects refer to the child's eliciting responses from others that are influenced by his or her genotype. For example, an irritable child is responded to differently than a well-tempered child, and an infant who likes to cuddle receives a different type of attention than an infant who does not want to be held. During early childhood, an attentive and cooperative child receives more positive interactions from parents and teachers than an uncooperative, distractible child. Evocative effects presumably remain constant throughout development.

Active effects refer to one's genotype affecting the type of environments one chooses to experience. A person actively selects an environment in which he or she feels comfortable. Accordingly, people with different genotypes choose to interact in different environments and thus have different experiences that influence their development. Active effects increase with age as children become increasingly independent of their parents.

How does Scarr and McCartney's model relate to individual differences in intelligence? For one thing, it suggests that parents' environmental influence on children should be greatest during the early childhood years and decrease with age as active genotype → environment effects increase. Evidence for this position comes from an adoption study by Scarr and Weinberg (1978, 1983). They reported that the average correlations of samples of adopted siblings (that is, genetically unrelated children living together), measured in early childhood, ranged from .25 to .39. However, the correlation of IQs for adopted siblings measured late in adolescence was 0! That is, the longer these genetically unrelated siblings lived together, the *less* alike in terms of IQ scores they became. Similar findings of reduced correlations with age have been reported for dizygotic (nonidentical) twins. Correlations of the IQs of dizygotic twins computed during the preschool years ranged from .60 to .75 but were reduced to .55 when measured later in childhood (Matheny, Wilson, Dolan, & Krantz, 1981). Following Scarr and McCartney's model, passive genotype → environment effects, as reflected by the type of environments parents provide for their children, decrease with age, and active genotype → environment effects increase; with age, children are increasingly able to select environments that suit their particular needs, and such selection is determined primarily by one's genotype.

Scarr and McCartney's model illustrates how genetic and environmental factors might interact to produce different patterns and levels of intelligence. What is particularly attractive about this model is its consideration of developmental effects. Genetic and environmental effects are not viewed as constants but as dynamic factors that have different effects on intelligence at different points in development. Their theory, in effect, postulates a transaction between developmental function and individual differences. As children become more autonomous with age, the influence of genetic and environmental factors on individual differences changes. As a developmental psychologist, I believe such approaches will be most fruitful in understanding the nature of human intelligence.

☐ Summary

Intelligence is generally understood to reflect goal-directed and adaptive functioning, involving sets of problem solving, verbal, and social skills. The primary approach to the study of individual differences in intelligence has been the *psychometric approach*. Intelligence is described in terms of *factors*, or sets of related abilities that can be discerned on tests by the statistical technique of *factor analysis*. The number of factors that has been proposed to constitute intelligence has varied considerably from two (Spearman's general *g* factor along with less important specific factors) to 180 in Guilford's structure-of-the-intellect model. The impact of the psychometric approach has been most strongly expressed in *IQ tests*. IQ tests assess intellectual abilities relative to a normative population. By knowing a child's IQ score, one knows where that child falls on a continuum with respect to other children his or her age at that particular time. Many researchers and theorists have argued that IQ tests are not theory based and are limited in the type of mental functioning they assess, and they have suggested that alternative means of evaluating intelligence be obtained..

Information processing approaches to intelligence provide researchers with well-developed theories and methods for assessing individual differences in intelligence. Differences in rate of processing, encoding, strategy use, knowledge base, metacognition, and other information processing components have been suggested as the basis for individual differences in children's thinking. Developmental psychologists often use information processing paradigms to explain differences in the thinking of children of different IQ levels (retarded or nonretarded) and children of comparable IQ but differential academic abilities (learning disabled versus nondisabled).

Piagetian approaches have viewed differences in rate of development as an important component of individual differences in intelligence. A number of researchers have correlated children's performance on Piagetian tasks with academic performance and IQ and have generally found significant relations. The research seems to indicate that both Piagetian and psychometric tests assess the same, general form of intelligence but that each also measures aspects of intelligence not measured by the other.

Sternberg's *triarchic theory* is a new approach to the study of intelligence. There are three subtheories in the triarchic theory: *contextual*, *experiential*, and *componential*. The contextual subtheory states that intelligence must be evaluated in the environment in which the individual lives. The experiential subtheory proposes that how people deal with *novelty* and the extent to which they can *automatize* cognitive functioning are important aspects in intelligence. The componential subtheory provides the universal information processing mechanisms by which knowledge is acquired and manipulated. The theory is an attempt to go beyond earlier approaches by viewing intelligence from a wider scope.

One issue central to the study of intelligence is the extent to which it is influenced by genetic or environmental factors. Studies examining *elementary cognitive tasks* (ECTs) have shown that response times for making relatively simple decisions are related to psychometric estimates of *g*, suggesting to some that these simple, and presumably inherited cognitive operations, are the basis for a broader intelligence. Others disagree, asserting that other, higher-order cognitive operations such as strategies and metacognition must also be considered.

Familial studies of intelligence, comparing the IQs of people of varying genetic relations (monozygotic twins, siblings), have been the major tool for assessing the *heritability* of intelligence. Studies show that the correlations of IQs between groups of people increase as genetic similarity increases. The current estimate of the heritability of intelligence is .50, meaning that, on average, 50% of the difference in IQ scores among people in a population can be attributed to inheritance. Heritability is a population statistic and varies with differences in environment. As environments among people become more homogeneous (more similar), the heritability of intelligence increases.

Scarr and McCartney's *genotype → environment theory* proposes that genotype drives experience. They describe three genotype → environment effects: *passive*, where biological parents rear the child; *evocative*, where characteristics of the child elicit responses from others; and *active*, where children select environments in which they choose to interact. Passive effects decrease in influence over time, while active effects increase. Data supporting their theory show that parents' environmental influence on their children's intelligence is greatest during the early years and wanes as the children approach adolescence.

11

Experience and Intelligence
with Marc T. Frankel

Establishing Intellectual Competence

☐ Institutionalization Studies   ☐ A Transactional Approach to the Study of Parent/Child Interaction
☐ Parents as Teachers   ☐ The Home Environment   ☐ The Role of Family Configuration

Modification and Maintenance of Intellectual Functioning

☐ Modification of Retardation Caused by Early Experience
☐ Maintenance of the Beneficial Effects of Early Experience on Intelligence
☐ How Modifiable Is Human Intelligence?

Summary

Most of the material presented thus far has concerned *endogenous*, or internal, influences on development, that is, those originating within children themselves. Following from the behaviorist tradition, it seems logical that there are also *exogenous*, or external, influences on a child's developing intellect and that these factors are highly variable among children. As noted in the preceding chapter, genetic factors can account for some but not all of the individual differences in intelligence among people. Differences in children's environments have been postulated by many as contributing substantially to individual differences in children's thinking, with parents playing the most critical role in affecting intellectual development, both directly by interacting with their children and indirectly by providing an environmental context in which the children develop. Children grow up in a range of environments that differ profoundly in the amount of cognitive stimulation they offer. One home may hold a rich array of books, magazines, newspapers, and art works, whereas a second home may be rather sterile with regard to such materials. Likewise, parents may differ radically in the importance they attach to their children's becoming immersed in intellectual pursuits or in the behaviors they use when teaching and playing. Does a childhood in the more literate atmosphere stimulate cognitive and intellectual skills?

The earliest scientific theories about the nature of intelligence, prevalent in the latter part of the 19th century and the early decades of the 20th, assumed that intelligence was *fixed* and *predetermined*. The nature/nurture controversy is a dynamic and constantly changing one, however, and the pendulum slowly shifted to the nurture side. The theorizing of Freud, with his emphasis on the role of early experience in the establishment of personality, contributed greatly to this shift. But it was the publication in 1961 of J. McVicker Hunt's book *Intelligence and Experience* that focused attention on the role of experience in the development of intelligence. Hunt presented the hypothesis that intelligence is fluid and modifiable through the early years of life. His book had a profound effect on the way psychologists and educators viewed intelligence and intellectual development, and its impact on theory and research

is still felt today. To a large extent as a result of Hunt's book, a vast body of literature has emerged that focuses directly on environmental influences on children's developing intelligence.

The role of experience in affecting children's intelligence is examined in this chapter. In discussing experience and intelligence, it is useful to distinguish among the establishment, modification, and maintenance of intelligence (see Cairns, 1979). What factors are responsible for establishing intellectual competence? Once a certain level of intellectual functioning has been achieved, what is necessary to maintain that level? Finally, to what extent can an established level of intelligence be modified, either positively or negatively? Factors that influence the establishment of intelligence most certainly also exert an influence on its maintenance and modification. But it is important to recognize that these three aspects of the intelligence/experience relationship can be distinct. Once intellectual competence is established, the child will not necessarily maintain that same relative level of intelligence independent of his or her surroundings. That is, establishing some level of intellectual ability does not guarantee that that level will be maintained or that it cannot be modified.

☐ Establishing Intellectual Competence
Institutionalization Studies

Studies examining the effects of early environment on children's intelligence are not a recent invention. Investigations assessing the effects of "maternal deprivation," the separation of infants from their unwed mothers and the rearing of them in overcrowded and understaffed institutions, have been reported from the 1930s (Dennis, 1973; Skeels & Dye, 1939; Spitz, 1945). For example, Dennis (1973) contrasted the outcomes of children reared in an orphanage in Beirut, Lebanon, called the Crèche, with those of infants placed in adoptive homes. The Crèche was a charity-run institution for illegitimate children. Infants received little direct stimulation in the form of play or other social interactions. They spent much of their day in small cribs without toys and with sheets covering the sides, limiting substantially what they could see. Life was more varied for older children, but opportunities for intellectual stimulation and the development of normal patterns of adult/child interaction were minimal. Furthermore, many of the primary caretakers were "graduates" of the Crèche themselves and were characterized by low IQ scores and a general unresponsiveness toward their young wards. Dennis reported that infants who remained institutionalized displayed signs of severe retardation within their first year and that their average IQs by age 16 ranged between 50 and 80. In contrast, infants leaving the Crèche for adoptive homes before the age of 2 years regained normal intellectual functioning, having average IQ scores of about 100. Children adopted following their second birthday also demonstrated gains in intellectual performance, but they typically performed several years below their age level on all subsequent testings.

Dennis's study and others like it are natural experiments and demonstrate how extremes in early environment can affect children's intellectual development. But such studies, although informative, lack the experimental rigor that psychologists like. (For example, there was no random assignment of children to an orphanage or to adoption.) Furthermore, such early deprived environments probably represent an extreme of child rearing and may not be applicable to the vast majority of parent/child interaction styles.

A Transactional Approach to the Study of Parent/Child Interaction

One critical aspect of the early studies investigating the effect of environment on children's intelligence is that most examined only the effects of parents or caretakers on children, ignoring the role that children may have in influencing significant others in their environment. In recent years, psychologists have come to view children as playing a critical role in their own development by influencing their parents' behavior, which, in turn, affects their subsequent growth. Bell (1968) emphasized the notion that parent and child have equal abilities to contribute to a social exchange and that each affects the other. With respect to intellectual development,

this viewpoint holds that cognitive influences are *transactional* (Sameroff, 1975; Sameroff & Chandler, 1975), for not only do the parents act to produce behavior in their children, but the children also modify their parents' behaviors.

Arnold Sameroff (1975) has distinguished the transactional model of development from nativist (that is, genetic), nurturist (that is, environmental), and interactionist models. Schematic representations of these various models are shown in Figure 11-1 (from Sameroff, 1975). Unlike the main-effect models (that is, either nature alone or nurture alone), the interactional and transactional models view both the environment and a child's biological constitution as having significant impacts on the course of development. In the interactional model, the environment is perceived as having a moderating effect on a child's congenital constitution, with the combined effects of constitution and environment being averaged to yield the expected outcome. In contrast, the transactional model views the child's constitution as having a continuous effect on his or her environment, which, in turn, affects the child (and the child's constitution). From this viewpoint, then, development is seen as *the continuous and bidirectional interaction between an active organism with a unique biological constitution and a changing environment.* Although Sameroff used the transactional model primarily to explain the long-term effects of biological impairments during early infancy in different environments, the model, in general form, can be applied to explain parent/child interactions in a wide range of contexts.

The transactional model has been used to understand the nature of differences in intelligence among children as a function of socioeconomic status. Socioeconomic status (SES) is customarily defined in terms of level of family income, occupational status, and years of parental education. Research has consistently shown that a significant portion of the differences in IQ and academic achievement among children can be attributed to SES factors (Lavin, 1965; Miner, 1957), with children from lower-class homes faring worse than children from more advantaged homes.

Variables such as SES do not influence children

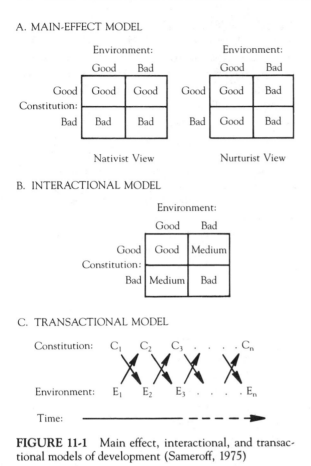

A. MAIN-EFFECT MODEL

Environment: Environment:

Good   Bad   Good   Bad

	Good	Bad
Good	Good	Good
Constitution: Bad	Bad	Bad

	Good	Bad
Good	Good	Bad
Constitution: Bad	Good	Bad

Nativist View   Nurturist View

B. INTERACTIONAL MODEL

Environment:

Good   Bad

	Good	Bad
Good	Good	Medium
Constitution: Bad	Medium	Bad

C. TRANSACTIONAL MODEL

Constitution: C_1 C_2 C_3 . . . . C_n

Environment: E_1 E_2 E_3 . . . . E_n

Time: ———————— – – – – ➤

FIGURE 11-1 Main effect, interactional, and transactional models of development (Sameroff, 1975)

independently of other factors. Thus, there is a high correlation between SES and home environment, friend selection, neighborhood, academic expectation, and academic opportunities, among others (Henderson, 1981). One factor related to SES is trauma suffered early in infancy, such as prematurity, fetal malnutrition, and anoxia (oxygen deprivation). Pasamanick and Knobloch (1966) proposed a *continuum of reproductive casualty*, with degree of biological impairment at birth influencing the level of cognitive functioning later in life. Not surprisingly, infants born of lower-class parents are more likely to experience such trauma than infants born to middle-class parents. However, perinatal distress influences not only the biological system of a child but also the type of environment the child experiences. Sameroff and Chandler (1975) proposed a *continuum*

of caretaker casualty to include environmental risk factors that may lead to poor developmental outcomes. Basically, they proposed that some caretaking environments (middle-class homes) are more likely to produce intellectually and socially competent children than others (lower-class homes). Furthermore, children who experience perinatal trauma were proposed to be especially susceptible to nonsupportive caretaking, so that the negative consequences of early biological impairment are exacerbated in such environments. That is, they proposed a transaction between infants' biological constitution and their environment, as reflected by differences in SES.

Support for Sameroff and Chandler's model was provided by an examination of the outcomes of children experiencing stress at birth (anoxia) as a function of their SES level. Although differences in developmental level between normal and biologically impaired infants are obvious at birth in both lower- and middle-class groups, these differences are diminished and often eliminated by age 6 or 7 years in middle-class homes. In contrast, these differences are maintained or increase with age in lower-class homes. Sameroff and Chandler speculated that distressed infants, characterized by more aversive cries, slower attainment of social-developmental milestones such as smiling and vocalization, and a sickly appearance, receive different types of treatment in different environments. In reasonably affluent and well-educated families, these distressed children may receive lavish attention and stimulation, facilitating the amelioration of their impaired condition. In deprived, stressed, and poorly educated families, these same infant characteristics result in a pattern of reduced attention and stimulation and, thus, continued cognitive and social deficits. That is, there is a transaction between parent and child, with the particular characteristics of the child interacting with the particular characteristics of the parents, yielding distinct patterns of development.

Recently, Zeskind (1986), expanding on Sameroff and Chandler's model, has emphasized the particular effect that the aversive cries of infirm infants can have on different parents. The sickly, piercing cry of a premature or anoxic baby is likely to be a signal to better educated and more affluent parents that their child needs special nurturing. This realization should result in a positive parent/child interaction pattern and a generally healthy outcome for the child. The same aversive cry may serve as a stressor for less well educated and impoverished parents, leading to a cycle of neglect and even abuse, neither of which is conducive to good intellectual development.

The effects of different caretaking environments as a function of infants' biological status were assessed experimentally in a series of studies by Zeskind and Ramey (1978, 1981). Infants from poor, rural environments who had been classified as at "high risk" for mental retardation were assigned to one of two care-giving environments. Infants in one group received medical care and nutritional supplements and participated in an educationally oriented day-care program beginning at approximately 3 months of age (experimental group). Infants in a control group received the medical care and nutritional supplements but did not partake in the day-care program. Within each group, approximately half of the infants were classified as being fetally malnourished at birth, whereas the remaining infants were described as being biologically normal. Fetal malnourishment typically produces infants who are developmentally delayed and lethargic and who have aversive cries.

At 3 months of age, fetally malnourished infants in both the control and experimental groups had lower developmental scores on the Bayley Mental Developmental Index than the nonmalnourished (normal) infants. However, Stanford-Binet IQ scores at 24 and 36 months demonstrated (1) overall higher IQ scores for the experimental than for the control children, (2) no difference in IQ scores between the normal and fetally malnourished infants in the experimental group, and (3) higher IQ scores for the normal than for the fetally malnourished infants in the control group. IQ scores at 36 months are shown for the four groups of this experiment in Table 11-1. In general, the pattern of IQ change observed in this experiment is similar to that observed by Sameroff and Chandler (1975), with the effects of a nonsupportive environment (the control group) being especially deleterious for the biologically distressed children.

Zeskind and Ramey also measured the degree of mother/child interaction in the home. They reported that in the experimental group there was no difference in the amount of maternal attention received by fetally malnourished and normal infants. In the control group, however, fetally malnourished infants were receiving less maternal attention by 24 months than the normal children. The researchers proposed, consistent with Sameroff's transactional interpretation, that the increased responsivity of fetally malnourished infants receiving the educational day care resulted in increased attention from their mothers and a generally positive developmental outcome. In contrast, the withdrawn and sickly behavior of the fetally malnourished infants in the control group resulted in less maternal attention, exaggerating the injurious effects of their biological impairment.

One problem with theories and research regarding socioeconomic effects is that they do not reflect unitary factors. This is made obvious in the Zeskind and Ramey experiments, in which children from impoverished homes were observed to suffer greater perinatal stress (fetal malnutrition) as well as less supportive home environments than would be expected in middle-class families. Family environment and socioeconomic level are aggregate variables that are themselves made up of many separate but strongly related items. To say that SES has a profound effect on intellectual development tells us nothing about the particular aspects of SES that account for the variance in performance. The central question when studying SES or related factors thus becomes "What aspects of experience are most important in the unfolding of intelligence?" Clearly,

TABLE 11-1   Mean Stanford-Binet IQ Scores at 36 Months for Fetally Malnourished and Biologically Normal Children as a Function of Participation in Educational Day Care (adapted from Zeskind and Ramey, 1981)

	Biologically normal	Fetally malnourished
Experimental (day-care) group	98.1	96.4
Control group	84.7	70.6

as reflected by Zeskind and Ramey's results, how parents interact with their children influences intellectual development. In the sections to follow, both laboratory and naturalistic research designed to investigate more precisely how parents influence their children's intelligence are examined.

Parents as Teachers

Parental Teaching Styles

One implicit assumption of the research on parents' roles in influencing their children's intelligence is that how parents (particularly mothers) instruct their children in intellectual tasks is probably important in how the children's intelligence develops. Pioneering work examining how mothers teach their children (*maternal teaching styles*) was conducted by Hess and Shipman (1965). In their initial study, they asked mothers from a wide range of SES levels to teach their children how to perform some simple tasks, among them an oddity problem. In oddity problems, a child is shown a set of items, one of which is different in some way from the others. For example, children may be shown pictures of a dog, a horse, a cow, and a flower and asked which picture does not belong with the other three. The mothers were to explain the task to their children so that they could later solve similar problems on their own.

When tested by an experimenter, middle-class children performed better after being taught by their mothers than did children from lower-class families. More important, however, were differences in how the mothers taught their children the tasks. In general, the cognitive environments created by the middle-class women were more advanced than those created by the lower-class women, most notably in terms of the use of language. Hess and Shipman isolated what they called a *restricted verbal code* in the maternal teaching styles of the lower-income mothers as opposed to the *elaborated verbal code* typical of the middle-income mothers (see also Bernstein, 1960). In effect, the lower-income mothers used brief, impersonal verbal messages with their children, thus limiting action and thought on the part of the child (for example, "Which one is different?" or "Is this one different? This one?"). Conversely, the middle-income mothers used specific, individualized messages that allowed a wider and more complex range of thought on their children's part, such as analyzing the task for various strategic options ("Look at all the pictures first before you pick one") and breaking down big tasks into smaller components ("Are *dog* and *horse* alike in any way? How about *horse* and *cow?*"). The assumption that differences in maternal teaching styles are causally related to children's intelligence is reflected in Hess and Shipman's statement that "teaching styles of the mothers induce and shape learning styles and information processing strategies in the children" (1965, p. 885).

Working with 5- and 6-year-old children, Rollins (1979) had mothers teach their children to organize a set of pictures according to conceptual categories (for example, sorting pictures into groups such as ANIMALS, TOYS, and FRUIT) and prepare them to remember those pictures for a later memory test. Rollins found that some mothers were strategy oriented; that is, they focused on the hierarchical nature of the sorting task (for example, *blocks, ball*, and *balloon* are all TOYS). These women also provided approval and feedback to their children contingent upon what the children had done. Children of these mothers asked many strategy-oriented questions (for example, "Is a *stool* FURNITURE?") and responded appropriately to their mothers' requests. By contrast, Rollins identified a second group of mothers who communicated in a highly concrete and declarative manner ("Show me the *dog*" or "That's a *banana*"), emphasizing individual cards as opposed to categories ("Try to remember *dog*" rather than "Try to remember all the ANIMALS"). Such mothers were predominantly disapproving when evaluating their children's behaviors during the session. The children of these mothers gave fewer strategy-oriented responses and, like their mothers, tended to be more concrete and declarative when initiating communication. As might be expected given the difference in maternal teaching styles, the children in the first group (whose mothers were strategic and positive) performed the memory task better than those in the second group.

Most of the early work on maternal teaching styles assumed that parents' behavior drove children's actions and, thus, their intelligence. Children were viewed as being relatively passive recipients in the exchange, a view no longer shared by most developmental psychologists. Consistent with the contemporary view of children as playing an active role in their own development, Davis and Lange (1973) found that parents modified their teaching styles to accommodate to their children's level of cognitive functioning. For instance, they found that parents adjusted their linguistic styles and strategic preferences in a block sorting task according to how they perceived their children's level of understanding. Similarly, Rogoff, Ellis, and Gardner (1984) demonstrated that middle-class mothers adjust their instructions when teaching children a classification task, based on their child's age and the demands of the task. For instance, 6-year-old children received a greater number of directives, open-ended questions, and reviews than did older children. Moreover, these changes in parental communication style were accompanied by better performance by the children.

Parental Teaching Style Research: Strengths and Weaknesses

In general, the way in which mothers (and presumably fathers) interact with their young children in teaching situations varies with socioeconomic level and is related to how the children perform on cognitive tasks. Although most of the research has focused on mothers interacting with their children, some research has been done looking at father/child interaction, with the findings generally being similar to those reported for mother/child dyads (Easterbrooks & Goldberg, 1984; Frankel & Rollins, 1983; Moore, Mullis, & Mullis, 1986).

One favorable aspect of the parental teaching paradigm is that of experimental control. Children from a wide range of backgrounds can be given the same task, and their performance and that of their parents can be assessed under controlled conditions. The disadvantage of such a paradigm is that it may not reflect what happens in real life. Women (and men) may have certain expectations of how they are supposed to behave in these artificial environments, and the types of problems examined in the lab may not reflect the teaching parents do at home. *Naturalistic studies*, examining parent/child interactions

in the home, are critical for understanding the effect that environment has on children's intelligence. Such studies are not without problems either; but the issue of how parents affect their children's intellectual development is not a simple one and must be approached from a variety of research perspectives.

The Home Environment

Naturalistic Studies of Parent/Child Interaction

One of the earliest studies to examine in detail SES differences in the interactions of mothers and their children in a naturalistic setting was that of Tulkin and Kagan (1972). In their study, two groups of mothers and their 10-month-old daughters were observed in their homes. The mothers were told that the investigator was interested in normal child behavior and that it was important for them to behave as normally as possible during these observations. One group of families was described as *working class*, with at least one parent not having graduated from high school and the father having a semiskilled or unskilled job. The second group was described as *middle class*, with at least one of the parents having completed college and the father having a professional occupation.

Tulkin and Kagan noted the characteristics of the physical environment and recorded the behaviors of the mothers toward their infants. With respect to the physical environment, the infants from the middle-class homes had more objects available for play and spent less time being restricted by barriers such as gates, playpens, or highchairs than the infants from the working-class families. The television set was more likely to be on in the working-class homes, and more adults were present.

Most critical for Tulkin and Kagan were the mothers' behaviors toward their children. To the researchers' surprise, there were no differences between the two groups of women in the amount of time spent in close proximity to their infants, in physical contact (holding, kissing), in prohibitions, or in responses to their infants' nonverbal behaviors. However, differences between the middle- and working-class mothers were dramatic for verbal behaviors. The middle-class women were more likely to talk to their preverbal infants than were the working-class women. Although Tulkin and Kagan did not assess the children's cognitive abilities years later, one of the most consistent findings of cognitive differences between children of different socioeconomic levels is in terms of language ability. Apparently, this difference has its origins in early mother/child interactions.

Differences in the verbal behavior of the middle- and working-class women were mirrored by differences in their attitudes about child development. In interviews that followed the completion of the study, many working-class women said they believed that it was not necessary to talk to children until they began to speak themselves and that it was foolish and socially inappropriate to carry on a conversation with a preverbal infant. Additionally, many of these women did not believe that they could have a significant impact on the intellectual development of their children. Like the psychologists at the turn of the century, they believed that intelligence is primarily a result of heredity, with parents playing only a minor role in their children's cognitive development. These views were not shared by the middle-class women.

The Tulkin and Kagan study is informative but limited, given its selection of subjects (10-month-old girls) and the fact that the long-term consequences of early parenting behavior were not assessed. One of the more impressive longitudinal projects evaluating the quality of parent/child interactions and later intelligence is that conducted by Caldwell, Bradley, and Elardo. They developed an inventory for assessing the quality of the home environment, called the Home Observation for Measurement of the Environment (HOME) (Caldwell & Bradley, 1978). The HOME scale is divided into six subscales and is used to code aspects of a child's home environment that relate to intellectual development:

1. Emotional and Verbal Responsivity of the Mother. Sample items:
   a. Mother spontaneously vocalizes to child at least twice during visit (excluding scolding).
   b. Mother responds to child's vocalizations with a vocal or verbal response.
   c. Mother caresses or kisses child at least once during visit.

2. Avoidance of Restriction and Punishment. Sample items:
   a. Mother does not shout at child during visit.
   b. Mother neither slaps nor spanks child during visit.
   c. Mother does not interfere with child's actions or restrict child's movement more than three times during visit.

3. Organization of the Physical and Temporal Environment. Sample items:
   a. Someone takes the child to the grocery store at least once a week.
   b. When mother is away, care is provided by one of three regular substitutes.
   c. The child's environment appears safe and free of hazards.

4. Provision of Appropriate Play Materials. Sample items:
   a. Child has a pull or push toy.
   b. Mother provides toys or interesting activities for child during interview.
   c. Mother provides toys for literature and music (books, records).

5. Maternal Involvement with the Child. Sample items:
   a. Mother tends to keep child within visual range and to look at him or her often.
   b. Mother "talks" to child while doing her work.
   c. Mother structures child's play period.

6. Opportunities for Variety in Daily Stimulation. Sample items:
   a. Father provides some care giving every day.
   b. Mother reads stories to child at least three times weekly.
   c. Child has at least three or more books of his or her own.

Subsequent studies, in which researchers coded mother/child interactions in the homes using the HOME scale, revealed moderate correlations (.30–.60) between these scores and IQ measures (Bee et al., 1982; Bradley & Caldwell, 1976, 1980; Elardo, Bradley, & Caldwell, 1977). More specifically, mothers who were emotionally and verbally more responsive to their infants, who provided more play materials for their children, and who were generally more involved with their children during observations when their infants were 6 and 24 months of age, had children with higher Stanford-Binet IQ scores at 54 months of age than mothers who provided less stimulation for their youngsters (Bradley & Caldwell, 1976). Table 11-2 presents the correlations between 6-month and 24-month HOME scores and 54-month IQ scores for children in this study. Investigators have also reported significant correlations between HOME subtest scores during infancy and subsequent scores on Piagetian cognitive measures (Wachs, Uzgiris, & Hunt, 1971) and tests of psycholinguistic ability (Elardo et al., 1977).

Another major longitudinal study examining the long-term consequences of early parenting styles is the Harvard Preschool Project, directed by Burton White (White, 1978; White et al., 1973). Based on socioeconomic measures, White and his colleagues identified groups of children who were predicted to differ in intellectual abilities by the beginning of the first grade. Commencing at 12 months of age, the children and their mothers were observed on repeated occasions in their homes, and the children were administered tests of cognitive and social skills (including Wechsler IQ tests at age 5) at regular intervals over their preschool years.

White speculated that the most critical time in development for establishing intellectual competence is between the ages of approximately 10 and 18 months. During this time, White proposed, mothers must deal with several changes in their children, and how they handle these changes determines, to a large extent, the course of intellectual development. One major change occurring during this period is *increased locomotion*. Most children are walking by the midteen months or are crawling sufficiently well to be able to get into everything. Infants are born curious, but babies at this age have the motor abilities to do something about it, and toddlers tend to explore their environments to their fullest abilities. How do mothers deal with this increased locomotion and the potential dangers that accompany it? Second, children's *language skills* increase considerably during this period. On average, children do not start putting two words together to make sentences until about 18 months (see Chapter 7). However, children's receptive language—what they can understand—increases dramatically over the first half of the second year. How do mothers handle this increased language ability of their children? Third, children during this period develop a greater sense of *autonomy* and *independence*. (Recall Piaget's description of toddlers during the tertiary circular reaction stage.) Accompanying this independence is the realization that they are distinct from their parents and that they need not comply with every request their parents make. As a result, the word *no* is used fre-

TABLE 11-2 Correlations between 54-Month Stanford-Binet Performance and Scores on the HOME Scale Obtained at 6 and 24 Months (Bradley and Caldwell, 1976)

	Correlations	
Home Observation for Measurement of the Environment	6 months	24 months
1. Emotional and Verbal Responsivity of Mother	.27	.50**
2. Avoidance of Restriction and Punishment	.10	.28*
3. Organization of Physical and Temporal Environment	.31*	.33*
4. Provision of Appropriate Play Materials	.44**	.56**
5. Maternal Involvement with Child	.28*	.55**
6. Opportunities for Variety in Daily Stimulation	.30*	.39**
Total score	.44**	.57**
Multiple correlation[a]	.50*	.63**

[a]This represents the correlation of all HOME subscales with Binet scores.
*$p < .05$.
**$p < .01$.

quently by the toddler. How do mothers deal with this negativism?

Based on analyses of their observations and the IQ level of the children at 5 years of age, White and his colleagues concluded that mothers who reared intellectually competent children tended to do three things particularly well. First, these women structured the physical environment so that it facilitated exploration on the part of their children. They provided a large variety of play objects and permitted their toddlers access to most of the living area of the house. The homes of these women were child-proofed and often not spic and span. There seemed to be a realization that a tidy house and a toddler were incompatible.

Second, these mothers served as "consultants" to their children. When their children were faced with a problem and asked for help, they assisted them, talked to them, often using language a bit more complex than they could comprehend, and suggested some alternative approaches to the problem. They tried to share their children's enthusiasm ("Wow, isn't it wonderful the way these soup cans roll!") but did not take over the activity from the child. Generally, it was the child who initiated the interaction and the child who terminated it. Most of these mother/child encounters lasted less than 30 seconds. These women also engaged in more long one-on-one interactions with their children than women who reared less intellectually competent children (for example, doing puzzles together or reading stories), but most of the interactions were of the abbreviated type described above.

The third thing women who reared intellectually competent children did particularly well concerned discipline. White reported that these women had presented a structured environment for their children with reasonably well-defined rules that were enforced firmly and consistently. However, these women simultaneously displayed deep love for their children and respect for their interests.

The results of naturalistic studies are generally consistent in their findings. Mothers who provide their children with a rich variety of objects with which to interact and who frequently talk to and provide intellectually stimulating tasks for their chil-

dren tend to have brighter children than women who provide less such stimulation. These parenting styles are correlated with SES level, although there are many parents from lower-class homes who do an excellent job of giving their children cognitively rich experiences, and there are middle-class parents who do a less than adequate job of providing their children the intellectual stimulation associated with academic success.

The Role of Children in Affecting Their Own Development

One criticism of the observational studies reviewed above is that they are correlational in nature, making any definitive statement about cause and effect impossible. For example, White reported that placing children behind barriers, such as in a playpen, for long periods is not conducive to good intellectual development. Given White's findings, it is tempting to conclude that restricting a child's exploration by extensive use of a playpen *causes* lower levels of intellectual functioning at a later time. Although this may be true, the role of the child must also be considered. Some children are easier to keep in a playpen than others. Some children are content sitting and playing with a few favorite toys and rarely complain about their confinement. Other children make it very difficult for their parents to make frequent use of the playpen, letting them know in no uncertain terms that life behind bars is not for them. The end result may be the same: The child given more freedom to explore develops a sharper intellect than the child who spends more time in the playpen. However, factors inherent in the child (that is, tolerance for confinement) may be just as critical as the parents' behavior in affecting the course of development. Again, parent/child interaction must be viewed as transactional, and we should not lose track of the child's role in influencing the structure of his or her own environment.

A home observational study that considered the possible role of children in influencing their own development was conducted by Carew (1980). Carew observed the behaviors of mothers and their children in their homes when the children were between the ages of 12 and 33 months and related her observations to children's IQ scores at 36 months. In findings similar to those of White and of Caldwell and her colleagues, Carew reported that mothers' behaviors (for example, providing highly intellectual stimulation) when their children were between 12 and 27 months of age best predicted IQ level at 36 months. However, mothers' behaviors toward their children for the 30- to 33-month observation period were less predictive of IQ. During this time, solitary, child-initiated activities accounted for more of the individual differences in IQ level at 36 months than did mothers' behaviors. This finding suggests that the direct influence of parents on children's behavior diminishes with age, as children take an increasingly active role in guiding their own development (see Scarr & McCartney, 1983). This decline, of course, in no way implies that how parents behave toward their children has no impact on them after 30 months of age. What must be kept in mind, however, is that children play a crucial role in influencing their *own* development at an early age and that parental influences must be evaluated in terms of a continuous transaction between children and their parents, both of whom are changed as a result of the interactions.

Parent/Child Effects in Later Childhood

As an examination of the studies reviewed thus far indicates, the bulk of research concerned with environmental effects on children's intelligence has focused on the early preschool years. This concentration is based on the implicit assumption that experiences early in life set the stage for later development and are thus of particular importance. As the findings of Carew indicate, however, it may be that intellectual performance during the early preschool years is more under the direct influence of a child's parents than performance during later childhood. With children's increasing age and their development of interests outside the home, their parents' influence on their intellectual functioning wanes. In fact, recall from Scarr and McCartney's (1983) theory that active genotype → environment effects are proposed to increase again in later childhood and adolescence as children become increasingly able to choose their own environments in which to experience life (see Chapter 10).

Some support for this position was obtained in a study by McCall, Applebaum, and Hogarty (1973). As part of the Fels study, a longitudinal project assessing aspects of psychological functioning from infancy into adulthood, children and their parents were evaluated on a variety of behavioral and attitudinal factors over a 15-year period (IQ tests were given to children between the ages of 2½ and 17 years). The McCall team examined aspects of parents' child-rearing practices, including their attitudes toward discipline and academic achievement. Children having the highest overall IQ levels and showing the greatest increases in test scores over childhood (between ages 3 and 12) were characterized as having parents who were "accelerating," in that they strove to increase their children's mental or motor development. These parents also tended to have clear household policies, were rewarding, and had medium to severe penalties for their children's transgressions. The researchers described these parents as providing an encouraging and rewarding environment with some structure and enforcement of rules. These findings are consistent with the notion that increases in IQ over the early school years are at least partially attributable to the influence of academically oriented parents. However, these children experienced a decline in IQ beginning in early adolescence, when their parents' influence on their day-to-day lives diminished. This study will be discussed in greater detail in Chapter 12.

The Effects of Experience on Intelligence from a Developmental Perspective

The studies by Carew and by McCall and his colleagues suggest that the contributions of home environment to individual differences in children's intelligence vary at different times in development. That is, there is not a constant relation between environment and intelligence but, rather, a dynamic one, changing over time. Along similar lines, the possibility that genetic and environmental factors influence children's intellects differently at different ages was investigated in a longitudinal study by Yeates, MacPhee, Campbell, and Ramey (1983). They examined the intellectual development of lower-class children classified as at high risk for mental retardation. Children were given Stanford-Binet

IQ tests at ages 24, 36, and 48 months. Their mothers were also administered an IQ test, and the investigators assessed the quality of the home environment and mother/child interactions at various points over the course of the study, using the HOME scale of Caldwell and her colleagues.

Using maternal IQ level as a measure of genetic influence on children's intelligence, Yeates and his colleagues reported that at 24 months, measures of maternal IQ and of home environment combined accounted for only 11% of the differences in children's IQ scores, with the presumably genetic influence of maternal IQ accounting for almost all of this variance. The picture changed, however, by 48 months. At this time, the combined effects of maternal IQ level and home environment accounted for nearly three times as much of the differences in children's Stanford-Binet scores as was the case at 24 months (29%), with maternal IQ level and the HOME measure contributing equally to individual differences.

Following a theory proposed by McCall (1981), Yeates and his associates suggested that neither genetic nor environmental differences have much effect on children's mental development over the first 2 years. McCall had asserted that infant development is highly *canalized*, meaning that it follows a species-typical pattern in all but the most limited environments. For instance, nearly all children babble (even deaf babies), walk, and acquire object permanence sometime before their second birthday. These patterns of development are relatively unaffected by all but the most adverse effects of genetics and environment. With the advent of symbolic functioning, the quality of cognition changes, and, according to McCall, children's intellects are more affected by variations in *both* genetics and environment. Although they were speculating, the Yeates team suggested that genetic influences on intelligence are most pronounced immediately after this sensorimotor-to-symbolic shift (between 2 and 3 years) but that environmental effects increase in influence after this point. In other words, the effects of individual differences in environment (and genetics) seem to have different impacts on children's intelligence at different times in development. The picture is further complicated when children's self-initiated activities are also considered (see Carew, 1980; McCall et al., 1973; Scarr & McCartney, 1983).

This developmental analysis of the effects of experience on intelligence forces a re-examination of some of the interpretations of the studies reviewed earlier in this chapter. For example, White (1978) proposed that the role of parents in affecting children's intellectual development was most critical for the 10- to 18-month age period. However, his study did not take into consideration children's environments much beyond this period. Supportive and nurturing parents of toddlers are likely to be similarly supportive when their children are 3, 4, and 5 years old. Thus, the significant correlations between parental behaviors during the second year of life and IQ at age 5 cannot be easily interpreted. Although environmental causes are clearly indicated, the exact nature of the relationship is not apparent. Competent parenting when the child is older may be equally or even more important than "good" parenting early in a child's life. Alternatively, the supportive behaviors of mothers when their children are 15 months old may produce competent 3-year-olds, and it may be the self-directed behavior of children from this point on that is mainly responsible for high IQs at age 5.

Although the overall picture is somewhat murky, it is apparent that experiences during the preschool years set the stage for later intellectual accomplishments. Supportive and responsive environments tend to produce intelligent and competent children. It is impossible at this time to specify *when*, during childhood, these experiences are most important or to be precise concerning the role children have in affecting their own development. Rather, from the available literature one can conclude that early experience is important but so is later experience. Also, from infancy, children play an important role in their own development, helping to shape their own intellects. One cannot put any numbers or percentages on "how much" of intellectual growth is influenced by nature or nurture or "how much" is child initiated or parent initiated. From the current perspective, in fact, "how much" is the wrong question. The better question concerns how nature and nurture interact to yield a particular pattern of development, always keeping in mind that the child plays an active role in shaping his or her own life course.

The Role of Family Configuration

A very different approach to explaining individual differences from an experiential perspective has been proposed by Zajonc and his colleagues (Zajonc & Markus, 1975; Zajonc, Markus, & Markus, 1979). Zajonc has reintroduced an old idea to modern psychology: that the size and configuration of one's family contribute significantly to one's intelligence. In general, researchers over the years have reported that one's IQ decreases as family size increases and that intellectual performance varies as a function of one's birth order (see Cicirelli, 1978). Zajonc and his colleagues developed a framework called *confluence theory* to explain the assumed relationship between cognitive functioning and family configuration. His theory holds that the intellectual environment of the family has a direct and formative effect on the intellectual development of children. He defined intelligence as an absolute level of functioning not corrected for age (similar to the concept of mental age) and thus unlike the traditional IQ scores. Likewise, he construed the intellectual environment of the family to be the average of the intelligence of all its members. In effect, the confluence model predicts that the greater the combined intelligence of family members surrounding a child, the greater will be that child's own intelligence. For example, the more young children there are in a family, the lower is the overall "intelligence" of that family. As children get older and more intelligent, the intellectual average of the family increases. Thus, a child born into a five-member family including three toddlers would live in a less cognitively sophisticated environment than a child born into a three-member family or a child born into a five-member family with teenage (and thus more intelligent) siblings.

Another important factor in Zajonc's model is having the opportunity to play the role of teacher. Children benefit intellectually by teaching younger siblings. Thus, an only child's intellectual level will not be so great as that of a first-born in a two- or three-child family, because he or she will not have

the opportunity to instruct a younger brother or sister. Last-born children suffer similarly.

Zajonc originally tested his model by analyzing IQ data from 386,114 men from the Netherlands who turned 19 between the years 1963 and 1966 (Belmont & Marolla, 1973). The IQ patterns of these men, as a function of family size and birth order, are shown in Figure 11-2. As can be seen, the data fit Zajonc's model well. Average IQs generally decrease both with increasing family size and ascending birth order.

Zajonc's theory has stimulated substantial research interest over the last decade. However, the results of many studies question the appropriateness of his model (Brackbill & Nichols, 1982; Rodgers & Rowe, 1985). Researchers have generally found that most of their data fall in the direction predicted by the confluence model, but simpler mathematical models can often account for the results (Rodgers, 1984). Also, as can be seen from Figure 11-2, the absolute magnitude of IQ differences is often quite small, so that the model can account for only a relatively small proportion (about 15%) of IQ differences among people (Galbraith, 1982). Others, however, have found substantial support for Zajonc's theory, contending that most of the researchers whose data dispute the confluence model have not had access to adequate data samples or failed to perform the proper statistical analyses (Berbaum & Moreland, 1985). In any case, the interest in the relationship between family configuration variables such as birth order remains high, and the confluence model has served as a good starting point for renewed investigation into an old topic.

☐ Modification and Maintenance of Intellectual Functioning

It seems clear from the preceding discussion that individual differences in intelligence can be influenced by a child's early environment. A related series of questions concerns the modification and maintenance of intelligence. Will the elevated or depressed IQ levels found in some populations still

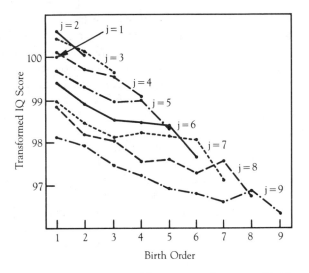

FIGURE 11-2 Average IQ scores as a function of birth order and family size (Zajonc and Markus, 1975)

be present decades later, or can people's level of intellectual functioning be modified by subsequent experiences?

In the sections to follow, the modification and maintenance of intellectual functioning will be considered for two related sets of conditions. First, to what extent are the intellectual deficits resulting from an impoverished early environment permanent? Can the deleterious effects of deprivation be ameliorated? And second, to what extent are the intellectual benefits resulting from enriched early environments permanent? Are intellectual skills that have been acquired during the preschool years maintained into later childhood?

Modification of Retardation Caused by Early Experience

As noted previously in this chapter, an early impoverished environment often results in reduced mental functioning. Based on the results of institutionalization studies of the type described earlier (Dennis, 1973; Goldfarb, 1947), it was assumed that the deleterious effects of stimulus and social deprivation were permanent (Hunt, 1961). Nevertheless, evidence suggesting the reversibility of the negative consequences of early deprivation surfaced from time to

time. Observations of children reared in relative isolation, for example, have indicated some plasticity of intellectual functioning with rehabilitation. One of the best-documented studies of the mental growth of isolated children is that of Koluchova (1972, 1976). A set of monozygotic twins, who were physically and psychologically normal at 11 months, experienced abuse, neglect, and malnutrition until discovered at 7 years 2 months. The children had no language and had an estimated mental age of about 3 years. They were placed in foster care and provided an educational program in the hope that they would attain some semblance of intellectual normalcy. The program was far more successful than originally expected, with the twins having WISC scores of 93 and 95 by 11 years of age and of 101 and 100 by 14 years. Several other studies have similarly reported normal intellectual or language functioning following educational intervention for children initially classified as retarded due to neglect or isolation over the preschool years (Clarke & Clarke, 1976; Davis, 1947; Mason, 1942). It must be noted, however, that these are exceptions. Not all children who experience severe deprivation early in life show such reversibility as a result of later education (Curtiss, 1977).

Related to the findings of the "isolation" studies are more recent reports of the intellectual performance of Asian children adopted into American homes. With the political turmoil in Southeast Asia during the 1970s, many abandoned and sickly children were adopted by American families. Generally, follow-up interviews of adopted Asian children who were malnourished and socially deprived as infants revealed that their intellectual and social development was at or above normal by early childhood (Clark & Hanisee, 1982; Winick, Meyer, & Harris, 1975). In the 1982 study by Clark and Hanisee, for example, 25 adopted Asian children were given a test of verbal intelligence, the Peabody Picture Vocabulary Test (PPVT), and a test of social competence, the Vineland Social Maturity Scale (VSMS). The average age of the children at the time of testing was 44 months, and all the children had been in their adoptive homes for at least 23 months before testing. Before being adopted, most of the children had experienced physical and psychological deprivation. Sixteen of them were reported to have been malnourished sometime during infancy, with many displaying dehydration and muscle weakness. Despite their inauspicious beginnings, the children fared exceptionally well on the tests of verbal and social competencies. The national average on both the PPVT and the VSMS is 100. The adopted children's average scores were 120 on the PPVT and 137 on the VSMS. These children, impoverished and malnourished as infants, showed no residual signs of their early deprivation within 2 years of having been placed in upper-middle-class homes.

One controversial study concerning the reversibility of the negative effects of early experience was reported by Skeels (1966). An initial study (Skeels & Dye, 1939) described the conditions of young inmates at an orphanage. The orphanage was similar to many other Depression-era institutions, overcrowded and understaffed, and it was the type of institution that had been associated with reduced mental functioning by as early as 4 months of age (Spitz, 1945).

Two baby girls who were malnourished and had been neglected by their families were committed to the orphanage and were assessed by the institution's staff. The girls (ages 13 and 16 months) were deemed to be severely retarded and were transferred to a school for the mentally retarded. They were placed on the wards of some of the older, brighter girls and women in the school and were the only preschool children on their wards. As such, they received heavy attention from the other inmates. Upon reexamination only 6 months later, the girls were classified as near normal in intelligence. Skeels believed the stimulation that the developmentally delayed children received from the mentally retarded women was responsible for their dramatic turnaround, and a larger-scale project was planned to evaluate this possibility.

Over the course of several years, 13 children (10 girls and 3 boys) from the orphanage were transferred to a school for the mentally retarded and placed on the wards of the brighter women inmates. These infants all showed signs of retardation at time of placement. Their IQ scores ranged from 35 to 89, with an average of 64.3. The average age at place-

ment was 19 months, with a range from 7 to 36 months. These 13 children made up the experimental group. A contrast group was chosen from children who remained in the orphanage until at least the age of 4, 8 boys and 4 girls. The mean IQ score of the children in this group was 86.7 when first tested (mean age at first test = 16 months), with a range from 50 to 101.

As with the two original girls described previously, the children in the experimental group received loving attention from the mentally retarded women. There was competition between wards to see who would have the first baby to walk or to talk. The attendants also spent much time with the youngsters, and the children were generally the recipients of constant attention. In almost every case, a single adult (inmate or attendant) became closely attached to a child, resulting in an intense one-to-one relationship that was supplemented by less intense but frequent interactions between the child and other adults.

Experimental children remained in the institution for an average of 19 months and were then returned to the orphanage, with most being subsequently placed in adoptive homes. Upon their removal from the school for the mentally retarded, each child was administered an IQ test; the average score was 91.8, an increase of 27.5 points. Children in the contrast group were tested at approximately 4 years of age and had an average IQ score of 60.5 points, a decline of 26.2 points. Children were retested approximately 2½ years later, with the experimental group having an average score of 95.9 and the contrast group an average of 66.1.

The results of this study are very impressive and demonstrate that toddlers characterized as severely retarded can realize significant gains in intelligence when placed in certain environments. Skeels extended his study, following these people into adulthood when they were between 25 and 35 years old. IQ tests were not given, but information was obtained concerning the occupational and educational levels of the subjects, as well as information pertinent to social adjustment. Of the 13 people in the experimental group, all had married, whereas only 2 of the 11 surviving members of the contrast group had married. The median number of years of formal education completed by the experimental group was 12 (that is, high school education), whereas the contrast group had completed a median of only 2.75 years. With respect to employment, most experimental subjects or their spouses were employed in skilled or semiskilled jobs. The range of socioeconomic status, based on income and occupation, was comparable to regional norms. In contrast, with 1 exception, subjects in the contrast group were in the lowest two socioeconomic levels. Four of the subjects in the contrast group remained institutional inmates, 5 held menial jobs such as dishwashers or cafeteria help, and only 1 had a skilled occupation (compositor and typesetter). Although IQ tests were not administered to the subjects as adults, IQ scores were available for some of the 28 children of the experimental subjects. IQ levels of these children ranged from 86 to 125, with an average of 103.9. In general, the experimental group, who started life with a severe disadvantage, were, by a variety of intellectual, occupational, and social standards, normal.

The Skeels study demonstrates the potential plasticity of human intelligence. However, the study is not without its detractors. As an experiment, it leaves much to be desired. Skeels took advantage of a naturally occurring situation and assessed the effects of early environments within the constraints imposed upon him by ethical and institutional considerations. As a result, there is much to fault with the methodology of the study, and, although the study has been widely praised, its serious shortcomings have also been noted (see Longstreth, 1981). One problem with the results was that they did not make sense given the predominant theoretical perspective of the time. The developmentally delayed children had experienced deleterious rearing conditions for too long to expect so dramatic a reversal, particularly at the hands of mentally retarded women.

One interpretation consistent with the transactional view of development that is popular today is that the intellectual immaturity of the retarded women may actually have facilitated social interaction with the orphans, providing them with stimulation they would not normally have received in the orphanage. In most situations, the characteristics of the severely retarded children in the experimental group would not produce lavish attention from adults. Most well-intending adults who direct their attention to a child expect some response in return. Children who are nonresponsive and generally lethargic tend not to elicit continued stimulation from adults, particularly adults from highly stressed or lower-class backgrounds (Sameroff & Chandler, 1975; Zeskind, 1986). This presumably would be especially true of overburdened members of an institution staff. Because of the limited mental capacity of the inmates, however, their attention may have been repeatedly directed to the children even in the absence of appropriate responses. After prolonged stimulation, the children may have become more responsive and begun the climb back to normal intellectual functioning. That is, it is possible that the intellectual immaturity of the institutionalized women in the Skeels study matched the needs of the children. Of course, highly responsive women of normal or above-normal intelligence could also have served as appropriate "therapists" for these children, as was apparently the case in the Asian adoption studies cited above (Clark & Hanisee, 1982). But this is not the type of experience that these children could have expected from the orphanage staff. Moreover, had the children remained in the institution for the mentally retarded for considerably longer, their intellectual gains would surely have been lost. As their intelligence increased, so would their needs for intellectual stimulation, quickly exceeding the boundaries of what the mentally retarded women could have provided.

Another controversial study purporting to illustrate the reversibility of the effects of impoverished early experience is a cross-cultural project by Kagan and Klein (1973). They evaluated the rearing environments and intellectual development of children living in an isolated farming village in Guatemala called San Marcos. During the first year of life, infants were tightly bundled and restricted to the inside of a windowless hut. The babies were frequently ill, and some suffered from malnutrition. There were very few toys or objects with which to play, and adults were minimally interactive with the infants, spending most of their waking hours working outside and away from the hut. The children remained restricted to the hut until they were able to locomote well, usually between 13 and 16 months.

Similar to institutionalized children (Spitz, 1945), the infants in San Marcos displayed retarded intellectual and social development during their first 2 years. One-year-olds were quiet, motorically flaccid, and inactive. They rarely smiled. In comparison to middle-class American infants, the San Marcos babies showed poorer visual and auditory attention and were behind developmental norms for achieving such skills as object permanence. These infants were slower to develop fear-of-stranger reactions, and they were retarded with respect to language development. All in all, the early restricted experiences of the babies seemed to result in serious developmental delays.

The world of the infants changed, however, once they were able to walk. Upon leaving the confinement of the hut, they encountered a complex world of people, domestic animals, and other children. Children in San Marcos are assigned adult tasks at an early age, so that 8-year-olds may be responsible for cooking meals, helping their fathers in the fields, cleaning, or taking care of infants. This drastic change in environment was accompanied by a similar change in the outward appearance of the children. The passive and unresponsive toddlers became alert and active children and gave the impression of possessing a normal level of intelligence.

Kagan and Klein tested this hypothesis by administering the San Marcos children (ages 5 through 12 years) a series of cognitive tests and comparing their performance with that of other Guatemalan children who had not been restricted as infants and to American children of the same age. The tests included recall of familiar objects, recognition memory for photographs of faces, perceptual analysis as reflected by performance on the Embedded Figures Test, and perceptual and conceptual inferences (for example, how accurately children can identify an object when given only partial information describing it). In general, by the age of 10 the children of San Marcos performed as well on these tasks as did middle-class American children, despite the deprived conditions of their first year of life and their early signs of retardation.

Kagan and Klein interpreted their data as indicating that the intellectually harmful results of early experience can be reversed when children encounter more stimulating and challenging environments beginning in their second year. Special educational intervention is not necessary, so long as the environment is sufficiently stimulating to permit the development of the complex cognitive skills that are the basis for successful functioning in all human societies.

Although Kagan and Klein's data indicated comparable intellectual functioning between Guatemalan Indian and American children by 10 years of age, a more recent study by the same authors has questioned that conclusion (Kagan, Klein, Finley, Rogoff, & Nolan, 1979). These researchers tested Guatemalan children from impoverished San Marcos and children from the more prosperous town of San Pedro on a variety of intelligence-related tasks and compared their performance with that of American children. The tasks used in this study involved more complex cognitive operations than those used in the earlier investigation and included classifying objects into conceptual categories, conservation of liquid and matter, and several memory span tasks, some requiring a series of cognitive operations for their successful completion. Counter to the results of the previous study, the Guatemalan children, and particularly those of San Marcos, performed significantly worse than their American counterparts.

The researchers suggested that the poorer performance of the San Marcos children on these more complex tasks was probably not due to experiences in infancy. Educational opportunities for the San Marcos children were minimal, and performance on the type of cognitive tests used in this study has been shown to be greatly influenced by formal schooling (Rogoff, 1981; Sharp, Cole, & Lave, 1979; Stevenson, Parker, Wilkinson, Bonnevaux, & Gonzalez, 1978). In general, the major difference in the interpretation of the two Guatemalan studies is one of degree. The deleterious consequences of restricted infant experience can be modified by adequate postinfancy stimulation. What is adequate is dependent upon what particular cognitive skills one is dealing with. The more complex the skills, the more intense the experiential intervention must be.

What seems to be a general conclusion from the work described in this section is that negative early experiences need not limit a child's level of intelligence in later life. Early experience is important and can drastically influence the course of development. But later experience is also important. Human intelligence is malleable early in life, although special educational intervention may be necessary in order to modify the effects of a severely restricted environment.

Along these lines, the short-term effectiveness of compensatory education has been well documented by a number of projects designed to provide preschool children from low-income homes with the intellectual skills necessary to do well in school (Bereiter & Englemann, 1966; Klaus & Gray, 1968; Ramey, Campbell, & Finkelstein, 1984). Such programs have raised the IQ scores of high-risk children by 10 to 15 points over the course of the program. These experimental programs, most of which were begun in the 1960s, varied considerably in the organization of their curricula, ranging from programs based on Piagetian theory to those using behavior modification techniques as advocated by B. F. Skinner and other behaviorists. What most programs did have in common was an emphasis on language and problem-solving skills and a low student/teacher ratio, allowing substantial individual attention to children. Generally, the greatest gains were demonstrated by children in the more rigorous, highly structured programs. In some, large gains in IQ level were noted relative to control subjects and to the children's performance before they entered the programs (Bronfenbrenner, 1974; Klaus & Gray, 1968). In other studies, intervention began shortly after birth, with children demonstrating high IQ scores relative to control subjects at every age tested, thus never needing compensation for below-average intellectual achievement (Ramey et al., 1984).

How pliable are we humans? At what age is plasticity lost? Unfortunately, we are not able to answer these questions. We do know from animal research that plasticity is reduced with age (Scott, 1968) and that we are most malleable as infants. As was mentioned earlier in this chapter, human development has been proposed to be highly canalized during the

first 18 or 24 months of life, meaning that all children follow the species-typical path "under a wide range of diverse environments and exhibit strong self-righting tendencies following exposure to severely atypical environments" (McCall, 1981, p. 5; see also Scarr-Salapatek, 1976; Waddington, 1957). In other words, although infants may be adversely affected by early maladaptive environments, there is a strong tendency to return to a course of normalcy, given an appropriate environment. This plasticity is progressively reduced later in life, beginning as early as 18 or 24 months of age. In general, the earlier intervention is begun, the greater its chance of reversing an established behavior pattern, if for no other reason than that older children and adults are more reluctant than younger children to accept the imposition of a drastically changed environment.

If the effects of a negative early environment can be reversed, what about the effects of a beneficial early environment? If intelligence can be modified for the better by experiences later in childhood, can later-childhood environment also modify a child's intellectual functioning for the worse? This issue will be discussed in the following section.

Maintenance of the Beneficial Effects of Early Experience on Intelligence

For the most part, evidence for the long-term effects of positive early environments comes from follow-up studies of preschool compensatory education programs. Although, as mentioned above, the initial reports of these programs were favorable, doubts concerning their long-term effectiveness began to surface shortly thereafter. The initial gains in IQ and academic performance shown by program graduates were slowly lost, and by the end of the fourth grade, levels of intellectual attainment were comparable between children who had participated in the programs and those who had not (Bereiter & Englemann, 1966; Klaus & Gray, 1968). The lack of long-term consistency in intellectual achievement caused Jensen (1969) to assert that compensatory education had failed and to question whether intelligence can be altered significantly by early intervention.

Despite these findings, researchers were not ready to dismiss the role of early compensatory education on the later intellectual functioning of high-risk children, and several investigators inquired into the long-term (from middle school and beyond) consequences of the preschool experience. Perhaps the most ambitious of these projects to date is that of Lazar and his colleagues (Lazar, Darlington, Murray, Royce, & Snipper, 1982). They collaborated with the investigators of 11 compensatory preschool programs. Graduates of these programs ranged in age from 9 to 19 years at the time of the follow-up, and assessments were made of children's IQ scores, academic achievements (as measured by standardized tests), school competence (as measured by assignment to special education classes and retention in grade), and attitudes concerning their school performance and their likelihood of future success.

Although different programs yielded slightly different patterns of results, the findings among the 11 programs were relatively consistent. With respect to levels of IQ and academic achievement, compensatory preschool programs had minimal long-term effects. Although the programs had an initial impact on children's IQ scores, few reliable differences were found between experimental and control subjects by 10 years of age. Preschool graduates did score higher on some achievement tests than control children, but this effect was not widespread. Similar findings of minimal long-term IQ and achievement differences between experimental and control children for four preschool programs have been reported in a more recent study by Miller and Bizzell (1984).

The findings of Lazar and his colleagues were more encouraging for school competence. For example, the median rate of assignment to special education classes was 13.8% for children who had participated in preschool programs and 28.6% for control children. Although less dramatic, there were also significant group differences in the percentage of children who were held back in grade. The median grade-retention rate was 30.5% for children in the control group and 25.8% for children who had participated in the preschool programs. Differences were also found in children's attitudes toward achievement. Program graduates were more likely to give achievement-related reasons for being proud of themselves, and the mothers of the experimental children

felt more positively about their children and their likelihood for success than the mothers of the control subjects.

The findings of Lazar and his colleagues (1982) cause mixed reactions. On the one hand, there were no long-lasting benefits of early education with respect to IQ scores and performance on standard academic tests. The elevated levels of IQ and school achievement noted for graduates shortly after leaving the programs had disappeared by grade four. On the other hand, the study demonstrated significant and important long-term benefits of compensatory education. The difference in assignment to special education classes alone represents a significant saving in tax dollars, justifying the cost of the preschool programs. Furthermore, differences in grade retention (and presumably the probability of completing high school) and in personal and maternal attitudes suggest that program graduates will be more likely to succeed economically in the years to come than children in the control conditions.

In sum, most of the benefits of the preschool programs were noncognitive. Although the programs had a significant impact on school competence, the impact was apparently not mediated by intelligence (as measured by IQ scores) but rather by social factors associated with program participation. Thus, the results of Lazar and his colleagues suggest that intellectual benefits realized during the preschool years will be lost if the program responsible for the gains is discontinued. Once intellectual competence is attained, it must be maintained. Apparently, the intellectual environment for most of the low-income children in these studies was not sufficiently supportive to maintain the level of intelligence established during the preschool years.

What if the compensatory preschool program had been extended into the early elementary school years? Might there then have been long-term effects of early education? This question was evaluated by Becker and Gersten (1982). They examined the academic performance of fifth- and sixth-grade children who had participated in Project Follow Through, a program designed to take over where the federally funded preschool Project Head Start left off. In Project Follow Through, low-income children are provided with compensatory education through the third grade. Becker and Gersten evaluated the effectiveness of five different Follow Through programs, comparing children's performance with that of control groups and with national norms on a series of achievement tests.

Children in the study had been administered portions of the Wide Range Achievement Test (WRAT) or the Metropolitan Achievement Test (MAT). Significant differences were found between the Follow Through and control children in both the fifth and sixth grades. Most striking were differences in reading level on the WRAT and differences on the spelling and math-problem-solving subscales of the MAT, all in favor of the Follow Through children. Of 180 statistical comparisons made between the control and the Follow Through children from the five different programs, 76 (42%) favored the Follow Through children, whereas only 2 (1%) favored the control subjects. Thus, compensatory education programs that are continued beyond the preschool years have beneficial effects on academic achievement.

Becker and Gersten also compared the performance of the Follow Through children on the WRAT and MAT with national norms. Mean percentile ranks for the Follow Through children for tests given in the third, fifth, and sixth grades are presented in Table 11-3 for the WRAT Reading, MAT Reading, MAT Math, and MAT Spelling subscales. The percentiles are based on national averages for the WRAT and MAT, with a score of 50 representing average performance. Tests given in the third grade reflect the children's performance while they were

still participating in Project Follow Through, whereas scores in the fifth and sixth grades reflect performance 2 and 3 years after termination of the program.

The most striking aspect of these data is the steady decline in percentile standing as a function of grade. These high-risk children were performing close to or above the national average on three of these four tests in the third grade (the exception being MAT reading, 38th percentile). Two years after they had left Follow Through, only their WRAT Reading was comparable to the national average, and by the sixth grade they declined to the 38th percentile. These results indicate that, although the Follow Through children maintained an academic advantage relative to matched sets of control children, they showed a decrement relative to national averages upon leaving the program. Again, the social and educational benefits of the program are significant. However, as with the findings of Lazar and his associates (1982) and Miller and Bizzell (1984), intellectual gains diminished once the children left the program.

How Modifiable Is Human Intelligence?

In general, the results of the studies reviewed in the previous section indicate that the beneficial effects of an early, stimulating environment can be altered by experiences that follow it. Human intelligence is modifiable in both positive and negative directions. Earlier in the chapter, research was examined indicating that the negative effects of early experience could be reversed. Given these findings, it is not surprising that one's relative level of cognitive functioning can also decline as a result of experience.

TABLE 11-3 Mean Percentile for Children Participating in Project Follow Through for Subtests of the Wide Range Achievement Test (WRAT) and the Metropolitan Achievement Test (MAT) (adapted from Becker and Gersten, 1982)

Time of test	WRAT reading	MAT reading	MAT math	MAT spelling
Last year of Follow Through: Grade 3	63rd	38th	62nd	47th
After completion of Follow Through: Grade 5	53rd	22nd	29th	37th
Grade 6	38th	20th	27th	37th

Intelligence is not something that once you "get it," you necessarily keep it. Intelligence, as measured by IQ tests, is a reflection of a person's intellectual functioning at a given time. Once established, intelligence (or any other complex behavior, for that matter) must be maintained. If the environmental supports responsible for establishing cognitive competence are removed, one should not be surprised that intelligence suffers.

The results of these studies reflect a flexible cognitive system that, over the course of childhood, can be greatly modified by changes in the environment. However, the research cited can be criticized for not being representative of the way the world is structured for most children. Fortunately, few children spend their early years restricted to closets, and most children who are provided stimulating environments as preschoolers can expect comparably stimulating environments in the years to come. These studies indicate what *can* happen to levels of intelligence over childhood and not necessarily what actually does happen.

Maintenance in level of intelligence is most likely to be found when a child's environment remains stable. However, the environments in which children find themselves change over time. One such change is the shift from home to school. Another related shift is from a family-centered life-style to a peer-centered life-style. Such a shift does not occur all at once, but with increasing age, children become more independent from their families' influence and more dependent upon their peers or their own inherent traits in determining the type of activities they choose (Scarr & McCartney, 1983). To the extent that these changes in environments do not represent major shifts in intellectual emphasis, levels of intelligence can be expected to be maintained. The more diverse the changing environments are from one another, the greater the change in level of intelligence that can be expected.

☐ Summary

Over the last several decades, research concerning the role of experience in affecting children's intellec-

tual development has proliferated. When examining environmental effects on intelligence, we should make a distinction among the establishment, modification, and maintenance of intelligence.

Early approaches to assessing the effects of experience on intelligence used human institutionalization studies, demonstrating that intellectual functioning can be seriously impaired under conditions of physical and social deprivation. It was assumed that the effects of such deprivation were permanent. Most early investigators assumed that parents and significant others affected the child, but they ignored the role of the child in affecting his or her own development. A *transactional approach* to development, emphasizing the interactive and bidirectional relations of children and their environments, has generally replaced the earlier unidirectional viewpoint.

Studies of socioeconomic status (SES) have examined the effects that this broad variable has on the development of intelligence. Differences in intelligence as a function of a child's SES have been reported for decades, with recent evidence pointing to the transaction between the caretaker and the child as an important mediator of SES-related differences in intelligence.

Laboratory studies of *parental teaching styles* have found that the way in which parents interact with their children in teaching situations varies with SES and is related to children's performance on cognitive tasks. *Naturalistic studies* of parent/child interaction generally find that mothers who provide their children with a variety of objects to play with and who are verbally responsive have brighter children than mothers who provide less intellectual stimulation.

The role of the child in affecting the parent/child relation must also be investigated, with more competent children possibly eliciting more competent parenting. Because of age-related changes in children's abilities, the role of environmental factors in intellectual development is likely to be different at different times in development.

Zajonc introduced the *confluence model* to account for differences in intelligence as a function of family size and birth order. Zajonc proposed that the intellectual level of a family, as measured by the average intelligence of family members, influences individual intelligence, as does the opportunity to play the role of teacher. Subsequent research has been divided, with some investigators finding support for the confluence model and others asserting that the model accounts for only a small portion of the variance of individual differences in intelligence.

Although the effects of early deprivation were once assumed to be permanent, research has indicated that early environmentally induced retardation can be reversed under certain conditions. Similarly, children from intellectually impoverished, low-income homes who receive cognitively enriched early experi-

ence through intensive compensatory education display immediate gains in IQ scores. However, follow-up data indicate that many of the gains manifested by these children are lost after the program ends. Once intellectual accomplishments are established, they must be maintained by subsequent environments. If the contexts of early, middle, and later childhood are highly similar, the relative level of intelligence is likely to be comparable across these years. Modifications in environment and experience, however, can foster modifications in intellectual attainments, for better or for worse.

12

Stability of Intelligence over Infancy and Childhood

The Relationship between Developmental Function and Individual Differences

Predicting Later Intelligence from Tests in Infancy
  □ Discontinuity with Instability   □ Continuity with Stability
  □ Can Later Intelligence Be Predicted from Infancy?

Stability of IQ Scores over Childhood
□ Prediction of Adult IQ Level from Childhood Data   □ Patterns of IQ Change over Childhood

Summary

We like to believe that the world we live in is relatively stable and predictable. This predilection includes some implicit beliefs concerning the stability of mental functioning. A smart 5-year-old does not turn into a dullard at 6, and a child functioning two standard deviations below the mean does not become a genius overnight. Two people may hold very different perspectives about the role of heredity or environment in establishing intellectual competence but still believe that once you "get it," intelligence remains relatively stable, assuming no drastic changes in your environment (see Chapter 11).

Developmental psychologists have been especially susceptible to this bias, for our profession specializes in investigating conditions in early life that predict later behavior or prepare the child for subsequent accomplishments. Despite our commonsense assumptions of the stability of intelligence and our professional biases that cause us to look for stability over time, what is the evidence? To what extent are individual differences in intellectual functioning stable over infancy and childhood?

Before looking at any evidence, we must first define what is meant by *stability*. Surely stability does not mean that intelligence stays the same over time. Many of the preceding chapters dealt with ways in which children become more intelligent with age—with changes in their *developmental function*, the form that cognition takes over the course of development. Stability, as used here, refers to the relative constancy of *individual differences*: the extent to which patterns of individual differences among a set of people remain constant over time. Is the valedictorian of her kindergarten class likely to be among the top students when her high school class graduates? Is the highly attentive 4-month-old likely to be a better reader than his less attentive peer?

Stability, when used in this sense, is measured by correlations of rank order. If a group of children is given IQ tests at age 5, for example, it can be ranked in terms of IQ score from highest to lowest. If that same group is tested again at age 10, we can compare the rankings of the children's IQ scores at the two ages. If the rankings are similar, the correlation will be positive and high. If there is no stability of

individual differences in IQ scores between ages 5 and 10, the correlation will be close to 0. It is also possible, although seemingly unlikely, that the brightest children at age 5 will be, on the average, the less bright children at age 10, resulting in a negative correlation. Note that the correlations used to assess stability are unrelated to the actual level of performance. Correlations may be high, implying stability, although the average level of performance may have systematically increased (or decreased) for most members of the sample.

Let me provide an example of the levels of IQ at two ages and the correlation of these scores. The IQ scores of six children at age 5 may be 90, 92, 101, 107, 112, and 122 for children A through F, respectively, an average of 104. The scores of these same children at age 10 may be 95, 98, 105, 112, 117, and 127, an average of 109, or a 5-point gain over the five years. Despite the improvement in IQ scores, each child maintained his or her rank order in the group, resulting in a perfect correlation of 1. Similarly, if half of the children showed *increases* in IQ scores over the 5-year period (95, 97, and 105 for children A, B, and C, for example), and the scores of the other three children showed a *decrease* (106, 110, and 118 for children D, E, and F, for example), the cross-age correlation would still be 1 because all children in this example maintained their relative rank order across the two testings. The correlation would be less than 1 only if there were some change in the rank order of the children over time.

In this chapter, the stability of individual differences in intelligence over time is examined. For the most part, IQ data will be used as a measure of intellectual functioning, although several studies will be reported that used other measures of cognition. In addition to investigating stability of intelligence via cross-age correlations, I will also examine patterns of change. That is, although there may be high correlations between measures of intelligence at two ages, that does not mean that intelligence has not changed over that period. In other words, the relationship between developmental function—patterns of change that characterize the species—and the stability of individual differences will be evaluated.

☐ The Relationship between Developmental Function and Individual Differences

Although developmental function and individual differences are conceptually and statistically distinct, they may be linked empirically. A major issue concerning the nature of developmental function, for example, is whether changes in the form that cognition takes over time are continuous or discontinuous (see Chapter 1). *Continuous* functions refer to those for which the target behaviors do not change substantially with age. Changes are mainly quantitative (changes in rate or amount) and not qualitative (changes in type or kind). Differences in memory span, for instance, can be attributed to quantitative increases in mental capacity, with the processes underlying memory span at different ages being generally the same. *Discontinuous* functions, in contrast, refer to those for which the nature of the target behavior changes substantially over time.

Piaget's theory, for example, posits discontinuity of developmental function. Concerning individual differences, they may be either stable over time (that is, similar rank orderings at different points in development) or unstable. The dimensions of developmental function and individual differences can be combined, and we can speak of developmental patterns with respect to both continuity/discontinuity and stability/instability (Emmerich, 1964; McCall, Eichorn, & Hogarty, 1977).

Table 12-1 presents some possible ways in which developmental function and individual differences may interact (from McCall et al., 1977). In the column titled Symbolic Developmental Progression, the letters refer to the form of cognition at a particular time, with the subscripts representing different points in development. Stability of individual differences is represented by lines connecting the various letters. When letters are not connected, individual differences are not stable between those developmental levels. In Case I, the same basic behavior (A)

TABLE 12-1   Some Types of Developmental Progressions (McCall et al., 1977)

Case	Symbolic developmental progression	Description	Implication
I	$A_1-A_2-A_3-A_4$	The same behavior (A) correlates with itself over age periods.	There is stability of individual differences in the same overt behavior: "homotypic" development.
II	$A_1-B_2-C_3-D_4$	Different behaviors (A–D) correlate over age periods.	There is stability of individual differences across a changing set of behaviors: "heterotypic" development.
III	$A_1-A_2-A_3-B_4-B_5-B_6$	There are two related periods of weak homotypic development.	There are brief periods of homotypic and heterotypic development; stability of individual differences spans only adjacent ages, involving similar or different behaviors.
IV	A_1, B_2, C_3, D_4	A sequence of different behaviors develops, with no correlation among them over age.	Different behaviors emerge in a fixed sequence (a discontinuous developmental function), and individual differences are not the same across these behaviors.
V	$A_1-B_2, C_3-C_4-D_5-D_6$	There is a sequence of unrelated periods of homotypic and heterotypic development.	This is a combination of Cases III and IV, indicating a sequence of brief periods of homotypic and heterotypic development; transitions include A_1-B_2, C_4-D_5, and B_2, C_3.
VI	$A_1-A_2-B_3-B_4, D_5-D_6-D_7$ $C_3-C_4-C_5$	There are two sequential, independent, but overlapping strings of heterotypic development (A_1-B_4 and C_3-D_7).	There are sequential and overlapping periods of heterotypic development (Case III).

is found at four different points in development and correlates with itself over time. Thus we have continuity of developmental function with stability of individual differences. Kagan (1971) has referred to this type of developmental progression as *homotypic*. Given that the behavior remains basically the same across development, we would be surprised if individual differences did not remain stable, although, hypothetically, this would be possible. In Case II there are changes in the nature of behavior over time, but correlations are still high between each point. Here we have discontinuity of developmental function with stability of individual differences. Kagan (1971) has referred to this type of developmental progression as *heterotypic*. In this situation, the assumption is that although the overt behavior changes with age, the processes underlying cognition remain constant, accounting for stability of individual differences. In Case III there are periods of both continuity and discontinuity, with stability of individual differences apparent only between adjacent points, and Case IV reflects discontinuity and instability. Cases V and VI reflect two other possible combinations of developmental function and individual differences.

The purpose of discussing all this is to illustrate that although developmental function and individual differences are conceptually independent, they may be related to each other in real life. For example, we would expect to find stability of individual differences in intelligence if the nature of intelligence were invariant over time. This is basically the position taken by writers such as Spearman, who postulate a general intelligence factor (g) that is constant across development. In contrast, people who believe that changes in intelligence are discontinuous are not so surprised to find instability of individual differences. Why should individual differences be stable over developmental periods when the nature of cognition changes so drastically? Why should an attentive, responsive, preverbal baby necessarily become an articulate, verbal 6-year-old? Note that discontinuity theorists do not necessarily predict instability (Piaget made no explicit hypotheses about stability of individual differences). It is quite possible that an advanced sensorimotor

child will become an advanced concrete operational thinker. The point is, people who believe that development is discontinuous do not necessarily expect to find stability of individual differences and thus rarely predict them. To a large extent, what one believes concerning the nature of developmental function will influence one's hypotheses about the nature of individual differences; these hypotheses, in turn, will affect one's research questions and methods in the quest for stability (or instability) of individual differences in intelligence.

☐ Predicting Later Intelligence from Tests in Infancy

There are, not surprisingly, two schools of thought concerning the prediction of intelligence in childhood from measures taken in infancy. One holds that there is some general aspect of intelligence (g) that remains constant throughout one's lifetime; therefore, measures of intelligence from infancy should predict intellectual functioning in later childhood (continuity with stability). The other position holds that the nature of cognition changes drastically over infancy and into childhood; because of these changes, measures of intelligence in infancy should not predict later intellectual functioning (discontinuity with instability).

For most of this century, the majority of data pertinent to this issue came from infant psychometric tests. Tests such as the Bayley Scales of Infant Development (Bayley, 1969), the Gesell Developmental Schedules (Gesell & Amatruda, 1954), the Neonatal Behavioral Assessment Scale (Brazelton, 1973), and their precursors are based on evaluations of individual differences in sensory and motor abilities. These tests have been well standardized, are reliable (that is, there is high test/retest and intertester agreement), and describe important differences among infants (McCall, Hogarty, & Hurlburt, 1972). See Table 12-2 on page 252 for examples of items in infant psychometric tests.

However, when babies who were given the Bayley and other scales are later administered IQ tests in early childhood, the correlations are disappointingly low. Prediction is only slightly greater for high-risk infants (that is, those with congenital health problems). Table 12-3 (from Fagan & Singer, 1983) summarizes the results of studies examining the relationship between sensorimotor tests of development and later IQ scores for both normal and high-risk samples as a function of age of testing (both in infancy and in childhood). As can be seen, the correlations are uniformly low, with the average correlation between infant tests and IQ scores at age 6 being .11 for normal infants. Prediction of childhood IQ scores from infancy measures is often considerably higher for infants scoring very low on the tests (for example, below 80), suggesting some power of these tests to predict pathology in limited situations (see McCall et al., 1972).

People favoring the continuity-with-stability view have not been daunted by these findings, however. There still may be stability of individual differences in intelligence from infancy onward; we just have not tapped it yet. The problem lies in the tests.

There is something wrong with infant intelligence scales. The measures used are not appropriate for evaluating g, and new tests must be developed that assess this general intellectual factor.

People favoring the discontinuity-with-instability view have been satisfied with the psychometric findings. There is nothing wrong with the tests, they contend. These tests have been developed over the last 60 years, and despite differences in the theoretical orientation of the tests' constructors, the content of the scales is very similar. These tests assess individual differences in what babies actually do, and they do not predict later intelligence because there is no connection between infant cognitive abilities and those of later childhood. Although accepting the null hypothesis is usually not considered to be good science, there comes a point when you can no longer ignore the data and must admit that the relationship between two variables is close to 0.

This, basically, is where the argument stood until the 1980s, when new research was reported provid-

TABLE 12-2 Examples of Items on the Bayley Scales of Infant Development (Adapted from Bayley, 1969)

Items typifying infants between 1 and 3 months	*Items typifying infants between 5 and 7 months*	*Items typifying infants between 9 and 12 months*	*Items typifying infants between 14 and 17 months*
Responds to sound of bell	Smiles at mirror image	Responds to verbal requests (Can child perform some act upon request, such as waving in response to "bye-bye" or clapping hands in response to "pat-a-cake"?)	Scribbles spontaneously (Will child attempt to scribble before it is demonstrated by examiner?)
Regards red ring (Does infant attend to a red ring suspended by string 8 inches from infant's eyes?)	Turns head after fallen spoon (Does infant turn head in direction of a spoon that falls to the floor and makes a noise?)		Says two words (Does child say two recognizable words during the interview?)
Vocalizes once or twice (Does infant coo, gurgle, squeal during examination period?)	Shows interest in sound production (Does infant intentionally use objects to make noise?)	Puts cube in cup on demand (Will infant place a cube in a cup when asked to do so?)	Shows shoes or other clothing (Will child point to his or her shoes in response to question "Where are your shoes?")
Demonstrates circular eye coordination: red ring (Does infant follow circular path of red ring moved above infant's eyes?)	Picks up cube deftly and directly (Does child pick up small cube?)	Stirs with spoon in imitation (Will infant imitate the examiner who makes a stirring motion in a cup?)	Builds a tower of three cubes
Displays social smile (Does infant smile or laugh in response to smile from examiner?)	Vocalizes four different syllables	Attempts to scribble (After examiner demonstrates scribbling on a piece of paper, will infant attempt to scribble when given the chance?)	Attains toy with stick (When small toy is placed out of reach of child, will child use stick to attempt to attain it?)
		Turns pages of book	

ing evidence for stability of intelligence from infancy to childhood. As will become clear below, however, there is no single answer to this issue, with proponents of both the continuity/stability and the discontinuity/instability positions having compelling data to support their arguments.

Discontinuity with Instability

As noted, the argument made by people favoring the discontinuity/instability position is that cognition goes through drastic changes over the course of infancy and that, because of these discontinuities, there is little or no long-term prediction of intelligence. Although this position is consistent with the low correlations found between sensorimotor tests and later IQ scores, these data themselves do not prove the hypothesis. Similarly, Piaget's (1952) observations of changes in developmental function across infancy are consistent with this interpretation, but they, too, do not confirm the hypothesis that the poor prediction from infancy tests is due to the discontinuous nature of development.

The most compelling evidence supporting the discontinuity/instability argument comes from the work of McCall and his colleagues (1977). They re-analyzed data from the Berkeley Growth Study, which consisted of 72 people who were tested at monthly intervals through infancy using a precursor of the Bayley Infant Scales. These people were later given IQ tests as children and adults. Rather than using total scores from the Bayley Scales, however, the researchers performed *principal component analyses* on the data, separately at each month. Principal component analysis is a form of factor analysis that derives a set of test items (the principal component) that accounts best for the performance of subjects at a particular age level (that is, the single set of items that accounts for most of the variance). For example, the items that constituted the first principal component at 2 months were (1) demonstrates horizontal, vertical, and circular eye following; (2) looks, reaches, closes on red ring; (3) displays social smile; (4) vocalizes to social stimulus; and (5) turns eyes to light. The pattern changes over time, so by 7 months, for example, the only 2-month item that was still included in the first principal component was (2) looks, reaches, closes on red ring. Other items that made up the first principal component at 7 months included (1) recovers rattle, (2) manipulates and rings bell, (3) interest in sound production, and (4) turns, looks at fallen spoon, among others. Items that constitute the principal component are those that, for a given age, best describe what infants do and best reflect individual differences among infants at that age.

McCall and his colleagues computed cross-age correlations among the principal components. As with total psychometric test scores, high correlations between principal components at two ages reflect

TABLE 12-3 Median Correlations between Conventional Tests of Infant Sensorimotor Development and Later IQ Scores for Normal and High-Risk Samples (Fagan and Singer, 1983)

| Infant test (months) | Normal sample | | | | High-risk sample | | | |
| | Age at follow-up test (years) | | | | Age at follow-up test (years) | | | |
	3	4–5	6+	Mean	3	4–5	6+	Mean
3–4	.04 (4)*	.06 (2)	.07 (3)	.06	.14 (2)	.08 (4)	.07 (2)	.10
5–7	.25 (14)	.20 (5)	.06 (6)	.15	.27 (5)	.24 (13)	.28 (3)	.26
8–11	.20 (8)	.23 (5)	.21 (3)	.21	.29 (6)	.23 (10)	.29 (6)	.27
Mean	.16	.16	.11		.23	.18	.21	

*Numbers in parentheses represent number of studies in each median correlation.

stability of individual differences, and low correlations reflect instability. The researchers reported periods of instability (when, on the average, the cross-age correlations were low) at five points in their data: 2, 8, 13, 21, and 30–36 months. These breaks in the pattern of correlations correspond roughly to Piagetian stage boundaries during the sensorimotor period (see Chapter 5). That is, there was instability of individual differences (low correlations) *between* stages, whereas correlations were generally high *within* a stage. In other words, when developmental differences were quantitative (that is, within a stage), there was stability of individual differences; when developmental differences were qualitative (that is, between stages), there was instability of individual differences.

The data of McCall and his colleagues (1977) demonstrate both discontinuity of developmental function and instability of individual differences over infancy within the same data set. In general, these findings illustrate that discontinuities in infancy are "responsible" for the inability of infant measures to predict later intelligence. Sensorimotor measures taken at 6 months do not even correlate well with measures taken at 14 months. It is little wonder that they do not correlate well with IQ tests administered in childhood.

Continuity with Stability

Although the interpretation of McCall and his colleagues appears clear-cut, it need not be the final word on the issue. It is possible that their data are valid, yet incomplete. There may be instability for the behaviors they measured, but other indices of infant intelligence may still exist for which there is stability of individual differences.

In a recent study by Messer and his colleagues, for example, mastery behavior during infancy was proposed to be a precursor of cognitive competence in early childhood (Messer et al., 1986). Mastery behavior in infants at 6 and 12 months was measured by their response to a variety of tasks. For example, to what extent do infants manipulate the task objects, relate two or more objects together, or persist in solving the problem despite previous setbacks? In many ways, these behaviors reflect *styles* of prob-

lem solving and differ from analyses that merely look at successful or unsuccessful completion of the task. Individual differences in mastery behaviors at 6 and 12 months were correlated with scores on the McCarthy Scales of Children's Ability administered at 30 months. Whereas correlations with the McCarthy scores for general cognitive and memory functioning were nonsignificant for Bayley tests given during infancy, significant correlations were reported for mastery scores obtained at 6 and 12 months. The researchers concluded that how infants go about solving problems (as reflected by the mastery scores) is more predictive of later cognitive functioning than infants' levels of competence (as reflected by the Bayley scores).

Other researchers, looking for specific cognitive processes in infancy that may predict later intellectual competence, have suggested that infants' preferences for novelty as measured by visual recognition tasks may be the stable cognitive phenomenon psychologists have been searching for. Experiments examining infants' visual perception have found that when babies 2 months of age and older are shown a visual display for a series of trials, the amount of time they look at the stimulus declines (habituation). When a new stimulus is then presented, however, they look longer at it than at the original one (dishabituation; see Chapters 4 and 8 for a more in-depth discussion of infant visual perception and memory). Methods for assessing this preference for novelty vary among investigations, but all involve repeated or prolonged exposure to one stimulus followed by the presentation of a new stimulus (either alone or paired with an "old" stimulus). Increased attention to the novel stimulus has been interpreted as reflecting discrimination and memory. The differential attention to the novel stimulus indicates that babies can discriminate it from the original stimulus. The discrimination between the two stimuli, however, is often made when only one is physically present, with the other being present only memorially, or after a significant delay period, reflecting memory for the original stimulus. Individual differences in preference for novelty are typically indicated by the percentage of time infants attend to the novel stimulus.

Fagan (1984a) has argued that such preferences

for novelty involve the ability to detect similarities among diverse stimuli and the related skill of forming schemas, or prototypes. The visual recognition task requires infants to encode a stimulus, compare it with previously experienced events, and categorize it as similar to or different from past events. Unlike many of the sensorimotor skills assessed on infant scales of intelligence, these abilities are also characteristic of cognition in later life and thus may serve as a basis for the continuity of intelligence.

Along similar lines, Sternberg (1985; Berg & Sternberg, 1985) has argued that response to novelty may be a major element of individual differences in intelligence that is constant across the life span (see Chapter 10). He proposes that how people react to novel situations is central to most definitions of intelligence. Even Piaget's concepts of assimilation and accommodation, for example, are essentially means for dealing with novel environmental events. In a similar vein, Rheingold (1985) has stressed the importance of novelty in development. She asserts that the development of behavior, including mental processes, can be viewed as becoming familiar with our world (both internal and external). As we gain knowledge, what was once novel becomes familiar. With increased knowledge, however, comes an increased ability to recognize novelty, something that is similar but not identical to that which we already know. Rheingold asserts that without the appearance of new stimuli and experiences, there can be no learning or development and that it is only through the process of becoming familiar with objects and events in life that the new can be discerned. Thus, like Sternberg, Rheingold sees the process of acquiring new knowledge—of making the novel familiar—to be a central aspect of development that is continuous throughout life.

Fagan and Singer (1983) reviewed evidence consistent with the above proposal. They noted that visual recognition differs among groups of infants who are expected to vary in later intelligence. For example, Fantz and Nevis (1967) reported a greater preference for novelty among 1- to 6-month-old infants of highly intelligent parents than among infants of parents with average intelligence. Similarly, differences in novelty preferences have been demonstrated between normal infants and those with

Down's syndrome (Miranda & Fantz, 1974) and between full-term and preterm infants (Rose, 1980), groups that are known to differ in IQ level in childhood.

More telling, however, are the predictive data. Fagan and Singer (1983) reviewed the results of previously published experiments concerning the prediction of childhood intelligence from infants' preferences for novelty via visual recognition, and they also reported the results of their own longitudinal study. The ages of infants assessed ranged from 3 to 7 months, and assessments of childhood IQ for 12 sets of data ranged from 2 to 7.5 years. The range of correlations between infants' preferences for novelty and later IQ was .33 to .66, with a mean value of .44. Compare this with the values given in Table 12-3, where average correlations between sensorimotor tests and IQ scores for normal infants ranged from .16 (for IQ tests given between the ages of 3 and 5 years) and .11 (for IQ tests given at age 6 and beyond).

Since Fagan and Singer's (1983) publication, at least four other longitudinal studies of infants' preferences and later IQ scores have been reported. Fagan (1984b) found that the correlation between novelty preferences at 7 months and scores on a verbal measure of intelligence at age 5 was .42 for a group of 38 children. In two studies by Rose and Wallace (1985a, 1985b), correlations between recognition memory at ages 6 and 12 months and IQ scores at ages 3, 3½, and 6 years ranged from .45 to .66 for a group of children who had been born prematurely. Similarly, a study by O'Connor, Cohen, and Parmelee (1984) found a correlation of .60 between a preference for novelty in the auditory modality at 4 months and Stanford-Binet scores at 5 years. Taken together, research over the past 5 years has demonstrated convincingly that indices of infants' preferences for novelty predict later intelligence far better than standard sensorimotor scales.

Preference for novelty is not the only candidate for an aspect of intelligence that is stable and continuous over infancy and childhood. Bornstein and Sigman (1986) have suggested that *rate of habituation of attention* in infancy, in addition to preference for novelty, predicts later intelligence. As noted, habituation of attention refers to the decreased amount of attention an infant gives to a stimulus as a result of repeated presentation of that stimulus. The work of Fagan and others cited previously in which infants were presented with novel stimuli following familiarization with a previous stimulus all thus involved habituation. Fagan and others emphasized the *increased* attention of infants when a new stimulus was shown (dishabituation). Bornstein and Sigman concur with Fagan about the power of infant dishabituation (preference for novelty) in predicting later intelligence; however, they also propose that individual differences in *rate* of habituation predict later intelligence. Support for their position comes from a number of studies in which rate of habituation (that is, how quickly infants decrease their visual attention to a repeatedly presented stimulus) was assessed in infancy (newborns to 5 months), with these same children given IQ tests later in childhood (2 to 5 years). Correlations between measures of infant habituation and childhood IQ scores were of a similar magnitude to those reported for the preference-for-novelty measures, ranging from .29 to .61 (Bornstein, 1985; Lewis & Brooks-Gunn, 1981; Miller et al., 1979; Rose, Slater, & Perry, 1986; Sigman, 1983).

The studies cited above indicate that there is a moderate degree of continuity of developmental function and stability of individual differences from infancy to early childhood. Given these findings, how might continuity of developmental function be interpreted? Bornstein and Sigman (1986) suggested three possible models to account for the continuity (and stability) in cognition observed from infancy:

Model 1: continuity of identical behavior
Model 2: continuity of developmental status
Model 3: continuity of underlying process

The first model, that of continuity of identical behavior, does not fit the data. The habituation or dishabituation of attention in infancy is not similar in form to the typically verbal IQ tests given in childhood.

The second model, continuity of developmental status, is also not a likely candidate, according to Bornstein and Sigman. This model states that the significant correlations between two different sets of behaviors over several years reflect continuity in the rate of development. Infants whose attentional abili-

ties mature first, in this view, become children whose verbal abilities likewise are quick to develop. If this were the case, one would also expect high correlations with infant psychometric tests such as the Bayley, because such tests should show the same continuity of developmental status as do tests of visual attention. As was noted earlier in this chapter, correlations between infant psychometric test scores and later intelligence are low.

The third model, continuity of underlying process, is much more likely. This model proposes that there is a constant process that underlies both individual differences in the allocation of infant attention and later tests of intelligence. The question is, what might that process be? Fagan (1984a) has suggested that the cognitive processes involved in infants' preferences for novelty are the foundation for a general intellectual factor, or *g*. These basic processes have a high heritability. However, Fagan noted that other factors such as birth order, race, and parents' education are not related to preferences for novelty, although they are significantly related to children's intellectual functioning. Thus, although Fagan believes that a general intellectual factor has been identified, he asserts that other environmental variables also influence children's intelligence and that these are independent of the genetically determined *g* factor.

Bornstein and Sigman are less confident that the underlying process reflects some global aspect of intelligence (that is, *g*), because although individual differences in habituation and dishabituation correlate significantly with later IQ tests (most of which have been verbal), they do not correlate well with other aspects of intelligent behavior (for example, discrimination learning, recognition memory). Thus, Bornstein and Sigman argue, we should look for more specific cognitive abilities in searching for the basis of the continuity of early intelligence.

If a general intellectual factor is not responsible for the continuity and stability of individual differences that are found, what is? Is it the ability to encode an object in detail? The ability to retain a mental image of a seen (or heard) object over long delays? Although none of the experiments done so far can determine the exact locus of these effects, one popular candidate is subjects' response to novelty. In many of the studies reviewed herein, infants' recognition performance was measured in terms of their reactions to a novel stimulus. As mentioned previously, Sternberg (1985) has proposed that how people respond to novelty is a major element of individual differences in intelligence and one that is invariant over the course of development (see also Rheingold, 1985). The findings of Fagan and others concerning the long-term prediction of intelligence from infants' recognition-memory performance provide additional support for Sternberg's position.

Related to the preference-for-novelty interpretation is Bornstein and Sigman's (1986) suggestion that it is motivation to explore new environments that underlies the stability of cognitive functioning over infancy and early childhood. Infants high in such motivation would tire quickly from repeated presentation of a single stimulus and thus display a rapid rate of habituation. Similarly, such infants should be eager to inspect a new stimulus when one is presented, displaying strong preferences for novelty (dishabituation). Likewise, infants high in mastery motivation (Messer et al., 1986) would have a disposition for acquiring new knowledge, again showing a preference for novelty.

Can Later Intelligence Be Predicted from Infancy?

The findings of Fagan, Bornstein, Sigman, and others seem to be directly contradictory to the earlier reported findings of McCall and his colleagues. Who is right? Given the state of our science, we are in no position to declare that either viewpoint represents absolute truth. However, it is not necessary for one to be wrong for the other to be right.

McCall and his associates proposed that development through infancy and into early childhood is discontinuous and, because of this, there is little stability of individual differences. In contrast, Fagan and Bornstein and Sigman proposed that there is continuity of intelligence and, as a result, stability of individual differences. There is no reason to doubt the validity of either's data. What we have here are different definitions of infant intelligence. Intelligence is not a single, well-defined dimension. If a g factor does exist, it reflects only part of the picture, a

position that Fagan (1984a) acknowledges. Furthermore, even if future research replicates the high correlations (about .60) between infant measures of rate of habituation or preference for novelty and later intelligence, these correlations would account for less than 40% of the variance in the distribution of intelligence scores. If response to novelty and motivation to explore new environments are the developmentally constant factors that account for this long-term prediction, they are only two of several critical aspects that determine intelligence (see Sternberg, 1985). The intelligence studied by McCall and his colleagues is every bit as real and as important as the intelligence studied by Fagan and by Bornstein and Sigman. The fact that one remains relatively stable over time and one does not, does not reduce the significance of either. Intelligence is a multifaceted thing, and we must interpret very cautiously any global pronouncements concerning its development.

☐ The Stability of IQ Scores over Childhood

Prediction of Adult IQ Level from Childhood Data

Although infant psychometric measures do not predict later IQ scores well, the stability of individual differences in intelligence as measured by IQ tests increases dramatically by age 2. Table 12-4 summarizes the findings of longitudinal studies by Bayley

TABLE 12-4 Cross-Age Correlations between IQ Tests Given in Childhood and Adult IQ Scores

Age of testing	Honzik, MacFarlence, and Allen (1948)	Bayley (1949)
1 year	—	−.14
2–3 years	.33	.40
4–5 years	.42	.52
6–7 years	.67	.68
8–9 years	.71	.80
10–11 years	.73	.87
12–13 years	.79	—
14–15 years	.76	.84

(1949) and Honzik, MacFarlence, and Allen (1948), and it presents the correlations between scores on intelligence tests given at various times during childhood and IQ scores as young adults (17 or 18 years of age). Whereas the correlations between intelligence tests given at 12 months and at 18 years are approximately 0 (Bayley, 1949), the correlations rise quickly by the beginning of the third year. In fact, recent research has yielded high correlations (in excess of .50) between infant tests given at 18 months and childhood IQ scores (O'Connor et al., 1984). The correlations with adult IQ scores rise rapidly until early childhood and are relatively stable from age 8 or so on. In fact, Kopp and McCall (1982) have stated that "following age 5, IQ is perhaps the most stable, important behavioral characteristic yet measured" (p. 39).

Why should there be such a high degree of stability in IQ scores over childhood, especially when predictions from infant psychometric tests are so poor? In all likelihood, the reason for the increased stability of IQ scores beginning around age 2 is the increasing similarity of the test items and of the nature of intelligence for children 2 years of age and beyond. Following Piaget, there is a qualitative change in intelligence occurring sometime between 18 and 30 months of age. Children become symbol users and will remain symbol users throughout their lives. IQ tests are constructed to reflect meaningful dimensions of intelligence for people of a given age, and, accordingly, the ability to retrieve and manipulate symbols is a central aspect of most if not all intelligence tests from the 2-year level onward. There is thus a continuity of developmental function, to the extent that symbolic functioning is involved in the measurement of intelligence at all ages. Although continuity of developmental function does not necessitate stability of individual differences, it can be seen from the earlier discussion of IQ prediction from infancy data that such a relationship probably exists.

The correlations with adult IQ scores increase again sometime after 5 years of age, and these correlations represent another qualitative change in thinking (Piaget & Inhelder, 1969; White, 1965). The similarity in cognitive operations and in the IQ test items that reflect such operations are greater between the 7- and the 18-year-old than between the 4- and the 18-year-old, accounting for the elevated correlations. That is, logical operations (taking Piaget's perspective for the moment) typify the thinking of both the 7- and the 18-year-old, and children who excel at such operations are likely to continue to perform well when more complex but qualitatively similar tests are administered 10 years later (that is, continuity with stability). Increases in the correlations with adult IQ scores are small beyond age 9 or so, but increases are nonetheless observed. These increases may, in part, be attributed to another qualitative shift in developmental function (concrete to formal operations). However, this rise in the correlations may also be due to the relatively brief time intervals between testings, for, in general, the closer in time two test administrations are to each other, the higher the correlation tends to be (Bloom, 1964).

In general, because IQ tests assess intellectual skills that characterize children at a particular age, the items that constitute a test for any two ages should increase in similarity as the cognitive abilities of children at those ages become more alike. This increased similarity in the contents of the tests should, in turn, yield stability of rank orders in test scores. When there is continuity of developmental function, there is similarity of test items, yielding stability of individual differences.

Patterns of IQ Change over Childhood

Despite the impressive stability of rank order of IQ scores from the early school years, there is still room for change, particularly change in level of IQ. Recall that correlations of rank order are statistically independent of average values. So, for example, the average level of IQ scores could vary substantially for a particular sample of children and affect the correlations of rank order only minimally.

One study that extensively examined patterns of IQ change over childhood was that of McCall, Applebaum, and Hogarty (1973). They analyzed IQ data from the Fels Longitudinal Study (see Kagan & Moss, 1962). In their study, the data of 80 people (38 males, 42 females) who had been administered a Stanford-Binet IQ test at 17 points in development (ages 2½, 3, 3½, 4, 4½, 5, 5½, 6, 7, 8, 9, 10, 11, 12, 14, 15, and 17 years) were examined for changes in amount and pattern of IQ scores over time.

First, let us examine the amount of change observed in this sample. The range of IQ scores for a given child was obtained, and the difference between a child's highest score during the 17 testing sessions and his or her lowest score was computed. Note that this is not the difference between a child's IQ score at 17 years and his or her score at 2½ years, but the difference between the highest and lowest scores a child received, independent of age. The average shift in IQ score for children in this sample was 28.5 points. The range for 21% of the children in this sample was 20 points or fewer, and 43% shifted between 21 and 30 points sometime between 2½ and 17 years of age. Slightly greater than one-third of the sample (36%) showed shifts of more than 30 points, with one child displaying an amazing increase of 74 points. Although such a drastic change is rare, shifts of over 50 points had been reported by other researchers (Honzik et al., 1948; Moore, 1967). In general, the levels of children's IQ scores in the study by McCall and his colleagues were not consistent over these repeated testings.

One potential problem with longitudinal studies is that children may become "test wise" as a result of repeated testings. It is possible that the large shifts in IQ scores observed in this study were due to practice effects, with children getting better at taking the tests with experience, resulting in elevated levels of performance as they grew older. This explanation, although reasonable, was not supported by the data. McCall and his colleagues subjected the IQ scores to *cluster analysis*, a statistical technique that discerns common patterns among sets of data. Thus, children showing similar patterns of IQ change over time would be grouped together in a single cluster. The cluster analysis yielded five distinct patterns of IQ change, and these are presented in Figure 12-1. The first thing to note is that the general trend is not consistently increasing IQ scores with each subsequent testing, making unlikely the hypothesis that the large IQ shifts observed for this sample were due to practice effects.

The largest cluster was Cluster 1 (45%), with children displaying minimal systematic variation from a

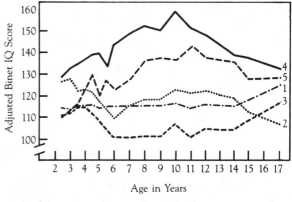
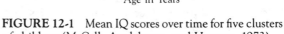

FIGURE 12-1   Mean IQ scores over time for five clusters of children (McCall, Applebaum, and Hogarty, 1973)

slightly rising pattern over childhood. Cluster 2 (11% of the sample) showed a sharp decline in IQ between the ages of 4 and 6 years, with a slight recovery in middle childhood, followed by a decrease in adolescence. Cluster 3 (13%) also showed a decline in IQ scores during the preschool years, followed by relatively stable performance from 6 to 14 years and an increase to age 17. Cluster 4 (9%) demonstrated a rapid rise in IQ scores, peaking between 8 and 10 years, followed by a comparably sharp decline. Cluster 5 (6%) showed a steady rise in IQ scores until age 8 or 10 years, much like children in Cluster 4, but displayed less of a subsequent drop in scores. The data for 16% of the sample followed no consistent pattern.

Note from Figure 12-1 that the children having the highest IQ scores (Cluster 4) also displayed the greatest amount of IQ change. This result is consistent with the findings of other investigators, who have similarly reported that very bright children tend to change more in test scores over time than children with lower scores (Terman & Merrill, 1937). Along these same lines, it is interesting to observe that for the two groups of children showing the overall highest levels of IQ (Clusters 4 and 5), scores increased until 8 or 10 years of age and then declined. Although speculative, one interpretation of this pattern is that at 8 to 10 years there is a transition in cognitive functioning (concrete to formal operations, for example) and that bright concrete operational thinkers, although making the transition to formal operations sooner than less bright children, do not maintain their high level of performance for this qualitatively different style of thought. A possibility suggested by McCall and his colleagues is that children's intellectual performance during the early school years is under the direct influence of their parents, who emphasize acquiring basic skills in math and reading. As children grow older and develop interests outside the home, parents' influence on their intellectual functioning wanes, and IQ scores drop accordingly.

Some support for this latter position was obtained by McCall and his colleagues. As part of the Fels Longitudinal Study, children and their parents were evaluated on a variety of behavioral and attitudinal factors during the course of the project. McCall and his associates examined aspects of parents' child rearing, including their attitudes toward discipline and academic achievement. The children having the highest overall IQ scores and showing the most change in test scores over childhood (Clusters 4 and 5) were characterized by having parents who were classified as accelerating, in that they strove to increase their children's mental or motor development. These parents also tended to have clear household policies, were rewarding, and had medium to severe penalties for children's transgressions. The researchers described these parents as providing an encouraging and rewarding environment with some structure and enforcement of the rules. These findings are consistent with the researchers' view that the children's increase in IQ scores over the early school years was due to the influence of their academically oriented parents.

Children in the two clusters showing decreasing preschool IQ scores (Clusters 2 and 3) tended to have parents who were minimally accelerating. Cluster 2 children were the least severely penalized, whereas Cluster 3 children were the most severely punished of any group. Children in Cluster 1 were the least homogeneous with respect to IQ pattern (relative to Clusters 2–5), and their parents showed a wide range of attitudes and behaviors.

The study by McCall and his colleagues (1973) indicates that substantial changes in IQ scores occur over childhood for some children, with the average shift being 28.5 points. These findings should be considered with respect to the very high stability of individual differences reported in the literature. How can rank order of individual differences be so high, yet actual levels of IQ vary so drastically for some children? One clue to this paradox can be found by examining Figure 12-1. Note that the lines depicting IQ change for the five clusters remain relatively distinct over the 15-year period. After age 7, there are only three points at which any line crosses another. Thus, despite the substantial variability in IQ scores that these lines reflect, the rank order of the various clusters remained essentially unchanged for most testings. Moreover, recall again that the children who showed the greatest amount of change were high-IQ children. Because of the way IQ tests are constructed, a change in IQ score from 130 to 160 is not the same as a 30-point shift from 75 to 105. In the former case, a child's relative rank order changes from approximately the 97th to the 99th + percentile. In both cases, a child would be brighter than all but a small minority of his age mates. In contrast, a change in IQ from 75 to 105 represents a change in relative rank order from about the 5th to the 63rd percentile, a change from borderline mentally retarded to slightly above normal! As the data indicate, changes of the former type are more common than are changes of the latter type, leaving the impression, both statistically and intuitively, that intelligence is relatively stable over time (McCall et al., 1973).

The data of McCall and his colleagues raise the question "When there are substantial changes in levels of IQ among groups of children, might there also be differences in the stability of IQ scores among the groups?" If level of IQ is viewed as reflecting developmental function, we can rephrase this question and ask, "Do different patterns of developmental function influence the stability of individual differences?" A study by Ramey, Yeates, and Short (1984) investigated this possibility.

These researchers examined IQ data from a longitudinal project that was designed to provide compensatory education to a group of preschool children from low-income homes who were classified as being at risk for mental retardation. Children in the control group were provided with nutritional supplements and received regular medical attention commencing shortly after birth. In addition to the nutritional and medical aid, children in the experimental group were enrolled in an academically oriented preschool program beginning by 3 months of age. Children in both groups were given infant psychometric tests at 6, 12, and 18 months and the Stanford-Binet at 24, 36, and 48 months.

Examination of test scores at 6 and 12 months indicated no difference in level of IQ between the control and experimental groups. Test scores were differentiated, however, for the remaining testings, with children in the experimental group having higher IQ scores than children in the control group at each age. For example, Stanford-Binet scores for the experimental group at 36 and 48 months were 102 and 103, respectively; in contrast, comparable scores for the control group were 84 and 89. These data indicate that an academically oriented preschool program can have a substantial effect on the intellectual functioning of a group of high-risk children, altering the level of developmental function relative to children in a control condition (see Chapter 11).

Ramey and his colleagues next asked whether the different patterns of developmental function would result in different patterns of stability of rank orders. They computed cross-age correlations of IQ scores separately for children in the experimental and control groups. Correlations of IQ scores at 6 through 36 months with the 48-month scores are presented for the experimental and control groups in Table 12-5. As can be seen, the pattern of correlations was highly similar between the two groups, despite the fact that their average IQ scores differed significantly.

The data indicate that level of intellectual functioning can be modified substantially by environmental intervention without influencing the pattern of individual differences within a group (Ramey et al., 1984). In other words, given a group of children, the rank order will remain relatively constant if all the children within that group experience basically the same environment. If the environment is relatively impoverished (as was the case for children in the control group), the overall level of IQ will be low. If the environment is relatively enriching (as was the case for children in the experimental group), the overall level of IQ will be high. Thus, although developmental function (with respect to IQ scores, anyway) can be influenced by specific experiences, these same experiences seem not to influence the stability of individual differences.

☐ Summary

Stability of intelligence refers to the degree to which the rank order of *individual differences* remains constant over time. Stability is evaluated by cross-age correlations, with high correlations reflecting stability of individual differences. The stability/instability dimension of individual differences is conceptually and statistically distinct from the continuity/discontinuity dimension of *developmental function*, although the two dimensions may be related empirically. Specifically, when developmental function is continuous, stability of individual differences is expected;

TABLE 12-5 Cross-Age Correlations with Stanford-Binet at 48 Months for Experimental and Control Children (Adapted from Rame, et al., 1984)

Age of testing	Experimental group (mean 48-month IQ = 102.7)	Control group (mean 48-month IQ = 89)
6 months	.25	.33
12 months	.31	.21
18 months	.46	.52
24 months	.65	.66
36 months	.75	.78

when developmental function is discontinuous, instability of individual differences is predicted.

Evidence from the psychometric literature indicates that the relationship between sensorimotor tests given in infancy and IQ scores later in childhood is low. Theorists such as McCall and his colleagues proposed that the low correlations can be attributed to the fact that developmental function over infancy and early childhood is discontinuous, resulting in instability of individual differences. McCall and his associates (1977), examining infant psychometric data, demonstrated stability of individual differences *within* stages but instability of individual differences *between* stages, supporting the discontinuity-with-instability hypothesis. In contrast, research by Fagan and by Bornstein and Sigman, among others, produced significant correlations between infant measures of preference for novelty and rate of habituation and later IQ scores. Fagan suggested that there is a general intellectual factor (g) that remains constant with development and that when infant intelligence is measured in

terms of this factor, individual differences are stable (continuity with stability). Infant intelligence is multifaceted, with some aspects presumably developing in a discontinuous fashion and others developing in a continuous fashion.

Stability of individual differences in intelligence over childhood increases with age. These increases are attributed to age-related increases in the similarity of cognitive functioning between children and adults (that is, continuity with stability). Despite the high cross-age correlations, however, there are significant changes in level of IQ over age. Results from McCall and his colleagues (1973) illustrated that the average shift in IQ scores over a 15-year period was 28.5 points. Five distinct patterns of change were noted, with high-IQ children showing greater changes in IQ scores over time than average or low-IQ children. Other research by Ramey and his colleagues indicates that groups of children who differ considerably in level of intelligence show comparable patterns with respect to the stability of individual differences.

Cognitive Styles
with Daniel D. Curtiss

Why Study Cognitive Styles?

Field Dependence/Field Independence

☐ The Definition and Measurement of FD/FI   ☐ Developmental Change and Stability of FD/FI
☐ Implications of FD/FI for Children's Intellectual Performance

Reflection and Impulsivity: The Significance of Conceptual Tempo

☐ Definition, Measurement, and Development of Reflection/Impulsivity
☐ Implications of Conceptual Tempo for Children's Task Performance

Convergent and Divergent Thinking

☐ Definitions and Distinctions   ☐ Measurement of Divergent Thinking
☐ Stability of Divergent Thinking over Childhood
☐ Correlates and Consequences of Divergent Thinking
☐ Is the Distinction between Convergent and Divergent Thinking a Distinction of Cognitive Style?

Hemisphericity: Left-Brain versus Right-Brain Processing

☐ Cerebral Lateralization   ☐ Successive versus Simultaneous Processing
☐ Hemisphericity and Creativity   ☐ Is Hemisphericity a Cognitive Style?

Summary

Cognitive styles refer to individual differences in the ways people process information. We are all aware that people go about doing things differently. They solve problems in diverse ways with varying strategies and approaches. Some people may try to create a new dinner dish by carefully following the step-by-step directions in a recipe. Others may buy the raw ingredients and throw a few things together to see what happens, perhaps creating their own recipe along the way. Both methods can result in a good or a bad dinner, and both reflect the style of the person doing the cooking; neither approach is inherently better than the other, only different. Perhaps cognitive styles help convey a flavor of the richness in the human intellectual experience.

Cognitive styles reflect relatively stable individual differences in information processing. Thus, many differences in how children process information could be considered to reflect their cognitive styles. There are many theoretical models of how individual differences in information processing affect children's learning. Whether one classifies some of these differences in children's thinking as cognitive styles is often a matter of personal perspective.

☐ Why Study Cognitive Styles?

Cognitive styles are of interest not only to cognitive psychologists studying individual differences in children's thinking but also to psychologists and educators seeking to improve the assessment techniques and remedial approaches for children with learning difficulties. For example, a child's cognitive style may mask certain abilities by affecting his or her performance on traditional psychometric tests (Kaufman & Kaufman, 1983). Also, a better understanding of cognitive styles may improve the way teachers instruct children, helping them develop alternative models for viewing learning (Keogh, 1973). Perhaps the importance of cognitive styles was best articulated in 1964 by Kagan and his colleagues, who noted that "pedagogical procedures should acknowledge the interactions between the dispositions of the learner and the material, and tailor presentations to the preferred strategies of the

child" (Kagan, Rosman, Day, Albert, & Philips, 1964, pp. 35–36).

Psychologists and educators have taken this pronouncement seriously and have searched for stable differences in how children process information, with an eye toward remediation. Observations made by veteran teachers in the classroom led Kenneth and Rita Dunn to coin the term *learning styles* to denote how individual differences within the student interact with elements in the classroom environment to either facilitate or impede academic achievement. The Dunns and their colleagues proposed that learning styles remain relatively stable regardless of the age, ability level, socioeconomic status, or achievement level of the student (Dunn & Dunn, 1978; Valle et al., 1986). They also stated that a child will do better in school when his or her preferred learning style is matched to a teacher's instructional style and the proper combination of elements in the classroom. In their model, characteristics of the environment (temperature, noise, lighting) and the social situation (working alone, in pairs, in groups) are proposed to affect children's learning. Also important are individual differences in physical factors (What perceptual mode do they learn best in? At what time of day do they learn best?); psychological factors (Are they impulsive or reflective? left-hemisphere dominant or right-hemisphere dominant?); and what are referred to as emotional factors (their feelings and behaviors with respect to motivation, persistence, responsibility, and the need for structure). According to the Dunns, a knowledge of children's learning styles can help a teacher modify instruction to best suit the needs of the student.

As can be seen from the description of the Dunns' model, a cognitive style (or learning style) can refer to almost any variation that influences a child's learning and cognition. One problem with models such as the Dunns' is assessment. How does one determine a child's inclination with respect to each of these diverse factors? The Dunns use a paper-and-pencil test, relying on a child's self-reports to determine his or her classification for each learning style. This approach has been appropriately criticized as attributing too much in the way of metacognitive knowledge to young children (Fischer & Fischer, 1979). Thus, there is controversy not only over what actually constitutes a cognitive style but also over how one is measured.

In this chapter, only four categories of cognitive styles are reviewed, and some people would disagree that each represents a "true" dimension. The distinction between field-dependent and field-independent children will be examined, followed by a look at reflective and impulsive children. These have been the two most studied categories of cognitive styles in the developmental literature, although there is even controversy over whether these much-studied phenomena represent stable and important cognitive dimensions. Much more controversial, however, are the last two topics that are discussed in this chapter: the difference between convergent and divergent thinkers and individual differences in hemisphericity, that is, right-brain versus left-brain processing. Much less developmental research has been conducted on these topics than on field dependence/field independence and reflection/impulsivity. Furthermore, what research has been done is often viewed as having been insufficiently rigorous. One reviewer reading a preliminary version of this chapter argued against including these topics in this textbook, lest they be given the tacit seal of legitimacy, which, in his opinion, they do not deserve. They are included, however, not primarily because of their significance in understanding individual differences in children's thinking. Rather, they are included because they have caught the attention of educators who work daily with children. Therefore, these cognitive styles warrant a close evaluation in the hope that future research will determine their ultimate value for understanding human cognition.

☐ Field Dependence/ Field Independence

The Definition and Measurement of FD/FI

The most studied category of cognitive styles is that of field dependence/field independence (FD/FI). The concept of FD/FI has its origins in adult perception. Herman Witkin and his associates observed

FIGURE 13-1 Example of items requiring subjects to find a simple form within a complex figure. Find the "termite" in these pictures. Field-dependent people have more difficulty on tasks of this sort than field-independent people.

individual differences in adults' abilities to abstract visual information (Witkin, Dyk, Faterson, Goodenough, & Karp, 1962; Witkin et al., 1954). Some people had a difficult time perceiving component parts of a visual field separately from the whole; Witkin referred to such people as *field dependent*. In contrast, others could analyze the perceptual field into its discrete parts; Witkin referred to these people as *field independent*. An example of a task that assesses the FD/FI dimension is one in which a person must find a figure embedded in a larger picture. An example of an *embedded figures test* is shown in Figure 13-1. Field-independent people discover the disguised object much more quickly than field-dependent people. In other words, the perception of field-dependent people is influenced by the entire perceptual field, so that they find it difficult to analyze any specific component of the field. Field-independent people are less affected by the global characteristics of a display and find it easier to discover the individual parts that make up the whole.

Field-dependent people are more easily misled by salient perceptual aspects of a situation than are field-independent people. This distinction is reminiscent of Piaget's notion of perceptual centration, which characterizes the thinking of preschool children. In conservation-of-liquid problems, for example, young children cannot ignore the difference in the height of the water level in the two glasses, failing to consider the corresponding differences in width (see Chapter 2). That field-dependent adults have analogous deficits for more complex tasks has been shown by Ehri and Muzio (1974). Field-dependent and field-independent college students were told to think about a merry-go-round with two circles of horses, one on the inside of the platform and the other on the outside. One child, they were told, chose a horse to ride on the inside circle, and another child chose a horse on the outside. Which child, if either, would be going faster? (The answer is the child on the outside.) After answering the question, the subjects were presented with some additional information to help them focus their attention on relevant aspects of the situation. For example, they were asked to trace the routes of the horses, to consider the mathematical formula for speed, and to think of a group of children holding hands and swinging around a post. Do some children run faster than others? Following this focusing activity, the subjects were asked to reconsider their answers.

Ehri and Muzio reported a significant correlation between FD/FI and performance on the reasoning task (− .49), with the field-independent students performing better than the field-dependent subjects. Most of the field-independent students solved the problem correctly the first time, and of those who did not, two-thirds corrected their responses after the focusing activity. In contrast, only 1 of 15 field-dependent college students correctly answered the problem initially, with only 3 others (20%) changing their responses when asked at the conclusion of the experiment. The performance of subjects scoring in the middle range on the FD/FI tests was inter-

mediate between that of the field-independent and the field-dependent subjects. Ehri and Muzio concluded that the field-independent adult subjects "were able to analyze the stimulus contexts, extract the relevant variables, and coordinate them appropriately," whereas "the thinking of field-dependent subjects tended to be dominated by the perceptible physical properties of the total stimulus configuration, and these subjects were most resistant to the influence of prompts hinting at another line of reasoning" (p. 571). Although these field-dependent adults are analogous to perceptually centered preschoolers, one can be confident that they could divorce themselves from the perceptual field sufficiently well to solve traditional conservation problems. Yet, the field-dependent people's reliance on the perceptual field in making judgments reminds one of the thinking of preoperational children, although the difficulty of the tasks does vary considerably.

Since its inception in the 1950s (Witkin et al., 1954), FD/FI has been proposed to influence more than just visual perception. FD/FI has been construed as a personality dimension, with field-dependent people relying primarily on external physical and social referents in processing information about themselves as well as about the environment. In contrast, field-independent people are more affected by internal sources of information. Field-dependent people have been hypothesized to be reliant on other people's judgments and opinions, whereas field-independent people have been viewed as being more autonomous in their decision making (see Kogan, 1983; Witkin, 1978). In the sections to follow, the "personality" side of FD/FI is avoided; the focus instead is on the information processing consequences of being field dependent or field independent.

A number of tests have been devised to assess FD/FI, but the two most widely used are the *Rod-and-Frame Test* and the *Embedded Figures Test* (Witkin et al., 1962). In the Rod-and-Frame Test, the subject is seated in a darkened room and is shown a tilted, luminous rod that is centered within a tilted frame. The subject's job is to adjust the rod so that it is upright. The frame remains tilted throughout the task. Over a series of trials, the rod and frame are tilted to

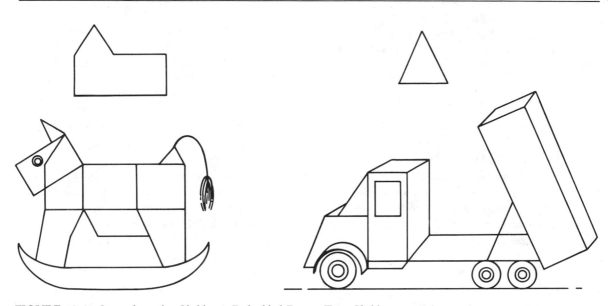

FIGURE 13-2 Items from the Children's Embedded Figures Test. Children are to locate the geometric form on top within the figure below it (Karp and Konstadt, 1971).

various degrees. The question of interest here is the degree to which the orientation of the frame affects a person's judgment of what is upright. By definition, field-dependent people are more affected by the orientation of the frame in determining upright than are field-independent people.

In the Embedded Figures Test, subjects must locate a specified geometric design within a complex figure. Separate versions of the Embedded Figures Test have been developed for preschool (Coates, 1972) and school-age children (Karp & Konstadt, 1971), and an example from this latter test is shown in Figure 13-2. Performance on the Embedded Figures Test is measured in terms of the total amount of time a person spends solving a series of problems. As mentioned above, field-dependent people take longer to solve such problems than field-independent people.

Developmental Change and Stability of FD/FI

Overall performance on tasks assessing FD/FI generally improves with age, in that older children and adults take less time to identify objects in the Em-

bedded Figures Test and are less influenced by the orientation of the frame in the Rod-and-Frame Test than are younger children (Witkin, Goodenough, & Karp, 1967). In other words, there is a general developmental trend toward increasing field independence. Witkin and his colleagues (1967) reported results from a longitudinal sample of males, who were followed from 10 to 24 years of age. They found a steady decrease in error estimation on the Rod-and-Frame Test from 10 to 17 years. Error rates stabilized, however, at this point, showing no further decrement at the age-24 testing, causing the researchers to propose that a child's developmental function with respect to FD/FI is completed by 17 years.

Although the tendency toward greater field independence with age is dramatic, individual differences with respect to FD/FI are found at all ages. Witkin and his colleagues computed cross-age correlations for scores on the Rod-and-Frame Test for different groups of children of both sexes who had been tested at intervals ranging from 4 to 14 years. They reported significant and high correlations for all comparisons, ranging from .48 to .92. The correlation over the longest period of time (between 10 and 24 years) was .66. These results indicate that children generally maintain their FD/FI orientation over development, despite substantial shifts toward field independence.

Implications of FD/FI for Children's Intellectual Performance

FD/FI and Children's Performance on Cognitive Tasks

Numerous studies have compared the cognitive and intellectual abilities of field-dependent and field-independent children. With few exceptions, field-independent children perform at higher levels than do field-dependent children. This difference has been demonstrated for a variety of tasks over a broad age range. For example, a significant relationship has been found between children's visual perspective taking and FD/FI (Okonji & Olagbaiye, 1975). Children between 7 and 10 years of age were administered a version of Piaget and Inhelder's (1967) three-mountain problem, in which children are to describe the view of a doll placed at various positions around a model of three mountains (see Chapter 2). The children's performance on this perspective-taking problem was strongly correlated with scores on the Children's Embedded Figures Test (average correlation = .90). Piaget and Inhelder suggested that the three-mountain problem involves the active restructuring of one's perspective, something that field-dependent children would have trouble doing, given their difficulty in separating parts from the whole. Field-dependent children have similarly fared worse than field-independent children on other Piagetian tasks, including conservation (Kalyan-Masih, 1985) and scientific reasoning problems (Case, 1974; Linn, 1978).

FD/FI and Intelligence

A number of studies have demonstrated a strong relationship between children's performance on FD/FI tasks and standard measures of intelligence (Case, 1974; Case & Globerson, 1974; Goodenough & Karp, 1961; Witkin et al., 1962). In a study by Case and Globerson (1974), for example, 8-year-old children were administered two tests of intelligence: the Raven Progressive Matrices Test, a nonverbal test of intelligence; and the Block Design subtest of the Wechsler Intelligence Scale for Children. In addition, children were administered the Rod-and-Frame Test and the Children's Embedded Figures Test. Correlations between the intelligence and FD/FI measures were high (ranging from .41 to .68), with field-independent children scoring higher on the intelligence tests than field-dependent children.

Other work has examined the factors that tests of FD/FI have in common with tests of intelligence, particularly the WISC (Goodenough & Karp, 1961). Factor analyses of the WISC generally result in three major factors (Cohen, 1959). Factor 1 is verbal comprehension and includes the Vocabulary, Information, and Comprehension subtests (see Chapter 10 for a description of these subtests). Factor 2 reflects attention and concentration and includes the subtests of Digit Span, Arithmetic, and Coding. Factor 3 reflects spatial processing or an "analytical field approach" (Kagan & Kogan, 1970) and includes the subtests of Picture Completion, Block Design, and Object Assembly. When similar analyses were performed on a series of tests assessing FD/FI, strong loadings were found for this third factor (Goodenough & Karp, 1961). Witkin and his colleagues (1962) suggested that the FD/FI measures and the subtests of the WISC that load heavily on Factor 3 all require overcoming some embedding context. In other words, measures of FD/FI assess the same cognitive skills that are measured by subtests of the WISC, suggesting that FD/FI reflects an important aspect of intelligence. Other researchers have shown similar relationships between measures of FD/FI and subtests of Wechsler IQ tests that assess spatial/analytic intelligence (Kalyan-Masih, 1985; MacLeod, Jackson, & Palmer, 1986). In fact, the similarity with respect to the type of cognition assessed by measures of FD/FI and the WISC Block Design subtest is so great that some researchers have used the subtest as an independent measure of FD/FI (Globerson, 1983, 1985; Globerson, Weinstein, & Sharabany, 1985). In addition, performance on the FD/FI tasks loads heavily on a general intelligence factor, suggesting that FD/FI may be less of a measure of cognitive style and more of a measure of general intelligence (Vernon, 1972).

Cognitive Style or Cognitive Development?

The significant relationship between measures of FD/FI and other tests of cognition and intelligence raises the possibility that FD/FI is merely an artifact and that what such tests measure is actually some aspect of general intelligence or development. As noted earlier, children become more field independent with age, further suggesting the possibility that the FD/FI tests are not assessing cognitive style but, rather, some developmental variations in thinking. In other words, FD/FI may merely be a reflection of a child's level of cognitive development and not a reflection of a cognitive style per se.

The distinction between FD/FI as a cognitive style and as a measure of cognitive development has been investigated by Globerson and her colleagues in a series of studies (Case & Globerson, 1974; Globerson, 1983, 1985, 1987; Globerson et al., 1985). Globerson examined FD/FI and cognition in terms of the developmental model of Pascual-Leone (1970; see Chapter 3). Basically, Pascual-Leone proposed that children's information processing is limited by the availability of mental capacity, or M-capacity. M-capacity is chiefly under the control of maturation and increases developmentally. With increasing M-capacity, children can activate more cognitive schemes to solve problems. Actual M-capacity cannot be affected by training, although other aspects of information processing such as knowledge and specific strategies are amenable to modification through instruction. Globerson reasoned that if FD/FI reflects a child's general level of cognitive development, it should vary directly with estimates of M-capacity and not be subject to training. If, however, FD/FI reflects an information processing strategy, it should be susceptible to training, unlike M-capacity itself.

Globerson and her colleagues (1985) tested this hypothesis by training 6- and 8-year-old field-dependent and field-independent children on tests of scientific reasoning, similar to the pendulum problem

used by Inhelder and Piaget (1958), described in Chapter 2. In tests of scientific reasoning, children must determine what factor or set of factors is responsible for a particular outcome. In the bending rods problem, for example, children are shown an apparatus holding two rods that vary on a number of dimensions (length, diameter, material, weight applied to them, and point of leverage). The children are to determine what factor or combination of factors is responsible for the relative bending of the rods. Earlier work by Case (1974) had shown that field-independent 8-year-olds performed this task better than field-dependent 8-year-olds after a brief training session. Globerson and her colleagues argued that Case's training might not have matched the cognitive style of the field-dependent children, accounting for their lower level of performance.

Globerson and her associates defined three groups of children: field-independent 8-year-olds, field-dependent 8-year-olds, and field-independent 6-year-olds. Some children were given training on scientific reasoning problems following the procedures used by Case (nonexplicit training), whereas others received more detailed instructions (explicit training). More specifically, because field-dependent children have difficulty attending to relevant perceptual cues when they are not perceptually salient, the researchers trained the children to be aware of cues that might be "hidden." For example, the children were trained to discern which of several factors was responsible for the "bounciness" of two balls. Training began by dropping the two balls at vastly different heights and then gradually minimizing the difference in heights from which the balls were dropped. Throughout training, the experimenter reminded the child that some differences were more subtle than others and that one must look carefully to detect the hidden causes. After the training, the children were administered different tests of scientific reasoning (for example, the bending rods test) to assess the effectiveness of training.

The results indicated that field-dependent children can indeed benefit from training in scientific reasoning. The results of the nonexplicit training replicated those of Case (1974). The field-independent 8-year-olds performed best, followed by the field-dependent 8-year-olds, with the field-independent 6-year-olds performing the worse. A different pattern of results was found for children receiving the explicit training. Differences in scientific reasoning were eliminated between the field-independent and field-dependent 8-year-olds, both of whom showed better performance than the field-independent 6-year-olds. Globerson and her colleagues interpreted these results as indicating that "field-dependent children are not inferior to their field-independent peers in their developmentally related cognitive performance" (1985, p. 689). The comparable performance under explicit training for the two groups of 8-year-olds indicates that these children had comparable amounts of mental effort (M-capacity) available. The typical superiority of field-independent children on tasks of this type stems from the different strategies they use and not from different cognitive capacity. In contrast, the lower performance of the 6-year-old field-independent children can be attributed to their lack of sufficient M-capacity to solve the scientific reasoning problems. Following Pascual-Leone's model, performance deficits attributable to insufficient M-capacity cannot be overcome by training, because developmental changes in M-capacity are governed by maturational and not environmental factors.

In related research, Globerson (1985) compared M-capacity and FD/FI for groups of 8-, 10-, and 12-year-olds. Tests of M-capacity (introduced in Chapter 3) are similar to tests of memory span but involve a further transformation of the stimuli. In Globerson's study, for example, children learned specific motor responses (raise hand, clap hands) to specific perceptual stimuli (a square, a red patch). Once the perceptual stimuli/motor response patterns had been learned, the children were shown a series of figures that included varying numbers of stimuli. They saw each figure for 5 seconds and then were to make all the appropriate motor responses (for example, clap hands, touch head, and raise hand, for the appropriate three-stimuli figure). Globerson reported that estimates of M-capacity increased with age. But there were no differences in estimates of M-capacity between the field-dependent and field-independent

children at any age. In other words, consistent with the findings of Globerson and her colleagues (1985), field-dependent and field-independent children have comparable amounts of mental capacity available to them. Differences in their task performance can more parsimoniously be attributed to differences in information processing styles than to differences in cognitive capacity itself.

☐ Reflection and Impulsivity: The Significance of Conceptual Tempo

We all know people who, when presented with a question, arrive at an answer quickly, sometimes even before the entire question is posed. This response is very impressive when the answer is a good one. We are less impressed, and sometimes annoyed, when the answer is considerably off the mark and possibly not even relevant to the question at hand. People who make quick decisions about complex problems and who make many errors in the process have been labeled *impulsives*. At the other extreme are people who methodically evaluate all the potential options, venturing a response only after giving considerable thought to the query. Individuals displaying such a deliberate procedure usually arrive at correct solutions. They have been labeled *reflectives*.

Not all quick responders are error prone, nor does everyone who follows the slow and steady path always arrive at sage decisions. Nevertheless, there is a well-established relation between speed of responding and error rate for many cognitive tasks. This *speed/accuracy trade-off* is manifested in simple tasks, such as rapidly determining whether the letters flashed on a screen constitute a word, and in more complex tasks, such as deciding which of six similar pictures exactly matches a seventh. The rate at which people typically make complex decisions has been referred to as their *conceptual tempo*, and because the speed of decision making is related to the likelihood of choosing correct alternatives, individual differences in conceptual tempo can have important implications for cognitive processing in general. Much research with children has investigated the consequences of individual differences in conceptual tempo on a variety of cognitive tasks, with most research emphasizing the differences between reflective and impulsive children.

Definition, Measurement, and Development of Reflection/Impulsivity

Jerome Kagan and his colleagues introduced the concept of reflection/impulsivity in the 1960s (Kagan, 1965a, 1966; Kagan, et al., 1964). Reflection/impulsivity refers to the tendency to respond quickly (or slowly) on tasks for which there is high response uncertainty. Latencies to answer simple questions, such as "How much is 2 + 2?" or "Who was the first president of the United States?" do not reflect this dimension. Answers to such questions probably reflect one's ability to retrieve well-established information from long-term memory. Reflection/impulsivity is assessed by more complex tasks for which the correct solution is not immediately obvious. Multiple-choice tests often provide good indices of reflection/impulsivity. For example, a re-

flective style would probably be more successful for the question "How many U.S. presidents have been assassinated?" with the alternatives being two, four, eight, and ten. Although one would not be likely to know the answer immediately, one can think of all the assassinated presidents one knows and select the alternative closest to but not below that number. This process takes time. An impulsive response would involve selecting the first alternative that seems "right." Similarly, the task of selecting the nine best baseball players from a child's class would seemingly benefit from a reflective approach to the problem. An impulsive child could wind up with a team loaded with outfielders and devoid of pitchers.

The Matching Familiar Figures Test

The task most frequently used to assess reflection/impulsivity is the *Matching Familiar Figures Test* (MFFT) (Kagan et al., 1964). Two examples from the MFFT are given in Figure 13-3. Children are shown a single standard picture and told that one of the six pictures on the adjoining page is exactly like

FIGURE 13-3 Examples from the Matching Familiar Figures Test. Children are to find the alternative that exactly matches the top picture (thanks to Kagan).

the standard. Their job is to find that picture. If a first response is incorrect, the children are told so and are asked to "find the picture on the bottom page that is exactly like the picture on the top page." There are 12 items on the MFFT, although a revised version includes 20 items (Cairns & Cammock, 1978). The amount of time it takes children to make their first response on each picture (their latencies) is recorded, as are their errors. Response latencies and errors are negatively correlated on the MFFT (average correlation being about −.50), with children who respond quickly making, on the average, more errors than children who respond slowly (Messer, 1976; Salkind & Nelson, 1980).

Based on the latency and error data, children are divided into four groups. The median response latency and the median number of errors are determined and are combined to yield a 2 × 2 matrix (see Figure 13-4). Children who are above the median in response latencies (slow) and below the median in errors (accurate) are classified as reflectives. Children who are below the median in response latencies (fast) and above the median in errors (inaccurate) are classified as impulsives. Approximately two-thirds of children fall into the reflective or impulsive classifications. The remaining one-third of the children are classified as fast-accurates (below median in both latencies and errors) and slow-inaccurates (above median in both latencies and errors). Although these latter two groups of children have not been totally ignored by researchers (Ault, Crawford, & Jeffrey, 1972; Block, Block, & Harrington, 1974), most studies have concentrated on the characteristics of reflective and impulsive children.

		MFFT Errors	
		Below Median	Above Median
MFTT Latencies	Below Median	Fast-Accurates	Impulsives
	Above Median	Reflectives	Slow-Inaccurates

FIGURE 13-4 Classification of children on the MFFT. Median rates are obtained for both total number of errors and latencies of children's first response on each MFFT item. Children are classified as impulsives, reflectives, fast-accurates, or slow-inaccurates as a function of whether they fall above or below the median rate for their group with respect to both errors and latencies.

The Development and Stability of Reflection/Impulsivity

Children become less impulsive with age. Salkind and Nelson (1980) tabulated MFFT latency and error data for a sample of over 2800 children ranging in age from 5 to 12 years. (The data had been collected by more than 90 individual researchers over a decade's time.) Average MFFT error and latency scores over this age period are shown in Figure 13-5, separately for boys and girls. As can be seen, errors showed a steady decline until age 10, when performance stabilized. Similarly, response latencies increased (became slower) over the 5- to 10-year period but decreased some at ages 11 and 12. Salkind and Nelson speculated about the decrease in response latencies, suggesting that around this time children realize that the trade-off between speed and errors is maximized. That is, going any more slowly will not improve performance. Children then select a mode of responding that is most appropriate for them. Keep in mind that slower is not always better and that children who can respond relatively quickly and still maintain their accuracy probably have the most desirable approach of all (see Salkind & Wright, 1977).

Although children tend to respond more slowly and to make fewer errors with age, this change does not reflect age-related changes in the stability of reflection/impulsivity. What is important is the relationship between errors and latencies and not the absolute number of errors that children make or the absolute number of seconds they take to respond. Impulsive children are defined as those who respond quickly and make many errors relative to their peers, whereas reflectives are defined as those who respond slowly and make few errors relative to their peers. With age, the median values of errors and latencies change, yet the relationship between errors and latencies may themselves be stable (see Chapter 12).

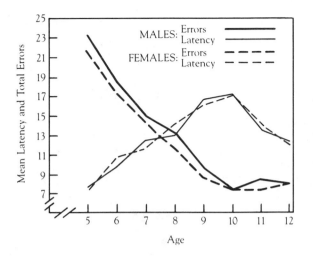

FIGURE 13-5   Total errors and average latencies to first response on the MFFT for males and females by age (Salkind and Nelson, 1980)

There has been considerable controversy over the stability of cognitive tempo. Will children who are classified as reflective at one time be similarly classified years later? One way of assessing the stability of reflection/impulsivity is by cross-age correlations (see Chapter 12). Generally, researchers have reported significant cross-age correlations for MFFT errors, typically ranging between .25 and .50 over 1- to 3-year periods. These correlations have been reported for preschool and young school-age children (see Messer, 1976) and for adolescents (Messer & Brodzinsky, 1981). One study has reported a significant correlation (.50) for MFFT errors for boys between 3 and 11 years of age (Gjerde, Block, & Block, 1985). The correlation over a similar time period for girls was not significant, however (.17). The picture looks different for MFFT latencies. Cross-age correlations are generally low during the preschool years (Gjerde et al., 1985; Messer, 1976) and increase somewhat when children are first tested in early grade school (Messer, 1976). Results for older children have been mixed. Messer and Brodzinsky (1981) tested children at 11 and 14 years, for example, and reported significant correlations for MFFT latencies (about .45). In contrast, few significant cross-age correlations were found for MFFT latencies

for children tested at the ages of 3, 4, 5, and 11 years (Gjerde et al., 1985).

The Generality of Conceptual Tempo

Reflection/impulsivity has been shown to be relatively consistent across a variety of tasks that involve a high degree of response uncertainty. For example, correlations of errors and latencies are high between children's performance on the visual MFFT and a similar test given in the haptic (active touch) modality (Butter, 1979; Kagan, 1965a, 1966). That is, children who are classified as reflective or impulsive when administered a visual match-to-sample task (the MFFT) are similarly classified when their job is to manually explore irregularly shaped forms, finding the one alternative that matches the standard. Somewhat less consistency has been reported for an auditory test of impulsivity (Kennedy & Butter, 1978), although even here, more than 50% of fourth-grade children tested were similarly classified on the auditory and visual tasks.

Conceptual Tempo or Intellectual Competence?

Does conceptual tempo reflect a stable and important cognitive style, or is it merely a measure of intelligence? The lack of stability of MFFT latencies and children's tendencies to become increasingly reflective with age call into question the significance of reflection/impulsivity as a cognitive style. The Blocks and their colleagues have been most critical of the MFFT as a test assessing conceptual tempo (Block, 1987; Block et al., 1974; Block, Gjerde, & Block, 1986; Gjerde et al., 1985). They point out, for example, that MFFT latencies are minimally predictive of children's personality or intelligence. In contrast, MFFT errors have been shown to correlate significantly with measures of both personality and intelligence (Block et al., 1986; Gjerde et al., 1985). In one study, children were administered the MFFT at ages 3, 4, 5, and 11 and Wechsler IQ tests at ages 4 and 11 (Gjerde et al., 1985). Correlations between MFFT latencies and IQ scores were generally low (median correlation = .08). Of 48 correlations (separate correlations were computed for the Verbal, Performance, and Full-Scale IQ scores for boys and girls), only 4 were statistically significant. In comparison, correlations between MFFT errors and IQ scores were higher (median correlation = −.30), with 17 of the 48 being significant. These and other data led the Blocks and their colleagues to speculate that performance on the MFFT can best be interpreted as reflecting children's intellectual *competence* rather than conceptual tempo (Block et al., 1986; Gjerde et al., 1985). In fact, Block (1987) is so adamant in this belief that he has stated that it is "correct to say that the MFFT should not now be employed as a measure of reflection-impulsivity" (p. 741). Not surprisingly, other psychologists maintain that conceptual tempo is an important and relatively stable cognitive style that has important educational implications (Kagan, 1987; Kogan, 1983; Messer & Brodzinsky, 1981).

Regardless of what the MFFT is assessing, the concept of reflection/impulsivity has attracted the attention of psychologists and educators. As a result, the role of children's conceptual tempo in information processing has been examined on a variety of cognitive and educational tasks. Some of the effects that conceptual tempo has on children's cognitive performance are examined in the following section.

Implications of Conceptual Tempo for Children's Task Performance

Reflectives versus Impulsives

Since the inception of research on conceptual tempo, comparisons have been made between children classified as reflectives and those classified as impulsives on cognitive tasks. In most cases, the benefits went to the reflectives, suggesting to many that an impulsive conceptual tempo was an educational handicap. Initial research indicated that impulsives showed poorer performance on a variety of reading-related tasks (Egeland, 1974; Erickson & Otto, 1973; Kagan, 1965b). However, other researchers failed to find connections between reading ability and a child's conceptual tempo (D. Denney, 1974; Hood & Kendal, 1975; Margolis, Peterson, & Leonard, 1978).

One reason for these discrepancies may be the way in which reflection/impulsivity is measured. For example, Butter, Kennedy, and Shoemaker-Kelly (1982) reported that third-graders' reading ability was differentially predicted by different measures of reflection/impulsivity. They administered third-grade children a variant of the visual MFFT and also an auditory task designed to assess reflection/impulsivity. In the *Auditory Impulsivity Task* children are shown a panel containing seven buttons, one at the top (standard) and six below in two rows of three (alternatives). When each button is pressed, it emits a sequence of tones and pauses. Children must find the one button of the six alternatives that plays the same tonal sequence as the standard. Using this task, the researchers reported that children's performance predicted reading comprehension and vocabulary test scores better than the visual match-to-sample task. They hypothesized that performance on the auditory task assesses some of the specific skills related to reading, making it a more sensitive predictor of reading ability than the visual MFFT.

One area in which differences between reflectives and impulsives has recently been investigated is *metacognition*, children's knowledge of their own cognitive abilities. For example, Stober (1985) reported a significant relationship between conceptual tempo and metacognition for a sample of 8-year-olds. Reflective children illustrated greater awareness of the objectives of cognitive tasks than impulsive children, as well as greater awareness of the benefits of planning and strategy evaluation. However, this relationship was not significant for a group of 11-year-olds. Similar research by Borkowski and his colleagues has found a relationship between reflection/impulsivity and metamemory (Borkowski, Peck, Reid, & Kurtz, 1983; Kurtz & Borkowski, 1987). In general, first- through third-grade reflective children showed greater metamemory knowledge than did impulsives in the same grades. Furthermore, reflective children displayed higher levels of recall and greater evidence of strategy use on the memory tasks than did impulsive children. Borkowski and his colleagues (1983) hypothesized that an impulsive conceptual tempo impedes metamemory development.

More specifically, they proposed that conceptual tempo "is a setting condition that dictates the level and depth of a child's metamemory" (p. 471), which, in turn, influences children's strategy use and, thus, memory performance (that is, conceptual tempo → metamemory → strategy use).

Because impulsive conceptual tempo has been associated with poor performance on a variety of cognitive tasks, many researchers have suggested that impulsive children can and should be taught to be more reflective in their approaches to problems. A variety of procedures has been developed to train impulsive children to become more reflective. The most successful modification studies have been those that draw impulsive children's attention to stimulus details and require them to examine all possibilities before making a decision (Butter, 1979; Egeland, 1974; Meichenbaum & Goodman, 1971; Zelniker, Jeffrey, Ault, & Parsons, 1972). In general, impulsive children can be trained to use a reflective strategy, although the durability of such training is questionable.

Reflective and Impulsive Children's Use of Strategies

It would seem obvious that reflective and impulsive children use different strategies on problem-solving tasks. Impulsive children's quick response times and accompanying high error rates would imply an incomplete evaluation of alternatives, whereas the slow and generally correct performance of reflectives would imply that a more thorough and exhaustive strategy was applied in solving the problems. This interpretation has been supported in several studies. One study examined the visual scanning of 9-year-old children as they solved the MFFT (Ault et al., 1972). The children classified as reflectives and fast-accurates made more systematic comparisons between the standard and the alternatives than did the impulsive or the slow-inaccurate children (see also Siegelman, 1969). In a more recent study, Cameron (1984) presented children in grades two, four, and six with a pattern matching task, in which they were to determine which of four dot patterns was con-

cealed behind a problem board. To find the answer, the children were to open shutters on the board, revealing the presence or absence of a dot in a particular location. With such a task, some moves by a child are more informative than others. For example, some moves will make it possible to eliminate one-half of the available alternatives by opening a single shutter. Other moves prove to be uninformative (that is, children open a shutter that could not help them differentiate among the four patterns), whereas still others will provide useful information only if a dot is behind the shutter but will be uninformative (and thus wasted) if a dot is not there. Cameron rated children's *quality of strategy* and related their responses to their conceptual tempo as measured by the MFFT. Cameron reported significant correlations between quality of strategy and MFFT latencies and errors for children at each grade level, with the benefits going to the reflective children. These findings are consistent with the interpretation that reflectives tend to use effective problem-solving strategies better than impulsives (see also Haskins & McKinney, 1976; Mitchell & Ault, 1979).

A somewhat different approach to reflective and impulsive children's use of strategies was taken by Zelniker and Jeffrey (1976). They proposed that the strategies used by impulsive children are not necessarily deficient but merely different from those used by reflective children. They proposed that the difference in strategy use revolves around the difference between *global* and *detail* processing of information. Tasks such as the MFFT require attention to stimulus detail. Specific components of individual stimuli must be identified and compared with details of the standard stimulus. Reflectives are better able to perform such detailed analyses than are impulsives. Zelniker and Jeffrey also hypothesized that impulsive children may have a greater tendency to attend to global or total stimulus characteristics and may perform well on tasks that emphasize global as opposed to detailed visual analysis.

Zelniker and Jeffrey developed two sets of visual match-to-sample tasks similar to the MFFT. One set required the analysis of detail for its successful completion (similar to the MFFT), whereas the other

Detail Problem   Global Problem

FIGURE 13-6   Examples of detailed and global stimuli used in experiments by Zelniker and Jeffrey assessing strategies of impulsive and reflective children (Zelniker and Jeffrey, 1976)

involved analysis of global stimulus characteristics. An example of each type of task is shown in Figure 13-6. Fourth-grade children were classified as reflective or impulsive on the MFFT, and they were administered 20 additional match-to-sample problems that required detailed analysis and 20 that required global analysis. The impulsives responded faster than the reflectives on both the detailed and the

global tasks. However, patterns for *errors* varied between the reflectives and impulsives as a function of which type of problem the children were performing (see Figure 13-7). As can be seen in Figure 13-7, the difference in errors was substantial for the detailed task, in favor of the reflectives. This pattern would be expected, in that the detailed task is similar in construction to the MFFT. Results were markedly different for the global task, however. Here, differences between the two groups were eliminated, with the impulsives actually making slightly fewer errors than the reflectives. Zelniker and Jeffrey interpreted these and other similar results as indicating that, under some situations, the strategies employed by impulsives may actually prove to be more efficient than those used by reflectives. In other words, an impulsive cognitive style is not always a sign of inefficient cognitive processing.

☐   Convergent and Divergent Thinking

Definitions and Distinctions

There are times, when faced with a problem, that one collects all the relevant information, defines all the aspects of the task that need defining, and converges on the proper solution. There are other times, however, when such a convergent orientation may not be so successful. When the goal is only vaguely defined and the means to arrive at this ambiguous

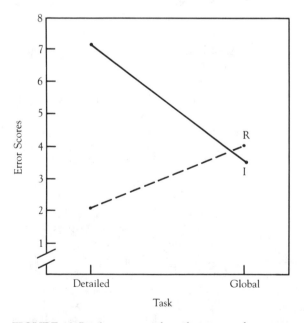

FIGURE 13-7   Average number of errors as a function of cognitive style (reflective versus impulsive) and type of task (global versus detailed) (Zelniker and Jeffrey, 1976)

end are uncertain, a better approach would involve considering possible alternatives to achieve a variety of similar outcomes. This, basically, is the distinction between *convergent* and *divergent* thinking. This distinction stems originally from the work of Guilford (1967). Guilford proposed that tasks that assess convergent thinking have only one correct answer. Answers to conventional arithmetic problems, word definitions, and most analogies are all examples of convergent tasks. In general, items on IQ tests assess convergent processes. In comparison, tasks that assess divergent thinking have more than one acceptable answer. For example, listing uses for a cork, thinking of words that begin with *K*, and discovering how many words can be made from the letters in CARE BEAR (a task found on the back of a recent menu from Pizza Hut) are all examples of tasks that assess divergent thinking.

Some people are better at convergent tasks than they are at divergent tasks, and vice versa. Adults and children who excel at convergent tasks are rated as being intelligent, as reflected by their scores on IQ tests. In contrast, children scoring high on tasks of divergent thinking are judged to be creative. Thus, the convergent/divergent distinction is essentially one between the conventional, focusing processes associated with intelligence (as assessed by IQ tests) and the "free-flowing" thought processes associated with creativity. In a sense, most of this book has dealt with the processes of convergent thinking. The sections to follow will deal with divergent thought processes in children.

Measurement of Divergent Thinking

Unfortunately, creativity has meanings that go beyond the way it is used in child developmental and educational research. When one thinks of creativity, one often thinks of creative geniuses of our culture. Thomas Edison, Albert Einstein, and Leonardo da Vinci may come to mind, or perhaps Pablo Picasso, Ludwig von Beethoven, or Isadora Duncan. These people were all geniuses and all highly creative. However, creativity comes in smaller packages and is used for more mundane tasks. It does not require genius. Rather, as assessed by tests of divergent

thinking, creativity is typically measured by the number of responses that children make to open-ended questions such as "Tell me all the different ways you could use a newspaper" or "Name all the things you can think of that move on wheels" (Torrance, 1966; Wallach & Kogan, 1965). These are tasks of *ideational fluency* (Wallach, 1970).

How does one determine how creative a child is on the basis of tasks such as these? One can evaluate the originality of the child's responses, the number of categories of items represented in the responses, the "quality" of each response, or just the total number of responses. Kogan (1983) has reviewed the pertinent literature examining the use of these various measures and has concluded that the sheer number of responses that children make is the single best measure of creativity. Frequency of response is highly correlated with these other measures and yields fewer problems in scoring than do measures such as uniqueness or quality of response. These latter measures are cumbersome, time consuming, and less reliable than simple frequency counts.

There are other indices of divergent thinking and creativity besides tests of ideational fluency. For example, *word fluency* refers to the ability to think of words that meet certain requirements, such as all the words beginning with the letter *J*, or the ability to solve anagrams. *Redefinition* refers to the ability to relinquish old ways of thinking about familiar objects and think of new uses for those objects (Wallach, 1970). Basically, tests of divergent thinking require people to show flexibility in their thought and to take multiple approaches to problems.

Such cognitive flexibility, required for successful performance on tests of divergent thinking, would seem to be a characteristic of intelligence in general. There has been considerable controversy in the research literature concerning the uniqueness of skills in divergent thinking. Some researchers report that performance on tests of divergent thinking are correlated as highly with tests of convergent thinking as they are with themselves (see Wallach, 1970). Yet, others have demonstrated that tests of divergent thinking assess intellectual skills that are separable from those assessed by tests of convergent thinking (Hattie & Rogers, 1986; Wallach & Kogan, 1965).

As with psychometric tests (see Chapter 10), different forms of factor analysis will produce slightly different patterns when comparing tests of convergent and divergent thinking. Hattie and Rogers (1986) have argued that when the "appropriate" factor-analytic model is chosen, distinct factors emerge for creativity and intelligence. Other studies have shown that how the creativity tests are administered influences the relationship that is found between creativity and intelligence. Distinct factors, or patterns, for children's performance on convergent and divergent tasks are found when the tests of divergent thinking are administered in a game-like setting. This uniqueness often disappears when the tasks are administered under "testing" conditions, however, with tests of convergent and divergent thinking being significantly correlated with each other (Milgram & Milgram, 1976; Nichols, 1971; Wallach & Kogan, 1965). Also, although measures of creativity and intelligence may be statistically independent under some conditions, Wallach (1971) has speculated that a certain moderate level of intelligence (as measured by IQ tests) is necessary for high levels of divergent thinking. In other words, being at least moderately intelligent is a necessary but not sufficient condition to demonstrate high levels of divergent thinking.

Stability of Divergent Thinking over Childhood

Although creativity (and thus divergent thinking) has been of great concern to educators and researchers for 30 years (Torrance, 1975), there has been relatively little study of the long-term stability of divergent thinking, and those studies assessing its stability over childhood have reported mixed results. For example, Kogan and Pankove (1972) administered children tests of creativity in the fifth grade and again in the tenth grade. Both the number of responses (productivity scores) and the uniqueness of their responses (uniqueness scores) were obtained, using tests developed by Wallach and Kogan (1965). Kogan and Pankove reported moderate levels of stability over the 5-year period but only under certain testing conditions. The tenth-grade children at one school were given the creativity tests in groups, whereas the children at another school were given

them individually. For the boys who were given the tests in a group setting, moderate stability of creativity scores was found (cross-age correlations for different subtests ranged from .38 to .52). However, these correlations were not significant for the boys who were administered the tests individually (cross-age correlations = .10 for productivity scores and .39 for uniqueness scores). Interestingly, the pattern was exactly reversed for the girls, who showed greater stability when the tests were administered individually. However, the magnitude of these correlations was less than that reported for the boys (correlations of productivity and uniqueness scores from the fifth to the tenth grades were .07 and .19 when the tenth-grade tests were group-administered, and .13 and .35 when the tests were individually administered). Kogan and Pankove speculated that the face-to-face contact might have inhibited adolescent boys' divergent thinking responses, whereas the social setting might have facilitated such responses in adolescent girls. As evidenced by the relatively low magnitude of the correlations, however, any facilitation for girls in the face-to-face interactions was minimal.

In two studies examining the stability of creativity over the teenage years, slightly higher cross-age correlations were reported. Cropley and Clapson (1971) administered two tests of creativity to children in grade 7 and again in grade 12. They reported significant correlations over this 5-year period ranging from .27 to .58, with the correlations being higher for boys than for girls. Similarly, Magnusson and Backteman (1978) reported cross-age correlations of .46 for boys and .42 for girls for creativity tests given at 13 and 16 years of age.

In more recent research, Harrington, Block, and Block (1983) reported significant correlations between tests of divergent thinking administered when children were 4 and 5 years of age and teacher estimates of children's creativity when they were in the sixth grade. Correlations were not significant for all contrasts, with the highest correlation being between creativity scores at 4 and 5 years and teachers' evaluations of children for the statement "[The child] is creative in perception, thought, work, or play." This correlation was .45, with other significant correlations ranging in magnitude between .26 and .35. In general, what little work has been done indicates only marginal stability of skills in divergent thinking over childhood.

Correlates and Consequences of Divergent Thinking

Divergent thinking may have different consequences at different ages. One area that has received substantial research attention is play, with children who score high on tests of divergent thinking (creative children) being more "playful" than other children (Dansky, 1980; Dansky & Silverman, 1973, 1975; Liberman, 1977; Wallach, 1970). Preschool children who engage in high amounts of fantasy play have been found to score higher on tests of divergent thinking than those who do not (Dansky, 1980; Johnson, 1976). Dansky and Silverman (1973) have pointed to Piaget's (1962) belief that children at play assimilate reality into their structures, distorting the world as they do. Piaget also suggested that play can be a source of "creative imagination." Dansky and Silverman (1973, 1975) proposed that opportunities to play may result in a higher incidence of divergent thinking responses in preschool children. In their studies, preschool children who had been given the opportunity to play with sets of objects before receiving a test of divergent thinking ("Think of all the ways you can use a ————") made a greater number of unusual responses than children not given the opportunity to play before testing. However, later work by Dansky (1980) indicated that *how* children play is probably important in affecting creativity. In this study, preschoolers who had engaged in make-believe during a free-play session demonstrated higher levels of performance on an immediately subsequent test of divergent thinking than those who had not (see also Pepler & Ross, 1981). Thus, it is the quality of play that is related to divergent thinking. These findings suggest that the processes that influence symbolic, fantasy play may be similar to those that influence divergent thinking, rather than suggesting that one phenomenon is the cause of the other.

Tests of divergent thinking supposedly assess creativity. A reasonable question is "Do they?" Are children's scores on divergent thinking tasks related to real-life evidence of creative activity? The answer

here is a qualified yes. Wallbrown and Huelsman (1975) administered tests of divergent thinking to third- and fourth-grade children. The children were also assigned three specific projects in an art class, two crayon drawings and one clay sculpture, which were judged in terms of originality and effectiveness of expression. Their performance on the tests of divergent thinking were significantly correlated with judgments of both their originality and effectiveness of expression in their clay sculptures (correlations ranged between .43 and .67). Correlations were smaller between tests of divergent thinking and judgments of the creativity of the crayon drawings, however, with only one of four correlations reaching statistical significance. These findings indicate that tests of divergent thinking predict some aspects of children's creative art, despite the very different nature of the tasks.

Other research has found small but significant correlations between children's performance on tests of divergent thinking and evidence of creativity such as creative writing, science (performing simple "experiments"), and dramatics (Rotter, Langland, & Berger, 1971). Research by Torrance (1972, 1975) has reported that performance on creativity tests given in high school are predictive of adult creative achievements (up to 12 years later), suggesting that when these tests are administered in young adulthood, they can predict subsequent performance.

Is the Distinction between Convergent and Divergent Thinking a Distinction of Cognitive Style?

Do tests of divergent thinking really assess creativity? The answer would seem to be that they do, but far from perfectly. There are individual differences in divergent thinking among children. There is only moderate stability of patterns of divergent thinking over childhood, and divergent thinking is marginally related to some aspects of real-life creative activity. Creativity is an illusive concept and one not easily measured by paper-and-pencil tests. Tests of divergent thinking as developed by Guilford (1967), Torrance (1966), and Wallach and Kogan (1965) do assess some processes that characterize the creative thinker. One must be cautious, however, not to rely too heavily on these tests as *the* assessment of creativity. The best predictor of future behavior is past behavior, and this would seem especially true for creativity.

Do individual differences in convergent and divergent thinking reflect differences in a cognitive style? On the one hand, it would seem so. The ways in which convergent and divergent thinkers go about solving problems seem clearly different and likely to produce drastically different outcomes. On the other hand, it is certainly simplistic to state that a person can be characterized as either a convergent or a divergent thinker. Each of us is capable of both types of thinking, and it appears that people who are good at divergent thinking are also likely to be good at convergent thinking (Wallach, 1970). Furthermore, the relatively poor stability and predictability of tests of creativity make it clear that attributing individual differences in divergent thinking to a cognitive style must be done tenuously. Differences among children do exist, and these differences have important implications for education. Individual differences in styles of divergent thinking warrant serious investigation by psychologists and educators. But these differences must be viewed as reflecting contemporaneous functioning and not as reflecting a style of thinking that is likely to remain stable over long periods of time or to predict performance in many related tasks.

☐ Hemisphericity: Left-Brain versus Right-Brain Processing

One area of individual differences that has stimulated considerable interest among educators and laypeople alike is known as *hemisphericity*. This controversial dimension of cognitive style relates to a child's supposed preference for processing information and solving problems using primarily the left cerebral hemisphere (left brain) or the right cerebral hemisphere (right brain). Despite inconclusive research support, many educators and parents concerned about children's learning difficulties have uncritically adopted the idea of hemisphericity to explain why some students underachieve. Anyone mingling with some groups of educators for any

length of time is sure to hear of an unfortunate "right-brain" child having difficulty learning in a "left-brain" world. There is no clear experimental evidence, however, documenting either the validity of hemisphericity or its usefulness in diagnosing children's learning problems. Yet, many aspects of hemisphericity are interesting and provocative and may someday provide reliable information about individual differences in children's thinking.

Cerebral Lateralization

Before the notion of hemisphericity evolved, breakthroughs in brain research had produced extensive neuropsychological data. Studies with brain-damaged patients indicated that certain basic behavioral functions are located within particular areas of the brain. Also, convincing research with subjects whose left and right hemispheres had been surgically disconnected showed that each hemisphere is specialized to process different types of information. These cerebral lateralization studies revealed that, in right-handed people, the left hemisphere is specialized for processing language and other analytic, logical, or temporal information, whereas the right hemisphere is best suited for processing nonverbal, visual, and spatial information. Although the concepts of cerebral localization and cerebral specialization are generally accepted, it is important to note that the subjects' brains in these early studies were injured or surgically altered, making it difficult to generalize the results to people with intact brains. While an extensive review of this research is beyond the scope of this chapter, you may wish to consult one of several sources for an in-depth look at the fascinating research underlying the concept of hemisphericity (Corballis & Beale, 1983; Gazzaniga, 1985; Springer & Deutsch, 1985).

The idea that a person's preference for information processing style and his or her approach to problem solving can be attributed to one side of the brain or the other is overly simplistic. Actually, both hemispheres in neurologically intact people are involved in most if not all learning tasks; however, the left or right side may be more involved, depending on the nature of the stimuli and the processing demands of the task (Kaufman & Kaufman, 1983).

Following are some of the characteristics often associated with the left and right hemispheres:

Left Hemisphere	*Right Hemisphere*
verbal	nonverbal
sequential	simultaneous
temporal	visual/spatial
logical	Gestalt
analytic	intuitive
convergent	divergent

Despite the absence of a clear dichotomy, researchers have used the idea of hemispheric specialization to develop models of information processing. One such model refers to a child's cognitive style preference for either successive (left-brain) or simultaneous (right-brain) processing.

Successive versus Simultaneous Processing

The dichotomy between successive and simultaneous processing is based on brain research by the neuropsychologist Alexander Luria (1966) as interpreted by Das, Kirby, and Jarman (1975). Successive, or sequential, processing orders stimuli into sequences to solve a problem, whereas simultaneous, or holistic, processing synthesizes separate elements into spatial groupings. These researchers developed neuropsychological tests to assess children's hemispheric cognitive style, and they have provided factor-analytic support for their theory and how it might affect children's school achievement (Das et al., 1975; Das & Molloy, 1975; Kirby & Das, 1977). The successive/simultaneous dichotomy has not been accepted by all researchers and educators, and much controversy exists concerning the validity of such a distinction (Springer & Deutsch, 1985; Sternberg, 1984). Nevertheless, the limited and controversial research base has not dampened the enthusiasm of researchers who have long been searching for a theory-based measure of intelligence that could be applied to teaching strategies to remediate the learning problems of individual students. The most ambitious educational instrument arising from the successive/simultaneous distinction to date is the Kaufman Assessment Battery for Children (K-ABC), a theory-based test of intelligence (Kaufman & Kaufman, 1983).

Rather than using the traditional IQ score, the K-ABC yields a Mental Processing Composite score that is a combination of the Sequential Processing scale (left brain) and the Simultaneous Processing scale (right brain). The Sequential scale of the K-ABC is composed of three subtests, with tasks that can be solved by arrangement of the stimuli into serial orders. The Hand Movements subtest, for example, requires the child to reproduce (in the proper sequence) a series of hand taps that increase in number with each trial. The Number Recall subtest, similar to the Digit Span subtest of the Wechsler scales, requires the child to repeat a series of digits in the exact order in which they were heard. The Word Order subtest is a type of serial recall task in which the child must point to the silhouettes of common objects in the same order in which they were spoken by the examiner.

The right-brain tasks that make up the seven subtests on the Simultaneous Processing scale use spatial stimuli that must be integrated and synthesized to produce the appropriate solutions. Although important at the perceptual level for forming the Gestalts (perceptual wholes) necessary to learn the shapes of letters and numbers, simultaneous processing is also proposed to be important for integrating diverse stimuli from many sources as needed for complex problem-solving tasks such as reading comprehension. In the Gestalt Closure subtest, the child must "fill in the gaps" to name objects in partially completed inkblot drawings. The Triangles subtest requires the child to construct an abstract design from several identical triangles. In the Spatial Memory subtest, the child is presented small, colorful drawings placed on a page. After viewing the drawings for 5 seconds, the child must correctly recall the spatial location of the drawings.

Some general relationships between hemispheric cognitive style and measures of academic achievement have been reported. For example, Das and Molloy (1975) found that high levels of both successive and simultaneous processing were necessary to attain the higher reading-comprehension scores in an average group of fourth-grade boys. Students who were significantly higher in either successive or simultaneous processing attained only moderate scores. In the Interpretation Manual for the K-ABC, the Kaufmans cite numerous studies demonstrating that reading problems in learning disabled students are related to lower levels of successive processing. They also present research to support their remedial program based on using the students' processing strengths. Although research into this approach to remediation shows promise (Kaufman & Kaufman, 1983), this research is in its neonatal stage, and much more needs to be done.

The K-ABC has received considerable criticism on many theoretical, methodological, and statistical grounds. For example, Das (1984a) asserted that the K-ABC does not measure sequential processing properly and that the distinction between simultaneous and sequential processing could just as easily be described as one between verbal and nonverbal processing. More critical is the contention by Sternberg (1984) and Goetz and Hall (1984) that the successive/simultaneous dichotomy proposed by the Kaufmans is not supported by the psychological literature. The same data that Kaufman and Kaufman use as evidence for hemispheric specialization can be explained by other information processing models.

The K-ABC is a relatively new and seemingly popular instrument to assess children's intelligence. Its reliance on the successive/simultaneous distinction gives it a theoretical basis often lacking in earlier tests of intelligence (see Chapter 10). However, the research basis for this distinction has been questioned, which essentially questions the validity of the K-ABC.

Hemisphericity and Creativity

One factor that has been proposed to be affected by hemisphericity is creativity. Because the right hemisphere is supposedly more intuitive and less involved in serial, convergent processes than the left hemisphere, right-brain functioning has been proposed to be associated with creative functioning (Krueger, 1976; Torrance, Reynolds, Riegel, & Ball, 1977). Torrance and his colleagues developed a test called Your Style of Learning and Thinking to assess hemisphericity with paper and pencil (Torrance et al., 1977). A modified version of this test was developed for use with children (Reynolds, Kaltsounis, &

Torrance, 1979). In this test, subjects are given a series of statements in sets of three and are to choose the one that best describes them. One statement reflects supposed right-hemispheric processing, another left-hemispheric processing, and a third integrated- or balanced-hemispheric processing. Several examples of items from the children's form of Your Style of Learning and Thinking (Reynolds et al., 1979) are shown:

1. a. I am good at remembering faces. [right hemisphere]
   b. I am good at remembering names. [left hemisphere]
   c. I am just as good at remembering names and faces. [integrated]
2. a. I answer best to directions when I have someone show me. [right hemisphere]
   b. I answer best to directions that are told to me or written for me. [left hemisphere]
   c. I follow directions just as well either way. [integrated]

Subjects are classified as using right-, left-, or integrated-hemispheric processing based on their responses to the 40-item test.

Several studies using Your Style of Learning and Thinking have found a creative advantage for people classified as right- or integrated-hemispheric. For example, Torrance and Mourad (1979) reported that graduate students classified as right-hemispheric were more creative and reported a greater number of creative achievements than graduate students classified as left-hemispheric. Few differences were found between the right- and integrated-hemispheric subjects (see also Torrance, 1982). In a study of gifted adolescents, Torrance and Reynolds (1978) reported that children with right-hemispheric styles produced more creative future career images and more frequently provided creative solutions to hypothetical conflicts than children with left-hemispheric styles. Again, children with integrated-hemispheric styles were similar to the right-hemispheric children. In a more recent study by Kershner and Ledger (1985), gifted and nongifted children in grades four, five, and six were classified with respect to hemisphericity and were administered tests of intelligence and creativity. They reported that the nongifted children preferred the left-hemispheric style more than did the gifted children, although there were no differences in the number of right- or integrated-hemispheric responses between the gifted and nongifted children. Counter to the findings of Torrance and his colleagues for older children and adults, creativity was not associated with right-hemispheric processes. Rather, highly creative children made more integrated-hemispheric choices than did less creative children.

The number of studies using Your Style of Learning and Thinking is small. There does seem to be a relationship between hemisphericity and creativity, with more creative adolescents and adults displaying a right-hemispheric advantage. However, the magnitude of these differences is small, and a different pattern of results has been reported for preadolescent children (Kershner & Ledger, 1985). As of now, there are too few data to make any definitive conclusions. The validity of the paper-and-pencil test used to assess hemisphericity needs to be examined further. This is especially critical for research with children, whose poor metacognitive skills may result in inaccurate or unreliable responses. In addition, tests of hemisphericity need to be further modified so that they can be easily and reliably administered to younger children. (The youngest children tested by Reynolds and his colleagues (1979) for the children's form of Your Style of Learning and Thinking were 9 years old.) Questions concerning the stability of hemisphericity and its developmental relation to other measures of cognition such as creativity can then be better assessed.

Is Hemisphericity a Cognitive Style?

Individual differences in hemispheric specialization have been accepted by many educators and laypeople as fact. Seminars and popular books abound attempting to teach people to make better use of one hemisphere or the other, or helping "right-brain" people cope in a "left-brain" world. In his book *The Social Brain*, Gazzaniga (1985) discusses the left-brain/right-brain mania that has inundated California and the country as a whole. Machines have been advertised that purport to harmonize the electrical patterns of each hemisphere, producing relaxation (for a mere $8000), and an ABC-TV reporter at the 1984 Olympics mentioned how running helps build up the right side of the brain. As Gazzaniga sees it, outrageous claims have been based on highly technical and limited experimental data.

The left-brain/right-brain dichotomy is based on solid experimental and neuropsychological evidence. But the more subtle distinction of individual differences in people's hemispheric dominance is less well founded. The ideas and data of Das, the Kaufmans, Torrance, and their colleagues are provocative and may have important implications for education. It seems too early, however, to jump on a bandwagon that proposes that individual differences in hemisphericity reflect a potent cognitive style. Nevertheless, it is also too early to dismiss hemisphericity as an unimportant aspect of individual differences in children's learning and thinking.

☐ Summary

Cognitive styles refer to individual differences in the way people process information that are relatively consistent over tasks and stable over time. Much of the research into children's cognitive styles has been done in the hope of improving instruction for children, particularly those with learning disabilities.

Field dependence refers to the extent to which a person is able to evaluate individual components of a perceptual field independently from the whole. Field-dependent people have a difficult time perceiving component parts of a visual field separately from the whole, whereas *field-independent* people can more easily analyze the perceptual field into its component parts. Field dependence/field independence (FD/FI) is measured by the *Embedded Figures Test*, in which a person must find a geometric figure embedded within a complex figure, and the *Rod-and-Frame Test*, in which a person must adjust a rod located within a tilted frame so that it is upright. Children become increasingly field independent with age, although there is substantial stability of individual differences in one's FD/FI classification over childhood and into young adulthood. Field-independent children have been found to perform better than field-dependent children on a variety of tasks, including various tests of Piagetian reasoning and IQ. Tests of FD/FI have been found to assess a form of spatial/analytical intelligence similar to that measured by certain subtests of the Wechsler intelligence scales.

There has been speculation that FD/FI is merely a reflection of cognitive development rather than a reflection of a cognitive style. Globerson and her colleagues have demonstrated that FD and FI children at any given age have comparable amounts of mental effort available for the execution of cognitive tasks and that FD/FI is a true cognitive style and not merely an indicant of level of cognitive development.

Conceptual tempo refers to individual differences in the speed with which one responds on problems of high response uncertainty. *Reflectives* respond slowly and make few errors. *Impulsives* respond quickly and make many errors. Reflection/impulsivity is assessed by the *Matching Familiar Figures Test* (MFFT) developed by Kagan and his colleagues. MFFT performance is relatively consistent across a variety of tasks involving a high degree of response uncertainty, with patterns of errors being relatively stable over development. Patterns of latencies are less stable over time. Significant correlations between MFFT performance and IQ scores have been found, causing some to speculate that individual differences in conceptual tempo can best be understood as differences in general intelligence.

Reflective children perform better on a variety of academic-type tasks than impulsive children. These measures include reading, memory, and meta-memory tasks. Impulsive children have been trained to increase their latencies and to respond more accurately. Impulsive children display inefficient problem-solving strategies. However, research by Zelniker and Jeffrey indicated that reflectives' strategies are best suited for tasks requiring analysis of *detail*, whereas impulsives' strategies are best suited for tasks requiring *global* analysis.

The distinction between *convergent* and *divergent* thinking is basically one between the type of intelligence that requires focusing on a specific answer and the type that involves originating several possible alternatives to a particular problem. Divergent thinking is viewed as a reflection of *creativity*. Tests of divergent thinking typically require thinking of as many different responses as one can to a particular problem ("How many different ways can you think of to use a brick?"). Such tests have been referred to as tasks of *ideational fluency*. Research has shown that divergent thinking shows only marginal stability over childhood. Tests of divergent thinking have been found to correlate with fantasy play during the preschool years and with some measures of creativity during childhood (for example, quality of art work).

Hemisphericity refers to the degree to which a person's preferred information processing style involves the left or right cerebral hemisphere. The left hemisphere has been associated with linguistic, analytical, and sequential processing, whereas the right hemisphere has been associated with nonverbal, visual/spatial, and simultaneous processing. The distinction between successive (left-hemisphere) and simultaneous (right-hemisphere) processing of information has been emphasized by some researchers, and Kaufman and Kaufman have developed an intelligence test based on this dichotomy (the K-ABC). The Kaufmans propose that individual differences in processing style can be compensated for by specific remediation. The K-ABC has been criticized on a number of grounds, with some asserting that the successive/simultaneous distinction is not well established in the research literature. Other researchers have proposed that right-hemispheric processing is related to creativity. Some support for this position has been found by Torrance and his colleagues, although the evidence is weak and opposite trends are reported for preadolescent children. Hemispheric differences have received much attention over the last decade, with many people overstating the significance of hemisphericity for individual differences in thinking.

Sex Differences

with Marc T. Frankel

Some Background on the Study of Sex Differences

Sex Differences in Cognition
☐ Sex Differences in Mathematical Ability   ☐ Sex Differences in Spatial Abilities
☐ Sex Differences in Verbal Behavior

Theories of the Origins of Sex Differences
☐ Gender Differentiation and the Effect of Prenatal Hormones on Cognitive Functioning
☐ Pubertal Hormones and Changes in Cognitive Functioning
☐ Patterns of Hemispheric Specialization   ☐ Sex-Linked Inheritance
☐ The Interaction of Biological and Experiential Factors in Sex Differences in Children's Thinking

How Important Are Sex Differences in Cognition?

Summary

Note

The study of sex differences in behavior has bridged many academic disciplines and has consumed the attention of scholars across several centuries. One reason for this interest is that sex (or gender) is an important aspect of our social lives. Our gender helps to define who we are, both for ourselves and for others, and it is one of only a few aspects of our social status that (with a handful of notorious exceptions) do not change with time. We progress from infancy to childhood to adulthood to old age; we change our marital status (some of us repeatedly), change jobs, get promoted and demoted, and become parents and grandparents; but our gender remains constant. Also, most people have some intuitive notions about differences in behavior between men and women and boys and girls, providing another impetus for research into sex differences.

☐ Some Background on the Study of Sex Differences

A popular theory of the late nineteenth century held that males were more likely than females to vary from the norm in their physical and mental characteristics. In other words, more males than females were expected to show behaviors at the extremes. To researchers such as Havelock Ellis, a turn-of-the-century sexologist, it followed that this *variability hypothesis* could explain why males displayed more diverse traits, both good (for example, genius) and bad (for example, criminal behavior). Ellis's landmark 1894 book, *Man and Woman: A Study of Human Secondary Sexual Characters*, proposed the variability hypothesis to account for the finding that males, as a group, scored higher on intelligence tests than females.

An early attempt to disprove the variability hypothesis can be found in the work of Hollingsworth (1916, 1918). Rather than attributing the overrepresentation of boys among those tested for suspected retardation or mental disability to inherently greater male variability, Hollingsworth proposed that this disparity was due to selective observation on the part of community officials. She asserted that this disproportion developed because the authorities were less likely to notice retarded girls until they became widows or prostitutes.

In a reversal of earlier findings, Wechsler, developer of the Wechsler intelligence scales, found that females scored higher than males on his 1943 IQ test. However, males and females were equivalent on the 1955 revision of the same test and on all subsequent revisions. This change is more likely to have been caused by modifications of test content than by changes in intelligence within the general population.

More recently, psychologists have abandoned the study of gender effects on IQ scores in favor of analyses of specific abilities that are important to intelligent functioning. A critical review of research into sex differences was published in 1974 by Maccoby and Jacklin in their highly influential book, *The Psychology of Sex Differences*. Maccoby and Jacklin based their synthesis primarily on pre-1970 child data. They concluded that evidence in support of sex differences in cognition could be found in three areas: *mathematical ability, spatial ability,* and *verbal ability*. Because of this conclusion, most of the data collected since 1974 have concerned these three areas, which will be the focus of the remainder of this chapter.

☐ Sex Differences in Cognition

Although sex differences can be found at any point along the age continuum, in theory, the point at which such differences first appear has major implications for our understanding of developmental causes. Sex differences observed early in life, for example, have presumably come under minimal environmental influence and suggest biological origins. At the same time, it does not require a Ph.D. in developmental psychology to realize that boys and girls are treated differently from earliest infancy (see Perry & Bussey, 1984). In comparison, differences that are not observed until late childhood might suggest an environmental explanation, particularly if the relevant academic experiences of boys and girls differed. Yet, such late-developing differences may reflect underlying biological factors that are not expressed until puberty. The age when the sexes diverge on a particular skill provides insights into the underlying causes of gender differences; but knowing the age of onset alone is not sufficient, for both biological and environmental factors can influence cognitive functioning at different times in development.

It is important to keep in mind throughout this chapter that sex differences do not imply *sexual dimorphism*. Sexual dimorphism is a state in which merely knowing the biological sex of an individual leads to perfect predictions about that person's behavior. Although humans do express some physical signs of sexual dimorphism (for example, genitalia), knowing a person's sex cannot lead to accurate predictions about intellectual performance. As will be seen, the magnitude of cognitive differences between the sexes is small and highly variable, rendering precise predictions of cognitive functioning based solely on sex impossible.

Sex Differences in Mathematical Ability

Maccoby and Jacklin (1974) reviewed the findings of 27 studies in which sex differences in quantitative (mathematical) ability had been assessed. Of the studies reporting significant differences between the sexes, the vast majority favored boys. Studies with pre-adolescent children, however, found either no sex differences in mathematics or small but significant differences *favoring* girls. Boys did not achieve quantitative superiority until 10 to 12 years of age, and after midadolescence, no findings were reported in which girls outscored boys.

Following Maccoby and Jacklin's review, there was an increase in research into sex differences in mathematical ability. One impetus to this research was the observation that men were statistically overrepresented in scientific and mathematical professions. The Maccoby and Jacklin data were considered evidence that this disparity stemmed from real differences in aptitude and skill level (that is, biologically based differences).

A different interpretation was made by Sells (1974), who noted the disparity in mathematical background between men and women. Males are more likely than females to enroll in advanced math-

ematics courses, for example, and during the 1950s and 60s, when most of the data reviewed by Maccoby and Jacklin were collected, boys took more extra courses involving math-related skills than girls (for example, mechanical shop). To Sells, the lack of sufficient academic background served as a filter to select against females pursuing occupations requiring mathematical ability.

Subsequent work by Fennema and Sherman (1977) and by Benbow and Stanley (1980, 1983) directly assessed the hypothesis that the differences in mathematical abilities between the sexes were due to differences in biologically induced aptitudes and not to experience. Fennema and Sherman assessed the mathematics achievement of 1233 male and female students from four high schools while controlling for course background and general intelligence. The statistical method of *covariation* allowed Fennema and Sherman to judge whether observed differences in math ability between the sexes were a function of previous courses taken or of specific cognitive capabilities. When math background, visual/spatial ability, and sociocultural factors were covaried with sex, previously significant sex differences in math scores became small and were statistically significant in only two of the four schools. Thus, Fennema and Sherman's data indicate that biological factors cannot account for sex differences in mathematical ability in all situations. Rather, both environmental (as reflected here by academic background) and biological factors influence mathematical ability, although the precise extent that each factor affects performance is unknown.

Stronger evidence for a biological basis of sex differences in mathematical skills is presented by Benbow and Stanley (1980), who reported significant sex differences in mathematical ability apparently independent of course background. Benbow and Stanley examined the verbal and mathematic Scholastic Aptitude Test (SAT) scores of a group of seventh- and eighth-grade children selected to participate in a study of mathematically skilled youth conducted at Johns Hopkins University. The students were selected in a series of "talent searches" conducted between 1972 and 1979 and scored in the top 5% of students taking the exam. The data revealed consistent sex differences favoring boys. Further, the students were essentially equivalent in verbal SAT scores and in math-course background. Benbow and Stanley (1983) reported similar findings in a second investigation with a much larger number of students (nearly 40,000). In this second study, they found that the disparity between the sexes was greater at the higher ability levels. For example, the ratio of boys to girls scoring 420 or more on the Math SAT was 1.5:1. In contrast, this boy-to-girl ratio was 4.1:1 for children scoring 600 or more and 13:1 for the small number of children scoring 700 or more.

Benbow and Stanley's subjects were selected in advance for exceptional math ability. It is possible that comparisons of scores in their sample have limited generalizability to the remaining 95% of the population. Moreover, their data reveal nothing about the sources of the observed sex differences in SAT scores. Although the findings are probably not rooted in differences in academic background, there is also no compelling reason to conclude that SAT scores reflect innate differences in aptitude or capacity. In fact, Fox (1976) underscored the fact that teachers, parents, and peers all have negative feelings about mathematically talented girls. Likewise, children's books, magazines, and the popular media often present females in stereotypic ways that militate against stronger interest in mathematics.

Fox's observations suggest that there are different expectations about the appropriateness of mathematical achievement for boys and girls. Math is typically seen as a male activity; that is, math is a sex-typed activity, and children learn that it is socially more acceptable for boys to do well than it is for girls (see Chapter 9). Conversely, children may learn that it is all right for girls *not* to excel in math, whereas more is expected of boys in this area.

This alternative was investigated by Raymond and Benbow (1986) in a study that assessed the relationship between parental attitudes, sex typing, and mathematical ability for groups of adolescents scoring high on the quantitative and verbal portions of the SAT. They reported that mathematically talented students received greater parental encouragement in mathematics than did verbally talented students and that this pattern did not differ with sex.

Related to this, the amount of encouragement in mathematics that children received was comparable for boys and girls, regardless of their area or level of talent (that is, high verbal or high math). Finally, mathematically talented girls were no more sex typed as masculine than were verbally talented girls, and there was no relationship between sex typing and SAT scores. Raymond and Benbow concluded that parental-socialization practices during adolescence could not account for mathematical ability in this group of mathematically talented children. The obvious interpretation, then, is that these sex differences have their origins in biology. However, Raymond and Benbow noted that cause and effect cannot be clearly separated in studies such as theirs.

Sex Differences in Spatial Abilities

A second area in which Maccoby and Jacklin reported sex differences favoring males was spatial ability. Two broad categories of spatial ability are distinguished here: *spatial orientation* and *spatial visualization*. Spatial orientation refers to how people understand the placement of objects in space with themselves as the reference point. Spatial orientation tasks include ones in which subjects are asked to distinguish geographic directions in an unfamiliar locale or to draw their way from point A to point B on a map. In contrast, spatial visualization tasks involve visual operations, such as mentally rotating a figure or adjusting a tilted object to bring it to an upright position. Developmental research on each of these topics will be reviewed briefly.

Sex Differences in Spatial Orientation

A colleague who conducts research on spatial orientation in children often hears stories of people who "can't tell their left from their right." As Harris (1981) points out, such anecdotes almost always originate from men who are describing women's seeming confusion over direction. More formal self-report data support these anecdotes, suggesting that a larger proportion of women than men have a poor sense of direction.

Money and his associates, in an early study of sex differences in spatial direction, asked 7- to 18-year-old boys and girls to follow a marked route on an outline map of city streets (Money, Alexander, & Walker, 1965). Without physically rotating the map, subjects were to tell whether each turn would be to their right or left. Boys were significantly more accurate than girls at every age.

Of course, subjects in this experiment still needed to mentally rotate the map, even though they were prohibited from physically doing so. Several researchers have argued that sex differences in spatial orientation will be most marked when such manipulations or transformations of spatial information are required for task solution (Anooshian & Young, 1981; Harris, 1981; Herman, Shiraki, & Miller, 1985).

Research investigating children's transformation of spatial information has been conducted by Herman, Siegel, and their colleagues. Herman and Siegel (1978) reported sex differences in situations in which children must form "cognitive maps" of an area. In one study, kindergarten and second- and fifth-grade children walked repeatedly through a large display of a model town consisting of buildings, streets, railroad tracks, and trees. Following the walks, the children were asked to re-create the layout from memory. The second- and fifth-grade boys were significantly more accurate than the same-aged girls, although no sex differences were found for kindergarten children. Similarly, Siegel and Schadler (1977) questioned 4- to 6-year-old children about their classrooms, a far more familiar place than the model town used by Herman and Siegel. Despite this enhanced familiarity, Siegel and Schadler found that boys were more accurate than girls. However, the stability of such sex differences has been questioned. For example, in at least one study similar to those described above, no sex differences among college undergraduates in memory for campus routes or building configurations were found (Herman, Kail, & Siegel, 1979).

More recently, Herman and his colleagues asked preschool children (3 to 5½ years of age) to walk through their own nursery school building, memorizing the locations of five specific target objects (Herman et al., 1985). After becoming familiarized with the building, each child was placed at one of three sighting locations and asked to point to each of

the targets, some of which were behind walls out of view. The experiment continued until each child had been tested at each of the three sighting locations.

Herman and his colleagues reported that boys had a higher accuracy rate than girls as measured by degrees of deviation from the correct direction (see Table 14-1). Although these data reflect sex differences in spatial orientation, at least two similar studies by Hazen and her colleagues found no sex effects (Hazen, 1982; Hazen, Lockman, & Pick, 1978). Unlike Herman and his associates, Hazen controlled for children's experience with the environment (for example, prior familiarity and "practice"). One explanation for the discrepancies between the findings of the Herman and the Hazen studies is that boys have greater exposure to the environment than girls because of tendencies toward greater amounts of exploration (see Hazen, 1982) and that it is this greater exposure that is responsible for their superior performance.

The preceding data illustrate some of the difficulties inherent in making generalizations about sex differences from psychological experiments. The studies of Herman and Siegel seem to support sex-stereotypic notions about sense of direction. However, these effects may be less the product of sex per se and more the product of exposure and experience stemming from other sex-related differences (for example, exploration).

Sex Differences in Spatial Visualization

As noted, some tasks require performing visual operations such as rotating a figure in order to identify it or adjusting a tilted object to a prescribed position. Maccoby and Jacklin (1974) distinguished two types of visual/spatial skills: *visual/nonanalytic* and *analytic/spatial*. Visual/nonanalytic skills involve mentally

TABLE 14-1 Degrees of Deviation from Correct Direction as a Function of Age and Sex (Herman et al., 1985)

	Boys	Girls
3-year-olds	41.32	45.80
5-year-olds	22.61	46.21

rotating an object or figure without accompanying verbal mediation. Because silent verbalization may be occurring without the experimenter's knowledge, such tasks are usually done under instructions to respond as rapidly as possible, with the assumption that entirely visual performance will be measurably quicker than verbally mediated activity.

Analytic/spatial skills incorporate verbal mediation in addition to visual processing. Tasks such as the Embedded Figures Test, in which a subject must find a simple figure embedded in a more complex one, or the Rod-and-Frame Test, in which a subject must adjust a rod situated within a tilted frame to the horizontal position, measure analytic/spatial ability (Witkin et al., 1954; see Chapter 13). One problem with such tasks is that sex differences may be attributed to *either* verbal or spatial skills or to some combination of the two.

Maccoby and Jacklin reported consistent sex differences favoring males on spatial visualization tasks. Closer inspection of the studies that Maccoby and Jacklin reviewed, however, indicates that such differences were not detected universally. Of 30 research studies of visual/nonanalytic abilities, 9 found differences favoring males, 2 found differences favoring females, and 19 reported no significant sex differences. Similarly, of 47 investigations of analytic/spatial skills, Maccoby and Jacklin reported 21 cases of male superiority, 3 studies in which females performed better, and 23 instances of no differences. In short, although the "box score" tally of differences favors males, there are actually more studies failing to confirm male superiority in spatial visualization skills.

A typical test of spatial visualization ability is the Rod-and-Frame Test, which Maccoby and Jacklin classified as indicative of analytic/spatial ability. The Rod-and-Frame Test requires a subject to move a lighted rod so that it remains horizontal, even though a surrounding frame, or in some cases the subject's chair, may be tilted. Errors on the test (that is, failures to make the rod horizontal) are considered evidence of deficits in analytic/spatial skill. Several studies have reported that males make fewer errors on the test than females (Harris, 1978; Witkin, Goodenough, & Karp, 1967). Further, the

test has been associated with the cognitive style construct of field dependence/field independence (Witkin, Dyk, Faterson, Goodenough, & Karp, 1962; see Chapter 13). According to this theory, females make more errors because they are comparatively more field dependent, meaning that they rely more heavily on the "field" surrounding the rod (that is, the frame) for cues. In contrast, males are deemed to be field independent, which allows them to ignore the frame and focus on the rod's relative position in space.

A simple test of spatial visualization ability that has consistently yielded sex differences in performance is Piaget and Inhelder's (1967) water level problem (see Figure 14-1). In this problem, subjects are shown tipped bottles and asked to judge the position of the water. The correct answer involves a knowledge of the horizontality of the water; that is, the subjects should indicate (usually by drawing a line) that the level of the water will be horizontal across the bottle. In Piaget and Inhelder's work, preoperational children had difficulty with the task, often indicating that the water level should be parallel to the bottom of the bottle and not parallel to the ground.

Piaget and Inhelder's data suggested that knowledge of invariant horizontality (and verticality) develops in late childhood. Other researchers noted, however, that many adolescents and young adults have difficulty with the concept, with a disproportionate number of females experiencing such difficulties (Liben, 1978; Thomas, Jamison, & Hummel, 1973; Willemsen & Reynolds, 1973). In a pioneer-

FIGURE 14-1 A water level problem. Subjects are to draw the water line in each bottle to represent how it would look if it were half-filled with water.

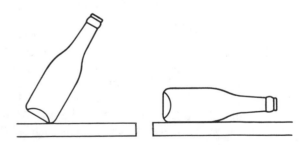

ing study, college women were first presented with a variant of the water level problem (Thomas et al., 1973). The women who consistently made errors in estimation (average estimation being greater than 4 degrees from the horizontal) were then given training in solving such problems. (Approximately 73% of all the women made errors greater than 4 degrees in the pretest.) Training in two experiments consisted of the subjects being permitted to see the actual water level in a bottle tilted identically to the bottle on which they were to make their predictions. Following the training, the subjects were given eight posttests on which they were to make predictions of water level, identical in form to the pretest. The performance of these women was compared with those of samples of men and women who had "passed" the pretest. In general, the training was ineffective in modifying these women's performance. Their predictions were significantly more inaccurate than those of the control subjects, and they were unable to verbalize a correct strategy.

More recent research by Liben and Golbeck (1980, 1984) has demonstrated that female children and adults can improve their performance on horizontality problems when the task demands are modified or when they are given explicit information about the concepts dealt with in the tasks. These findings indicate that females have the ability to construct mature spatial representations and that some of the sex differences on these tasks "reflect males' and females' differential knowledge of the relevant physical phenomena" (Liben & Goldbeck, 1984, p. 605). Yet, sex differences are seemingly robust on this task, suggesting that some of these differences have their roots in biology.

Given the research findings, to what extent can sex differences in spatial ability be attributed to experiential factors? Fennema and Sherman (1977), in addition to their work with mathematics, obtained scores on a test of spatial relations for children in grades 9 through 12. They reported significant differences in scores, favoring boys, at two of the four schools used in their study, suggesting, as with mathematics, that the differences were not robust. Further, boys at the two schools where sex differences

were reported were found to have taken courses with significantly more space-related content (for example, graphic arts and mechanical shop). When statistically controlling for differences in academic background, Fennema and Sherman found that the difference in spatial skills between the sexes disappeared.

More recently, Newcomb and her colleagues found that differences in spatial *experience* accounted for observed differences in spatial *performance* (Newcombe, Bandura, & Taylor, 1983). They created a list of everyday activities that might occur in a population of high school and college students. In the first part of the study, college students were asked to classify the activities as masculine, feminine, or neutral. The raters typically selected those tasks judged to have high spatial content as masculine and as having more male participants:

Masculine	*Neutral*	*Feminine*
touch football	bowling	figure skating
baseball	softball	field hockey
basketball	advanced	baton twirling
darts	tennis	gymnastics
hunting	table tennis	ballet
skateboarding	diving	disco dancing
shooting pool	drawing	embroidery
car repair	sculpting	tailoring
electrical	photography	touch typing
circuitry	navigating	knitting
sketching	in car	
house plans	marching	
	in band	

Subsequently, the researchers found small but significant sex differences among college students on a psychometric test with strong spatial components. They also reported a significant correlation between spatial activities and aptitude scores, particularly for females. That is, the more spatial activities in which one engages, the higher one's spatial ability is likely to be. Working with preschool children, Connor and Serbin (1977) similarly reported differences in visual/spatial play activities between boys and girls. They further reported that the amount of boys' visual/spatial play correlated significantly with their performance on the Block Design subtest of the WISC and the Preschool Embedded Figures Test, suggesting that sex differences in play activity are responsible in part for boys' generally greater spatial skills.

Sex Differences in Verbal Behavior

"Female superiority on verbal tasks has been one of the more solidly established generalizations in the field of sex differences." So wrote Maccoby and Jacklin (1974, p. 75) in introducing their section on sex differences in verbal ability. Despite these strongly stated opening remarks, Maccoby and Jacklin followed with the observation that the magnitude of such differences is small and often insignificant; but when differences do appear in the data, they usually favor females.

Sex differences in the rate of language acquisition have been found (Clarke-Stewart, 1973; Moore, 1967), although most studies have failed to observe any significant sex differences (McCarthy, 1954). In related research, Lewis and his colleagues reported greater vocalization by infant girls than by boys. For example, 3-month-old girls were found to vocalize more than boys in response to their mother's initiation to "talk" (Lewis & Freedle, 1973), and infant girls between the ages of 3 and 13 months vocalized more to facial stimuli than did boys of the same age (Lewis, 1969).

A more recent experiment by Roe and her colleagues proposed that early sex differences in vocal responsiveness are due to differences in parental behaviors and not to biological differences between boys and girls (Roe, Drivas, Karagellis, & Roe, 1985). They compared the vocal responsiveness of home-reared and institutionally-reared 3-month-old infants in Greece. The researchers cited evidence that male children are more valued than female children in Greece, and they speculated that this bias may result in findings opposite to those reported by Lewis for American infants. Infants were spoken to by a female experimenter and by their mothers or caretakers for a series of 3-minute intervals in an attempt to elicit vocalizations. No sex differences were noted in vocal responsiveness for the institutionally-reared infants. Differences were found for

the home-reared group, however, favoring the *boys*. Home-reared boys were more vocally responsive to their mothers than to the stranger, whereas this difference was not significant for the home-reared girls. The researchers proposed that this sex difference in vocal responsiveness "is influenced very early in life by environmental factors . . . related to the fact that male children in Greece are more valued and desired by parents than female children" (Roe et al., 1985, p. 375).

Differences in verbal ability past infancy are primarily limited to early adolescence and beyond. When sex differences are found during the preschool and school years, according to Maccoby and Jacklin, they again typically favor girls and, for the most part, are limited to children from impoverished families. Such differences are not universal, however. In U.S. studies, girls excel at reading through the elementary school years, and, during this same time, boys are more likely to be assigned to remedial reading classes. Yet, most studies from Great Britain show no consistent sex differences in reading ability, and girls are more likely to be illiterate than boys in Germany, Nigeria, and India (see Gibson & Levin, 1975). These findings suggest that sex differences in reading ability during the school years are probably due to differences in rearing or educational practices and not to differences in biology.

Sex differences in verbal abilities are more pronounced beginning about age 10 or 11, when "girls begin to come into their own in verbal performance" (Maccoby & Jacklin, 1974, p. 84). As a group, girls are likely to be better readers than boys and to solve verbal problems such as anagrams more easily. Such effects are not robust, however, and there have been more studies failing to find sex differences in verbal abilities during adolescence and adulthood than there have been studies finding them (Maccoby & Jacklin, 1974).

More recently, Cox and Waters (1986) have reviewed research into memory development and have concluded that reliable sex differences are found, favoring girls, in the use of *organizational strategies* in free recall. Organization in free recall refers to the extent to which a person takes advantage of conceptual relations existing among items to be remembered in order to aid memory, such as remembering all the pictures of ANIMALS together or recalling all the FURNITURE words in a single cluster (see Chapter 8). The strategy of organization would seem to be related to the structure of semantic memory (see Chapters 7 and 8) and to verbal processing in general. Cox and Waters pointed out that sex differences in organization and memory have generally *not* been analyzed by researchers, making the absolute number of studies investigating this issue small. Of those analyzing sex differences, about half report no significant differences in organization and memory between the sexes. For those studies reporting sex differences, all favor girls, with differences being found over a broad age range (from 6-year-olds to adults).

As with mathematical and spatial skills, it is difficult to determine the origins of sex differences in verbal abilities. The study of Roe and her colleagues suggests that the early sex difference in vocal responsiveness is due to the behaviors of parents, not to differences in biology. Boys and girls are socialized differently, generally being encouraged to display sex-appropriate behavior. Reading and the expression of feelings (both verbal tasks) are viewed as stereotypic female activities (see Perry & Bussey, 1984) and may contribute to girls' superior verbal skills. Also, many of the stories in children's reading books are not inherently interesting to children (Blom, Waite, & Zimet, 1968), and there is evidence that boys are particularly motivated by the interest level of the reading material. For example, Asher and Markel (1974) reported that fifth-grade boys displayed better comprehension for stories of high interest than for those of low interest. This difference in reading level was much smaller for fifth-grade girls (see Table 14-2). As can be seen from the table, sex differences in reading ability were small and insignificant for high-interest stories but large and significant in favor of girls for low-interest stories.

☐ Theories of the Origins of Sex Differences

Numerous theories have been advanced to explain sex differences in cognitive functioning. In the final analysis, however, most explanations fall into one of two categories: nature or nurture. Experiential (nurture) explanations for sex differences have been presented throughout this chapter. Boys may be superior to girls in spatial and mathematical skills because they are encouraged to partake in activities emphasizing spatial processing, both in play and in the classroom; girls may be more verbal than boys because adults speak to them differently than they do to boys and encourage them to express their thoughts verbally.

On the nature side of the debate, the different biologies of males and females may affect thought patterns in a variety of ways. Differences may be genetic, attributed to specific genes unique to or characteristic of one sex. Alternatively, the differences may arise because of *hormonal* differences between the sexes. Although both sexes have male hormones (androgens) and female hormones (estrogens) pulsing through their bloodstreams, the distributions vary. Hormonal differences between the sexes are most pronounced at two times during the preadult years: before birth and at adolescence. It has been proposed that the presence of male hormones in large amounts alters the brain and, thus, the course of cognitive functioning (Money & Ehrhardt, 1972). Such effects may occur before birth, at puberty, or at both times.

This section begins with a brief overview of sexual differentiation during the prenatal period. Specific biological explanations for sex differences in cognition are then examined, and the chapter concludes with a brief look at possible interactions between biology and environment that may contribute to sex differences in children's thinking.

TABLE 14-2 Average Reading Scores for Fifth-Grade Children as a Function of Sex and Interest Level of Material (Asher and Markel, 1974)

Interest level	Sex of child	
	Boys	Girls
High	9.33	10.71
Low	5.57	9.32

Gender Differentiation and the Effects of Prenatal Hormones on Cognitive Functioning

A normal human being has 46 chromosomes in each cell of his or her body, excepting the sex cells (ova and sperm), which have 23. The full complement of 46 chromosomes occurs in 23 pairs, each member of which is genetically similar to its mate, with the exception of the 23rd pair. This pair has been termed the *sex chromosomes*. In all normal females, the 23rd pair consists of two X chromosomes; in all normal males, the 23rd pair consists of one X chromosome and a smaller Y chromosome. At conception, the 23 chromosomes in the father's sperm join with the 23 chromosomes of the mother's ovum to begin a new person. From the mother, the child receives an X chromosome, because she has only X chromosomes to contribute (all women being XX). From the father, the child will receive either an X or a Y chromosome, because half of males' sperm cells carry the X chromosome and the other half the Y. An offspring receiving an X chromosome from her father is a genetic female (XX); an offspring receiving a Y chromosome is a genetic male (XY).

As the embryo develops over the first 2 months of life, there are no apparent physical differences between males and females. However, differences are taking place beneath the surface. In girls, genes on the two X chromosomes are directing the construction of ovaries; in boys, genes on the XY chromosomes are directing the construction of testes. Once these organs begin functioning, they produce hormones. From this point it is the hormones, specifically the androgens, that (primarily) determine further sexual differentiation.

When estrogen is produced, or in the absence of any prenatal hormones, the embryo develops into a female. In the genetic anomaly of Turner's syndrome, for example, there is only a single X chromosome. In such cases no functioning ovaries develop, and no estrogen is produced. Yet, at birth the child is easily recognized as a girl. That is, in the absence of any hormone or in the presence of estrogen, nature produces a girl. It is the presence of an androgen (most particularly, testosterone) that is responsible for maleness. As androgens are produced by the testes (and later the adrenal glands), they are ab-

sorbed into the embryonic and fetal tissues. When they are absorbed into the tissues that are destined to become the sexual organs (for example, penis and vagina), feminization is halted and masculinization is begun. That is, prenatal androgens inhibit the construction of female sex organs and direct construction of the corresponding male structures.

The presence of androgens affects not only the physical structure of the organism but also its behavior. In nonhuman mammals, females given large doses of androgens prenatally show characteristic male social and sexual behavior, despite the presence of female genitalia. Similarly, males who are castrated early in life or given drugs that prevent the further absorption of androgens display classic female behavior, such as nest building and nurturing of pups (see Money & Ehrhardt, 1972).[1] Analogous situations occur in humans. Genetic girls who are exposed to excessive amounts of androgens during the fetal period because of malfunctioning adrenal glands or an androgen-producing tumor in the mother are born as normal girls. Compared with unexposed females, however, these girls are more likely to be classified as "tomboys" during childhood. They tend to prefer high-energy activities over more sedentary pursuits; they show little maternalism in the form of doll play or interest in baby-sitting when older; and their aspirations for the future are more typical of boys their age than of girls (Ehrhardt & Baker, 1974; Ehrhardt & Money, 1967).

One hypothesis for the origins of these differences involves the effects of fetal hormones on the brain. More specifically, the presence of androgens during the fetal period "masculinizes" the brain, in particular the hypothalamus. The hypothalamus plays a critical role in the regulation of behavior, including appetitive and sexual behaviors. It may also have a role in information processing. This is a position taken by Reinisch and her colleagues (Reinisch, 1974; Reinisch, Gandelman, & Speigel, 1979). In general, the hypothalamus influences the release of sex hormones during all stages of life, which may affect certain aspects of information processing. Reinisch and her colleagues suggest that prenatal exposure to sex hormones affects perception, particularly with respect to olfaction and taste, and may be responsible for sex differences in spatial and mathematical abilities.

Pubertal Hormones and Changes in Cognitive Functioning

During puberty, the bodies of both boys and girls change in proportion and function. For the most part, these changes are mediated by the presence of sex hormones. Just as sex hormones prior to birth influence the structure of the body and brain of the fetus, hormones circulating through adolescent veins produce analogous changes. As we have observed, many sex differences in cognition are not reliably found until adolescence. Although one explanation for such late-occurring effects is differential experience, another is sex differences in adolescent hormones. For example, a relationship between the physical manifestation of sex hormones and cognitive functioning was reported in a longitudinal sample of adolescents (Petersen, 1976). The patterns of performance varied for boys and girls, but, for both sexes, the degree of masculinization predicted spatial abilities.

A related hypothesis that has attracted substantial research attention was introduced by Waber (1976, 1977). Waber proposed that *rate of maturation* is the key factor affecting sex differences in adolescent cognition. As is well documented, girls mature at a faster rate than boys, on average (Tanner, 1962). Waber reported that children who showed late pubertal onset, regardless of sex, had better spatial ability than early maturers. This is the typical pattern of boys (late maturation, good spatial skills). Waber also hypothesized that early maturers (usually girls) should show superior verbal skills relative to late maturers (usually boys). This latter hypothesis was not supported.

A number of other studies have reported findings similar to Waber's, suggesting that rate of maturation is indeed an important factor in cognitive differences between the sexes (Diamond, Carey, & Back, 1983; Newcombe & Bandura, 1983; Sanders & Soares, 1986). But other research has failed to find the predicted differences (Newcombe, Dubas, & Moore, 1985; Rovet, 1983; Waber, Mann, Merola,

& Moylan, 1985). There is something about adolescent hormones and their timing that influences sex differences in cognition. That "something" is elusive, and it apparently accounts for only a small portion of individual differences in thinking. "The inference that sex differences in cognitive abilities are attributable to the sex-related variation in maturation rate, therefore, should be viewed with some caution pending further study" (Waber et al., 1985, p. 680).

Patterns of Hemispheric Specialization

The notion that the two hemispheres of the brain function differently is probably as old as the finding that the brain comprises two relatively symmetrical halves. A popular (and simplified) description of the roles that the two hemispheres play in cognition (at least for right-handed people) is that the left hemisphere specializes in verbal and analytical kinds of thinking, whereas the right hemisphere excels at spatial, Gestalt problems (see Kinsbourne & Smith, 1974; Milner, 1971; Chapter 13). *Hemispheric dominance* refers to the speed with which the appropriate hemisphere takes control of various tasks, with the dominant hemisphere being the one that achieves control first.

Buffery and Gray (1972) proposed that left-hemisphere dominance occurs at an earlier age in girls than in boys, giving girls advanced mastery over verbal problems. According to Buffery and Gray, however, this mastery in verbal processing is achieved at the expense of mastery on spatial tasks, because spatial tasks are proposed to be represented in both hemispheres. In effect, the early *hemispheric lateralization* (specialization) typical of girls limits the practice that children's left hemispheres have with spatial (and perhaps mathematical) kinds of problems. Maccoby and Jacklin made a similar assertion, proposing that girls are verbally precocious because of their early left-hemispheric dominance.

Subsequent work has provided some support for sex differences in hemispheric dominance. For example, Waber (1976, 1977) argued that the reason late maturers excel at spatial tasks is that their brains do not become lateralized until late, allowing them to develop their spatial abilities more fully. Early maturers' brains become lateralized before they have an opportunity to develop spatial thinking skills more acutely. Research has indicated that the hemispheres of males are more clearly differentiated than female brains with respect to cognitive processing (Levy & Reid, 1978), providing some indirect support for Waber's hypothesis. More recent research has been inconsistent, however, with some studies providing partial support for Waber's hypothesis (Newcombe et al., 1985; Rovet, 1983) and others finding no evidence of differences in lateralization as a function of timing of puberty (Newcombe & Bandura, 1983; Waber et al., 1985). As with other sex differences, those in hemispheric specialization seem to play some role in the pattern of cognitive functioning, but absolute differences are small, and the phenomenon is not robust.

Sex-Linked Inheritance

The male Y chromosome is smaller than the female X chromosome and has fewer genes on it. Thus, boys not only have some genes that differ from those of girls but also lack some genetic information that girls have on their X chromosome.

In most cases, two genes, one on each member of a pair of chromosomes, determine a particular characteristic. For example, a gene for blue eyes provided by the mother may be matched with a gene for brown eyes provided by the father. In situations where the two genes do not express exactly the same information (for example, blue eyes and brown eyes), one gene may be *dominant* over the other. In the example above, the gene for brown eyes is dominant relative to the *recessive* gene for blue eyes, and the offspring will have brown eyes. The only way the recessive characteristic can be expressed in the phenotype (the actual observed characteristic) is if the individual has two recessive genes, in this case two genes for blue eyes.

Sex-linked (or X-linked) inheritance is an exception to this rule. A recessive gene on the X chromosome may have no mate on the Y chromosome in males. Thus, whereas a girl requires recessive genes on both of her X chromosomes before that trait will

be expressed, a boy needs only to have one recessive gene. This is because a single recessive gene in the absence of corresponding genetic material will be expressed in the phenotype. Accordingly, recessive characteristics associated with the sex chromosomes are found more frequently in boys than in girls. Color blindness, hemophilia, and some forms of baldness are all sex linked and are rarely found in females.

Recent efforts at documenting sex-linked inheritance of cognitive abilities have centered on specific mental operations, particularly spatial processing. Evidence pertaining to this hypothesis has been obtained in studies investigating children with genetic abnormalities such as Turner's syndrome (23rd chromosome pair = XO) and triple X syndrome (Rovet & Netley, 1982, 1983); twin studies (Vandenberg, 1969); and familial studies, assessing patterns of spatial ability as a function of genetic relationship (Bock & Kolakowski, 1973; Bouchard & McGee, 1977). As will be no surprise to anyone by now, the findings are mixed. However, the majority opinion is that many studies finding evidence for X-linked inheritance of spatial ability are flawed or are based on too-small sample sizes and that there is no conclusive evidence for the validity of the X-linked hypothesis (see Boles, 1980; Halpern, 1986; Sherman, 1978).

The Interaction of Biological and Experiential Factors in Sex Differences in Children's Thinking

The extent to which differences in biology are responsible for sex differences in cognition is much debated. Given that some reliable sex differences in cognitive functioning do exist (something that not all researchers accept: see Caplan, MacPherson, & Tobin, 1985), to what extent can they be attributed to biological (genetics, hormones, hemispheric specialization) or experiential factors? Some authors have proposed a distinction between *sex differences*, those attributable mainly to biological factors, and *gender differences*, those attributable mainly to experiential factors (Deaux, 1985). Such a dichotomy seems artificial, and the most fruitful approach to understanding sex differences in any realm is to examine how nature and nurture interact (or transact) to yield a particular pattern of development.

In the preceding sections research was examined investigating *direct* effects of biology on cognition. For example, hormonal differences between boys and girls produce different brain structures that are hypothesized to be responsible for different patterns of mental abilities (Reinisch et al., 1979). It is possible that such direct effects on information processing play only a small role in sex differences in thinking. In fact, nearly all researchers who propose biologically determined sex differences in cognition stress that environment also plays a critical role (Petersen, 1976). Yet, there may be other biologically induced characteristics whose effects on cognition are only *indirect*. For example, Newcombe and Bandura (1983) reported that adolescent girls' responses on personality inventories assessing gender roles correlated with cognitive abilities independent of rate of maturation. It is possible that individual differences in personality traits cause people to choose activities more consistent with those traits (see Scarr & McCartney, 1983). To the extent that personality characteristics have a genetic component (Bouchard, 1985; Plomin, 1986), children's biology may indirectly influence their style of thinking.

One noncognitive area in which reliable sex differences have been found is general activity level, with boys being more active than girls (Pedersen & Bell, 1970). This difference is found even during the first days of life, when individual experiences are not likely to have had a strong impact on behavior (Phillips, King, & DuBois, 1978). As a result of this inherent difference in activity levels, boys and girls, on the average, may explore the environment differently and engage in different types of play activities (DiPietro, 1981; Halverson & Waldrop, 1973). Such a biologically based difference would affect the types of experiences boys and girls have, which, in turn, might affect their patterns of thinking (Connor & Serbin, 1977; Hazen, 1982). Similarly, children with sex-stereotypic physical characteristics (for example, the athletic teenage boy or the early maturing teenage girl) may be treated in a more sex-stereotypic fashion than their less sex-stereotypic-looking peers. Children who look the role may

be expected to play the role, with biology affecting how others treat them and how children perceive themselves (see Nash, 1979).

Possible biological differences between the sexes with respect to cognition cannot be dismissed out of hand. It is equally clear that environment plays a crucial role in influencing differences that are found between the sexes in cognitive functioning. Studies examining how biology and experience interact to yield various patterns of performance are necessary to explicate the nature of sex differences in children's thinking, with indirect biological effects being considered alongside direct effects.

☐ How Important Are Sex Differences in Cognition?

There are several potential markets for data on sex differences in cognition. For one, vocational and educational counselors may base recommendations to clients on the conclusions drawn from sex-difference research. Hence, if a counselor were to read Maccoby and Jacklin's (1974) book or any of a dozen recent textbooks on child or developmental psychology, he or she might suggest that males pursue careers involving extensive quantitative or spatial thinking. Likewise, the same counselor would probably be biased toward recommending more verbally oriented professions for female clients.

The research cited in this chapter has shown that sex differences in cognition vary as a function of both biology and experience; furthermore, the percentage of studies reporting such differences has dwindled steadily since 1980. How does one evaluate the importance of the various investigations of sex differences in children's thinking, some of which find sex differences and some of which do not? One technique, used by Hyde (1981) is *meta-analysis*. Meta-analysis is a statistical technique that allows an investigator to evaluate the magnitude of a significant effect across a large number of studies.

Hyde re-analyzed the findings of studies reviewed by Maccoby and Jacklin, focusing on those showing "well-established" sex differences favoring boys in mathematical and spatial abilities and favoring girls in verbal skills. She examined 16 studies of quantitative performance, 10 of spatial skills, and 27 of verbal ability. Hyde reported that the sex of the child alone accounted for approximately 1% of the variance in verbal performance. Differences in visual/spatial ability attributed to the sex of the child were slightly greater, but even here sex accounted for less than 5% of the difference in performance. For those readers without a background in statistics, these findings mean that the differences, although statistically significant, are small in absolute magnitude. To give an idea of the magnitude of these differences, the idealized distributions of verbal and visual/spatial skills between males and females are shown in Figure 14-2 (expressed in terms of standard scores from Hyde, 1981). As can be seen, there is substantial overlap of performance between the sexes, and the absolute differences in the means are small.

Three other meta-analyses of sex differences have been published since Hyde's paper, and all find that sex accounts for only a small proportion of the differences in performance between males and females. Plomin and Foch (1981) reported that sex differences in verbal abilities for the studies reviewed by Maccoby and Jacklin accounted for only 1% of the variance. Linn and Petersen (1985) reported that only between 1% and 5% of differences in spatial abilities can be attributed to sex, depending on the particular task. One exception noted by Linn and Petersen was mental rotation, in which males at all ages performed better than females. Rosenthal and Rubin (1982) similarly reported small differences between the sexes in their meta-analysis of 40 studies investigating sex differences that were published between 1975 and 1978. Furthermore, they found that sizes of effect diminished across the years, with females showing a substantial gain in cognitive performance (relative to males) in recent years.

Given the small magnitude of sex differences in cognition, one must be cautious in interpreting the importance of sex differences in children's thinking. From a perspective of individual differences, it is as interesting and important to explore patterns of variation in performance within the sexes as those between them. Nevertheless, sex differences, although small, are apparently reliable, making them a po-

Verbal Ability

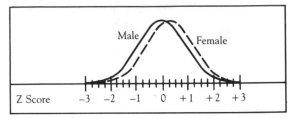

Visual/Spatial and Quantitative Abilities

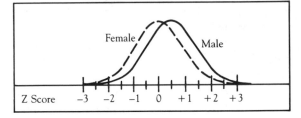

FIGURE 14-2 Idealized distribution of performance of males and females for verbal ability and visual/spatial and quantitative abilities expressed in standard scores (Hyde, 1981).

tentially useful candidate for understanding the mechanisms of individual differences and their development in general. Our culture's fascination with sex differences and their possible import will not diminish soon, and thus we can expect the topic to remain of interest to researchers for decades to come.

☐ Summary

Although early research into sex differences in cognition concentrated on overall differences in intelligence and achievement, recent work has dealt with more specific aspects of thinking. Maccoby and Jacklin, in their 1974 book, *The Psychology of Sex Differences*, reviewed the existing literature and concluded that there were three areas in which sex differences in cognition had been found: *mathematics*, *spatial ability*, and *verbal ability*, the former two favoring males and the latter favoring females.

With respect to mathematics, differences between boys and girls are typically not manifested until early adolescence, with many studies failing to find significant sex differences. More recent work indicates that adolescent boys outperform adolescent girls in mathematics. These effects are small, but they are maintained even when controlling for differences in course background or parental attitudes and expectations.

Differences in spatial skills, involving such tasks as mental rotation, Embedded Figures Tests, and Piaget and Inhelder's water level problem, again favor males, although many studies report no significant sex differences. Research suggests that, for some spatial tasks, males show superior performance because they have greater knowledge of relevant aspects of the tasks and that females' performance can be modified when they are given such knowledge. Differences in play and exploration activities between the sexes may result in different patterns of experience, contributing to differences in spatial abilities.

Differences in verbal abilities are small during infancy and the preschool and school-age years. Female superiority is most pronounced beginning at 10 to 11 years of age, but many studies fail to find significant sex differences even during this period. Recent research concerning the use of *organizational strategies* in free recall suggests female superiority beginning as young as 6 years of age, although the number of studies investigating sex differences in memory ability is still small. Sex differences in verbal skills have been attributed to differences in parental behavior and to differences in school curriculum with respect to the teaching of reading.

In addition to experiential explanations for sex differences in children's thinking, several researchers have proposed biological explanations. Differential prenatal exposure to sex *hormones* (particularly the male androgens) has been proposed to affect the fetal brain and to influence information processing. Similarly, hormones during puberty have been suggested as a cause for sex differences in cognition. *Rate of maturation* has been proposed as a factor in sex differences, with slow maturers (usually boys) having the time to develop spatial skills more fully, and fast maturers (usually girls) not having this opportunity. Related to rate of maturation is the hypothesis that the two hemispheres of the brains of boys and girls are differentially specialized (*hemispheric lateralization*). Finally, *sex-linked* (or X-linked) inheritance has been suggested as a mechanism whereby a recessive gene for spatial ability is more likely to be expressed in boys than in girls. Although there is support in the literature for each of these positions, there are many contradictory data, making it impossible to state definitively how biological factors influence sex differences in cognition.

Indirect biological effects should also be investigated. For example, boys' greater activity levels may lead them to different types of experiences than girls have, producing different patterns of cognitive abilities. Similarly, genetic disposition toward certain personality characteristics can influence the types of environments one chooses to experience and, in turn, may affect the development of intellectual skills.

Sex differences in children's thinking have been studied extensively over the years, and the findings have been mixed. The technique of *meta-analysis* involves the examination of numerous experiments investigating the same phenomenon and determining the size of the effect. Meta-analyses of sex differences in children's thinking indicate that although significant differences between girls and boys are found, overall, sex alone usually accounts for between 1% and 5% of the variance. That is, even when differences are real, their magnitude is small.

☐ Note

1. If androgens are given in sufficiently large amounts while the female is physically immature, or if they are totally prevented from being absorbed into the tissues of male animals, the external genitalia of the opposite sex will be manifested. That is, the physical characteristics of the animal will be different from its genetic characteristics. Behavioral differences attributed to prenatal hormones such as those described in the text occur when androgens are present in large amounts in females (or not absorbed in males) after the external genitalia have formed (see Money & Ehrhardt, 1972).

References

ABRAVANEL, E., & GINGOLD, H. (1985). Learning via observation during the second year of life. *Developmental Psychology, 21,* 614–623.

ABRAVANEL, E., LEVAN-GOLDSCHMIDT, E., & STEVENSON, M. B. (1976). Action imitation: The early phase of infancy. *Child Development, 47,* 1032–1044.

ABRAVANEL, E., & SIGAFOOS, A. D. (1984). Explaining the presence of imitation during early infancy. *Child Development, 55,* 381–392.

ACKERMAN, B. P. (1984). Item specific and relational encoding effects in children's recall and recognition memory for words. *Journal of Experimental Child Psychology, 37,* 426–450.

ACKERMAN, B. P. (1985a). Children's retrieval deficit. In C. J. Brainerd & M. Pressley (Eds.), *Basic processes in memory development: Progress in cognitive development research.* New York: Springer.

ACKERMAN, B. P. (1985b). Constraints on retrieval search for episodic information in children and adults. *Journal of Experimental Child Psychology, 40,* 152–180.

ACKERMAN, B. P. (1986). Retrieval search for category and thematic information in memory by children and adults. *Journal of Experimental Child Psychology, 42,* 355–377.

ACREDOLO, L. P., PICK, H. L., & OLSEN, M. G. (1975). Environmental differentiation and familiarity as determinants of children's memory for spatial location. *Developmental Psychology, 11,* 495–501.

ADAMS, G. R., & JONES, R. M. (1981). Imaginary audience behavior: A validation study. *Journal of Early Adolescence, 1,* 1–10.

ADAMS, R. J., MAURER, D., & DAVIS, M. (1986). Newborns' discrimination of chromatic from achromatic stimuli. *Journal of Experimental Child Psychology, 41,* 262–281.

AINSWORTH, M. D. S. (1967). *Infancy in Uganda: Infant care and the growth of love.* Baltimore: Johns Hopkins University Press.

AINSWORTH, M. D. S. (1979). Infant–mother attachment. *American Psychologist, 34,* 932–937.

AINSWORTH, M. D. S., BELL, S. M., & STAYTON, D. J. (1971). Individual differences in strange situation behavior of one-year-olds. In H. R. Schaffer (Ed.), *The origins of human social relations.* London: Academic Press.

AINSWORTH, M. D. S., BLEHAR, M. C., WATERS, E., & WALL, S. (1978). *Patterns of attachment: A psychological study of the Strange Situation.* Hillsdale, NJ: Erlbaum.

AINSWORTH, M. D. S., & WITTIG, D. S. (1969). Attachment and exploratory behavior of one-year olds in a strange situation. In B. M. Foss (Ed.), *Determinants of infant behavior* (Vol. 4). London: Methuen.

ANDERSON, J. R. (1976). *Language, memory, and thought.* Hillsdale, NJ: Erlbaum.

ANGLIN, J. M. (1970). *The growth of word meaning.* Cambridge, MA: MIT Press.

ANGLIN, J. M. (1977). *Word, object, and conceptual development.* New York: Norton.

ANNETT, M. (1959). The classification of instances of four common class concepts by children and adults. *British Journal of Psychology, 29,* 233–236.

ANOOSHIAN, L. J., & YOUNG, D. (1981). Developmental changes in cognitive maps of a familiar neighborhood. *Child Development, 52,* 341–348.

ANTELL, S. E., & KEATING, D. P. (1983). Perception of numerical invariance in neonates. *Child Development, 54,* 695–701.

AREND, R., GOVE, F., & SROUFE, L. A. (1979). Continuity of individual adaptation from infancy to kindergarten: A predictive study of ego-resiliency and curiosity in preschoolers. *Child Development, 50,* 950–959.

ARLIN, M., & BRODY, R. (1976). Effects of spatial presentation and blocking on organization and verbal recall at three grade levels. *Developmental Psychology, 12,* 113–118.

ASHCRAFT, M. H. (1982). The development of mental

arithmetic: A chronometric approach. *Developmental Review, 2,* 213–236.

ASHCRAFT, M. H. (1983). Procedural knowledge versus fact retrieval in mental arithmetic: A reply to Baroody. *Developmental Review, 3,* 231–235.

ASHCRAFT, M. H., & FIERMAN, B. A. (1982). Mental addition in third, fourth, and sixth grades. *Journal of Experimental Child Psychology, 33,* 216–234.

ASHER, S. R., & MARKEL, R. A. (1974). Sex differences in comprehension of high- and low-interest reading material. *Journal of Educational Psychology, 66,* 680–687.

ASHMEAD, D. H., & PERLMUTTER, M. (1980). Infant memory in everyday life. In M. Perlmutter (Ed.), *New directions for child development: Children's memory.* San Francisco: Jossey-Bass.

ASLIN, R. N. (1977). Development of binocular fixation in human infants. *Journal of Experimental Child Psychology, 23,* 133–156.

ASLIN, R. N., & JACKSON, R. W. (1979). Accommodative convergence in young infants: Development of a synergistic sensory–motor system. *Canadian Journal of Psychology, 33,* 222–231.

ASLIN, R. N., PISONI, D. B., & JUSCZYK, P. W. (1983). Auditory development and speech perception in infants. In M. M. Haith & J. J. Campos (Eds.), *Infancy and developmental psychobiology: Vol. 2.* P. H. Mussen (Gen. Ed.), *Handbook of child psychology* (4th ed.). New York: Wiley.

ATKINSON, R. C., & SHIFFRIN, R. M. (1968). Human memory: A proposed system and its control processes. In K. W. Spence & J. T. Spence (Eds.), *The psychology of learning and motivation: Advances in research and theory* (Vol. 2). New York: Academic Press.

ATKINSON, R.C., & SHIFFRIN, R. M. (1971). The control of short-term memory. *Scientific American, 225,* 82–90.

AULT, R. L., CRAWFORD, D. E., & JEFFREY, W. E. (1972). Visual scanning strategies of reflective, impulsive, fast-accurate, and slow-inaccurate children on the Matching Familiar Figures Test. *Child Development, 43,* 1412–1417.

BACH, M. J., & UNDERWOOD, B. J. (1970). Developmental changes in memory attributes. *Journal of Educational Psychology, 61,* 292–296.

BAHRICK, L. E., & WATSON, J. S. (1985). Detection of intermodal proprioceptive–visual contingency as a potential basis of self-perception in infancy. *Developmental Psychology, 21,* 963–973.

BAKER-WARD, L., ORNSTEIN, P. A., & HOLDEN, D. J. (1984). The expression of memorization in early childhood. *Journal of Experimental Child Psychology, 37,* 555–575.

BALDWIN, J. M. (1895). *Mental development in the child and the race.* New York: Macmillan.

BANDURA, A. (1977). *Social learning theory.* Englewood Cliffs, NJ: Prentice-Hall.

BANKS, M. S. (1980). The development of visual accommodation during early infancy. *Child Development, 51* 646–666.

BANKS, M. S., & GINSBURG, A. P. (1985). Early visual preferences: A review and a new theoretical treatment. In H. W. Reese (Ed.), *Advances in child development and behavior.* New York: Academic Press.

BANKS, M. S., & SALAPATEK, P. (1981). Infant pattern vision: A new approach based on the contrast sensitivity function. *Journal of Experimental Child Psychology, 31,* 1–45.

BANKS, M. S., & SALAPATEK, P. (1983). Infant visual perception. In M. M. Haith & J. J. Campos (Eds.), *Infancy and developmental psychobiology: Vol. 2.* P. H. Mussen (Gen. Ed.), *Handbook of child psychology* (4th ed.). New York: Wiley.

BARRERA, M. E., & MAURER, D. (1981). Recognition of mother's photographed face by the three-month-old infant. *Child Development, 52,* 714–716.

BARTLETT, F. C. (1932). *Remembering: A study in experimental and social psychology.* Cambridge, England: Cambridge University Press.

BAUER, R. H. (1979). Memory, acquisition, and category clustering in learning-disabled children. *Journal of Experimental Child Psychology, 27,* 365–383.

BAUER, R. H. (1982). Information processing as a way of understanding and diagnosing learning disability. *Topics in Learning and Learning Disabilities, 2,* 33–45.

BAYLEY, N. (1949). Consistency and variability in the growth of intelligence from birth to eighteen years. *Journal of Genetic Psychology, 75,* 165–196.

BAYLEY, N. (1969). *The Bayley Scales of Infant Development.* New York: Psychological Corporation.

BEAL, C. R. (1985). Development of knowledge about the use of cues to aid prospective retrieval. *Child Development, 56,* 631–642.

BEAL, C. R., & FLAVELL, J. H. (1982). Effects of increasing salience of message ambiguities on kindergarteners' evaluations of communicative success and message adequacy. *Developmental Psychology, 10,* 43–48.

BEAL, C. R., & LOCKHART, M. E. (in press). The effect of proper name and appearance change on children's reasoning about gender constancy. *International Journal of Behavioral Development.*

BECKER, W. C., & GERSTEN, R. (1982). A follow-up of Follow Through: The later effects of the direct instruction model on children in fifth and sixth grades. *American Educational Research Journal, 19,* 75–92.

BEE, H. L., BARNARD, K. E., EYRES, S. J., GRAY, C. A., HAMMOND, M. A., SPIETZ, A. L., SNYDER, C., & CLARK, B. (1982). Prediction of IQ and language skill from prenatal status, child performance, family characteristics, and mother–infant interaction. *Child Development, 53,* 1134–1156.

BEHREND, D., ROSENGREN, K., & PERLMUTTER, M. (in press). A new look at the effects of age, task difficulty, and parents' presence on children's private speech. *International Journal of Behavioral Development*.

BELL, R. Q. (1968). A reinterpretation of the direction of effects in studies of socialization. *Psychological Review, 75*, 81–95.

BELLUGI, U. (1967). *The acquisition of negation*. Unpublished doctoral dissertation, Harvard University.

BELMONT, J. M., BUTTERFIELD, E. C., & BORKOWSKI, J. G. (1978). Training retarded people to generalize memorization methods across memory tasks. In M. M. Grunberg, P. E. Morris, & R. N. Sykes (Eds.), *Practical aspects of memory*. London: Academic Press.

BELMONT, J. M., FERRETTI, R. P., & MITCHEL, D. W. (1982). Memorizing: A test of untrained mildly retarded children's problem solving. *American Journal of Mental Deficiency, 87*, 197–210.

BELMONT, L., & MAROLLA, F. A. (1973). Birth order, family size and intelligence. *Science, 182*, 1096–1101.

BEM, S. (1981). Gender schema theory: A cognitive account of sex-typing. *Psychological Review, 88*, 354–364.

BENBOW, C. P., & STANLEY, J. C. (1980). Sex differences in mathematical ability: Fact or artifact? *Science, 210*, 1262–1264.

BENBOW, C. P., & STANLEY, J.C. (1983). Sex differences in mathematical reasoning: More facts. *Science, 222*, 1029–1031.

BERBAUM, M. L., & MORELAND, R. L. (1985). Intellectual development within transracial adoptive families: Retesting the confluence model. *Child Development, 56*, 207–216.

BEREITER, C., & ENGLEMANN, S. (1966). *Teaching disadvantaged children in the preschool*. Englewood Cliffs, NJ: Prentice-Hall.

BERG, C. A., & STERNBERG, R. J. (1985). Response to novelty: Continuity versus discontinuity in the developmental course of intelligence. In H. W. Reese & L. P. Lipsitt (Eds.), *Advances in child development and behavior* (Vol. 19). New York: Academic Press.

BERK, L. E. (1986). Relationship of elementary school children's private speech to behavioral accompaniment to task, attention, and task performance. *Developmental Psychology, 22*, 671–680.

BERK, L. E., & GARVIN, R. A., (1984). Development of private speech among low-income Appalachian children. *Developmental Psychology, 20*, 271–286.

BERLIN, B., & KAY, P. (1969). *Basic color terms: Their universality and evolution*. Berkeley: University of California Press.

BERNARD, J., & SONTAG, L. W. (1947). Fetal reactivity to tonal stimulation: A preliminary report. *Journal of Genetic Psychology, 70*, 205–210.

BERNSTEIN, B. (1960). Language and social class. *British Journal of Sociology, 11*, 271–276.

BEST, D. L., & ORNSTEIN, P. A. (1986). Children's generation and communication of mnemonic organizational strategies. *Developmental Psychology, 22*, 845–853.

BINET, A., & SIMON, T. (1905). Methodes nouvelles pour le diagnostic du niveau intellectuel des anormaux. *L'Année Psychologique, 11*, 245–336.

BINET, A., & SIMON, T. (1908). Le développement de l'intelligence chez les enfants. *L'Année Psychologique, 14*, 1–90. (Reprinted in A. Binet & T. S. Simon, *The development of intelligence in children*. Baltimore: Williams & Wilkins, 1916.)

BIRCH, H. G., & BELMONT, L. (1965). Auditory–visual integration, intelligence and reading ability in school children. *Perceptual and Motor Skills, 20*, 295–305.

BIRCH, H. G., & LEFFORD, A. (1963). Intersensory development in children. *Monographs of the Society for Research in Child Development, 32* (Serial No. 110).

BISANZ, J., DANNER, F., & RESNICK, L. (1979). Changes with age in measures of processing efficiency. *Child Development, 50*, 131–141.

BJORK, E. L., & CUMMINGS, E. M. (1984). Infant search errors: Stage of concept development or stage of memory development. *Memory and Cognition, 12*, 1–19.

BJORKLUND, D. F. (1985). The role of conceptual knowledge in the development of organization in children's memory. In C. J. Brainerd & M. Pressley (Eds.), *Basic processes in memory development: Progress in cognitive development research*. New York: Springer.

BJORKLUND, D. F. (1987a). How age changes in knowledge base contribute to the development of children's memory: An interpretive review. *Developmental Review, 7*, 93–130.

BJORKLUND, D. F. (1987b). A note on neonatal imitation. *Developmental Review, 7*, 86–92.

BJORKLUND, D. F., & BERNHOLTZ, J. E. (1986). The role of knowledge base in the memory performance of good and poor readers. *Journal of Experimental Child Psychology, 41*, 367–373.

BJORKLUND, D. F., & DE MARCHENA, M. R. (1984). Developmental shifts in the basis of organization in memory: The role of associative versus categorical relatedness in children's free recall. *Child Development, 55*, 952–962.

BJORKLUND, D. F., & HARNISHFEGER, K. K. (1987). Developmental differences in the mental effort requirements for the use of an organizational strategy in free recall. *Journal of Experimental Child Psychology, 44*, 109–125.

BJORKLUND, D. F., & HOCK, H. S. (1982). Age differences in the temporal locus of memory organization in children's recall. *Journal of Experimental Child Psychology, 32*, 347–362.

BJORKLUND, D. F., & JACOBS, J. W. (1985). Associative and categorical processes in children's memory: The role of automaticity in the development of organization in free recall. *Journal of Experimental Child Psychology, 39,* 599–617.

BJORKLUND, D. F., & MUIR, J. E. (1988). Children's development of free recall memory: Remembering on their own. In R. Vasta (Ed.), *Annals of child development* (Vol. 5). Greenwich, CN: JAI Press.

BJORKLUND, D. F., ORNSTEIN, P. A., & HAIG, J. R. (1977). Development of organization and recall: Training in the use of organizational techniques. *Developmental Psychology, 13,* 175–183.

BJORKLUND, D. F., THOMPSON, B. E., & ORNSTEIN, P. A. (1983). Developmental trends in children's typicality judgments. *Behavior Research Methods & Instrumentation, 15,* 350–356.

BJORKLUND, D. F., & ZEMAN, B. R. (1982). Children's organization and metamemory awareness in their recall of familiar information. *Child Development, 53,* 799–810.

BLACK, M. M., & ROLLINS, H. A., JR. (1982). The effects of instructional variables on young children's organization and free recall. *Journal of Experimental Child Psychology, 33,* 1–19.

BLOCK, J. (1987). Misgivings about the Matching Familiar Figures Test: Premature or overdue? *Developmental Psychology, 23,* 740–741.

BLOCK, J., BLOCK, J. H., & HARRINGTON, D. M. (1974). Some misgivings about the Matching Familiar Figures Test as a measure of reflection–impulsivity. *Developmental Psychology, 10,* 611–632.

BLOCK, J., GJERDE, P. F., & BLOCK, J. H. (1986). More misgivings about the Matching Familiar Figures Test as a measure of reflection–impulsivity: Absence of construct validity in preadolescence. *Developmental Psychology, 22,* 820–831.

BLOM, G. E., WAITE, R. R., & ZIMET, S. (1968). Content of first grade reading books. *The Reading Teacher, 21,* 317–323.

BLOOM, B. S. (1964). *Stability and change in human characteristics.* New York: Wiley.

BOCK, R. D., & KOLAKOWSKI, D. (1973). Further evidence of sex-linked major gene influence on human spatial ability. *American Journal of Human Genetics, 25,* 1–14.

BOLES, D. (1980). X-linkage of spatial ability: A critical review. *Child Development, 51,* 625–635.

BOMBA, P. C., & SIQUELAND, E. R. (1983). The nature and structure of infant form categories. *Journal of Experimental Child Psychology, 35,* 294–328.

BORKE, H. (1973). The development of empathy in Chinese and American children between three and six years of age. *Developmental Psychology, 9,* 102–108.

BORKE, H. (1975). Piaget's mountains revisited: Changes in the egocentric landscape. *Developmental Psychology, 11,* 240–243.

BORKOWSKI, J. G. (1985). Signs of intelligence: Strategy generalization and metacognition. In S. R. Yussen (Ed.), *The growth of reflection in children.* New York: Academic Press.

BORKOWSKI, J. G., & CAVANAUGH, J. C. (1979). Maintenance and generalization of skills and strategies by the retarded. In N. R. Ellis (Ed.), *Handbook of mental deficiency* (2nd ed.). Hillsdale, NJ: Erlbaum.

BORKOWSKI, J. G., & MAXWELL, S. E. (1985). Looking for Mr. Good-g: General intelligence and processing speed. *The Behavioral and Brain Sciences, 8,* 221–222.

BORKOWSKI, J. G., & PECK, V. A. (1986). Causes and consequences of metamemory in gifted children. In R. J. Sternberg & J. C. Davidson (Eds.), *Conceptions of giftedness.* Cambridge, England: Cambridge University Press.

BORKOWSKI, J. G., PECK, V. A., REID, M. K., & KURTZ, B. E. (1983). Impulsivity and strategy transfer: Metamemory as mediator. *Child Development, 54,* 459–473.

BORKOWSKI, J. G., REID, M. K., & KURTZ, B. E. (1984). Metacognition and retardation: Pragmatic, theoretical and applied perspectives. In P. H. Brooks, R. Sperber, & C. McCauley (Eds.), *Learning and cognition in the mentally retarded.* Hillsdale, NJ: Erlbaum.

BORNSTEIN, M. H. (1985). Habituation of attention as a measure of visual information processing in human infants: Summary, systematization, and synthesis. In G. Gottlieb & N. A. Krasnegor (Eds.), *Measurement of audition and vision in the first year of postnatal life: A methodological overview.* Norwood, NJ: Ablex.

BORNSTEIN, M. H., FERDINANDSEN, K., & GROSS, C. G. (1981). Perception of symmetry in infancy. *Developmental Psychology, 17,* 82–86.

BORNSTEIN, M. H., KESSEN, W., & WEISKOPF, S. (1976). Color vision and hue categorization in young infants. *Journal of Experimental Psychology: Human Perception and Performance, 2,* 115–129.

BORNSTEIN, M. H., & SIGMAN, M. D. (1986). Continuity in mental development from infancy. *Child Development, 57,* 251–274.

BOTVIN, G. J., & MURRAY, F. B. (1975). The efficacy of peer modeling and social conflict in the acquisition of conservation. *Child Development, 46,* 796–799.

BOUCHARD, T. J., JR. (1985). Twins reared together and apart: What they tell us about human diversity. In S. W. Fox (Ed.), *The chemical and biological bases of individuality.* New York: Plenum.

BOUCHARD, T. J., JR., & McCUE, M. (1981). Familial studies of intelligence: A review. *Science, 212,* 1055–1059.

BOUCHARD, T. J., JR., & McGEE, M. G. (1977). Sex differences in human spatial ability: Not an X-linked recessive gene effect. *Social Biology, 24,* 332–335.

BOVET, M. (1976). Piaget's theory of cognitive development and individual differences. In B. Inhelder &

H. H. Chapman (Eds.), *Piaget and his school: A reader in developmental psychology*. New York: Springer.

BOWER, G. H. (1970). Organizational factors in memory. *Cognitive Psychology, 1,* 18–46.

BOWER, T. G. R. (1971). The object in the world of the infant. *Scientific American, 225,* 30–38.

BOWER, T. G. R. (1982). *Development in infancy*. San Francisco: W. H. Freeman.

BOWER, T. G. R., BROUGHTON, J. M., & MOORE, M. K. (1971). The development of the object concept as manifested by changes in the tracking behavior of infants between 7 and 20 weeks of age. *Journal of Experimental Child Psychology, 11,* 182–193.

BOWER, T. G. R., & PATERSON, J. G. (1972). Stages in the development of the object concept. *Cognition, 1,* 47–55.

BOWER, T. G. R., & WISHART, J. G. (1972). The effects of motor skill on object permanence. *Cognition, 1,* 28–35.

BOWLBY, J. (1969). *Attachment and loss: Vol. 1. Attachment*. London: Hogarth.

BRACKBILL, Y., & NICHOLS, P. L. (1982). A test of the confluence model of intellectual development. *Developmental Psychology, 18,* 192–198.

BRADLEY, R. H., & CALDWELL, B. M. (1976). Early home environment and changes in mental test performance in children from 6 to 36 months. *Developmental Psychology, 12,* 93–97.

BRADLEY, R. H., & CALDWELL, B. M. (1980). The relation of home environment, cognitive competence, and IQ among males and females. *Child Development, 51,* 1140–1148.

BRADLEY, R. H., CALDWELL, B. M., & ELARDO, R. (1977). Home environment, social status, and mental test performance. *Journal of Educational Psychology, 69,* 697–701.

BRAINERD, C. J. (1974). Training and transfer of transitivity, conservation, and class inclusion of length. *Child Development, 45,* 324–334.

BRAINERD, C. J. (1977a). Cognitive development and concept learning: An interpretive review. *Psychological Bulletin, 84,* 919–939.

BRAINERD, C. J. (1977b). Effects of spatial cues on children's cardinal number judgments. *Developmental Psychology, 13,* 425–430.

BRAINERD, C. J. (1978a). *Piaget's theory of intelligence*. Englewood Cliffs, NJ: Prentice-Hall.

BRAINERD, C. J. (1978b). The stage question in cognitive-developmental theory. *The Behavioral and Brain Sciences, 2,* 173–213.

BRAINERD, C. J. (1983). Working-memory systems and cognitive development. In C. J. Brainerd (Ed.), *Recent advances in cognitive developmental theory: Progress in cognitive development research*. New York: Springer.

BRAINERD, C. J., & ALLEN, T. W. (1971). Training and generalization of density conservation: Effects of feed-

back and consecutive similar stimuli. *Child Development, 42,* 693–704.

BRAINERD, C. J., & BRAINERD, S. H. (1972). Order of acquisition of number and liquid quantity conservation. *Child Development, 43,* 1401–1405.

BRAINERD, C. J., & KASZOR, P. (1974). An analysis of two proposed sources of children's class inclusion errors. *Developmental Psychology, 10,* 633–643.

BRAINERD, C. J., & KINGMA, J. (1984). Do children have to remember to reason? A fuzzy-trace theory of transitivity development. *Developmental Review, 4,* 311–377.

BRAINERD, C. J., & KINGMA, J. (1985). On the independence of short-term memory and working memory in cognitive development. *Cognitive Psychology, 17,* 210–247.

BRAINERD, C. J., KINGMA, J., & HOWE, M. L. (1986). Spread of encoding and the development of organization in memory. *Canadian Journal of Psychology, 40,* 203–223.

BRAINERD, C. J., & PRESSLEY, M. (EDS.) (1985). *Basic processes in memory development: Progress in cognitive development research*. New York: Springer.

BRANSFORD, J. D., & FRANKS, J. J. (1971). The abstraction of linguistic ideas. *Cognitive Psychology, 2,* 331–350.

BRAY, N. W., JUSTICE, E. M., FERGUSON, R. P., & SIMON, D. L., (1977). Developmental changes in the effects of instructions on production-deficient children. *Child Development, 48,* 1019–1026.

BRAY, N. W., & TURNER, L. A. (1986). The rehearsal deficit hypothesis. In N. R. Ellis & N. W. Bray (Eds.), *International review of research in mental retardation* (Vol. 14). New York: Academic Press.

BRAZELTON, T. B. (1973). Neonatal behavioral assessment scale. *Clinics in Developmental Medicine, No. 50.* Philadelphia: Lippincott.

BRAZELTON, T. B., KOSLOWSKI, B., & MAIN, M. (1974). The origins of reciprocity: The early mother–infant interaction. In M. Lewis & L. Rosenblum (Eds.), *The effect of the infant on its caregiver*. New York: Wiley.

BREMNER, J. G. (1985). Object tracking and search in infancy: A review of data and a theoretical evaluation. *Developmental Review, 5,* 371–396.

BRENNAN, W. M., AMES, E. W., & MOORE, R. W. (1966). Age differences in infants' attention to patterns of different complexity. *Science, 151,* 354–356.

BRETHERTON, I. (1980). Young children in stressful situations: The supporting role of attachment figures and unfamiliar categories. In G. V. Coelho & P. Ahmed (Eds.), *Uprooting and development*. New York: Plenum.

BRETHERTON, I. (1985). Attachment theory: Retrospect and prospect. In I. Bretherton & E. Waters (Eds.), *Growing points of attachment theory and research. Monographs of the Society for Research in Child Development, 50* (Serial No. 209).

BRETHERTON, I., & RIDGEWAY, D. (1987, April). *3-year olds' internal working models of attachment*. Paper presented at the meeting of the Society for Research in Child Development, Baltimore.

BRIARS, D., & SIEGLER, R. S. (1984). A featural analysis of preschoolers' counting knowledge. *Developmental Psychology, 20,* 607–618.

BRONFENBRENNER, U. (1974). *Is early intervention effective? A report on longitudinal evaluations of preschool programs* (Vol. 2). Washington, DC: Department of Health, Education and Welfare, Office of Child Development.

BRONSON, G. (1974). The postnatal growth of visual capacity. *Child Development, 45,* 873–890.

BROOKS, P. H., SPERBER, R., & McCAULEY, C. (EDS.). (1984). *Learning and cognition in the mentally retarded.* Hillsdale, NJ: Erlbaum.

BROWN, A. L. (1975). The development of memory: Knowing, knowing about knowing, and knowing how to know. In H. W. Reese (Ed.), *Advances in child development and behavior* (Vol. 10). New York: Academic Press.

BROWN, A. L. (1978). Knowing when, where, and how to remember: A problem of metacognition. In R. Glasser (Ed.), *Advances in instructional psychology.* New York: Halstead Press.

BROWN, A. L., BRANSFORD, J. D., FERRARA, R. A., & CAMPIONE, J. C. (1983). Learning, remembering, and understanding. In J. H. Flavell & E. M. Markman (Eds.), *Cognitive development: Vol. 3.* P. H. Mussen (Gen. Ed.), *Handbook of child psychology* (4th ed.). New York: Wiley.

BROWN, A. L., & DeLOACHE, J. S. (1978). Skills, plans and self-regulation. In R. S. Siegler (Ed.), *Children's thinking: What develops?* Hillsdale, NJ: Erlbaum.

BROWN, A. L., & SCOTT, M. S. (1971). Recognition memory for pictures in preschool children. *Journal of Experimental Child Psychology, 11,* 401–412.

BROWN, A. L., & SMILEY, S. S. (1978). The development of strategies for studying texts. *Child Development, 49,* 1076–1088.

BROWN, A. L., SMILEY, S. S., DAY, J. D., TOWNSEND, M. A. R., & LAWTON, S. C. (1977). Intrusion of a thematic idea in children's comprehension and retention of stories. *Child Development, 48,* 1454–1466.

BROWN, R., & FRASER, E. (1964). The acquisition of syntax. In U. Bellugi & R. Brown (Eds.), The acquisition of language. *Monographs of the Society for Research in Child Development, 29* (Serial No. 92).

BRUNER, J. S. (1966). On cognitive growth. In J. S. Bruner, R. R. Olver, & P. M. Greenfield (Eds.), *Studies in cognitive growth.* New York: Wiley.

BRUNER, J. S., OLVER, R. R., & GREENFIELD, P. M. (EDS.). (1966). *Studies in cognitive growth.* New York: Wiley.

BRYANT, P. E., & TRABASSO, T. (1971). Transitive inference and memory in young children. *Nature, 232,* 456–458.

BUFFERY, A., & GRAY, J. (1972). Sex differences in the development of spatial and linguistic skills. In C. Ounsted & D. Taylor (Eds.), *Gender differences, their ontogeny and significance.* Edinburgh: Churchill Livingstone.

BULLOCK, M. (1985). Animism in children's thinking: A new look at an old question. *Developmental Psychology, 21,* 217–225.

BUSHNELL, E. W. (1981). The ontogeny of intermodal relations: Vision and touch in infancy. In R. D. Walk & H. L. Pick, Jr. (Eds.), *Intersensory perception and sensory integration.* New York: Plenum.

BUTTER, E. J. (1979). Visual and haptic training and cross-modal transfer of reflectivity. *Journal of Educational Psychology, 71,* 212–219.

BUTTER, E. J., KENNEDY, C. B., & SHOEMAKER-KELLY, K. E. (1982). Prediction of third grade reading ability as a function of performance on visual, auditory, and visual–auditory cognitive style tasks. *The Alberta Journal of Educational Research, 28,* 347–359.

BUTTERWORTH, G., & LIGHT, P. (EDS.). (1982). *Social cognition: Studies of the development of understanding.* Chicago: University of Chicago Press.

BYRD, D. M., & GHOLSON, B. (1985). Reading, memory, and metacognition. *Journal of Educational Psychology, 77,* 428–436.

CAIRNS, E., & CAMMOCK, T. (1978). Development of a more reliable version of the Matching Familiar Figures Test. *Developmental Psychology, 14,* 555–560.

CAIRNS, R. B. (1979). *Social development: The origins and plasticity of interchanges.* San Francisco: W. H. Freeman.

CALDWELL, B. M., & BRADLEY, R. H. (1978). *Home Observation for Measurement of the Environment.* Little Rock, AR: University of Arkansas at Little Rock.

CALLANAN, M. A., & MARKMAN, E. M. (1982). Principles of organization in young children's natural language hierarchies. *Child Development, 53,* 1093–1101.

CAMERON, R. (1984). Problem-solving inefficiency and conceptual tempo: A task analysis of underlying factors. *Child Development, 55,* 2031–2041.

CAMPIONE, J. C., & BROWN, A. L. (1977). Memory and metamemory development in educable retarded children. In R. V. Kail, Jr. & J. W. Hagen (Eds.), *The development of memory and cognition.* Hillsdale, NJ: Erlbaum.

CAMPIONE, J. C., & BROWN, A. L. (1984). Learning ability and transfer propensity as sources of individual differences in intelligence. In P. H. Brooks, R. Sperber, & C. McCauley (Eds.), *Learning and cognition in the mentally retarded.* Hillsdale, NJ: Erlbaum.

CAMPIONE, J. C., BROWN, A. L., FERRARA, R. A., JONES, R. S., & STEINBERG, E. (1985). Breakdowns in flexible use of information: Intelligence related differences in transfer following equivalent learning performance. *Intelligence, 9,* 297–315.

CAMPOS, J. J., HIATT, S., RAMSAY, D., HENDERSON, C., & SVEJDA, M. (1978). The emergence of fear on the visual cliff. In M. Lewis & L. A. Rosenblum (Eds.), *The development of affect.* New York: Plenum.

CAMPOS, J. J., LANGER, A., & KROWITZ, A. (1970). Cardiac responses on the visual cliff in pre-motor human infants. *Science, 170,* 195–196.

CANTOR, D. S., ANDREASSEN, C., & WATERS, H. S. (1985). Organization in visual episodic memory: Relationships between verbalized knowledge, strategy use, and performance. *Journal of Experimental Child Psychology, 40,* 218–232.

CAPLAN, P. J., MACPHERSON, G. M., & TOBIN, P. (1985). Do sex-related differences in spatial abilities exist? *American Psychologist, 40,* 786–799.

CAPON, N., & KUHN, D. (1979). Logical reasoning in the supermarket: Adult females' use of a proportional reasoning strategy in an everyday context. *Developmental Psychology, 15,* 450–452.

CAREW, J. V. (1980). Experience and the development of intelligence in young children at home and in day care. *Monographs of the Society for Research in Child Development, 45* (Serial No. 187).

CAREY, S. (1977). The child as a word learner. In M. Halle, J. Bresnan, & G. A. Miller (Eds.), *Linguistic theory and psychological reality.* Cambridge, MA: MIT Press.

CAREY, S. (1985a). Are children fundamentally different kinds of thinkers and learners than adults? In S. F. Chapman, J. W. Segal, & R. Glaser (Eds.), *Thinking and learning skills* (Vol. 2). Hillsdale, NJ: Erlbaum.

CAREY, S. (1985b). *Conceptual changes in childhood.* Cambridge, MA: MIT Press.

CARLSON, J. S., JENSEN, C. M., & WIDAMAN, K. F. (1983). Reaction time, intelligence and attention. *Intelligence, 7,* 329–344.

CARMICHAEL, L. (1970). The onset and early development of behavior. In P. Mussen (Ed.), *Carmichael's manual of child psychology* (Vol. 1) (3rd ed.). New York: Wiley.

CARON, A. J., CARON, R. F., & CARLSON, V. R. (1979). Infant perception of the invariant shape of objects varying in slant. *Child Development, 50,* 716–721.

CARPENTER, T. P., & MOSER, J. M. (1982). The development of addition and subtraction problem-solving skills. In T. P. Carpenter, J. M. Moser, & T. A. Romberg (Eds.), *Addition and subtraction: A cognitive perspective.* Hillsdale, NJ: Erlbaum.

CARSON, M. T., & ABRAHAMSON, A. (1976). Some members are more equal than others: The effect of semantic typicality on class-inclusion performance. *Child Development, 47,* 1186–1190.

CASE, R. (1974). Mental strategies, mental capacity and instruction: A neo-Piagetian investigation. *Journal of Experimental Child Psychology, 18,* 382–397.

CASE, R. (1984). The process of stage transition: A neo-Piagetian view. In R. J. Sternberg (Ed.), *Mechanisms of cognitive development.* New York: W. H. Freeman.

CASE, R. (1985). *Intellectual development: Birth to adulthood.* New York: Academic Press.

CASE, R., & GLOBERSON, T. (1974). Field dependence and central computing space. *Child Development, 15,* 772–778.

CASE, R., KURLAND, M., & GOLDBERG, J. (1982). Operational efficiency and the growth of short-term memory span. *Journal of Experimental Child Psychology, 33,* 386–404.

CASSIDY, J. (1987, April). *An assessment of the working model of the self within the attachment relationship.* Paper presented at the meeting of the Society for Research in Child Development, Baltimore.

CATTELL, R. B. (1963). Theory of fluid and crystalized intelligence: A critical experiment. *Journal of Educational Psychology, 54,* 1–22.

CATTELL, R. B. (1971). *Abilities: Their structure, growth and action.* Boston: Houghton Mifflin.

CAVANAUGH, J. C., & BORKOWSKI, J. G. (1980). Searching for metamemory–memory connections: A developmental study. *Developmental Psychology, 16,* 441–453.

CAVANAUGH, J. C., & PERLMUTTER, M. (1982). Metamemory: A critical examination. *Child Development, 53,* 11–28.

CECI, S. J. (1980). A developmental study of multiple encoding and its relationship to age-related changes in free recall. *Child Development, 51,* 892–895.

CECI, S. J. (1983). Automatic and purposive semantic processing characteristics of normal and language/learning disabled (L/LD) children. *Developmental Psychology, 19,* 427–439.

CECI, S. J. (1984). A developmental study of learning disabilities and memory. *Journal of Experimental Child Psychology, 38,* 352–371.

CECI, S. J., & BRONFENBRENNER, U. (1985). "Don't forget to take the cupcakes out of the oven": Prospective memory, strategic time-monitoring, and context. *Child Development, 56,* 152–164.

CECI, S. J., & HOWE, M. J. A. (1978). Semantic knowledge as a determinant of developmental differences in recall. *Journal of Experimental Child Psychology, 26,* 230–245.

CHECHILE, R. A., & RICHMAN, C. L. (1982). The interaction of semantic memory with storage and retrieval processes. *Developmental Review, 2,* 237–250.

CHENG, P. W. (1985). Restructuring versus automaticity: Alternative accounts of skill acquisition. *Psychological Review, 92,* 414–423.

CHI, M. T. H. (1977). Age differences in memory span. *Journal of Experimental Child Psychology, 23,* 266–281.

CHI, M. T. H. (1978). Knowledge structure and memory

development. In R. Siegler (Ed.), *Children's thinking: What develops?* Hillsdale, NJ: Erlbaum.

CHI, M. T. H. (1981). Knowledge development and memory performance. In M. Friedman, J. P. Das, & N. O'Connor (Eds.), *Intelligence and learning*, New York: Plenum.

CHI, M. T. H. (1985). Interactive roles of knowledge and strategies in the development of organized sorting and recall. In S. F. Chipman, J. W. Segal, & R. Glaser (Eds.), *Thinking and learning skills: Vol. 2. Research and open questions.* Hillsdale, NJ: Erlbaum.

CHI, M. T. H., FELTOVICH, P. J., & GLASER, R. (1981). Categorization and representation of physics problems by experts and novices. *Cognitive Science, 5,* 121–152.

CICIRELLI, V. G. (1978). Relationship of sibling structure to intellectual abilities and achievement. *Review of Educational Research, 48,* 365–379.

CLARK, E. A., & HANISEE, J. (1982). Intellectual and adaptive performance of Asian children in adoptive American settings. *Developmental Psychology, 18,* 595–599.

CLARK, E. V. (1973). What's in a word? On the child's acquisition of semantics in his first language. In T. E. Moore (Ed.), *Cognitive development and the acquisition of language.* New York: Academic Press.

CLARK, E. V. (1983). Meanings and concepts. In J. H. Flavell & E. M. Markman (Eds.), *Cognitive development: Vol. 3.* P. H. Mussen (Gen. Ed.), *Handbook of child psychology* (4th ed.). New York: Wiley.

CLARK, H. H., & CLARK, E. V. (1977). *Psychology and language: An introduction to psycholinguistics.* New York: Harcourt Brace Jovanovich.

CLARKE, A. D. B., & CLARKE, A. M. (1976). Formerly isolated children. In A. M. Clarke & A. D. B. Clarke (Eds.), *Early experience: Myth and evidence.* London: Open Books.

CLARKE-STEWART, A. K. (1973). Interactions between mothers and their young children: Characteristics and consequences. *Monographs of the Society for Research in Child Development, 38* (Serial No. 153).

COATES, D. L., & LEWIS, M. (1984). Early mother–infant interaction and infant cognitive status as predictors of school performance and cognitive behavior in six-year-olds. *Child Development, 55,* 1219–1230.

COATES, S. (1972). *Preschool Embedded Figures Test.* Palo Alto, CA: Consulting Psychologist Press.

COHEN, J. (1959). The factorial structure of the WISC at ages 7-6, 10-6, and 13-6. *Journal of Consulting Psychology, 23,* 285–299.

COHEN, L. B., & GELBER, E. R. (1975). Infant visual memory. In L. B. Cohen & P. Salapatek (Eds.), *Infant perception: From sensation to cognition* (Vol. 1). New York: Academic Press.

COHEN, L. B., & STRAUSS, M. S. (1979). Concept ac-

quisition in the human infant. *Child Development, 50,* 419–424.

COHEN, L. B., & YOUNGER, B. A. (1983). Perceptual categorization in the infant. In E. K. Scholnick (Ed.), *New trends in conceptual representations: Challenges to Piaget's theory?* Hillsdale, NJ: Erlbaum.

COHEN, S. E., & BECKWORTH, L. (1979). Preterm infant interaction with the caregiver in the first year of life and competence at age two. *Child Development, 50,* 767–776.

COLE, M., FRANKEL, F., & SHARP, D. (1971). Development of free recall learning in children. *Developmental Psychology, 4,* 109–123.

COLE, M., & SCRIBNER, S. (1977). Cross-cultural studies of memory and cognition. In R. V. Kail, Jr. & J. W. Hagen (Eds.), *Perspectives on the development of memory and cognition.* Hillsdale, NJ: Erlbaum.

COLLINS, A. M., & LOFTUS, E. F. (1975). A spreading activation theory of semantic processing. *Psychological Review, 82,* 407–428.

COLOMBO, J. (1986). Recent studies in early auditory development. In G. J. Whitehurst (Ed.), *Annals of child development* (Vol. 3). Greenwich, CN: JAI Press.

CONDON, W., & SANDER, L. (1974). Synchrony demonstrated between movements of the neonate and adult speech. *Child Development, 45,* 456–462.

CONNOR, J. M., & SERBIN, L. A. (1977). Behaviorally based masculine and feminine activity-preference scales for preschoolers: Correlates with other classroom behaviors and cognitive tests. *Child Development, 48,* 1411–1416.

CORBALLIS, M. C., & BEALE, I. L. (1983). *The ambivalent mind: The neuropsychology of left and right.* Chicago: Nelson-Hall.

CORMAN, H., & ESCALONA, S. (1969). Stages of sensorimotor development: A replication study. *Merrill-Palmer Quarterly, 15,* 351–361.

CORNELL, E. (1974). Infants' discrimination of photographs of faces following redundant presentations. *Journal of Experimental Child Psychology, 18,* 98–106.

CORSALE, K., & ORNSTEIN, P. A. (1980). Developmental changes in children's use of semantic information in recall. *Journal of Experimental Child Psychology, 30,* 231–245.

COWAN, N., & DAVIDSON, G. (1984). Salient childhood memories. *The Journal of Genetic Psychology, 145,* 101–107.

COWART, B. J. (1981). Development of taste perception in humans: Sensitivity and preference throughout the life span. *Psychological Bulletin, 90,* 43–73.

COX, D., & WATERS, H. S. (1986). Sex differences in the use of organization strategies: A developmental analysis. *Journal of Experimental Child Psychology, 41,* 18–37.

CRAIK, F. J. M., & LOCKHART, R. S. (1972). Levels of processing: A framework for memory research. *Journal of Verbal Learning and Verbal Behavior, 11,* 671–684.

CRONBACH, L. J. (1957). The two disciplines of scientific psychology. *American Psychologist, 12,* 671–684.

CROPLEY, A. J., & CLAPSON, L. G. (1971). Long-term test–retest reliability of creativity tests. *British Journal of Educational Psychology, 41,* 206–208.

CURTISS, S. (1977). *Genie: A psycholinguistic study of a modern day "wild child."* New York: Academic Press.

CUVO, A. J. (1975). Developmental differences in rehearsal and free recall. *Journal of Experimental Child Psychology, 19,* 265–270.

DAEHLER, M. W., & BUKATKO, D. (1977). Recognition memory for pictures in very young children: Evidence from attentional preferences using a continuous presentation procedure. *Child Development, 48,* 693–696.

DALE, P. S. (1976). *Language development: Structure and function* (2nd ed.). New York: Holt, Rinehart & Winston.

DALLAGO, M. L. P., & MOELY, B. E. (1980). Free recall in boys of normal and poor reading levels as a function of task manipulations. *Journal of Experimental Child Psychology, 30,* 62–78.

DANNER, F. W., & DAY, M. C. (1977). Eliciting formal operations. *Child Development, 48,* 1600–1606.

DANSKY, J. L. (1980). Make-believe: A mediator of the relationship between play and associative fluency. *Child Development, 51,* 576–579.

DANSKY, J. L., & SILVERMAN, I. W. (1973). Effects of play on associative fluency in preschool-aged children. *Developmental Psychology, 9,* 38–43.

DANSKY, J. L., & SILVERMAN, I. W. (1975). Play: A general facilitator of associative fluency. *Developmental Psychology, 11,* 104.

DANST, C. J., BROOKS, P. H., & DOXSEY, P. A. (1983). Characteristics of hiding places and the transition to stage IV performance in object permanence tasks. *Developmental Psychology, 18,* 671–681.

DAS, J. P. (1984a). Simultaneous and successive processes and K-ABC. *The Journal of Special Education, 18,* 229–338.

DAS, J. P. (1984b). Cognitive deficits in mental retardation: A process approach. In P. H. Brooks, R. Sperber, & C. McCauley (Eds.), *Learning and cognition in the mentally retarded.* Hillsdale, NJ: Erlbaum.

DAS, J. P., KIRBY, J., & JARMAN, R. F. (1975). Simultaneous and successive syntheses: An alternative model for cognitive abilities. *Psychological Bulletin, 82,* 87–103.

DAS, J. P., & MOLLOY, G. N. (1975). Varieties of simultaneous and successive processing in children. *Journal of Educational Psychology, 67,* 213–220.

DAVIDSON, J. E., & STERNBERG, R. J. (1984). The role of insight in intellectual giftedness. *Gifted Child Quarterly, 28,* 58–64.

DAVIS, A. J., & LANGE, G. (1973). Parent–child communication and the development of categorization styles in preschool children. *Child Development, 44,* 624–629.

DAVIS, K. (1947). Final note on a case of extreme isolation. *American Journal of Sociology, 53,* 432–437.

DEAUX, K. (1985). Sex and gender. *Annual Review of Psychology, 36,* 49–81.

DECASPER, A. J., & FIFER, W. P. (1980). Of human bonding: Newborns prefer their mother's voice. *Science, 208,* 1174–1176.

DECASPER, A. J., & SPENCE, M. J. (1986). Prenatal maternal speech influences newborns' perception of speech sounds. *Infant Behavior and Development, 9,* 133–150.

DELOACHE, J. S. (1986). Memory in very young children: Exploitation of cues to the location of a hidden object. *Cognitive Development, 1,* 123–138.

DELOACHE, J. S., & BROWN, A. L. (1983). Very young children's memory for the location of objects in a large scale environment. *Child Development, 54,* 888–897.

DELOACHE, J. S., CASSIDY, D. J., & BROWN, A. L. (1985). Precursors of mnemonic strategies in very young children's memory for the location of hidden objects. *Child Development, 56,* 125–137.

DEMARIE-DREBLOW, D., & MILLER, P. H. (in press). The development of children's strategies for selective attention: Evidence for a transitional period. *Child development.*

DEMPSTER, F. N. (1978). Memory span and short-term memory capacity: A developmental study. *Journal of Experimental Child Psychology, 26,* 419–431.

DEMPSTER, F. N. (1981). Memory span: Sources of individual and developmental differences. *Psychological Bulletin, 89,* 63–100.

DEMPSTER, F. N. (1985). Short-term memory development in childhood and adolescence. In C. J. Brainerd & M. Pressley (Eds.), *Basic processes in memory development: Progress in cognitive development research.* New York: Springer.

DENNEY, D. R. (1974). Relationship of three cognitive style dimensions to elementary reading abilities. *Journal of Educational Psychology, 66,* 702–709.

DENNEY, N. W. (1974). Evidence for developmental changes in categorization criteria for children and adults. *Human Development, 17,* 41–53.

DENNEY, N. W., & ACITO, M. A. (1974). Classification training in two- and three-year old children. *Journal of Experimental Child Psychology, 17,* 37–48.

DENNIS, W. (1973). *Children of the Crèche.* New York: Appleton-Century-Crofts.

DETTERMAN, D. (1982). Does "g" exist? *Intelligence, 6,* 99–108.

DE VILLIERS, J. G., & DE VILLIERS, P. A. (1978). *Language acquisition.* Cambridge, MA: Harvard University Press.

DE VILLIERS, P. A., & DE VILLIERS, J. G. (1979). *Early language.* Cambridge, MA: Harvard University Press.

DE VRIES, R. (1969). Constancy of generic identity in the years three to six. *Monographs of the Society for Research in Child Development, 34* (Serial No. 127).

DIAMOND, A. (1985). Development of the ability to use recall to guide action as indicated by infants' performance on AB̄. *Child Development, 56,* 868–883.

DIAMOND, R., CAREY, S., & BACK, K. J. (1983). Genetic influences on the development of spatial skills during early adolescence. *Cognition, 13,* 167–185.

DIPIETRO, J. A. (1981). Rough and tumble play: A function of gender. *Developmental Psychology, 17,* 50–58.

DIRKS, J., & NEISSER, U. (1977). Memory for objects in real scenes: The development of recognition and recall. *Journal of Experimental Child Psychology, 23,* 315–328.

DODGE, K. A. (1986). A social information processing model of social competence in children. In M. Perlmutter (Ed.), *Minnesota symposium on child psychology* (Vol. 18). Hillsdale, NJ: Erlbaum.

DODGE, K. A., PETTIT, G. S., McCLASKEY, C. L., & BROWN, M. M. (1986). Social competence in children. *Monographs of the Society for Research in Child Development, 51* (Serial No. 213).

DOLGIN, K. G., & BEHREND, D. A. (1984). Children's knowledge about animates and inanimates. *Child Development, 55,* 1646–1650.

DOWD, J. M., & TRONICK, E. F. (1986). Temporal coordination of arm movements in early infancy: Do infants move in synchrony with adult speech? *Child Development, 57,* 762–776.

DRACHMAN, D. B., & COULOMBRE, A. J. (1962). Experimental clubfoot and arthrogryposis multiplex congenita. *Lancet,* September 15, 1962, 523–526.

DUNCAN, E. M., & KELLAS, G. (1978). Developmental changes in the internal structure of semantic categories. *Journal of Experimental Child Psychology, 26,* 328–340.

DUNN, R., & DUNN, K. (1978). *Teaching students through their individual learning styles: A practical approach.* Reston, VA: Reston.

EASTERBROOKS, M. A., & GOLDBERG, W. A. (1984). Toddler development in the family: Father involvement and parenting characteristics. *Child Development, 55,* 740–752.

EATON, W. O., & VON BARGEN, D. (1981). Asynchronous development of gender understanding in preschool children. *Child Development, 52,* 1020–1027.

EGELAND, B. (1974). Training impulsive children in the use of more efficient scanning techniques. *Child Development, 45,* 165–171.

EGELAND, B., & FARBER, E. A. (1984). Infant–mother attachment: Factors related to its development and changes over time. *Child Development, 55,* 753–771.

EHRHARDT, A. A., & BAKER, S. W. (1974). Fetal androgens, human central nervous system differentiation, and behavior sex differences. In R. C. Friedman, R. M. Richart, & R. L. Vande Wiele (Eds.), *Sex differences in behavior.* New York: Wiley.

EHRHARDT, A. A., & MONEY, J. (1967). Progestin-induced hermaphroditism: IQ and psychosexual identity in a study of ten girls. *Journal of Sex Research, 3,* 83–100.

EHRI, L. C., & MUZIO, I. M. (1974). Cognitive style and reasoning about speed. *Journal of Educational Psychology, 66,* 569–571.

EILERS, R. E., GAVIN, W. J., & WILSON, W. R. (1979). Linguistic experience and phonemic perception in infancy: A cross-linguistic study. *Child Development, 50,* 14–18.

EIMAS, P. D., SIQUELAND, E. R., JUSCZYK, P., & VIGORITO, J. (1971). Speech perception in infants. *Science, 71,* 303–306.

ELARDO, R., BRADLEY, R. H., & CALDWELL, R. H. (1977). A longitudinal study of the relation of infants' home environments to language development at age three. *Child Development, 48,* 595–603.

ELKIND, D. (1967). Egocentrism in adolescence. *Child Development, 38,* 1025–1033.

ELKIND, D., & BOWEN, R. (1979). Imaginary audience behavior in children and adolescents. *Developmental Psychology, 15,* 38–44.

ELLIS, H. (1894). *Man and woman: A study of human secondary sexual characters.* London: Walter Scott.

EMERSON, H. F., & GEKOWSKI, W. L. (1976). Interactive and categorical grouping strategies and the syntagmatic–paradigmatic shift. *Child Development, 47,* 1116–1121.

EMMERICH, W. (1964). Continuity and stability in early social development. *Child Development, 35,* 311–322.

ENNIS, R. H. (1975). Children's ability to handle Piaget's propositional logic: A conceptual critique. *Review of Educational Research, 45,* 1–41.

ENNIS, R. H. (1976). An alternative to Piaget's conceptualization of logical competence. *Child Development, 47,* 903–919.

ERICKSON, L. G., & OTTO, W. R. (1973). Effect of intralist similarity and impulsivity–reflectivity on kindergarten children's word recognition performance. *Journal of Educational Research, 66,* 466–470.

ERICKSON, M. F., SROUFE, L. A., & EGELAND, B. (1985). The relationship between quality of attachment and behavior problems in preschool in a high-risk sample. In I. Bretherton & E. Waters (Eds.), Growing points of attachment theory and research. *Monographs of the Society for Research in Child Development, 50* (Serial No. 209).

ERLENMEYER-KIMLING, L., & JARVIK, L. R. (1963). Genetics and intelligence: A review. *Science, 142,* 1477–1479.

EVANS, M. A. (1985). Self-initiated speech repairs: A reflection of communicative monitoring in young children. *Developmental Psychology, 21,* 365–371.

EYSENCK, H. J. (1982). The psychophysiology of intelligence. In C. D. Speilberger & J. N. Butcher (Eds.), *Advances in personality assessment* (Vol. 1). Hillsdale, NJ: Erlbaum.

EYSENCK, H. J. (1985). The nature of cognitive differences between blacks and whites. *The Behavioral and Brain Sciences, 8,* 229.

EYSENCK, M. W., & BARON, C. R. (1974). Effects of cuing on recall from categorized word lists. *Developmental Psychology, 10,* 665–666.

FABRICIUS, W. V., & WELLMAN, H. M. (1983). Children's understanding of retrieval cue utilization. *Developmental Psychology, 19,* 15–21.

FAGAN, J. F., III. (1973). Infants' delayed recognition memory and forgetting. *Journal of Experimental Child Psychology, 16,* 424–450.

FAGAN, J. F., III. (1974). Infant recognition memory: The effects of length of familiarization and type of discrimination task. *Child Development, 45,* 351–356.

FAGAN, J. F., III. (1976). Infants' recognition of invariant features of faces. *Child Development, 47,* 627–638.

FAGAN, J. F., III. (1984a). The intelligent infant: Theoretical implications. *Intelligence, 8,* 1–9.

FAGAN, J. F., III. (1984b). The relationship of novelty preferences during infancy to later intelligence and recognition memory. *Intelligence, 8,* 339–346.

FAGAN, J. F., III, & SINGER, J. T. (1983). Infant recognition memory as a measure of intelligence. In L. P. Lipsitt & C. K. Rovee-Collier (Eds.), *Advances in infancy research* (Vol. 2). Norwood, NJ: Ablex.

FAGOT, B. I., LEINBACH, M. D., & HAGAN, R. (1986). Gender labeling and the adoption of sex-typed behaviors. *Developmental Psychology, 22,* 440–443.

FANTZ, R. L. (1958). Pattern vision in young infants. *Psychological Record, 8,* 43–47.

FANTZ, R. L. (1961). The origin of form perception. *Scientific American, 204,* 66–72.

FANTZ, R. L., & MIRANDA, S. B. (1975). Newborn attention to form of contour. *Child Development, 46,* 224–228.

FANTZ, R. L., & NEVIS, S. (1967). The predicted value of changes in visual preferences in early infancy. In J. Hellmuth (Ed.), *Exceptional Infant: Vol. 1. The normal infant.* New York: Brunner/Mazel.

FANTZ, R. L., ORDY, J. M., & UDELF, M. S. (1962). Maturation of pattern vision in infants during the first six months. *Journal of Comparative and Physiological Psychology, 55,* 907–917.

FELZEN, E., & ANISFELD, M. (1970). Semantic and phonetic relations in the false recognition of words by third- and sixth-grade children. *Developmental Psychology, 3,* 163–168.

FENNEMA, E., & SHERMAN, J. (1977). Sex-related differences in mathematics achievement, spatial visualization, and affective factors. *American Educational Research Journal, 4,* 51–71.

FIELD, D. (1987). A review of preschool conservation training: An analysis of analyses. *Developmental Review, 7,* 210–251.

FIELD, T. M., WOODSON, R., COHEN, D., GREENBERG, R., GARCIA, R., & COLLINS, K. (1983). Discrimination and imitation of facial expressions by term and preterm neonates. *Infant Behavior and Development, 6,* 485–489.

FIELD, T. M., WOODSON, R., GREENBERG, R., & COHEN, D. (1982). Discrimination and imitation of facial expression by neonates. *Science, 218,* 179–181.

FISCHER, B. B., & FISCHER, L. (1979). Styles in teaching and learning. *Educational Leadership, 36,* 245–254.

FISCHER, K. W. (1980). A theory of cognitive development: The control and construction of hierarchies of skills. *Psychological Review, 87,* 477–531.

FISCHER, K. W., & BULLOCK, D. (1981). Patterns of data: Sequence, synchrony and constraint in cognitive development. In K. W. Fischer (Ed.), *New directions for child development: Cognitive development.* San Francisco: Jossey-Bass.

FISCHER, K. W., & PIPP, S. L. (1984). Processes of cognitive development: Optimal level and skill acquisition. In R. J. Sternberg (Ed.), *Mechanisms of cognitive development.* New York: W. H. Freeman.

FISHER, C. B., FERDINANDSEN, K., & BORNSTEIN, M. H. (1981). The role of symmetry in infant form discrimination. *Child Development, 52,* 457–462.

FIVUSH, R., HUDSON, J., & NELSON, K. (1984). Children's long-term memory for a novel event: An exploratory study. *Merrill-Palmer Quarterly, 30,* 303–316.

FLAVELL, J. H. (1963). *The developmental psychology of Jean Piaget.* Princeton, NJ: Van Nostrand.

FLAVELL, J. H. (1970a). Developmental studies of mediated memory. In H. W. Reese & L. P. Lipsitt (Eds.), *Advances in child development and child behavior* (Vol. 5). New York: Academic Press.

FLAVELL, J. H. (1970b). Concept development. In P. Mussen (Ed.), *Carmichael's manual of child psychology* (Vol. 1) (3rd ed.). New York: Wiley.

FLAVELL, J. H. (1971). Stage-related properties of cognitive development. *Cognitive Psychology, 2,* 421–453.

FLAVELL, J. H. (1978a). Developmental stage: Explanans or explanandum? *The Behavioral and Brain Sciences, 2,* 187.

FLAVELL, J. H. (1978b). Metacognitive development. In J. M. Scandura & C. J. Brainerd (Eds.), *Structural/process theories of complex human behavior.* Alphen a. d. Rijn, the Netherlands: Sijthoff and Noordhoff.

FLAVELL, J. H. (1982). On cognitive development. *Child Development, 53,* 1–10.

FLAVELL, J. H., BEACH, D. R., & CHINSKY, J. H. (1966). Spontaneous verbal rehearsal in a memory task as a function of age. *Child Development, 37,* 283–299.

FLAVELL, J. H., BOTKIN, P. T., FRY, C. L., WRIGHT, J. W., & JARVIS, P. E. (1968). *The development of role-taking and communication skills in children.* New York: Wiley.

FLAVELL, J. H., EVERETT, B. A., CROFT, K., & FLAVELL, E. R. (1981). Young children's knowledge about visual perception: Further evidence for level 1–level 2 distinction. *Developmental Psychology, 17,* 99–107.

FLAVELL, J. H., FLAVELL, E. R., & GREEN, F. L. (1983). Development of the appearance–reality distinction. *Cognitive Psychology, 15,* 95–170.

FLAVELL, J. H., FRIEDRICHS, A. G., & HOYT, J. D. (1970). Developmental changes in memorization processes. *Cognitive Psychology, 1,* 324–340.

FLAVELL, J. H., GREEN, F. L., & FLAVELL, E. R. (1986). Development of knowledge about the appearance–reality distinction. *Monographs of the Society for Research in Child Development, 51* (Serial No. 212).

FLAVELL, J. H., & ROSS, L. (EDS.). (1981). *Social cognitive development: Frontiers and possible futures.* New York: Cambridge University Press.

FLAVELL, J. H., SPEER, J. R., GREEN, F. L., & AUGUST, D. L. (1981). The development of comprehension monitoring and knowledge about communication. *Monographs of the Society for Research in Child Development, 46* (Serial No. 192).

FLAVELL, J. H., & WELLMAN, H. M. (1977). Meta-memory. In R. V. Kail, Jr. & J. W. Hagen (Eds.), *Perspectives on the development of memory and cognition.* Hillsdale, NJ: Erlbaum.

FLAVELL, J. H., & WOHLWILL, J. F. (1969). Formal and functional aspects of cognitive development. In D. Elkind & J. H. Flavell (Eds.), *Studies in cognitive development.* London: Oxford University Press.

FLAVELL, J. H., ZHANG, X-D, ZOU, H., DONG, Q., & QI, S. (1983). A comparison between the development of the appearance–reality distinction in the People's Republic of China and the United States. *Cognitive Psychology, 15,* 459–466.

FONTAINE, R. (1984). Imitative skill between birth and six months. *Infant Behavior and Development, 7,* 323–333.

FORD, N. E., & KEATING, D. P. (1981). Developmental and individual differences in long-term memory retrieval: Process and organization. *Child Development, 52,* 234–241.

FOX, L. H. (1976). Sex differences in mathematical precocity: Bridging the gap. In D. P. Keating (Ed.), *Intellectual talent: Research and development.* Baltimore: Johns Hopkins University Press.

FRANKEL, M. T., & ROLLINS, H. A., JR. (1983). Does mother know best? Mothers and fathers interacting with preschool sons and daughters. *Developmental Psychology, 19,* 698–702.

FRANKEL, M. T., & ROLLINS, H. A., JR. (1985). Associative and categorical hypotheses of organization in the free recall of adults and children. *Journal of Experimental Child Psychology, 40,* 304–318.

FRAUENGLASS, M. H., & DIAZ, R. M. (1985). Self-regulatory functions of children's private speech: A critical analysis of recent challenges to Vygotsky's theory. *Developmental Psychology, 21,* 357–364.

FREUD, S. (1938). *An outline of psychoanalysis.* London: Hogarth.

FRIEDMAN, S. (1972). Habituation and recovery of visual response in the alert human newborn. *Journal of Experimental Child Psychology, 13,* 339–349.

FURTH, H. G. (1969). *Piaget and knowledge: Theoretical foundations.* Englewood Cliffs, NJ: Prentice-Hall.

FURTH, H. G., & MILGRAM, N. A. (1973). Labeling and grouping effects in the recall of pictures by children. *Child Development, 44,* 511–518.

FUSON, K. C. (1979). The development of self-regulating aspects of speech: A review. In G. Zivin (Ed.), *The development of self-regulation through private speech.* New York: Wiley.

FUSON, K. C., PERGAMENT, G. G., LYONS, B. G., & HALL, J. W. (1985). Children's conformity to the cardinality rule as a function of set size and counting accuracy. *Child Development, 56,* 1429–1436.

FUSON, K. C., SECADA, W. G., & HALL, J. T. (1983). Matching, counting, and conservation of numerical equivalence. *Child Development, 54,* 91–97.

GALBRAITH, R. C. (1982). Sibling spacing and intellectual development: A closer look at the confluence model. *Developmental Psychology, 18,* 151–173.

GARDNER, J., & GARDNER, H. (1970). A note on selective imitation by a six-week-old infant. *Child Development, 41,* 1209–1213.

GAZZANIGA, M. S. (1985). *The social brain: Discovering the networks of the mind.* New York: Basic Books.

GEIS, M. F., & HALL, D. M. (1976). Encoding and incidental memory in children. *Journal of Experimental Child Psychology, 22,* 58–66.

GELMAN, R. (1969). Conservation acquisition: A problem of learning to attend to relevant attributes. *Journal of Experimental Child Psychology, 7,* 167–187.

GELMAN, R. (1972). Logical capacity of very young children: Number invariance rules. *Child Development, 43,* 75–90.

GELMAN, R., & GALLISTEL, R. (1978). *The child's understanding of number.* Cambridge, MA: Harvard University Press.

GELMAN, R., MECK, E., & MERKIN, S. (1986). Young children's numerical competence. *Cognitive Development, 1,* 1–30.

GESELL, A., & AMATRUDA, C. (1954). *Developmental diagnosis.* New York: Paul B. Holber.

GEWIRTZ, J. L. (1972). Attachment, dependence, and a distinction in terms of stimulus control. In J. L. Gewirtz (Ed.), *Attachment and dependency.* New York: Wiley.

GHATALA, E. S. (1984). Developmental changes in incidental memory as a function of meaningfulness and encoding condition. *Developmental Psychology, 20,* 208–211.

GHATALA, E. S., CARBONARI, J. P., & BOBELE, L. Z. (1980). Developmental changes in incidental memory as a function of processing level, congruity and repetition. *Journal of Experimental Child Psychology, 29,* 74–87.

GHATALA, E. S., LEVIN, J. R., PRESSLEY, M., & GOOD-WIN, D. (1986). A componential analysis of the effects of derived and supplied strategy-utility information on children's strategy selections. *Journal of Experimental Child Psychology, 41,* 76–92.

GIBSON, E. J. (1969). *Principles of perceptual learning and development.* New York: Appleton-Century-Crofts.

GIBSON, E. J. (1971). Perceptual learning and the theory of word perception. *Cognitive Psychology, 2,* 351–368.

GIBSON, E. J., & LEVIN, H. (1975). *The psychology of reading.* Cambridge, MA: MIT Press.

GIBSON, E. J., & SPELKE, E. S. (1983). The development of perception. In J. H. Flavell & E. M. Markman (Eds.), *Cognitive development: Vol. 3.* P. H. Mussen (Gen. Ed.), *Handbook of child psychology* (4th ed.). New York: Wiley.

GIBSON, E. J., & WALK, R. D. (1960). The "visual cliff." *Scientific American, 202,* 64–71.

GIBSON, J. J. (1966). *The senses considered as perceptual systems.* Boston: Houghton Mifflin.

GINSBURG, H. (1977). *Children's arithmetic: The learning process.* New York: Van Nostrand.

GITOMER, D. H., & PELLEGRINO, J. W. (1985). Developmental and individual differences in long-term memory retrieval. In R. Dillon (Ed.), *Individual differences in cognition* (Vol. 2). Orlando, FL: Academic Press.

GJERDE, P. E., BLOCK, J., & BLOCK, J. H. (1985). Longitudinal consistency of Matching Familiar Figures Test performance from early childhood to preadolescence. *Developmental Psychology, 21,* 262–271.

GLOBERSON, T. (1983). Mental capacity and cognitive functioning: Developmental and social class differences. *Developmental Psychology, 19,* 225–230.

GLOBERSON, T. (1985). Field dependence/independence and mental capacity: A developmental approach. *Developmental Review, 5,* 261–273.

GLOBERSON, T. (1987). Confusing developmental and individual differences: A reply to Anderson. *Developmental Review, 7,* 142–144.

GLOBERSON, T., WEINSTEIN, E., & SHARABANY, R. (1985). Teasing out cognitive development from cognitive style: A training study. *Developmental Psychology, 21,* 682–691.

GLUCKSBERG, S., KRAUSS, R. M., & WEISBERG, R. (1966). Referential communication in nursery school children: Method and some preliminary findings. *Journal of Experimental Child Psychology, 3,* 333–342.

GOETZ, E. T., & HALL, R. J. (1984). Evaluation of the Kaufman Assessment Battery for Children from an information-processing perspective. *The Journal of Special Education, 18,* 281–296.

GOLDFARB, W. (1947). Variations in adolescent adjustment of institutionally reared children. *American Journal of Orthopsychiatry, 17,* 449–457.

GOLDSTEIN, D., HASHER, L., & STEIN, D. K. (1983). Processing of occurrence-rate and item information by children of different ages and abilities. *American Journal of Psychology, 96,* 229–241.

GOODENOUGH, D. R., & KARP, S. A. (1961). Field dependence and intellectual functioning. *Journal of Abnormal and Social Psychology, 63,* 241–246.

GOTTFRIED, A. W., ROSE, S. A., & BRIDGER, W. H. (1977). Cross-modal transfer in human infants. *Child Development, 48,* 116–123.

GOTTLIEB, G. (1973). Introduction to behavioral embryology. In G. Gottlieb (Ed.), *Studies on the development of behavior and the nervous system: Vol. 1. Behavioral embryology.* New York: Academic Press.

GOUZE, K. R., & NADELMAN, L. (1980). Constancy of gender identity for self and others in children between the ages of three and seven. *Child Development, 51,* 275–278.

GOVE, F. L., & KEATING, D. P. (1979). Emphatic role-taking precursors. *Developmental Psychology, 15,* 594–600.

GRATCH, G. (1975). Recent studies based on Piaget's view of object concept development. In L. B. Cohen & P. Salapatek (Eds.), *Infant perception: From sensation to cognition* (Vol. 4). New York: Academic Press.

GRATCH, G., APPEL, K. J., EVANS, W. F., LeCOMPTE, G. K., & WRIGHT, N. A. (1974). Piaget's stage IV object concept error: Evidence of forgetting or object conception? *Child Development, 45,* 71–77.

GRAY, W. M., & HUDSON, L. M. (1984). Formal operations and the imaginary audience. *Developmental Psychology, 20,* 619–627.

GREEN, B. L., BJORKLUND, D. F., & QUINN-COBB, C. (1988, March). *Development of meta-imitation.* Paper presented at the meeting of the Conference on Human Development, Charleston, SC.

GREENFIELD, D. B., & SCOTT, M. S. (1986). Young children's preferences for complementary pairs: Evidence against a shift to a taxonomic preference. *Developmental Psychology, 22,* 19–21.

GROEN, G. J., & PARKMAN, J. M. (1972). A chronometric analysis of simple addition. *Psychological Review, 79,* 329–343.

GROEN, G. J., & RESNICK, L. B. (1977). Can preschool children invent addition algorithms? *Journal of Educational Psychology, 69,* 645–652.

GUILFORD, J. P. (1967). *The nature of human intelligence.* New York: McGraw-Hill.

GUILFORD, J. P. (1988). Some changes in the structure-of-the-intellect model. *Educational and Psychological Measurement, 48,* 1–4.

GUILLAUME, P. (1971). *Imitation in children.* Chicago: University of Chicago Press.

GUTTENTAG, R. E. (1984). The mental effort requirement of cumulative rehearsal: A developmental study. *Journal of Experimental Child Psychology, 37,* 92–106.

GZESH, S. M., & SURBER, C. F. (1985). Visual perspective-taking skills in children. *Child Development, 56,* 1204–1213.

HAITH, M. M. (1966). The response of the human new-born to visual movement. *Journal of Experimental Child Psychology, 3,* 235–243.

HAITH, M. M. (1980). *Rules that babies look by: The organization of newborn visual activity.* Hillsdale, NJ: Erlbaum.

HALFORD, G. S. (1982). *The development of thought.* Hillsdale, NJ: Erlbaum.

HALFORD, G. S. (1984). Can young children integrate premises in transitivity and serial order tasks? *Cognitive Psychology, 16,* 65–93.

HALPERN, D. F. (1986). *Sex differences in cognitive abilities.* Hillsdale, NJ: Erlbaum.

HALVERSON, C. F., & WALDROP, M. F. (1973). The relations of mechanically recorded activity level to varieties of preschool play behavior. *Child Development, 44,* 678–681.

HAMANN, M. S., & ASHCRAFT, M. H. (1985). Simple and complex mental addition across development. *Journal of Experimental Child Psychology, 40,* 49–72.

HARLOW, H. F., DODSWORTH, R. O., & HARLOW, M. K. (1965). Total isolation in monkeys. *Proceedings of the National Academy of Science, 54,* 90–97.

HARRINGTON, D. M., BLOCK, J., & BLOCK, J. H. (1983). Predicting creativity in preadolescence from divergent thinking in early childhood. *Journal of Personality and Social Psychology, 45,* 609–623.

HARRIS, L. J. (1978). Sex differences in spatial ability: Possible environmental, genetic and neurological factors. In M. Kinsborne (Ed.), *Asymmetrical function of the brain.* New York: Cambridge University Press.

HARRIS, L. J. (1981). Sex-related variations in spatial skill. In L. S. Liben, A. H. Patterson, & N. Newcombe (Eds.), *Spatial representation and behavior across the lifespan.* New York: Academic Press.

HARRIS, P. L. (1973). Perseverative errors in search by young infants. *Child Development, 44,* 26–33.

HARRIS, P. L. (1975). Development of search and object permanence during infancy. *Psychological Bulletin, 82,* 332–344.

HARVEY, S., & SEELEY, K. (1984). An investigation of the relationships among intellectual and creative abilities, extracurricular activities, achievement, and giftedness in a delinquent population. *Gifted Child Quarterly, 28,* 135–139.

HASHER, L., & ZACKS, R. T. (1979). Automatic and effortful processes in memory. *Journal of Experimental Psychology: General, 108,* 356–388.

HASKINS, R., & MCKINNEY, J. D. (1976). Relative effects of response tempo and accuracy on problem solving and academic achievement. *Child Development, 47,* 690–696.

HATTIE, J., & ROGERS, H. J. (1986). Factor models for

assessing the relation between creativity and intelligence. *Journal of Educational Psychology, 76,* 482–485.

HAWKINS, J., PEA, R. D., GLICK, J., & SCRIBNER, S. (1984). "Merds that laugh don't like mushrooms": Evidence for deductive reasoning by preschoolers. *Developmental Psychology, 20,* 584–594.

HAYES, L. A., & WATSON, J. S. (1981). Neonatal imitation: Fact or artifact? *Developmental Psychology, 17,* 655–660.

HAYNES, H., WHITE, B. L., & HELD, R. (1965). Visual accommodation in human infants. *Science, 148,* 528–530.

HAZEN, N. L. (1982). Spatial exploration and spatial knowledge: Individual and developmental differences in very young children. *Child Development, 53,* 826–833.

HAZEN, N. L., & DURRETT, M. E. (1982). Relationship of security of attachment to exploration and cognitive mapping abilities in 2-year olds. *Developmental Psychology, 18,* 751–759.

HAZEN, N. L., LOCKMAN, J. J., & PICK, H. L., JR. (1978). The development of children's representations of large-scale environments. *Child Development, 49,* 623–636.

HEIDENHEIMER, P. (1978). A comparison of the roles of exemplar, action, coordinate, and superordinate relations in the semantic processing of 4- and 5-year old children. *Journal of Experimental Child Psychology, 25,* 143–159.

HEIDER, E. R. (1972). Universals in color naming and memory. *Journal of Experimental Psychology, 93,* 10–20.

HEISEL, B. E., & RITTER, K. (1981). Young children's storage behavior in a memory for location task. *Journal of Experimental Child Psychology, 31,* 250–264.

HENDERSON, R. W. (1981). Home environment and intellectual performance. In R. W. Henderson (Ed.), *Parent–child interaction: Theory, research, and prospects.* New York: Academic Press.

HENDRICKSON, D. E., & HENDRICKSON, A. E. (1980). The biological basis of individual differences in intelligence. *Personality and Individual Differences, 1,* 3–33.

HERMAN, J. F., KAIL, R. V., JR., & SIEGEL, A. W. (1979). Cognitive maps of college campus: A new look at freshman orientation. *Bulletin of the Psychonomic Society, 13,* 183–186.

HERMAN, J. F., SHIRAKI, J. H., & MILLER, B. S. (1985). Young children's ability to infer spatial relationships: Evidence from a large, familiar environment. *Child Development, 36,* 1195–1203.

HERMAN, J. F., & SIEGEL, A. W. (1978). The development of cognitive mapping of the large scale environment. *Journal of Experimental Child Psychology, 26,* 389–406.

HESS, R. D., & SHIPMAN, V. C. (1965). Early experience and the socialization of cognitive modes in children. *Child Development, 36,* 869–886.

HIGGINS, E. T., RUBLE, D. N., & HARTUP, W. W. (EDS.). (1983). *Social cognition and social development: A sociocultural perspective.* New York: Cambridge University Press.

HOCHBERG, J. E. (1962). Nativism and empiricism in perception. In L. Postman (Ed.), *Psychology in the making.* New York: Knopf.

HOCK, H. S., ROMANSKI, L., GALIE, A., & WILLIAMS, C. S. (1978). Real-world schemata and scene recognition in adults and children. *Memory & Cognition, 6,* 423–431.

HOFFMAN, M. L. (1975). Developmental synthesis of affect and cognition and its implications for altruistic motivation. *Developmental Psychology, 11,* 607–622.

HOLLINGSWORTH, L. (1916). Sex differences in mental traits. *Psychological Bulletin, 13,* 377–385.

HOLLINGSWORTH, L. (1918). Comparison of the sexes in mental traits. *Psychological Bulletin, 25,* 427–432.

HOMA, D., CROSS, J., CORNELL, D., GOLDMAN, D., & SCHWARTZ, S. (1973). Prototype abstraction and classification of new instances as a function of number of instances defining the prototype. *Journal of Experimental Psychology, 101,* 116–122.

HONZIK, M. P., MACFARLENCE, J. W., & ALLEN, L. (1948). Stability of mental test performance between 2 and 18 years. *Journal of Experimental Education, 17,* 309–324.

HOOD, J., & KENDAL, J. R. (1975). A qualitative analysis of oral reading errors of reflective and impulsive second graders: A follow-up study. *Journal of Reading Behavior, 7,* 269–281.

HOROBIN, K., & ACREDOLO, L. (1986). The role of attentiveness, mobility history, and separation of hiding sites on Stage IV search behavior. *Journal of Experimental Child Psychology, 41,* 114–127.

HOVING, K. L., SPENCER, T., ROBB, K. Y., & SCHULTE, D. (1978). Developmental changes in visual information processing. In P. A. Ornstein (Ed.), *Memory development in children.* Hillsdale, NJ: Erlbaum.

HOWE, M. L., BRAINERD, C. J., & KINGMA, J. (1985). Development of organization in recall: A stages-of-learning analysis. *Journal of Experimental Child Psychology, 39,* 230–251.

HUDSON, J., & FIVUSH, R. (1983). Categorical and schematic organization and the development of retrieval strategies. *Journal of Experimental Child Psychology, 36,* 32–42.

HUDSON, J., & NELSON, K. (1983). Effects of script structure on children's story recall. *Developmental Psychology, 19,* 625–635.

HUDSON, J., & NELSON, K. (1986). Repeated encounters of a similar kind: Effects of familiarity on children's autobiographical memory. *Cognitive Development, 1,* 253–272.

HUMPHREY, G. K., HUMPHREY, D. E., MUIR, D. W., & DODWELL, P. C. (1986). Pattern perception in infants: Effects of structure and transformation. *Journal of Experimental Child Psychology, 41,* 128–148.

HUMPHREYS, L. G. (1980). Me thinks they do protest too much. *Intelligence, 4,* 179–183.

HUMPHREYS, L. G., & PARSONS, C. K. (1979). Piagetian tasks measure intelligence and intelligence tests assess cognitive development. *Intelligence, 3,* 369–382.

HUMPHREYS, L. G., RICH, S. A., & DAVEY, T. C. (1985). A Piagetian test of general intelligence. *Developmental Psychology, 21,* 872–877.

HUNT, E. (1978). Mechanics of verbal ability. *Psychological Review, 85,* 109–130.

HUNT, E., DAVIDSON, J., & LANSMAN, M. (1981). Individual difference in long-term memory access. *Memory & Cognition, 9,* 599–608.

HUNT, E., LUNNEBORG, C., & LEWIS, J. (1975). What does it mean to be high verbal? *Cognitive Psychology, 7,* 194–227.

HUNT, J. McV. (1961). *Intelligence and experience.* New York: Ronald Press.

HYDE, J. S. (1981). How large are cognitive gender differences? A meta-analysis using ω^2 and d. *American Psychologist, 36,* 892–901.

INHELDER, B., & PIAGET, J. (1958). *The growth of logical thinking from childhood to adolescence.* New York: Basic Books.

INHELDER, B., & PIAGET, J. (1964). *The early growth of logic in the child.* New York: Norton.

INHELDER, B., SINCLAIR, H., & BOVET, M. (1974). *Learning and the development of cognition.* Cambridge, MA: Harvard University Press.

JACKSON, E., CAMPOS, J. J. & FISCHER, K. W. (1978). The question of décalage between object permanence and person permanence. *Developmental Psychology, 14,* 1–10.

JACOBSON, S. W. (1979). Matching behavior in the young infant. *Child Development, 50,* 425–430.

JAMES, W. (1890). *The principles of psychology.* New York: Henry Holt.

JENSEN, A. R. (1969). How much can we boost IQ and scholastic achievement? *Harvard Educational Review, 39,* 1–123.

JENSEN, A. R. (1981). Reaction time and intelligence. In M. P. Friedman, J. P. Das, & N. O'Connor (Eds.), *Intelligence and learning.* New York: Plenum.

JENSEN, A. R. (1985). The nature of the black–white difference on various psychometric tests: Spearman's hypothesis. *The Behavioral and Brain Sciences, 8,* 193–263.

JOHNSON, E. C., & JOSEY, C. C. (1931–32). A note on the development forms of children as described by Piaget. *Journal of Abnormal and Social Psychology, 26,* 338–339.

JOHNSON, J. E. (1976). Relations of divergent thinking and intelligence test scores with social and non-social make-believe play of preschool children. *Child Development, 47,* 1200–1203.

JUSTICE, E. M. (1985). Categorization as a preferred memory strategy: Developmental changes during elementary school. *Developmental Psychology, 21,* 1105–1110.

KAGAN, J. (1965a). Impulsive and reflective children: Significance of conceptual tempo. In J. D. Krumholtz (Ed.), *Learning and the educational process.* Chicago: Rand McNally.

KAGAN, J. (1965b). Reflection–impulsivity and reading ability in primary grade children. *Child Development, 36,* 609–628.

KAGAN, J. (1966). Reflection–impulsivity: The generality and dynamics of conceptual tempo. *Journal of Abnormal Psychology, 71,* 17–24.

KAGAN, J. (1971). *Change and continuity in infancy.* New York: Wiley.

KAGAN, J. (1974). Discrepancy, temperament, and infant distress. In M. Lewis & I. Rosenblum (Eds.), *The origins of fear.* New York: Wiley.

KAGAN, J. (1976). New views on cognitive development. *Journal of Youth and Adolescence, 5,* 113–129.

KAGAN, J. (1987). Misgivings about the Matching Familiar Figures Test: A brief reply to Block, Gjerde, and Block (1986). *Developmental Psychology, 23,* 730–739.

KAGAN, J., KEARSLEY, R. B., & ZELAZO, P. R. (1975). The emergence of initial apprehension to unfamiliar peers. In M. Lewis & L. Rosenblum (Eds.), *Friendship and peer relations.* New York: Wiley.

KAGAN, J., & KLEIN, R. E. (1973). Cross-cultural perspectives on early development. *American Psychologist, 28,* 947–961.

KAGAN, J., KLEIN, R. E., FINLEY, G. E., ROGOFF, B., & NOLAN, E. (1979). A cross-cultural study of cognitive development. *Monographs of the Society for Research in Child Development, 44* (Serial No. 180).

KAGAN, J., & KOGAN, N. (1970). Individual variations in cognitive processes. In P. H. Mussen (Ed.), *Carmichael's manual of child psychology* (Vol. 1) (3rd ed.). New York: Wiley.

KAGAN, J., & MOSS, H. A. (1962). *Birth to maturity: A study of psychological development.* New York: Wiley.

KAGAN, J., ROSMAN, B. L., DAY, D., ALBERT, J., & PHILIPS, W. (1964). Information processing in the child: Significance of analytic and reflective attitudes. *Psychological Monographs, 78* (No. 578).

KAIL, R. V., JR. (1984). *The development of memory in children* (2nd ed.). San Francisco: W. H. Freeman.

KAIL, R. V., JR. (1986). Sources of age differences in speed of processing. *Child Development, 57,* 969–987.

KAIL, R. V., JR., & HAGEN, J. W. (1977). *Perspectives on the development of memory and cognition.* Hillsdale, NJ: Erlbaum.

KALLIO, K. D. (1982). Developmental change on a five-term transitive inference. *Journal of Experimental Child Psychology, 33,* 142–164.

KALYAN-MASIH, V. (1985). Cognitive performance and cognitive style. *International Journal of Behavioral Development, 8,* 39–54.

KAMIN, L. J. (1974). *The science and politics of IQ.* Potomac, MD: Erlbaum.

KAPLAN, N. (1987, April). *Internal representations of attachment in 6-year-olds.* Paper presented at the meeting of the Society for Research in Child Development, Baltimore.

KARMEL, B. Z. (1969). The effect of age, complexity, and amount of contour on pattern preferences in human infants. *Journal of Experimental Child Psychology, 7,* 339–354.

KARMEL, B. Z., & MAISEL, E. B. (1975). A neuronal activity model for infant visual attention. In L. B. Cohen & P. Salapatek (Eds.), *Infant perception: From sensation to cognition* (Vol. 1). New York: Academic Press.

KARP, S. A., & KONSTADT, N. (1971). *Children's Embedded Figures Test.* Palo Alto, CA: Consulting Psychologists Press.

KARZON, R. G. (1985). Discrimination of polysyllabic sequences by one- to four-month-old infants. *Journal of Experimental Child Psychology, 39,* 326–342.

KAUFMAN, A. S., & KAUFMAN, N. L. (1972). Tests built from Piaget's and Gesell's tasks as predictors of first-grade achievement. *Child Development, 43,* 521–535.

KAUFMAN, A. S., & KAUFMAN, N. L. (1983). *Kaufman Assessment Battery for Children (K-ABC).* Circle Pines, MN: American Guidance Service.

KAYE, D. B. (1986). The development of mathematical cognition. *Cognitive Development, 1,* 157–170.

KAYE, K. (1982). *The mental and social life of babies: How parents create persons.* Chicago: University of Chicago Press.

KAYE, K., & MARCUS, J. (1981). Infant imitation: The sensory–motor agenda. *Developmental Psychology, 17,* 258–265.

KEATING, D. P. (1975). Precocious cognitive development at the level of formal operations. *Child Development, 46,* 276–280.

KEATING, D. P., & BOBBITT, B. L. (1978). Individual differences in cognitive processing: Components of mental ability. *Child Development, 49,* 155–167.

KEATING, D. P., KENISTON, A. H., MANIS, F. R., & BOBBITT, B. L. (1980). Development of the search processing parameter. *Child Development, 51,* 39–44.

KEE, D. W., & BELL, T. S. (1981). The development of organizational strategies in the storage and retrieval of categorical items in free-recall learning. *Child Development, 52,* 1163–1171.

KEENEY, T. J., CANNIZZO, S. R., & FLAVELL, J. H. (1967). Spontaneous and induced verbal rehearsal in a recall task. *Child Development, 38*, 953–966.

KEIL, F. C., & BATTERMAN, N. (1984). A characteristic-to-defining shift in the development of word meaning. *Journal of Verbal Learning and Verbal Behavior, 23*, 221–236.

KELLAS, G., McCAULEY, C., & McFARLAND, C. E. (1975). Developmental aspects of storage and retrieval. *Journal of Experimental Child Psychology, 19*, 51–62.

KELLER, D. (1982). Developmental effects of typicality and superordinate property dominance on sentence verification. *Journal of Experimental Child Psychology, 33*, 288–297.

KELLER, D., & KELLAS, G. (1978). Typicality as a dimension of encoding. *Journal of Experimental Psychology: Human Learning and Memory, 4*, 78–85.

KENDLER, H. H., & KENDLER, T. S. (1962). Vertical and horizontal processes in problem solving. *Psychological Review, 69*, 1–16.

KENNEDY, C. B., & BUTTER, E. J. (1978). Cognitive style in two modalities: Vision and audition. *Journal of Educational Psychology, 70*, 193–199.

KEOGH, B. K. (1973). Perceptual and cognitive styles: Implications for special education. In L. Mann & D. A. Sabatino (Eds.), *The first review of special education.* Philadelphia: Buttonwood Farms.

KERSHNER, J. R., & LEDGER, G. (1985). Effect of sex, intelligence, and style of thinking on creativity: A comparison of gifted and average IQ children. *Journal of Personality and Social Psychology, 48*, 1033–1040.

KESSEN, W., & NELSON, K. (1978). What the child brings to language. In B. Z. Presseison, D. Goldstein, & M. H. Appel (Eds.), *Topics in cognitive development: Vol. 2. Language and operational thought.* New York: Plenum.

KILLEN, M., & UZGIRIS, I. C. (1981). Imitation of actions with objects: The role of social meaning. *Journal of Genetic Psychology, 138*, 219–229.

KINGMA, J. (1984). Traditional intelligence, Piagetian tasks, and initial arithmetic in kindergarten and primary school grade one. *Journal of Genetic Psychology, 145*, 49–60.

KINGSLEY, P. R., & HAGEN, J. W. (1969). Induced versus spontaneous rehearsal in short-term memory in nursery school children. *Developmental Psychology, 1*, 40–46.

KINSBOURNE, M., & SMITH, W. L. (EDS.). (1974). *Hemispheric disconnection and cerebral function.* Springfield, IL: Thomas.

KIRBY, J. R., & DAS, J. P. (1977). Reading achievement, IQ, and simultaneous–successive processing. *Journal of Educational Psychology, 69*, 564–570.

KLAGSBURN, M., & BOWLBY, J. (1976). Responses to separation from parents: A clinical test for young children. *British Journal of Projective Psychology, 21*, 7–21.

KLAHR, D., & WALLACE, J. G. (1976). *Cognitive develop-*

ment: An information processing view. Hillsdale, NJ: Erlbaum.

KLAPP, S. T., MARSHBURN, E. A., & LESTER, P. T. (1983). Short-term memory does not involve the "working memory" of information processing: The demise of a common assumption. *Journal of Experimental Psychology: General, 112*, 240–264.

KLAUS, R. A., & GRAY, S. (1968). The early training project for disadvantaged children: A report after five years. *Monographs of the Society for Research in Child Development, 33* (Serial No. 120).

KLIMA, E., & BELLUGI, U. (1966). Syntactic regularities in the speech of children. In T. Lyons & R. Wales, *Psycholinguistic papers.* Edinburgh: Edinburgh University Press.

KOBAK, R. R. (1987, April). *Attachment in late adolescence: Working models affect regulation and representation of self and others.* Paper presented at the meeting of the Society for Research in Child Development, Baltimore.

KOBASIGAWA, A. (1974). Utilization of retrieval cues by children in recall. *Child Development, 45*, 127–134.

KOBASIGAWA, A. (1977). Retrieval strategies in the development of memory. In R. V. Kail, Jr. & J. W. Hagen (Eds.), *Perspectives on the development of memory and cognition.* Hillsdale, NJ: Erlbaum.

KOEPKE, J. E., HAMM, M., LEGERSTEE, M., & RUSSELL, M. (1983). Neonatal imitation: Two failures to replicate. *Infant Behavior and Development, 6*, 97–102.

KOGAN, N. (1983). Stylistic variation in childhood and adolescence: Creativity, metaphor, and cognitive style. In J. H. Flavell & E. M. Markman (Eds.), *Cognitive development: Vol. 3.* P. H. Mussen (Gen. Ed.), *Handbook of child psychology* (4th ed.). New York: Wiley.

KOGAN, N., & PANKOVE, E. (1972). Creativity ability over a five-year span. *Child Development, 43*, 427–442.

KOHLBERG, L. (1966). A cognitive-developmental analysis of children's sex-role concepts and attitudes. In E. E. Maccoby (Ed.), *The development of sex differences.* Stanford, CA: Stanford University Press.

KOHLBERG, L. (1969). Stage and sequence: The cognitive-developmental approach to socialization. In D. A. Goslin (Ed.), *Handbook of socialization theory and research.* Chicago: Rand McNally.

KOHLBERG, L., YAEGER, J., & HJERTHOLM, E. (1968). Private speech: Four studies and a review of theories. *Child Development, 39*, 691–736.

KOLUCHOVA, J. (1972). Severe deprivation in twins: A case study. *Journal of Child Psychology and Psychiatry, 13*, 107–114.

KOLUCHOVA, J. (1976). A report on the further development of twins after severe and prolonged deprivation. In A. M. Clarke & A. D. B. Clarke (Eds.), *Early experience: Myth and evidence.* London: Open Books.

KOPP, C. B., & McCALL, R. B. (1982). Predicting later mental performance for normal, at-risk, and handicapped infants. In P. B. Baltes & O. G. Brim (Eds.), *Life-span development and behavior* (Vol. 4). New York: Academic Press.

KOPP, C. B., SIGMAN, M., & PARMELEE, A. H. (1974). Longitudinal study of sensorimotor development. *Developmental Psychology, 10,* 687–695.

KORNER, A. F., & THOMAN, E. B. (1972). The relative efficacy of contact and vestibular-proprioceptive stimulation in soothing neonates. *Child Development, 43,* 433–454.

KOSSLYN, S. M. (1978). The representational-developmental hypothesis. In P. A. Ornstein (Ed.), *Memory development in children.* Hillsdale, NJ: Erlbaum.

KOSSLYN, S. M. (1981). The medium and the message in mental imagery: A theory. *Psychological Review, 88,* 46–66.

KRAMER, J. A., HILL, K. T., & COHEN, L. B. (1975). Infants' development of object permanence: A refined methodology and new evidence for Piaget's hypothesized ordinality. *Child Development, 46,* 149–155.

KRATOCHWILL, T. R., & GOLDMAN, J. A. (1973). Developmental changes in children's judgments of age. *Developmental Psychology, 9,* 358–362.

KREUTZER, M. A., LEONARD, C., & FLAVELL, J. H. (1975). An interview study of children's knowledge about memory. *Monographs of the Society for Research in Child Development, 40* (Serial No. 159).

KRUEGER, T. (1976). *Visual imagery in problem solving and scientific creativity.* Derby, CT: Seal Press.

KUCZAJ, S. A. (1982). The acquisition of word meaning in the context of the development of the semantic system. In C. Brainerd & M. Pressley (Eds.), *Progress in cognitive development research: (Vol. 2). Verbal processes in children.* New York: Springer.

KUHN, D. (1976). Relation of two Piagetian stage transitions to IQ. *Developmental Psychology, 12,* 157–161.

KUHN, D., & BRANNOCK, J. (1977). Development of the isolation of variable scheme in experimental and "natural experiment" contexts. *Developmental Psychology, 13,* 9–14.

KUHN, D., LANGER, J., KOHLBERG, L., & HAAN, N. S. (1977). The development of formal operations in logical and moral judgment. *Genetic Psychology Monographs, 95,* 97–188.

KUHN, D., NASH, S. C., & BRUCKEN, L. (1978). Sex role concepts of two- and three-year-olds. *Child Development, 49,* 445–451.

KURTZ, B. E., & BORKOWSKI, J. G. (1987). Development of strategic skills in impulsive and reflective children: A longitudinal study of metacognition. *Journal of Experimental Child Psychology, 43,* 129–146.

LABARBA, R. C. (1981). *Foundations of developmental psychology.* New York: Academic Press.

LABORATORY OF COMPARATIVE HUMAN COGNITION. (1983). Culture and cognitive development. In W.

Kessen (Ed.), *History, theory, and methods: Vol. 1.* P. H. Mussen (Gen. Ed.), *Handbook of child psychology* (4th ed.). New York: Wiley.

LAMB, M. E., & SHERROD, L. R. (EDS.). (1981). *Infant social cognition: Empirical and theoretical considerations.* Hillsdale, NJ: Erlbaum.

LANE, D. M., & PEARSON, D. A. (1982). The development of selective attention. *Merrill-Palmer Quarterly, 28,* 317–337.

LANE, M. K., & HODKIN, B. (1985). Role of atypical exemplars of social and nonsocial superordinate categories within the class inclusion paradigm. *Developmental Psychology, 21,* 909–915.

LANGE, G. W. (1973). The development of conceptual and rote recall skills among school age children. *Journal of Experimental Child Psychology, 15,* 394–407.

LANGE, G. W., & JACKSON, P. (1974). Personal organization in children's free recall. *Child Development, 45,* 1060–1067.

LANGLOIS, J. H., RUGGMAN, L. A., CASEY, R. J., RITTER, J. M., A. REISER-DANNER, & JENKINS, V. Y. (1987). Infant preferences for attractive faces: Rudiments of a stereotype? *Developmental Psychology, 23,* 363–369.

LASKY, R. E., SYRDAL-LASKY, A., & KLEIN, R. E. (1975). VOT discrimination by four to six-and-a-half-month-old infants from Spanish environments. *Journal of Experimental Child Psychology, 20,* 215–225.

LAURENCE, M. W. (1966). Age differences in performance and subjective organization in the free-recall learning of pictorial material. *Canadian Journal of Psychology, 20,* 388–399.

LAURENDEAU, M., & PINARD, A. (1962). *Causal thinking in children.* New York: International Universities Press.

LAVIN, D. (1965). *The prediction of academic performance.* New York: Russell Sage Foundation.

LAZAR, I., DARLINGTON, R., MURRAY, H., ROYCE, J., & SNIPPER, A. (1982). Lasting effects of early education: A report from the Consortium for Longitudinal Studies. *Monographs of the Society for Research in Child Development, 47* (Serial No. 195).

LEAL, L., CRAYS, N., & MOELY, B. E. (1985). Training children to use a self-monitoring study strategy in preparation for recall: Maintenance and generalization effects. *Child Development, 56,* 643–653.

LEMPERS, J. D., FLAVELL, E. R., & FLAVELL, J. H. (1977). The development in very young children of tacit knowledge concerning visual perception. *Genetic Psychology Monographs, 95,* 3–53.

LESTER, B. M., KOTELCHUCK, M., SPELKE, E., SELLERS, M. J., & KLEIN, R. E. (1974). Separation protest in Guatemalan infants: Cross cultural and cognitive findings. *Developmental Psychology, 10,* 79–85.

LEVY, J., & REID, M. (1978). Variations in cerebral organization as a function of handedness, hand posture in writing, and sex. *Journal of Experimental Psychology: General, 107*, 119–144.

LEWIS, M. (1969). Infants' responses to facial stimuli during the first year of life. *Developmental Psychology, 1*, 75–86.

LEWIS, M., & BROOKS-GUNN, J. (1981). Visual attention at three months as a predictor of cognitive functioning at two years of age. *Intelligence, 5*, 131–140.

LEWIS, M., & FREEDLE, R. O. (1973). Mother–infant dyad: The cradle of meaning. In P. Pilner, L. Krames, & T. Alloway (Eds.), *Communication and affect: Language and thought*. New York: Academic Press.

LEWIS, M., & SULLIVAN, M. W. (1985). Imitation in the first month of life. *Merrill-Palmer Quarterly, 31*, 315–333.

LIBEN, L. S. (1978). Performance in Piagetian spatial tasks as a function of sex, field dependence, and training. *Merrill-Palmer Quarterly, 24*, 97–110.

LIBEN, L. S. (1981). Copying and reproducing pictures in relation to subjects' operative levels. *Developmental Psychology, 17*, 357–365.

LIBEN, L. S., & GOLBECK, S. L. (1980). Sex differences in performance on Piagetian spatial tasks: Differences in competence or performance? *Child Development, 51*, 594–597.

LIBEN, L. S., & GOLBECK, S. L. (1984). Performance on Piagetian horizontality and verticality tasks: Sex-related differences in knowledge of relevant physical phenomena. *Developmental Psychology, 20*, 595–606.

LIEBERMAN, J. N. (1977). *Playfulness: Its relationship to imagination and creativity*. New York: Academic Press.

LINDBERG, M. (1980). The role of knowledge structures in the ontogeny of learning. *Journal of Experimental Child Psychology, 30*, 401–410.

LINN, M. C. (1978). Influence of cognitive style and training on tasks requiring the separation of variables schema. *Child Development, 49*, 874–877.

LINN, M. C., & PETERSEN, A. C. (1985). Emergence and characterization of sex differences in spatial ability: A meta-analysis. *Child Development, 56*, 1479–1498.

LINN, S., REZNICK, J. S., KAGAN, J., & HANS, S. (1982). Salience of visual patterns in the human infant. *Developmental Psychology, 18*, 651–657.

LIST, J. A., KEATING, D. P., & MERRIMAN, W. E. (1985). Differences in memory retrieval: A construct validity investigation. *Child Development, 56*, 138–151.

LODICO, M. G., GHATALA, E. S., LEVIN, J. R., PRESSLEY, M., & BELL, J. A. (1983). The effects of strategy-monitoring on children's selection of effective memory strategies. *Journal of Experimental Child Psychology, 35*, 263–277.

LOFTUS, E. F. (1975). Leading questions and the eyewitness report. *Cognitive Psychology, 7*, 560–572.

LONGSTRETH, L. E. (1981). Revisiting Skeels' final study: A critique. *Developmental Psychology, 17*, 620–625.

LOOFT, W. R. (1971). Children's judgments of age. *Child Development, 42*, 1282–1284.

LOOFT, W. R., & BARTZ, W. H. (1969). Animism revived. *Psychological Bulletin, 71*, 1–19.

LORENZ, K. Z. (1973). The comparative study of behavior. In K. Lorenz & P. Leyhausen (Eds.), *Motivation of human and animal behavior: An ethological view*. New York: Van Nostrand.

LOVELL, K. (1961). A follow-up study of Inhelder and Piaget's "The growth of logical thinking." *British Journal of Psychology, 52*, 143–153.

LOVELL, K., MITCHELL, B., & EVERETT, I. R. (1962). An experimental study of the growth of some logical structures. *British Journal of Psychology, 53*, 175–188.

LUCARIELLO, J., & NELSON, K. (1985). Slot-filler categories as memory organizers for young children. *Developmental Psychology, 21*, 272–282.

LUNZAR, F. A., DOLAN, T., & WILKINSON, J. E. (1976). The effectiveness of measures of operativity, language and short-term memory in the prediction of reading and mathematical understanding. *British Journal of Educational Psychology, 46*, 295–305.

LURIA, A. R. (1961). *The role of speech in the regulation of normal and abnormal behavior*. New York: Liveright.

LURIA, A. R. (1966). *Higher cortical functions in man*. New York: Liveright.

LURIA, A. R. (1976). *Cognitive development: Its cultural and social foundations*. Cambridge, MA: Harvard University Press.

LUTKENHAUS, P., GROSSMANN, K. E., & GROSSMANN, K. (1985). Infant–mother attachment at twelve months and style of interaction with a stranger at the age of three. *Child Development, 56*, 1538–1542.

MACCOBY, E. E., & JACKLIN, C. N. (1974). *The psychology of sex differences*. Stanford, CA: Stanford University Press.

MACFARLANE, A. (1975). Olfaction in the development of social preferences in the human neonate. *CIBA Foundation Symposium 33: Parent–infant interaction*. Amsterdam: Elsevier.

MACKAIN, S. (1987, April). *Gender constancy: A realistic approach*. Paper presented at the meeting of the Society of Research in Child Development, Baltimore.

MACLEOD, C. M., JACKSON, R. A., & PALMER, J. (1986). On the relation between spatial ability and field dependence. *Intelligence, 10*, 141–151.

MAGNUSSON, D., & BACKTEMAN, G. (1978). Longitudinal stability of person characteristics: Intelligence and creativity. *Applied Psychological Measurement, 2*, 481–490.

MAIN, M. (1987, April). *States of mind with respect to attachment in adulthood: Why the relationship to infant attachment classification?* Paper presented at the meeting of the Society for Research in Child Development, Baltimore.

MAIN, M., KAPLAN, N., & CASSIDY, J. (1985). Security in infancy, childhood, and adulthood: A move to the level of representation. In I. Bretherton & E. Waters (Eds.), Growing points of attachment theory and research. *Monographs of the Society for Research in Child Development*, 50 (Serial No. 209).

MANDLER, G. (1967). Organization and memory. In K. W. Spence & J. T. Spence (Eds.), *The psychology of learning and motivation* (Vol. I). New York: Academic Press.

MANDLER, J. M. (1978). A code in the node: The use of a story scheme in retrieval. *Discourse Processes, 1,* 14–35.

MANDLER, J. M. (1983). Representation. In J. H. Flavell & E. M. Markman (Eds.), *Cognitive development: Vol. 3.* P. H. Mussen (Gen. Ed.), *Handbook of child psychology* (4th ed.). Wiley: New York.

MANDLER, J. M., & ROBINSON, C. A. (1978). Developmental changes in picture recognition. *Journal of Experimental Child Psychology, 26,* 122–136.

MANDLER, J. M., & STEIN, N. L. (1974). Recall and recognition of pictures by children as a function of organization and distractor similarity. *Journal of Experimental Psychology, 102,* 657–669.

MARATOS, O. (1973). *The origin and development of imitation in the first six months of life.* Ph.D. thesis, University of Geneva.

MARATSOS, M. (1983). Some current issues in the study of the acquisition of grammar. In J. H. Flavell & E. M. Markman (Eds.), *Cognitive development: Vol. 3.* P. H. Mussen (Gen. Ed.), *Handbook of child psychology* (4th ed.). New York: Wiley.

MARCUS, D. E., & OVERTON, W. F. (1978). The development of cognitive gender constancy and sex role preferences. *Child Development, 49,* 434–444.

MARGOLIS, H., PETERSON, N., & LEONARD, H. S. (1978). Conceptual tempo as a predictor of first-grade reading achievement. *Journal of Reading Behavior, 10,* 359–362.

MARKMAN, E. M. (1981). Comprehension monitoring. In W. P. Dickson (Ed.), *Children's oral communication skills.* New York: Academic Press.

MARKMAN, E. M. (1983). Two different kinds of hierarchical organization. In E. K. Scholnick (Ed.), *New trends in conceptual representation: Challenges to Piaget's theory?* Hillsdale, NJ: Erlbaum.

MARKMAN, E. M. (1984). The acquisition and hierarchical organization of categories by children. In C. Sophian (Ed.), *Origins of cognitive skills.* Hillsdale, NJ: Erlbaum.

MARKMAN, E. M., COX, B., & MARCHIDA, S. (1981). The standard object-sorting task as a measure of conceptual organization. *Developmental Psychology, 17,* 115–117.

MARKMAN, E. M., HORTON, M. S., & McLANAHAN, A. G. (1980). Classes and collections: Principles of organization in the learning of hierarchical relations. *Cognition, 8,* 227–241.

MARKMAN, E. M., & SEIBERT, J. (1976). Classes and collections: Internal organization and resulting holistic properties. *Cognitive Psychology, 8,* 561–577.

MARR, D. B., & STERNBERG, R. J. (1986). Analogical reasoning with novel concepts: Differential attention of intellectually gifted and nongifted children to relevant and irrelevant novel stimuli. *Cognitive Development, 1,* 53–72.

MARTIN, C. L., & HALVERSON, C. F. (1981). A schematic processing model of sex-typing and stereotyping in children. *Child Development, 49,* 1119–1134.

MASANGKAY, Z. S., McCLUSKEY, K. A., McINTYRE, C. W., SIMS-KNIGHT, J., VAUGHN, B. E., & FLAVELL, J. H. (1974). The early development of inferences about the visual percepts of others. *Child Development, 45,* 357–366.

MASON, M. K. (1942). Learning to speak after six and one-half years of silence. *Journal of Speech Disorders, 7,* 295–304.

MASTEN, A. S. (1986). Humor and competence in school-aged children. *Child Development, 57,* 461–473.

MASUR, E. I., McINTYRE, C. W., & FLAVELL, J. H. (1973). Developmental changes in apportionment of study time among items in a multitrial free recall task. *Journal of Experimental Child Psychology, 15,* 237–246.

MATAS, L., AREND, R. A., & SROUFE, L. A. (1978). Continuity of adaptation in the second year: The relationship between quality of attachment and later competence. *Child Development, 49,* 547–556.

MATHENY, A. P., JR., WILSON, R. S., DOLAN, A. B., & KRANTZ, J. Z. (1981). Behavioral contrasts in twinships: Stability and patterns of differences in childhood. *Child Development, 52,* 579–598.

MAURER, D., & SALAPATEK, P. (1976). Developmental changes in the scanning of faces by young infants. *Child Development, 47,* 523–527.

MAURER, D., SIEGEL, L. S., LEWIS, T. L., KRISTOFFERSON, M. W., BARNES, R. A., & LEVY, B. (1979). Long-term memory improvement? *Child Development, 50,* 106–118.

McCABE, A. E., SIEGEL, L. S., SPENCE, I., & WILKINSON, A. (1982). Class-inclusion reasoning: Patterns of performance from three to eight years. *Child Development, 53,* 780–785.

McCABE, M. A., & UZGIRIS, I. C. (1983). Effects of model and action on imitation in infancy. *Merrill-Palmer Quarterly, 29,* 69–82.

McCALL, R. B. (1981). Nature–nurture and the two realms of development: A proposed integration with respect to mental development. *Child Development, 52,* 1–12.

McCALL, R. B., APPLEBAUM, M. I., & HOGARTY, P. S. (1973). Developmental changes in mental performance. *Monographs of the Society for Research in Child Development*, 38 (Serial No. 150).

McCall, R. B., Eichorn, D. H., & Hogarty, P. S. (1977). Transitions in early mental development. *Monographs of the Society for Research in Child Development*, 42 (Serial No. 171).

McCall, R. B., Hogarty, P. S., & Hurlburt, N. (1972). Transitions in infant sensori-motor development and the prediction of childhood IQ. *American Psychologist*, 27, 728–748.

McCall, R. B., & Kennedy, C. B. (1980). Subjective uncertainty, variability of experience, and the infant's response to discrepancies. *Child Development*, 51, 285–287.

McCall, R. B., Kennedy, C. B., & Applebaum, M. I. (1977). Magnitude of discrepancy and the distribution of attention in infants. *Child Development*, 48, 772–785.

McCall, R. B., Parke, R. D., & Kavanaugh, R. D. (1977). Imitation of live and televised models by children one to three years of age. *Monographs of the Society for Research in Child Development*, 42 (Serial No. 173).

McCarthy, D. (1954). Language development in children. In L. Carmichael (Ed.), *A manual of child psychology* (2nd ed.). New York: Wiley.

McCauley, C., Weil, C. M., & Sperber, R. D. (1976). The development of memory structure as reflected by semantic-priming effects. *Journal of Experimental Child Psychology*, 22, 511–518.

McConaghy, M. J. (1979). Gender permanence and the genital basis of gender: Stages in the development of constancy of gender identity. *Child Development*, 50, 1223–1226.

McCue, M., Bouchard, T. J., Jr., Lykken, D. T., & Feuer, D. (1984). Information processing abilities in twins reared apart. *Intelligence*, 8, 239–258.

McGhee, P. E. (1974). Cognitive mastery and children's humor. *Psychological Bulletin*, 81, 721–730.

McGhee, P. E. (1976). Children's appreciation of humor: A test of the cognitive congruency principle. *Child Development*, 47, 420–426.

McGhee, P. E. (1979). *Humor: Its origins and development*. San Francisco: W. H. Freeman.

McKenzie, B., & Over, R. (1983). Young infants fail to imitate facial and manual gestures. *Infant Behavior and Development*, 6, 85–96.

McNamara, T. P., & Sternberg, R. J. (1983). Mental models of meaning. *Journal of Verbal Learning and Verbal Behavior*, 22, 449–474.

Meeker, M. (1969). *The structure of intellect: Its interpretation and uses*. Columbus, OH: Charles E. Merrill.

Meichenbaum, D. H., & Goodman, J. (1971). Training impulsive children to talk to themselves: A means of developing self-control. *Journal of Abnormal Psychology*, 77, 115–126.

Melkman, R., & Deutsch, C. (1977). Memory functioning as related to developmental changes in bases of organization. *Journal of Experimental Child Psychology*, 23, 84–97.

Meltzoff, A. N. (1985). Immediate and deferred imitation in fourteen- and twenty-four-month-old infants. *Child Development*, 56, 62–72

Meltzoff, A. N., & Borton, R. W. (1979). Intermodal matching by human neonates. *Nature*, 282, 403–404.

Meltzoff, A. N., & Moore, M. K. (1977). Imitation of facial and manual gestures by human neonates. *Science*, 198, 75–78.

Meltzoff, A. N., & Moore, M. K. (1983). Newborns imitate adult facial gestures. *Child Development*, 54, 702–709.

Meltzoff, A. N., & Moore, M. K. (1985). Cognitive foundations and social functions of imitation and intermodal representation in infancy. In J. Mehler & R. Fox (Eds.), *Neonate cognition: Beyond the booming buzzing confusion*. Hillsdale, NJ: Erlbaum.

Mendelson, M. J., & Haith, M. M. (1976). The relation between audition and vision in the human newborn. *Monographs of the Society for Research in Child Development*, 41 (Serial No. 167).

Mervis, C. B., & Crisafi, M. A. (1982). Order of acquisition of subordinate-, basic-, and superordinate-level categories. *Child Development*, 53, 250–266.

Mervis, C. B., & Rosch, E. (1981). Categorization of natural objects. *Annual Review of Psychology*, 32, 89–115.

Messer, D. J., McCarthy, M. E., McQuiston, S., MacTurk, R. H., Yarrow, L. J., & Vietze, P. M. (1986). Relation between mastery behavior in infancy and competence in early childhood. *Developmental Psychology*, 22, 366–372.

Messer, S. B. (1976). Reflection–impulsivity: A review. *Psychological Bulletin*, 83, 1026–1053.

Messer, S. B., & Brodzinsky, D. M. (1981). Three-year stability of reflection–impulsivity in young adolescents. *Developmental Psychology*, 17, 848–850.

Milgram, R. M., & Milgram, N. A. (1976). Group versus individual administration in the measurement of creative thinking in gifted and nongifted children. *Child Development*, 47, 563–565.

Miller, D. J., Ryan, E. B., Aberger, E., McGuire, M. D., Short, E. J., & Kenny, D. A. (1979). Relationships between assessments of habituation and cognitive performance in the early years of life. *International Journal of Behavioral Development*, 2, 159–170.

Miller, L. B., & Bizzell, R. P. (1984). Long-term effects of four preschool programs: Ninth- and tenth-grade results. *Child Development*, 55, 1570–1587.

Miller, L. C., Lechner, R. E., & Rugs, D. (1985). Development of conversational responsiveness: Preschoolers' use of responsive listener cues and relevant comments. *Developmental Psychology, 21,* 473–480.

MILLER, P. H. (1985). Metacognition and attention. In D. L. Forrest-Pressley, G. E. MacKinnon, & T. G. Waller (Eds.), *Metacognition, cognition, and human performance* (Vol. 2). New York: Academic Press.

MILLER, P. H., & HARRIS, Y. R. (in press). Preschoolers' strategies of attention on a same–different task. *Developmental Psychology.*

MILLER, P. H., HAYNES, V. F., DeMARIE-DREBLOW, D., & WOODY-RAMSEY, J. (1986). Children's strategies for gathering information in three tasks. *Child Development, 57,* 1429–1439.

MILLER, P. H., & WEISS, M. G. (1982). Children's and adults' knowledge about what variables affect selective attention. *Child Development, 53,* 543–549.

MILNER, B. (1971). Interhemispheric differences in the localization of psychological processes in man. *British Medical Journal, 27,* 272–277.

MINER, J. B. (1957). *Intelligence in the United States.* New York: Springer.

MIRANDA, S. B., & FANTZ, R. L. (1974). Recognition memory in Down's syndrome and normal infants. *Child Development, 45,* 651–660.

MISCHEL, W. (1970). Sex typing and socialization. In P. H. Mussen (Ed.), *Carmichael's manual of child psychology* (Vol. 2) (3rd ed.). New York: Wiley.

MISTRY, J. J., & LANGE, G. W. (1985). Children's organization and recall of information in scripted narratives. *Child Development, 56,* 953–961.

MITCHELL, C., & AULT, R. L. (1979). Reflection–impulsivity and the evaluation process. *Child Development, 50,* 1043–1049.

MOELY, B. E. (1977). Organizational factors in the development of memory. In R. V. Kail, Jr. & J. W. Hagen (Eds.), *Perspectives on the development of memory and cognition.* Hillsdale, NJ: Erlbaum.

MOELY, B. E., OLSON, F. A., HAWLES, T. G., & FLAVELL, J. H. (1969). Production deficiency in young children's clustered recall. *Developmental Psychology, 1,* 26–34.

MONEY, J., ALEXANDER, D., & WALKER, H. T., JR. (1965). *A standardized road-map test of direction sense.* Baltimore: Johns Hopkins University Press.

MONEY, J., & EHRHARDT, A. A. (1972). *Man and woman, boy and girl.* Baltimore: Johns Hopkins University Press.

MONTEPARE, J. M., & McARTHUR, L. B. (1986). The influence of facial characteristics on children's age perceptions. *Journal of Experimental Child Psychology, 42,* 303–314.

MOORE, J. J., MULLIS, R. L., & MULLIS, A. K. (1986). Examining metamemory within the context of parent–child interactions. *Psychological Reports, 59,* 39–47.

MOORE, T. (1967). Language and intelligence: A longitudinal study of the first eight years. Part 1. Patterns of development in boys and girls. *Human Development, 10,* 88–106.

MORRISON, F. J., HOLMES, D. L., & HAITH M. M. (1974). A developmental study of the effects of familiarity on short-term visual memory. *Journal of Experimental Child Psychology, 18,* 412–425.

MORRISON, F. J., & LORD, C. (1982). Age differences in recall of categorized material: Organization or retrieval? *Journal of Genetic Psychology, 141,* 233–241.

MOSHER, F. A., & HORNSBY, J. R. (1966). On asking questions. In J. S. Bruner, R. R. Olver, & P. M. Greenfield (Eds.), *Studies in cognitive growth.* New York: Wiley.

MOYNAHAN, E. D. (1973). The development of knowledge concerning the effect of categorization upon free recall. *Child Development, 44,* 238–246.

MUNROE, R. H., SHIMMIN, H. S., & MUNROE, R. L. (1984). Gender understanding and sex role preference in four cultures. *Developmental Psychology, 20,* 673–682.

MURCHISON, C., & BORING, E. G. (1952). *A history of psychology in autobiography* (Vol. 4). Worcester, MA: Clark University Press.

MYERS, M., & PARIS, S. G. (1978). Children's metacognitive knowledge about reading. *Journal of Educational Psychology, 70,* 680–690.

MYERS, N. A., CLIFTON, R. K., & CLARKSON, M. G. (1987). When they were very young: Almost threes remember two years ago. *Infant Behavior and Development, 10,* 123–132.

NAKAZIMA, S. (1962). A comparative study of the speech developments of Japanese and American English in children. *Studies in Phonology, 2,* 27–39.

NASH, S. C. (1979). Sex roles as a mediator of intellectual functioning. In M. A. Wittig & A. C. Petersen (Eds.), *Sex-related differences in cognitive functioning.* New York: Academic Press.

NAUS, M. J., & ORNSTEIN, P. A. (1983). Development of memory strategies: Analysis, questions and issues. In M. T. H. Chi (Ed.), *Trends in memory development research: Vol. 9. Contributions to human development.* Basel: S. Karger.

NEIMARK, E., SLOTNIK, N. S., & ULRICH, T. (1971). Development of memorization strategies. *Developmental Psychology, 5,* 427–432.

NEISSER, U. (1979). The concept of intelligence. *Intelligence, 3,* 217–227.

NELSON, K. (1973). Structure and strategy in learning to talk. *Monographs of the Society for Research in Child Development, 38* (Serial No. 149).

NELSON, K. (1974). Variations in children's concepts by age and category. *Child Development, 45,* 577–584.

NELSON, K. (1983). The derivation of concepts and categories from event representatives. In E. K. Scholnick (Ed.), *New trends in conceptual representation: Challenges to Piaget's theory?* Hillsdale, NJ: Erlbaum.

NELSON, K. (1986). *Event knowledge: Structure and function in development.* Hillsdale, NJ: Erlbaum.

NELSON, K., FIVUSH, R., HUDSON, J., & LUCARIELLO, J. (1983). Scripts and the development of memory. In M. T. H. Chi (Ed.), *Trends in memory development research: Vol. 9. Contributions to human development.* Basel: S. Karger.

NELSON, K., & ROSS, G. (1980). The generalities and specifics of long-term memory in infants and young children. In M. Perlmutter (Ed.), *New directions for child development: Children's memory.* San Francisco: Jossey-Bass.

NETTELBECK, T., & KIRBY, N. H. (1983). Measures of timed performance and intelligence. *Intelligence, 7,* 39–52.

NEWCOMBE, N., & BANDURA, M. M. (1983). Effects of age at puberty on spatial ability in girls: A question of mechanism. *Developmental Psychology, 19,* 215–244.

NEWCOMBE, N., BANDURA, M. M., & TAYLOR, D. C. (1983). Sex differences in spatial ability and spatial activities. *Sex Roles, 9,* 377–386.

NEWCOMBE, N., DUBAS, J. S., & MOORE, M. (1985, April). *Association of timing of puberty with spatial ability, lateralization and personality: Do they persist in adulthood?* Paper presented at the meeting of the Society for Research in Child Development, Toronto.

NICHOLS, J. G. (1971). Some effects of testing procedure on divergent thinking. *Child Development, 42,* 1647–1651.

O'CONNOR, J. J., COHEN, S., & PARMELEE, A. H. (1984). Infant auditory discrimination in preterm and full-term infants as a predictor of 5 year intelligence. *Developmental Psychology, 20,* 159–165.

OKONJI, O., & OLAGBAIYE, O. O. (1975). Field dependence and the coordination of perspectives. *Developmental Psychology, 11,* 520.

OLSON, S. L., BATES, J. E., & BAYLES, K. (1984). Mother–infant interactions and the development of individual differences in children's cognitive competence. *Developmental Psychology, 20,* 166–179.

OLVER, R. R., & HORNSBY, J. R. (1966). On equivalence. In J. S. Bruner, R. R. Olver, & P. M. Greenfield (Eds.), *Studies in cognitive growth.* New York: Wiley.

OPPENHEIM, D. (1987, April). *Preschoolers' representations of attachment issues in a doll play interview.* Paper presented at the meeting of the Society for Research in Child Development, Baltimore.

OPPENHEIM, R. W. (1981). Ontogenetic adaptations and retrogressive processes in the development of the nervous system and behavior. In K. J. Connolly & H. F. R. Prechtl (Eds.), *Maturation and development: Biological and psychological perspectives.* Philadelphia: International Medical Publications.

ORNSTEIN, P. A., BAKER-WARD, L., & NAUS, M. J. (1988). The development of mnemonic skill. In M. Weinert & M. Perlmutter (Eds.), *Memory development: Universal changes and individual differences.* Hillsdale, NJ: Erlbaum.

ORNSTEIN, P. A., HALE, G. A., & MORGAN, J. S. (1977). Developmental differences in recall and output organization. *Bulletin of the Psychonomic Society, 9,* 29–32.

ORNSTEIN, P. A., & NAUS, M. J. (1978). Rehearsal processes in children's memory. In P. A. Ornstein (Ed.), *Memory development in children.* Hillsdale, NJ: Erlbaum.

ORNSTEIN, P. A., & NAUS, M. J. (1985). Effects of the knowledge base on children's memory strategies. In H. W. Reese (Ed.), *Advances in child development and behavior* (Vol. 19). New York: Academic Press.

ORNSTEIN, P. A., NAUS, M. J., & LIBERTY, C. (1975). Rehearsal and organizational processes in children's memory. *Child Development, 46,* 818–830.

ORNSTEIN, P. A., NAUS, M. J., & STONE, B. P. (1977). Rehearsal training and developmental differences in memory. *Developmental Psychology, 13,* 15–24.

OWENS, R. E., JR. (1984). *Language development: An introduction.* Columbus, OH: Charles E. Merrill.

PARASKEVOPOULOS, J., & HUNT, J. McV. (1971). Object construction and imitation under differing conditions of rearing. *Journal of Genetic Psychology, 119,* 301–321.

PARIS, S. G. (1973). Comprehension of language connectives and propositional logical relationships. *Journal of Experimental Child Psychology, 16,* 278–291.

PARIS, S. G. (1978). The development of inference and transformation as memory operations. In P. A. Ornstein (Ed.), *Memory development in children.* Hillsdale, NJ: Erlbaum.

PARIS, S. G., & LINDAUER, B. K. (1976). The role of inference in children's comprehension and memory for sentences. *Cognitive Psychology, 8,* 217–227.

PARIS, S. G., & LINDAUER, B. K. (1977). Constructive aspects of children's comprehension and memory. In R. V. Kail, Jr. & J. W. Hagen (Eds.), *Perspectives on the development of memory and cognition.* Hillsdale, NJ: Erlbaum.

PARIS, S. G., NEWMAN, R. S., & McVEY, K. A. (1982). Learning the functional significance of mnemonic actions: A microgenetic study of strategy acquisition. *Journal of Experimental Child Psychology, 34,* 490–509.

PARIS, S. G., & OKA, E. R. (1986). Children's reading strategies, metacognition, and motivation. *Developmental Review, 6,* 25–56.

PARSONS, C. (1960). Inhelder and Piaget's "The growth of logical thinking." II. A logician's viewpoint. *British Journal of Psychology, 51,* 75–84.

PASAMANICK, B., & KNOBLOCH, H. (1966). Retrospective studies on the epidemiology of reproductive causality: Old and new. *Merrill-Palmer Quarterly, 12,* 7–26.

PASCUAL-LEONE, J. (1970). A mathematical model for the transition rule in Piaget's developmental stages. *Acta Psychologia, 32,* 301–345.

PEDERSEN, F. A., & BELL, R. Q. (1970). Sex differences in preschool children without histories of complications of pregnancy and delivery. *Developmental Psychology, 3,* 10–15.

PEPLER, D. J., & ROSS, H. S. (1981). The effects of play on convergent and divergent problem solving. *Child Development, 52,* 1202–1210.

PERLMUTTER, M., & LANGE, G. (1978). A developmental analysis of recall–recognition distinctions. In P. A. Ornstein (Ed.), *Memory development in children.* Hillsdale, NJ: Erlbaum.

PERLMUTTER, M., & MYERS, N. A. (1979). Development of recall in 2- to 4-year-old children. *Developmental Psychology, 15,* 73–83.

PERLMUTTER, M., SCHORK, E. J., & LEWIS, D. (1982). Effects of semantic and perceptual orienting tasks on preschool children's memory. *Bulletin of the Psychonomic Society, 19,* 65–68.

PERRY, D. G., & BUSSEY, K. (1984). *Social development.* Englewood Cliffs, NJ: Prentice-Hall.

PERRY, D. G., WHITE, A. J., & PERRY, L. C. (1984). Does early sex typing result from children's attempts to match their behavior to sex role stereotypes? *Child Development, 55,* 2114–2121.

PETERSEN, A. C. (1976). Physical androgyny and cognitive functioning in adolescence. *Developmental Psychology, 12,* 524–533.

PHILLIPS, S., KING, S., & DuBOIS, L. (1978). Spontaneous activities of female versus male newborns. *Child Development, 49,* 590–597.

PIAGET, J. (1952). *The origins of intelligence in children.* New York: Norton.

PIAGET, J. (1954). *The construction of reality in the child.* New York: Basic Books.

PIAGET, J. (1955). *The language and thought of the child.* New York: World Publishing.

PIAGET, J. (1962). *Play, dreams, and imitation in childhood.* New York: Norton.

PIAGET, J. (1965a). *The child's conception of number.* New York: Norton.

PIAGET, J. (1965b). *The moral judgment of the child.* New York: Free Press.

PIAGET J. (1967). Genesis and structure in the psychology of intelligence. In J. Piaget, *Six psychological studies.* New York: Vintage Book.

PIAGET, J. (1968). *On the development of memory and identity.* Worcester, MA: Clark University Press.

PIAGET, J. (1969a). *The child's conception of the world.* Totowa, NJ: Littlefield & Adams.

PIAGET, J. (1969b). *Judgment and reasoning in the child.* London: Routledge.

PIAGET, J. (1971). *Biology and knowledge.* Chicago: University of Chicago Press.

PIAGET, J., & INHELDER, B. (1967). *The child's conception of space.* New York: Norton.

PIAGET, J., & INHELDER, B. (1969). *The psychology of the child.* New York: Basic Books.

PIAGET, J., & INHELDER, B. (1973). *Memory and intelligence.* New York: Basic Books.

PIEN, D., & ROTHBART, M. K. (1976). Incongruity and resolution in children's humor: A re-examination. *Child Development, 47,* 966–971.

PIEN, D., & ROTHBART, M. K. (1980). Incongruity, humor, play, and self-regulation of arousal in young children. In P. E. McGhee & A. J. Chapman (Eds.), *Children's humor.* Chichester: Wiley.

PLOMIN, R. (1986). Behavioral genetic methods. *Journal of Personality, 54,* 226–261.

PLOMIN, R., & DeFRIES, J. C. (1980). Genetics and intelligence: Recent data. *Intelligence, 4,* 15–24.

PLOMIN, R., & FOCH, T. T. (1981). Sex differences and individual differences. *Child Development, 52,* 383–385.

POSNER, M., BOIES, S., EICHELMAN, W., & TAYLOR, R. (1969). Retention of visual and name codes of single letters. *Journal of Experimental Psychology, 79,* 1–16.

POSNER, M. I., & KEELE, S. W. (1970). Retention of abstract ideas. *Journal of Experimental Psychology, 83,* 304–308.

PRESSLEY, M. (1982). Elaboration and memory development. *Child Development, 53,* 296–309.

PRESSLEY, M., BORKOWSKI, J. G., & O'SULLIVAN, J. T. (1984). Memory strategy instruction is made of this: Metamemory and durable strategy use. *Educational Psychologist, 19,* 94–107.

PRESSLEY, M., FORREST-PRESSLEY, D. L., ELLIOT-FAUST, D., & MILLER, G. (1985). Children's use of cognitive strategies: How to teach strategies, and what to do if they can't be taught. In M. Pressley & C. J. Brainerd (Eds.), *Cognitive learning and memory in children: Progress in cognitive development research.* New York: Springer.

PRESSLEY, M., & LEVIN, J. R. (1977). Task parameters affecting the efficacy of a visual imagery learning strategy in younger and older children. *Journal of Experimental Child Psychology, 24,* 53–59.

PUFALL, P. B., SHAW, R. E., & SYRDAL-LASKY, A. (1973). Development of number conservation: An examination of some predictions from Piaget's stage analysis and equilibration model. *Child Development, 44,* 21–27.

QUINE, W. V. (1972). *Methods of logic.* New York: Holt, Rinehart & Winston.

RABINOWITZ, M. (1985, April). *An alternative approach to memory development.* Paper presented at the meeting of the Society for Research in Child Development, Toronto.

RABINOWITZ, M., & CHI, M. T. H. (1987). An interactive model of strategic processing. In S. J. Ceci (Ed.), *Handbook of cognitive, social, and neuro-psychological aspects of learning disabilities.* Hillsdale, NJ: Erlbaum.

RABINOWITZ, M., & MANDLER, J. M. (1983). Organization and information retrieval. *Journal of Experi-*

mental Psychology: Learning, Memory and Cognition, 9, 430–439.

RADER, N., SPIRO, D. J., & FIRESTONE, P. B. (1979). Performance on a stage IV object-permanence task with standard and nonstandard covers. *Child Development, 50,* 908–910.

RAMEY, C. T., CAMPBELL, F. A., & FINKELSTEIN, N. W. (1984). Course and structure of intellectual development in children at risk for developmental retardation. In P. H. Brooks, R. Sperber, & C. McCauley (Eds.), *Learning and cognition in the mentally retarded.* Hillsdale, NJ: Erlbaum.

RAMEY, C. T., YEATES, K. O., & SHORT, E. J. (1984). The plasticity of intellectual development: Insights from preventive intervention. *Child Development, 55,* 1913–1925.

RAYMOND, C. L., & BENBOW, C. P. (1986). Gender differences in mathematics: A function of parental support and student sex typing? *Developmental Psychology, 22,* 808–819.

REESE, H. W. (1962). Verbal mediation as a function of age level. *Psychological Bulletin, 59,* 502–509.

REINISCH, J. M. (1974). Fetal hormones, the brain and human sex differences: A heuristic, integrative review of the recent literature. *Archives of Sexual Behavior, 3,* 51–90.

REINISCH, J. M., GANDELMAN, R., & SPEIGEL, F. S. (1979). Prenatal influence on cognitive abilities: Data from experimental animals and human genetic and endocrine syndromes. In M. A. Wittig & A. C. Petersen (Eds.), *Sex-related differences in cognitive functioning.* New York: Academic Press.

RESNICK, L. B. (1983). A developmental theory of number understanding. In H. P. Ginsberg (Ed.), *The development of mathematical thinking.* New York: Academic Press.

REVELLE, G. L., WELLMAN, H. M., & KARABENICK, J. D. (1985). Comprehension monitoring in preschool children. *Child Development, 56,* 654–663.

REYNOLDS, C. R., KALTSOUNIS, B., & TORRANCE, E. P. (1979). A children's form of your style of learning and thinking: Preliminary norms and technical data. *Gifted Child Quarterly, 23,* 757–766.

REZNICK, J. S., & KAGAN, J. (1983). Category detection in infancy. In L. P. Lipsitt & C. K. Rovee-Collier (Eds.), *Advances in infancy research* (Vol. 2). Norwood, NJ: Ablex.

RHEINGOLD, H. L. (1985). Development as the acquisition of familiarity. *Annual Review of Psychology, 36,* 1–17.

RHEINGOLD, H. L., HAY, D. F., & WEST, M. J. (1976). Sharing in the second year of life. *Child Development, 47,* 1148–1158.

RICE, M. L., & KEMPER, S. (1984). *Child language and cognition: Contemporary issues.* Baltimore: University Park Press.

RICHMAN, C. L., NIDA, S., & PITTMAN, L. (1976). Effects of meaningfulness on child free-recall learning. *Developmental Psychology, 12,* 460–465.

RILEY, C. A. (1976). The representation of comparative relations and the transitive inference task. *Journal of Experimental Child Psychology, 22,* 1–22.

RILEY, C. A., & TRABASSO, T. (1974). Comparatives, logical structures, and encoding in a transitive inference task. *Journal of Experimental Child Psychology, 17,* 187–203.

RINGEL, B. A., & SPRINGER, C. J. (1980). On knowing how well one is remembering: The persistence of strategy use during transfer. *Journal of Experimental Child Psychology, 29,* 322–333.

ROBERTS, K., & HOROWITZ, F. D. (1986). Basic level categorization in seven- and nine-month-old infants. *Journal of Child Language, 13,* 191–206.

ROBERTSON, J., & ROBERTSON, J. (1971). Young children in brief separation: A fresh look. *Psychoanalytic Study of the Child, 26,* 264–315.

RODGERS, J. L. (1984). Confluence effects: Not here, not now! *Developmental Psychology, 20,* 321–331.

RODGERS, J. L., & ROWE, D. C. (1985). Does continuity breed similarity? A within-family analysis of nonshared sources of IQ differences between siblings. *Developmental Psychology, 21,* 743–746.

ROE, K. V., DRIVAS, A., KARAGELLIS, A., & ROE, A. (1985). Sex differences in vocal interaction with mother and stranger in Greek infants: Some cognitive implications. *Developmental Psychology, 21,* 372–377.

ROGOFF, B. (1981). Schooling's influence on memory test performance. *Child Development, 52,* 260–267.

ROGOFF, B., ELLIS, S., & GARDNER, W. (1984). Adjustment of adult–child instruction according to child's age and task. *Developmental Psychology, 20,* 193–199.

ROGOFF, B., NEWCOMBE, N., & KAGAN, J. (1974). Planfulness and recognition memory. *Child Development, 45,* 972–977.

ROHWER, W. D., JR., & LITROWNIK, J. (1983). Age and individual differences in the learning of a memorization procedure. *Journal of Educational Psychology, 75,* 799–810.

ROHWER, W. D., JR., RAINES, J. M., EOFF, J., & WAGNER, M. (1977). The development of elaborative propensity during adolescence. *Journal of Experimental Child Psychology, 23,* 472–492.

ROLLINS, H. A., JR. (1979, April). *The relationship of mother's teaching style to children's response, family socioeconomic status, and cognitive competence.* Paper presented at the meeting of the Southeastern Psychological Association, New Orleans.

ROSCH, E. (1973). On the internal structure of perceptual and semantic categories. In T. E. Moore (Ed.), *Cognitive development and the acquisition of language.* New York: Academic Press.

ROSCH, E. (1975). Cognitive representations of semantic categories. *Journal of Experimental Psychology: General, 7,* 192–233.

ROSCH, E., & MERVIS, C. B. (1975). Family resemblances: Studies in the internal structure of categories. *Cognitive Psychology, 7,* 573–605.

ROSCH, E., MERVIS, C. B., GRAY, W. D., JOHNSON, D. M., & BOYES-BRAEM, P. (1976). Basic objects in natural categories. *Cognitive Psychology, 8,* 382–439.

ROSE, D. H., SLATER, A., & PERRY, H. (1986). Prediction of children's intelligence from habituation in early infancy. *Intelligence, 10,* 251–263.

ROSE, S. A. (1980). Enhancing visual recognition memory in preterm infants. *Developmental Psychology, 16,* 85–92.

ROSE, S. A., GOTTFRIED, A. W., & BRIDGER, W. H. (1981). Cross-modal transfer in 6-month-old infants. *Developmental Psychology, 17,* 661–669.

ROSE, S. A., GOTTFRIED, A. W., & BRIDGER, W. H. (1983). Infants' cross-modal transfer from solid objects to their graphic representations. *Child Development, 54,* 686–694.

ROSE, S. A., & WALLACE, I. F. (1985a). Cross-modal and intramodal transfer as predictors of mental development in full-term and preterm infants. *Developmental Psychology, 21,* 949–962.

ROSE, S. A., & WALLACE, I. F. (1985b). Visual recognition memory: A predictor of later cognitive functioning in preterms. *Child Development, 56,* 843–856.

ROSENTHAL, R., & RUBIN, D. B. (1982). Further meta-analytic procedures for assessing cognitive gender differences. *Journal of Educational Psychology, 74,* 708–712.

ROTH, C. (1983). Factors affecting developmental changes in the speed of processing. *Journal of Experimental Child Psychology, 35,* 509–528.

ROTTER, D. M., LANGLAND, L., & BERGER, D. (1971). The validity of tests of creative thinking in seven-year-old children. *Gifted Child Quarterly, 43,* 471–480.

ROVEE-COLLIER, C. K., & FAGEN, J. W. (1981). The retrieval of memory in early infancy. In L. P. Lipsitt & C. K. Rovee-Collier (Eds.), *Advances in infancy research* (Vol. 1). Norwood, NJ: Ablex.

ROVET, J. (1983). Cognitive and neuropsychological test performance of persons with abnormalities of adolescent development: A test of Waber's hypothesis. *Child Development, 54,* 941–950.

ROVET, J., & NETLEY, C. (1982). Processing deficits in Turners syndrome. *Developmental Psychology, 18,* 77–94.

ROVET, J., & NETLEY, C. (1983). The triple X chromosome syndrome in childhood: Recent empirical findings. *Child Development, 54,* 831–845.

RUBIN, K. H., & KRASNOR, L. R. (1986). Social cognitive and social behavior perspectives on problem solving. In M. Perlmutter (Ed.), *Minnesota symposium on child psychology* (Vol. 18). Hillsdale, NJ: Erlbaum.

RUBLE, D. N., BALABAN, T., & COOPER, J. (1981). Gender constancy and the effects of sex-typed televised toy commercials. *Child Development, 52,* 667–673.

RUFF, H. A., & BIRCH, H. G. (1974). Infant visual fixation: The effect of concentricity, curvilinearity, and number of directions. *Journal of Experimental Child Psychology, 17,* 460–473.

RUSHTON, J. P., BRAINERD, C. J., & PRESSLEY, M. (1983). Behavioral development and construct validity: The principle of aggregation. *Psychological Bulletin, 94,* 18–38.

RUSSELL, R., & DENNIS, W. (1939). Studies in animism. I. A standardized procedure for the investigation of animism. *Journal of Genetic Psychology, 55,* 389–400.

SABIN, E. J., CLEMMER, E. J., O'CONNELL, D. C., & KOWAL, S. (1979). A pausological approach to speech development. In A. W. Siegman & S. Feldstein (Eds.), *Of speech and time: Temporal speech patterns in interpersonal contexts.* Hillsdale, NJ: Erlbaum.

SALAPATEK, P. (1975). Pattern perception in early infancy. In L. B. Cohen & P. Salapatek (Eds.), *Infant perception: From sensation to cognition* (Vol. 1). New York: Academic Press.

SALAPATEK, P., & KESSEN, W. (1966). Visual scanning of triangles by the human newborn. *Journal of Experimental Child Psychology, 3,* 155–167.

SALATAS, H., & FLAVELL, J. H. (1976). Behavioral and metamnemonic indicators of strategic behavior under remember instructions in first grade. *Child Development, 47,* 81–89.

SALKIND, N. J., & NELSON, C. F. (1980). A note on the developmental nature of reflection–impulsivity. *Developmental Psychology, 16,* 237–238.

SALKIND, N. J., & WRIGHT, J. C. (1977). The development of reflection–impulsivity and cognitive efficiency. *Human Development, 20,* 377–387.

SALTZ, E., CAMPBELL, S., & SKOTKO, D. (1983). Verbal control of behavior: The effects of shouting. *Developmental Psychology, 19,* 461–464.

SALTZ, E., SOLLER, E., & SIGEL, I. E. (1972). The development of natural language concepts. *Child Development, 43,* 1191–1202.

SAMEROFF, A. J. (1975). Early influences on development: Fact or fancy? *Merrill-Palmer Quarterly, 21,* 267–294.

SAMEROFF, A. J., & CHANDLER, M. J. (1975). Reproductive risk and the continuum of caretaking causality. In F. D. Horowitz (Ed.), *Review of child development research* (Vol. 4). Chicago: University of Chicago Press.

SAMUEL, A. G. (1978). Organizational vs. retrieval factors in the development of digit span. *Journal of Experimental Child Psychology, 26,* 308–319.

SAMUELS, C. A., & EWY, R. (1985). Aesthetic perception of faces during infancy. *British Journal of Developmental Psychology, 3,* 221–228.

SANDERS, B., & SOARES, M. P. (1986). Sexual maturation and spatial ability in college students. *Developmental Psychology, 22,* 199–203.

SAXE, G. B. (1979). Developmental relations between notational counting and number conversation. *Child Development, 50,* 180–187.

SCARR, S., & MCCARTNEY, K. (1983). How people make their own environments: A theory of genotype→environment effects. *Child Development, 54,* 424–435.

SCARR, S., & WEINBERG, R. A. (1976). IQ test performance of black children adopted by white families. *American Psychologist, 31,* 726–739.

SCARR, S., & WEINBERG, R. A. (1978). The influence of "family background" on intellectual attainment. *American Sociological Review, 43,* 674–692.

SCARR, S., & WEINBERG, R. A. (1983). The Minnesota Adoption Studies: Genetic differences and malleability. *Child Development, 54,* 260–267.

SCARR-SALAPATEK, S. (1976). An evolutionary perspective on infant intelligence: Species pattern and individual variations. In M. Lewis (Ed.), *Origins of intelligence.* New York: Plenum.

SCARR-SALAPATEK, S., & SALAPATEK, P. (1970). Patterns of fear development during infancy. *Merrill-Palmer Quarterly, 16,* 86–99.

SCHAFFER, H. R., & EMERSON, P. E. (1964). The development of social attachments in infancy. *Monographs of the Society for Research in Child Development, 29* (Serial No. 94).

SCHANK, R. C., & ABELSON, R. P. (1977). *Scripts, plans, goals and understanding.* Hillsdale, NJ: Erlbaum.

SCHIFF, A. R., & KNOPF, I. J. (1985). The effect of task demands on attention allocation in children of different ages. *Child Development, 56,* 621–630.

SCHMIDT, C. R., & SCHMIDT, S. R. (1986). The use of themes as retrieval cues in children's memory for stories. *Journal of Experimental Child Psychology, 42,* 237–255.

SCHNEIDER, W. (1985). Developmental trends in the metamemory–memory behavior relationship: An integrated review. In D. L. Forrest-Pressley, G. E. MacKinnon, & T. G. Waller (Eds.), *Cognition, metacognition, and human performance* (Vol. 1). New York: Academic Press.

SCHNEIDER, W. (1986). The role of conceptual knowledge and metamemory in the development of organizational processes in memory. *Journal of Experimental Child Psychology, 42,* 318–336.

SCHNEIDER, W., KORKEL, J., & WEINERT, F. E. (1987, April). *The knowledge base and memory performance: A comparison of academically successful and unsuccessful learners.* Paper presented at the meeting of the American Educational Research Association, Washington, DC.

SCHWANENFLUGEL, P. J., GUTH, M. E., & BJORKLUND, D. F. (1986). A developmental trend in the understanding of concept attribute importance. *Child Development, 57,* 421–430.

SCHWARTZ, M., & DAY, R. H. (1979). Visual shape per-

ception in early infancy. *Monographs of the Society for Research in Child Development, 44* (Serial No. 182).

SCOTT, J. P. (1968). *Early experience and the organization of behavior.* Belmont, CA: Brooks/Cole.

SCOTT, M. S., GREENFIELD, D. B., & STERENTAL, E. (1986). Abstract categorization ability as a predictor of learning disability classification. *Intelligence, 10,* 377–387.

SCOTT, M. S., SERCHUK, R., & MUNDY, P. (1982). Taxonomic and complementary picture pairs: Ability in two- to five-year-olds. *International Journal of Behavioral Development, 5,* 243–256.

SELLS, L. W. (1974). Critical points for affirmative action. In L. W. Sells (Ed.), *Toward affirmative action: New directions for institutional research.* San Francisco: Jossey-Bass.

SELMAN, R. L. (1976). Social-cognitive understanding: A guide to educational and clinical practice. In T. Lickona (Ed.), *Moral development and behavior.* New York: Holt, Rinehart & Winston.

SELMAN, R. L., SCHORIN, M. Z., STONE, C. R., & PHELPS, E. (1983). A naturalistic study of children's social understanding. *Developmental Psychology, 19,* 82–102.

SERBIN, L. A., & SPRAFKIN, C. (1986). The saliency of gender and the process of sex typing in three- to seven-year-old children. *Child Development, 57,* 1188–1199.

SHANTZ, C. U. (1975). The development of social cognition. In E. M. Hetherington (Ed.), *Review of child development research* (Vol. 3). New York: Wiley.

SHANTZ, C. U. (1983). Social cognition. In J. H. Flavell & E. M. Markman (Eds.), *Cognitive development: Vol. 3.* P. H. Mussen (Gen. Ed.), *Handbook of child psychology* (4th ed.). New York: Wiley.

SHAPIRO, S. I., & MOELY, B. E. (1971). Free recall, subjective organization, and learning to learn at three age levels. *Psychonomic Science, 23,* 189–191.

SHARP, D., COLE, M., & LAVE, C. (1979). Education and cognitive development: The evidence from experimental research. *Monographs of the Society for Research in Child Development, 44* (Serial No. 170).

SHATZ, M. (1983). Communication. In J. H. Flavell & E. M. Markman (Eds.), *Cognitive development: Vol. 3.* P. H. Mussen (Gen. Ed.), *Handbook of child psychology* (4th ed.), New York: Wiley.

SHATZ, M., & GELMAN, R. (1973). The development of communication skills. *Monographs of the Society for Research in Child Development, 38* (Serial No. 152).

SHEINGOLD, K. (1973). Developmental differences in intake and storage of visual information. *Journal of Experimental Child Psychology, 16,* 1–11.

SHEINGOLD, K., & TENNEY, Y. (1982). Memory for a salient childhood event. In U. Neisser (Ed.), *Memory observed: Remembering in natural contexts.* San Francisco: W. H. Freeman.

SHEPARD, R. N. (1967). Recognition memory for words, sentences, and pictures. *Journal of Verbal Learning and Verbal Behavior, 6,* 156–163.

SHERMAN, J. A. (1978). *Sex-related cognitive differences: An essay on theory and evidence.* Springfield, IL: Charles C Thomas.

SHIFFRIN, R. M., & SCHNEIDER, W. (1977). Controlled and automatic human information processing. II. Perceptual learning, automatic attending, and a general theory. *Psychological Review, 84,* 127–190.

SHIRLEY, M. M. (1933). *The first two years: A study of 25 babies* (Vol. 2) (Institute of Child Welfare Monograph Series No. 7). Minneapolis: University of Minnesota Press.

SHULTZ, T. R. (1972). Role of incongruity and resolution in children's appreciation of cartoon humor. *Journal of Experimental Child Psychology, 13,* 456–477.

SHULTZ, T. R., & HORIBE, F. (1974). Development of the appreciation of verbal jokes. *Developmental Psychology, 10,* 13–20.

SHULTZ, T. R., & PILON, R. (1973). Development of the ability to detect linguistic ambiguity. *Child Development, 44,* 728–733.

SHULTZ, T. R., & ROBILLARD, J. (1980). The development of linguistic humor in children: Incongruity through rule violation. In P. E. McGhee & A. J. Chapman (Eds.), *Children's humor.* Chichester: Wiley.

SIEGEL, A. W., & SCHADLER, M. (1977). The development of young children's spatial representations of their classrooms. *Child Development, 48,* 388–394.

SIEGEL, L. S., McCABE, A. E., BRAND, A. J., & MATHEWS, J. (1978). Evidence for the understanding of class inclusion in preschool children: Linguistic factors and training effects. *Child Development, 49,* 688–693.

SIEGELMAN, E. Y. (1969). Reflective and impulsive observing behavior. *Child Development, 40,* 1213–1222.

SIEGLER, R. S. (1981). Developmental sequences within and between concepts. *Monographs of the Society for Research in Child Development, 46* (Series No. 189).

SIEGLER, R. S. (1983). How knowledge influences learning. *American Scientist, 71,* 631–683.

SIEGLER, R. S. (1986). *Children's thinking.* Englewood Cliffs, NJ: Prentice-Hall.

SIEGLER, R. S. (1987). The perils of averaging data over strategies: An example from children's addition. *Journal of Experimental Psychology: General, 116,* 250–264.

SIEGLER, R. S., & LIEBERT, R. M. (1972). Effects of presenting relevant rules and complete feedback on the conservation of liquid quantity task. *Developmental Psychology, 7,* 133–138.

SIEGLER, R. S., ROBINSON, M., LIEBERT, D. E., & LIEBERT, R. M. (1973). Inhelder and Piaget's pendulum problem: Teaching preadolescents to act as scientists. *Developmental Psychology, 9,* 97–101.

SIEGLER, R. S., & SHRAGER, J. (1984). Strategy choices in addition and subtraction: How do children know what to do? In C. Sophian (Ed.), *Origins of cognitive skills.* Hillsdale, NJ: Erlbaum.

SIGEL, I. E. (1953). Developmental trends in the abstraction ability of children. *Child Development, 24,* 131–144.

SIGMAN, M. (1983). Individual differences in infant attention: Relations to birth status and intelligence at five years. In T. Field & A. Sostek (Eds.), *Infants born at risk: Physiological, perceptual, and cognitive processes.* New York: Grune & Stratton.

SKEELS, H. M. (1966). Adult status of children with contrasting early life experiences. *Monographs of the Society for Research in Child Development, 31* (Serial No. 105).

SKEELS, H. M., & DYE, H. B. (1939). A study of the effects of differential stimulation on mentally retarded children. *Program of the American Association of Mental Deficiency, 44,* 114–136.

SKODAK, M., & SKEELS, H. M. (1945). A follow-up study of children in adoptive homes. *Journal of Genetic Psychology, 66,* 21–58.

SLABY, R. G., & FREY, K. S. (1975). Development of gender constancy and selective attention to same-sex models. *Child Development, 46,* 849–856.

SLATER, A., EARLE, D. C., MORISON, V., & ROSE, D. (1985). Pattern preferences at birth and their interaction with habituation-induced novelty preferences. *Journal of Experimental Child Psychology, 39,* 37–54.

SLATER, A. M., & KINGSTON, D. J. (1981). Competence and performance variables in the assessment of formal operational skills. *British Journal of Educational Psychology, 51,* 163–169.

SLOBIN, D. I. (1970). Universals of grammatical development in children. In G. B. Flores, J. Arcais, & W. J. M. Levelt (Eds.), *Advances in psycholinguistics.* Amsterdam: North-Holland Publishing.

SMILEY, S. S., & BROWN, A. L. (1979). Conceptual preference for thematic or taxonomic relations: A nonmonotonic age trend from preschool to old age. *Journal of Experimental Child Psychology, 28,* 249–257.

SMITH, C. L. (1979). Children's understanding of natural language categories. *Journal of Experimental Child Psychology, 30,* 191–205.

SMITH, E., SHOBEN, E., & RIPS, L. (1974). Structure and process in semantic memory: A featural model for semantic decisions. *Psychological Review, 81,* 214–241.

SMITH, L. B. (1983). Development of classification: The use of similarity and dimensional relations. *Journal of Experimental Child Psychology, 36,* 150–178.

SMITH, L. B., & KEMLER, D. G. (1977). Developmental trends in free classification: Evidence for a new conceptualization of perceptual development. *Journal of Experimental Child Psychology, 24,* 279–298.

SODIAN, B., SCHNEIDER, W., & PERLMUTTER, M. (1986). Recall, clustering, and metamemory in young children. *Journal of Experimental Child Psychology, 41,* 395–410.

SOLKOFF, N., YAFFE, S., WEINTRAUB, D., & BLASE, B. (1969). Effects of handling on the subsequent development of preterm infants. *Developmental Psychology, 1,* 765–768.

SONNENSCHEIN, S. (1986). Development of referential communication: Deciding that a message is informative. *Developmental Psychology, 22,* 164–168.

SONSTROEM, A. M. (1966). On the conservation of solids. In J. S. Bruner, R. R. Olver, & P. M. Greenfield (Eds.), *Studies in cognitive growth.* New York: Wiley.

SOPHIAN, C. (1980). Habituation is not enough: Novelty preferences, search, and memory in infancy. *Merrill-Palmer Quarterly, 26,* 239–257.

SOPHIAN, C. (1985). Perseveration and infants' search: A comparison of two- and three-location tasks. *Developmental Psychology, 21,* 187–194.

SPEAR, N. E. (1984). Ecologically determined dispositions control the ontogeny of learning and memory. In R. V. Kail, Jr. & N. E. Spear (Eds.), *Comparative perspectives on the development of memory.* Hillsdale, NJ: Erlbaum.

SPEARMAN, C. (1927). *The abilities of man.* New York: Macmillan.

SPELKE, E. S. (1976). Infants' intermodal perception of events. *Cognitive Psychology, 5,* 553–560.

SPERBER, R. D., DAVIES, D., MERRILL, E. C., & McCAULEY, C. (1982). Cross-category differences in the processing of superordinate–subordinate relationships. *Child Development, 53,* 1249–1253.

SPERLING, G. (1960). The information available in brief visual presentations. *Psychological Monographs, 74,* No. 11.

SPITZ, H. H., & BORYS, S. V. (1984). Depth of search: How far can retarded search through an internally represented problem space? In P. H. Brooks, R. Sperber, & C. McCauley (Eds.), *Learning and cognition in the mentally retarded.* Hillsdale, NJ: Erlbaum.

SPITZ, R. (1945). Hospitalism: An inquiry into the genesis of psychiatric conditions in early childhood. *Psychoanalytic Study of the Child, 1,* 53–74.

SPRINGER, S. P., & DEUTSCH, G. (1985). *Left brain, right brain* (2nd ed). New York: W. H. Freeman.

STARK, R. (1978). Features of infant sounds: The emergence of cooing. *Journal of Child Language, 5,* 1–12.

STARKEY, P., & GELMAN, R. (1982). The development of addition and subtraction abilities prior to formal schooling in arithmetic. In T. P. Carpenter, J. M. Moser, & T. A. Romberg (Eds.), *Addition and subtraction: A cognitive perspective.* Hillsdale, NJ: Erlbaum.

STEIN, N. L., & GLENN, C. G. (1979). An analysis of story comprehension in elementary school children. In R. O. Freedle (Ed.), *New directions in discourse processes* (Vol. 2). Norwood, NJ: Ablex.

STEIN, N. L., & MANDLER, J. M. (1975). Development of detection and recognition orientation of geometric and real figures. *Child Development, 46,* 379–388.

STEINBERG, E. R., & ANDERSON, R. C. (1975). Hierarchical semantic organization in 6-year-olds. *Journal of Experimental Child Psychology, 19,* 544–553.

STEINER, J. E. (1979). Human facial expressions in response to taste and smell stimulation. In H. W. Reese & L. P. Lipsitt (Eds.), *Advances in child development and behavior* (Vol. 13). New York: Academic Press.

STERN, D. N., SPIEKER, S., & MACKAIN, K. (1982). Intonation contours as signals in maternal speech to prelinguistic infants. *Developmental Psychology, 18,* 727–735.

STERNBERG, R. J. (1977). *Intelligence, information processing, and analogical reasoning: The componential analysis of human abilities.* Hillsdale, NJ: Erlbaum.

STERNBERG, R. J. (1980). Sketch of a componential subtheory of human intelligence. *Behavioral and Brain Sciences, 3,* 578.

STERNBERG, R. J. (1984). The Kaufman Assessment Battery for Children: An information processing analysis and critique. *Journal of Special Education, 18,* 267–279.

STERNBERG, R. J. (1985). *Beyond IQ: A triarchic theory of human intelligence.* Cambridge, England: Cambridge University Press.

STERNBERG, R. J., CONWAY, B. E., KETRON, J. L., & BERNSTEIN, M. (1981). People's conceptions of intelligence. *Journal of Personality and Social Psychology, 41,* 37–55.

STERNBERG, R. J., & SLATER, W. (1982). Conceptions of intelligence. In R. J. Sternberg (Ed.), *Handbook of human intelligence,* Cambridge, England: Cambridge University Press.

STERNBERG, S. (1969). High-speed scanning in human memory. *Science, 153,* 652–654.

STEVENSON, H. W., PARKER, T., WILKINSON, A., BONNEVAUX, B., & GONZALEZ, M. (1978). Schooling, environment, and cognitive development: A cross-cultural study. *Monographs of the Society for Research in Child Development, 43* (Serial No. 175).

STOBER, S. F. (1985, April). *A metacognitive perspective of conceptual tempo.* Paper presented at the meeting of the Society for Research in Child Development, Toronto.

STODDART, T., & TURIEL, E. (1985). Children's concepts of cross-gender activities. *Child Development, 56,* 1241–1252.

STONE, C. A., & DAY, M. C. (1978). Levels of availability of a formal operational strategy. *Child Development, 49,* 1054–1065.

STONE, L. J., & CHURCH, J. (1973). *Childhood and adolescence: A psychology of the growing person.* New York: Random House.

STRAUSS, M. S. (1981, April). *Infant memory of prototypical information.* Paper presented at the meeting of the Society for Research in Child Development, Boston.

SULLIVAN, M. W., ROVEE-COLLIER, C. K., & TYNES, D. M. (1979). A conditioning analysis of infant long-term memory. *Child Development, 50,* 152–162.

SUOMI, S., & HARLOW, H. (1972). Social rehabilitation of isolate-reared monkeys. *Developmental Psychology, 6,* 487–496.

TANNER, J. M. (1962). *Growth at adolescence.* Oxford: Blackwell Scientific Publications.

TANNER, J. M. (1970). Physical growth. In P. H. Mussen (Ed.), *Carmichael's manual of child psychology* (Vol. 1) (3rd ed.). New York: Wiley.

TATARSKY, J. H. (1974). The influence of dimensional manipulations on class-inclusion performance. *Child Development, 45,* 1173–1175.

TAYLOR, M., & FLAVELL, J. H. (1984). Seeing and believing: Children's understanding of the distinction between appearance and reality. *Child Development, 55,* 1710–1720.

TERMAN, L. M., & MERRILL, M. A. (1937). *Measuring intelligence.* Boston: Houghton Mifflin.

THOMAS, H., JAMISON, W., & HUMMEL, D. D. (1973). Observation is insufficient for discovering that the surface of still water is invariantly horizontal. *Science, 101,* 173–174.

THOMPSON, J. G. (1941). The ability of children of different grade levels to generalize on sorting tests. *Journal of Psychology, 11,* 119–126.

THORNDIKE, R. L., HAGEN, E. P., & SATTLER, J. M. (1986). *The Stanford-Binet Intelligence Scale: Guide for administering and scoring* (4th ed.). Chicago: Riverside.

THURSTONE, L. L. (1938). *Primary mental abilities.* Chicago: University of Chicago Press.

TIGHE, T. J., TIGHE, L. S., & SCHECHTER, J. (1975). Memory for instances and categories in children and adults. *Journal of Experimental Child Psychology, 20,* 22–37.

TINBERGEN, N. (1951). *The study of instinct.* New York: Oxford University Press.

TINSLEY, V. S., & WATERS, H. S. (1982). The development of verbal control over motor behavior: A replication and extension of Luria's findings. *Child Development, 53,* 746–753.

TORGESEN, J. K. (1977). Memorization processes in reading-disabled children. *Journal of Educational Psychology, 79,* 571–578.

TORRANCE, E. P. (1966). *Torrance tests of creative thinking.* Princeton, NJ: Personnel Press.

TORRANCE, E. P. (1972). Predictive validity of the Torrance tests of creative thinking. *Journal of Creative Behavior, 6,* 236–252.

TORRANCE, E. P. (1975). Creativity research in education: Still alive. In I. A. Taylor & J. W. Getzels (Eds.), *Perspectives in creativity.* Chicago: Aldine.

TORRANCE, E. P. (1982). Hemisphericity and creative functioning. *Journal of Research and Development in Education, 15,* 29–37.

TORRANCE, E. P., & MOURAD, S. (1979). Role of hemisphericity in performance on selected measures of creativity. *Gifted Child Quarterly, 23,* 44–55.

TORRANCE, E. P., & REYNOLDS, C. R. (1978). Images of the future of gifted adolescents: Effects of alienation and specialized cerebral functioning. *Gifted Child Quarterly, 22,* 40–54.

TORRANCE, E. P., REYNOLDS, C. R., RIEGEL, T., & BALL, O. (1977). Your style of learning and thinking, Forms A and B: Preliminary norms, abbreviated technical notes, scoring keys, and selected references. *Gifted Child Quarterly, 21,* 563–557.

TRABASSO, T. (1975). Representation, memory, and reasoning: How do we make transitive inferences? In A. D. Pick (Ed.), *Minnesota symposia on child psychology* (Vol. 9). Minneapolis: University of Minnesota Press.

TRABASSO, T., RILEY, C. A., & WILSON, E. G. (1975). The representation of linear order and spatial strategies in reasoning: A developmental study. In R. J. Falmagne (Ed.), *Reasoning: Representation and process.* Hillsdale, NJ: Erlbaum.

TREHUB, S. E. (1976). The discrimination of foreign speech contrasts by infants and adults. *Child Development, 47,* 466–472.

TREHUB, S. E., SCHNEIDER, B. A., & ENDMAN, M. (1980). Developmental changes in infants' sensitivity to octave-band noises. *Journal of Experimental Child Psychology, 29,* 282–293.

TREVARTHEN, C. (1977). Descriptive analyses of infant communicative behavior. In H. R. Schaffer (Ed.), *Studies in mother–infant interaction.* London: Academic Press.

TULKIN, S. R., & KAGAN, J. (1972). Mother–child interaction in the first year of life. *Child Development, 43,* 31–41.

TULVING, E. (1972). Episodic and semantic memory. In E. Tulving & W. Donaldson (Eds.), *Organization of memory.* New York: Academic Press.

TULVING, E. (1985). How many memory systems are there? *American Psychologist, 40,* 385–398.

TVERSKY, A., & KAHNEMAN, D. (1983). Extensional versus intuitive reasoning: The conjunction fallacy in probability judgment. *Psychological Review, 90,* 293–315.

URBERG, K. A., & DOCHERTY, E. M. (1976). Development of role-taking skills in young children. *Developmental Psychology, 12,* 198–203.

UYEDA, K. M., & MANDLER, G. (1980). Prototypicality norms for 28 semantic categories. *Behavior Research Methods and Instrumentation, 12,* 567–595.

UZGIRIS, I. C. (1964). Situational generality of conservation. *Child Development, 35,* 831–841.

UZGIRIS, I. C. (1973). Patterns of cognitive development in infancy. *Merrill-Palmer Quarterly, 19,* 181–204.

UZGIRIS, I. C. (1983). Organization of sensorimotor intelligence. In M. Lewis (Ed.), *Origins of intelligence: Infancy and early childhood* (2nd ed.). New York: Plenum.

UZGIRIS, I. C. (1984). Imitation in infancy: Its interpersonal aspects. In M. Perlmutter (Ed.), *Minnesota symposia on child psychology* (Vol. 17). Hillsdale, NJ: Erlbaum.

UZGIRIS, I. C., & HUNT, J. McV. (1975). *Assessment in infancy: Ordinal scales of psychological development.* Urbana: University of Illinois Press.

VALLE, J. D., DUNN, K., DUNN, R., GEISERT, G., SINATRA, R., & ZENHAUSERN, R. (1986). The effects of matching and mismatching students' mobility preferences on recognition and memory tasks. *Journal of Educational Research, 79,* 267–272.

VANDENBERG, S. G. (1969). A twin study of spatial ability. *Multivariate Behavioral Research, 4,* 273–294.

VANDER LINDE, E., MORRONGIELLO, B. A., & ROVEE-COLLIER, C. (1985). Determinants of retention in 8-week-old infants. *Developmental Psychology, 21,* 601–613.

VELLUTINO, F. R., & SCANLON, D. M. (1985). Free recall of concrete and abstract words in poor and normal readers. *Journal of Experimental Child Psychology, 39,* 363–380.

VERNON, P. A. (1983). Spread of information processing and general intelligence. *Intelligence, 5,* 345–355.

VERNON, P. E. (1972). The distinctiveness of field independence. *Journal of Personality, 40,* 366–391.

VINTER, A. (1986). The role of movement in eliciting early imitations. *Child Development, 57,* 66–71.

VYGOTSKY, L. S. (1962). *Thought and language.* Cambridge, MA: MIT Press.

WABER, D. P. (1976). Sex differences in cognition: A function of maturation rate? *Science, 192,* 572–574.

WABER, D. P. (1977). Sex differences in mental abilities, hemispheric lateralization, and rate of physical growth at adolescence. *Developmental Psychology, 13,* 29–36.

WABER, D. P., MANN, M. B., MEROLA, J., & MOYLAN, P. (1985). Physical maturation rate and cognitive performance in early adolescence: A longitudinal examination. *Developmental Psychology, 21,* 666–681.

WACHS, T., UZGIRIS, I. C., & HUNT, J. McV. (1971). Cognitive development in infants of different age levels and from different environmental backgrounds: An exploratory investigation. *Merrill-Palmer Quarterly, 17,* 283–317.

WADDINGTON, C. H. (1957). *The strategy of the genes.* London: Allen & Sons.

WALK, R. D. (1981). *Perceptual development.* Pacific Grove, CA: Brooks/Cole.

WALK, R. D., & GIBSON, E. J. (1961). A comparative and analytical study of visual depth perception. *Psychological Monographs, 75* (15, Whole No. 519).

WALLACH, M. A. (1970). Creativity. In P. H. Mussen (Ed.), *Carmichael's manual of child psychology* (Vol. 1) (3rd ed.). New York: Wiley.

WALLACH, M. A. (1971). *The intelligence/creativity distinction.* Morristown, NJ: General Learning Press.

WALLACH, M. A., & KOGAN, N. (1965). *Modes of thinking in young children.* New York: Holt, Rinehart & Winston.

WALLBROWN, F. H., & HEULSMAN, C. D., JR. (1975). The validity of the Wallach–Kogan creativity operations for inner-city children in two areas of visual art. *Journal of Personality, 43,* 109–126.

WALLEY, A. C., PISONI, D. B., & ASLIN, R. N. (1981). The role of early experience in the development of speech perception. In R. N. Aslin, J. R. Alberts, & M. R. Petersen (Eds.), *Development of perception: Psychobiological perspectives: Vol. 1. Audition, somatic perception, and chemical senses.* New York: Academic Press.

WASON, P. C., & JOHNSON-LAIRD, P. N. (1972). *Psychology of reasoning: Structure and content.* Cambridge, MA: Harvard University Press.

WATERS, E., WIPPMAN, J., & SROUFE, L. A. (1979). Attachment, positive effect, and competence in the peer group: Two studies in construct validation. *Child Development, 50,* 821–829.

WAXMAN, S., & GELMAN, R. (1986). Preschoolers' use of superordinate relations in classification and language. *Cognitive Development, 1,* 139–156.

WEAVER, S. L., & CUNNINGHAM, J. G. (1985, April). *Young children's implicit and explicit knowledge of their memory.* Paper presented at the meeting of the Society for Research in Child Development, Toronto.

WECHSLER, D. (1967). *Manual for the Wechsler Preschool and Primary Scale of Intelligence.* New York: Psychological Corp.

WECHSLER, D. (1974). *Manual for the Wechsler Intelligence Scale for Children—Revised.* New York: Psychological Corp.

WEGNER, D. M., & VALLACHER, R. R. (1977). *Implicit psychology: An introduction to social cognition.* New York: Oxford University Press.

WEINRAUB, M., CLEMENS, L. P., SOCKLOFF, A., ETHRIDGE, T., GRACELY, E., & MYERS, B. (1984). The development of sex-role stereotypes in the third year: Relationships to gender labeling, gender identity, sex-typed toy preference, and family characteristics. *Child Development, 55,* 1493–1503.

WELLMAN, H. M. (1977). Tip of the tongue and feeling of knowing experiences: A developmental study of memory monitoring. *Child Development, 48,* 13–21.

WELLMAN, H. M. (1983). Metamemory revisited. In M. T. H. Chi (Ed.), *Trends in memory development research: Vol. 9. Contributions to human development.* Basel: S. Karger.

WELLMAN, H. M. (1988). The early development of memory strategies. In F. Weinert & M. Perlmutter (Eds.), *Memory development: Universal changes and individual differences.* Hillsdale, NJ: Erlbaum.

WELLMAN, H. M., COLLINS, J., & GLIEBERMAN, J. (1981). Understanding the combination of memory variables. Developing conceptions of memory limitations. *Child Development, 52,* 1313–1317.

WELLMAN, H. M., FABRICIUS, W. V., & SOPHIAN, C. (1985). The early development of planning. In H. M. Wellman (Ed.), *Children's searching: The development of search skills and spatial representation.* Hillsdale, NJ: Erlbaum.

WELLMAN, H. M., RITTER, K., & FLAVELL, J. H. (1975). Deliberate memory behavior in the delayed reactions of very young children. *Developmental Psychology, 11,* 780–787.

WELLMAN, H. M., & SOMERVILLE, S. C. (1980). Quasi-naturalistic tasks in the study of cognition: The memory-related skills of toddlers. In M. Perlmutter (Ed.), *New directions for child development: Children's Memory.* San Francisco: Jossey-Bass.

WELLS, G. L., & LOFTUS, E. F. (1984). *Eyewitness testimony: Psychological perspectives.* New York: Cambridge University Press.

WERKER, J. F., GILBERT, J. H. V., HUMPHREY, K., & TEES, R. C. (1981). Developmental aspects of cross-language speech perception. *Child Development, 52,* 349–355.

WHITE, B. L. (1978). *Experience and environment: Major influences on the development of the young child* (Vol. 2). Englewood Cliffs, NJ: Prentice-Hall.

WHITE, B. L., CAREW-WATTS, J., BARNETT, I. C., KABAN, B., MARMOR, J., & SHAPIRO, B. (1973). *Environment and experience: Major influences on the development of the young child.* Englewood Cliffs, NJ: Prentice-Hall.

WHITE, J. L., & LABARBA, R. C. (1976). The effects of tactile and kinesthetic stimulation on neonatal development in the preterm infant. *Developmental Psychobiology, 9,* 569–577.

WHITE, R. W. (1959). Motivation reconsidered: The concept of competence. *Psychological Review, 66,* 297–333.

WHITE, S. H. (1965). Evidence for a hierarchical arrangement of learning processes. In L. P. Lipsitt & C. C. Spiker (Eds.), *Advances in child development and behavior* (Vol. 2). New York: Academic Press.

WHITE, S. H., & PILLEMER, D. B. (1979). Childhood amnesia and the development of a socially accessible memory system. In J. F. Kihlstrom & F. J. Evans (Eds.), *Functional disorders of memory.* Hillsdale, NJ: Erlbaum.

WHITE, T. (1982). Naming practices, typicality and underextension in child language. *Journal of Experimental Child Psychology, 33,* 324–346.

WHITEHURST, G. J., & SONNENSCHEIN, S. (1985). The development of communication: A functional analysis. In G. J. Whitehurst (Ed.), *Annals of child development* (Vol. 2). Greenwich, CT: JAI Press.

WHITNEY, P. (1986). Developmental trends in speed of semantic memory retrieval. *Developmental Review, 6,* 57–79.

WHITNEY, P., & KUNEN, S. (1983). Development of hierarchical conceptual relationships in children's semantic memories. *Journal of Experimental Child Psychology, 35,* 278–293.

WICKELGREN, L. (1967). Convergence in the human newborn. *Journal of Experimental Child Psychology, 5,* 74–85.

WILKINSON, A. (1976). Counting strategies and semantic analysis as applied to class inclusion. *Cognitive Psychology, 8,* 64–85.

WILLEMSEN, E., & REYNOLDS, B. (1973). Sex differences in adults' judgment of the horizontal. *Developmental Psychology, 8,* 309.

WILLIAMS, K. G., & GOULET, L. R. (1975). The effects of cueing and constraint instructions on children's free recall performance. *Journal of Experimental Child Psychology, 19,* 464–475.

WINER, G. A. (1974). An analysis of verbal facilitation of class-inclusion reasoning. *Child Development, 45,* 224–227.

WINER, G. A. (1980). Class-inclusion reasoning in children: A review of the empirical literature. *Child Development, 51,* 309–328.

WINICK, M., MEYER, K. K., & HARRIS, R. C. (1975). Malnutrition and environmental enrichment by early adoption. *Science, 190,* 1173–1175.

WITKIN, H. A. (1978). Cognitive styles in personal and cultural adaptation. *The 1977 Heinz Werner lectures.* Worcester, MA: Clark University Press.

WITKIN, H. A., DYK, R. B., FATERSON, H. F., GOODENOUGH, D. R., & KARP, S. A. (1962). *Psychological differentiation.* New York: Wiley.

WITKIN, H. A., GOODENOUGH, D. R., & KARP, S. A. (1967). Stability of cognitive style from childhood to young adulthood. *Journal of Personality and Social Psychology, 7,* 291–300.

WITKIN, H. A., LEWIS, H. B., HERTZMAN, M., MACHOVER, K., MEISSNER, P., & WAPNER, S. (1954). *Personality through perception.* New York: Harper.

WORDEN, P. E. (1983). Memory strategy instruction with the learning disabled. In M. Pressley & J. R. Levin (Eds.), *Cognitive strategy research: Psychological foundations.* New York: Springer.

WOZNIAK, R. H. (1972). Verbal regulation of motor behavior: Soviet research and non-Soviet replications. *Human Development, 15,* 13–57.

YEATES, K. O., MacPHEE, D., CAMPBELL, F. A., & RAMEY, C. T. (1983). Maternal IQ and home environment as determinants of early childhood intellectual competence: A developmental analysis. *Developmental Psychology, 19,* 731–739.

YOUNGER, B. A., & COHEN, L. B. (1983). Infant perception of correlations among attributes. *Child Development, 54,* 858–867.

YUSSEN, S. R. (1974). Determinants of visual attention and recall in observational learning by preschoolers and second graders. *Developmental Psychology, 10,* 93–100.

YUSSEN, S. R., & BIRD, J. E. (1979). The development of metacognitive awareness in memory, communication, and attention. *Journal of Experimental Child Psychology, 28,* 300–313.

YUSSEN, S. R., & LEVY, V. M., JR. (1975). Developmental changes in predicting one's own span of short-term memory. *Journal of Experimental Child Psychology, 19,* 502–508.

ZAJONC, R. B., & MARKUS, G. B. (1975). Birth order and intellectual development. *Psychological Review, 82,* 74–88.

ZAJONC, R. B., MARKUS, H., & MARKUS, G. B. (1979). The birth order puzzle. *Journal of Personality and Social Psychology, 37,* 1325–1341.

ZELAZO, P. R., ZELAZO, N. A., & KOLB, S. (1972). "Walking" in the newborn. *Science, 176,* 314–315.

ZELNIKER, T., & JEFFREY, W. E. (1976). Reflective and impulsive children: Strategies of information processing underlying differences in problem solving. *Monographs of the Society for Research in Child Development, 41* (Serial No. 168).

ZELNIKER, T., JEFFREY, W. E., AULT, R., & PARSONS, J. (1972). Analysis and modification of search strategies of impulsive and reflective children on the Matching Familiar Figures Test. *Child Development, 43,* 321–335.

ZEMBER, M. I., & NAUS, M. J. (1985, April). *The combined effects of knowledge base and mnemonic strategies on children's memory.* Paper presented at the meeting of the Society for Research in Child Development, Toronto.

ZESKIND, P. S. (1986, April). *Infant crying: A biobehavioral synchrony between infants and caregivers.* Paper presented at the Conference on Human Development, Nashville.

ZESKIND, P. S., & RAMEY, C. T. (1978). Fetal malnutrition: An experimental study of its consequences on infant development in two caregiver environments. *Child Development, 49,* 1155–1162.

ZESKIND, P. S., & RAMEY, C. T. (1981). Sequelae of fetal malnutrition: A longitudinal, transactional, and synergistic approach. *Child Development, 52,* 213–218.

ZIMMERMAN, B. J., & ROSENTHAL, T. L. (1974). Observational learning of rule-governed behavior by children. *Psychological Bulletin, 81,* 29–42.

Author Index

Abelson, R. P., 148
Abrahamson, A., 120, 146
Abravanel, E., 96–99, 109
Acito, M. A., 114
Ackerman, B. P., 56, 116, 148, 149, 163, 165
Acredolo, L., 104, 105, 169
Adams, G. R., 35
Adams, R. J., 70
Ainsworth, M. D. S., 191, 194, 196, 198
Albert, J., 264
Alexander, D., 289
Allen, L., 257, 258
Amatruda, C., 251
Ames, E. W., 73
Anderson, J. R., 149
Anderson, R. C., 119
Andreassen, C., 170
Anglin, J. M., 80, 115, 116, 146, 147
Anisfeld, M., 110
Annett, M., 119
Anooshian, L. J., 289
Antell, S. E., 124
Appel, K. J., 104
Applebaum, M. I., 75, 236, 258, 259
Arend, R. A., 197
Arlin, M., 163
Ashcraft, M. H., 128–130
Asher, S. R., 293
Ashmead, D. H., 109, 193
Aslin, R. N., 70, 76, 81, 82
Atkinson, R. C., 46, 47, 153
August, D. L., 138
Ault, R. L., 272, 275

Bach, M. J., 110
Back, K. J., 295
Backteman, G., 278
Bahrick, L. E., 83
Baker, S. W., 294
Baker-Ward, L., 60, 63, 164, 166, 169
Balaban, T., 184
Baldwin, J. M., 87, 89, 96

Ball, O., 282
Bandura, A., 185
Bandura, M. M., 291, 295–297
Banks, M. S., 70, 73
Baron, C. R., 164
Barrera, M. E., 71
Bartlett, F. C., 18, 159, 166
Bartz, W. H., 65
Bates, J. E., 196
Batterman, N., 144, 150
Bauer, R. H., 209
Bayles, K., 196
Bayley, N., 96, 251, 252, 257, 258
Beach, D. R., 161
Beal, C. R., 138, 164, 185
Beale, I. L., 280
Becker, W. C., 244, 245
Beckworth, L., 196
Bee, H. L., 233
Behrend, D. A., 65, 142
Bell, J. A., 170
Bell, R. Q., 228, 297
Bell, S. M., 196
Bell, T. S., 164
Bellugi, U., 137
Belmont, J. M., 208
Belmont, L., 11
Bem, S., 188
Benbow, C. P., 287, 288
Berbaum, M. L., 238
Bereiter, C., 243
Berg, C. A., 218, 255
Berger, D., 279
Berk, L. E., 142
Berlin, B., 80
Bernard, J., 69
Bernholtz, J. E., 210
Bernstein, B., 231
Bernstein, M., 200
Best, D. L., 163
Binet, A., 16, 203
Birch, H. G., 11, 74, 98, 192

Bird, J. E., 169
Bisanz, J., 211
Bizzell, R. P., 244, 245
Bjorke, E. L., 104, 105
Bjorklund, D. F., 55, 60–64, 100, 120, 132, 144, 145,
     147–150, 158, 163, 164, 166–168, 192, 209, 210, 218
Black, M. M., 163
Blase, B., 69
Blehar, M. C., 194
Block, J., 272–274, 278
Block, J. H., 272, 273, 278
Blom, G. E., 293
Bloom, B. S., 258
Bobbitt, B. L., 56, 211, 219
Bobele, L. Z., 111
Bock, R. D., 296
Boies, S., 220
Boles, D., 296
Bomba, P. C., 80
Bonneraux, B., 242
Boring, E. G., 43
Borke, H., 28, 59, 64
Borkowski, J. G., 170, 202, 207, 212, 220, 274
Bornstein, M. H., 74, 80, 255–257, 262
Borton, R. W., 83, 98
Borys, S. R., 207
Botkin, P. T., 137, 174
Botvin, G. J., 29, 30
Bouchard, T. J., Jr., 219, 221, 296, 297
Bovet, M., 30, 213
Bowen, R., 34, 35
Bower, G. H., 163
Bower, T. G. R., 102–104
Bowlby, J., 190, 194, 195
Boyes-Braem, P., 145
Brackbill, Y., 238
Bradley, R. H., 233, 234
Brainerd, C. J., 17, 26, 29–32, 38, 54, 57, 58, 105, 119, 120,
     125, 128, 129, 132, 163, 165, 170
Brainerd, S., 26, 29
Brand, A. E., 119
Brannock, J., 35
Bransford, J. D., 18, 160, 168
Bray, N. W., 207
Brazelton, T. B., 192, 251
Bremner, J. G., 105
Brennan, W. M., 73
Bretherton, I., 194, 195
Briars, D., 126
Bridger, W. H., 83, 98
Brody, R., 163
Brodzinsky, D. M., 273, 274
Bronfenbrenner, U., 169, 243
Bronson, G., 76
Brooks, P. H., 105, 208
Brooks-Gunn, J., 256
Broughton, J. M., 103
Brown, A. L., 55, 60, 61, 116, 118, 130, 156, 160, 161, 165,
     168, 171, 207, 208, 212
Brown, M. M., 177
Brown, R., 136
Brucken, L., 187

Bruner, J. S., 27, 56, 108, 110, 111, 132, 140, 161
Bryant, P. E., 31
Buffery, A., 295
Bukatko, D., 156
Bullock, M., 40, 65
Bushnell, E. W., 83
Bussey, K., 286, 293
Butter, E. J., 273–275
Butterworth, G., 174
Byrd, D. M., 213

Cairns, E., 272
Cairns, R. B., 100, 227
Caldwell, B. M., 233, 234, 236, 237
Callanan, M. A., 121
Cameron, R., 275
Cammock, T., 272
Campbell, F. A., 236, 243
Campbell, S., 140
Campione, J. C., 168, 207, 208
Campos, J., 78, 105
Cannizzo, S. R., 162
Cantor, D. S., 170
Caplan, P. J., 296
Capon, N., 37
Carbonari, J. P., 111
Carew, J. V., 235–237
Carey, S., 38, 61, 65, 143, 295
Carlson, J. S., 219
Carlson, V. R., 79
Carmichael, L., 69
Caron, A. J., 79
Caron, R. F., 79
Carpenter, T. P., 128
Carson, M. T., 120, 146
Case, R., 20, 38, 52–54, 56, 108, 113, 131, 154, 161, 166, 168
     218, 220, 268, 269
Cassidy, D. J., 60, 165
Cassidy, J., 195
Cattel, R. B., 202, 206
Cavanaugh, J. C., 168, 170, 207
Ceci, S. J., 56, 149, 165, 169, 208, 209, 211
Chandler, M. J., 228–230, 241
Chechile, R. A., 166
Cheng, P. W., 48
Chi, M. T. H., 31, 53, 61, 62, 64, 146, 154, 166, 167, 209, 220
Chinsky, J. H., 161
Church, J., 184
Cicirelli, V. G., 238
Clapson, L. G., 278
Clark, E. A., 239, 241
Clarke, E. V., 135, 143, 239
Clarke, H. H., 135, 239
Clarke-Stewart, A. K., 292
Clarkson, M. G., 161
Clemmer, E. J., 139
Clifton, R. K., 161
Coates, D. L., 196
Coates, S., 267
Cohen, D., 98
Cohen, J., 268

Cohen, L. B., 71, 79, 102, 146, 155
Cohen, S. E., 196, 255
Cole, M., 117, 158, 241
Collins, A. M., 47, 149
Collins, J., 164
Collins, K., 98
Colombo, J., 82
Condon, W., 82
Connor, J. M., 187, 188, 291, 297
Conway, B. E., 200
Cooper, J., 184
Corballis, M. C., 280
Corman, H., 93, 102
Cornell, D., 80
Cornell, E., 79
Corsale, K., 163
Coulombre, A. J., 5
Cowan, N., 161
Cowart, B. J., 69
Cox, B., 116
Cox, D., 163, 292
Craik, F. J. M., 111
Crawford, D. E., 272
Crays, N., 170
Crisafi, M. A., 145
Croft, K., 28
Cronbach, L. J., 2
Cropley, A. J., 278
Cross, J., 80
Cummings, E. M., 104, 105
Cunningham, J. G., 169
Curtiss, S., 239
Cuvo, A. J., 162

Daehler, M. W., 156
Dale, P. S., 135
Dallago, M. L. P., 209
Danner, F. W., 35, 211
Dansky, J. L., 279
Danst, C. J., 105
Darlington, R., 244
Das, J. P., 205, 207, 281–284
Davey, T. C., 214
Davidson, G., 161
Davidson, J. E., 211, 216
Davis, A. J., 232
Davis, D., 56, 211
Davis, K., 239
Davis, M., 70
Day, D., 264
Day, J. D., 160
Day, M. C., 35
Day, R. H., 79, 80
Deaux, K., 296
DeCasper, A. J., 69, 70, 81, 192
DeFries, J. C., 221
DeLoach, J. S., 60, 61, 164
de Marchena, M. R., 150, 167
DeMarie-Dreblow, D., 60, 168
Dempster, F. N., 51–53, 56, 154
Denney, D. R., 274

Denney, N. W., 114, 116, 117
Dennis, W., 9, 65, 227, 228, 239
Detterman, D., 202
Deutsch, C., 115
Deutsch, G., 280, 281
de Villiers, J. G., 135, 143
de Villiers, P. A., 135, 143
De Vries, R., 122, 183, 184
Diamond, A., 104, 105, 154
Diamond, R., 295
Diaz, R. M., 142
DiPietro, J. A., 297
Dirks, J., 156, 157
Docherty, E. M., 176
Dodge, K. A., 174, 176–179, 197, 198
Dodsworth, R. O., 9
Dodwell, P. C., 74
Dolan, A. B., 224
Dolan, T., 213
Dolgin, K. G., 65
Dong, Q., 123
Dowd, J. M., 82
Doxsey, P. A., 105
Drachman, D. B., 5
Drivas, A., 292
Dubas, J. S., 295
DuBois, L., 297
Duncan, E. M., 148
Dunn, K., 264
Dunn, R., 264
Durrett, M. E., 196
Dye, H. B., 9, 227, 240
Dyk, R. B., 265, 290

Earle, D. C., 78
Easterbrooks, M. A., 232
Eaton, W. O., 184
Egeland, B., 196, 197, 274, 275
Ehrhardt, A. A., 293, 294, 299
Ehri, L. C., 266
Eichelman, W., 220
Eichorn, D. H., 20, 93, 250
Eilers, R. E., 81
Eimas, P. D., 81
Elardo, R., 233, 234
Elkind, D., 34, 35
Elliot-Faust, D., 161
Ellis, H., 286
Ellis, S., 232
Emerson, H. F., 116
Emerson, P. E., 191
Emmerich, W., 250
Endman, M., 69, 192
Englemann, S., 243
Ennis, R. H., 44
Eoff, J., 164
Erickson, L. G., 274
Erickson, M. F., 197
Erlenmeyer-Kimling, L., 221
Escalona, S., 93, 102
Evans, M. A., 139

Evans, W. F., 104
Everett, B. A., 28
Everett, I. R., 119
Ewy, R., 75
Eysenck, H. J., 202, 219, 222, 223
Eysenck, M. W., 164

Fabricius, W. V., 164, 165
Fagan, J. F., III, 79, 155, 253–257, 262
Fagen, J. W., 155
Fagot, B. L., 188
Fantz, R. L., 71, 72, 74, 84, 255
Farber, E. A., 196
Faterson, H. F., 265, 290
Feltovich, P. J., 146
Felzen, E., 110
Fennema, E., 287, 291
Ferdinandsen, K., 74
Ferrara, R. A., 168, 208
Ferretti, R. P., 208
Feuer, D., 219
Field, D., 29
Field, T. M., 98
Fierman, B. A., 128
Fifer, W. P., 69, 70, 81
Finkelstein, N. W., 243
Finley, G. E., 242
Firestone, P. B., 105
Fischer, B. B., 265
Fischer, C. B., 74
Fischer, K. W., 20, 38–43, 105, 108, 113, 131
Fischer, L., 265
Fivush, R., 112, 148, 149
Flavell, E. R., 28, 123, 124
Flavell, J. H., 6, 7, 28, 29, 38, 39, 55, 59, 116, 123, 124, 130, 137, 138, 161–164, 168, 169, 171, 174, 212
Foch, T. T., 298
Fontaine, R., 98, 192
Ford, N. E., 211
Forest-Pressley, D. L., 161
Fox, L. H., 288
Frankel, F., 158, 167
Frankel, M. T., 167, 232
Franks, J. J., 18, 160
Fraser, E., 136
Frauenglass, M. H., 142
Freedle, R. O., 292
Freud, S., 9, 17, 190
Frey, K. S., 184–188
Friedman, S., 78, 155
Fry, C. L., 137, 174
Furth, H. G., 20, 163
Fuson, K. C., 126, 127, 140

Galbraith, R. C., 238
Galie, A., 156
Gallistel, R., 126, 130
Gandelman, R., 294
Garcia, R., 98
Gardner, H., 98
Gardner, J., 98

Gardner, W., 232
Garvin, R. A., 142
Gavin, W. J., 81
Gazzaniga, M. S., 280, 283
Geiss, M. F., 111
Gekowski, W. L., 116
Gelber, E. R., 155
Gelman, R., 29–31, 59, 119, 125, 126, 128, 130, 131, 139, 175
Gersten, R., 244, 245
Gesell, A., 251
Gewirtz, J. L., 190
Ghatala, E. S., 111, 166, 170
Gholson, B., 213
Gibson, E. J., 68, 76, 77, 110, 144, 150, 292
Gibson, J. J., 68
Gilbert, J. H. V., 81
Gingold, H., 96, 97, 109
Ginsberg, H., 73, 128
Gitomer, D. H., 211
Gjerde, P. E., 273, 274
Glaser, R., 146
Glenn, C. G., 149
Glick, J., 36
Glieberman, J., 164
Globerson, T., 268–270
Glucksberg, S., 137, 138, 175
Goetz, E. T., 282
Goldbeck, S. L., 291
Goldberg, J., 52, 54, 220
Goldberg, W. A., 232
Goldfarb, W., 9, 239
Goldman, D., 80
Goldman, J. A., 27
Goldstein, D., 209
Gonzales, M., 242
Goodenough, D. R., 265, 267, 268, 290
Goodman, J., 142, 275
Goodwin, D., 170
Gottfried, A. W., 83, 98
Gottlieb, G., 19
Goulet, L. R., 164
Gouze, K. R., 184, 187, 188
Gove, F. L., 176, 197
Gratch, G., 104, 105
Gray, J., 295
Gray, S., 243
Gray, W. D., 145
Gray, W. M., 35
Green, B. L., 55
Green, F. L., 123, 138
Greenberg, R., 98
Greenfield, D. B., 116, 210
Greenfield, P. M., 27
Groen, G. J., 128
Gross, C. G., 74
Grossman, K., 197
Grossman, K. E., 197
Guilford, J. P., 201, 202, 277, 279
Guillaume, P., 96
Guth, M. E., 144, 145
Guttentag, R. E., 168

Gzesh, S. M., 28

Haan, N. S., 37
Hagan, R., 188
Hagen, E. P., 203
Hagen, J. W., 59, 162
Haig, J. R., 163
Haith, M. M., 192
Hale, G. A., 166
Halford, G. S., 31, 32, 108, 113
Hall, D. M., 111
Hall, J. T., 127
Hall, J. W., 126
Hall, R. J., 282
Halpern, D. F., 296
Halverson, C. F., 188, 297
Halwes, T. G., 163
Hamann, M. S., 128, 129
Hamm, M., 98
Hanisee, J., 239, 241
Hans, S., 75
Harlow, H. F., 9
Harlow, M., 9
Harnishfeger, K. K., 60, 61, 168
Harrington, D. M., 272, 278
Harris, L. J., 288–290
Harris, P. L., 104, 105
Harris, R. C., 239
Harris, Y. R., 60
Hartup, W. W., 174
Harvey, S., 206
Hasher, L., 48, 209
Haskins, R., 275
Hattie, J., 277, 278
Hawkins, J., 36
Hay, D. F., 28, 175
Hayes, L. A., 98
Haynes, H., 70, 192
Haynes, V. F., 60
Hazen, N. L., 196, 289, 297
Heidenheimer, P., 112, 113
Heider, E. R., 80
Heisel, B. E., 164
Held, R., 70, 192
Henderson, C., 78
Henderson, R. W., 229
Hendrickson, A. E., 219
Hendrickson, D. E., 219
Herman, J. E., 289
Hess, R. D., 231
Heulsman, C. D., Jr., 279
Hiatt, M. M., 51, 68, 72, 78, 82
Higgins, E. T., 174
Hill, K. T., 102
Hjertholm, E., 141
Hock, H. S., 156, 157, 166
Hockberg, J. E., 71
Hodkin, B., 120
Hoffman, M. L., 28
Hogarty, P. S., 20, 93, 236, 250, 251, 258, 259
Holden, D. J., 60, 164
Hollingsworth, L., 286

Holmes, D. L., 51
Homa, D., 80
Honzik, M. P., 257, 258
Hood, J., 274
Horibe, F., 181, 182
Hornsby, J. R., 11, 12, 116
Horobin, K., 104, 105
Horowitz, F. D., 80
Horton, M. S., 121
Hoving, K. L., 51
Howe, M. J. A., 56–58, 149, 165
Howe, M. L., 163
Hudson, J., 112, 148, 149
Hudson, L. M., 35
Hummel, D. D., 290
Humphrey, D. E., 74
Humphrey, G. K., 74
Humphrey, K., 81
Humphreys, L. G., 213, 214
Hunt, E., 211, 219, 220
Hunt, J. McV., 8, 93, 96, 102, 227, 234, 239
Hurlburt, N., 251
Hyde, J. S., 297, 298

Inhelder, B., 17, 23, 28, 30–33, 35, 36, 39, 43, 44, 64, 91, 114, 118, 119, 159, 175, 213, 258, 268, 269, 290

Jacklin, C. N., 185, 286–290, 292, 295, 297, 298
Jackson, E., 105
Jackson, P., 163
Jackson, R. A., 268
Jackson, R. W., 70
Jacobs, J. W., 167
Jacobson, S. W., 98–100
James, W., 69
Jamison, W., 290
Jarman, R. F., 281
Jarvik, L. R., 221
Jarvis, P. E., 137, 174
Jeffrey, W. E., 272, 275, 276, 284
Jensen, A. R., 202, 219, 243
Jensen, C. M., 219
Johnson, D. M., 145
Johnson, E. C., 65
Johnson, J. E., 279
Johnson-Laird, P. N., 38
Jones, R. M., 35
Jones, R. S., 208
Josey, C. C., 65
Jusczyk, P., 81
Justice, E. M., 169

Kagan, J., 9, 10, 75, 84, 146, 169, 179, 190, 193, 198, 232, 233, 241, 242, 251, 258, 264, 268, 271, 273, 274, 284
Kahneman, D., 121, 122
Kail, R. V., Jr., 53, 56, 59, 168, 289
Kallio, K. D., 31
Kaltsounis, B., 282
Kalyan-Masih, V., 268
Kamin, L. J., 8
Kaplan, N., 195

Karabenick, J. D., 139
Karagellis, A., 292
Karmel, B. Z., 73
Karp, S. A., 265, 267, 268, 290
Karzon, R. G., 82
Kaszor, P., 119, 120
Kaufman, A. S., 204, 213, 264, 280–284
Kaufman, N. L., 204, 213, 264, 280–284
Kavanaugh, R. D., 96
Kay, P., 80
Kaye, D. B., 129
Kaye, K., 96, 99
Kearsley, R. B., 193
Keating, D. P., 56, 124, 176, 211, 213, 219
Kee, D. W., 164
Keele, S. W., 80, 166
Keeny, T. J., 162
Keil, F. C., 144, 150
Kellas, G., 147, 148, 162
Keller, D., 147, 148
Kendal, J. R., 274
Kendler, H. H., 59
Kendler, T. S., 59
Keniston, A. H., 56
Kennedy, C. B., 75, 273, 274
Keogh, B. K., 264
Kershner, J. R., 282, 283
Kessen, W., 72, 73, 80, 109, 192
Ketron, J. L., 200
Killen, M., 96
King, S., 297
Kingma, J., 32, 54, 57, 58, 66, 163, 165, 213
Kingsley, P. R., 162
Kingston, D. J., 35
Kinsbourne, M., 295
Kirby, J., 281
Kirby, N. H., 219
Klagsburn, M., 195
Klahr, D., 38
Klapp, S. T., 54
Klaus, R. A., 243
Klein, R. E., 81, 193, 241, 242
Klima, E., 137
Knobloch, H., 229
Knopf, I. J., 57, 58
Kobak, R. R., 195
Kobasigawa, A., 57, 164
Koepke, J. E., 98
Kogan, N., 266, 268, 274, 277–279
Kohlberg, L., 37, 141, 142, 183, 188, 198
Kolakowski, D., 296
Kolb, S., 99
Koluchova, J., 239
Konstadt, N., 267
Kopp, C. B., 93
Korkel, J., 210
Korner, A. E., 69
Koslowsky, B., 192
Kosslyn, S. M., 56, 110
Kotelchuck, M., 193
Kowal, S., 139

Kramer, J. A., 102
Krantz, J. Z., 224
Krasnor, L. R., 177, 179
Kratochwill, T. R., 27
Krauss, R. M., 137, 138, 175
Kreutzer, M. A., 168, 169
Krowitz, A., 78
Krueger, T., 282
Kuczaj, S. A., 135
Kuhn, D., 35, 37, 187, 213, 214
Kunen, S., 148
Kurland, M., 52, 54, 220
Kurtz, B. E., 212, 274

LaBarba, R. C., 69, 99
Laboratory of Comparative Human Cognition, 215
Lamb, M. E., 174
Lane, D. M., 57
Lane, M. K., 120
Lange, G. W., 156, 163, 164, 232
Langer, A., 78
Langer, J., 37
Langland, L., 279
Langlois, J. H., 74, 75
Lansman, M., 211
Lasky, R. E., 81
Laurence, M. W., 166
Laurendeau, M., 65
Lave, C., 242
Lavin, D., 228
Lawton, S. C., 160
Lazar, I., 244, 245
Leal, L., 170
Lechner, R. E., 137
LeCompte, G. K., 104
Ledger, G., 282, 283
Lefford, A., 98
Legerstee, M., 98
Leinbach, M. D., 188
Lempers, J. D., 28
Leonard, C., 168
Leonard, H. S., 274
Lester, B. M., 193
Lester, P. T., 54
Levan-Goldschmidt, E., 96
Levin, H., 292
Levin, J. R., 164, 170
Levy, J., 296
Levy, V. M., Jr., 55, 169
Lewis, D., 111
Lewis, J., 211
Lewis, M., 98, 196, 256, 292
Liben, L. S., 159, 290, 291
Liberman, J. N., 279
Liberty, C., 158, 162, 207
Liebert, D. E., 30, 35
Light, P., 174
Lindauer, B. K., 160
Lindberg, M., 167
Linn, M. C., 268, 298
Linn, S., 75

List, J. A., 211
Litrowink, J., 168
Lockhart, M. E., 185
Lockhart, R. S., 111
Lockman, J. J., 289
Lodico, M. G., 170
Loftus, E. F., 18, 47, 149
Longstreth, L. E., 241
Looft, W. R., 27, 65
Lord, C., 163
Lorenz, K. Z., 99
Lovell, K., 35, 119
Lucariello, J., 112, 148
Lunneborg, C., 211
Lunzar, F. A., 213
Luria, A. R., 117, 140, 281
Lutkenhaus, P., 197
Lykken, D. T., 219
Lyons, B. G., 126

Maccoby, E. E., 185, 286, 287, 289, 292, 295, 297, 298
Macfarlane, A., 69, 192
MacKain, K., 82
MacKain, S., 185
MacLeod, C. M., 268
MacPhee, D., 236
MacPherson, G. M., 296
Magnusson, D., 278
Main, M., 192, 195
Maisel, E. B., 73
Mandler, G., 120, 147, 149, 163, 166
Mandler, J. M., 116, 156, 157
Manis, F. R., 56
Mann, M. B., 295
Maratos, O., 98
Maratsos, M., 135, 136
Marchida, S., 116
Marcus, D. E., 184
Marcus, J., 96
Margolis, H., 274
Markel, R. A., 293
Markman, E. M., 116, 119, 121, 139
Markus, G. B., 238, 239
Markus, H., 238
Marolla, F. A., 238
Marr, D. B., 216, 217
Marshburn, E. A., 54
Martin, C. L., 188
Masangkay, Z. S., 28
Mason, M. K., 239
Masten, A. S., 182
Masur, E. I., 169
Matas, L., 197
Matheny, A. P., Jr., 224
Mathews, J., 199
Maurer, D., 70–73, 159
Maxwell, S. E., 202, 220
McArthur, L. B., 27
McCabe, M. A., 96
McCall, R. B., 20, 75, 93, 96, 236, 237, 243, 250–254, 258–260, 262

McCarthy, D., 149, 292
McCartney, K., 223, 236, 237, 246, 297
McCauley, C., 56, 150, 162, 167, 208, 211
McClaskey, C. L., 176, 177
McCluskey, K. A., 28
McConaghy, M. J., 184, 185
McCue, M., 219–221
McFarland, C. E., 162
McFarlence, J. W., 257, 258
McGhee, M. G., 296
McGhee, P. E., 179, 180
McIntyre, C. W., 28, 169
McKenzie, B., 98
McKinney, J. D., 275
McLanahan, A. G., 121
McNamara, T. P., 143
McVey, K. A., 170
Meck, E., 126
Meeker, M., 202
Meichenbaum, D. H., 142, 275
Melkman, R., 115
Meltzoff, A. N., 83, 96–98, 100, 109, 192
Mendelson, M. J., 82
Merkin, S., 126
Merola, J., 295
Merrill, E. C., 56, 211
Merill, M. A., 259
Merriman, W. E., 211
Mervis, C. B., 143, 145, 146
Messer, D. J., 254, 257
Messer, S. B., 272–274
Meyer, K. K., 239
Milgram, N. A., 163, 278
Milgram, R. M., 278
Miller, B. S., 289
Miller, D. J., 256
Miller, G., 161
Miller, L. B., 244, 245
Miller, L. C., 137
Miller, P. H., 55, 60, 168
Milner, B., 295
Miner, J. B., 228
Miranda, S. B., 74, 255
Mischel, W., 185
Mistry, J. J., 164
Mitchell, B., 119
Mitchell, C., 275
Mitchell, D. W., 208
Moely, B. E., 62, 163, 170, 209
Molloy, G. N., 281
Money, J., 288, 289, 293, 294, 299
Montepare, J. M., 27
Moore, J. J., 232
Moore, M., 295
Moore, M. K., 97, 98, 100, 103, 192
Moore, R. W., 73
Moorc, T., 259, 292
Moreland, R. L., 238
Morgan, J. S., 166
Morrison, F. J., 51, 163
Morrison, V., 78

Morrongiello, B. A., 15
Moser, J. M., 128
Mosher, F. A., 11, 12
Moss, H. A., 258
Mourad, S., 282
Moylan, P., 295
Moynahan, E. D., 169
Muir, D. W., 74
Muir, J. E., 158, 164
Mullis, A. K., 232
Mullis, R. L., 232
Mundy, P., 116
Munroe, R. H., 184
Munroe, R. L., 184
Murchison, C., 43
Murray, F. B., 29, 30
Murray, H., 244
Muzio, I. M., 266
Myers, M., 169
Myers, N. A., 161, 166

Nadelman, L., 184, 187, 188
Nakazima, S., 135
Nash, S. C., 187, 297
Naus, M. J., 62, 63, 158, 161, 162, 166, 167, 207
Neisser, U., 156, 157, 215
Nelson, C. F., 272, 273
Nelson, K., 109, 112, 143, 144, 148–150, 161
Netley, C., 296
Nettelbeck, T., 219
Nevis, S., 255
Newcombe, N., 169, 291, 295–297
Newman, R. S., 170
Nichols, J. G., 278
Nichols, P. L., 238
Nida, S., 166
Nolan, E., 242

O'Connell, D. C., 139
O'Connor, J. J., 255
Oka, E. R., 55
Okonji, O., 268
Olagbaige, O. O., 268
Olsen, M. G., 169
Olson, F. A., 163
Olson, S. L., 196
Olver, R. R., 27, 116
Oppenheim, R. W., 100, 195
Ordy, J. M., 71
Ornstein, P. A., 60, 62–64, 120, 147, 158, 161–164, 166, 167, 207, 210
O'Sullivan, J. T., 170
Otto, W. R., 274
Over, R., 98
Overton, W. F., 184
Owens, R. E., Jr., 135

Palmer, J., 268
Pankove, E., 278
Paraskevopoulous, J., 96
Paris, S. G., 37, 55, 160, 169, 170

Parke, R. D., 96
Parker, T., 242
Parkman, J. M., 128
Parmelee, A. H., 93, 255
Parsons, C., 44
Parsons, C. K., 214
Parsons, J., 275
Pasamanick, B., 229
Pascual-Leone, J., 51, 52, 154, 269
Paterson, J. G., 103
Pea, R. D., 36
Pearson, D. A., 57
Peck, V. A., 212, 274
Pedersen, F. A., 297
Pellegrino, J. W., 211
Pepler, D. J., 279
Pergament, G. G., 126
Perlmutter, M., 109, 111, 142, 156, 163, 166, 168, 170, 193
Perry, D. G., 188, 286, 293
Perry, H., 256
Perry, L. C., 188
Petersen, A. C., 295, 297, 298
Peterson, N., 274
Pettit, G. S., 176
Phelps, E., 176
Philips, W., 264
Phillips, S., 297
Piaget, J., 5, 6, 13, 16–44, 46, 52, 64–66, 87–97, 100–103, 113, 118, 122, 124, 125, 127, 137, 141, 159, 174, 180, 193, 213, 268, 269, 279, 290
Pick, H. L., Jr., 169, 289
Pien, D., 179, 182
Pillemer, D. B., 161
Pilon, R., 181
Pinard, A., 65
Pipp, S. L., 40, 41
Pisoni, D. B., 81, 82
Pittman, L., 166
Plomin, R., 221, 297, 298
Posner, M., 80, 166, 220
Pressley, M., 161, 164, 170, 212
Pufall, P. B., 125

Qi, S., 123
Quine, W. V., 35
Quinn-Cobb, C., 55

Rabinowitz, M., 116, 167
Rader, N., 105
Raines, J. M., 164
Ramey, C. T., 230, 236, 243, 260, 261
Ramsay, D., 78
Raymond, C. L., 288
Reese, H. W., 59
Reid, M., 296
Reid, M. K., 212, 274
Reigel, T., 282
Reinisch, J. M., 294, 297
Resnick, J. M., 294, 297
Resnick, L. B., 128, 129, 211
Revelle, G. L., 139

Reynolds, B., 290
Reynolds, C. R., 282, 283
Reznick, J. S., 75, 146
Rheingold, H. L., 28, 75, 175, 215, 225, 257
Rich, S. A., 214
Richman, C. L., 166
Ridgeway, D., 195
Riley, C. A., 31
Ringel, B. A., 169
Rips, L., 143
Ritter, K., 164
Robb, K. Y., 51
Roberts, K., 80
Robertson, J., 195
Robillard, J., 177
Robinson, C. A., 156, 157, 166
Robinson, M., 35
Rodgers, J. L., 238
Roe, A., 292
Roe, K. V., 292
Rogers, H. J., 277, 278
Rogoff, B., 169, 232, 242
Rohwer, W. D., Jr., 164, 168
Rollins, H. A., Jr., 163, 167, 231, 232
Romanski, L., 156
Rosch, E., 80, 120, 143, 145–148
Rose, D. H., 78, 256
Rose, S. A., 83, 98, 255
Rosengren, K., 142
Rosenthal, R., 298
Rosenthal, T. L., 30
Rosman, B. L., 264
Ross, G., 149, 161
Ross, H. S., 279
Ross, L., 174
Roth, C., 56, 62, 211
Rothbart, M. K., 177, 182
Rotter, D. M., 279
Rovee-Collier, C. K., 155
Rovet, J., 295, 296
Rowe, D. C., 238
Royce, J., 244
Rubin, D. B., 298
Rubin, K. H., 177, 179
Ruble, D. N., 174, 184, 186–188
Ruff, H. A., 74, 192
Rugs, D., 137
Rusell, M., 98
Rushton, J. P., 170
Russell, R., 65

Sabin, E. J., 139
Salapatek, P., 72, 73, 192, 193
Salatas, H., 163
Salkind, N. J., 272, 273
Saltz, E., 140, 147
Sameroff, A. J., 228–230, 241
Samuel, A. G., 52
Samuels, C. A., 75
Sander, L., 82
Sanders, B., 295

Sattler, J. M., 203
Saxe, G. B., 127
Scanlon, D. M., 210
Scarr, S., 221–225, 236, 237, 246, 297
Scarr-Salapatek, S., 193, 243
Schadler, M., 289
Schaffer, H. R., 191
Schank, R. C., 148
Schechter, J., 58
Schiff, A. R., 57, 58
Schmidt, C. R., 164
Schmidt, S. R., 164
Schneider, B. A., 69, 192
Schneider, W., 48, 163, 167, 168, 170, 171, 210, 211, 215
Schorin, M. Z., 176
Schork, E. J., 111
Schulte, D., 51
Schwanenflugel, P. J., 144, 145
Schwartz, M., 79, 80
Schwartz, S., 80
Scott, J. P., 243
Scott, M. S., 116, 156, 210
Scribner, S., 36, 117
Secada, W. G., 127
Seeley, K., 206
Seibert, J., 119, 121
Sellers, M. J., 193
Sells, L. W., 287
Selman, R. L., 175, 176, 197
Serbin, L. A., 187–189, 291, 297
Serchuck, R., 116
Shantz, C. U., 174
Sharabany, R., 268
Sharp, D., 158, 241
Shatz, M., 138, 175
Shaw, R. E., 125
Sheingold, K., 50, 51, 161
Shepard, R. N., 155
Sherman, J. A., 287, 291, 296
Sherrod, L. R., 174
Shiffrin, R. M., 46–48, 153, 215
Shimmin, H. S., 184
Shipman, V. C., 231
Shiraki, J. H., 289
Shirley, M. M., 193
Shoben, E., 143
Shoemaker-Kelley, K. E., 274
Short, E. J., 260
Shrager, J., 129, 130
Shultz, T. R., 177, 181, 182
Siegel, A. W., 289
Siegel, L. S., 119
Siegelman, E. Y., 275
Siegler, R. S., 30, 35, 64, 126, 129, 130
Sigafoos, A. D., 97–99
Sigel, I. E., 115, 147
Sigman, M. D., 93, 255–257, 262
Silverman, I. W., 279
Simon, T., 16, 203
Sims-Knight, J., 28
Sinclair, H., 30

Singer, J. T., 253, 255
Siqueland, E. R., 80, 81
Skeels, H. M., 9, 222, 227, 240, 241
Skodak, M., 222
Skotko, D., 140
Slaby, R. G., 184–188
Slater, A., 78
Slater, A. M., 35, 256
Slater, W., 200
Slobin, D. I., 137
Smiley, S. S., 116, 118, 130, 160
Smith, C. L., 119, 120
Smith, E., 143, 146, 147
Smith, L. B., 68
Smith, W. L., 295
Snipper, A., 244
Soares, M. P., 295
Sodian, B., 163
Solkoff, N., 69
Soller, E., 147
Sommerville, S. C., 169
Sonnenschein, S., 55, 138
Sonstroem, A. M., 111, 112
Sontag, L. W., 69
Sophian, C., 104, 154, 165
Spear, N. E., 161
Spearman, C., 201, 202, 224, 251
Speer, J. R., 138
Speigel, F. S., 294
Spelke, E. S., 68, 82, 83, 193
Spence, I., 119
Spence, M. J., 70, 81, 192
Spencer, T., 51
Sperber, R. D., 56, 150, 167, 208, 211
Sperling, G., 50
Spieker, S., 82
Spiro, D. J., 105
Spitz, H. H., 207
Spitz, R., 9, 227, 240, 241
Sprafkin, C., 189
Springer, C. J., 169
Springer, S. P., 280, 281
Sroufe, L. A., 197
Stanley, J. C., 287, 288
Stark, R., 135
Starkey, P., 128
Stayton, D. J., 196
Stein, D. K., 209
Stein, N. L., 149, 156
Steinberg, E. R., 119, 208
Steiner, J. E., 69
Sterental, E., 210
Stern, D. N., 82
Sternberg, R. J., 48, 54, 55, 58, 66, 143, 200, 203, 205, 206,
    212, 214–218, 220, 255, 257, 281, 282
Stevenson, H. W., 242
Stevenson, M. B., 96
Stober, S. F., 274
Stoddart, T., 189
Stone, B. P., 162
Stone, C. A., 35

Stone, C. R., 176
Stone, L. J., 184
Strauss, M. S., 71, 79, 80
Sullivan, M. W., 98, 155
Suomi, S., 9
Surber, C. F., 28
Svejda, M., 77
Syrdal-Lasky, A., 81, 125

Tanner, J. M., 295
Tatarsky, J. H., 120
Taylor, D. C., 291
Taylor, M., 123
Taylor, R., 220
Tees, R. C., 81
Tenney, Y., 161
Terman, L. M., 8, 203, 259
Thoman, E. B., 69
Thomas, H., 290, 291
Thompson, B. E., 120, 147, 210
Thompson, J. G., 115
Thorndike, R. L., 203
Thurstone, L. L., 201, 202
Tighe, L. S., 58
Tighe, T. J., 58
Tinbergn, N., 99
Tinsley, V. S., 140
Tobin, P., 296
Torgesen, J. K., 209
Torrance, E. P., 227–279, 282–284
Townsend, M. A. R., 160
Trabasso, T., 31, 32
Treharthen, C., 193
Trehub, S. E., 69, 81, 192
Tronick, E. F., 82
Tulkin, S. R., 232, 233
Tulving, E., 153, 154
Turiel, E., 189
Turner, L. A., 207
Tversky, A., 121, 122
Tynes, D. M., 155

Udelf, M. S., 71
Underwood, B. J., 110
Urberg, K. A., 176
Uyeda, K. M., 120, 147
Uzgiris, I. C., 26, 93, 94, 96, 97, 102, 234

Vallacher, R. R., 174
Valle, J. D., 264
Vandenberg, S. G., 296
Vander Linde, E., 155
Vaughn, B. E., 28
Vellutino, F. R., 210
Vernon, P. A., 219
Vernon, P. E., 269
Vigorito, J., 81
Vinter, A., 98
VonBargen, D., 184
Vygotsky, L. S., 114, 140, 141

Waber, D. P., 295, 296
Wachs, T., 234
Waddington, C. H., 243
Wagner, M., 164
Waite, R. R., 293
Waldrop, M. F., 297
Walk, R. D., 70, 76, 77
Walker, H. T., Jr., 289
Wall, S., 194
Wallace, J. G., 38
Wallach, M. A., 277–280
Wallbrown, F. H., 279
Walley, A. C., 82
Wason, P. C., 38
Waters, E., 194, 197
Waters, H. S., 140, 163, 170, 292
Watson, J. S., 83, 98
Waxman, S., 119
Weaver, S. L., 169
Wechsler, D., 187, 203–205
Wegner, D. M., 174
Weil, C. M., 150, 167
Weinberg, R. A., 221, 222, 224
Weinert, F. E., 210
Weinraub, M., 187
Weinstein, E., 268
Weintraub, D., 69
Weisberg, R., 137, 138, 175
Weiskopf, S., 80
Weiss, M. G., 55
Wellman, H. M., 55, 60, 139, 164, 165, 168–170
Wells, G. L., 18
Werker, J. F., 81
West, M. J., 28, 175
White, A. J., 188
White, B. L., 70, 192, 234–237
White, J. L., 69
White, R. W., 177
White, S. H., 161, 258
Whitehurst, G. J., 55, 138
Whitney, P., 56, 148, 211
Wickelgren, L., 70
Widaman, K. F., 219

Wilkinson, A., 119, 120, 242
Wilkinson, J. E., 213
Willemsen, E., 290
Williams, C. S., 156
Williams, K. G., 164
Wilson, E. G., 31
Wilson, R. S., 224
Wilson, W. R., 81
Winer, G. A., 118–120
Winick, M., 239
Wippman, J., 197
Wishart, J. G., 103
Witkin, H. A., 265–268, 290
Wittig, D. S., 191, 196
Wohlwill, J. F., 7
Woodson, R., 98
Woody-Ramey, J., 60
Worden, P. E., 209
Wozniak, R. H., 140
Wright, J. C., 272
Wright, J. W., 137, 174
Wright, N. A., 104

Yaeger, J., 141
Yaffe, S., 69
Yeates, K. O., 236, 260
Young, D., 289
Younger, B. A., 79, 146
Yussen, S. R., 55, 164, 169

Zacks, R. T., 48
Zajonc, R. B., 238, 239, 246
Zelazo, N. A., 99
Zelazo, P. R., 99, 193
Zelniker, T., 275, 276, 284
Zeman, B. R., 62, 63, 166, 167
Zember, M. I., 167
Zeskind, P. S., 229, 230, 241
Zhang, X. D., 123
Zimet, S., 293
Zimmerman, B. J., 30
Zou, H., 123

Subject Index

Abstract representation, 112, 113
Abstract tier, in Fischer's theory, 40, 41, 113, 131
Accommodation:
  in imitation, 20, 94, 95
  in Piaget's theory, 20–22, 26, 41, 88, 89, 94, 95
  as response to novelty, 255
  during sensorimotor period, 88, 89, 94
  in vision (focusing of lens), 70
Active effects, in Scarr and McCartney's genotype → environment theory, 223, 224
Active intermodal mapping, as explanation for neonatal imitation, 98, 99
Active rehearsal; *see* Cumulative rehearsal
Activity level, sex differences in, 297
Acuity, in infancy, 70, 71, 73, 74, 76
Adaptation (*see also* Accommodation; Assimilation):
  in Piaget's theory, 20, 21, 88
  during sensorimotor period, 88
  in Sternberg's contextual subtheory, 214
Adolescence:
  egocentricity in, 34, 35
  and formal operations, 32–38
  and humor appreciation, 182
  pubertal hormones and sex differences in cognition, 295
Analytic/spatial skills, 289, 290, 295
  and Embedded Figures Test, 290
  and field dependence/field independence, 268, 290
  and Rod-and-Frame-Test, 290
Androgen:
  effects on brain, 294
  and sex differences, 293
Animism, 64, 65
Anticipatory images, 109
Appearance/reality distinction, 122–124, 131
  and dual encoding, 124, 131
  and gender constancy, 123
  and generic identity, 122
  and intellectual realism errors, 123
  and phenomenism errors, 123, 124
Arithmetic, 24, 124, 127–130
  development of mental, 128–130, 215
  and fact retrieval, 128–130

Arithmetic (*continued*)
  min model, 128–130
  in Piaget's theory, 127, 128
  and private speech, 142
  and procedural knowledge, 129
Assimilation:
  functional (reproductive), 89
  generalizing, 89
  in Piaget's theory, 20–22, 26, 41, 88–90, 94
  recognitory, 88
  as response to novelty, 255
  during sensorimotor period, 88–90
Attachment, 190–197
  and cognitive changes, 191–194
  and effects on intelligence, 195–197
  mental models of, 194, 195
  nature of, 190, 191
  perceptual and cognitive bases of, 191–193
  quality of, 191, 196, 197
Attention:
  allocation of, 48
  in conservation, 30
  and habituation, 74, 78, 79, 155, 156
  in iconic store, 51
  knowledge of, 55
  and primary and secondary visual systems, 76
  to same-sex models, 185, 186
  selective, 57, 58, 168
  to visual patterns in infancy, 71–76, 82
Attractive faces, in infants' visual preferences, 74, 75
Audio-visual integration, 11
Auditory Impulsivity Task, 274
Auditory perception:
  in infancy, 81, 82, 135
  in newborns, 69
  role in attachment, 192
Automaticity (automatic processing), 12, 47–49, 62–64
  and knowledge base, 62–64, 166, 167
  in learning-disabled children, 208, 209
  and memory strategies, 166, 167
  and mental arithmetic, 129
  in Sternberg's experiential subtheory, 215, 216

Babbling, 135
Balance-scale problem, 64
Basic level categories, 145, 146
Bayley Scales of Infant Development, 251, 252
Bidirectionality of structure and function, 5, 19
Bifoveal fixation, in depth perception, 76
Binocular cues, in depth perception, 76
Birth order, and intelligence, 238
Body orientation senses, 69

Canalization, of early cognitive abilities, 237, 243
Capacity (limited mental), 39, 46, 49–54, 56, 58, 60, 61
    of iconic store, 50, 51
    and speed of processing, 53, 56
    and strategy use, 60, 168
Categorization (*see also* Classification: Natural language
        categories):
    in infancy, 78–81
    and prototypes, 80
Causality:
    magical-phenomenalistic, 91, 92
    in Piaget's sensorimotor period, 91–93
Centration, 27, 34
    and field dependence/field independence, 266
Cerebral lateralization, 280, 281
    sex differences in, 295, 296
Characteristic features of words, 144, 150
Chemical senses, 69
Chromosomes, sex, 294
Chunking, and memory span, 52, 53
Circular reactions:
    defined, 89
    in Piaget's theory, 89–92
Classification, 113–122
    class inclusion, 118–122
    complementary, 114–117, 130, 132
    conceptual, 114–117, 130, 132
    and cultural differences, 117
    graphic collections, 114, 118, 119
    idiosyncratic, 114
    multiple classifications, 118, 119
    nongraphic collections, 118, 119
    perceptual, 114, 116
    in Piaget's theory, 118, 119
    preferences, 116, 117
    styles of, 113–117
    and symbolic functioning, 117, 118
Class inclusion, 118–122
    adults' reasoning in, 121, 122
    and collections, 121
    development of, 119, 120
    factors affecting, 120, 121
    training of, 119, 120
    and typicality, 120, 121
Cluster analysis, of IQ data, 259
Clustering:
    and associative strength, 167
    development of, 163
    of gifted, 212
    of learning-disabled, 209
    as measure of organization in free recall, 61–63, 163

Cognition, defined, 3, 4
Cognitive maps, 289
Cognitive styles, 263–283
    convergent/divergent thinking, 276–280
    field dependence/field independence, 265–270
    hemisphericity, 280–283
    reflection/impulsivity (conceptual tempo), 270–276
Collections, as alternatives to classes, 121
Collective monologues, 138
Color perception
    in infancy, 80, 81
    in newborns, 70
Communication skills, 137–140
    and collective monologues, 138
and egocentricity, 28, 137–139, 141, 175
    and metacognition, 138–140
    in Piaget's theory, 137, 138, 141
Compensatory education:
    long-term effects, 243–245
    short-term effects, 243, 260, 261
    and stability of individual differences, 260, 261
Complementary classification, 114–117, 130, 132
Complexity, role in infants' visual preferences, 73, 74
Componential theory (Sternberg's), 48, 58, 59, 216, 218
    knowledge-acquisition components, 48, 49, 54, 55, 57,
        58, 216
    metacomponents, 48, 49, 54, 55, 216
    performance components, 48, 49, 54, 55, 216
Conceptual classification, 114–117, 130, 132
Conceptual (cognitive) tempo, 270, 273 (*see also* Reflection/
        impulsivity)
    generality of, 273
    and intelligence, 273, 274
    and metacognition, 212, 274, 275
    and reading, 274
    stability of, 273
    training studies of, 142, 275
Concrete operations, 22–29, 31–33, 38, 52, 59, 159
    in comparison to formal operations, 32, 33, 35, 38
    in comparison to preoperations, 24–29
    and imagery, 109
    and M-space, 52
    and patterns of IQ change, 259
    and production deficiencies, 59
    and reconstructive memory, 159
Conditioning:
    in infants, 155, 157
    prenatal, 70
Confluence theory, 238
Conservation, 24–27, 29–31, 41, 59
    and attention, 30
    and Bruner's theory, 111, 112
    and Fischer's theory, 131
    and humor, 179, 180
    and M-space, 52
    of number, 124–127
    as opposed to identity, 122
    and recognition memory, 157
    and rule assessment, 64
    training studies of, 30

Constructive memory, 158–161
  and early childhood memories, 160, 161
  and inferences, 160
  Piagetian perspective, 159, 160
Constructive nature of cognition, in Piaget's theory, 18, 19
Contextual subtheory, in Sternberg's theory, 214, 215, 218
Continuity of development, 6, 7, 10, 17, 250
  and attachment, 195
  and relation to individual differences, 250–258
Continuum of caretaker causality, 229
Continuum of reproductive causality, 229
Contour, role in infants' visual preferences, 72, 73
Contrast, role in infants' visual preferences, 72
Contrast sensitivity function, 73
Controlled processes, 46–48
Convergence of eyes, 70
Convergent thinking:
  and IQ, 277
  as opposed to divergent, 276–278
Coordination of eyes, 70
Coordination of secondary circular reactions, 91, 92
Counting:
  and conservation, 127
  and early arithmetic, 128, 129
  principles of, 126
Creativity:
  and divergent thinking, 277–280
  and hemisphericity, 282, 283
Cross-age correlations, as measure of stability, defined, 249
Cross-modal matching, 83
Crystallized abilities (intelligence), 202, 203, 206
Cued recall, 57, 153, 157
Cumulative (active) rehearsal, 162, 168, 207
  in retarded children, 207, 208
Curvature, role in infants' visual preferences, 74

Decentration, 27, 34
Deep-structure ambiguity, in appreciation of jokes, 182
Deferred imitation, see Imitation
Defining features of words, 144, 150
Depth perception, 76–78
Detail processing, and reflection/impulsivity, 275, 276
Development, defined, 4, 5
Developmental function, 2, 10, 13, 17, 200, 249
Deviation IQ, 205, 206
Discontinuity of development, 6, 7, 10, 17, 38, 250
  relation to individual differences, 250–254, 257
Discrepancy principle:
  with respect to humor, 179
  with respect to visual attention, 75, 76
Discrimination:
  of depth, 77–78
  in vision, 71, 79
Discrimination learning, 30, 58, 59
Disequilibrium, 26
  in Piaget's theory (equilibration), 21, 26
Dishabituation, see Habituation
Distinctive features, in perceptual learning, 68
Divergent thinking, 276–280
  and children's artwork, 279
  correlates of, 279

Divergent thinking (continued)
  defined, 277
  distinction between convergent and, 277–280
  and intelligence, 278
  and play, 279
  stability of, 278, 279
Dual encoding, and appearance/reality distinction, 124, 131

Early childhood memories, 160, 161
Early experience, effects on intelligence, 8–10, 227, 228
Ease of item identification, as reflection of speed of processing, 53
Efficiency of cognitive processing:
  developmental differences in, 53, 54
  and memory span, 154
  and memory strategies, 165, 167, 168
  and mental arithmetic, 129, 130
  and strategy use, 61
  and symbol systems, 132
Effortful processing, 47–49, 61
  and humor, 179, 180
Egocentricity, 26–29, 39
  in adolescents, 34–36
  in communication, 28, 137–139, 141, 175
  and fall-back rule, 64
  and field dependence/field independence, 268
  and private speech, 141, 142
  in social perspective, 174–176
  in visual perspective, 28, 29, 39
Egocentric speech, see Private speech
Elaborated verbal code, 231
Elaboration, 164, 168, 212
Elementary cognitive tasks (ECTs), and intelligence, 219, 220
Embedded Figures Test, 265–267
  and analytic/spatial skills, 290
Empiricists' position (see also Environment; Experience):
  with respect to intelligence, 8, 227
  with respect to vision, 71
Enactive representation, 108
Encoding, 10, 11, 49, 55, 56
  and dual encoding, 124
  of early childhood memories, 161
  in iconic store, 51
  influence on memory strategies, 165, 166
  item-by-item, 165
  and organization in memory, 165, 166
  and reconstructive memory, 159, 160
  and retrieval, 163, 164
  selective, 49
  of social cues, 177, 178
  of word features, 110, 111
Environment (see also Experience):
  and differences in intelligence, 232–238
  effect on development, 5, 7–9, 18
  importance in maintaining intelligence level, 243–246
  in transactional model, 228–231
Epigenesis, in Piaget's theory, 19, 20, 22, 41, 100, 108
Episodic memory, 153, 154
Equilibration, in Piaget's theory, 21, 22
Estrogen, and sex differences, 293

Evocative effects, in Scarr and McCartney's genotype → environment theory, 223
Experience:
  as cause for development, 5, 9
  early, 8–10, 227, 228
  in Fischer's theory, 40, 41
  and heritability of intelligence, 218, 222
  importance of later, 236, 237, 243
  and intelligence, 227–246
  and patterns of IQ change, 260
  in Scarr and McCartney's genotype → environment theory, 223
  and sex differences in cognition, 287, 291–293, 297
Experiential subtheory, in Sternberg's theory, 215, 216, 218
Exploration:
  motivation for and stability of intelligence, 257
  and quality of attachment, 196
  and sex differences in spatial orientation, 289
Externality effect, in infants' vision, 73, 74

Factor analysis:
  and principal component analysis, 253
  in psychometric approach to intelligence, 201
  and tests of divergent thinking, 278
  and tests of hemisphericity, 281
  of WISC and field dependence/field independence, 268
Factors of intelligence, 200–203, 206
Fact retrieval, in arithmetic, 128–130
Fall-back strategies, 64
Familial studies of intelligence, 220–224
Family configuration variables, and intelligence, 238, 239
Fantasy, in children's humor, 180
Field dependence/field independence (FD/FI), 265–270
  and analytic/spatial skills, 290
  definition and measurement of, 265–267
  developmental change and stability of, 267, 268
  and implications for intelligence, 268, 269
  and M-capacity, 269, 270
Fischer's skills theory, 40–42, 113, 131
Fixed-action patterns, as explanation for neonatal imitation, 98–100
Fluid abilities, 202, 203, 206
Formal education:
  effects on classification, 117
  effects on intelligence, 242
Formal operations, 22–24, 32–38
  and giftedness, 213
  and M-space, 52
  and patterns of IQ change, 259, 270
  and realtion to IQ, 213
Free recall, 153, 157–170
  and expenditure of mental effort, 60, 61
  and retrieval strategies, 57
Function, in development, 4, 5
Functional (reproductive) assimilation, 89
Functional core, in Nelson's theory, 112
Functional features, 112, 148, 150
Functional invariants, in Piaget's theory, 20

g (Spearman's):
  and elementary cognitive tasks (ECTs), 219, 220

g (Spearman's) (continued)
  and field dependence/field independence, 268, 269
  as general factor of intelligence, 201–203, 214
  heritability of, 256
  and stability of intelligence, 251, 252, 256
Gender consistency, 184, 185
Gender constancy:
  and appearance/reality distinction, 123
  consequences for gender identification, 185, 186
  development of, 183–185
  and intelligence, 186–188
  and sex-stereotypic behavior, 186–188
Gender identification, 183–190
Gender identity, 122, 184, 185
Gender schemes, 188, 189
Gender stability, 184, 185
Generalizing assimilation, 89
Generic identity, 122
Genesis, in Piaget's theory, 19
Genetic epistemology, 16
Genetics:
  as responsible for individual differences, 8, 218–222
  in Scarr and McCartney's genotype → environment theory, 222–224
Genevan psychology, 16
Genotype → environment theory of Scarr and McCartney, 222–224, 236, 246
Gesell Developmental Schedules, 251
Gifted children:
  and creativity and hemisphericity, 282, 283
  and metacognition, 212
  sex differences in mathematical ability of, 287, 288
  and Sternberg's theory, 216–218
Global processing, and reflection/impulsivity, 275, 276
Goal-directed behavior:
  in sensorimotor period, 91
  and strategies, 11, 161, 165
Grammar, 136
Graphic collections, 114, 118, 119

Habituation:
  of attention, 74, 78, 79
  in cross-modal matching, 83
  as measure of categorization, 78–81
  as measure of memory, 78, 80, 154
  in preference for novelty tasks, 254
  rate of and prediction of later intelligence, 255–257
Head Start, 8, 244
Hearing, sense of, see Auditory perception
Hemisphericity, 280–283
  and cerebral lateralization, 280, 281
  characteristics associated with two hemispheres, 281
  and creativity, 282, 283
  sex differences in, 295, 296
Heritability of intelligence, 8, 218–224, 256
  definition, 218, 219
  and ECTs, 219, 220
  and familial studies, 220–224
Heterogeneity of cognitive function, 40
Heterotypic developmental progression, 250, 251
Hierarchization, 22

Holophrastic speech, 136
Homogeneity of cognitive function, 6, 7, 24, 38–41
Homotypic developmental progression, 250, 251
Horizontal décalage, 26
Hormonal sex differences, 293–295
    prenatal, 295
    pubertal, 295
Humor, 179–182
    appreciation of in adolescence, 182
    and cognitive development, 180–182
    and mental effort, 179,180
Hypothalamus, and sex differences in cognition, 294
Hypothetico-deductive reasoning, 32, 36, 37, 113

Iconic store, see Sensory register
Ideational fluency, as measure of divergent thinking, 277
Identity, as qualitative constancy, 122
Idiosyncratic classification, 114
Ikonic representation, in Bruner's theory, 110
Imagery:
    anticipatory images, 109
    in encoding, 56
    as memory strategy, 59
    reproductive images, 109
    and symbolic function, 109, 111
    and symbol system, 10, 93
Imaginary audience, 34
Imitation:
    and active intermodal mapping, 98, 99
    deferred, 93, 95–97, 108
    as form of accommodation, 20, 94, 95
    and innate releasing mechanisms, 98, 99
    of invisible gestures, 94, 96, 98
    mutual, 94, 97
    in neonates, 97–100
    role in attachment, 192
    during sensorimotor period, 94–100
    and transient ontogenetic adaptations, 100
Impulsivity (impulsive conceptual tempo), see Conceptual
    tempo; Reflection/impulsivity
Incongruity, role in humor, 179, 180, 182
Independent processes model of working memory, 54
Individual differences (see also Intelligence):
    in cognitive styles, 264–283
    defined, 2, 4, 200, 249
    in divergent thinking, 276–280
    in field dependence/field independence, 265–270
    in hemisphericity, 280–283
    in language, 292, 293
    in mathematics, 287, 288, 297, 298
    in refection/impulsivity, 270–276
    with respect to nature/nurture, 8
    and sex, 286–298
    in spatial skills, 288–292, 297, 298
    stability of, 8, 249–261, 267, 268, 273, 278, 279
Inductive reasoning, 33
Infancy (infants):
    and attachment, 190–197
    and memory, 75, 79, 154, 155
    and perception, 68–85, 192
    prediction of later intelligence from, 251–257

Infancy (infants) (continued)
    and sensorimotor development, 20, 22, 23, 87–105
Infantile amnesia, 161
Inferences:
    memory and, 160
    transitive, 31, 32, 38, 59
Inflections, in children's language, 136
Information processing, 13
    as approach to cognitive development, 46–65
    as approach to individual differences, 206–213
    model of attachment, 194, 195
    social, 176–179
    and symbolic functioning, 131
Inheritance:
    of intelligence, 8, 9, 218–222
    sex-linked, 296
Innate releasing mechanism, as explanation for neonatal imita-
    tion, 98–100
Inner speech, 141–143
Institutionalization studies, 9, 227, 228, 240, 241
Intellectual realism, and appearance/reality distinction, 123
Intelligence (individual differences in):
    analytic/spatial, 268, 288–290
    and attachment, 195–197
    and changes in IQ pattern, 258–261
    and conceptual tempo (reflection/impulsivity), 273, 274
    defined, 200
    and early experience, 8–10, 227, 228
    effects of formal education on, 242
    familial studies of, 220–224
    and family configuration variables, 238, 239
    and field dependence/field independence, 268–270
    and gender constancy, 186–188
    heritability of, 218–224
    information processing approach to, 206–213
    maintenance of, 243–246
    modification of, 238–243, 245, 246
    Piagetian approaches to, 213, 214
    prediction of from infancy to childhood, 251–257
    prediction of IQ over childhood, 257–261
    psychometric approaches to, 200–206
    relation to parenting, 231–237
    role of environment, 227–246
    Scarr and McCartney's genotype → environment theory,
        222–224
    and SES, 228–231
    stability of, 248–261
    Sternberg's triarchic theory of, 214–218
Intentionality, during sensorimotor period, 87–93, 100
Intermodal integration:
    cross-modal matching, 83
    in infancy, 82–84
    as necessary for imitation, 98, 99
Intrinsic activity:
    and functional assimilation, 89
    in Piaget's theory, 17, 18
Invention of new means, in Piaget's sensorimotor period, 92, 93
Invisible gestures, see Imitation
IQ:
    changes in pattern of, 258–261
    and cluster analysis, 259

IQ *(continued)*
  and convergent thinking, 277
  defined, 205
  deviation IQ, 205, 206
  and extreme scores, 260
  heritability of, 218–224
  as measure of intelligence, 8, 203, 206
  and mental age, 205, 206
  predicted from infancy, 251–257
  and relation to information processing tasks, 220
  and relation to Piagetian tasks, 213, 214
  and sex differences, 286
  stability of over childhood, 257, 258, 260, 261

Jokes, appreciation of, 180–182

Kaufman Assessment Battery for Children (K-ABC), 204–206
  and simultaneous/successive processing, 281, 282
Knowledge-acquisition components, in Sternberg's theory, 48, 49, 54, 57, 216
Knowledge base:
  automaticity and, 62–64
  contributions to cognitive development, 61–65
  differences between good and poor readers, 209, 210
  and individual differences in cognition, 209–211
  and inferences, 160
  and judgments of animism, 64, 65
  of learning-disabled children, 210
  and memory span, 61, 62
  and memory strategies, 62–64, 165–167
  and sex differences in spatial visualization, 291
  and Siegler's rule assessment approach, 64
  and speed of processing, 56, 62, 211, 220
  and Sternberg's theory, 216

Language:
  acquisition of, 135–137
  babbling, 135
  changes between 10 and 18 months and parenting, 234
  and communication skills, 137–140
  grammar, 136
  holophrastic speech, 136
  infants' preparedness for, 81, 82
  inflections, 136
  overregularization, 136
  Piaget's view of, 93, 108
  rules, 136
  and semantic memory, 143–150
  SES differences in, 233
  sex differences in, 292, 293
  and symbolic function, 108, 110, 111
  syntax, 136
  telegraphic speech, 136
Learning:
  contrasted with development, 4
  perceptual, 68
  as unlikely explanation for neonatal imitation, 98
Learning-disabled children:
  and automaticity, 208, 209
  and knowledge base, 210
  and speed of retrieval, 211

Learning-disabled children *(continued)*
  and strategies, 208, 209
Learning styles, 264
Levels of processing model, 111
Lexical ambiguity, in appreciation of jokes, 181
Logic:
  in Piagetian theory, 24, 38
  propositional, 35, 37
Logico-mathematical knowledge, 113
Long-term store, 46, 47, 49, 153, 154

Magical-phenomenalistic causality, 91, 92
Maintenance of intelligence, 243–246
Mastery behavior in infancy, 254
  prediction of later intelligence, 254, 257
Matching Familiar Figures Test (MFFT), 271–276
Maternal teaching styles, 231, 232
Mathematical ability:
  biological basis of, 287, 288
  and parental expectations, 289
  role of experience, 287
  sex differences in, 287, 288, 297, 298
Maturation, 21
  in information processing capacity, 51–53, 56, 270
  rate of and sex differences in cognition, 295–297
Mediational deficiency, 59
Memory:
  constructive, 158–161
  of early childhood, 160–161
  and encoding, 159, 165, 166
  episodic, 153, 154
  of good and poor readers, 210
  in infants, 75, 79, 154, 155
  and inferences, 160
  of learning-disabled children, 209
  long-term, 46, 47, 49, 153, 154
  memory span, 51–53, 55, 61, 62, 153, 169
  metamemory, 165, 168–171
  and object permanence, 103–105
  and organization, 60, 62, 162, 163
  recall, 153, 157–170
  recognition, 110, 153, 155–157, 163, 166
  reconstructive, 159, 160
  and reflection/impulsivity, 274
  and rehearsal, 51–53, 57, 59, 62, 161, 162, 167, 168, 207, 208
  and retrieval, 53, 56, 57, 128, 129, 161, 163, 164
  semantic, 47, 49, 62, 63, 143–150, 153, 154, 166, 167, 209–211
  short-term, 46–48, 50, 51, 53, 54, 154
  and strategies, 51–54, 57, 59, 60, 62, 158, 161–171, 207, 208
  in young children, 60
Memory span, 51, 53
  and knowledge base, 61, 62
  prediction of, 55, 169
  and strategies, 52, 53
Mental age, and IQ, 205, 206
Mental models of attachment, 194, 195
Meta-analysis, of sex differences, 297, 298
Metacognition, 49, 55
  and assessment of learning styles, 264, 265

Metacognition (continued)
  and communication, 138–140
  individual differences in, 212, 213
  and memory, 165, 168–171
  and reflection/impulsivity, 274
Metacommunication, 138–140
Metacomponents, in Sternberg's theory, 48, 54, 216 (see also Metacognition)
Metamemory, 165, 168–171
  individual differences in, 212
  and reflection/impulsivity, 275
Min model of arithmetic, 128–130
M-space (M-capacity, M-power), 51, 52
  and field dependence/field independence, 269, 270
  and maturation, 270
Modification of intelligence, 238–243, 245, 246
Moro reflex, 69, 99
"Motherese," 82, 136
Multiple classification, 118
Multistore models, 46, 153
Mutual imitation, see Imitation

Nativist position (see also Genetics; Heritability; Inheritance):
  with respect to intelligence, 8
  with respect to vision, 71, 72
Naturalistic studies, of effects of experience on intelligence, 232–236
Natural language categories:
  and basic level categories, 145, 146
  and category prototypes, 146–148
  and category typicality, 146–148
  development of, 144–149
  and scripts, 148, 149
Nature and nurture, 2, 5, 7–9, 227
Neonatal Behavioral Assessment Scale, 251
Newborns (neonates):
  active intermodal mapping, 98, 99
  basic perceptual abilities, 68–71
  color perception, 70
  cross-modal integration, 83
  imitation, 97–100
  memory, 79, 155
  in sensorimotor period, 87–89
Nodes, in semantic memory, 47
Nongraphic collections, 118, 119
Novelty:
  influence on memory, 156, 157
  preference for, in infant memory, 155
  preference for and prediction of current intelligence in infants, 255
  preference for and prediction of later intelligence, 254–257
  in Sternberg's theory, 215, 216, 255, 257
  in visual preferences, 72, 75, 76
Number concept, 124–127, 130
  and conservation, 124–127

Object permanence, 100–105
  and the "A not B" task, 102, 104, 105
  and attachment, 193
  and attentional deficits, 104, 105
  and invisible displacement, 102

Object permanence (continued)
  and manual search skills, 103
  and memory, 103–105, 154
Olfaction, see Smell, sense of
Operating space, in Case's theory, 53
Operations, in Piaget's theory, definition, 23, 24 (see also Concrete operations; Formal operations; Preoperations)
Optimal level, in Fischer's theory, 40, 131
Organization (in memory), 59–63, 161–163
  and clustering, 61–63, 163
  and efficiency of cognitive processing, 168
  individual differences in, 209, 292, 293
  and knowledge base, 62, 63, 167
  role of encoding, 165, 166
  sex differences in, 292, 293
  training of, 163, 169, 170
Organization (in Piaget's theory), 20
Overextensions, 143
Overregularization, 136

Paired-associate procedure, 164
Parental teaching styles, 231, 232
Parenting:
  and changes in IQ pattern, 260
  and relation to intelligence, 231–236
Partial report technique, with respect to sensory register, 50
Passive effects, in Scarr and McCartney's genotype → environment theory, 222–224
Passive rehearsal, 162
  in retarded children, 207
Perception
  in infancy, 68–84
  role in attachment, 192
Perceptual centration, see Centration
Perceptual classification, 114, 116
Perceptual learning, 68
Performance components, in Sternberg's theory, 48, 49, 54, 55, 216
Personal fable, 35
Perspective taking:
  in communication, 28, 137–139
  and field dependence/field independence, 268
  social, 174–176
  visual, 28, 29, 39
Phenomenism errors, and appearance/reality distinction, 123, 124
Phonemes, and infant perception, 81, 135
Phonological ambiguity, in appreciation of jokes, 181
Piagetian theory:
  accommodation, 20–22, 26, 41, 87–89, 94, 95, 255
  adaptation, 20, 21, 88
  and animism, 64, 65
  approach to individual differences, 213–214
  and arithmetic, 127, 128
  assimilation, 20–22, 26, 41, 255
  bidirectionality of structure and function, 19
  centration, 27, 34, 266
  circular reactions, 89–92
  classification, 118, 119
  communication, 137, 138

Piagetian theory (*continued*)
    concrete operations, 22–29, 31–35, 38, 52, 59, 109, 159, 259
    conservation, 24–27, 29–31, 41, 52, 59, 64
    constructive nature of cognition, 18, 19
    coordination of secondary circular reactions, 91, 92
    decentration, 27, 34
    disequilibrium, 26
    egocentricity, 27–29, 34–36, 39, 64, 137, 138, 175, 176, 268
    epigenesis, 19, 20, 22, 41
    equilibration, 21, 22
    and field dependence/field independence, 268
    formal operations, 22–24, 32–38, 52, 259, 260
    functional invariants, 20
    and gender identity, 183
    genesis, 19
    genetic epistemology, 16
    Genevan psychology, 16
    hierarchization, 22
    horizontal dècalage, 26
    hypothetico-deductive reasoning, 32, 36, 37
    and imitation, 20, 94–100, 109
    inductive reasoning, 33
    intrinsic activity, 17, 18
    invention of new means, 92, 93
    and IQ tests, 214, 258
    logic, 24, 35, 37, 38
    magical-phenomenalistic causality, 91
    object permanence, 100–105, 193
    organization, 20
    and play, 20, 279
    and prediction of stability of intelligence, 251
    preoperations, 22–33, 38, 52, 159
    primary circular reactions, 89, 90, 94
    and reflective abstraction, 34
    reflexes, 87–89
    reversibility, 24–27
    schemes, 17, 20, 21, 24, 26, 37, 41, 88, 89
    secondary circular reactions, 90, 91
    sensorimotor period, 6, 22, 23, 28, 87–106, 108, 253
    stages, 17, 22–41
    states versus transformations, 29
    structures, 17–22, 26, 40
    structures of the whole, 24, 38, 41
    tertiary circular reactions, 92
    thinking about thinking, 34
    training studies, 29–32, 35, 269, 291
    transitive inferences, 21, 32, 38, 59
    and water level problem, 290, 291
Plasticity of intelligence, 8–10, 243
Play:
    and divergent thinking, 279
    as form of assimilation, 20
    symbolic, 93, 108, 109
Prediction of intelligence:
    from infancy to childhood, 251–257
    from parents' behavior, 233–237
    over childhood, 257–261
Preoperations, 22–33, 38
    and M-space, 52
    and reconstructive memory, 159

Primacy effect, 158
    and learning-disabled children, 209
    and rehearsal training, 162
Primary circular reactions, 89, 90, 94
Primary memory, 46
Primary mental abilities, in Thurstone's theory, 201, 202
Primary visual system, 76
Principal component analysis, 253
Private speech, 141, 142
Procedural knowledge, and arithmetic, 129
Processing efficiency, *see* Efficiency of cognitive processing
Production deficiency, 59, 60, 162
Project Follow Through, 244, 245
Proprioception:
    in intermodal integration, 83
    in newborns, 69
Prototypes, category:
    development of, 146–148
    in infants' categories, 80
    as reflected by preference for novelty tasks, 255
Psychometric approach, 200–206 (*see also* Intelligence; IQ)
Puberty, hormonal differences, 295, 296
Pupillary reflex, 70, 71

Qualitative differences:
    and cross-age correlations of IQ scores, 258
    with respect to stages, 6, 7, 10, 11, 16–18, 38
Quantitative differences, with respect to stages, 6, 7, 10, 11, 16, 18, 38
Quantity identity, 122

Reading:
    and reflection/impulsivity, 274
    and relation to operativity, 213
    sex differences in, 292, 293
    and speed of processing, 212
Recall, 153, 157–170 (*see also* Cued recall; Free recall; Memory)
    of good and poor readers, 210
    of learning-disabled children, 209
    and reflection/impulsivity, 274
Recency effect, 158
    in learning-disabled children, 209
Recognition memory, 110, 153, 155–157, 163, 166
    in infants, prediction of later intelligence, 254–256
Recognitory assimilation, 88
Redefinition, as measure of divergent thinking, 277
Reflection/impulsivity, 270–276
    and Auditory Impulsivity Task, 274
    and cognitive task performance, 274–275
    definition of, 271
    and detail processing, 275, 276
    development of, 272
    and global processing, 275, 276
    and intelligence, 273, 274
    and Matching Familiar Figures Test (MFFT), 274–276
    and metacognition, 212, 274
    and reading, 274
    and recall, 274
    stability of, 272, 273
    and strategies, 274–276

Reflection/impulsivity (*continued*)
  training studies of, 142, 275
  visual scanning, 275
Reflective abstraction, 34
Reflexes:
  Moro, 69, 99
  and neonatal imitation, 97–100
  in sensorimotor period, 87–90
Rehearsal:
  cumulative, 162, 168, 207
  frequency and recall, 161, 162
  and knowledge base, 62, 167
  in inconic store, 51
  and memory span, 52, 53, 59
  overt rehearsal procedure, 162, 207
  passive, 162
  of retardates, 207, 208
  style of, 162, 167
  training of, 162, 168, 208
Representation, 10, 11, 108–113, 117, 130–132
  abstract, 112, 113
  action-based, 111, 112
  conceptual, 111, 112
  enactive, 108
  and functional core, 112
  ikonic, 110
  language-based, 110, 111
  literal, 109, 110, 117, 180, 181
  and schematic organization, 112
  in semantic memory, 47
  symbolic, 108, 109
Representational tier, in Fischer's theory, 40, 41, 131
Reproductive images, 109
Restricted verbal code, 231
Retardation:
  contrast of retarded and nonretarded children, 207, 208, 212
  and institutionalization, 228, 240, 241
  and transactional model, 230
Retrieval, 56, 57, 153
  in arithmetic, 128–130
  in memory, 161, 163, 164
  in memory span tests, 53
  role of encoding in, 163, 164
  of stories, 164
Reversibility, in Piaget's theory, 24–27
  and arithmetic, 127
  compensation (reciprocity), 24, 26
  negation (inversion) 24, 26, 27
Reversibility of intelligence, *see* Modification of intelligence
Rod-and-Frame Test, 266, 277
  and analytic/spatial skills, 290
Rules:
  in acquiring language, 136
  in gender identification, 184
  in neonates' vision, 68
  in Siegler's rule assessment approach, 64
  in social information processing, 177
Rule assessment approach, in Siegler's theory, 64

Schemas:
  gender, 188, 189

Schemas (*continued*)
  and models of attachment, 194
  as reflected by preference for novelty tasks, 255
  for scenes, 157
  as sensory representations, 75, 76
Schematic organization:
  in representation, 112
  and scripts, 148, 149
  and slot fillers, 148
Schemes, in Piaget's theory, 17, 20, 21, 24, 26, 37, 41, 88, 89
  during sensorimotor period, 88–90, 96
Scholastic Achievement Test (SAT), and sex differences in mathematics, 287, 288
Scripts, 148, 149
Secondary circular reactions, 90, 91
Secondary visual system, 76
Selective attention, 57, 58, 168
  to same-sex models, 185, 186
Selective comparisons, 49, 58
Self-monitoring, 55, 139
Semantic memory, 47, 49, 62, 63, 143–150, 153, 154
  basic level categories, 145, 146
  and category prototypes, 146
  and category typicality, 146–148
  characteristic features, 144
  defining features, 144
  development of, 149, 150
  and development of natural language categories, 144–149
  and development of scripts, 148, 149
  and development of semantic features, 143, 144
  and early words, 143
  and free recall, 166, 167
  of good and poor readers, 209, 210
  and overextensions, 143
  sex differences in, 293
  and speed of retrieval, 211
  and underextensions, 143
Semantic word features, 10, 110
  characteristic features, 144
  defining features, 144
  development of, 143, 144
Semiotic function, 108
Sensorimotor period, 6, 22, 23, 28, 86–106, 108
  accommodation in, 88, 89, 94
  adaptation in, 88
  assimilation in, 88–90
  and changes in attachment behaviors, 193
  coordination of secondary circular reactions, 91, 92
  and imitation, 94–100, 192
  invention of new means, 92, 93
  magical-phenomenalistic causality, 91
  object permanence, 100–105, 193
  and prediction of later intelligence, 253–255
  primary circular reactions, 89, 90, 94
  and principal component analysis, 253, 254
  reflexes, 87–90
  secondary circular reactions, 90, 91
  tertiary circular reactions, 92
Sensorimotor tier, in Fischer's theory, 40, 41, 131
Sensory register, 46–48, 50, 51, 153, 154
Serial position, 158, 162

Serial position (continued)
  of learning-disabled children, 209
Sex differences, in cognition, 286–298
  importance of, 297, 298
  and IQ, 286
  and mathematical ability, 287, 288, 297, 298
  and parental expectations, 288
  in spatial abilities, 288–292, 297, 298
  theories of, 293–297
  and variability hypothesis, 286
  in verbal behaviors, 292, 293, 297, 298
Sex-linked inheritance, and sex differences in cognition, 296
Sexual differentiation, 293–295
Short-term store, 46–48, 50, 51, 53, 54, 154
  and IQ, 203
  and recency effects, 158
Skill theory, see Fischer's skills theory
Skin senses, 69
Slot-filler categories, 148
Smell, sense of:
  in newborns, 69
  sex differences in, 294
Social cognition, 174–197
  and early social functioning, 190–197
  gender identification, 183–190
  humor, 179–182
  perspective taking, 174–176
  social information processing, 176–179
Social information processing, 176–179
Socioeconomic status (SES):
  and compensatory education, 243
  and parenting, 231–235
  and relation to environments experienced, 229–231
  and relation to intelligence, 228–231
Spatial abilities:
  and hemispheric lateralization, 294–296
  and rate of maturation, 295
  sex differences in, 288–292, 297, 298
  and spatial orientation, 288, 289
  and spatial visualization, 289–292
Spatial/analytic abilities, see Analytic/spatial skills
Spatial orientation:
  and cognitive maps, 289
  and exploration, 289
  sex differences in, 288, 289
Spatial visualization:
  analytic/spatial, 289, 290
  sex differences in, 289–292
  visual/nonanalytic, 289, 290
Speed/accuracy trade-off, 270
Speed of processing, 52, 53, 56
  and individual differences, 220
  and knowledge base differences, 56, 62, 211, 220
Speed of retrieval, and individual differences in intelligence, 211, 212, 219, 220
Stability of individual differences, 2, 5, 8–10
  of divergent thinking, 278, 279
  of field dependence/field independence, 267, 268
  of intelligence, 249–261
  of reflection/impulsivity, 273

Stages (see also Concrete operations; Formal operations; Piagetian theory; Preoperations; Sensorimotor period):
  in conservation of number, 124, 125
  continuity versus discontinuity, 6, 7, 10, 17
  definition, 5–7, 38, 39
  homogeneity of cognitive function, 6, 7, 24, 38–41
  invariant order, 22
  in Piaget's theory, 17, 22–41
  and representation, 130, 131
Stanford-Binet, 203, 205–207
States versus transformations, in Piaget's theory, 29
Sternberg's triarchic theory, 214–218
  and adaptation, 214
  componential subtheory, 48, 49, 54, 55, 57–59, 216, 218
  contextual subtheory, 214, 215, 218
  experiential subtheory, 215, 216, 218
  and gifted children, 216–218
Storage space, in Case's theory, 53
Strategies:
  arithmetic, 128–130
  constraint seeking, 11, 12
  definition, 11, 12
  as effortful processes, 64
  elaboration, 164, 168, 212
  fall-back, 64
  of good and poor readers, 210
  hypothesis scanning, 12
  imagery, 59
  individual differences in, 207–209
  influence of encoding on, 165, 166
  and knowledge base, 62–64, 163, 166, 167
  of learning-disabled children, 208–209
  mediational deficiency, 59, 60
  memory, 51–54, 57, 59, 60, 62–64, 158, 161–171, 207, 209
  and memory span, 52, 53
  and metamemory, 168–171
  and M-space, 53
  organizational, 62, 63, 161–163, 167, 292, 293
  production deficiency, 59, 60, 162
  and reflection/impulsivity, 274–276
  rehearsal, 51–53, 59, 161, 162, 167, 168, 207, 208
  retrieval, 53, 56, 57, 128, 129, 161, 163, 164, 167
  role in cognitive development, 59–61
  and serial position effect, 158
  sex differences in organizational, 292, 293
  in short-term store, 46–48
  social, 174
  utilization deficiency, 60
  young children's use of, 164, 165
Structure:
  in development, 4, 5, 19
  in Piaget's theory, 17–22, 26, 40
Structure/function, 5, 19
  bidirectionality of, 5
Structure-of-the-intellect theory (Guilford), 201, 202
Structures d'ensemble, see Structures of the whole
Structures of the whole, 24, 38, 41
Successive/simultaneous processing, 281, 282
  and the K-ABC, 281, 282
Surface-structure ambiguity, in appreciation of jokes, 182
Syllogisms, 36

Symbolic function, 108, 109, 130, 131
  in Bruner's theory, 110
  in classification, 117, 118
Symbols, 6, 11, 23, 24, 258
  and humor, 180
  and hypothetico-deductive reasoning, 32
  and representation, 108–113
  and training studies, 130
  and transition to preoperational thought, 92, 93
Symmetry, role in infants' visual preferences, 74
Syntax, 136

Taste, sense of:
  in newborns, 69
  sex differences in, 294
Telegraphic speech, 136
Tertiary circular reactions, 92
Testosterone, 294
Thinking about thinking, 34
Total processing space, in Case's theory, 53
Touch:
  in cross-modal matching, 83
  in newborns, 69
Training studies:
  and action-based representation, 111, 112
  and classification, 117, 130
  and class-inclusion, 119, 120
  and discovery learning, 29, 30
  and elaboration, 164, 168, 212
  and field dependence/field independence, 266, 269
  and gifted, 212
  and impulsive conceptual tempo, 142
  and memory, 162–164, 168, 208, 212
  and metamemory, 169, 170
  and organization, 163, 168, 208
  and Piaget's theory, 29–32, 35, 269, 291
  and reflection/impulsivity, 142, 275
  and rehearsal, 162, 168, 208
  and retarded children, 208
  and retrieval, 164
  and scientific reasoning, 269, 270
  and use of symbols, 130
  and water level problem, 291
Transactional view of development, 8, 228–231, 235
  in Scarr and McCartney's genotype → environment theory, 224
Transient ontogenetic adaptation, and neonatal imitation, 100
Transitive inferences, 31, 32, 38, 59
Triarchic theory, see Sternberg's triarchic theory
Turner's syndrome, and cognitive differences, 294, 296
Typicality, category:
  and class inclusion, 120, 121
  and good and poor readers, 210

Typicality (continued)
  and infants' categories, 80
  and natural language categories, 146–148

Underextensions, 143
Unidirectionality of structure and function, 5
Utilization deficiency, 60

Variability hypothesis, with respect to sex differences, 286
Verbal behavior, sex differences in, 292, 293
Vestibular senses, 69
Vision, in neonates, 68, 70, 71 (see also Visual information processing)
Visual cliff, 77
Visual information processing:
  and attention, 71–76
  and depth perception, 76–78
  and discrimination, 71
  in infancy, 71–81
  and infant categorization, 78–81
  and intermodal integration, 83
  and visual preferences, 71–76
Visual/nonanalytic skills, 289–291
Visual preferences (in infancy), 71–77
  and contrast sensitivity function, 73, 74
  and physical stimulus characteristics, 72–75
  and psychological stimulus characteristics, 75–77
  role in attachment, 192
  role of attractiveness, 74, 75
  role of complexity, 73, 74
  role of contrast (contour), 72, 73
  role of curvature, 74
  role of movement, 72
  role of novelty, 72, 75
  role of symmetry, 74
Visual scanning:
  in infants, 72, 73
  in newborns, 68
Visual tracking, in newborns, 70

Wechsler Intelligence Tests, 203–206 (see also IQ)
  factor analysis of, 268
  WAIS-R, 203
  WISC-R, 203–206
  WPPSI, 203
Word fluency, as measure of divergent thinking, 277
Working memory, 46, 47, 54

X-linked inheritance, see Sex-linked inheritance

Your Style of Learning and Thinking, 282, 283

☐ Source Notes

CHAPTER 1. **12,** Figure 1-1 adapted from "On Asking Questions," by F. A. Mosher and J. R. Hornsby. In S. Bruner, R. R. Olver, and P. M. Greenfield (Eds.), *Studies in Cognitive Growth.* Copyright 1966 by John Wiley & Sons. Reprinted by permission of Jerome Bruner.

CHAPTER 2. **30,** Figure 2-4 adapted from "Conservation Acquisition: A Problem of Learning to Attend to Relevant Tributes," by R. Gelman, *Journal of Experimental Child Psychology,* 1969, *7,* 167–187. Copyright 1969 by Academic Press. Reprinted with permission. **33,** Figure 2-5 from *The Growth of Logical Thinking from Childhood to Adolescence,* by B. Inhelder and Jean Piaget. Copyright 1958 by Basic Books. Reprinted with permission. **36,** Syllogisms adapted from "Evidence for Deductive Reasoning by Preschoolers," by J. Hawkins, R. D. Pea, J. Glick, and S. Scribner, *Developmental Psychology,* 1984, *20,* 584–592. Copyright 1984 by the American Psychological Association. Reprinted with permission. **41,** Table 2-3 adapted from "Processes of Cognitive Development: Optimal Level and Skill Acquisition," by K. W. Fischer and S. L. Pipp. In R. J. Sternberg (Ed.), *Mechanisms of Cognitive Development.* Copyright 1984 by W. H. Freeman and Company. Reprinted with permission.

CHAPTER 3. **47,** Figure 3-1 from "The Control of Short-Term Memory," by R. C. Atkinson and R. M. Shiffrin, *Scientific American,* 1971, *225,* 66–72. Copyright © 1971 by Scientific American, Inc. All rights reserved. Reprinted by permission. **47,** Figure 3-2 from "A Spreading Activation Theory of Semantic Processing," by A. M. Collins and E. F. Loftus, *Psychological Review,* 1975, *82,* 407–428. Copyright 1975 by the American Psychological Association. Reprinted with permission. **50,** Figure 3-4 from "Sketch of a Componential Sub-Theory of Human Intelligence," by Robert J. Sternberg, *Behavioral and Brain Sciences,* 1980, *3.* Reprinted with the permission of Cambridge University Press. **51,** Figures 3-5 and 3-6 from "Developmental Differences in Intake and Storage of Visual Information," by K. Sheingold, *Journal of Experimental Child Psychology,* 1973, *16,* 1–11. Copyright 1973 by Academic Press. Reprinted by permission. **52,** Table 3-1 from "Mental Strategies, Mental Capacity, and Instruction: A NeoPiagetian Investigation," by R. Case, *Journal of Experimental Child Psychology,* 1974, *18,* 382–397. Copyright 1974 by Academic Press. Reprinted with permission. **54,** Figure 3-8 from "Operational Efficiency and the Growth of Short-Term Memory Span," by R. Case, D. M. Kurland, and J. Goldberg, *Journal of Experimental Child Psychology,* 1982, *23,* 386–404. Copyright 1982 by Academic Press. Reprinted with permission. **57,** Figure 3-9 from "Utilization of Retrieval Cues by Children in Recall," by A. Kobasigawa, *Child Development,* 1974, *45,* 127–134. Copyright 1974 by *Child Development.* Reprinted with permission. **62,** Figure 3-10 from "Knowledge Structures and Memory Development," by M. T. H. Chi. In R. Siegler (Ed.), *Children's Thinking: What Develops?* Copyright 1978 by Lawrence Erlbaum Associates, Inc. Reprinted with permission.

CHAPTER 4. **72,** Figure 4-1 from "The Origin of Form Perception," by R. L. Fantz, *Scientific American,* 1961, *204,* 66–72. Copyright © 1961 by Scientific American, Inc. All rights reserved. **73,** Figure 4-2 from "Visual Scanning of Triangles by the Human Newborn," by P. Salapatek and W. Kessen, *Journal of Experimental Child Psychology,* 1966, *3,* 155–

167. Copyright 1966 by Academic Press. Reprinted with permission. **73,** Figure 4-3 adapted from "Pattern Perception in Infancy," by P. Salapatek. In L. B. Cohen and P. Salapatek (Eds.), *Infant Cognition: From Sensation to Perception.* Copyright 1975 by Academic Press. **74,** Figure 4-4 from "Infant Visual Fixation: The Effect of Concentricity, Curvilinearity, and Number of Directions," by H. Ruff and H. G. Birch, *Journal of Experimental Child Psychology,* 1974, *17,* 460-473. Copyright 1974 by Academic Press. Reprinted with permission. **75,** Figure 4-5 from "Magnitude of Discrepancy and the Distribution of Attention in Infants," *Child Development,* 1977, *17,* 772–785. Copyright 1977 by Academic Press. Reprinted with permission.

CHAPTER 5. **94–95,** Excerpts from *Play, Dreams, and Imitation in Childhood,* by J. Piaget. Copyright © 1962 by W. W. Norton, pp. 10 and 63. Reprinted by permission. **98,** Photo 5-1 from "Imitation of Facial and Manual Gestures by Human Neonates," by A. N. Meltzoff and M. K. Moore, *Science,* 1977, *198,* 75–78. Copyright 1977 by the AAAS. Reprinted with permission. **99,** Table 5-3 from "Matching Behavior in the Young Infant," by S. Jacobson, *Child Development,* 1979, *50,* 425–430. © 1979 by The Society for Research in Child Development. Reprinted with permission. **105,** Figure 5-1 from "Development of the Ability to Use Recall to Guide Performance, as Indicated by Infants' Performance on AB," by A. Diamond, *Child Development,* 1985, *56,* 868–883. © 1985 by The Society for Research in Child Development. Reprinted with permission.

CHAPTER 6. **112,** Table 6-2 from "A Comparison of the Roles of Exemplar, Action, Coordinate, and Superordinate Relations in the Semantic Processing of 4- and 5-Year-Old Children," by P. Heidenheimer, *Journal of Experimental Child Psychology,* 1978, *25,* 143–159. Copyright 1978 by Academic Press. Reprinted with permission. **127,** Table 6-3 from "Developmental Relations between Notational Counting and Number Conservation," by G. Saxe, *Child Development,* 1979, *50,* 189–197. © 1979 by the Society for Research in Child Development. Reprinted with permission. **129,** Figure 6-3 from "Working-Memory Systems and Cognitive Development," by C. J. Brainerd, in C. J. Brainerd (Ed.), *Recent Advances in Cognitive-Developmental Theory: Progress in Cognitive Development Research,* 1983, p. 192. Copyright 1983 by Springer Verlag Publishing Company. Reprinted with permission. **131,** Figure 6-4 from "A Theory of Cognitive Development," by K. W. Fischer, *Psychological Review,* 1980, *87,* 477–531. Copyright 1980 by the American Psychological Association. Reprinted with permission.

CHAPTER 7. **138,** Figure 7-1 from "Referential Communication in Nursery School Children: Method and Some Preliminary Findings," by G. Glucksberg, R. M. Krauss, and R. Weisberg, *Journal of Experimental Child Psychology,* 1966, *3,* 333–342. Copyright 1966 by Academic Press. Reprinted with permission. **144,** Text in column one from "A Characteristic-to-Defining Shift in the Development of Word Meaning," by F. C. Keil and N. Baterman, *Journal of Verbal Learning and Verbal Behavior,* 1984, *23,* 221–236. Copyright 1984 by Academic Press. Reprinted by permission. **145,** Table 7-1 and Figure 7-2 from "A Developmental Trend in the Understanding of Concept Attribute Importance," by P. J. Schwanenflugel, M. E. Guth, and D. F. Bjorklund, *Child Development,* 1986, *57,* 421–

430. © 1986 by the Society for Research in Child Development. Reprinted with permission. **147,** Figure 7-3 from "Developmental Trends in Children's Typicality Judgments," by D. F. Bjorklund, B. E. Thompson, and P. A. Ornstein, *Behavior Research Methods and Instrumentation*, 1983, *15*, 350–356. Copyright 1983 by Behavior Research Methods and Instrumentation. Reprinted with permission.

CHAPTER 8. **156,** Figures 8-1 and 8-2 from "Developmental Changes in Picture Recognition," by J. M. Mandler and C. A. Robinson, *Journal of Experimental Child Psychology*, 1978, *26*, 122–136. Copyright 1978 by Academic Press. Reprinted with permission. **159,** Figure 8-5 from "Copying and Reproducing Pictures in Relation to Subjects' Operative Levels," by L. S. Liben, *Developmental Psychology*, 1981, *17*, 357–365. Copyright 1981 by the American Psychological Association. Reprinted with permission. **162,** Table 8-1 from "Rehearsal and Organizational Processes in Children's Memory," by P. A. Ornstein, M. J. Naus, and C. Liberty, *Child Development*, 1975, *46*, 818–830. © 1975 by The Society for Research in Child Development. Reprinted with permission.

CHAPTER 9. **177,** Figure 9-1 from "Social Competence in Children," by Dodge et al., *Monographs of the Society for Research in Child Development*, 1986, *51*, (Serial No. 213). © 1986 by the Society for Research in Child Development. Reprinted with permission. **187,** Figure 9-2 from "Gender Constancy and the Effects of Sex-Typed Television Toy Commercials," by Ruble, et al., *Child Development*, 1981, *52*, 667–673. © 1981 by The Society for Research in Child Development. Reprinted with permission. **194,** Figure 9-3 from "Attachment Theory: Retrospect and Prospect," by I. Bretherton. In I. Bretherton and E. Waters (Eds.), *Growing Points of Attachment Theory and Research, Monographs of the Society for Research in Child Development*, 1985, *50*, (Serial No. 209.) © 1985 by The Society for Research in Child Development. Reprinted with permission.

CHAPTER 10. **202,** Figure 10-1 from "The Structure-of-the-Intellect Model," by J. P. Guilford. In B. B. Wolman (Ed.), *Handbook of Intelligence*. Copyright 1985 by John Wiley & Sons. Reprinted with permission. **203,** Table 10-1 adapted from *The Stanford-Binet Intelligence Scale: (4th Edition) Guide for Administering and Scoring*, by R. L. Thorndike, E. P. Hagen, and J. M. Sattler. Copyright 1986 by The Riverside Publishing Company. Reprinted with permission. **208,** Figure 10-3 from "Breakdown of Flexible Use of Information: Intelligence-Related Differences in Transfer Following Equivalent Learning Performance," by J. C. Campione, A. L. Brown, R. A. Ferrara, R. S. Jones, and E. Steinberg, *Intelligence*, 1985, *9*, 297–315. Copyright 1985 by *Intelligence*. Reprinted with permission. **217,** Table 10-2 from "Analogical Reasoning with Novel Concepts: Differential Attention of Intellectually Gifted and Nongifted Children to Relevant and Irrelevant Novel Stimuli," by D. B. Marr and R. J. Sternberg, *Cognitive Development*, 1986, *1*, 53–72. Copyright 1986 by *Cognitive Development*. Reprinted with permission. **223,** Figure 10-4 from "The Nature of Cognitive Differences between Blacks and Whites," by H. J. Eysenck, *Brain and Behavioral Science*, 1985, *8*, 229. Copyright 1985 by *Brain and Behavioral Science*. Reprinted with permission. **223,** Figure 10-5 adapted from "How People Make Their Own Environments: A Theory of Genotype—Environment Effects," by S. Scarr and K. McCartney, *Child Development*, 1983, *54*,

424–435. © 1983 by The Society for Research in Child Development. Adapted with permission.

CHAPTER 11. **229,** Figure 11-1 adapted from "Early Influences on Development: Fact or Fancy?", by A. J. Sameroff, *Merrill-Palmer Quarterly*, 1975, *21*, 267–294. Copyright 1975 by *Merrill-Palmer Quarterly*. Reprinted with permission. **230,** Table 11-1 adapted from "Preventing Intellectual and Interactional Sequelae of Fetal Malnutrition: A Longitudinal, Transactional, and Synergistic Approach," by P. S. Zeskind and C. T. Ramey, *Child Development*, 1981, *52*, 213–218. © 1981 by The Society for Research in Child Development, Inc. Reprinted with permission. **233,** HOME Scale adapted from "Home Observation for Measurement of the Environment," by B. M. Caldwell and R. H. Bradley, 1978, University of Arkansas at Little Rock. Reprinted with permission of the authors. **234,** Table 11-2 adapted from "Home Observation for Measurement of the Environment," by B. M Caldwell and R. H. Bradley, 1978, University of Arkansas at Little Rock. Reprinted with permission. **239,** from "Birth Order and Intellectual Development," by R. B. Zajonc and G. B. Markus, *Psychological Review*, 1975, *82*, 74–88. Copyright 1975 by the American Psychological Association. Reprinted with permission. **245,** Table 11-3 from "The Relation of Infants' Home Environment to Mental Test Performance at Fifty-Four Months: A Follow-Up Study," by R. H. Bradley and B. M. Caldwell, *Child Development*, 1976, *47*, 1172–1174. © 1976 by The Society for Research in Child Development, Inc. Reprinted with permission.

CHAPTER 12. **250,** Table 12-1 from "Transitions in Early Mental Development," by R. B. McCall, D. H. Eichorn, and P. S. Hogarty, *Monographs of the Society for Research in Child Development*, 1977, *42*, (Serial No. 171). © 1977 by The Society for Research in Child Development, Inc. Reprinted with permission. **252,** Table 12-2 adapted from *Manual of the Bayley Scales of Infant Development*, by N. Bayley, 1969. Copyright 1969 by The Psychological Corporation. Adapted with permission. **253,** Table 12-3 from "Infant Recognition Memory as a Measure of Intelligence," by J. F. Fagan and L. T. Singer, in L. P. Lipsitt and C. K. Rovee-Colleir (Eds.), *Advances in Infancy Research*, Vol. 2, pp. 31–89. Copyright 1983 by Ablex Publishing Corporation. Reprinted with permission. **257,** Table 12-4 adapted from "Stability of Mental Test Performance between 2 and 18 Years," by M. P. Honzik, J. W. McFarlence, and L. Allen, *Journal of Experimental Education*, 1948, *17*, 309–324; and "Consistency and Variability in the Growth of Intelligence from Birth to Eighteen Years," by N. Bayley, *Journal of Genetic Psychology*, 1949, *75*, 165–196. **259,** Figure 12-1 from "Developmental Changes in Mental Performance," by R. B. McCall, M. I. Applebaum, and P. S. Hogarty, *Monographs of the Society for Research in Child Development*, 1973, *38*, (Serial No. 150). © 1973 by The Society for Research in Child Development. Reprinted with permission. **261,** Table 12-5 from "The Plasticity of Intellectual Development: Insights from Preventive Intervention," by C. T. Ramey, K. O. Yeates, and E. J. Short, *Child Development*, 1984, *55*, 1913–1925. © 1984 by The Society for Research in Child Development. Reprinted with permission.

CHAPTER 13. **267,** Figure 13-2 reproduced by special permission of the publisher, Consulting Psychologists Press, Inc., Palo Alto, CA 94306 from "The Children's Embedded Figures Test," by S. A. Karp and N. Konstadt. © 1971. Further

reproduction is prohibited without the publisher's consent. **273,** Figure 13-5 from "A Note on the Developmental Nature of Reflection-Impulsivity," by N. J. Salkind and C. F. Nelson, *Developmental Psychology*, 1980, *16*, 237–238. Copyright 1980 by the American Psychological Association. Reprinted with permission. **276,** Figures 13-6 and 13-7 from "Reflective and Impulsive Children: Strategies of Information Processing Underlying Differences in Problem Solving," by T. Zelniker and W. E. Jeffrey, *Monographs of the Society for Research in Child Development*, 1976, *41*, (Serial No. 168). © 1976 by The Society for Research in Child Development. Reprinted with permission.
CHAPTER 14. **289,** Table 14-1 from "Young Children's Ability to Infer Spatial Relationships: Evidence from a Large, Familiar Environment," by J. F. Herman, J. H. Shiraki, and B. S. Miller, *Child Development*, 1985, *56*, 1195–1203. © 1985 by The Society for Research in Child Development. Reprinted with permission. **291,** Insert adapted from "Sex Differences in Spatial Ability and Spatial Activities," by N. Newcombe, M. M. Bandura, and D. C. Taylor, *Sex Roles*, 1983, *9*, 377–386. Copyright 1983 by Plenum Press. Adapted with permission of the author. **293,** Table 14-2 adapted from "Sex Differences in Comprehension of High- and Low-Interest Reading Material," by S. R. Asher and R. A. Markel, *Journal of Educational Psychology*, 1974, *66*, 680–687. Copyright 1974 by the American Psychological Association. Adapted with permission. **298,** Figure 14-2 from "How Large are Cognitive Gender Differences? A Meta-Analysis Using ω^2 and d," by J. S. Hyde, *American Psychologist*, 1981, *36*, 892–901. Copyright 1981 by the American Psychological Association. Reprinted with permission.